Dragons & Butterflies

Sentenced to Die, Choosing to Live

Dragons & Butterflies

Sentenced to Die, Choosing to Live

Shani Krebs

JONATHAN BALL PUBLISHERS

JOHANNESBURG & CAPE TOWN

First published in 2014 by
JONATHAN BALL PUBLISHERS
a division of Media24 Limited
PO Box 33977
Jeppestown
2043

ISBN 978-1-86842-575-4
Also available as an ebook
ISBN 978-1-86842-576-1

Design and typesetting by Triple M Design, Johannesburg
Cover design by Publicide
Set in 11/15pt Roitis Serif Std
Printed and bound by Paarl Media, Paarl
All photographs are reproduced by kind permission of the author.

Twitter: www.twitter.com/JonathanBallPub
Facebook: www.facebook.com/pages/Jonathan-Ball-Publishers/298034457992
Blog: http://jonathanball.bookslive.co.za/

To view examples of the author's artwork, visit www.shanikrebs.com

Contents

Author's Note

During my time in prison in Thailand, although I never formally mastered the Thai language, I learnt to speak it fairly fluently. The Thai used among inmates and guards was colloquial, regional and mixed with street and prison slang. I did not read the language, nor did I learn to write it. The mixture I have used in the book comes from my experience and an ear that is attuned to phonetics.

Everything I have described in these pages is true. However, for reasons that will be clear to the reader, some people's names have been changed in order to protect their identities.

Prologue

Although it was furnished, and nobody had made me feel in any way unwelcome, the room I had been shown into seemed desolate to the point of being menacing. The double window frames were barred. There was a security gate across the door. Already I felt anxious and confined, restricted, and yet there was also a sense of security and comfort. On the way, all that had registered in my mind were the high walls, the electrified fences, everything gated and closed off. Where was I? What was this place?

They had left me alone, to have some time to myself, probably to come to terms with everything that had happened over the past week. I looked around, but I felt weak and disoriented, and slightly dizzy. I realised that I must be mentally, emotionally and physically exhausted. The past days had taken their toll. I needed to give myself time to get to grips with my strange new circumstances. I went to the washbasin to brush and floss my teeth, looking for the ordinary routines that were familiar to me and felt safe. Then I forced myself to climb onto the bed. Although I couldn't shake a clammy feeling of uneasiness, it wasn't long before I slipped into a deep sleep.

It couldn't have been more than ten minutes later when I woke up with a lurch of fear. My chest was tight. I couldn't breathe. I felt the walls and ceiling closing in on me like a vice. I jumped up, startled, immediately on the defensive, blood pounding in my ears. For a moment I didn't know where I was. Everything was strange. I felt panic rising.

Later, when I felt calmer, I allowed myself to drift off again, only to go through the same ordeal. I had barely fallen asleep when I woke up, drenched in cold sweat and gasping for air.

Once again I lay down, taking deep breaths, trying to slow my pounding heart. I told myself that I would come through this as I had come through so many difficult times in my life. I whispered the Master of the Universe prayer, the prayer that had given me strength to overcome so much adversity, and the very same prayer that I believed had saved my life: 'Hear, O Israel, the Lord our G-d, the Lord is One.' I said the comforting words over and over.

The window in the small bathroom was slightly ajar. Although the bars across it were thick and sturdy, for some reason I became uncomfortable knowing it was open. Outside, in the shadows, I felt as if something or someone was lurking, an unknown force waiting and watching, biding its time. I don't know what made me imagine this. All I knew was that I had to shut the window, and so I got up and went and pulled it firmly closed. I secured the catch and stood back. It wasn't enough. I stood looking at it, barefoot, in the new clothes that didn't feel right on me. I remembered that I had a few lengths of string in the side compartment of my travel bag. String had come in useful where I had just been.

I took a piece and tied it around the handle of the window, then looped it through and around the bars until I was satisfied that it was really tight and that the window wouldn't budge. Then I took a towel and, using the pegs I also carried with me, attached it to the bars. Somehow, just doing this made me feel more at ease, and I could feel my breathing slowing down and becoming more regular. I did the same in the other room, attaching string to fasten the window closed and snug against the bars that kept me in and everyone else out.

A wave of exhaustion swept over me. I lay down on the mattress, but no matter what I did I couldn't get comfortable. I stretched out my arms, straightened my legs, stared at the ceiling. Carefully I looked around, to familiarise myself with everything in the room, hoping that I would fall asleep while doing it. Would I ever get used to this kind of bed? Maybe that was the problem.

There was a bright light on the small bedside table. I switched it off and the room fell into an eerie darkness. I closed my eyes, but all I could see was a series of disturbing lights flashing against my eyelids. When I opened my eyes again, I was back in darkness, but the darkness scared me more. I switched the light on again, then switched it off. Then I got off the bed and went into the passage and turned the light on there instead. That felt a bit better. I tossed and turned, still wrestling with the bedding.

At 2am I was still awake, but so tired I wanted to cry. Finally, out of sheer exhaustion my eyes closed and stayed closed until 5am, when nature called. When I lifted my head I found that I was sprawled on my back, with a pillow, nothing else, between my body and the hard floor.

What I had been dreading most since coming here was using the toilet, and up till now I had successfully avoided having to face it. I couldn't delay any longer. I approached the unfamiliar style of toilet nervously, uncertain how to use it or how I would keep my balance. I took a deep breath. Fortunately I managed and didn't slip off. I felt quite pleased with myself, as if I had won a little victory. Perhaps I could learn to cope with it in time. Another foreign thing to master. There was so much I was going to have to learn in this alien world.

I looked out into the yard outside, with the early morning light filtering through the windows, and felt myself relaxing for the first time. I teased loose the tangle of string securing the bedroom window, pushed gently on the pane until it opened, and felt the cool breeze against my skin. I would have to come to terms with this place, no matter how hard it was, I told myself firmly. Nothing had changed; only the playing field was different.

In the street outside I caught a glimpse of the yellow ribbons that friends and family had tied around the trees that lined the route through the neighbourhood that was so strange and yet so familiar to me.

I felt a surge of emotion I couldn't identify. But I knew one thing for sure: after 18 years in Thailand's high-security prison, the notorious Bangkwang, I was home.

Adjusting was not going to be easy.

Chapter 1

The Beginning

During the 1956 Hungarian Revolution, a young couple, Fritz and Katalin Krebs, with Katalin's ten-year-old daughter Marika from a previous marriage and a group of 15 others, made their way by train to the Austrian border in the hope of escaping the Soviet invasion. For three hours they plodded through the heavy snow that blanketed the countryside until eventually they were picked up by a truck. They were taken to a nearby town where they were given shelter in a large warehouse together with hundreds of other refugees, all waiting to be relocated to other countries.

A few weeks later, Fritz, Katalin and Marika boarded a flight for South Africa. This was to be their land of milk and honey, a land of sunshine with an endless coastline waiting to be explored. Katalin was full of hopes and dreams for their sweet new life, the start, as she saw it, of their future as a family.

After a stop in the Belgian Congo, where they changed planes, they touched down at Jan Smuts airport in Johannesburg. From there they caught a bus to Vanderbijlpark, an industrial city south of Johannesburg.

It was Christmas Eve.

To begin with, Katalin and Fritz stayed with fellow Hungarian immigrants. Then they made their way to the prosperous gold-mining town of Slurry, 260km west of Johannesburg, in what is now North West, where the young Fritz got a job in a cement factory. But they did not stay there long. Within a year the family moved to nearby Mafeking (now Mahikeng). In the years that followed, the family was to relocate several times from one dull town to the next, but they adjusted relatively easily in a country of diverse ethnicity.

In 1957 Katalin and Fritz were blessed with a beautiful baby girl, Joan Barbara, my sister, a first-generation South African.

My own story begins early in 1959, when my parents were still living in Mafeking. Katalin, now a young housewife, loved to sing and dance. Oblivious to the tiny heart that was already beating in her womb, one morning, as she went about her chores, bobbing her head and moving her hips to 'Blue Suede Shoes' crackling out of the speakers of an old record player, she found herself facing a dilemma.

Fritz had begun to drink excessively, and the rages and physical violence that went with his drinking, and of which she bore the brunt, were taking their toll on her. She wasn't sure how much more she could take. When she looked in the mirror on the wall at the entrance to their living room, she still saw a woman of unassuming beauty. She was aware of how men gazed at her wherever she went and that other women were envious of her looks. Today, as she paused in her housework and caught sight of her reflection, she gently touched her cheekbone where a slight discoloration of the skin had begun to appear. Her eyes welled with tears. How much more humiliation could she endure? How much more physical abuse could she cope with when Fritz was drunk and became violent?

Although Katalin had threatened to leave Fritz many times, until that day she hadn't had it in her heart to actually pack up and go. When he broke down, as he routinely did afterwards, and begged for her forgiveness, promising never to raise his hand to her again, she always forgave him, but always against her better judgement. No more, she vowed, as she looked into her eyes reflected in the mirror. This time would be the last.

For a while, the situation at home seemed to improve, and, when they did fight, the make-up sex with Fritz was more passionate than before. She believed that her husband was genuinely making an effort, and it helped that he was trying to limit his drinking to weekends only.

And then Katalin discovered she was pregnant – with me.

The last thing she needed in her life was another child, especially in such a rocky home environment, but she was firmly opposed to abortion. In her culture it was considered the greatest of blessings to have as many children as possible, and so she began to come round to the prospect of a third child, and hopefully a boy this time – a son for Fritz.

On 14 October 1959, as the sun began to set, Katalin lay resting in the hospital ward where she was soon to give birth. She placed her hands softly on her swollen belly. Startled by the sudden rustling of tree branches scratching against the windows, she looked outside. The leaves moved about in a gusty wind and the sky on the distant horizon was a deep sullen grey. Perhaps there would be a storm that night.

Csodalatos latvany, she thought wistfully, what an awesome sight, as the waning rays of the sun filtered through her window, casting a pattern of shadows on the walls and accentuating shades of glowing vermilion. Suddenly there was a blinding lightning flash, followed by a series of deafening rolls of thunder.

She watched, mesmerised by the kaleidoscopic display outside and the crashing and rumbling of thunder echoing over the low hills. Nature was putting on a dramatic display for her new arrival. It must be a boy, she thought. At the precise moment that the heavens parted and torrents of rain sheeted down, my mother's own waters broke and she went into labour. Eight hours later, I gulped my first breath of life. With the snipping of the umbilical cord, the moment when we are no longer an extension of our mothers but a separate entity, Alexander Shani Krebs gave a high-pitched cry. Perhaps if I had had an idea of the wretched childhood that awaited me, I might very well have wormed my way back into my mother's womb. But there was no going back for me!

The most intimate of human relationships is that between a child and a parent, and the most impressionable time is the years between birth and cognitive emotional response, although we do not consciously remember this period. We know that these early stages of a child's development begin to form and mould the fundamental aspects of those intrinsic behaviour patterns that we will carry through to adulthood. In fact, this goes even further back – to when we are still in the womb. This could very well have been the time when my later problems originated, but they were all still ahead of me on that wild and stormy night.

During my mother's pregnancy, Fritz had unfortunately returned to his old antics. He seemed to be forever drunk, and on many occasions would stay out all night, returning the next morning with the fragrance of another woman's perfume lingering on his skin. My parents were constantly at each other's throats, screaming and shouting. I am surprised I wasn't born with a hearing impediment because of the brutal, unthinking way my father treated Katalin during her pregnancy. So much for my mother's wishful thinking; instead of her pregnancy being a portent of better things to come, there must have been times when she thought I was more of a curse than a blessing.

One night, when I was a mere infant, my father, intoxicated of course, attacked my mother with a milk bottle. While she was attempting to wrestle it from his hand, the bottle slipped and crashed to the floor, shattering into razor-sharp pieces. In her frenzy to escape, Katalin accidentally stood on a jagged shard, which deeply lacerated the sole of her bare foot. Instinctively she pulled the glass from the soft tissue in which it had lodged and, limping painfully, with blood spurting from the wound, she scooped up my sister in one arm, plucked me out of my cot with the other, darted out of the house, and ran to our neighbours.

Our neighbours were typical, middle-class, church-going Afrikaners. Shocked by the state of my injured, frightened mother, they rushed her to the hospital. When she returned home, Katalin arrived with a police escort because she believed that her life and those of her children were in danger.

My father was arrested and charged, and divorce proceedings soon commenced. By the time I was a year old, Katalin and Fritz were officially divorced.

Marika, my half-sister, had eloped at the age of 16, at around the time I was born, and married a Hungarian guy, Bela Gurics. By the time of the divorce, she was already long gone.

Being an immigrant and now a single parent with two kids in a foreign country wasn't exactly the life my mother had envisaged for herself when she escaped from Hungary. Even after the divorce my father wasn't a very responsible person; he was always either late with his maintenance payments or else he couldn't pay the amount agreed upon for one reason or another. Providing for her children was beginning to prove an almost impossible task for Katalin, but she was still young and beautiful, and, as fate would have it, it wasn't too long or very surprising before she surrendered to the beguiling charms of another ultra-egotistical Hungarian man. Janos Horvath was ten years Katalin's junior and a contemptible charmer who turned out to be nothing more than an ill-mannered peasant.

Perhaps it was love at first sight, but they married before they really got to know each other properly. We all moved into Janos's house in Orkney, a mining town run by the Vaal Reefs gold-mining group.

Because I was so young when my mother remarried, I actually thought that Janos was my real father, and so I grew up calling him 'Dad'. As the years went by, though, it became apparent that my step-father was even more psychotic than my biological father.

In those early years, life at home was pretty much 'normal', probably not very different to the modest stereotypical families we were friendly with. Normal, that is, except that Joan and I had an abusive stepfather along with a mother who, coming from a family of Hungarian bureaucrats, was an obstinate disciplinarian and who firmly believed that the opinions of children counted for nothing. Joan and I were severely chastised for the slightest transgression. My parents were sticklers for discipline and never hesitated to inflict as much physical pain as they thought was appropriate for whatever they perceived as a wrongdoing. We were only too aware of the repercussions if we neglected to meet the standards set by our parents. But, besides the authoritarian conditions we had to endure, we were nevertheless content and healthy, and we never went hungry. My mom was an excellent cook and she prepared lavish traditional Hungarian dishes for the family.

Unlike other families, we didn't employ domestic helpers and so, as soon as we were old enough, my sister and I were required to help with the chores around the house. We became domesticated. Personal hygiene was of particular importance to my mother and was vigorously administered. I often found myself subjected to one of her severe scrubbing sessions, and as a result I hated taking a bath. She would go to work on me with one of those huge brushes whose bristles were so hard they left scratch marks on your skin.

At the time I was too young to understand this, but my mother was a woman of exceptional faith, who had secretly embarked on a spiritual path of her own. Although as children we were well acquainted with stories from both the Old and New Testaments, we had a limited knowledge of other faiths outside of Christianity. Religion, in the traditional sense of worship and adherence, was never practised in our home but was rather enforced by the more fundamental principles of what was morally right or unethical and wrong, as set down in the Ten Commandments.

Although Katalin might to outsiders have appeared to be complacent and happy, she was strict in her ways. Beneath what she allowed to appear on the surface there lurked a deeply sad soul. Every year, in the private confines of her bedroom, my mother would light candles, cover her head with a shawl and pray. Although I was intrigued by this ritual, I was too preoccupied with being a child to give it much thought, and I couldn't really have been bothered with what I saw as one of my mother's eccentricities. Nor did she offer any explanation. It was only years later that I learnt my mother was lighting a Yahrzeit candle in memory of her dearly loved family, who had all perished at the hands of the Nazis in Budapest during 1944.

My memories of my early years are patchy. Although I couldn't have known it at the time, it became evident that I was 'different' and destined not to have a normal life. I do recall suffering from terrible nightmares, when I would wake up crying hysterically to the point of being inconsolable. I developed an intense fear of the dark and had acute claustrophobia. In addition, I was already showing symptoms of the insomnia that would be a problem for me all my life. My sister Joan, whom we called Babi, was quite the opposite: she was a sleepwalker and an adventurous little girl who, besides often roaming around the house in her sleep, was on occasion found strolling in the streets at all hours of the night – fast asleep.

One memory that does still live with me, vividly so, is of an incident that occurred when I was about four years old. I must have just started primary school. My stepfather Janos had transformed the back yard of the property we lived on into a regular animal kingdom. We had chickens, ducks, guinea fowl, turkeys and even a couple of pigs, with their squealing piglets running around. His pride and joy, however, were his racing pigeons.

I was given the task of tending to his birds. This primarily entailed ensuring that they had water and cleaning their cages, and also making sure that the gate leading into their enclosure was bolted at all times. Janos himself took care of feeding them. I guess this had something to do with the master bonding with his birds.

One afternoon, our neighbour's cat managed to get over the 2m-high wall that separated our properties and somehow worked the bolt on the pigeons' cage free from the latch. The cat then proceeded methodically to devour a couple of Janos's most prized birds.

Janos routinely checked all the animals just before dusk.

I was peacefully sorting through my silkworm boxes in my room when I heard Janos repeatedly shouting my name. At first I pretended not to hear him, but when my mother told me that my father required my attention I had no choice. I couldn't fathom what on earth Janos was going on about, as I generally fulfilled all my duties as he instructed. But there was no mistaking from his furious tone, firstly, that something was seriously wrong and, secondly, that I was in trouble. I was frightened, but I reluctantly went to find him.

I walked through the kitchen and out the back door. I passed beneath the mulberry tree where our two German shepherds were stretched out in the late afternoon sunshine. For a moment I wished I could have traded places with one of them. They looked at me soulfully, almost as if they understood what was about to happen. It couldn't have been for more than a few seconds that I allowed my mind to drift. I was just standing there, gazing up at the sky, when Janos's shriek startled me back into reality.

Trembling, I hesitantly approached him. He yelled all sorts of profanities at me in Hungarian – even now I would be embarrassed to repeat them. Next, in a single motion, he grabbed me by my collar, lifted me into the air, and proceeded to shove my face against the fence, pointing with his free hand at the dismembered bodies of the dead pigeons, the remains of which were scattered over the floor of the cage. He accused me of negligence and even threatened to kill me. In his anger he had tightened his grip around my throat and I could feel myself choking and then beginning to black out. All of a sudden, he hurled me to the ground. The next thing I knew I was being punched and kicked repeatedly, and then Janos was beating me with a wooden plank. Half-unconscious, I could hear our dogs barking like crazy. If they hadn't been chained to their kennels, I think they would have ripped Janos to pieces. Those dogs were my best and only friends.

Alerted to the commotion coming from the yard, my mother came running out of the house.

'Leave him alone!' she screamed. 'Have you lost your mind, beating a defenceless child?'

Thank G-d my mother intervened when she did, or I might very well have met the same fate as those wretched pigeons that day. Many years later, when my mother related the incident to me, she told me that I was beaten so badly that I soiled and wet my pants. She kept me at home in bed for nearly a month before I made a full recovery, while my stepfather went about his daily routine as if nothing had happened. The only difference was that from then on he took responsibility for his stupid birds.

I couldn't understand his fascination with his racing pigeons. We would load them into specially designed bird crates and drive in whatever direction for about 30km. Then he would release the birds and, while driving, watch them head directly back home. What was the big deal? I could never get it.

Janos had devised some sort of plan to catch the cat, a ginger tom, that had caused all the trouble, and he waited patiently for it to appear.

One afternoon it returned, and Janos's eyes lit up with excitement. He dashed out of the house and went to the shed, where he pulled on a pair of elbow-length asbestos gloves. Then he took a corn sack and stealthily made his way to the cages, where the cat had already found a way into the coop.

Driven by a mixture of rage and revenge, Janos swooped down on the unsuspecting feline. After what seemed like quite a struggle, he subdued and bagged the shrieking cat. Once inside the sack, the poor animal went berserk. It made me think of a game my sister and I would play in our parents' double bed; we would crawl under the blanket from the bottom end and race to see who could reach the top of the bed first. Sometimes my sister would only pretend to participate and then, as I crept under the blanket, she would pounce on top of me, holding and pressing the blanket down while I wriggled frantically beneath it. The feeling of being trapped was horrible and I would be overcome with claustrophobia. I imagined that was what the poor cat must have been feeling. I couldn't help feeling sorry for it and wondering what awful fate awaited it.

Noticing me watching from a distance, Janos gave me a sort of complacent, psychotic grin that sent a chill up my spine. He walked towards me, holding the sack in one hand, and gestured to me to follow him. As we walked, he said to me in an almost paternal tone that I shouldn't worry, as the cat would never devour another pigeon again. He put his arm round my shoulder, dragging the squirming sack along the gravel behind him. At four years old, I interpreted this unusual display of affection as my being exonerated for the loss of his pigeons. I had no idea what Janos planned to do with the cat.

Janos had two cars. Usually he drove one of his slick, pearl-white two-door Zodiacs, but he had also recently acquired a bakkie. I walked with him into the garage, where he hurled the doomed cat into the back of the bakkie. Then he picked up a 5-litre jerry can of petrol and placed it alongside the sack. We both climbed into the bakkie and Janos drove to an abandoned mine dump. By now it was virtually dark and I could barely make out the surroundings. I didn't understand what was going on, but I remember feeling desperately uncomfortable.

There was something eerily quiet about this place. Without warning Janos slammed on the brakes and the bakkie came to a lurching halt in a cloud of dust. I just about hit my head on the dashboard.

While we waited for the dust to settle we could hear the muffled sounds of the cat still desperately trying to free itself. Janos got out of the bakkie, ordering me to sit tight and wait. Then he removed the jerry can and seized the hessian sack. I watched as he strolled about 5m ahead of where we were parked, directly in my line of vision. He threw the sack onto the ground with violent force. Then he slowly doused it with petrol, struck a match and let it fall.

I watched in fascinated horror as the match seemed to descend in slow motion. I saw the flicker of the flame on contact, and then a huge fireball, so sudden and so big it almost caught Janos's face. The next instant there was the most ghastly screeching from the sack, and after that – silence. Janos stood by, tittering and grunting to himself, while I sat in the cab, frozen in shock and disbelief. In the days, weeks and months that followed, the images of that night never left my mind.

Our house in Orkney was close to all the local amenities. Diagonally opposite us was the predominantly English-speaking Vaal Reef Primary School, which Joan and I attended. A further 100m up the road was the Afrikaans high school, General Smuts Hoërskool. It was massive, and boasted about 1 500 pupils, as well as two rugby fields and an Olympic-size swimming pool.

One of the few boys I made friends with in the neighbourhood lived just up the road from me. His name was Dantjie, and of course Janos, being a great tease, called him 'donkey'. Dantjie was slightly older than me, quite tall and hardly spoke a word of English. Although I spoke fluent Hungarian, my command of English was still shaky, but I knew enough Afrikaans to be able to communicate with him. As we were both bent on getting into mischief at every available opportunity, we made a great team. One of our preferred stunts was shooting our cata-pults at street lights, road signs and birds.

It goes without saying that the odd human being made an enticing target for us, too, and that in most instances, I'm afraid to say, it would be an elderly African man plodding home with his bicycle. Armed with our catapults, we would roam through the open areas of bush at the back of the two schools and follow the dozens of well-worn footpaths that stretched for miles. As we became bolder and more adventurous, Dantjie and I would follow these paths for hours. For the most part we encountered wild rabbits, occasional snakes and meerkats, and we'd pass many Africans travelling by foot from the farms and mines in the area, going to the shops for supplies or visiting friends or relatives in the towns.

Back in those days, security was not as rigorous as it would be today. My school was enclosed by a 2.5m-high perimeter fence of a type typical of the average home at that time. The rear of the school looked onto the bush, which provided refuge for the occasional vagrant and served as a thoroughfare for a constant flow of foot traffic. To prevent intruders from entering the school premises, a barbed-wire barrier, similar to those used by mining companies and factories, was erected on top of the fence. The only other deterrents were a security guard and bold red and white warning boards announcing 'TRESPASSERS WILL BE PROSECUTED' attached to the fence at 50m intervals around the whole of the property.

I knew of one particular classroom in the primary school where all sorts of interesting things were kept. These ranged from antique silver and wooden objects to stuffed animals and jars containing preserved reptiles, and included a vast collection of unfamiliar insects. The place fascinated me, and I'd described the room to Dantjie on a few occasions. One Saturday, as we were heading home after an uneventful excursion into the neighbouring fields, I brought up the subject again. If we could somehow get into that classroom, I suggested to Dantjie, there was a possibility of hidden treasures. The prospect of finding something valuable was all the motivation Dantjie needed.

Unperturbed by the possibility of being caught, we breached the property's defences with relative ease. Once we were inside the empty and quiet building, we made our way to what was actually the biology laboratory. The guard who regularly patrolled the school grounds was nowhere to be seen. Once we reached the classroom, we pressed our faces and hands against the window, hoping that the door might have been left unlocked. As we anticipated, though, it was locked, and none of the windows had been left open either. I knew that Dantjie always carried a penknife with him. Half in English and half in Afrikaans, I urged him to hand it to me. He looked a bit puzzled, but handed it over. I then motioned him to keep lookout and to warn me if he saw any-body coming. With the bigger blade of the penknife I began to remove the putty around the edge of the window that secured the pane of glass to the metal frame. The putty was so dry it came away easily.

Although at the age of five or six I had a fairly good idea of what was right and what was forbidden, I could never have foreseen that this, my first act of breaking and entering, innocently naughty as it was, would be my first step along the path to a life of crime. I guess fate has its way of securing the course that our lives are to follow.

Within a few minutes I had removed the pane of glass. I reached inside and opened the window. Dantjie and I climbed through and then each of us went in our own direction. My attention was drawn to a display of butterflies. I remember being overcome with sadness, see-ing these beautiful creatures reduced to lifeless ornaments. I had never seen a butterfly close up before and I was fascinated by the intricate patterns and brilliant colours of their wings.

I was so spellbound by the various things exhibited around the class-room that I completely lost track of time. Then, as if from a distance, I heard Dantjie's voice telling me in a hushed tone that we had to leave. When I turned around I was astonished to see him clutching tightly in his arms a fairly large replica of a Voortrekker wagon, probably just like the one his ancestors had travelled in. Seeing my expression of disbelief and disapproval, Dantjie's features became set in a mixture of defiance and national pride. It was as if stealing the wagon would, in a sense, be retrieving a part of the heritage that had been surrendered to the English at the turn of the century. Shaking his head in a swift motion, and without saying a word, my friend's resolve was clear. He was asserting ownership of the wagon, irrespective of how I felt.

And who was I to argue? In my child's mind it seemed only fair now that I, too, should help myself to something. Besides knowing full well that if I was caught I would get a severe beating from my parents, I also knew that I was contemplating breaking one of the Ten Commandments. The excitement of taking some sort of a trophy away with me outweighed the fear of being beaten, and any moral sense instilled by my discipline-minded parents vanished in an instant. And, of course, there *was* the likelihood that we might even get away with it. The criminal mind is not much more than a trained opportunist.

My eyes darted around the classroom looking for something I could take as a souvenir. My attention was caught by a fluffy, snow-white rabbit skin. Without giving it a second thought, I grabbed it and stuffed it down the front of my khaki shorts. Then my friend and I left the school property unnoticed. Before parting ways to go to our respective homes, we shook hands and swore each other to secrecy. No matter what, we told each other solemnly, we would never tell anybody what we had done. Satisfied by our agreement, we went our separate ways and home to supper.

During the day our front door was hardly ever locked, so getting into the house was easy, but traversing the oak floors without making a noise was another story altogether. As light-footed as I was, I had barely taken a few steps when the floorboards squeaked loudly.

'Is that you, Shani?'

Unfortunately for me, my mom had acute hearing. Nothing escaped her ears.

'Yes,' I responded innocently, although my heart was thumping. Without paying much attention to me, she told me to go get washed up. Normally, when I returned from one of my escapades in the veld, I would be dirty and my clothes would be covered in the needle-sharp blackjacks that clung to your socks and jersey when you brushed through them. I rushed to my bedroom and hid the rabbit skin under my mattress.

The evening passed without incident. Joan and I ate supper together at the dining room table while my mother waited on us. That night it was Hungarian goulash, a beef and vegetable stew flavoured with red paprika – one of my favourite dishes. Delicious though it was, my mother had a habit of dishing up huge quantities of food, which we almost always found impossible to finish. One of the rules in our house, however, was that we children had to eat everything on our plates, down to the last morsel, before we could be excused from the table. I recall one time when I had eaten so much I was literally choking, and before I could dash to the bathroom I vomited into my plate. My mother forced me to eat the remainder of the food on my plate, along with what I had just regurgitated. I never looked forward to meals, especially supper. Sometimes they felt like torture.

The next day, Sunday, just before lunch, I was in the back yard playing with our Alsatians, my head in the clouds as usual. Yesterday's event was the furthest thing from my mind. By now my rabbit skin was safely stashed away in the old servants' quarters on our property, which had been transformed into a makeshift storeroom.

The people of Orkney were predominantly God-fearing folk who worked on the mines. The town had more churches than supermarkets. Every Sunday, at exactly 10am, the sound of church bells could be heard from every direction. I remember being told by my mom that if I was asked at school what religion we were, to say we were Roman Catholics. Apparently, I had been baptised a Catholic, although we practised no religion in our home. It struck me as strange that neither of my parents nor any of their Hungarian friends ever attended church, but I assumed it was just part of the white South African culture. No Africans worshipped in the white people's churches either.

On weekends our meals were served at a fixed time, which only varied if we had visitors or if Janos decided to braai. Because Janos generally worked night shift, this was the only time that the family ate together.

The hour was fast approaching for Sunday lunch, and then it passed. There was no sign of anybody. Eventually, overcome by pangs of hunger, I decided to go inside to investigate the delay. My mother was not in the kitchen, although the pots on the stove seemed to indicate that lunch was ready. I could hear the faint murmur of conversation coming from the lounge.

Oblivious to the arrival of unexpected guests, I ran into the lounge calling out, in Hungarian, '*Anyu, nagyon ehjes vagyok*' (Mom, I'm starving). Before I could finish my sentence, I skidded to a halt. There, in our lounge, sat Dantjie's parents, staring coldly at me. And resting in the centre of our marble coffee table was the Voortrekker wagon Dantjie had stolen. It looked bigger than I remembered it. Mouth agape, I stood there paralysed and terrified at the same time.

Deep in the pit of my stomach I could feel my insides twisting and knotting. Whenever my wellbeing was threatened, my instinct was to run. My brain and body seemed to be at variance today. There was no-where to go and I knew it. All I could wish for was that whatever my punishment was going to be, that it be swift. The next thing I knew my mother's towering frame was millimetres from my face. I felt a fleeting sense of relief that it was my mother in a fit of rage and not my step-father. Heaven knows what would have befallen me then.

Surprisingly, Janos was beaming. He seemed unusually amused by what was going on. I could have sworn his partiality was a sign that, in an absurd way, he was actually proud of me, but I didn't have time to think this through. My mother grabbed hold of my ear, gave it a sharp twist and violently jerked my head from one shoulder to the other. Was it true, she demanded, that I had broken into the school? She pointed accusingly at the wagon on the coffee table. 'Is it true that you stole that thing? Is it?'

Still tightly holding onto my ear and jerking my head painfully to and fro, she yelled in Hungarian, '*Valaszolj nekem!*', pulling my ear even harder, if that was possible. 'Answer me!'

I looked out of the window, where I could see Dantjie sitting wide-eyed in the rear of his parents' car, which was parked in our driveway. Although the reflection of the sun on the windscreen obscured my view, his diminutive figure portrayed great shame for having betrayed my trust. Strangely, I felt no animosity towards him. I realised, how-ever, that I could no longer be his friend. I was beginning to learn one of the underlying principles that reflect the true nature of a person.

Since I'd run into the lounge neither of Dantjie's parents had uttered a single word, but their silent scrutiny made me feel far worse than the torrents of scorn and anger that were pouring out of my mother's mouth. After being firmly reprimanded and warned that Dantjie and I were never to see each other again, I was dismissed and told that I would be dealt with later.

Once our visitors had left, I was instructed to fetch the rabbit skin from its hiding place. Armed with the largest wooden spoon we had in the kitchen, my mother followed me outside to the storeroom. Before I could even open the door, she had taken hold of my arm and begun to hit me on my tender buttocks with the spoon. I jumped and danced around her in circles, crying out with every lash. The pain was terrible. Eventually, the wooden spoon broke, but this didn't stop her from exacting further punishment by slapping me around with her hands.

All things considered, perhaps in the end I got off relatively lightly. On Monday morning my mother accompanied my sister and me to school. She met with the principal, returned the wagon and the rabbit skin and apologised for my behaviour. She explained that I had already been punished, adding that, in the event that he had any trouble with me in the future, he had my parents' permission to deal with me in whatever manner he saw fit.

After this episode, the humiliation and embarrassment of being labelled a thief did deter me from stealing again – for a while. Despite the fact that we learn many of life's lessons the hard way, I continued to be a difficult child. I constantly misbehaved and refused to comply with the rigid regulations imposed by my parents, although I think, for the most part, they just misunderstood me.

As Joan and I got older, our parents became more innovative with their forms of punishment. These varied from being lashed with a steel coat hanger to being locked inside a wardrobe for hours. The coat hanger was Janos's favourite device because it inflicted the most pain, leaving bruises and at times drawing blood. But I found the confined space in the cupboard the most traumatic and I feared this punishment more than any other.

My mother, after having to replace many a wooden spoon, introduced a more practical measurement of punishment, which involved very little effort on her part but turned out to be more effective than any of the other more physical measures she and Janos employed in keeping us in line. She would take a soup bowl, fill it to the brim with uncooked rice, and pour the grains onto the tiled kitchen floor. There she would carefully arrange the rice into two mounds on which my sister and I were required to kneel, our arms crossed, for whatever length of time matched the severity of the misdeed. It's difficult to describe the discomfort and pain of kneeling on rice. Suffice it to say that, when the allotted time was up, I recall having literally to scratch and pick out the grains that had embedded themselves in my skin.

Another punishment Janos liked to use when Joan and I were naughty or our clothes got dirty would be to force us to wear these huge sacks that were normally used for mielies. He had cut holes in the top to make openings for our arms, and, with no clothes on underneath, we'd have to put on these rough, scratchy sacks and walk around in them until he told us we could take them off.

Although my parents were unrelenting in their assertion of authority and exercise of discipline, our lives seemed no different really from those of the other suburban families who were our neighbours and friends. Remember that, in the 1960s, attitudes towards children were archaic in comparison to today's more progressive outlook, especially among the Eastern European immigrant community.

When I was growing up, if a kid was naughty nobody in his right mind would consider that kid to have some kind of psychological problem that might require therapy. Kids were considered to be resilient and were largely left to develop on their own. It was unheard of for a child to see a psychologist or to take medication. Conditions such as ADD (attention deficit disorder) went completely undiagnosed. Problems at school, such as poor concentration, learning difficulties and hyperactivity were usually regarded as behavioural problems, for which children were punished. From age five I was probably already showing signs of having ADD, but I didn't think I was any different from most kids that age, and presumed I would improve as I got older.

In all fairness to our parents, who might have failed as our guardians because they lacked some basic parenting skills, and whose attempts to nurture and educate us weren't always effective, equally there were happy and exciting moments in my childhood, and extended periods of normal family life. There was always food in plenty and we were never short of anything. Janos made good money on the mines. An outsider would probably have said we were an ideal family.

One memorable moment when I was happy as a kid was when I got my first bicycle. Another time, Janos built me a go-kart using a wooden frame and the wheels from my old pram. When we were old enough, my sister and I went everywhere on our bikes. My mother was a gardening enthusiast and our front garden flourished with a variety of indigenous flowers and fruit trees while the driveway was lined with rose bushes – which we crashed into many a time trying too fast to negotiate the turn on our bikes.

Janos had a distillery in which he made a drink called *pálinka* (like schnapps, and really strong) from apricots. From when I was about five he used to encourage me to drink it.

A few months after the school incident, while out on my bicycle I decided to make a turn at Dantjie's house, in the hope of a chance meeting. To my surprise and dismay, the house was empty and the garden neglected, with weeds growing everywhere. I felt a deep sense of loss, knowing that I would probably never see my friend again.

It wasn't too long after that that Janos was transferred.

Moving house was a headache. Everything had to be packed into cardboard boxes, and breakable items had to be padded in newspaper. My mom had a collection of rare porcelain dishes, along with other glass ornaments and vases that she proudly displayed in an antique cabinet. My sister and I were required to help wrap these items, which inevitably resulted in breakages. Tensions ran high and everybody seemed on edge, especially my mother, who supervised the whole move. In the interim one of our German shepherds, Nero, the smaller of the two, had contracted rabies and had to be put down. The other dog, Pajtas, was given to the police.

I was heartbroken about leaving our dog behind, but at the same time I was excited at the prospect of moving to another town. And the thought of no longer being required to work in Janos's little animal kingdom – he reluctantly gave his pigeons to one of his friends – was an added bonus.

We moved to Westonaria, a mining town on the West Rand. Part of the benefits of working for mining companies is that they provide subsidised housing. We were given a brand-new home in a modern housing development on top of the hill about 15km outside town. The roads were not even tarred, so new was this development, and although the house itself was slightly smaller than our old one, my mom was thrilled at the idea of having a new kitchen. This time, our school wasn't within walking distance and Joan and I had to catch a bus. After school, it would drop us at the bottom of the hill and we would have to walk the distance to our house, which after a long day at school was quite strenuous. I was about six years old.

Although I was not outstanding at school, I was showing signs of being intuitive and an above-average student. It was around the time I was in Standard 1, when a whole new range of subjects was introduced, that I have my earliest recollection of starting to express myself by scribbling with a pen or pencil on whatever surface was available. Drawing was an instinctive force within me. My peers and teachers began to recognise my talents. They were amazed by my illustrations and by my ability to blend colours. I was awarded gold stars for those subjects where we could illustrate our projects and our poems, such as Geography and English. Any subject that required us to draw or illustrate certain functions relating to the subject earned me high praise and recognition.

In the afternoons, while we waited for the bus, we would play games – marbles for the boys, hopscotch for the girls. Another favourite was a game called fly, where three sticks were placed on the grass about a metre apart and parallel to each other. You would run and leap over the first stick but you were only allowed one step before clearing the second stick and then the third. Taking off between the second and third stick, you would try to give a mighty jump to clear the third stick by as wide a margin as you could. Then you would move the third stick to the place you'd landed, thereby widening the distance between the sticks and making it more difficult for the next kid to clear. If you jumped and touched the stick, or landed with two feet or took more than one step in between the sticks, you were out.

One afternoon, when I was still very new at the school, I got so caught up playing fly with some of the other kids that I missed the bus. The bus usually came pretty late anyway, so by this time the school was deserted, and there was nobody around I could ask for a lift home. The only thing for it was to walk home, which I believed I could do even though I didn't know the area very well yet. All I could think about, though, was my mother's anger while she contemplated my punishment, so I set off as fast as my small legs could walk. Once I reached the outskirts of the town, the rest of the way was easy. All I had do was walk along two stretches of road that connected to the other at a T-junction. After a while my schoolbag felt really heavy on my back and my legs ached. Then an African commuter bus pulled up alongside me, and the driver leaned across and shouted out to me in Afrikaans, 'Waar gaan die kleinbaas?' (Where is the small boss going?)

I pointed towards the hill. Although I couldn't really see the driver, I could hear him encouraging me to jump on. I hurriedly clambered up the huge metal steps, thanking him, and then I stood there clinging to the railing as the bus jerkily moved forward. Once we reached the T-junction, the driver pulled over again. He was turning left and I was going in the opposite direction. I climbed down the steps and set off again on foot. There was a lot more traffic on this road, and cars whooshed past me in both directions. Then a woman stopped her car beside me and she gave me a lift home. Filled with a mixture of triumph at having successfully navigated the way from school to house and nervousness about my mother's reaction, I pushed open our front gate. It always made a screaming sound when you opened it, but before I had time to close it behind me Mom came flying out of the house. Tears streaming down her cheeks, she shrieked at me and swept me off my feet at the same time, holding me tightly against her chest with both arms. 'Don't ever do that again, Shani,' she pleaded. 'Don't you *ever* do that again.'

I was not accustomed to either of my parents displaying such affection and I found myself unable to control my own tears. My mother was just relieved that I was home and safe, and for once she didn't punish me. She was more angry with Babi, my sister Joan, who had neglected to make sure I was on the bus. From that moment on, Babi was given the responsibility of always keeping an eye on me, and, to my mind, she took her newly acquired maternal duties a little too seriously. Sometimes she made my life sheer hell with her bossiness.

After our move to Westonaria there was a distinct change in the atmosphere in our family. My mother and Janos hardly seemed to quarrel any more. Perhaps it had something to do with the highveld air, and we did all spend a lot of time outdoors. It was also around this time that I acquired a passion for building and flying kites.

My stepfather was a keen hunter and he would regularly go on overnight hunting expeditions, returning with all sorts of game, from which my mom prepared her range of lavish dishes. I was about eight years old when, after much pleading, Janos reluctantly agreed to take me with him on one of his hunting trips.

It was late afternoon when we set off, after loading the bakkie with supplies. Janos drove to an area of rugged terrain not too far from where we lived. He parked the van and we got out and looked around. He charged his gun belt with shotgun shells and I filled my pockets with pellets. I was hoping to shoot some rock pigeons with my air rifle. Janos took his double-barrelled shotgun and we trudged along in the direction of some forest, while he took me through the do's and don'ts of hunting. It was almost dark by the time we approached the cluster of dense trees. Janos instructed me to wait beside a huge decaying trunk that seemed to be the refuge of all sorts of creepy-crawlies, and I didn't much like the look of it. Sensing my apprehension, he placed his hand on the back of my neck, assuring me that he wouldn't be too far, and that I had nothing to worry about. His paternal gesture did very little to comfort me. Struggling to hide my indignation at being left behind, I grudgingly accepted that I had no choice but to wait, as apparently my presence on the hunt would be more of a hindrance than anything else.

Janos disappeared into the forest. As soon as he was out of sight, I was paralysed with fear. Holding tightly onto my air rifle, I did a quick reconnaissance of my surroundings, while my vivid imagination replayed numerous possible scenarios, most of which ended with me being devoured by some ferocious beast. I had never felt so scared, alone or vulnerable. I wondered what had possessed me to think hunting was fun. I anxiously looked around for a place to hide and noticed a large boulder a few metres away. It stuck up amid the dense bush and was shielded by a group of wild thorn trees. I thought it would offer a view of the dark landscape as well as provide safety from any prowling predators.

Silently perched on what I now considered my stronghold, my senses adapted to the darkness, and I took in all the enchanted and mystical undertones that emanated from the forest. The sounds ranged from the cooing of the rock pigeons, the flirting of small birds and the slithering motions of snakes to the musical chirping of the male African cricket. I imagined I heard the steps of some carnivorous animal, too, as well as the distinctive doleful howl of a hyena.

Then, after what seemed like hours, the harmony of nature was shattered by the loud thunder of a shotgun discharging. Birds that had nested for the night blindly rose up and scattered in every direction. I got the fright of my life. I had estimated Janos to be some distance from where he'd left me but it sounded like he was very close by. Despite the shock of the noise, I was also comforted by his presence. Then, at spaced intervals, sometimes firing two consecutive shots, I could hear that he was moving further and further away from me. I was scared, but it heightened my vigilance. I wondered if Janos would ever return.

Eventually, to my intense relief, my stepfather did come back. On his approach he gave a hoot that was a perfect imitation of the low, wavering call of an owl, and at the same time, in his usual bellicose manner, he called out to me in Hungarian.

'*Shani! Hol a fenebe vagy mar?*' (Where the fuck are you?)

Silently I descended from my hiding place. 'Here,' I replied nonchalantly, as I strolled towards him. 'I'm here.'

Janos held a couple of dead guinea fowl and pheasant in his hands.

'*Fogd mar meg ezt es menjunk a francba,*' he said, throwing them down at my feet (Grab these already and let's get the fuck out of here).

Although I was used to being around slain animals, having been taught to wring the neck of a chicken at age five, I was squeamish at the sight of blood. Whenever Janos brought home game he had shot, I couldn't help feeling pangs of remorse for the dead creatures.

The one positive result of my first hunting mission, however, which I wasn't aware of at the time, was that I overcame my fear of darkness and my nightmares ended. There were several occasions after this when Janos took me hunting, and each time my confidence grew, making these trips more interesting and adventurous for me. Janos even allowed me to fire his shotgun. The first time, I almost dislocated my shoulder. There were times when we would sleep out in the bush and Janos would skin and disembowel a rabbit and cook it over a fire for dinner. I felt at one with nature. Being outdoors produced in me a certain tranquillity and sense of inner peace. I remember these outings with fondness.

After we had been living in Westonaria for about three years, Janos got fed up with working on the mines. His restlessness was compounded by constantly having to work night shift. In addition, there had recently been a series of accidents in which miners had been trapped underground, with many dying of suffocation before rescue workers could reach them.

It was time for change, so once again we moved. This time we went to the fast-developing industrial town of Vanderbijlpark, where my mother and my biological father Fritz had first lived when they came to South Africa. The main reason for moving here, besides employment opportunities, was the presence of the Hungarian community. My half-sister Marika and her husband Bela lived in Vanderbijlpark, and they now had a new baby daughter, Zsuzsika, which meant that I was an uncle. Most of the Hungarians in the area either knew each other personally or had connected at one time or another, and everyone figured in the gossip that was so prevalent within that small European community.

There was also an intricate but reliable network that helped people to track down relatives or friends who, like my own parents, had fled the Soviet crackdown in 1956, in the course of which entire families had been split up. The need to reunite lost family members was still very much alive among Hungarian exiles.

Our family took up residence in a modern apartment block called Kronendaal Heights, where we occupied a two-bedroomed flat. This meant I had to share a room with Joan, not a happy situation for me. Our flat was on the ground floor directly adjacent to the entrance, where there was a suite of doctors' rooms. The smell of sterile liquid always seemed to hang in the passageway, which triggered in me a phobia of doctors and hospitals. In front of the building was a swimming pool encircled by a well-manicured, lush green lawn, a variety of tropical trees, ferns and bushes, and a steel fence.

The change from living in virtual isolation on the hill to the hustle and bustle of a large town was invigorating. Joan and I were enrolled in Oliver Lodge Primary School, which was right behind our building. Next door was a church. By now I was nine or ten years of age and in Standard 3.

There were many nationalities in Vanderbijlpark – Greek, Portuguese, Scots, Italian and English-speaking South Africans – and this made life so much more interesting at school. The kids were generally friendlier, and everyone seemed to know one another. Some of the kids in my class were already physically well developed; some even had facial hair.

Our teachers had a liberal attitude, as the majority of foreigners had difficulty keeping up with the rest of the class. The lax discipline gave the school a certain ambience that also encouraged a degree of unruliness.

One year, we went on a school tour to Rhodesia where we visited the Victoria Falls. A group of us were standing really close to the edge, looking down, when one of my friends slipped. I managed to grab his collar and prevent him from going over the edge. I didn't give it much thought at the time, but the memory of how lucky he was has always stuck with me.

Another time, while at the Wankie Game Reserve, I was in the toilet when I was confronted by three older kids. Although they were in my standard at school, they were all a good three years older than me. They cornered me and one of them took out his dick and tried to force himself on me. It was a terrifying experience, feeling all these hands trying to subdue me. I wrestled and wriggled, punched and kicked my way free. I never ever spoke about the incident to anyone.

In Vanderbijlpark social events were organised regularly on the weekend. There were private parties or discos, which were held at one of the many church halls, or people would meet up at the local movie house to see the latest Hollywood blockbuster. Then there was the renowned Mikado bioscope, also known as 'the bughouse', where two feature films were run and re-run the entire day. The bughouse attracted some fairly unsavoury customers – me being one of them – who would make a day of it.

The Mikado was owned by a Hungarian woman who was married to a Portuguese man. Her name was Manya and she was a good friend of my mother. She used to let me in for free. From a very young age I loved movies. When the lights dimmed and that big screen sputtered into life, I was propelled into a world of fantasy, and my own reality ceased to exist. My favourite films were Westerns, but somehow I always found myself identifying more with the Indian warriors who, though lacking the firepower of the cowboys, were far superior when it came to surviving in the bush. I loved especially the 'spaghetti Westerns' starring Clint Eastwood – *The Good, the Bad and the Ugly*, *For a Few Dollars More* and *A Fistful of Dollars*. I had a comprehensive personal collection of film posters, and these became my pride and joy.

In the diversity of the communities and nationalities in our town, we came to associate certain groups with certain things. For example, the Portuguese controlled all the fresh fruit and vegetable shops, the Greeks monopolised the corner café and fish and chip outlets, the Germans and Swiss exercised exclusive rights over the specialised engineering industries, the Lebanese had second-hand car dealerships, and the Afrikaners farmed the land and occupied most of the civil service positions.

The Italians, renowned for their culinary skills, introduced their cuisine through a fast-growing chain of classy restaurants, while our esteemed Jewish counterparts, noted for being astute businessmen but wrongly perceived as extortionist moneylenders, occupied the more distinguished positions in the medical profession, and also dominated the wholesale and clothing industries.

Hungarians were commonly known as being jacks of all trades and masters of none. While some of the men were qualified tradesmen, many were involved in less honourable professions and in shady dealings. These extended from prostitution, gambling and pornography to illegal trading in uncut diamonds. In a country where it was rumoured that diamonds the size of pebbles washed up on the shore and gold nuggets could be found in the street, the desire for success by whatever means possible could be easily justified. Besides providing for one's immediate family and establishing one's roots in a foreign country, there was the added moral obligation of financially assisting relatives back home in Budapest.

Although Hungarians played hard, partying was restricted to one night during the week and to the weekends.

One Sunday morning, when I was ten years old, my mother told Joan and me to put on our best clothes. She had a surprise for us. At first I thought she was taking us to church for some reason, although the only time G-d was mentioned in our home was when someone was cursing. It turned out that Janos was going to take us to meet some-one – and this someone turned out to be our real father, Fritz, who was living right there in Vanderbijlpark. I can't say I remember what I was feeling – probably nothing. My biological father had abandoned me at a very young age; Janos, although he was abusive and regularly beat the crap out of me, was more of a father presence in my life than anybody else. I suppose you could say I was nervous. All I knew about my dad was that, according to my mother, whenever I was angry with someone, I would say that that person was 'no better than my bastard pig father'. Not a great legacy so far.

Janos drove us in his car. We pulled up next to a three-storey apartment building above a café at an intersection on a main road. After telling us where to go, Janos drove off, leaving Joan and I standing on the pavement. For a moment we stood there in silence. Then Joan took my hand and said, 'Let's go meet our father.'

A half-drunk Hungarian man opened the door to us. We stepped into a flat filled with smoke. There were at least six other men present, sitting around a table playing cards. The lounge and dining room area was one room and quite spacious. My eyes darted around as I wondered which one of these men was my father. If I'd had a choice, I wouldn't have chosen any of them. It didn't matter anyway as he was as much of a stranger to me as all of them.

The man who had let us in called out, 'Hey, Fritz! Here are your kids.'

My father was slumped in one of the chairs in the lounge. It seemed to be a great effort for him to get up and greet us. I'm not sure if this was because he was drunk or whether it was out of a lack of interest. His breath reeked of alcohol and cigarettes. His attention went straight to Joan. He hugged and kissed her, saying how he couldn't believe how big she had grown. Then he looked at me, his eyes moving from my head to my toes. He stretched out his hand and, reluctantly, I shook it. I'm not sure why he didn't hug me. Joan sat on his knee while I sat down on the couch opposite them. He didn't look anything like me. He was balding, and what hair he had was combed back slickly with Brylcreem. And he was not a big man; for some reason I had thought he would be.

Fritz asked us about our mother, school and other stuff like that. Then he said, and I'm still not sure if he was joking or not, that Joan was his daughter but that I was not his son. He seemed to find this very funny. Apparently he was convinced that my mother had had an affair with Janos when they were still together and that I was the result. As the morning progressed, he did little to impress me. He was quick to tell us that he was getting remarried to an Afrikaner woman named Anna-Marie who had five of her own children, the youngest of whom was a boy my age, Christo. He said he had just got a job at the Iscor steelworks and would be staying in Vanderbijlpark and that we would be seeing a lot more of him. I don't think it was me that he wanted to see, but rather my sister, and I couldn't wait to get away from there.

When Janos came to fetch us, he asked how the visit had gone. I asked him if it was true that he was my father. He denied this, so the question was, who really *was* my father? At home my mother tried to convince me that Fritz was in fact my dad but I wasn't convinced. I didn't care. Fathers, in my opinion, were people the world could do without.

After that first time we visited Fritz fairly often; I became good friends with Christo, his stepson. We went to boxing classes together and generally got up to mischief. Fritz changed his attitude towards me after my mother talked to him, but neither of us ever expressed much recognition of our blood tie. I never could accept him as my father. I felt nothing for him. Besides Christo, Anna-Marie's other kids were already grown up. She and Fritz enjoyed drinking, as it turned out, and Fritz would bash her up every now and again. This would lead to him getting a hiding from one of her sons. How dysfunctional could you get?

Just as I was beginning Standard 5, my mother dumped Janos. At first it was strange not having him around, but I can't say I missed him.

Mom got a job at Iscor, where she ran the canteen, which meant that my sister and I had the run of the house while she was at work. That was disastrous. It seems we had inherited our parents' fighting spirit and we fought like cat and dog. My mother did her best to bring up two strong-willed individuals on her own, but being a single parent wasn't easy. We were difficult to control, and she constantly threatened to send us to boarding school if we didn't get along. Stubborn as we were, we paid no heed to her warnings.

In early December, in the summer of 1971, one day my mother left for work much earlier than normal and returned unusually late that evening. Besides the regular chitchat at dinner, she offered no explanation. Later in the evening, after taking our respective baths and just before bedtime, we were summoned to her bedroom, where she seated us one on either side of her. I had never before seen my mom so pensive and tormented. Her subdued posture made it obvious that we were in for something unpleasant. She took our hands, and, in a solemn and melancholy tone, she began to explain that, since her separation from Janos, it had become increasingly difficult for her to make ends meet, and that now she could no longer support us. In addition, she was on the verge of a nervous breakdown, worrying about us and our future.

She then revealed what she had been doing that day: she had been to Johannesburg to confirm and finalise our acceptance and admission into Arcadia, a Jewish orphanage. Then she told us that we would be leaving first thing in the morning. Joan began to cry, tearfully protesting that we were not orphans and that she couldn't send us away. We belonged with our mother.

My mother's eyes, in turn, filled with tears and I saw that her lips were quivering. There followed an awkward moment of silence as she did her best to compose herself. She wasn't finished. She said there was something else very important that we needed to know. We listened attentively as she told us how, when she was a young girl, in 1944, her parents, Margit Blanca Hecht and Shandor Sinkowitz, had been taken away by the Nazis in the dead of night. She had had three uncles, her father's brothers, who had all been killed before the war. She had witnessed her sisters, brothers, uncle and aunts and their children being taken away, loaded into cattle cars and sealed freight trains, and sent to the gas chambers where they, along with millions of other Jews, were exterminated. She also spoke of a stepsister who had been shot and killed for no reason other than that she was a Jew. My mother took refuge in the ghetto and managed to survive among the community there. She got some work in a shoe factory. Then the SS came and rounded up all the Jews in the factory. They lined them up and took them away to be shot. One of the soldiers, however, took a liking to her and pulled her out of the line. Eventually the war ended and, miraculously, my mother had survived its hell.

By this time, all three of us were in tears. My mom said that she hoped one day we would understand her reluctance to share the tragedy that had befallen her family, and she tried, too, to describe the apprehension she'd felt about teaching us the way of our forefathers, Abraham, Isaac and Jacob. But now that we were old enough, she'd decided, it was our right by birth to know the truth and seeing that we were about to embark on a new life, where we would be among our own people, we should be proud of our heritage, and free to learn the traditions of our religion which, G-d willing, we would one day hand down to our children and they to theirs.

Tears continued to fall from my mom's eyes as she hugged us tightly and begged us to forgive her for failing in her duties as a mother. She promised that she would be in constant contact with us and would visit regularly. She also stressed that Joan and I should always love and protect each other, no matter what, and that we should strive to be good and righteous. She told us never to forget that she loved us more than anything in this world, and that it broke her heart to let us go. To this day her words that night and the memory of that moment resonate in my head, and whenever I think of it the tears still come.

Chapter 2

Arcadia

The period of time between my mother's heart-rending disclosures and our arrival at Arcadia remains something of a blur for me, but I do remember the desolate moment at the orphanage when Joan and I tearfully wished her farewell. At the same time we were greeted and welcomed by the compassionate smiles of Doc and Ma Lichtigfeld. The trauma of being separated from my mother, the imposing buildings that were to be our new home, and the sheer size and grandeur of the property all rendered me speechless.

I felt so many emotions: abandoned, lost, confused and anxious about what sort of cruel and deprived existence awaited us beyond the huge double wooden doors that graced the entrance to Arcadia. Joan and I were ushered to our respective departments. She was taken to the junior girls' section; I went to the new boys' department, which was formerly the hospital. There I was received by the principal, Sydney Klevansky, aka Vicky, whose cheerful disposition immediately dismissed all notions of malevolence that, until then, I'd associated with boarding schools.

After the grand tour, Vicky showed me to my dormitory. I understood that the other occupants – David and Sammy Lasker, Charles Goldman and Glen Osher – were roughly my age. The December school holidays had already begun and some of the Arcadia children were on vacation with their parents, while the majority had either gone out for the day or were preparing to do so. Vicky introduced me to Charles, who was on his way out to the bioscope, and instructed him to help me settle in. Running late, Charles apologetically excused himself but casually pointed in the direction of his wardrobe, saying that he was in a hurry, but, if I felt like it, there was a pile of comics in his bottom drawer. I was welcome to help myself.

With all the excitement and upheaval of the past 14 hours, I was suddenly overcome with exhaustion. I think I was asleep even before my head hit the pillow. I couldn't have slept for more than an hour and a half, though, before I woke up. After freshening up, I set about to unpack my things. When my mom was arranging our admission to the Arc, as everyone called it, she had been told that we wouldn't need to bring anything with us besides the clothes on our backs, as they would take care of all our needs. Luckily, Joan and I had brought some clothing and toiletries with us, as it later became apparent that the only clothes supplied by the Arc were donated and second-hand items, most of them unwearable.

When I was finished unpacking I decided to check out Charles' comic books. I sat on the floor in front of the wardrobe, pulled open the bottom drawer and systematically began removing all the comics. I discovered that he had an extensive collection of some of my favourites, and I was drawn irresistibly into a sanctuary of make-believe.

All of a sudden, the swing door that led into our dormitory was flung violently open. Seconds later, a figure was towering over me aggressively and demanding to know what the hell I thought I was doing. I was stunned. Before I could answer, the boy began punching and kicking me and accusing me of being a thief. Instinctively, I raised my arm to protect my face and pulled my knees to my chest to block the blows and kicks, just as I did when I got a hiding from Janos. This beating wasn't too severe, though, nor did it last long. I had had far worse from my stepfather. It ended with me being hurled across the length of the room. As I crashed to the floor, it dawned on me that the beginning of my so-called new life rather closely resembled the world I thought I had left behind. I prepared myself for the worst.

I later learnt that the person responsible for my undeserved hiding was none other than the acting head boy, Danny Lasker, who from that day on became my sworn enemy. My sister was furious when she heard what had happened to me, and went at once to confront him. She strongly advised him to get his facts straight before he found it necessary to get physical, and warned him in no uncertain terms that if he ever dared lay a finger on her brother again, he would have to deal with her.

I cannot recall ever having any problems with Danny after that, although most of us juniors were roughed up by the seniors from time to time. We accepted this as part of life in Arcadia.

Those early days were hard. I had no knowledge of Judaism, and, having been brought up as a Hungarian, not to mention thinking that I was a Catholic, I was different. The other kids were more than willing to teach me and help me out. One day when I was showering I noticed something odd: all the other boys were circumcised, while I had a foreskin. I didn't know why but it made me feel uncomfortable, so much so that I tried to hide it and thereafter took my shower after everybody else was finished. In the event that somebody came to the bathroom, I would pull my foreskin back, which made it look as if I, too, were circumcised. Somebody must have noticed, though, and one of the seniors spoke to the principal. Before I knew it I was booked into the Brenthurst Clinic.

On a Saturday night a couple of days after my operation, we had a disco at Arcadia. The majority of the younger kids went to Saxonwold Primary School, and many of their friends came to the dance. It was here that I met a pretty girl named Andy Raven, who may have been slightly younger than me. She had long black hair that cascaded down her shoulders almost to her lower back. While we were slow dancing and she was really close, I became aroused and experienced an instant pain in my groin. Without saying a word to her, I ran to the toilet and pulled down my pants. My stitches were stretching and the wound had opened up. No more slow dancing for me that night! The revelation of me being Jewish was both painful and interestingly educational as I began to embrace the culture bestowed upon me by my maternal grandparents.

During school holidays the children in the orphanage who weren't able to spend the holidays with their loved ones had the choice of either going to Durban and staying with a Jewish family there (Joan chose this option) or attending Bnei Akiva youth camp down on the coast. From the first year at Arcadia this was what I opted for. Going to Bnei Akiva camp was the best thing that ever happened to me in those early days at Arcadia. Each of us at the home had, at some stage in our young lives, experienced things that were too painful to think about, let alone talk about. Those experiences would nevertheless have a profound impact on the way we thought and functioned. Not only did Bnei Akiva enable me suppress some difficult childhood memories, but it also gave me a sense of belonging and worth. Finally I could begin to embrace what appeared to represent the beginning of a more wholesome life.

Instruction in Judaism, and the requirement to keep Shabbos (the Sabbath) and daven (pray) three times a day, formed an integral part of our routine. I remember one year, on our return from camp, Danny had become much more religious and was influential in encouraging some of us to become more observant and devoted. It was also compulsory for all the children to learn basic Hebrew.

In 1972, Doc and Ma retired. The new incumbents at Arcadia were Philip and Sylvia Duzzy, and their arrival coincided with preparation for my Bar Mitzvah, the ceremony where a Jewish boy of 13 years old becomes recognised as an adult. There were three of us who were having our Bar Mitzvah. Mr Duzzy was an excellent *chazzan* (cantor) and he taught me my Bar Mitzvah portion, but, because my Hebrew wasn't up to scratch, I learnt it by rote. I dreaded my sessions with Mr Duzzy. He had the most terrible breath, which made me even more eager to learn my Torah portion as quickly as possible.

Then the big day finally arrived when I became a man and could now be counted as one of the *minyan*, the quorum of ten Jewish adults required for certain religious obligations when worshipping in the synagogue. The *shul* was packed. The only relatives of mine who were there were my mother and sister, but my good friend Harry from Parktown Boys' High School came along, too. I was dreading standing on the *bima* and singing in front of all the guests. My legs were shaking. When it came to my turn to sing, one of the senior Arc boys, Gary Joffee, attempted secretly to record me by trying to work between my legs a microphone attached to a cassette recorder. He kept touching me, and, as nervous as I already was, having him fiddling around between my legs made it even more difficult for me to concentrate.

The atmosphere in the *shul* was incredibly spiritual. Everybody was silent. I felt as if *Hashem* was there, watching and blessing me as I made my transition into manhood. After the reception, and when all the guests were gone, we boys sat on our beds checking out our gifts. Unlike the other boys, I received only a few envelopes with vouchers and cash.

A few months after Joan and I went to live at Arcadia, our mother went back to Hungary. She stayed in touch, but her visits during our time there were periodic and never for very long. After a couple of years she returned to South Africa and stayed for a while with friends in Vanderbijlpark and Johannesburg. Then she went back to Budapest again and would come out on holiday when she could. When she did come to see us, she brought gifts of clothing and toiletries. For her, these visits were always emotional, and I think they brought her as much pain as they did joy.

As for me, I loved it at Arcadia and it did not take me long to adjust to life there and to accept that this was my home. While I enjoyed my mother's visits, I didn't really understand the emotion around them or whether I needed to feel anything. The fact that she came to see us whenever she could, as she had promised, showed us that she cared, but I never wanted to leave when she left or to consider a life outside of the life I had made at Arcadia.

My two fathers – Fritz, my biological father, and Janos, whose negative influence in my tender years remains with me to this day – played no active role in my life. My sister Joan was my family.

Television came to South Africa in 1976, and I remember the occasion when Arcadia received its first set. It had been donated by a benefactor and there was a whole ceremony to mark its arrival. Many of us refused to pose for the photo because we saw the whole affair as a publicity stunt intended to glorify the benefactor and to an extent humiliate the recipients. Some Arcs were sensitive to this type of exhibitionism; in comparison to our peers from the different schools we attended, we led an underprivileged lifestyle and we didn't need to have it rubbed in. Nevertheless, this did not diminish our excitement and enthusiasm at actually having our very own TV.

On the first night that we were going to witness the debut of the new phenomenon, everyone scrambled to get to the library straight after dinner to try and get the best seats. The table where I ate was right next to the entrance to the dining room and adjacent to the committee room, and so I was the first to reach the door. I grabbed the door handle and yanked, expecting the door to fly open. It was locked. By then most of the kids were piling up behind me and a slight commotion of chatter and confusion ensued as we impatiently waited for the door to be opened. Then we heard the clanging of keys and an all too familiar voice, shouting with authority.

'Line, line, line up!'

It was Vicky.

The muttering of discontented kids persisted in a low moan as a few of us reluctantly began to form a semblance of a queue. Then, before I could stop myself, I yelled, 'Would you like us to buy tickets as well?' This was greeted with an outburst of laughter by the other children, but Vicky didn't appreciate my witticism.

'Get to your room! You are punished. No television for you!' he shouted, grabbing me by the arm.

'Who wants to watch stupid TV anyway?' I mumbled cockily under my breath as I made my exit.

As they watched me go, everyone fell silent. It was as if there was a collective realisation that, in future, this form of entertainment would also become an instrument of punishment.

Although the novelty of television had worn off even before I got to watch it, my spirits weren't that easily dampened. I was only too aware of the conveniences the TV room had to offer. I settled down in my dormitory, but before long I was summoned by Vicky. He put his arm around my neck, pulled me into his embrace, and in an apologetic tone said that I was welcome to go and watch TV if I wanted to. I thanked him and expressed my regret at my disrespectful outburst. I think I learnt a very important lesson that night: it didn't matter who was wrong or who was right in a confrontation: in order to pacify or bring about a cessation of hostilities between two parties, an apology went a long way. This would stand me in good stead many times in my life.

In the weeks and months that followed, the library, which officially became known as the TV room, became a refuge and a safe haven from the many distractions that were part of everyday life in Arcadia. For those of us who, on occasion, bunked out of the home, the TV room also became our alibi. When asked where we'd been we would innocently respond: 'We were watching TV.'

Watching TV also gave us the opportunity to get intimate with the girls. I mean, what could be more romantic than watching *The Brady Bunch* of a Friday evening while holding your girlfriend's hand?

When I was about 14 years old, puberty set in with a vengeance. My interest in the opposite sex was becoming fervently apparent. By then Sammy Lasker, Charles Goldman and I were well into our unrelenting reign of mischief, and there wasn't a single room in Arcadia or a building in its vicinity that we couldn't get into. However, most of our attention was focused on the girls, especially the seniors. One favourite activity was to target a girl and stalk her. Then one of us would distract her while the other would come from behind and look up her dress. Sometimes we even used this ploy on our female teachers.

The ideal focus for our prying adolescent eyes was the public telephone. Here, the girls seemed to spend hours on end talking to their boyfriends and not focusing on anything else. A pen-size flashlight became an indispensable commodity for us, and Charles Goldman also kept a small mirror permanently in his pocket. We eventually got bored with this game, though. We wanted to see the real thing – a completely naked woman. And so this became our mission.

At that time I was secretly in love with one of the girls at Arcadia. She oozed femininity and had all the qualities that appealed to me, so we began to devise a cunning plan to see her without her clothes on. After several failed attempts, we figured that the best time would be on a Saturday morning, just before lunch and before the senior girls returned from a morning basking in the sun at the swimming pool, which was a regular activity in summer. Sammy and I swam and sunbathed, the picture of innocence, while inconspicuously keeping an eye on her. She was the type of girl you couldn't help staring at anyway, and no doubt she was accustomed to it. After a while she began gathering her things together and preparing to go indoors. Sammy and I sprang into action. We sprinted to the senior girls' dormitory.

After some careful manoeuvring, we managed to sneak into her room unnoticed. I hid under her bed while Sammy crawled under my sister Joan's bed. And there we were, anxiously awaiting our target's arrival, hearts in our mouths. I was suddenly nervous and starting to become apprehensive. I wasn't sure that I could go through with our scheme, after all. I mean, what if we were caught? We were dead quiet, but the silence was almost deafening. Beads of sweat formed on my forehead. Then we heard the creaking of the wooden floorboards, which intensified with the approaching footsteps and seemed to reverberate with the pounding of my heart.

I suddenly decided I was too young for so much excitement. I desperately wanted to get out of there. How on earth had I got here in the first place, I berated myself. Much as I wanted to, I couldn't blame Sammy. I was in it as deep as he was. It was too late to abort the plan.

The door opened. I covered my eyes with both my hands and pulled my knees to my chest, panic setting in. I expected to be caught at any second. I vowed not to open my eyes nor to move a muscle.

Nothing happened. After a couple of minutes the sounds of the girl's distinct, methodical movements, together with sheer curiosity, got the better of me. I straightened my legs and removed my hands from my face. I took a peep across to Joan's bed where my eyes met Sammy's. He winked and gave me a thumbs up. My eyes slid towards a pair of dainty feet. Bare feet. I edged forward a little more and there, right before my very eyes, was a fully naked female body in all its splendour.

It was a breathtaking moment. She was everything I'd imagined, and more. She had obviously just taken a shower as the towel she was using to dry her hair covered her eyes. I could feel my breathing growing heavier. I wanted to touch her, but instead I retreated into the shadows under the bed. She took her time dressing, which allowed Sammy and me a few more good peeps, but soon she was dressed and then there was silence. I couldn't understand what she was doing that was taking so long so I edged forward again to look, accidentally moving the bedspread. She was busy applying mascara, her face close to the mirror. Unbeknown to me of course, from the angle of the mirror she had a clear view directly under the bed behind her ...

Her shriek was piercing. 'What the hell are you doing, you little brat?' she screamed, grabbing the bedspread and pulling it up. 'Are you mad?'

I almost had a heart attack. I had to do some quick thinking if I wasn't going to get myself killed.

'Shhhh!' I whispered, putting my index finger over my lips. 'Keep your voice down.' I looked up at her innocently, my eyes wide.

A mixture of confusion and bewilderment spread across her face.

'We're playing catches and I'm hiding from Charles,' I whispered again, even more softly.

'Oh,' she responded, her face going totally blank.

I decided to push my luck. 'Do me a favour? Could you go and check if Charles is anywhere outside or near the stairway?'

Almost as if she was in a trance, she agreed. She even told me stay where I was while she went to see if Charles was around. He wasn't – luck was on my side. By the time she returned and assured me that the coast was clear, I had come out from under the bed. I thanked her hurriedly and was out of there in a flash. By then, Sammy had made his own escape, undetected.

By lunchtime the girl had clearly realised what I'd actually been up to, and she was furious. She pointed an angry finger in my direction and warned, 'Watch out, my boy.'

So ended my secret one-sided romance, and also our peeping-tom days – not a bad thing, I suppose, although I guess boys will always be boys.

By the time I was 15, although I had never had any formal sex education, I had had several innocent relationships with various girls younger than me, but somehow it was always the more mature girls I was attracted to. This might, of course, have been because, during that era at the Arc, we boys were outnumbered by the girls, most of whom were our seniors.

One day, what started out as an average Monday evening unexpectedly took an interesting turn. One of the senior girls, Lisa, whom admittedly I had noticed and had on occasion fantasised about, cornered me as I was walking past the public telephone.

'Shani,' she called out, 'what is your problem?'

I was startled and a bit nervous, too. 'What do you mean?' I stuttered.

She looked at me, mildly annoyed. 'Do you think I'm stupid?' she replied.

Normally I could talk my way out of any situation, but that day, perhaps because of the age difference and because we both knew there was an attraction between us, I felt distinctly uneasy. For once I couldn't think of anything to say.

She smiled. I got the impression that she was taking great pleasure in teasing me. And then, with what seemed like a reconciliatory gesture, she stretched out her arm and rested her hand on my shoulder. 'Come on, Shani,' she said seductively, 'I've seen the way you look at me.' She gazed steadily into my eyes.

Besides being momentarily mesmerised, I was also consumed with desire. In my state of stupor I found myself staring at her exposed cleavage, and I could have sworn her breasts swelled in concert with every breath she took. I had an almost uncontrollable urge to touch and kiss her, and I nearly did, when suddenly we were interrupted by the approaching footsteps of one of the other girls coming down the stairs from the girls' department to use the phone.

That night I struggled to sleep, although being an insomniac didn't help either. Moreover, I found myself replaying the earlier incident over and over in my head. While touching myself, I kept rehearsing what I should have said to Lisa, and I could have kicked myself for not confessing that I was attracted to her.

It was very possible that she felt the same way, but, even so, I still had my doubts. Girls were generally unpredictable, and perhaps my indiscreet watching of her had actually been more annoying than welcome. I decided that I would do my best from then on to ignore her and refrain from staring. Satisfied with my plan, I fell asleep.

The next morning at breakfast I didn't see Lisa, as the places where we usually sat weren't near each other, and in fact she wasn't uppermost in my mind – until she walked past me carrying a pile of dirty dishes. I simply couldn't resist looking at her. She, on the other hand, now seemed blithely unaware of my presence, which came as a bit of a relief and to a degree confirmed my suspicions.

After school, before *shul* and dinner, we boys usually got together for a game of football. Some of the girls would congregate at the end of the veranda that ran along the rear of the main building, and that afternoon I couldn't help noticing Lisa there among the group. She appeared to be looking in our direction, but I couldn't be sure. I continued to concentrate on the game, and when next I looked up the girls had all disappeared.

During the week everybody except the matrics was required to attend homework sessions in the dining room between 7 and 8pm. Being a creature of habit, I always sat at the same table where I took my meals, although we could sit anywhere we liked to do our homework. That evening I arrived relatively early. Only a handful of kids were there. I got stuck into my homework and paid no attention to the scuffling noise of children filtering into the dining room at different intervals.

I was completely engrossed in my studies when, to my surprise, Lisa appeared. She pulled out the chair directly opposite mine and asked if I minded if she joined me. Although secretly delighted, I kept my expression neutral. Be my guest, I gestured casually. Needless to say, I found it difficult to concentrate on my work, and after a few minutes I excused myself. I went to the lavatory, where I washed my face and spent some time looking in the mirror and reciting what I was going to say to her. I knew I needed to broach the subject of what had happened between us the night before. Feeling more composed and confident, I went back to the dining room. Taking my courage in both hands, in a low voice I asked Lisa what last night had been all about and then I admitted I had been staring at her because I found her desirable. Then I promptly added that it wasn't a big deal.

Lisa looked amused, but she held my gaze and there was something definitely seductive in the way she looked at me. My heart skipped multiple beats. Then she told me amiably that she was flattered by the attention. If she wasn't flirting with me, then I didn't know anything. The tension between us was unmistakable.

I just smiled back at her and pretended to continue doing my homework, but after that it was almost impossible.

While I was busy wondering what my next move should be, Lisa began to pack up her things. As she left, she passed me a folded piece of paper. I looked around the room to see if anyone had noticed anything and then, satisfied that nobody had, hurriedly opened the note. It read: 'Meet me at the fishpond by the *shul* at 8.30. PS Don't be late.' I had to reread the note several times before the reality of what she was proposing registered in my mind. It was almost 8pm. I gathered up my things and, at breakneck speed, raced down to my dormitory, where I took a quick shower.

As the appointed time approached, I slipped out of the boys' department and stealthily made my way to the *shul*. The area around the fishpond was deserted and, except for the stars and the dim light from the rooms, it was very dark. I found the silence unsettling and, just to make matters worse, my old fear of the dark crept out of the shadows. It was already 8.35 and Lisa was nowhere in sight. It was beginning to dawn on me that perhaps I had fallen victim to a cruel prank.

Then I heard a soft voice calling out my name – 'Shani!' – and there she was. We touched hands and I think I tried to mumble something, but then we were in each other's arms, kissing passionately. After a minute, Lisa suggested we go to the Hebrew classroom.

Most of us kids at the Arc avoided being in this part of the grounds after dark. It was rumoured that ghosts roamed around here at night, and it wasn't a comfortable feeling. All the same, how could I resist Lisa? I took her hand and led her down the steps. Inside the building, it was pitch dark and it took some time for my eyes to adjust. I kept imagining that someone was lurking in the shadows and that at any moment we would be pounced on. Sensing my discomfort, Lisa beckoned me closer and began kissing me again, this time unbuttoning my shirt. Her tender touch on my exposed chest was exciting and I completely forgot where I was. I removed her blouse and then her bra and before long we were both naked. We piled our clothes on the floor and I gently laid her down on them.

Things really got wild and heated after that as we explored each other's bodies. I was in seventh heaven. Suddenly I heard a shuffling noise only a few metres away from where we were lying. I froze and tightened my grip on Lisa, and in a whisper asked her if she had heard anything. After a long silence, she started to giggle, accusing me of being a scaredy-cat.

I laughed and we continued to be intimate, but in a disturbed moment my mind flashed back to an incident when I was about five or six years old. I had been on holiday with my mother and Janos in Lourenço Marques (Maputo). The hotel room had a double bed. I remember being very hot, and in the middle of the night I was woken up by strange muffled noises. I was scared. I looked towards the bed where my parents were sleeping. My stepfather was on top of my mother and it looked like they were wrestling. I was sure he was hurting her, beating her as I'd seen him do many times before.

Frightened, I had cowered under my blanket and prayed that the noises would cease, before eventually falling into a deep slumber. I had blocked the incident from my mind until now.

Back in the Hebrew classroom, time became timeless, but, as we reached levels of ecstasy that transcended anything I'd ever experienced, without warning Lisa's head tilted back and her entire body started convulsing uncontrollably. This was accompanied by a short burst of a shrieking groan. I got the fright of my life. I thought she was having an epileptic fit. Panic-stricken, and not at all sure what to do, I stroked her long hair and did my best to soothe her, saying, 'It's okay, it's okay' over and over again.

This was a total freak-out, I thought. I mean, what if she died? How on earth was I going to explain myself? After a lot of stroking and reassuring, to my relief Lisa came round and seemed to have no recollection of anything unusual happening.

When I asked if she was okay, she appeared baffled by my question and insisted she was fine. By now it was late and I suggested we should get going, so we dressed hurriedly and made our way back to the main building. There we kissed again before going our separate ways.

In retrospect, losing my virginity was an extraordinary experience, even though it might not have carried the hallmark of true love. The spontaneous and exciting manner in which it happened makes it one of my most memorable sexual encounters. Just for the record, and to my embarrassment, later in life I discovered that what I thought were symptoms of epilepsy was just Lisa having an orgasm. As I said, my sex education was sketchy, to say the least.

M

Me and my friends at the Arc, all about 16 years old, entered a phase of night excursions. This added an element of danger to our normal adventures. Such outings comprised, among other things, 'borrowing' parked cars or anything with wheels, and housebreaking, which isn't altogether an appropriate description for what we did. It was more like trespassing, the challenge being to get in and out of buildings undetected; we never intended to steal anything. If we were caught, escape was imperative, and this was the ultimate adrenaline rush. It was all part of the game. Getting caught meant also a loss of face in front of the other boys.

On countless occasions we were chased by security guards, landlords, gardeners, the police and even milkmen, and as a result we became great athletes. At school, we Arcs always took first, second or third place in the cross-country races, which was a source of surprise to our other friends, who never saw us at training and couldn't fathom why the boys from Arcadia were always such formidable opponents.

Friday nights were bunking-out nights. By age 16, watching *The Brady Bunch* had lost its thrill for us. We were looking for something a bit more exciting. One night we unanimously decided to explore the buildings of the Johannesburg General Hospital, which was still under construction, as well as the area nearby, which happened also to be the location of a girls' boarding school, Roedean. The area itself was charming, with botanical gardens known as The Wilds bordering the school's property. This enhanced its splendour and tranquillity during the daytime, but at night it looked more like the setting for a horror movie. I recall at around that time a man's mutilated body was found in The Wilds, and a few incidents of rape had also taken place there. Crime was on the increase, and even usually quiet Killarney had become notorious as a playground for unsavoury characters. As a result, the police patrolled the area constantly.

And so, with the increased element of risk, when we went on our Friday night adventures – or night raids, as we called them – as a preventive measure we were now compelled to carry weapons. These took the form of batons, nunchakus and knives, and sometimes even baseball bats. We were resourceful and were renowned for our courage and determination. Our motto was 'Do or Die.' Little did I know then the impact and influence our comradeship was already having on my character.

On this particular Friday night, we were more in number than usual. It had been decided that certain junior boys would be allowed to join in the expedition as part of their initiation into manhood. Bar Mitzvahs were a spiritual thing and were for 'bagels'; survival in a precarious situation was the real test. Straight after dinner, our usual crew assembled in the driveway. This consisted of myself, Sammy Lasker, Charles Goldman, brothers Eric and Leo Niedermayr and Colin Coats, who wasn't actually an Arcadian but had proved his loyalty and become a staunch friend. The two junior boys joining us for the first time were David Graff and Steven Landsman, aka Fanny. Taking the junior boys with us was irresponsible, but nothing new for the harum-scarum boys we were. Our logic was that, sooner or later, they would be bunking out on their own anyway. None of us really considered the consequences of our actions.

Armed with our weapons, some of us even wearing balaclavas, we

49

stealthily made our way out of the grounds, via the hill, passing on the side of the Goldsmith residence. The hospital construction site provided a maze of adventure. Our relentless quest for excitement was insatiable, and the fact that we were fearless made us unpredictable. In addition, our defiance of authority was growing. It was a trait inherent in most Arcs.

Chained to one of the streetlights inside the hospital premises was a three-wheeled bicycle cart, the type with a large bin on the front, often used by milkmen to do their deliveries. Some of the boys tried to pull the chain apart, but without success.

'Let me have a go,' said Colin.

He grabbed the chain with both hands and pulled with all his strength, and to our amazement the lock popped open. Triumphantly, he mounted the saddle and gestured to us to jump into the bin. We all piled in and raced off down the hill, screaming our heads off. Because of the excessive weight and the speed we were travelling at, Colin lost control and crashed into the sidewalk, while we all went flying in different directions – what a gas! We laughed our heads off and bolted from the scene.

We then made our way to Roedean School, where, on previous outings, some of us had actually met a few of the girls, who seemed to quite fancy us. Already familiar with the terrain around the property, getting in and out was only a matter of manoeuvring from one side to the other. The only obstacle that presented any actual difficulty was the 2m-high steel fence topped with barbed wire, but this we climbed with relative ease. We entered the grounds, which were dimly lit, and made our way to the front of the building. I was feeling uncomfortable; there was something eerie about the place. The silence was unnatural. Unbeknown to us, lurking behind us in the shadows someone was watching our movements. We congregated in front of the main building and then, at the top of our voices and in concert, we began reciting the song 'Three German Officers Crossed the Line, Parlez-Vous', and so on. Lights started coming on in different sections of the building, and then we heard a dog barking. It wasn't a very convincing bark, so we paid it no attention. It sounded like a poodle maybe.

But then, rising above the barking, came a coarse masculine voice that sounded awfully close.

'What the hell are you doing here?!' I could have sworn it was a German accent. As one, we turned and streaked off across the grass. The next thing we heard was a gunshot. Colin was a little to my right, but we were pretty close to each other and I heard him swear under his breath.

'Ouch, my leg – I've been hit!' He doubled over, obviously in pain.

Then there was another shot.

'Nonsense,' I said, trying to reassure him. 'That was a cap gun or a firecracker. Come on!'

We had all run in different directions, but we had agreed beforehand that, if anything happened and we were separated, we would meet in The Wilds by the fishponds. I had taken the lead, and so far Colin was keeping up with me but again he pleaded that he had been hit. Fanny was further back and just off Colin's right side.

As I ran, I couldn't help wondering to myself what kind of lunatic would shoot at a bunch of kids. Minutes later we were all at our appointed rendezvous; everyone was accounted for, something of a victory all things considered, although one of us was not entirely un-scathed, it had to be said. I explained to the others that Colin had been shot and we proceeded to inspect his leg. True to his word, we could see with our own eyes that some damage had been done. A mixture of shock and surprise came over us as we crowded round to examine the wound. There was a hole in the rear of his jeans covered in blood, just below his right buttock. We guessed that the bullet had exited on the other side, travelling straight through his thigh. Colin pulled his jeans to his knees, and we all stared silently. It wasn't a pleasant sight. Red and white flesh was hanging out of the wound.

By now Colin was definitely in pain and we knew we needed to get back to the Arc before we could make an intelligent decision about what to do next. We also assumed that whoever had shot at us would have called the police by now. We quickly made our way through the back of The Wilds, which was quite a climb, and ran along the out-skirts of Killarney and around the Oppenheimers' property.

It wasn't very late, around 10pm, when we got back to the Arc. We sent the junior boys back to their dormitories while we smuggled Colin into the toilets under the stairway that led to the senior girls' section. I rushed up the stairs to call Joan, who just happened to be coming out of her room. I'm sure I was quite a sight, covered in blackjacks, panic-stricken and sweating like a pig. She asked what the hell we had done this time. I blurted out the story. Her expression was a mixture of anger and confusion. Then, without saying anything further, I grabbed her arm and pulled her back down the stairs with me.

Down in the toilets, Sammy explained in a controlled tone what had transpired. I'd always known Joan to be squeamish, but, to my surprise, she took charge of the situation. She started assigning duties: Sammy and I were instructed to keep a lookout for Vicky; Eric and Sandra Newstead were told to fetch towels, a bowl of hot water and some bandages; and Colin was ordered to remove his pants so that Joan could perform some basic first aid on him.

Despite our vigilance, we didn't hear Vicky coming. He appeared to have been making his way to the area that adjoined the toilet. As soon as we were aware of this I thought we were surely busted. Not only would he have a clear view of Colin's naked bum, but Joan's profile was in full view, too, through the slightly ajar toilet door. And then suddenly Vicky was right there, stamping his feet and demanding to know what was going on. He tried to push his way into the toilet, and instinctively I grabbed the handle and pulled it closed. Sammy and I told Vicky that Colin didn't have his pants on so he shouldn't come in. Vicky was startled. He had obviously seen Joan in there. He looked at us suspiciously, quite sure that something was wrong but not able to figure out what it was.

'Well, then finish whatever it is that you're doing and get back to the dormitory,' he said, and turned and left, while we sighed with relief.

By this stage Colin was in great pain, and Joan strongly suggested that we get him to a hospital. So we phoned a close friend of Colin's, Steven Penn, whose father was a pharmacist and lived in Greenside. Within 15 minutes they'd arrived and whisked Colin off to hospital. Fortunately he recovered without any complications, and even though we may literally have crossed the line that night, at least no one had got arrested. The incident didn't deter us from future escapades, however, and Colin remained a staunch friend.

In 1977, my matric year, I was the so-called head boy of Arcadia. Being a keen sportsman, I never smoked cigarettes, nor did I have the slightest inclination to experiment with marijuana. By now I was a strong and confident youngster. I didn't care what any of my peers thought of me. The kids at King David, the high school I attended, who were often seen as spoilt Jewish brats, were, in my eyes, my equals. I never begrudged them what they had, but nor did I allow the deprivations in my own life to affect my self-esteem. It didn't bother me that my dad didn't drive a Mercedes or a Jaguar. I didn't even *have* a dad. I was who I was, and nothing was going to change that. My life in Arcadia had, for the most part, turned out to be great.

The only forms of transport we Arcs had at our disposal were the Arcadia van and bus, and then only as passengers. A custom handed down to us by our predecessors, however, was to take the Arc van for a joyride in the late evening. David Lasker was an accomplished driver from an early age, and a mentor to those who followed in the years to come.

It was forbidden to leave the premises on Friday evening, as it was the Sabbath, but this never stopped us bunking out. Late one Friday evening, with a chill autumn wind gusting around the buildings, I lay restlessly on my bed. I decided that a night out and about in the Arc van was just what I needed to spice up what had been a mundane week. I encouraged a younger boy, Mark Wasserman, to join me.

Around midnight, after everyone had gone to sleep, Mark and I hijacked the Arc van and off we went, gallivanting aimlessly through the deserted suburbs. In retrospect, I can only wonder what possessed me to be so irresponsible: there I was, an unlicensed driver, putting both our lives in danger. While the thrill might elude us, the fact remains that my defiance of authority was a driving force in all my pleasure-seeking endeavours. Around 1am, somewhere in Bramley, we got stuck in a dead end, and what made matters worse was that we were at the bottom of a steep hill. And so began the arduous task of getting the van back up the hill. There was nothing for it but to push. Eventually, after what felt like hours, we managed to get it out. Finally we got back on a straight and level road, exhausted and sweating like animals.

Suddenly, a blue Valiant with dimmed lights appeared in the distance. We both spotted it at the same time.

'Shit, it's the police,' Mark said, while pushing from behind. 'Now what?'

My heart stopped for what seemed like an eternity. As the Valiant got closer, I leapt into the driver's seat of the van while Mark, who had remained at the rear, kept pushing, on my instruction. The Valiant pulled alongside us. It was the police all right.

'*Wat is die probleem with you ous?*' The policeman asked us, half in English and half in Afrikaans.

My chest was pounding. I tried to speak but no words came. Then, as if from a distance, I heard myself saying, 'She won't start, officer. Do you think you could help push?' (Talk about having chutzpah!)

I couldn't have been very convincing.

'Pull over and get out the car,' the cop ordered, his voice stern. He told me to park on the side of the road, although he had pulled the Valiant up in front of us, forcing me to a standstill anyway.

Before I fully realised what was going on, my door was flung open and I was blinded by the beam of his flashlight.

'Where are the keys, man?' he asked me in a much harsher tone, while shining his torch on the empty ignition. Then he asked to see my licence.

My whole body began to shake, and I began to stutter, too.

'I, uh, uh, uh ... well, there are no, uh, k-k-k-k-k-keys,' I told him.

A scuffle followed, during which he tried to pull me from my seat and I tried to push him away. Then all hell seemed to break loose. I heard shouting from the rear of the van.

'Put your hands in the air!' The second policeman had got to Mark.

At this stage I must have gone into shock. I began fighting both cops off and telling them that I could explain everything, but they kept coming at me. They still couldn't get me out of the van, though. Then one of them produced what looked like a 9mm automatic and stuck it between my eyes. I froze instantly. Then I was literally wrenched out of the driver's seat. Mark was already sitting in the back of the Valiant, his wrists cuffed. I've never forgotten the desperate look in his eyes.

We were taken to the Bramley police station. During the interrogation I was slapped and punched in the stomach. Mark, who was two or three years my junior, wasn't touched. After telling them that we were from Arcadia, it turned out that the sergeant on duty was familiar with the Arc and that he also knew Vicky. This was something of a mixed relief, as neither of us relished the prospect of spending the weekend in the cells but nor did we like the idea of seeing the expression on Vicky's face. At around 2am we were escorted back to Arcadia.

Vicky didn't say a single word, but his disappointment was obvious and I could see immediately that I had let him down. Before retiring to his room, he came to my dormitory. Without even looking at me, he said one simple sentence: 'I cannot understand your mentality.' Before he left the room, he repeated it. Just the look in his eyes made me realise the severity of my situation.

The following Monday, an emergency session was held by the senior members of the Arc committee, which, if I'm not mistaken, was chaired by Sidney Nochumson. Mr Nochumson and I enjoyed a mutual dislike of each other. On several occasions I had been brought in front of the chairman for various misdemeanours. One incident that was clearly still fresh in his mind was the mass uprising, instigated by yours truly, against the hypocritical rule of the Duzzys. A point had been reached where the Duzzys were losing control of the kids. At one stage we got so bold that we let down the rear tyres on Mrs Duzzy's car, and on another occasion I got one of the juniors to throw a stink bomb at the couple after lunch. Eventually they were afraid to come out of their flat, which was at the top of the stairway to the girls' department. It was even rumoured that the Duzzys felt their lives were in danger, and one day somebody went through my cupboards, possibly thinking that

I might have had some sort of weapon in my possession. In doing so, they had come across my journal, in which I used to write down my private thoughts. I had also sketched some pretty weird sexual stuff in there. My journal was then examined by several members of the Arcadia committee. I could only imagine their faces when they saw some of my diagrams.

With my having become a familiar figure for Mr Nochumson, leniency was far from our chairman's agenda when it came to me. The incident with the police, as it happened, was the final straw. I was formally expelled. It was decided that I be sent to Norman House, a reformatory or haven for juvenile delinquents.

During the period I was at Arcadia we enjoyed the privilege of attending the school of our choice, and the majority of us chose King David Victory Park. Once I was in the care of Arcadia, the committee had complete control over our education and our lives until we left school. My mother, who was living in Hungary for most of this period, was not consulted and nor did she involve herself in any way in these decisions.

The decision by the committee to expel me left me distraught. In fact, I was devastated. I felt a great injustice had befallen me, a view that was shared by my fellow matric students at school, headed by Roy Lotkin, then my best friend at King David. The students of King David drafted a petition pleading with the Arc committee to retract my punishment and allow me to complete my matric. Another meeting was arranged and Mr Jeffrey Wolf, who was the principal at King David, attended the meeting, by choice, in my defence.

Luckily, I had a good reputation at school. Not only was I in the swimming team, but I also played in the First XV rugby team for two consecutive years and was awarded half-colours for my performance. I was also a house captain, and during the year we had won all the inter-house sports activities, except for the rugby, where we took second place.

Thanks to Mr Wolf's intervention, I was given permission to stay on at Arcadia for the remainder of my matric, on the condition that I was gated for three months and my allowance be withheld for the same period. It was further agreed that I attend counselling with the psychologist at Arcadia, whose name was Vivienne Budlender. She turned out to be a lovely person and we formed a strong friendship. She was a compassionate woman, someone who never accepted anything at face value. We remained friends for years. Thanks to Mr Wolf, Vicky and the King David matrics, I had an opportunity to make amends.

Vicky informed me soon after the meeting that he had never before heard a person speak so highly of another individual as Mr Wolf had spoken of me. I was humbled by this. All the same, I didn't do very well in my matric prelims; however, I did pass and attained a distinction in Art.

Skateboarding had just become the new craze. Most of my time and energy during this period was channelled into skating. I had a Snowy Smith board with alpha wheels – the Mercedes of skateboards at the time. What a trip it was! Imagine skating down Oxford Road and overtaking double-decker buses – well, that's what we did. I had just turned 18. I was at the peak of my youth, invincible and ready to take on the world. Matric prelims, which made up 15 per cent of our final grades, were behind us. But instead of studying for the real thing still ahead, I was out perfecting my skills on my skateboard.

How I had made it to matric was a miracle in itself. My History teacher expected me to be the only student out of the entire matric group to fail outright, while my Economics teacher was confident I could obtain a distinction. Besides my Art teacher, though, as far as I was concerned, the rest of my teachers couldn't have been bothered. Whenever I arrived for English lessons, I was told: 'Mr Krebs, take your place at the back of the class and do whatever you wish, but don't disturb the rest of us.'

I never expected to pass at the end of the year. This wasn't because I wasn't academically inclined. I just had no interest whatsoever in schoolwork. I was actually of the opinion that school was hindering my education. I wanted to get out into the real world, the world being the true master of life's greatest lessons. Unlike my peers, most of whom would go on to university and had already chosen careers, I knew that my grades wouldn't be good enough for me to achieve a university pass, although I would have liked to have studied Fine Art.

Over and above this, I also wanted to get my spell in the army behind me. I didn't join up out of patriotism or a sense of obligation, but because military training in South Africa in the 1970s was compulsory. We would get our call-up papers while we were still at school and I had already received mine. I had been called up to serve 18 months at the signals unit in Heidelberg, from June 1978 to the end of 1979. I rather looked forward to being a soldier. As they said, you were not a man until you had been through the army.

In November, just before our finals, King David held a speech night at school. Everybody was required to attend. Awards would be presented and the principal would deliver a farewell speech, in which he would inform the matrics about their duties and responsibilities as the future guardians of their country, and the importance of furthering their education and becoming productive members of society. It was a tradition, and for most students speech night was also an inspiration. The door to adulthood was opening and we would be responsible for our own actions from then on. I couldn't have cared less about speech night. I couldn't wait to leave school and be free.

The morning before speech night, a close friend of mine, Craig, told me that he would fetch me an hour earlier as he and three of our teachers were getting together for a short private farewell, just before the evening's official events. He wanted me to join them. I wasn't quite sure what was going down, but the prospect of socialising with our mentors was an invitation too enticing to refuse.

As a keen sportsman, I didn't smoke cigarettes and I was totally anti-drugs. I knew Craig smoked weed whenever we went to parties, and invariably there was a small group of friends who would sneak away and smoke, but I was never in the least tempted. I just let them do their thing. I didn't question their choices, but I didn't show any interest in joining them.

Craig picked me up and we drove to the Emmarentia shops where he pulled up beside some guy on the street corner. Words and money were exchanged and we then drove around the block. When we got back to the same spot, another guy walked up to the car and dropped two matchboxes through the window onto Craig's lap, who at this stage seemed quite anxious and was nervously looking around to see whether anybody had seen or was watching us. Satisfied that the coast was clear, he handed me the matchboxes and we drove off. I had no idea what was going on, but I did understand that we had just done something forbidden. Being inquisitive by nature, I opened one of the two boxes.

'What the fuck?' I said, looking at Craig.

I recognised the contents immediately. Before I could prevent them, memories from my childhood began flashing through my mind. I tried to force them back down, out of my head, out of me altogether.

Craig said, 'Take it easy man – it's only weed.'

I knew what weed looked like. I knew what it smelt like. I knew the effect it had on people. I knew a lot of things I didn't want to know, and most of them I knew before I even had pubic hair.

'Oh, really?' I retorted. 'You're kidding. I know what the fuck it is, and you know very well that I don't approve of this shit.'

Craig said it was for our meeting with the school teachers, as if that would make things better.

'What?' I said. Man, I couldn't believe it! Here was my school friend doing weed with our teachers!

'Is that cool or what, china?' Craig said, looking to me for my approval.

I was still more than a little confused, but I settled down. And the more I thought about it, the cooler I actually began to think it was. Schoolteachers were the fount of knowledge, understanding and everything that was morally right. Teachers were responsible for instilling in us these very principles. Then surely it had to follow that, if they smoked weed, all the taboos surrounding its use must be false. Suddenly I felt a whole new respect for my friend; he seemed far better versed in the ways of the world than I was.

Maybe, I reasoned, weed wasn't so bad for you after all; in fact, there was no evidence that I knew of to prove that it was. It had become quite fashionable at our age to smoke weed. I did point out to Craig that, besides being illegal, I had heard that excessive smoking could cause temporary loss of memory and that it destroyed your brain cells. If nothing else, these two things should have been of some concern to him.

Craig just chuckled. 'That's bullshit, china,' he told me. 'It's only illegal because it makes you feel good.'

That kind of made sense as I recalled whenever my stepfather had smoked weed, which he did regularly, it did seem to alter his state of mind. Janos did seem more chilled when he was stoned.

'You'll see when you try, china,' Craig added, rolling down the window, 'it's such a buzz.'

The fresh air felt cool on my face, and I mulled over what Craig had been saying. He had a point, I thought. There was no harm in trying. I needed to find out for myself. We drove to the bird sanctuary, which was this beautiful tree-filled park with big open fields where people would walk their dogs. It was almost dark when we arrived. There was nobody in sight, no other parked cars.

Craig started crushing and cleaning the weed in the palm of one of his hands, going through exactly the same rituals that were now coming back to me vividly. He handed me a cigarette and asked me to empty the tobacco out; I had no problem doing it, and it must have looked like I had done it before. No sooner had we finished preparing a few joints than we became aware of two sets of headlights approaching in convoy. Nervously, Craig quickly hid the joints just behind the front wheel of the car and pretended to take a leak. Then, when both cars were well in our line of vision, he made a sign and said, 'Oh, it's Mr Fairchild and party.'

The cars pulled up next to us and everyone jumped out. Some looked a little surprised to see me, but were not in the least perturbed. Mr Fairchild was tall, with long greasy hair and a beard. He reminded me of a hippie from the 1960s. The three female teachers were all dressed up, but were different in every respect. Even before we had finished greeting one another, Craig had already lit up one joint and passed it to the women.

Then he lit another for us guys and we passed it around among us. For some reason, when people smoke joints they always seem to share them. I assume it's something to do with enhancing the bonding experience of doing something illegal, or perhaps it's just a drug culture thing. I had no idea what the effect would be or what 'it makes you feel good' meant. Generally, I felt good anyway – why did I need a substance to make me feel better about myself? All the same, I sucked hard on the joint, inhaling all the smoke. It tasted awful, burning my throat, and I coughed on that first drag. It also had an unusual taste. It was very harsh and the smell was slightly different to the weed Janos had smoked. I don't know why – maybe my expectations were too high – but nothing was happening to me.

We passed around another joint. I sucked even harder this time, and the next thing I knew Craig was saying, 'Stop, stop' and taking the joint away from me. He told me that he needed to doctor it because I'd been sucking so hard the joint had burned down the one side. He put spit on his finger and applied it to the area that was more burnt. I noticed that everybody's mood had changed. Our teachers were much more relaxed and cheerful now and they all seemed to be speaking at the same time.

I, on the other hand, was rather disappointed, and could feel only a slight headache creeping up on me. I couldn't understand why people made such a big deal about smoking weed or why it was referred to as an addictive substance. Anyway, everyone had a few good laughs, not that I could fathom what was so funny. I guessed being stoned turned you into something of a comedian. After a while our teachers bade us farewell and drove away. Craig then proceeded to put eye drops in his eyes and suggested I do the same.

'Shani, are you goofed?' he asked me.

'Not really, man,' I told him. I certainly didn't feel stoned. I'm not sure if I felt anything at all except for my headache. I looked in the car mirror and was shocked to see how red my eyes were.

By the time we got to King David, which was a two-minute drive from the bird sanctuary, thanks to the eye drops my eyes had cleared completely. There were cars parked all the way down the road and people were still arriving. On entering the assembly hall, which was by now packed with students and their parents, we were greeted by a clamour of conversation that echoed throughout the big room. This was, after all, a pivotal moment for most of my peers.

In my eyes, however, it was nothing more than a banal affair, and if it hadn't been for the fact that Craig and I were jointly being awarded the Art prize, I might very well not have even attended at all. Suddenly I felt a little light-headed. All eyes seemed to be on me, or was it my imagination? And all of a sudden my conscience was troubling me. What had I done? I had lost the innocence of my youth. Was this the beginning of the many evils that I was going to fall victim to? Was it possible that fate had its own plans for me?

I went to the toilet and splashed water on my face, looked in the mirror and thought to myself, you cool, my china, and went back to find my place in the hall.

The principal approached the podium. His speech seemed to go on forever. Most of what he said went straight in one ear and out the other for me, except for one thing, which did stick with me. This was something about the world being a very competitive, at times even ruthless, place where one needed all one's wits to survive. Everybody applauded at the conclusion of his talk and then our vice-principal, who was also head of the English department, was called to address the audience. By this stage I was already bored and nothing he could say would bear any significance on the way I anticipated my future was going to be. After his tiresome rambling, the awards were presented.

The Art prize was the last to be given out. Craig and I were called to the stage. I felt unusually self-conscious. I'm not sure whether it was the fact that I was perceived by most to be an underachiever or whether it was the lingering effects of the weed we had smoked. In my eyes, the prize was a farce as we were the only two who had taken Art as a subject out of the entire 1977 matric group. What was the point of an award?

Final exams were just around the corner. The least I could do, I decided, was to make a last attempt to pass. Failing would be an embarrassment.

I had always scraped through without studying, but I knew there was no way I could get through finals using the same strategy.

In the weeks leading up to finals, Craig would fetch me from the Arc and we would go to the library at Wits University. We managed to get our hands on the previous year's exam papers from Damelin College, and this turned out to be a huge advantage. I don't think I had read a single one of the setwork books during my school career, so I needed to take all the short-cuts available to me.

Early one evening, while I was waiting for Craig to fetch me for our regular study session at the library, one of the Arc girls, Melissa, who was also my ex-girlfriend and at that time my best friend Derek's chick, came to me and said she needed to speak to me when I got back. Derek was already away in the army.

'I may be back late, probably around midnight,' I told her, but she assured me she would wait up.

The thing was that I still had feelings for Melissa, and in a sense I had been upset that Derek was going out with her. It didn't seem right. Anyway, sure enough, there she was, waiting for me in the shadow of the stairway that led upstairs to the girls' department. It was close to midnight and very quiet. I watched Melissa come down the stairs. She had a beauty about her that could make any man irrational. I met her halfway up, took her by the hand and led her to what was then the movie room, which was adjacent to the dining room and next to the pantry. We didn't switch the lights on. We settled on the couch, and before I could say anything her arms were around me and she began to sob.

Stroking her hair and whispering in her ear, I told her it was okay to cry and encouraged her to just let it all out. Then I placed my hands on either side of her face and gently kissed her on the lips, reawakening feelings I realised I had been suppressing for a long time. From her reaction to my kiss, it was quite apparent that she still fancied me as well. We kissed, we touched and together we met and rode the crest of a wave that seemed never to end. I don't know how long we lay there afterwards in silence, but we both understood that there was no return from where we had just been. It was a special moment.

Once I was back in the boys' dorm and tucked into my bed, I felt guilt-ridden for having betrayed Derek, but at the same time I justified it by the fact that Melissa had been my girlfriend to begin with. I was only 16 when we first went steady, but when things began to get serious, I broke up with her. At 16 I was having too much fun, I reckoned, to have a serious relationship and girls were generally a headache. That night, however, I had fallen hopelessly in love all over again. The fact that, from then on, we had to sneak around and keep our romance a secret only added to the thrill and excitement. We became dangerously adventurous to the point of being careless.

Melissa shared a room with two other girls, and I started sneaking into her dorm late at night, where, as quietly as possible, we would make love. On one occasion we fell asleep in each other's arms and only woke up in the early hours of the morning. There was no way I could exit down the stairs. I had to make my way undetected to the girls' lounge, out onto the balcony and over the edge, which was a 3m drop. Fortunately, I somehow managed not to hurt myself.

Our relationship intensified over the weeks and Melissa agreed to dump Derek. We would be free to live and dance to the only way we knew, to lose ourselves in our own world. Melissa was forever on my mind and it was difficult for me to concentrate on my studies. Then one weekend Derek came home on his first army pass and we went on a double date. It was fucking awkward. Here I was, with another ex-girlfriend for whom I still had feelings, and Melissa, my current lover, was with her boyfriend, my supposed best friend. We went out for an early dinner and then to a movie. I ended up sitting between the two girls and, while holding the hand of my date, I also secretly held Melissa's hand. Derek fell asleep during the movie, which made it easier. I'm not sure what was going through my mind at the time, but love sure has a way of twisting our morals. Or perhaps it was that we were young – enough of an excuse to do as we pleased.

I studied hard in the run-up to our final exams. Subjects like History I learnt parrot fashion, preparing as much as I thought would see me through the exam. I began to think there was a good chance I might actually pass matric – and, despite all predictions to the contrary, I did.

It was official: my schooldays were behind me. I was ready to embrace everything the free world could throw at me – the good, the bad and the ugly.

Leaving Arcadia was a bittersweet moment for me, just as it would be, I imagined, for any normal kid leaving his parents' home. Vicky was forever telling us how tough it was in the real world and that we didn't appreciate how easy we had it in Arcadia. Delaying adulthood was not an option, however. There was a world out there that awaited a whole new generation of enthusiasts, and I topped the list. Saying goodbye to all the other kids was hard but, like so many other ex-Arcadians who had come and gone but who still visited regularly on weekends and attended the *shul* on festivals, I would be no different. Arcadia was our home. We were all part of something bigger.

I moved in with Joan, but December holidays were already upon us so I didn't settle there for long. Derek and I hitched a ride to Durban, where we met up with his brother Theo, who was staying there with their mother. Half of Johannesburg was in Durban, and we had the best time ever. What stands out the most for me was our adventurous, carefree spirit and how we embraced our newfound freedom. We came and went and did as we pleased, not having to answer to anybody. There were no set times for meals. We were free to be who we were. We were wild and we were invincible.

Our favourite hangout was the Elangeni Hotel, which was within walking distance of the beachfront. We sometimes slept ten people in a single room. Sometimes we even slept in the hotel toilet.

Durban was renowned for having the best weed in the southern hemisphere and we smoked pretty often. Theo smoked his first joint with us that holiday, and, after my initiation on speech night with Craig and our teachers, my aversion to getting stoned had melted away. I loved the feeling smoking weed gave me. But weed wasn't a priority for any of us the summer we finished school. We were just out to have fun.

Chapter 3

Soldiers We Are Not

Early in December 1977 I had received a letter from the army, telling me that my call-up had been changed: I was to be posted to 4 SAI Middelburg, and the period of training had been extended from 18 months to two years. The Border War had intensified, especially in Angola. Troops were being moved to the operational area and bodies were starting to come back in bags. The conflict was real. Our troops were dying out there, and nobody really knew what we were fighting about. Not that I gave a shit, but it disturbed me that we were fighting a war in another country. I thought fleetingly of becoming a Jehovah's Witness. Those guys were pacifists and did their two-year stints in detention barracks. The only problem was that they were looked down upon by the other soldiers as being chancers or *jippogat*s.

At 8am on Monday 9 January 1978 I presented myself at Milner Park (Milpark) in Johannesburg with all the other conscripts who had received orders to assemble there. Guys were arriving from all over South Africa. We made up an entire battalion. There were corporals, sergeants, sergeant majors, even lieutenants, all shouting at once.

'*Jou bliksem se moer!*'

'*Kom hier!*'

'*Troeper!*'

'*Roer jou gat!*'

After having our names taken, we were split up into groups and taken in Bedford army trucks to the Joburg central railway station. Our appointed corporal marched us to the platform. Some of the Afrikaans guys marched like they had been doing it forever. Generally the Afrikaners were very '*kop toe*' (the guys who felt a deep sense of duty towards South Africa). We boarded a train and I ended up sitting opposite two well-built Afrikaans guys who were both over 2m tall. They were also a good couple of years older than me.

It turned out that both these guys had degrees. Instead of joining the army first, they had gone to university, which meant that immediately after basic training they would be given the rank of second lieutenant. We instantly struck up a friendship and the trip to Middelburg passed quickly. As we pulled into the station, I looked out at the open landscape, struck by the bright crimson red colour of the sand. Once we disembarked, orders in Afrikaans came blasting from megaphones. Once again, we were loaded onto Bedford trucks and then transported to the camp. On arrival at our camp site, I was amazed to see rows of identical military tents stretching as far as the eye could see. Besides the mess hall and the toilets, there wasn't a single building.

We were divided into companies and then taken for a medical examination, after which we were all subjected to the ultimate induction for a soldier: a barber with an electric razor proceeded to shave my head, and I watched my blond curls cascade to the ground. The man basically reshaped my head, leaving nothing but bristles. I wanted to cry. I couldn't stop rubbing my hands all over my head.

In the army, 4 SAI Middelburg was known for being one of the toughest infantry units (it was almost a concentration camp, in my opinion). After being shorn, we were issued with uniforms, which included a beret, a heavy metal helmet, or *staaldak*, and a *baalsak*. We also received clean linen and two blankets. In my tent there were four iron-framed beds. I had discovered at Milpark that another guy from Arcadia had also been posted to Middelburg and coincidentally he was in the same tent as me. The following morning at breakfast I met up with a handful of other Jewish guys.

It didn't take long to realise that the South African army didn't much care about soldiers of the Jewish faith. For a start, there were no kosher meals and, secondly, we were expected to train on Shabbos. None of us Jewish guys in Middelburg were happy with this state of affairs. Knowing very well that they wouldn't or couldn't provide us with any, we decided to demand kosher food anyway. With any luck we hoped we might be transferred to Voortrekkerhoogte, outside Pretoria, where apparently there was a kosher kitchen. We also refused to train on Shabbos.

We went to talk to the corporal in charge, who was singularly unimpressed when he heard our requirements. '*Gaan na julle tente en vrek!*' (Go to your tents and die) he ordered. When I got back to our camp site, about 40 guys had congregated around the entrance to my tent. My friend from Arcadia was standing there, his face white as a sheet. He looked really nervous. He told me that, because we had refused to exercise, there were a few individuals making racial remarks.

I turned around and said loudly, 'What's the problem here? I will take on any one of you. Who wants to fight? I'll show you what a Jew can do!' Nobody said anything, but just as they were about to back away, this big, fat, dark-skinned guy came pushing his way through the crowd. He reminded me of a charging buffalo. Both thumbs pointing inward to his chest, he shouted, '*Ek sal jou opfok!*' (I will fuck you up).

I stood my ground, waited and when he was within punching distance I hit him with all my strength smack on the jaw. He just stood there, like nothing had happened. Then, angrier than before, he raised his arms and attempted to grab me around the throat, at which moment I felt myself being pulled from behind and yanked out of his reach.

The two guys I had met on the train stepped in front of me and, in a threatening tone, told the fat guy to get the fuck out of there. *Fok off.* And they made it quite clear that anybody who fucked with me or my friends in the tent would have them to deal with. The fat guy wasn't happy, but he backed off, rubbing his jaw ruefully, and the crowd dispersed. I thanked my two protectors, who had surely saved me from a good ass-kicking.

Later that afternoon, we Jews were all told to report to the first-aid tent. When we got there, the medic, who had the rank of lance corporal, said in a harsh tone, '*Hier is die fokken Jode – spuit hulle diep in*' (Here are the fucking Jews – inject them deep).

I was totally taken aback. Up until then, I had never really encountered anti-Semitism, and certainly not so blatantly. Fortunately for me, I was first in line for our tetanus injection. This fucking medic used the same syringe on each of us and he really thrust the needle into our arms. Afterwards all eight of us were marched around the parade ground for some three hours. I had hardly been in the army a couple of days and already I was hating every moment. How I wished I had gone to college. Even repeating matric would have been better than this!

I don't think that in the history of the SADF there had ever been a soldier or group of soldiers who'd refused to train on a Saturday or eat the food because it wasn't kosher. In addition, we demanded extra vegetables. We were certainly audacious, but we had also given them something to think about. By the end of the week, our transfer papers to 3 SAI in Potchefstroom, where there was a kosher kitchen, had been signed. Most of us had been hoping to be moved to Voortrekkerhoogte but we guessed Potchefstroom had to be better than where we were.

On the train ride to Potch, the eight of us fellow Jews really bonded; we had beaten the system, which seemed like an excellent start to our army experience. When we arrived at the Potchefstroom military base, the authorities didn't know the first thing about us or where we had come from, nor could they understand why we had been transferred so early into training. The new intake of conscripts was already into their second week of basic training. The fact that our heads were so closely shaven that we looked like convicts, compared to the moderate short back and sides of the 'roofies' (new recruits) at Potch, also made us stand out. Not knowing quite what to do with us, we were all put into a tent, where we lay around idly. It was quite a strange situation, watching the others training while we lazed about. After a week, they finally resolved the dilemma somehow and we were split up into different companies.

One good thing about the Potch camp was that there were very few tents; the new intake slept in bungalows. As I was making my way to my allocated spot in my bungalow, I exchanged greetings with a guy whose bed was close to the door. Mine was about six beds down on the opposite side. I had hardly reached my bed when I heard someone say in a loud voice: '*Hey, Joot!*' (Hey, Jew!)

'Fuck!' I said. I couldn't believe my ears. I hadn't even put my bag down and already I was about to lose my cool. What the fuck? Spinning around and dropping my *baalsak* at the same time, I saw the tall frame of this red-headed, freckle-faced 2m-tall Afrikaner. Fuck, I thought, why's it always the big guys getting in my face? I was about to open my mouth to retaliate and utter some profanity of my own when I re-alised he was not actually addressing me, but talking to the little guy I had just passed near the entrance a moment before. I walked up to this big Dutchman, jabbed my finger in his chest and, in Afrikaans, said, '*Ek is ook 'n Joot*' (I am also a Jew) 'and my name is Shani Krebs.' And pointing towards my Jewish brother, I continued, still in Afrikaans: '*Hy het ook 'n naam. Maak seker jy gebruik dit*' (He also has a name. Make sure you use it.)

My Afrikaans isn't so perfect but he got the message. I turned away and went back to my spot and proceeded to unpack my things. The little guy came up to me, shook my hand, introduced himself and thanked me.

Once I was settled, I couldn't believe how jacked-up this place was. Next door to our battalion was 4 Artillery Regiment, where there were also quite a few Jewish guys, and we all ate together in the mess hall. The two chefs there were Jewish, and the atmosphere at mealtimes was great and spirits were high. Basic training was quite tough, though. Every day we would run 2.4km with full kit, which meant with your webbing, magazines and ammunition, and your R1 rifle. Without fail, Stan Nathan, who was a marathon runner, came in first, winning by a good 50m. Depending on my mood, I usually ran in second, but Stan was the man to beat. Having two Jewish guys holding the best times for the 2.4 in our company gained us Jews a lot of respect.

Ironically, two of the slowest runners, who were always far behind the rest of the company, also happened to be Jewish. One was a lanky guy, quite skinny, but the other stood at around 1.8m and carried so much flab around his stomach I bet he struggled to see his toes. On a few occasions, while going on a 20km hike, which also entailed some running, my two Jewish brothers inevitably trailed far behind the rest of us. Sometimes the corporal would order, '*Gaan haal jou maatjie!*' (Go fetch your friend). Normally, a couple of the guys who were in the front (the fittest and the strongest and most '*kop toe*' (i.e. the arse-lickers) would run to the back to forcibly help along those who were trailing. On approaching they would slam their rifles into the chest of whomever it was who couldn't keep up, knocking them to the ground, then pulling them by either the scruff of their collars or their webbing until they got to their feet. They would then either push them from behind or drag them along until they caught up with the rest of the squad. On one or two such occasions, I would run and get to them before the others could and carry their rifles or their webbing for them. This would ease their load and enable them to keep up with the rest of us, and also save them from some humiliation.

Basic training was hard, but inspection parades in our barracks were the worst. Our beds had to be square, and starch was used to make the edges flush. The men took hours to prepare, and whenever there was a major inspection everybody slept on the floor.

Theory classes were held outdoors, and I would often be so exhausted that I literally fell asleep standing up. When the officer in charge caught you sleeping he would say: '*Haai, troep, sien jy daardie boom? Is jy al terug?*' (Hey, trooper, see that tree? Are you back already?). You would run to the tree as fast as possible, come back, only to be told it was the wrong tree, and then you had to run again. This could be repeated several times.

The soldiers who were there six months before us, from the previous year's call-up, filled most of the clerical or admin positions, and they were called '*ou manne*' (old men) – not that they were old, only that they required more respect as they had been there longer than us roofies. The food was not too bad and at least it was kosher. Everybody was required to line up as you entered the mess hall. There you helped yourself to a *varkpan*, a stainless-steel tray that had five divisions for your food. I don't know why, but many of the guys suffered from gyppo-guts (diarrhoea). It was rumoured that our coffee was laced with 'blue stone' to suppress sexual desire, and we suspected this may have been the cause.

A few days after joining the company, we were issued with two metal dog tags, which had our name, army number, blood group and religion inscribed on them. That was the moment when the realisation that I was being trained to be a soldier to fight a war really came home to me. It was then that I started mulling over the idea of trying to avoid going to the border.

On our first expedition to the shooting range, which was also part of a 10km hike, I devised a plan. At the range we were issued with live ammunition, and because of this there were strict safety measures in place. We were split up into groups of 20 men. We had full kit and were required to wear our *staaldakke*. Our faces were painted in 'Black is Beautiful', our nickname for the camouflage paint we had to use.

We were instructed to lie down in the firing position, and each soldier was given a specific target to fire on. I emptied my entire magazine at the target set for the guy who was next to me, hoping that being a bad shot would disqualify me from going to the front line. After all of us had finished target practice, we had to get into company formation for the regimental sergeant major (RSM) to address us.

It was already midday and the sun was beating down. A mixture of sweat and black camouflage paste was pouring down my face. Out of the whole company, two of us were ordered to remain behind, while the others started the long march back to camp. I knew I was in trouble. I was asked how it was possible that I hadn't managed to fire one single round into my target but had been consistently accurate when it came to the target next to mine. Perhaps this hadn't been such a clever move. I guessed the RSM might have seen that trick once or twice before. I decided to act dumb anyway, like I didn't know what he was talking about, but the RSM lost his temper and he ripped my rifle out of my arms. A corporal was appointed to take me for an *afkak* parade (a shitting-off parade). First I was made to leopard-crawl for about 20m, get up and run for another 20m, and then fall down and roll 20m. And then start the whole exercise all over again.

This carried on for at least 30 minutes. The heat was unbearable and

I felt myself on the verge of collapse. Every muscle in my body ached, my head was spinning, my eyes, nostrils and mouth were full of grass and dust, and my elbows were raw and bleeding.

I don't know why suddenly I needed to urinate – in fact, I almost pissed in my pants. I got up, proceeded to open my fly, and started to relieve myself. Aaaah, what a good feeling it was; it felt like I was in heaven. My eyes were actually closed when the corporal came running at me and, with my own rifle butt, hit me square in the chest, causing me literally to take off and land flat on my back. Dazed and gasping for air, I just lay there in the dirt. Then he threw my rifle at me and walked away. I think I must have passed out because when I came around there was nobody around.

Fuck, I thought, I could have died and they wouldn't have known.

Luckily I still had water in my water bottle. I sat up and drank, and then tried to pull myself together and start the long hot walk back to base. I was not even a quarter of the way back when a jeep with two MPs in it pulled up beside me. They took one look at me, no doubt immediately realising what had happened. They didn't ask and, anyway, I was too tired to explain. The lift back was a godsend, though. I stumbled into camp, not too long after the others, relieved to still be alive.

I missed civilian life. I thought about Melissa all the time. Whenever I had to do physical training, it was thinking of her that got me through. I wrote to her every week, and the anticipation of getting a letter from her in reply would keep me on tenterhooks. Our physical absence from each other's lives was driving me crazy and my need to be with her was sometimes simply overwhelming. Melissa, however, was still with Derek – she never had dumped him – and the idea that she was more than likely having sex with him hurt me badly. I thought she would have got rid of him by now, but it was becoming apparent that Derek was going nowhere. More than anything, it seemed, she was afraid to leave him. The way I got letters through to her at Arcadia and preserved our secret was to address the envelopes to myself c/o Arcadia and arrange that Melissa would 'keep' them for me. We kept writing to each other, and in every letter I wrote to Melissa I told her that she was to burn or discard it as soon as she had read it. Of course I didn't

73

realise how hard it would be for her to do that, and in the end it was those letters that were my undoing.

A few weeks before the end of basic training, I received the letter I had been dreading. Our secret was out.

Melissa and Derek had had an argument. In his anger, he had stormed upstairs to her dormitory and begun to pull all her clothes out of her wardrobe, tearing and ripping everything he had bought her. The next thing, all my letters, which Melissa had hidden between her clothes, came tumbling out onto the floor. I tried to imagine my best friend's confusion at all these envelopes addressed to me and how he would have ripped those open, too. When he read lines such as 'Dearest Darling Melissa' and, at the bottom, 'Lots of Love, Shani' our cover was completely blown and the depth of our deception revealed. I felt terrible, but in a way I was also relieved that the truth was out in the open. Now Melissa and I could get together properly.

Derek's reaction was understandable. He couldn't believe what I had done to him. I was no longer his friend. Instead I was his sworn enemy. My heart was in turmoil. I wasn't sure what the outcome would be, but it still looked like there was no way Derek would leave Melissa. He was really into her. Anyway, I would have to wait until my first weekend pass, after three months' basic training, to find out.

Actually, I couldn't wait to get back to Johannesburg to see my family and friends. The pass started on Friday afternoon from 4pm until our return to camp by 8pm on Sunday.

I got a lift back to Joburg with one of the Jewish guys from 14 Field Regiment, who drove a 2-litre Alfa Berlina. I couldn't have wished for a quicker ride home. Franco was a maniac on the road, but he got me to Joan's flat in record time. Because he was one of the *ou manne*, he only had to be back in camp on the Monday morning, which meant I would have to catch a bus back on Sunday night. Joan's flat was a one-bedroomed apartment in a block called Plumridge on the corner of Lily Road and Louis Botha Avenue. It had an enclosed balcony, which became my room.

Word was soon out that I was in town.

I arranged to meet Derek at Arcadia on Saturday afternoon to sort out the Melissa issue once and for all. Back in those days, not having your own car was not really a problem and we used to hitchhike everywhere. When I arrived at Arcadia, Derek's brother Theo was already waiting for me. He and I were good chinas. He wasn't about to take sides, as he had his own problems with Derek, but when he expressed his disapproval of me having fucked my best friend's chick and of blackmailing her into having sex with me, I couldn't believe what I was hearing. Blackmailing? What was he talking about? Fuck, man, Melissa and I were in love! Then he told me that Melissa had confessed to Derek that she had only slept with me because I threatened to tell Derek she'd been unfaithful to him if she didn't.

What a cock-and-bull story, if ever I heard one! Melissa might have had her own reasons for lying, but I held my tongue.

Then Derek arrived on his motorbike and we confronted each other. I could see in his eyes that he was really hurting. In fact, he could hardly speak and he broke down, asking me over and over how I could have done this to him when we were almost like brothers.

Eventually he said, 'Let's fight for her. Whoever wins gets to keep Melissa.'

By then I was having doubts about whether Melissa was *worth* fighting for, especially in the light of her accusing me of fucking her against her will.

'You know what, Derek?' I said. 'You can keep her.' And with that, I simply walked away.

I knew that Derek and I could never be friends again, at least not in the same way of deep friendship and mutual trust. Although I wasn't completely to blame for what had happened, I felt it was best just to move on.

Derek drove off on his motorbike. I was sad but, hey, Melissa had been my chick to start with!

That night a few of my chinas and me met at my sister's flat after she had gone out. We smoked a couple of joints, drank a few beers, and sat around and talked shit about the army. Then, at midnight, we all went to a club in Braamfontein. The place was pumping. As the night progressed I got drunker and even more stoned. Numbing my brain was one way of forgetting Melissa. Then, in the early hours of the morning, I got a lift back to Joan's flat (she wasn't impressed when I stumbled in out of my mind) and on Sunday I slept most of the day. By the time I got to the station I'd missed my bus back to Potch.

The next bus was only early on Monday morning. I imagined I would be in all sorts of shit, be put on extra guard duty or something. I arrived back at camp 20 hours late and was summoned to appear in front of Major Welgemoed, who reminded me of an SS officer. For some reason, this man disliked me intensely and I had a sneaking suspicion it probably had something to do with my being Jewish. I was informed that I was officially being charged with going AWOL and that my hearing would be the very next morning. To cut a long story short, I was sentenced to 21 days in DB (detention barracks).

The Potch DB, which was one of the toughest and most notorious in the country, was situated at the back of the parade ground, opposite the ammunition stores. Hidden by huge bushes and trees, the DB itself was enclosed by a 4.5m barbed-wire fence and it housed about 50 prisoners. It was rather like a POW camp, I thought. Just outside the front entrance was an intricate obstacle course, and on the left was a small gravel parade ground about 20m square. At the entrance to the building was a veranda where the guards would sit and shout orders. The one-stripe corporal with the baby face and big belly was a sadistic bastard I would get to know well. His name was Corporal Swanepoel.

When I arrived I was made to stand at attention on the gravel parade ground while Corporal Swanepoel walked in slow circles around me, whispering in my ear 'Ons gaan jou opfok, rooinek' (We are going to fuck you up, redneck). I was not permitted to budge. It was already 5pm. Everybody else seemed to be locked up already in the cells. After an hour of this psychological intimidation, they checked me in and I was thrown into a cell on my own. I don't think I slept much at all, and at 3.30am we were woken up anyway.

I watched in amazement as all the prisoners immediately got down on their hands and knees and began to clean the cells and corridors. I'd noticed how brightly the polished floors shone and now I knew why. Among us were two trustees, and these guys, who were a couple of the biggest motherfuckers I had seen, were in charge of us. They would torture the other prisoners by making them eat soap, and sometimes they would burn their chests with cigarette butts and make them do push-ups or beat them with their fists. Once the place was clean, a team of three prisoners would go to the mess hall to fetch breakfast.

Afterwards we were permitted to answer nature's call, and to shave and shower. On my first morning, while I was taking my shower, I found myself all on my own. Not thinking anything strange was going on, I went about getting washed up. The next thing I knew, I felt two hands grabbing me from behind, locking my neck in a deadly grip. Then I felt another man trying to wrestle me to the ground. Fortunately for me, I had soap all over my body, which made it difficult for my attackers to hold onto me. I started to shout, lashing out with my fists and elbows, and I managed to fight them off. What the fuck was going on? After delivering a few blows here and there, the two guys backed off and left me alone. I later learnt that this two-man assault team was notorious. Apparently they were allowed by the authorities to rape newcomers.

Everything in DB ran like clockwork. The system was designed to inflict as much discipline as possible, with the goal of breaking you, physically and mentally. After breakfast our *varkpanne* were collected and then a team of two or more guys was required to wash up. One of the corporals would stand next to you and hit you on your elbows and on the back of your head with a long steel dishing-up spoon, all the time shouting *'Maak gou! Maak gou!'* (Hurry up! Hurry up!).

By 6.30am we had to report to the parade ground for inspection in our green prison overalls and combat training boots. At 7 the DBI would arrive, and then for three straight hours we would do the most intensive exercises you could imagine. That first day, besides jogging around the parade ground carrying somebody piggy-back, I did over 1 000 push-ups, 1 000 sit-ups and as many feet-raisers. During the push-ups, I reached a point where my entire body was numb. I would rest my lower body on the floor, push up onto my arms, and collapse, hitting my chest on the hard gravel. It was a gruelling exercise session. Basic training was a walk in the park by comparison. If somebody fell behind, we were all punished and would have to start all over again.

Near the end of the third hour, we had to go down into a squatting position, hold onto the man in front of us, making a train formation, and then bunny-hop ten times around the parade ground. If the chain broke, we would have to start again. It seemed never-ending. It was impossible to bunny-hop without breaking the chain. Guys would get cramps in their calves, while others would just fall over and start puking. Some even collapsed and had to be taken to the hospital.

After our morning exercise session we were given time out and served a cup of tea. Prisoners were not allowed to keep cigarettes or matches on them. The guards had a cardboard box in which they kept everyone's smokes. Your packet would have your name on it. We were called one by one to collect a cigarette and the guard would give us a light, and all this time we would be standing at attention. Once your cigarette was lit, you did an about-turn and went to stand at one of the poles that made up the perimeter of the detention barracks. There you could stand at ease with one hand behind your back while you smoked. Once you were finished smoking you would come to attention, do a left turn and wait until everybody else was finished. Then you would march to the guard and throw your cigarette butt in a bucket. I later discovered the reason for this practice: if you took the filter, burnt it and pressed it flat, you could make a sharp-edged device that could be used to slit your wrists.

After tea, we were allowed to take another short break, and during this time some of the guys would do their laundry. Lunch was served in a small open area with a roof over it. Once lunch was finished, we were allowed another cigarette break, and then some of us were taken out to work on rubbish removal duty. I remember once we found battery acid in the rubbish. On the way back, a few of us rubbed it in our eyes, hoping to get out of PT. We succeeded in being taken to the hospital, where we were treated, but unfortunately they managed to clean our eyes out and we got out of nothing.

From 3pm we had to report to the parade ground again, where we were given full gear, complete with *staaldakke*. Inside our webbing were sandbags. We would then get into platoon formation and begin marching. Most of the orders were shouted in Afrikaans.

'*Links regs, links regs, ooooom ... keer*' (Left right, left right, abooout ... turn).

'*Makeer die pas*' (Mark time).

'Platoon halt!'

At first we marched at normal pace; we also did a lot of marking time marching on the spot. The corporal in charge would then up the pace, shouting the orders really fast. It was impossible to keep in step with the man in front of you, resulting in the corporal getting really pissed off. One corporal had a squeaky voice that rose to a high pitch: '*Julle troepe wil saamwerk nie!*' (You troops don't want to work together); '*Ons doen push-ups. Sak vir 'n honderd!*' (Drop for a hundred). What was supposed to be an hour's marching invariably turned into a vigorous shitting-off session. Twice a week we did the obstacle course, which was tough but mostly fun as we had to compete against each other.

Our two hated trustee friends used to leave the camp before the sun rose, and come back only after the afternoon exercise period. I found out that every morning they went to the bowling green. Bowls, aka old man's marbles, was a popular sport among the high-ranking elderly officers. The two trustees were required to be there before the sun rose and then, using a large piece of heavy sackcloth, they would wipe the dew off the grass before the sun's rays could damage the green. This way it was always kept fresh and smooth. They also had to ensure that the clubhouse and the grounds around the green were immaculately clean. Fuck, that was the ultimate privilege!

Once the day was over, we took our second shower of the day, and for this we had to strip naked and line up next to the barbed-wire fence. Two men had ten seconds to shower. While we were doing this, our friendly corporals, once again armed with the long steel dishing-up spoons, would hit us on sensitive bony spots, urging us to '*Maak gou! Maak gou!*' all the time. In the event that you were not pulling your weight in keeping up with the rest of the squad, news would filter through to you, minutes before shower time, to go stand at the end of the queue. Rumour had it that two guards would beat you up. Nobody wanted to be subjected to such brutality, so we would all push ourselves beyond our limits. Showering was a joke. Try to imagine

79

having only ten seconds to shower and having to dodge a few painful blows as you try to rinse off the soap! It must have been a comical sight, actually: all you could hear and see was 'Ouch! Ouch!' and men dancing around naked.

That first night, after supper, I was totally and utterly exhausted. I fell asleep even before my head hit the ground. At around 1am I woke up, still in a sort of trance. I couldn't bend my arms. Both arms had locked solid. They were also really swollen around the triceps and they hurt like hell. At first I thought I'd been bitten by a scorpion. I couldn't understand what the fuck was going on. Somehow I wriggled my body to the cell door and managed to get to my feet. Then, using the ball of my foot, I repeatedly kicked the door, calling out, 'Help! Help!' at the top of my voice.

That motherfucker Swanepoel was on night shift. Eventually, after about five minutes of my banging and shouting, he opened my cell.

'*Wat is jou fokken probleem?*' (What's your fucking problem?), he asked sarcastically.

'*Ek wiet nie, Corporal, ek dink my arm is gebreek*' (I don't know, Corporal; I think my arm is broken), I said. I turned my shoulder to show him.

He grabbed the top of my arm and at the same time pushed his thumb and fingers into my muscles, causing me to yelp in pain. He had a sadistic smirk on his face.

'Stop crying,' he told me. He said I could see the doctor in the morning. In the meantime, I should just go back to sleep.

Easy for him to say. So long as I didn't move, the pain seemed to subside and slowly I slipped into a deep sleep. The next morning, at 3.30, although my arms were still sore and I still couldn't bend them, somehow I managed to slip into my overalls. The pain was excruciating. Using only my feet and standing on a cloth, I shuffled around the floor of my cell, polishing it as best I could. It had to shine like a mirror or I'd be in shit. I couldn't shave because I couldn't raise my arms to my face, so one of the other inmates shaved me. When the breakfast was dished up, my plate was placed on the floor in front of me and, like a dog, I bent over and ate my food.

At 7am, just before the morning exercise session, Swanepoel walked around checking our hair and seeing whether we had shaved. Knowing that I couldn't bend my arms, I was the perfect sitting target for him. He walked up to me, looked in my eyes, took hold of my ear, twisted my head to the side and then, in a contemptuous manner, asked why I hadn't shaved properly. Then, before I even had time to answer him, he took the cigarette he was smoking and stubbed it out on my cheek. I could hear the hair on my skin sizzle. Then he dropped the butt down the front of my overalls, where it landed on top of my underpants right on my penis. I jumped up and down and somehow managed to undo the buttons of my overalls and get rid of the butt, which had by then already burned a small hole through the fabric of my underwear. While this was going on, Swanepoel had a good laugh. I gave him a dirty look and wished I could throttle him, but thought it better to bide my time. As the DBI arrived, so did the military doctor on his routine DB visit. All those who wanted to report sick were called to fall out. I was the first among the few to leave the parade ground.

I explained my problem to the doctor and he prescribed a muscle cream. On his report card he wrote that I could still do PT but was excused from doing push-ups and the obstacle course. I couldn't believe it. There I was, back in the squad being forced to exercise, and when everyone else was doing push-ups, I had to do sit-ups. How I got through that day I don't know.

At lunchtime, once again I had to eat my food from a plate on the floor. Nobody was allowed to feed me.

But Swanepoel wasn't finished with me yet. On the occasions when he didn't call me 'rooinek' or 'Joodjie', he referred to me as 'die man met die groot bors en die kort bene'. That night he arranged a small surprise for the man with the big chest and the short legs.

About an hour after supper Swanepoel, the two trustees and two other inmates entered my cell. In his hand Swanepoel held a tube of wintergreen cream. He explained that the only way to get the movement back in my arms, which had by now swollen to double their size, was to bend them by force. One of the guys rubbed wintergreen all over my arms and around my elbow joints, while the other held me down. Then Swanepoel himself began the patently enjoyable process of bending my arms. It was agonising. I yelled out in pain. For a single moment I thought saw a glimpse of sympathy in his eyes, but then it was gone, and he carried on methodically, first bending one arm and then the other. I almost passed out from the pain.

I did get back some movement in my arms, but the following morning they had swelled up even more. I looked like a bodybuilder. Gradually, however, as the days went by, I regained full movement.

I'd been in DB for about ten days when Rabie, one of the trustees, completed his sentence and was being returned to his unit. This meant that his job working at the bowling green was up for grabs. That afternoon, after the hour's *afkak* session with full gear and *staaldak*, we were told that all of us would be competing in a race and the winner would be given the coveted bowling green position. This job would mean no more hours of PT in the morning, nor in the afternoon. Toast and jam sandwiches for breakfast and as much coffee as you could drink. At that stage I was literally on the point of breaking down. Every night I cried silent tears. This place was pure hell and I had been pushed to my limit. I doubted I could last much longer. I was going to get that bowling green job if it killed me.

The race began. On your marks, get set, go! We all bolted around the parade ground at breakneck speed. I managed to stay in about tenth position. I was an experienced long-distance runner and I knew there was no reason why I couldn't win this. In times of desperation, like many people, I suppose, I always turned to G-d. Please G-d, let me win, I whispered silently.

The weather was hot, I was dog-tired and my *staaldak* was too big for my head. It bounced about, slipping over my eyes, and I had to hold it steady with one hand. After a few laps it really started to bother me. Legs pumping hard, I worked myself into a strong second position, and with only ten laps to go, I knew I could bag the race. By now the helmet was actually hurting my skull, besides irritating the shit out of me, so I ripped it off my head and threw it on the ground.

As I passed Swanepoel, he called me over. '*Wat die fok doen jy?*' he demanded. '*Gaan haal jou staaldak!*'

So I had to go back to fetch my *staaldak* and put it back on my head. I had now fallen into last position. The pressure was on. I picked up the pace almost to a sprint and, with only two laps to go, I was passing the other guys one by one. Then I was back in second position, and on the last lap the leader and I were neck and neck. I dug really deep; where I got the strength from I don't know, but, by some superhuman effort, I won the race.

Swanepoel wasn't happy. Neither were the others. And the fact that they had been beaten by a Jew made it that much worse. I fell to the ground and lay flat on my back, gasping for breath. I looked to the heavens and I thanked G-d for coming through for me in my time of need. Seven days left in this shithole, I thought, and I wouldn't be doing any more PT.

Working at the bowling green turned out to be a holiday in comparison to what I had gone through. My remaining days in DB would be a breeze. The afternoon before my seventeenth day, and the last day before my release, we arrived back at DB from the bowling green just as the guys were lining up for their shower. While I was standing naked along the fence, I was told by one of the other inmates that Swanepoel had instructed that I was to be the last to shower today. Fuck, I thought, what was going on? I hadn't done anything wrong, but my mind was all over the place. Why would Swanepoel want to beat up on me?

Then it dawned on me. I was getting out tomorrow. My original sentence was 21 days, but through good behaviour I had got a four-day reduction. Then I knew what Swanepoel was up to! Hitting an official carried a minimum of 90 days in detention. He wanted to provoke me into a fight.

The shower was at the back of an open brick construction. There were two water outlets a metre apart, with a wall on either side, but no doors. Beside them were four deep basins where the pots and *varkpanne* were washed.

Everybody had finished taking their shower when I showed up. Nobody was around except Swanepoel, who was waiting for me with a cigarette in his mouth. There was another MP standing with him. I stepped into the shower area. Swanepoel took a deep drag, flicked the butt onto the lawn behind him and began moving towards me. I waited, keeping a careful eye on him. Then he asked me why the *fok* I kept taking the squad out of step when I was marching. What the—? I realised this guy was fucking crazy. And I was working at the bowling green now anyway; I wasn't marching with any squad. As I opened my mouth to tell him he must have mistaken me for somebody else, he slapped me so hard that my ears rang.

Then he jabbed his finger in my chest and said, '*Jou fokken Joot, jy dink jy is sterk*' (You fucking Jew, you think you're strong).

Startled, I could taste blood in my mouth. I could also feel my blood pressure rising. Bang! Another slap across the other side of my face. Then Swanepoel had his fists up, openly challenging me. '*Jou bliksem, slaan my terug!*' (You fucking cunt, hit me back), he taunted. He moved in on me and punched me in the stomach.

I buckled over for a second, straightened up and looked directly into his eyes. 'Fuck you,' I said. 'I'm not going to fight.' Then I turned and walked out of the shower. Swanepoel mumbled something under his breath that I couldn't hear. The other MP was nowhere to be seen.

While I felt a sense of victory on the one hand, on the other I felt strangely humiliated. I knew Swanepoel's intention had been to provoke me, and I was surprised at my ability to control my temper. Under normal circumstances I wouldn't have hesitated. Even though I hated him, and all I wanted to do was smash his face, there was no way I wanted to spend a single minute longer in DB than I had to.

The next morning, when I was released, Swanepoel was not around. When I walked out through the gate in the barbed-wire fence, I felt hardened. I was a changed man. It felt strange, but this was yet another defining moment in my life. I had survived another challenge and had come out stronger.

I was warmly welcomed by my friends back at camp. When asked what it was like in DB, I joked and said that unless you had been there, you couldn't fully claim to have experienced the army. By now we were almost three weeks into second-phase counterinsurgency training. I wasn't given a choice about what field I wanted to specialise in and was placed with the platoon that had been trained to use a 91mm mortar. Just my luck; I had the responsibility of carrying the barrel, which weighed close to 20kg. We were put through a vigorous obstacle course that simulated a battlefield. Manoeuvring between the obstacles with the heavy barrel, along with my rifle and full kit, was no joke. Second phase was pretty intensive. Besides being taught to assemble and fire the 91mm mortar, we were also trained in bush warfare and one-on-one combat.

I started having visions of myself somewhere in the Angolan bush, dodging enemy fire and having to take care of this fucking mortar barrel. Jesus! What the fuck was I doing here? I had had my fair share of fights, but going to war and actually killing somebody was not me. Our generation was mostly anti-apartheid anyway and against the policies of the ruling National Party. The whole world was boycotting South Africa. I saw no reason why I should give my life for a government that violated human rights on such a large scale. I dreaded the thought of going to war and dying for a cause that I didn't believe in.

With every day that went by, however, the threat of going to the border became more real. There was no doubt about it: we were being trained to kill. It seemed as if my fate was being decided by the mere fact that I had made the choice to do my army training first rather than go to college to study. I cursed myself for not having the foresight to know better.

A week before the end of second phase and our deployment to the border, as if G-d had been reading my thoughts, an order came to our unit: North West Command was forming a marching band and they were looking for anybody who played a musical instrument. The timing couldn't have been better. Here was an opportunity I couldn't allow to pass. Four of us Jewish guys huddled together after the parade, excited by the prospect of getting out of going to the border. None of us had ever played a musical instrument before, never mind in a band, but back in my early days at Arcadia I had taken piano and guitar lessons, so maybe that counted. Because music lesson times had clashed with when we played soccer, and because I was tone deaf, my music career hadn't actually lasted more than two weeks. Now I could have kicked myself for not persevering.

We discussed all the possible scenarios. How difficult, we concluded, would it be to learn to blow a trumpet or play a drum? So we all gave our names to join the band. Three of us claimed to be able to play trumpet and the fourth guy said he played the drums. Within 24 hours we were transferred to headquarters and out of the fighting unit. As it turned out, another Jewish guy, from 14 Field Regiment just up the road, also joined, and with him a friend from Durban, Paul Bushmell. We were six Jews out of approximately 20 guys.

Every day we had to report to the main hall, which was also used as a cinema. Outside was the army canteen, where you could buy anything from hot pies and cold drinks to toiletries and other necessities. There were two pianos on the stage in the hall. The guy in charge of forming the band was Staff Sergeant Meintjies. His superior was Captain Henrico, who was there to welcome us all. He gave us a big speech about how important this band was to the 'Big Brass'. Fortunately for me, and for the rest of my friends, our musical instruments would only be issued in a week or two, and until then we were to remain in the hall and just chill. There was not much to do, so, while idling around, we found ourselves smoking weed and getting high almost every day. We were bored out of our skulls.

One morning, while fucked out of our heads, we decided to have races with the pianos on the stage. We were busy pushing the pianos around when the staff sergeant walked in. The man was so shocked he couldn't find the words to say anything. He just stared at us blankly and then he left.

Best of all was that we weren't required to do any guard duty. At the end of the day, we would drive to Joburg for a jol and return early in the morning. In fact, during my entire time in the band, none of us had a bed in the camp. Even while we were driving back at 5am we were getting high. It was like a never-ending party. Some of the

Afrikaans guys who were serious musicians were totally amazed by our behaviour and lack of respect for authority.

Then came the day that our instruments finally arrived. This was the moment of truth, and the moment I'd been dreading. Once we were issued with instruments and music books, we were briskly informed that we had two weeks to practise and prepare for the audition. The pressure was on. Every day we sat in the hall and practised. I tried, I really did, but I couldn't blow a single note on my trumpet. Smoking weed was much easier. At intervals we would jump into our cars, go for a drive and smoke a joint. By the end of the second week, with the help of some of the other band members, and to my surprise, every one of us Jewish guys had learnt to play – everyone except me.

D-day was upon us. One by one we had to go up on the stage where Staff Sergeant Meintjies was sitting, proudly waiting to audition us. Everybody made it through. I hung back to the very last, and then I couldn't delay any longer. I held the trumpet to my mouth, took a deep breath and blew with all my might. My cheeks puffed up and my eyeballs nearly popped, but, except for a farting sound, not a single musical note emanated from my instrument. Jesus, I was embarrassed. Staff Sergeant Meintjies turned red and then went pale. He looked like he was going to faint.

Thinking quickly, I said, '*My mond is nie gebou vir hierdie ding nie*' (My mouth is not built for this thing), and I pointed scornfully at the mouthpiece. I will never forget the expression on Meintjies' face. He was totally gobsmacked. I quickly added, in English, before he had a chance to say anything: 'Perhaps I could play the cymbals?'

Meintjies' face lit up immediately and regained its normal colour. He stretched out his hand and took my trumpet away from me, nodding curtly. There was no way he could return me to my unit. This would have been not only a loss of face for him, but also a sign of incompetence, over and above which was the fact that most of our battalion had already moved to the border. (Although the civil war in Angola had formally ended in 1975, guerrilla warfare was still being waged by UNITA forces who, supported by South Africa, were fighting the MPLA, who in turn were armed by the Soviet Union and Cuba.)

Over the next days and weeks, I would sit around and bang the cymbals together, which, I reckoned, could be done by any fool. Still, the best part of being in the band was that we could go home every night. Captain Henrico was really very fond of us. On one occasion I even brought my sister Joan to visit him, and he proudly escorted her onto the parade ground while inspecting the men.

We were having the time of our lives, on the jol almost every night, loafing about during the day. All I had to do was clash those cymbals now and again. Joan's flat had become a regular sleepover place for my friends; there were times when there were four or five of us crashing there, sprawled all over the lounge. One guy even slept in the bath one night. My sister, bless her soul, was very accommodating and never really complained until, one day, while we were smoking up a storm in her flat, one of my friends blew weed into her parrot's face. The poor creature then committed suicide. When Joan came home, she found that the bird had stuck its head through the bars of the cage and broken its neck. She went totally ballistic and immediately banned my friends from the premises. When Joan was out at work, though, we would still meet there and smoke weed.

It was around this time that I first thought of selling marijuana. Everybody was smoking and we were always looking to score, so one weekend, instead of heading for Joburg, I hitched from Potchefstroom, in my army uniform with a small travel bag, to Durban. In those days soldiers had no problem getting lifts. I got to Durban late at night. I had no idea where or how I was going to score. With my monthly allowance, I had a total of R200 on me. Somehow I found myself in Phoenix, an Indian area north of the city centre. The streets were well lit and the houses were far more upmarket than those in the townships of Joburg. As I was walking down a street I was approached by a young Indian guy. He couldn't have been much older than me.

'Hey, soldier boy, you must be lost,' he said in a cocky voice. 'This isn't a safe place for you to be walking around at this time of the night.'

'Well, maybe you can help,' I answered.

Durban's marijuana was world famous. While we were in Durban over the December holidays after finishing school, whenever we scored weed this would be mainly through the Indian waiters who worked at the hotels. Invariably, they had the best quality. The weed was rolled into brown paper about the length of an index finger and as thick as an earbud. There were 20 pencils to a roll.

'I'm looking to buy marijuana,' I told the guy before he could answer me.

For a moment he seemed hesitant. Understandably, he was wary. He wasn't to know if I could be trusted. He asked where I was from. I told him Joburg.

'My name is Shaun,' I said, sticking out my hand.

He took my hand. 'Cool, man,' he said. 'I think I like you – my name is Samir, but you can call me Sam.'

It was the beginning of a fruitful partnership. As it happened, Samir lived just around the corner, and within an hour he had organised me a big coffee can of loose marijuana, which cost me a mere R150. It was excellent quality. The heads were still slightly wet and had red hairs on them. I also met two of his brothers, maybe an uncle or two, and some friends. We all smoked a pipe together. I remember coughing like hell, which Samir found very funny. The weed was so potent that I almost hit a bummer. For a moment I forget where I was or what I was actually doing there. I couldn't move, the shit was so good. Sensing how stoned I was, Samir made me a cup of tea, after which he offered to drop me on the freeway as I needed to get back to Joburg as soon as possible. The coffee can fitted perfectly in my bag. It was close to midnight when I was picked up by a trucker in a huge Oshkosh truck, who took me as far as the Pietermaritzburg turn-off. Then, luckily, a travelling salesman who was driving all the way to Joburg stopped for me, and I was home just as the sun was rising. I couldn't believe it: I had made my first successful trip in just under 15 hours. When I arrived at the flat in Berea, Joan was still asleep, and I was soon asleep, too, still in my browns and boots.

By the time I woke up my sister had left for work, so I went to the kitchen and made myself a few cheese and apricot jam sandwiches. I phoned Derek and, in as few words as possible, told him about my trip. The eagle had landed, I announced proudly, and he should get his ass over to my place as soon as possible. A couple of months after the blow-up over Melissa, Derek and I had patched up our friendship. It was never quite the same and was sometimes a bit strained, but we got on fine most of the time. First on my list of things to do that day was to go to the bank to stock up on plastic bags (bankies) to pack the weed in. Out of the coffee can stash I managed to get about 70 bags. At R15 a bag, that was almost R1 000 – not a bad profit.

That Saturday night we hit the clubs, and by the end of the night I had sold almost half my stash. Fuck! Weed, I was discovering, was worth more than gold. Club Xanadu in Braamfontein was popular with the elite northern-suburbs Jewish youth. I bumped into a lot of my friends there. The word was out: we had the best weed in Joburg. By Monday morning I had only five bags left. I took one bag back to camp with me and shared it with the guys in the band.

Our first official parade was about to happen. We had practised marching and formations for weeks now, and the day was almost upon us when we were required to wear our step-outs and impress the Big Brass. My Jewish mates and I smoked a huge pipe before we were set to perform. I mean, how could we go to a music concert without getting stoned?

The band got together outside the stadium. Staff Sergeant Meintjies was there to lead as the conductor and to make sure everything ran smoothly. As we entered the stadium, flourishing a chopstick he introduced the first note. We all proudly played our instruments. Stoned out of my mind, I happily banged away at the cymbals. I was having the time of my life when I saw Staff Sergeant Meintjies yelling at me. I couldn't hear a thing, of course, but he seemed to be telling me to stop playing. How odd. And the bass drummer in the centre of the squad kept turning his head and giving me dirty looks. Apparently I was taking the whole band out of tune and out of step. Once this was established, I was given a new role: that of pretending to be playing but not actually playing my instrument at all. Fortunately, in a marching band there are two of you who play the cymbals, so nobody would be any the wiser if I was playing or not.

Fuck, it was funny!

After the parade, which by the way went off pretty well, the brass were very impressed with Meintjies' new marching band, although, sadly, I couldn't share in the glory or take any credit for our success. Meintjies later called me aside and told me in no uncertain terms not to come to practice any more. And when marching, he emphasised, I should please refrain from banging a single note.

This charade went on for a few months before some of us were eventually thrown out. After that, one of the other Jewish guys, Larry, and I became RPs (regimental police) at North West Command Headquarters. Imagine that! One of the biggest goofballs in the South African army was now a military policeman. It just got funnier by the day. The two of us were posted at the main entrance and we were required to check every vehicle that went out or came in. We had our own guardhouse at the gate; just behind us was a large parking lot that was more like a scrapyard for damaged military vehicles. There were Ratels, Buffels and Bedford trucks, all of which needed to be repaired or stripped for spare parts.

Whenever we wanted to smoke a joint, one of us would walk through the parking lot pretending to be checking the perimeter, while the other guarded the gate in the event that a military vehicle might want to come in. Our first few days on the job, we were very serious about it. Whenever the big brass entered, we would come to attention, salute, raise the boom and allow the vehicle to pass through. After a few weeks or so, we were old hands at the job.

By this time, I had also done three further trips to Durban and back. Samir never let me down. Instead of meeting him in Phoenix, we would now meet in the city centre. Derek and I had also organised, compliments of the Arcadia 'after care' (I'll explain later), a two-bedroomed flat in Joburg in a block situated diagonally across and approximately 150m away from the Hillbrow police station. The block was called Clarendon Place and it was on the corner of Louis Botha Avenue and Empire Road. It was a real dump by any standards. The wooden floorboards creaked, and the high ceilings had these intricate ornamental designs along the top. In my room all I had was an old wooden bed, a double-door wardrobe, a dressing table and curtains that I think were from the Second World War. The bathroom had one of those four-legged steel bathtubs that was so deep you could drown in it. The kitchen was something else; our fridge made such a noise it sounded like there were men at work with earth-moving machinery. I continued to live at my sister's place, but we would use this flat to meet our friends. Basically, it became the place where we sold dope.

I remember one Friday night, just before hitting the jol, there were about 30 people in my room, huddled in groups, everybody smoking. There was actually a halo of smoke in the form of a cloud just beneath the ceiling – it was a surreal sight.

Business was good. Derek and I had made enough money to buy a second-hand Datsun 1800 SSS, canary yellow in colour. It was a real Dutchman's car, but we had fun in it. Our reputation for having good weed was growing and our circle of friends was increasing rapidly. People would come and go from our flat in Hillbrow all day long. And whenever somebody came to buy weed, it was an excuse to smoke a joint with them.

Initially when we rented the flat, we had only the bare basics when it came to furniture. Often on weekends a group of us guys would meet at Arcadia, either to catch a game of football or touch rugby, or just to get together with other Arcadians. Some of the juniors were growing up fast and followed the traditions of their predecessors. One of the boys I had taken under my wing when I had lived there was a kid called Morris. Being the youngest of four siblings made it quite tough for him. At any given time we were no more than 20 to 50 kids at Arcadia so we forged an unusually strong bond. We were more like brothers and sisters than a whole lot of children in an institution. So when we needed something for our flat in Hillbrow, who better to turn to for help than our brothers at Arcadia? Morris and some of the other boys secured pots and pans, eating utensils and other items of kitchenware and we smuggled it all out of Arcadia. There were even times when we ex-Arcadians spent the day there, hanging out at the swimming pool or the soccer field and we had some ever-obliging kids sneaking food out to us.

Life in the city was fast-moving, and having to go back to the army every day was a pain. I was growing more and more restless. As regimental police, Larry and I were required to wear red armbands marked 'RP'. This gave us quite a bit of authority. To liven things up, one day we decided that, whenever any cars arrived, we would give them a thorough search – just for the hell of it and to relieve the boredom. I would run into the middle of the road, in front of the boom, and point my rifle directly at the driver, while my partner would check the identification and sometimes, when the mood took him, force the driver and passengers out of the vehicle, check inside, then make them open the boot and, lastly, check under their vehicle with a mirror. Then, one day, some high-ranking officer, who I think was a lieutenant general from Pretoria, came to North West Command dressed in civilian clothing. We put him through our standard vigorous checking procedure. I thought he was some retired staff sergeant or sergeant major and we didn't even bother to salute him. He wasn't impressed; in fact, he was quite annoyed. After allowing him in, not even five minutes later I was summoned to Sergeant Major Visagie's office. He was a short, stout man, probably in his mid-forties, and he had one of those handlebar moustaches that was so long I'm sure the ends could have met at the back of his head. He went ballistic! How could I point a rifle that had live ammunition in it, he demanded, and shake down the second-highest-ranking officer in the entire military? I was lucky he wasn't going to throw me into DB. From now on, I should conduct myself in a military fashion. Dismissed! When I told Larry back at the gate, we laughed so much I almost pissed myself.

Being an RP is like being on permanent guard duty. In a word, it was fucking boring, even when we were stoned. Some days just dragged. I couldn't wait for the day to finish so that I could get back to Joburg to smoke and sell my weed.

Then one particular day, around 1pm, I decided enough was enough. The army wasn't the place for me. I took my rifle, gave it to Larry, removed my RP armband and said: 'That's it, china, I've had enough. I'm not fucking guarding this gate any more. Please cover for me.'

Larry was shaken.

'What the fuck are you doing, man?' he said.

'I'm leaving,' I told him.

'Don't be crazy,' Larry said, but by then I was already walking away. I stood right outside headquarters, put my thumb out and hitched a ride to Joburg.

Although the original six friends from the band had been split up, we would still meet up regularly and we all kept in touch. The night I left the army, Larry came to the flat in Hillbrow looking to buy some weed. He told me everything was cool at the camp, and so far nobody had even missed me. I gave him a bank bag for free and asked him to continue covering for me. This went on for two weeks: I kept Larry happy by giving him free dope, and he made sure nobody noticed my absence. Into the third week, Larry phoned my sister's place saying that Visagie had finally asked where I was. I was having such a good time. We had just made a big trip to Durban in the SSS and had scored about five sacks of weed, each sack the size of an average pillow. Our reputation was growing and our circle of friends was widening.

By now our crew – me, Derek, Mark, Russell and a few other boys – were selling weed to most of our contemporaries who lived in the affluent northern suburbs of Johannesburg. At any given time, there were at least six of us. We were even looking to buy another car. In those days souped-up V8s were very popular, so while looking to purchase something much faster we came across what I think was a 1960 Cadillac Fleetwood limousine. Someone told us it used to belong to former prime minister John Vorster. We paid R3 000 for it.

So there we were, driving our newly acquired Cadillac, but first we had to perform an initiation ritual. We picked up a few friends, shut all the windows, closed the glass partition between the driver and the back seat, and smoked up a storm, forming what we called a hot-box. Stoned and happy, we cruised the streets aimlessly, looking to pick up girls and just generally causing havoc. Driving down Oxford Road near Rosebank, we came across a guy hitchhiking. He was wearing a suit and holding a briefcase. I mean, imagine a limo stopping for a hitchhiker? We pulled over, opened the door, smoke billowing out, and offered the guy a ride. He hesitated at first, but when he got a whiff of the weed, he jumped right in, smiling.

We had a lot of fun with that limo. Unfortunately, the thing guzzled petrol and it also had a serious oil leak. Eventually, it just wasn't practical to keep it and we sold it off.

There was no way I wanted to go back to the army. By now I had been gone for almost a month. Whenever Larry came to the flat in Hillbrow, I just used to give him one or two bags of weed, no questions asked. Then on one particular day, he declined the weed. He said he couldn't cover for me any more. He had run out of excuses. The authorities were beginning to suspect that I had gone absent without leave (AWOL). I didn't really care. Fuck it, man, I thought, let them catch me. The next day I got a message through Joan that my name had been distributed nationwide to all military police to try and apprehend me. I was going to be charged with desertion. At first, I didn't give a damn. Our flat in Hillbrow was as busy as a railway station. Business was good and I was stoned most of the time. I had also hooked up with this chick from Northview High School, Tessa. She was pretty and no more than 15 years old.

Life was great. I was free and running wild. Not a care in the world.

One night Larry arrived. His face was starting to bug me. 'What the fuck now?' I said to him.

'Shaun, you're my friend,' he said seriously. 'I advise you to come back. You are in deep shit, man. I was told that if you come back, they will be lenient with you.'

It seemed like the odds were against me, so, very reluctantly, the following morning I went back to the base with Larry. I reported straight to Visagie. By now my hair was quite long, longer than the average military-style haircut anyway. I definitely didn't look like a soldier.

I was charged with abandoning my post, being absent without leave, and something or other to do with my rifle, but because I had come back on my own steam, I was sentenced only to 90 days' DB, with immediate effect. It hadn't even been six months since my last stay there, but, thankfully, my friend Corporal Swanepoel had by then been transferred to Pretoria.

Apparently some guy had died in Upington DB and because of that there was an inquiry going on into the conditions and treatment of inmates around all the DBs in the country. Instead of the normal three-hour PT session in the morning, this had been cut down to one hour and then another hour in the afternoon. At least something about DB was in my favour.

I was checked in by a new corporal whose name was Naude, a good-looking guy with blond hair and a thin, wiry frame. He spoke fairly good English. He was holding my file. 'I see you are a troublemaker,' he said. Then he got to his feet, lifted his fists and starting throwing punches at me. Fuck! It seemed I was in for another hard time. Instinctively I dodged and blocked him and at the same time threw a few punches of my own. He was pretty quick and appeared to be enjoying our little sparring session. Once it was over, and after signing in, I walked around outside and noticed a whole bunch of guys in blue overalls sitting in the open-walled mess hall praying. Then I walked around the back to where the shower area was and met up with one of the regular inmates. He was an Afrikaans dude, and quite a friendly guy. I asked him who the blue-overalls boys were.

'Jehovah's Witnesses,' he said and added something about them being conscientious objectors who refused to do military training on moral and religious grounds. What else could the army do with them but throw them into DB to serve their two years. Lucky them, I thought.

Then I heard this voice from behind me saying, '*Wat die fok doen julle?*' (What the fuck are you doing?) '*Sak vir veertig!*' (Drop for forty).

The guy I'd been talking to instantly dropped to the ground and started doing push-ups. I turned around to see which corporal it was and I saw that it was actually a fellow detainee giving the orders.

'Fuck you,' I said in English. 'Who the fuck do you think you are?' I reached down and pulled the other guy up. 'Don't do it,' I told him.

This was my second stint in DB. I was an '*ou man*' now and there was no way I was going to allow anybody to order me around. I was also thoroughly irritated and in a bad mood. *And* dying to smoke a joint. The fucker gave me a dirty look but marched off. The Afrikaans dude looked anxious and hurriedly disappeared. So far, two people already thought I was trouble.

As I made my way to my cell, I passed the first cell in the building and was rushed by an inmate. He grabbed the front of my overalls, pulled me into his own cell and shoved me up against the wall in the corner. He was strong, but he couldn't wrestle me to the ground. We were locked arm in arm. The guy was my size, and as ugly as hell. After a minute or so of grappling on our feet, three MPs came running in. They pulled us apart and pushed me out into the passage.

My attacker pointed his stubby finger at me. '*Jy is dood!*' (You are dead) he yelled.

Fuck, I thought to myself, this is really a bad start. I might have been a lot better off doing the 40 push-ups. That night in my cell, the same guy who had been so quick to do the push-ups let me know that my new enemy was none other than the most feared guy in DB. Even the MPs were afraid of him. He was there for military car theft, going AWOL, resisting arrest and assaulting an officer. Over and above that, he was at least a good four years older than me. His name was Daisel. He was the main man. Daisel *ran* the DB.

I struggled to sleep that night, wondering what events daylight would bring. We were now woken at 4am, but the usual routine of polishing the floor and cleaning the toilets remained in place. Daisel wasn't around and the guys in his cell were fast asleep. During PT I realised I was getting dirty looks from everybody, especially from Daisel, but nothing happened. It was obvious he wanted to deal with me personally. When I took my place at the table for lunch, nobody sat anywhere near me except for Daisel, who took the seat directly opposite me. He just sat there, giving me foul looks. Any moment, I thought, he is going to mount the table and rip out my jugular.

Nowadays, before meals – and I assumed this might have had something to do with the Jehovah's Witnesses – prayers were said. I remember the words that lunch time: 'Close your eyes, in the name of Jesus ...' I didn't dare close mine. I noticed Daisel didn't close his eyes either.

Daisel was slightly shorter than me, about 1.7m tall, I reckoned, but he had an athletic build and must have weighed about 80kg. Both his front teeth were missing and he had unusually big canines. He also had pointy ears, which gave him the appearance of a wolf – not a great combination.

We sat there staring at each other. I never batted an eyelid. Then, in Afrikaans, I said to him, '*Dink jy miskien jy's sterk?*' (Do you think you are strong?).

Daisel turned red. I thought the veins in his forehead were going to burst. He was just about to stand up and, I'm sure, throw the table at me, when I stuck out my hand inviting him to an arm wrestle, adding, '*Soos manne*' (like men).

A smile spread across his face, and he nodded his head in approval. Then he rolled his shoulders around, moving his head from side to side and looking around at his followers as if to let them know this was a battle he had already won. Everybody gathered around, even the MPs. We locked hands, our eyes fixed on each other. Daisel's hands were slightly bigger than mine. I thought I might lose, and if I did, I understood that I would be in shit.

Jesus, the fucker was strong! And he used all his strength to push me. My arm started to bend millimetres at a time. I could see it dropping. But then, I don't know how, using all my strength I managed to get him back to the starting position. Arm to arm, eyes to eyes, I held on for dear life. Neither of us budged. I'm sure not more than a minute or two passed, but it seemed like an hour. I was aching, my arm felt numb, but I could see that Daisel was also starting to feel the strain. I knew I couldn't hold out much longer, so I said, 'Draw – *gelyk.*' Daisel agreed. He stood up and stretched out his hand, and I could see in his eyes that I had gained his respect. I was happy to shake his hand, even though I couldn't feel my own fingers by then.

Daisel wasn't very smart, but he turned out to be one of the most honourable guys I'd met in a very long time. After lunch he came to me, put his arm around me, and told me he wanted me to come and stay in his cell. We became instant friends. Daisel was so organised it was unbelievable. He had cartons of cigarettes, a guitar and coffee whenever he wanted, and as his 'china' I didn't have to do any work.

On weekends Daisel would actually be allowed to leave the DB, use one of the MPs' jeeps and go to town to the local disco, returning in the early hours of the morning.

The nights were long and lonely. Ever since the inquiry into DB conditions, things had got pretty lax. There were three bunk beds in our cell. I was given the bottom one. I wasn't sure that I was happy about someone sleeping above me, but it was better than sleeping on the concrete floor. Those first days were difficult. I had not smoked any weed and my throat was raw from nicotine. Besides struggling to sleep, which was nothing new, I was restless.

Foremost in my mind was how Derek was handling my share of the marijuana sales. And I couldn't stop thinking about Tessa, my schoolgirl girlfriend. Through Daisel, I arranged to have a note sent to a friend of mine, asking him to send me some weed. A couple of days later, a matchbox full of weed – 'Swazi reds' – was delivered to me in my cell.

Daisel's job was washing the inmates' overalls. The washing was done outside the actual DB in a shack made of corrugated iron. He arranged with an MP for me to work with him, which gave us an opportunity to smoke without anybody seeing us. On this particular day Daisel had prepared a broken bottle neck. At the mouth end he fitted a rolled-up piece of silver paper, which formed a filter. This was known as a *gerick*. We crushed the Swazi reds, separating the seeds from the leaves, mixed the weed with a little tobacco and loaded it into the broken bottle neck.

I gave Daisel the honours of busting the pipe. It was my first *skyf* since I had turned myself in. I sucked really hard. I could see the weed burn down the side of the bottle neck as smoke filled my lungs. I held it as long as my breath allowed, then slowly exhaled. My mind went into a spin and my perceptions of my immediate environment altered to the point where I didn't know where I was. My mood was one of absolute bliss. It didn't matter where I was. I could have been anywhere. At that moment in time and space, I lost myself within the realms of my being and just let myself be taken higher.

When Daisel and I were washing the overalls in what looked like a primitive steam bath, we used a coal fire to keep the water hot. Once the overalls were placed in the steaming water, Daisel took a piece of soap from a bucket full of broken-up pieces of deep-red Lifebuoy. He made some remark about the soap looking like Rooibart, which was a potent quality of weed, difficult to acquire, and he burst out laughing at his own joke. I couldn't help but laugh as well. I mean, when you're stoned, everything seems funny. And the more Daisel laughed, the uglier he looked. It really cracked me up.

In DB we were allowed visitors once a month. Joan had got engaged to a guy named Malcolm, and the two of them came to visit me, bringing Tessa with them. Tessa wasn't allowed in at first because she was only 15, but then the MPs relented. The visit area was just outside the DB and adjacent to the obstacle course. My head had been shaved completely and my sister was quite distraught at the sight of me. But even though none of them was used to seeing me without hair, they also couldn't help remarking how healthy I looked. The visit was over quite quickly and pretty soon we all had to return to our cells.

I felt alone and lost. Seeing my family and my girlfriend had unsettled me more than I had anticipated. A couple of days after that, Daisel was released. It was only after he had gone that I learnt that he'd spent time in almost every DB in the country. My friend was quite a notorious criminal in army circles. On his last day we embraced each other and said our farewells, and I reminded him to stay out of trouble – unlikely though that was.

My remaining days without Daisel were boring but, luckily for me, because of good behaviour, once again my term was adjusted. After spending a total of 45 days in DB, I, too, was released.

On my first weekend pass I went straight to our flat in Hillbrow. The place was deserted; you could see nobody had been there for weeks. The shelves of my wardrobe had been ransacked and my stuff was lying all over the floor. Someone had been here and conducted a very thorough search. Because nothing seemed to be missing, I immediately knew it had been the *boere*, a term we used in South Africa at that time for the police. When I had last been in the flat, the whole bathtub had been full of weed. Now of course it was empty.

During the past 45 days in DB I'd smoked weed only on two occasions and I looked forward to getting back into my routine. What was it about the green herb that made me a slave of my own desires? For a moment I felt a sense of loss, perhaps the loss of my innocence, the loss of youth. What did it matter, though? I was young and invincible and what better way to pass the time while in the army than getting stoned? I couldn't claim to be a victim of circumstances. I'd made a choice. Choices don't choose us ... or do they? But destiny always has an ulterior motive, I would come to discover, and don't let anybody tell you otherwise. Just when you think you have it all figured out, there's a twist in the road that, more often than not, will alter the course of your life. Nothing is set in concrete.

I had nothing of real value in the flat. It was basically just clothing, which I could collect at any time. I hitched a ride to my sister's flat and got in touch with Derek, who quickly filled me in on how the cops had raided the Hillbrow place. Fortunately, by the time they came most of our stash had been sold, and whatever remained had been moved to another flat before the raid. This was a flat in Yeoville that Derek rented. We had both known it was only a matter of time before the cops would get wind of what was going on in Clarendon Place, with so many people coming and going at all hours of the day and night. Our new flat, we decided, would be out of bounds to everybody.

Over New Year a few of us took our seven-day pass from the army and I drove down to Cape Town with four friends: Gerry, who was from Durban, Sam from Pretoria and Mark and me from Joburg. We drove in Sam's light blue Chevair and it took us just over 12 hours to get there. Our first destination was the renowned tattoo artists, Adams, in Woodstock. It was Gerry who had planted the idea in our heads. I wasn't all that keen.

All the way down to Cape Town, we smoked weed through a small clay pipe. Perhaps smoking weed at the coast is different to smoking on the highveld. You seemed to be on more of a buzz – or it could just have been that we all had that holiday feeling. When we got to Woodstock, we found Tattoo Adams totally fucked out of his head, but he claimed he worked best when he was stoned, so we trusted him. One of the reasons why I was against having a tattoo was because Jews are not allowed to mark their skin. If we do, then, when we die, we cannot be buried in a Jewish cemetery. However, once I was inside the studio I was mesmerised by the different designs stuck all over the walls, from floor to ceiling. What made it even more enticing was that I appreciated art. Suddenly I couldn't resist having a tattoo.

My friend Sam, also of strong faith, also succumbed to temptation. He had a small devil's fork tattooed just above his private parts. I decided to have an eagle done, explaining to Tattoo Adams that the eagle should look as if it was about to pounce on its prey. It goes without saying that my tattoo turned out to look nothing like I had envisaged. Gerry, on the other hand, had a small 'Hot Stuff' tattooed on his right arm and a beautiful eagle on his left, with an American flag.

We jolled in Cape Town for an exciting five days, visiting clubs and bars and picking up chicks. We had to get back to Potchefstroom before our pass expired, and, as it happened, time ran out the night before we made our way out of Cape Town. We hadn't been travelling for much more than an hour when, as dawn was breaking, Sam fell asleep at the wheel. As we were rounding a bend the car started to drift over into the oncoming lane. In the distance we could see a vehicle approaching. I tried to yell out from where I was sitting, behind the passenger seat, but, in that moment, I became paralysed. I couldn't move a muscle and the words that I uttered got lost somewhere between my brain and my vocal cords.

Sam's head dropped to the side and, fortunately for all of us, this small movement woke him up. He frantically corrected the steering, veering back from the wrong side of the road and avoiding a head-on collision. But there was quite a steep drop on our side and the Chevair went flying down the embankment, plummeted under a fence and plunged into a vineyard.

No one moved. We were all in shock. It took a while for us to realise what had happened. Then I rolled down my window and stretched out my arm. I turned to my friends. 'Grape, anyone?' I asked. I don't know whether it was shock or what, but at that we all burst out laughing and couldn't stop until tears were pouring out of our eyes. Eventually we got out of the car, gathered our bags together and hitched back to Cape Town. Sam phoned his family, who arranged a tow truck, and then he and Mark caught a plane back to Joburg. Gerry and I decided to hitch back because neither of us could afford a plane ticket.

After an abortive attempt at doing a physical instruction training course, I returned to my unit, where there were a couple of us *ou manne* who now had not very much to do. We were put in tents and given odd jobs here and there, such as maintaining the gardens and helping with the garbage disposal.

Meanwhile, back in civvy street, our weed enterprise was still growing. On weekends, during the day, when we were not playing football we would be running around selling our bank bags. At night we were at the clubs. By this stage I was popping Obex, a diet tablet that, when mixed with alcohol and weed, put you on quite a buzz.

Our crew had also gained some new members. In fact, there was a whole generation of girls and boys our age who were fast becoming part of the trendsetting drug culture of Johannesburg. And when you had drugs, there were always girls around.

I was 19 years old, almost 20, without a worry in the world. I lived in the moment and had no plans for the future. Why plan ahead when anything could happen? Enjoy the moment as if tomorrow will never come, that was my philosophy. Once caught up in the fast lane, the thrill was too exciting. I knew that I would keep pushing myself to the limit, and so far I had no idea what the limit was.

The year was almost over. It was 15 October 1979, the day I came into the world. Once again I was AWOL from the army. On my birthday about ten friends congregated in two cars on the soccer field at Arcadia, which was where we kept part of our stash. It was a central place, well concealed and was easily and quickly accessible. We made a couple of pipes. Then one of the guys offered me a pill. When I asked him what it was, he said, 'Don't worry, man, it'll make you feel good.'

What the heck, I thought, it's my birthday. What better way to celebrate than to get completely fucked out of my head. I popped the pill. We smoked a few more pipes.

One of my friends had driven there on a Yamaha XT 500 Thumper, which was a scrambler but also a road bike. We were about to leave when I asked him if I could take the bike and fetch my chick. I would meet them all at our prearranged rendezvous at the Killarney shopping mall. They all left before me, as I first wanted to make sure our sack of weed was well hidden in the dense foliage at the bottom of the driveway. By now the pill had kicked in; I felt light-headed and, compounded by the effects of the marijuana I had smoked, I was ready to rock and roll. I jumped onto the motorbike, kick-started it and pulled a slight wheelie, lifting the front end of the bike in the air and leaving a trail of dust and grass behind me. I turned onto Oxford Road. The engine beneath me roared like a beast. It was a powerful machine.

Man and machine racing together against the wind – it felt fantastic! I opened her up full throttle, through all the gears. I must have been clocking anything between 140 and 160kph, passing and overtaking cars at such a speed that they seemed to be standing still. All I was wearing was a pair of jeans, a T-shirt, my canvas tackies and an open-face helmet. The speed I was travelling at made tears stream from my eyes.

The next thing I knew, a woman in a midnight blue BMW turned in front of me without using her indicator ...

It happened right outside Temple Emanuel. Whether I was slow to react or not wouldn't have made a difference at the speed I was going, and I hit her squarely between the front wheel and the driver's seat. Luckily, the bike and I were airborne. I landed on the pavement to one side and crashed into the concrete wall, while the bike wrapped itself around a tree. Besides being grazed all over, I couldn't move. My left leg was twisted to one side in what anyone could see was an abnormal position. It was obviously broken. I was screaming from the pain. Then I heard a loud crashing sound. The BMW was blocking the traffic on the oncoming side of the road, and an Audi and a Mercedes had ploughed straight into the bitch's car.

I felt this hot liquid on my body; I looked down and saw blood, but I couldn't understand where it was all coming from. Then I saw that my baby finger had been almost completely severed. It was hanging by a piece of skin. This made me forget about my leg and start yelling, 'My finger, my finger!'

Then I heard my friend Mark, aka Long John, screaming my name.

My friends, who had been waiting for me, had obviously realised something was wrong and had come looking for me. Mark later told me that, when he saw the point of impact where the bike was and where my body lay in a twisted position on the pavement, he thought I was dead for sure. Mark was in a red Datsun 1200 with four of our other friends. I'd heard the screech of brakes, which was actually Mark driving into the back of the other two cars in the pile-up. Fortunately, only the front of his car got smashed.

I was taken by ambulance to the General Hospital in Hillbrow. I had to inform the clerk who checked me in that I was a soldier. This was a standard regulation for all soldiers in civilian clothes who were injured while on weekend passes.

The doctor told me that they couldn't treat me, that I would have to be moved immediately to 1 Military Hospital in Pretoria. I pleaded with him to at least give me something for pain. At first he refused, until my friends, who had followed the ambulance, almost fucked him up. He then quickly administered a shot of pethidine.

The ride to Pretoria was terrible. With every bump the ambulance went over, I felt a rush of pain from my leg to my brain. Once we got there I was rushed to theatre for surgery. When I woke up, I found myself in quite a big ward, but I was still only semi-conscious, and moaning and groaning. My entire body ached. My right leg was so stiff and sore it might as well have been broken, too. I was stretched out on my back, with the broken left leg in a full plaster cast and elevated on two pillows. It throbbed like I couldn't believe. I couldn't stop the tears from streaming down my cheeks.

In an attempt to distract myself and also to familiarise myself with my new surroundings, I half-lifted my head from my pillow and did a quick reconnaissance of the ward. The patient to my immediate left looked like he was from outer space: he had both his legs in some sort of contraption with all these pulley cables and protruding steel pins, which seemed to be holding his upper thighs together as well as his lower legs. Both his arms were broken, too, and they were also suspended from a complicated-looking steel structure. On top of that, his head was completely wrapped in bandages. I wanted to shrivel up in shame and crawl into a hole. This guy had injuries one thousand times worse than mine and he was lying there in silence. I wondered if maybe he was dead. I looked to my right and then all around me. In comparison to everybody else's injuries, I could consider myself very lucky. There, at that moment, life was teaching me another lesson, and only later on would I understand the full impact of it.

Later, I was given some painkillers and the tablets knocked me out. I don't know how long I'd been sleeping when I felt somebody hugging and kissing me, and wishing me happy birthday. It was my sister Joan, who had come to see me with some of my friends. Despite the pain I was in, I was pleased to have them around me, but I don't remember much after that because I passed out soon after being woken.

The following morning, an entourage of doctors and nurses came to do their rounds. I could see that the doctor who came to my bed wasn't at all happy with what he was seeing on my X-rays. He carefully explained that I had sustained a compound fracture of both my tibia and fibula and then strongly suggested that they operate immediately and insert a steel plate into the leg. If this wasn't put in, he said, I might walk with a limp for the rest of my life.

As a child, I'd had these visions of playing football in the English First Division for my favourite team, Manchester United, even maybe representing my country in the World Cup. I was a great footballer and a big fan of the game. One moment you are who you are, the next second everything you ever dreamt of is taken away from you. I cursed myself for taking that fucking red pill. What the fuck had I been thinking? One bad choice made on the spur of the moment had changed the course of the rest of my life.

In life, there are some choices that are not within our control. We can't choose who our parents are, for example, or who our children will be. But the other choices, the ones we deliberately make ourselves, ultimately define who we are. Perhaps taking that pill and getting on the bike was the beginning of a series of bad choices that would mould me and determine the course of my life. And even if I knew that such choices might lead to an untimely death for me, did I care? Truthfully? No, I did not.

Many of my idols, like James Dean, Jimi Hendrix, Jim Morrison and Janis Joplin, had all died before they reached the age of 30. Who wanted to live past 30 anyway? I mean, 30 was like fucking *old*, and I was just barely out of my teens.

Besides the bad news he'd just delivered, the doctor also wasn't happy with the way my leg had been set. I heard him instruct one of the nurses, in Afrikaans, to have the plaster removed so that my leg could be reset. I called out to the doctor and he came back over to my bed. I told him that under no circumstances did I want a steel plate, screws or any other foreign objects planted in my leg. Taken back and clearly disapproving, he reluctantly acquiesced and told me that the choice was mine.

After the doctors finished their rounds a nurse and a male assistant arrived, presumably a national serviceman doing his two years as a medic, and together they cut the plaster off my leg with a vibrating metal saw. I asked the medic what had happened to the guy in the bed next to me and, for that matter, most of the guys in the ward. It looked like they were all pretty fucked up.

He told me that I was in the same ward as all the casualties who were being flown back from the Angolan border and that the guy next to me had been in a vehicle that had hit a land mine. My conscience pricked me a little bit because I had managed to wangle my way out of fighting alongside these soldiers, but mostly I felt blessed. I could so easily have been a border war casualty myself, but, ironically, here I was anyway, a casualty from a different war, a war of recklessness that could have been avoided. What a fuck-up I was. It just went to show: you should never stop counting your blessings. No matter what your circumstances are, there is always somebody, somewhere, less fortunate than you.

The idea of using a bedpan (basically taking a crap in my bed) was something I couldn't tolerate, so, after a couple of days, with the assistance of a medic, the painful task of climbing out of my bed began. Just lowering my broken leg to the floor and the restoration of blood flow caused the most terrible pain; in fact, it was so sore that my whole body started shaking. I cried out to the medic, saying, 'I can't, I can't.'

This guy had no sympathy. He said, 'Man, it's up to you. Do you want to take a crap or not, because if you do, you have to *vasbyt*.'

And so, slowly, inch by inch, *vasbyt* I did.

A few days later I was getting around on crutches. At first this was really difficult, and painful, but it became easier with practice. The doctors had also managed to sew my baby finger back on. It had been severed at an angle from just behind the nail, shattering the bone. It was bandaged and kept immobile in an aluminium brace, which was held together by an adhesive bandage.

After two weeks I was moved to another ward that was full of soldiers who were well on their way to recovery or who had only minor injuries. Time in that ward just dragged. I spent most of my days sleeping and the nights reading whatever books happened to be circulating. One of my favourite books, strangely enough, was *Papillon*, the best-selling account by Henri Charrière of his incarceration and escape from prison in French Guiana. The title of the book takes its name from the butterfly – *papillon* – he had tattooed on his chest.

Although my finger had healed and the stitches had been removed, it looked deformed to me, a bit like the front end of a hammerhead shark. It looked almost as if someone had sewn a thumb onto it. It also felt clumsy, ugly, and I kept knocking it against everything. When the doctor did his rounds one morning, I told him my problem. He examined the finger and was convinced that he could fix it by replacing the bone with a pin and a little trim here and there. He told me confidently that he could reshape my finger and restore it to its former self.

I was totally unpersuaded. 'You know what, doc,' I said with bravado

I didn't really feel, 'let's just chop it off. It will be one less fingernail I'll need to cut.'

One thing about the military hospital, they didn't procrastinate, and I was booked the very next day for the procedure. I woke up back in my ward and had to keep my hand upright to prevent the flow of blood to the wound. Those first few nights, I found it very difficult to sleep, as my arm was suspended in a sling above my head. Within a couple of days, though, my finger had gone septic. It was dark in colour and smelt terrible.

The doctor was concerned. He told me that if the infection spread any further he might have to amputate the whole finger *and* part of my hand. Fuck, this couldn't be happening. The doctor then quickly added a 'but'. In life there is always a 'but', and invariably it's not a good sign. In this instance, though, the 'but' had a positive ring to it. The doctor said there was a chance that the finger could be saved, but I would have to clean it three to five times a day using Eusol, which is an antiseptic liquid, and bandage it up with penicillin gauze. So every day I cleaned my finger and dressed it. At first, there was so much pus that I would have to take a syringe, stick the needle quite far into my finger and drain the pus out. It wasn't pleasant, but within a week the infection had gone and I had saved my hand.

Even though I was recovering in hospital, I was still a conscript in the South African army and had to complete my time in the military. Because I'd been in DB, the time spent there, which totalled 62 days, had to be added to my original mandatory two years of service, which, in effect, meant I would have to do an extra two months. But still, I now had *min dae* (few days). My army service was coming to an end at last. Knowing this, and also knowing that I wasn't going to be returned to my unit, I started becoming belligerent and giving the nurses a hard time, undermining their authority at every opportunity. It got so bad that I was moved into a private ward. It had been almost a month since I'd smoked any weed. Maybe I was craving it, or maybe I just wanted to smoke for the hell of it, but, whatever it was, I needed to get my hands on something.

I had befriended one of the medics and I kept asking him to organise something for me. Finally he came through. Using a candle, I started to prepare a bottle neck in my room. I fitted some silver paper in the, bottom, gave it to the medic and told him to call me when everything was ready. We were going to smoke it outside, at the back of the ward. I hopped along to the rendezvous on my crutches. The medic was there, as well as two Afrikaans guys I didn't know, but who also wanted to smoke. So, being the gentleman that I was, I gave one of the strangers the pipe to bust. I gave him a light and, as he sucked, the weed started burning, smoke filling his lungs. There was a popping sound and then pieces of burning weed shot out of the bottle neck. The fucker who was supposed to have prepared the pipe hadn't separated the seeds from the leaves. As the guy exhaled the smoke, he drawled, 'This weed is so good, man, it even pops.' I was finished. I couldn't stop laughing. Obviously he had never smoked weed in his life before. In fact I could see by the colour, dryness and the way the stuff was burning that it was really shit quality. It was 'majut', the cheap weed smoked in the townships and the worst quality you could imagine. You bought it in matchboxes.

Having smoked the best-quality weed, I shouldn't have smoked the crap these guys had organised, but, being the fool I was, my logic said that a single hit was better than nothing and might even satiate my craving. I was my own worst enemy. The very reason I was in hospital was because I'd indulged in a mind-altering substance that had impaired my judgement. If I had had any sense I would never have taken another drag of a single joint. I mean, what was the point in numbing your brain? But there I was again, staring into nothingness. I had a splitting headache, a sore throat, a broken leg and was minus part of my finger – shouldn't that have been enough of a wake-up call? How long would it take before I realised that drugs were destructive and destroyed life?

After a month in 1 Mil, I was discharged not only from the hospital but also from the army. My family had organised me a room in a private house in Kernick Avenue, Melrose. The only problem was that my bedroom was upstairs and, still being on crutches, stairs were a real struggle for me, so, for the time being I was confined to my bed.

At first it wasn't too bad. A lot of my friends came to visit and made me a joint here and there. I even got laid once or twice. I don't know what it is about fucking a guy with a broken leg, but something about it seemed to turn girls on. Over the course of the seven months I was in plaster, I slept with a lot of chicks.

After a while, I started getting restless. I needed to get out of the house. One weekend I insisted that my friends come and fetch me and take me on the jol. They were only too eager to take me out. Theo, Derek's brother, was my best friend then. We were both ex-Arcadians and we were inseparable. We had some really great times. He was a black belt, wild as hell, fearless and always ready for a fight. He lived in Sandown in a cottage on his father's property and we would hang out there, smoking weed in a clay pipe, or chillum. While I lit the match and held it to the pipe, Theo would suck so hard he would finish the entire pipe on his own in one drag. This didn't impress me very much, so when we smoked his weed he would bust the pipe; when it was mine I would have the first hit.

While my leg was in plaster, Theo would fetch and carry me wherever I wanted to go. On that first weekend out, going down the stairs and climbing into the car wasn't too easy. As soon as we left the house, the first thing I said was 'Let's have a joint'. My friends laughed, and as one, three hands stretched out to me, each one clasping a joint. 'Thank you, guys,' I said, 'I have a lot of catching up to do. Where are we jolling?' I was told to sit back and enjoy the ride.

We were in three cars, numbering 12 strong. Derek had been invited to the 21st birthday party of an army friend named Greg, but he'd been told that the invitation strictly extended only to him. Greg specifically asked him not bring any of his wild friends – we had a reputation that stretched way back. Greg lived on the first floor of a block of flats. Before we went inside, Derek explained the situation. We were gatecrashing, he told us, and he asked us all to promise that whatever happened we wouldn't cause a fight.

The Chinese have a saying: 'Don't trouble trouble, unless trouble troubles you'. As much as we tried, and for reasons that only the powers above knew, trouble had a habit of following us wherever we went. When we entered the dimly lit apartment, which had a quaint furnished entrance hall, I could see that there were at least 30 people already in the flat. The lounge area was fairly big and there were streamers and balloons all over the walls. Hanging from the lights was a banner with the words 'HAPPY 21ST GREG' written on it. Oh how cute, I thought sarcastically. So a 21st might be a milestone in a person's life, but surely getting totally fucked out of your mind with the boys had to be better than some faggoty little party! In fact, I decided, Greg deserved to get fucked up.

When we showed up, there was a Bob Marley track playing and quite a few people were vibing to the song. You should have seen Greg's face when we waltzed in, with me hopping on my crutches. The expression on his face read: Disaster Waiting to Happen.

Derek went straight to Greg to wish him happy birthday, while the rest of us, before he could kick us out, quickly split up and mingled with the crowd. Not that Greg would have had the balls to throw us out, nor would we have gone without a fight. One of our crew, whose name was Fred, was from Durban and he had only recently joined us. He was renowned for being wild. Once Fred had a couple of drinks inside him it was guaranteed there would be a fight. He also became almost childlike when he was out of it and would often steal something, not because he was a thief but more out of sheer mischief.

Somehow most of us had worked our way to the bar, which was out on the balcony. As we usually did, we downed our drinks as fast as possible. As everyone knows, after a quick couple of shots, alcohol soon numbs the brain. We couldn't have been there for more than an hour when Fred tried to steal a bottle of whisky. I was standing inside the flat, but right by the balcony, when an argument broke out between one of our birthday boy's friends and Fred.

The next thing I knew, Fred started hitting anybody and everybody within his immediate radius. I don't know what the fuck happened then, but, probably because there were so many people on the balcony, the balustrade collapsed and Fred, along with a handful of other people, went over the edge and plummeted to the ground. Among the casualties were at least two girls, who were quite badly injured, and one guy who was bleeding profusely. I managed to get a glimpse over the edge, where I spotted Fred, who had landed on his back on top of the broken bricks. He struggled to his feet and I heard him say 'Where's my fucking flip-flop?' Then he plucked the shoe out of the rubble and walked off. The party had come to a sudden end. We all left before we were thrown out. Derek, who had got a mouthful from his friend, was the last to leave.

My close friend Mark was a tall, lanky fellow who was not at all aggressive, let alone physically strong. For some unknown reason, a while back Mark had badmouthed a guy named Jeffrey Anthony. Jeffrey was the leader of a Lebanese gang in Joburg at that time. Although we were rivals in the marijuana trade, generally there existed a mutual respect between us, and Jeffrey operated by a code of honour that most old-school gangsters adhered to back then. I still don't know why Mark did what he did, because Jeffrey was largely feared by his peers, and especially by those who were younger than him. In any event, the word was put out to have Mark fucked up.

One afternoon, when I was still on crutches, Mark and I were bored and so the two of us and Russell got in the car and started driving aimlessly around town. We were cruising down Louis Botha Avenue when Russell and Mark decided they wanted to play Space Invaders at Pan Burgers near Corlett Drive. I reminded them that Pan Burgers was where a lot of the younger Lebanese guys in Jeffrey Anthony's crew hung out. They said we'd just drive past, and if it wasn't too busy, we'd go and play. I was quite friendly with most of the Lebanese guys, so I wasn't too concerned about myself; it was Mark I was more worried about.

Apart from one or two youngsters, we found the place more or less deserted, so we went in and started playing on the machines. We'd hardly got started when the Lebanese boys gradually filtered in. Before we knew it, we were outnumbered by at least three to one. Two of the guys grabbed Mark and started threatening him. Leaning on my crutch, I grabbed the one guy by the shoulder. 'Take it easy, china!' I told him. He turned around and told me in no uncertain terms to keep out of it. This was not my problem, he said, and pointed out the obvious, namely, that I already had a broken leg. The next thing I knew, Russell was trying to make a run for it, but not before he got a punch in the face. He jumped into the car; I followed on my crutches, and by some miracle Mark also managed to get away. Before we could get moving, though, one of the senior Lebanese guys – I didn't know the guy myself – walked up to the car and motioned to Mark to open the window. I told Mark that he shouldn't but he did anyway, and this guy just gave him one punch square on his nose. I actually heard Mark's nose crack and break.

At that time, between the Lebanese and ourselves, the marijuana trade was divided fairly. I met up with some of the guys from my own crew and shared with them what had happened to Mark. We discussed whether we would take any action, but most of us knew that Mark had brought what had happened to him on himself, and so to involve all of us in retaliation would disrupt everything. A couple of days after that, about six of us were walking out of the Killarney shopping mall when out of the blue we bumped into Jeffrey. We stopped to talk and the subject of Mark came up. Jeffrey said bluntly that Mark had deserved what he'd got. We just let it ride and we went our separate ways.

Months later, after a full recovery, Mark was once again in a fight. He got beaten up so badly he ended up in hospital. When I visited him there, I was shocked at his condition. I told him that if I found the guy who'd done this to him, I was going to fuck him up.

As the days passed and Mark recovered, I got the name of the fucker who'd done the actual damage. I learnt he was an amateur boxer called Lance who was undefeated in ten fights, which pissed me off even more. Mark was really such a harmless guy. It was also rumoured that Lance had the reputation of being one of the to-do guys on the street. I already had told several people of my intention to fight him.

By now my schoolgirl girlfriend Tessa and I had parted ways and I had hooked up with my friend Russell's sister, Katy. One weekend, while I was at their place in Atholl Oaklands, Russell had one of his friends over, and who should it be but Lance, the very person who had fucked up Mark! The guy was right there in the living room and apparently, so Russell told me, had heard I was looking for him. I followed Russell to the living room. As I walked in, my adrenaline was pumping.

In situations like these, I'm not much of a one for words, but the guy was dressed in a suit!

'Are you the guy who beat up Mark?' I said to him without any preamble.

Lance nodded and gave me a challenging smirk.

Motherfucker, I thought, moving closer.

Then he quickly added that he lived around the corner and asked if I would mind if he went home to change into something more comfortable to fight in. What the fuck? Was this some kind of *date*? I was ready to take him out there and then, and I didn't think he'd given my mate Mark any chances. But being the gentleman that I was, I agreed, although with some reluctance.

And so Lance left. I still had a hangover from the jol the night before, so I decided to have a bath while I waited, and while I was happy and relaxed in a tub of hot water Russell came into the bathroom and rolled me a joint. He pleaded with me to go easy on his friend. Whatever happened, he said, please don't kick his head in. I didn't say anything, but I kept having visions of Mark's beaten face. Soon after my bath, Lance returned, dressed in tracksuit pants, sleeveless T-shirt and a pair of running shoes. I was dressed again, too, but now that the joint had taken effect, I was kind of mellow, and not nearly as angry as I'd been earlier.

Lance and I were about the same weight, although he may have been about an inch taller than me. I saw that he was sweating; he had clearly been warming up. My friend Derek was there, and Russell acted as referee. Russell stood between us, we squared up, and the next thing I knew Lance rushed me. He jumped up in the air and started throwing a series of punches to my head, one after the other. I held both my fists up to my face in an attempt to block his punches, but they just kept coming. What the fuck, I thought, what's this guy trying to do?

With my left hand I grabbed his hair on the side of his head and in one swift motion pulled him to the ground. Then with my right hand I pounded him exactly three times on the side of his face. Lance shouted, 'Stop! Stop!' just when I was thinking of finishing him off with a kick or two to the face, and I vaguely remember Russell asking me not to.

Fuck, I thought, the fool was surrendering already.

As a child, when I was in Arcadia, whenever we fought – and we fought a lot – if you were forced into submission and you uttered the words 'I give up', it signalled an immediate end to the fight. On principle you stopped as soon as your adversary admitted defeat.

I had no choice but to let the bastard go, but what the hell – at least I had kept my word to Mark. Revenge had been exacted. I remember wondering to myself how this guy had gained the reputation of someone you shouldn't fuck with when he'd capitulated so easily. Anyway, he apologised for what he had done to Mark and put out his hand, which I shook. Then he left, satisfyingly humiliated.

Russell, Derek and I wasted no time: we quickly made another pipe.

I hoped Mark would learn to stay out of trouble, but that was wishful thinking.

Chapter 4

Rags to Riches

Soon after recovering from my motorbike accident and coming to the end of my two years' military service, I got my first real job. I started working in the rag trade as a salesman. My chief motivation for pursuing this line of business was the company car that came with it. Strangely enough, Derek and I both applied for positions in clothing sales at the same time, although independently. We both got the job. Having my own wheels and being out on the road all day tied in well with my other line of business. So my life as a salesman at Terryvette clothing began. My hours were from 7am to 5pm five days a week. Before very long I was seeing and servicing up to 40 agents per day. I was earning good money, too: between R4 000 and R7 000 a month. Accountants weren't even earning that in those days.

And on the weekends I partied hard, drank, went to clubs and got high. Girlfriends came and went and generally life was good.

According to the doctors who had attended to me during my stay in hospital, I was probably going to have a limp for the rest of my life. Being a fighter, I was determined to prove them wrong. When the plaster was removed, my leg was as thin as my arms, the skin flaky and peeling. I was advised against playing any contact sport and it was also suggested that I see a physiotherapist. Instead I joined a martial arts club in Doornfontein called Goju Ryu Seiwakai. It was run by

Shihan Booth, a 7th dan who was married to a Japanese woman, also a black belt. My legs were weak, and at first I struggled to keep up with the class. Goju Ryu was full contact; at the end of every lesson we would have to free-fight, and Shihan Booth was not happy unless blood was drawn. If it wasn't, he would personally call one of the students up and draw blood himself.

With time, I grew stronger and I lost my limp. I attained the level of brown belt. My best friend at the club was a guy named Pat. He was a grade higher than me and had a lightning-fast roundhouse kick. We agreed that when we came up against each other in a free-fighting session we should use only our fists and not our feet. I knew I would have no chance against him otherwise. Then one day the occasion arose and we were pitted against each other. While we were fighting, out of the blue Pat kicked me square in the face. Luckily I managed to turn my head to the side, so most of the impact was on the side of my head and nose, but I still saw stars. Thinking that my nose was broken, I instinctively put both hands to my face. Shihan went mad. What would happen if I was being attacked in the street, he shouted. Would I tell my attackers to wait a second while I checked if my nose was okay?

So we had to start again. The instant Shihan gave the instruction to continue I delivered a lunge punch straight to Pat's face. He fell backwards and blood spurted from his cheek. As he dropped, I moved forward but found I just couldn't deliver another blow. He was my friend, after all, even though the fucker had hurt my nose. Instead I stood there feeling sorry for him. Shihan started shouting at me to finish him off. I couldn't believe that I was about to beat up my friend, so I just looked at Shihan and said, 'No'. Then I turned around and left the gym. I never went back.

I worked for Terryvette for over a year and I did really well there, earning decent money and jolling on weekends. It was a good time to be young, free and wild. Once I had gained strength in my leg and exercised carefully, I started a social football team, which we called Mandrax United, and we would play against other social teams, of which there were many around Joburg at that time. Friday and Saturday nights, my friends and I would move among the many clubs and restaurants in town – Charlie C's, Arlecchinos, Mike's Kitchen and the Turn 'n Tender in Greenside. The schwarmas at Mi-Vami's in Hillbrow were legendary, and Fontana's in Highpoint was open 24 hours – after a night of clubbing, buying a hot roast chicken there and eating it on your own was no problem. When we were stoned, sometimes we would head over to Wurstbude for German sausage served with sauerkraut, which was great when you had the munchies, or to Milky Lane, which had the best waffles in the world.

I was offered a job with one of Terryvette's competitors, Crystal Clothing, which I accepted, and I got into a relationship with a girl named Penelope. We became close and in December that year she planned a holiday for us to the Transkei. In the 1980s, this was a popular destination. The primary attraction for us was not the beautiful and undeveloped coastline, but rather the excellent weed you could get there. Penelope invited two of her best friends, Kiara and Andrea, to come along with us, and I asked Marco and Gerald to join us as well. Marco was a fellow Arcadian and Gerald was a mate who played in my football team. Our intention was to spend at least a week in the Transkei, then drive down the Garden Route and hit Cape Town. In the Transkei I would buy a stash of marijuana, sell it in Cape Town and use the profit to pay for my holiday.

We left Johannesburg the second week in December, driving in convoy – Marco in his white Kombi, Gerald in his Ford Escort and me in my Skyline. The girls had enough luggage with them for three months. They were real kugels and a whole lot of fun to be with. The drive down was a blast. Music blaring – Talking Heads or Bob Marley – all of us wearing our Ray-Bans; we were just so cool. We smoked weed the whole way and pulled over whenever we got a chance, to buy cold drinks.

Because I was responsible for the girls, around 11pm the first night I decided to pull over. I didn't want to risk driving at night while stoned out of my head. Heaven forbid that I should have an accident and something should happen to my valuable cargo. Already Penelope's father didn't exactly approve of me. So we pulled off the road and reversed into a thick covering of bushes, where we made a last pipe, after which we all passed out. It couldn't have been more than a couple of hours later when there was a knock on my side window and a torch was shining in our faces. It was the police, and there were two of them. I thought I was dreaming. We were in the middle of fucking nowhere; what the fuck was going on? I also had LSD in my wallet. I rolled my window down and asked if I could help them, and the officers very politely said that we needed to move our car to a rest area allocated for trucks and cars, which was only about 500m up the road. I thanked them just as politely and rolled my window back up again. A lucky break, that was for sure!

I woke up early in the morning just as the sun was rising and we continued on our journey. Naturally, first things first, I smoked a joint. The drive through the beautiful scenery of the Transkei interior was pretty uneventful and, surprisingly, there weren't any roadblocks. The gravel roads were slippery from recent rain and there were lots of potholes, so driving became quite dangerous. Marco's Kombi broke down and I had to tow him. It was hectic. There were these buses coming around corners at incredible speeds, almost wiping us out. I sobered up very quickly. Fortunately, we found a garage that was able to fix the Kombi.

At Port St Johns we stopped at a trading store that looked like a rundown shack from an old Western but was amazingly well stocked with camping equipment and food. As we pulled in our cars were surrounded by African kids no older than 13 or 14, who seemed to have come out of nowhere. We realised right away that these kids were looking for customers: in each one's outstretched hand was a sample of marijuana. One of the stronger-looking kids had the best quality out of the group, so I bought what he had and told him to come see us at the camp site. I didn't know exactly where we'd be, but he said no problem, he would find us. After buying supplies for the next few days we left the store and came to a fork in the road. If you took the right fork you would end up at the municipal camp site, where there were toilets and showers but you were required to pay; if you took the left fork you came to a beautiful camp site, but with no public amenities whatsoever. The road into the municipal camp site was so steep that we reckoned it would be impossible to get out if it rained, and we could be trapped there for days. We took a vote and the general consensus was to take the undeveloped camp site, which was more alluring anyway. Driving in was horrendous all the same. The road was wet, and several times our cars almost slid over the edge. No sooner had we found a cool spot to pitch our tent than a light drizzle began to fall and the wind picked up.

We had barely parked the cars when Andrea, in her nasal kugel tone, said, 'I need to use the loo, Shaun.' I just packed up laughing before reminding her that we *had* voted on this. 'Is it a number one or a number two you're wishing to do?' I enquired. 'If it's a number one, you see that bush about 30m away? That would be your best bet. If it's a number two, then that very same bush will provide enough cover for you, but take a toilet roll with you and the spade I have in the boot.'

Andrea stared at me in complete disbelief. 'ARE YOU MAD, SHAUN?' she snapped. 'In that case, I'm not going.'

'Baby,' I told her as I began unpacking our camping equipment, 'we are going to be stuck here for a few days, so you either go and do what you have to do, or hold it in – it's up to you.'

Marco and Gerald helped me pitch the tent. Sadly, it was too wet to make a fire but we settled in pretty nicely. Although it was still drizzling, we took a walk to see where the beach was. It was a beautiful sight. With the weather so overcast, though, we walked back and sat in the tent and smoked marijuana. Later that afternoon the kid we'd met at the trading store came and found us, bringing with him a bundle of the same weed we'd purchased earlier. What more could we wish for? Music, a light drizzle and the best weed. To cut a long story short, we were stuck there for two days, but our little friend made sure we never ran out of weed.

On the second day, the wind was so strong that it ripped my tent and we were forced to take shelter in the car. Everybody was miserable; by then we just wanted to get the hell out of there. Our fortunes took a turn for the better on the third day when a scorching-hot sun broke through the clouds. By lunchtime the road seemed reasonably dry, and we decided to leave while the going was good. With the poor condition of the road, I couldn't risk taking any passengers so the girls had to hike up the hill. They were *not* impressed. After that bit of adventure, we went and booked into a hotel. Gerald and Marco slept in the Kombi while the girls and I had beds. After showering for the first time in three days we all gathered around and smoked a Mandrax pipe. It was such a relief being back in civilisation.

Gerald and Marco decided to go and look for the kid who'd been keeping us in weed to find out if he could take us into the mountains. He said he could, and in fact he took us on a long drive along winding sand roads that weren't even safe for a cattle cart. We were taken to a tribesman named Julius, who was famous for making the best liquid hash in the world. He had a whole crop growing on the other side of the mountain. Apparently his hash was sold on the streets of Amsterdam, or so we'd heard. I had a little surprise for him. I doubted whether he'd ever smoked Mandrax.

To get to his hut, we had to leave the car 500m away and do the rest of the distance on foot. Julius, who looked like an old chief, met us at the entrance to his hut with a smile from ear to ear. He invited us inside. We all shook hands and introduced ourselves and then we sat on sections of logs cut into stools. Julius brought out what looked like a Turkish opium pipe, a bit like a hubbly-bubbly, and we smoked with him. Then I made him a Mandrax pipe. He was dizzy from that – hell, he was so stoned. We bought a 5kg coffee can of marijuana from him for R150 and assured him we'd be back in a few months' time.

While we were sitting there smoking, I was on cloud nine. No traffic, no buzz of people around, just pure tranquillity. I felt one with nature. The quiet, together with my altered state of mind and being so far removed from civilisation, really did something to me. While I was tripping out on the magnificence of nature, the sun disappeared behind these ominous black clouds. I remember pointing in their direction and saying to the guys that if we didn't get out of there, we'd get stuck like we had been at the camp site. We knew by then that the Transkei roads turned into rivers of clay as soon as the rain came down.

We said hurried farewells and left, but the clouds were moving faster than we were. Before we even reached the car, rain started bucketing down. We managed to drive down the mountain just ahead of it. For a while it was touch and go. No fucking around with nature.

Funnily enough, as we got to the bottom of the mountain, a BMW came around the corner. It was one of my mates from Joburg.

'Like, what the fuck are you doing here, man?' I asked him, laughing, as we drew up alongside each other.

'We're going to see Julius,' he answered, just like it was an everyday happening.

I advised him to come back another day because it was too dangerous to drive. He ignored my warning and drove up anyway, and I wished him luck.

We went back to the hotel, where I packed the marijuana into bank bags, leaving them slightly open in case the weed went mouldy. Sometimes if a crop is picked too early and stored, mould can set in very quickly and then the stuff is unsmokeable. That afternoon we relaxed at the hotel and walked on the beach. We planned to go the next day to Umngazi River Mouth, a popular holiday resort on the Wild Coast. It is set in a valley on the bank of a beautiful lagoon, with huge white sand dunes and deserted beaches around it. A perfect place for a great day out.

Early in the morning, just before we set off, we all swallowed half a cap of LSD. We took with us about three litres of vodka, orange juice, our ghetto blaster with lots of music, boogie boards, an ice cooler and some food. We were going all out for a day of partying. We also had enough marijuana for an army. Penelope had her Nikon camera. Marco and I had our firearms. We found a place to park our cars and proceeded to cross the river mouth on foot. It was low tide so there was only a few centimetres of water to wade through.

We found a good spot in among the sand dunes, settled in and made a fire. The music was going, and we started drinking vodka and orange juice. Once the LSD took effect, and after smoking marijuana, we were all totally fucked. Some of us took flattened cardboard boxes up the sand dunes and slid down on them, shrieking with laughter and landing in the lagoon, while some of us swam in the sea. Penelope and I decided to explore the area just behind the chalets at the resort. Actually, we were hiding from Marco. Everyone was hiding from Marco. Man, he was so out of it, he looked like his head was going to explode. He was joking, of course, but he kept running after the girls and he was pretty scary. The girls were actually frightened. When you take LSD your senses become heightened and physically you become abnormally strong. You also see things that you normally wouldn't. Everything becomes colourful and beautiful. Penelope and I came across a place where spiders had spun the most amazing webs and we were both completely captivated by the patterns. Through the foliage I got occasional glimpses of Marco on the beach, looking around desperately and obviously wondering where everyone had got to.

It was such an amazing day that we completely lost track of time, and by the time we all reconnected and had smoked some more weed, we'd been on the beach for about seven hours. By the time we got back to the river mouth, the tide had risen and there was now a raging river. I volunteered to wade across first to see if it was safe for the others to follow. At the forefront of my mind was the possibility of sharks, which are known to like river mouths. I was also concerned about Marco's condition, and so I told him to give me his gun. Getting across was no easy feat. I was tossed around by the current and cut my feet on the rocks. The water came up to my shoulders. Once I reached the other side, I left the guns on the embankment. In the meantime, Penelope had given Marco her camera to carry across for her – what on earth possessed her to do that, I don't know. I made my way back and instructed the guys to allow the girls to cross with me first before they followed. All three girls clung to my shoulders. It was frightening anyway, and it was made worse because all three of them were crying. At any moment we could have been swept out to sea; that's how strong the current was. Once we were safely on the other side, I looked back and saw that Marco was already in the middle of the river mouth.

He was waving Penelope's camera around above his head, asking how much it was worth. To him it was a joke, but I was worried. He was so fucked out of his head he was likely to drop the camera in the water, so I rushed back in, waded over to him and grabbed the thing out of his hand, and just in time, too. Eventually we were all safely on the other side, exhausted, all with cut feet, and we lay sprawled out on the sand. Nobody uttered a word, not even Marco.

We spent that day hanging around the hotel. The next day was Christmas Day. Someone told us about this long isolated beach where the sand was white and stretched as far as the eye could see, so we planned to go check it out the next day. We left early as usual, with all our beach luggage. We also took with us champagne, party caps, whistles and rattles – and of course I brought along the drugs.

As before, we all popped some LSD before we set off. We found the beach easily enough, but accessing it was more difficult. We ended up walking across some sort of parade ground that had a flagpole at the edge of it; it looked like a Scout camp. It was very isolated, though; there wasn't even a dog in sight. We still had to walk quite a distance along the shoreline to reach the beach we were looking for. While walking we noticed a barrier reef just off the coast. Already the LSD was starting to kick in, and Penelope and I decided to go out onto the rocks and explore.

While we were looking for shells among the rocks, I happened to look towards the coastline and saw Marco, waving frantically and calling my name. I couldn't understand what the fuck he wanted, so I chose to ignore him. Then he shouted so loud I nearly fell off the rocks. I turned around and saw Gerald holding his forearm. Something had happened. I assumed that maybe a snake had bitten him.

I made my way back to the beach. Marco looked so shocked I thought his eyeballs were going to pop out of his head. What the fuck was going on? Gerald looked down at his forearm; when I followed his gaze, he released his hand and, to my horror, revealed a huge hole in the flesh. I could see the muscle inside his arm. It was a gruesome sight.

What had happened was that he had taken the broken bottle neck we used as a pipe to smoke marijuana and stuck it in the pocket of his baggies, but had left the end sticking out. When he'd bent down to pick something up his forearm snagged on the jagged head of the glass, slicing his arm open so deeply that you could see the tendons.

Where the fuck was the hospital? What the fuck was *I* supposed to do? I was tripping on acid, we were in the middle of fucking nowhere, and I just couldn't believe it. It bummed me out immediately.

Even in my state of being high, I couldn't help noticing that there was no blood. Gerald was dark-skinned but his face was as white as snow. He was in deep shock. I tried to take stock of the situation and formulate a plan. It was decided that Marco would drive Gerald either back to the hotel, where I was hoping they would have a first-aid kit, or somehow get him to a fucking hospital. We would stay behind and wait. It was still early in the morning and there was no point in all of us going along. Once Marco and Gerald had left, I needed a joint. Then the girls and I opened the champagne, plonked ourselves where we were on the warm sand and started partying. There wasn't a soul around. We lay on our towels, switched on the music and just enjoyed the morning sun.

About three hours passed and we all started getting irritable because Gerald and Marco had not returned. Then Andrea freaked out and said she was leaving, so off she flounced. It was weird: the further she walked the smaller she became until only her head was visible, and then she simply disappeared. The whole scenario was repeated in reverse when she came back again. I thought I was seeing a mirage. Well, I suppose you might call it that.

By now we were more worried than irritated. We wanted to leave the beach but there was so much luggage it was impossible for me and the girls to carry it all on our own. Luckily, two couples came walking along the beach just then and they agreed to help us. Still raving out of our heads, we made our way up the embankment and onto the parade ground, where we walked slap-bang into a platoon of policemen who were marching there. It was bizarre. I was as high as a kite, but the shock of seeing the police jolted me back to reality. I had weed in my bag and LSD in my wallet. I thought I must have looked guilty as hell, but the police didn't even give us a second glance. Maybe we did look like regular holiday-makers.

Marco and Gerald eventually returned to the hotel. They had managed to find a local doctor, who had stitched up Gerald's cut.

As far as I was concerned, it was time to leave the Transkei, but there was one more stop to make: Coffee Bay, with its famous natural wonder, the Hole in the Wall. From there, we meandered down the coast – I was popping acid and everyone was smoking joints – and the view was magnificent. When we got to Cape Town, we stayed in Bantry Bay in an apartment overlooking the Atlantic Ocean. Cape Town was buzzing. It seemed like the whole of Johannesburg was down there. We hooked up with a bunch of our friends who were members of the Houghton Country Club, one of whom was Barney. He told us how he and his crew had spent a day in a nature reserve, Bain's Kloof, about 120km northeast of Cape Town, where there was apparently a beautiful waterfall. It sounded great, so we decided to head out there the following day.

There were about eight of us, all togged out in our Ray-Bans and beach gear, and a couple of us had eaten slivers of LSD. The waterfall wasn't all that exciting, but it was good to be out in a nature reserve on such a gorgeous summer's day. We put on our music and made ourselves comfortable around the picnic area. In my travel bag, which went with me wherever I went, I had ten plastic bank bags filled with weed. I settled down with my back against a rock, took a handful of weed, placed it in a Frisbee and proceeded to crush and separate the stalks and the seeds. We made a few joints for everybody; what remained in the Frisbee was enough to fill about half a matchbox.

Andrea came over and asked me if she and the other girls could have the remaining weed. I handed the Frisbee to her, warning her to be careful and not to leave it lying around. We guys were standing away from where the girls were sitting. We had just finished smoking when three park rangers turned up. In their green uniforms, armed with rifles that were so old they could have been from the Boer War, I couldn't help thinking they looked really funny. I was really high by then, of course. I pointed towards them and said loudly, 'Hey, guys, look, we're being attacked by Israeli paratroopers.'

Within seconds, the rangers came down the slope in a cloud of dust, rifles trained on us. We were told to freeze. Andrea still had the Frisbee and the marijuana in her hand. Luckily they didn't search us guys there and then. The rangers were more interested in catching Andrea than anyone else. We were ordered to follow them to the office, which was about 400m away. I deliberately walked slowly and managed to fall a little behind the others. I took out all ten bank bags, which were in a yellow plastic supermarket bag, folded them as tightly as I could and stuffed the bag down the front of my Bermudas. It was far too bulgy and anyone could have seen I was hiding something, so I tied my towel around my waist, but still the bag stuck out. So I let the travel bag hang from my shoulder and over the front of my pelvis and tried to look casual. When we got to the office, the rangers took Andrea inside while I walked to the car and, as nonchalantly as I could, opened the door. I pulled the plastic bag out from my crotch and placed it under the car. I threw my travel bag on the front seat. Then I walked back to the office, where by now the rangers had summoned the police from Worcester.

Andrea was crying. She asked me to take the rap. Normally, I might have owned up, but I had specifically warned her, and she'd been caught red-handed ... I mean, all she'd had to do was drop the Frisbee. We were all standing around waiting for the police when I happened to turn around; from where we were standing, the yellow shopping bag containing the ten plastic bank bags of weed was in full view. There was no other litter anywhere around. I almost crapped my pants. Apparently what had happened was that our friends from the Houghton Country Club, who'd been there the day before, had caused so much havoc that the rangers had immediately assumed we were the same group. And this time around they weren't going to let us get away with anything.

The rangers ordered us to bring our cars over to the office, but nobody spotted the yellow bag. As I got into the driver's seat, I scooped up the bag. I managed to park on a sand hump, so when I got out of the vehicle I hurriedly slipped the bag behind and in between the front wheel and the hump.

Two white boys in blues arrived soon afterwards in a police van. By now Andrea was on the verge of hysteria, so Penelope agreed to go with her to the police station. The police then conducted a thorough search of my vehicle. Clearly, they were not very well acquainted with drug paraphernalia. There was a broken bottle neck behind the driver's seat and a piece of silver paper rolled into a spiral filter, but they didn't seem to be bothered by these. When Andrea and Penelope were put into the back of the police van, I suddenly had visions of Andrea's parents, both of them pointing their fingers and scolding me. I imagined her father being so mad that he was practically frothing at the mouth, about to grab me by the throat and squeeze me to death, telling me he had trusted me with his only daughter, and now she was in jail. Andrea's whole protected little world was crumbling around her. Here was a good Jewish girl being busted, and that desperate look of innocence on her face, almost as if she was heading for the gallows, stayed in my mind for a long time. The police told us that we should come to the court in the morning, as the girls would appear first thing.

Fortunately, Andrea got off with a R150 fine, her father didn't kill me, and we all breathed a collective sigh of relief.

After that, we stuck to visiting the beaches and tourist attractions in Cape Town.

Come January, all my friends who were at university withdrew from the social scene, soon to be lost in their studies, and I went back to my job as a salesman. One night, after we had been out jolling and smoking weed till the early hours, Penelope's father put his foot down. As we opened the door to her house, he was standing there in his boxers, grandpa vest and these funny slippers. I pissed myself laughing, but he didn't see anything amusing in the situation. He grabbed Penelope by the hair and told her to go to her room. I started shouting at him, warning him not to touch her, but he slammed the door in my face. After that, I was banned from the house. Although I still cared deeply for her and we saw each other from time to time, Penelope became caught up with her studies and it was difficult to sustain our relationship. At the end of the year, her parents bought her a ticket to travel around the world. I was heartbroken. When Penelope left, I felt abandoned and I looked for consolation by smoking weed and getting high. This would become a pattern for me – living on the edge, danger-ously and destructively.

M

I went to work for a company called Fedgas. I was the youngest member of a strong sales team. The company put us through a vigorous training course, and it was a very challenging job. Proving to a manufacturing company that it was more cost-effective to use gas than electricity required a sharp mind. Negotiation took place at executive level. I loved that job; it was stimulating, and I envisaged myself having a good future with a company that was already well established in the industry. When I joined I was given a basic salary, a company car and a medical plan; I was also assured that in the months to come a commission package would be worked out on the sales I made.

I was young. There was no real rush to be successful, and during my time with Fedgas I cleaned up my act. While I was still selling weed on the side and partying and smoking at weekends, I had also saved enough to buy myself a CB900F Honda motorbike with a modified Kerker exhaust, and I was living in a spacious one-bedroomed apart-ment that led onto a garden with a communal swimming pool.

I had a steady girlfriend named Lana, whose father, Ronnie, was a partner in a top law firm. Lana was a good and stable influence in my life. Ronnie drove a Porsche 928S, which on occasion Lana and I stole while her parents were out of town. Anyone who drives a Porsche will know that keeping to the speed limit in a car like that is almost impos-sible. Lana was the worst backseat driver I had ever met, but she was surprised at how easily I was able to drive the car, when her father had been taught by the agent.

One Saturday night I took the Porsche at quite a speed through the infamous S-bend on Louis Botha Avenue, which was known as Death Bend. The car handled beautifully. Although she'd sat tight through the corners, Lana was having a fit. Unless I slowed down, she threatened, this would be the last time she'd ever allow me to drive the Porsche.

Actually, I didn't really care whether I drove it again or not, because that experience alone was worth it.

Anyway, we drove to a party at her friend's house where everybody was smoking weed and getting pissed. I didn't drink any alcohol that night because I felt a certain responsibility about getting the Porsche home unscratched.

Around midnight, we left the party, slightly stoned, but I still jumped behind the wheel. Lana was freaking out, but I stubbornly insisted I was fine to drive. On the freeway, I opened her up and clocked almost 300kph. If we'd gone any faster, we would have taken off. Amazingly, nothing happened and we got the car home safely, but even so Lana kept to her word: we never took the car out again.

Lana and I were crazy about each other, although our relationship was more physical than anything else. For a while during our time as a couple I was clean. She was a Scorpio, strong-willed and used to getting her way. Among her less appealing attributes, though, was a tendency to get jealous and be possessive. If she caught me looking at another woman, I would be accused of wanting to fuck her.

Lana had been blessed with breasts that were the envy of every girl, and men would fantasise over them. I would spend hours fondling and sucking them. Foreplay was never so exciting. Then one day, out of the blue, Lana decided to have a breast reduction. I was against the idea, but she went ahead and had the operation anyway. I couldn't believe what a mess they made. The fucking plastic surgeon deserved to be shot. Her breasts were half the size afterwards, and it looked as if a butcher, not a doctor, had gone to work on her. Also, her stitches came apart, causing an infection, so that was another disaster. Luckily, her nipples still matched, and I was actually quite surprised the surgeon had managed to line them up evenly. Still, Lana had a lot of pain. I would help her dress and clean her wounds and eventually she healed pretty well, but she was left with unsightly scarring. Sadly – and here I have to be truthful – after the operation I was no longer physically attracted to her, and this was probably the beginning of the end of our relationship.

At the time, my neighbour was a single mother from Mauritius. She was of French Creole descent, with dark skin and blonde hair. She had a beautiful daughter, Cherie, who was still at school. Whenever I went for a swim in the communal pool, the daughter always seemed to appear from nowhere and she would join me. She was probably no older than 16, and to begin with I paid her hardly any attention. It was her mother I would fantasise about when I was masturbating.

At this stage, Lana and I were arguing constantly. Sex had become less frequent, and it was obvious to both of us that we were on the verge of breaking up. One night, while I was home alone, I smoked a joint and was lying flat on my back on the carpet, eyes closed, my arms stretched out, and silently singing along to the lyrics of the song that was playing on my stereo. I had left the back door open. I was so caught up in the music that it took me a few moments to sense a presence in the room. Standing over me was Cherie. She was wearing these tight little shorts and, from where I was lying, her legs seemed so long I could have sworn they stretched all the way to heaven.

Covering her firm, voluptuous breasts was a flimsy little T-shirt, her nipples practically piercing through the fabric. Fuck, she was hot. I was not sure how to read the situation. Smiling apologetically by waving her hand, which had an unlit cigarette in it, she asked, 'Do you have a light?' in what was definitely a seductive tone.

'Well, hi there,' I said, pushing myself up on my arms. 'We have never formally been introduced. I'm Shaun, and you are?'

'I know who you are,' she laughed. 'I'm Cherie.'

I jumped to my feet. 'Just a minute, let me get you a lighter,' I said.

All I was wearing was a pair of jeans. While I made my way to the bedroom, I thought of putting on a shirt. My lighter and packet of Camels were on the bedside table. As I turned around, Cherie was there. She had followed me into my bedroom and was standing so close to me I could feel the warmth of her breath on my face. I felt dizzy. I reached out my hand and moved her hair back from her face, and pulled her towards me. As our lips touched, with my other hand I squeezed her breasts, then caressed them with both hands. Our tongues mingled hungrily, exploring each other's mouths. I placed my hands on her buttocks, pulling her tightly against my manhood. I literally ripped the little she was wearing off her taut muscular body and in a minute I was in bed with a little tigress.

In the middle of making passionate love to her, my conscience started troubling me. I was being unfaithful to Lana. I stopped moving my hips, still holding Cherie tightly, and let out a deep sigh. Fuck, what was I doing? I rolled off her, soaked in her wetness.

'I, uh, have a girlfriend,' I said lamely.

'And I have boyfriend,' Cherie said, lighting up a cigarette.

That may well be, I thought to myself, but the problem was that I could never look Lana in the eye as though nothing had happened. Too late! I had eaten the forbidden fruit and it was quite apparent that Cherie was not planning to leave my bed until she'd finished what we'd started. Sensing my hesitation, she put out her cigarette and moved her body onto mine, touching me all over. It felt good. We kissed, grabbed, groped.

Then she straddled me and with her hand guided me inside her soft, wet, hot pussy. Turning her over, I mounted her, lifting her legs until they almost touched the pillow. It was wild. Eventually she climaxed and I followed soon afterwards. Heaving and panting, we lay side by side on our backs. Then Cherie began to tell me that her boyfriend, Peter, used to score weed from me, and that she had seen me at nightclubs but had been too afraid to approach me.

We chatted and smoked a joint and later she left.

Feeling guilt-ridden about what had happened, in an attempt to clear my mind, I took a midnight dip in the pool. On the one hand, I felt guilty for cheating on Lana, but probably more because of her extreme jealousy of other women than for the fact that I had been unfaithful; on the other hand, knowing that a break-up was imminent, I didn't actually give a fuck, or so I thought. I didn't tell Lana about my infidelity, but women generally have a sixth sense about these things. Eventually she asked me if I had been fucking around, and I confessed. And so we broke up.

I was really distressed by the break-up. For a long time I couldn't accept that I had lost Lana, but there was no way she was going to give me a second chance. For weeks I would drive out on my motorbike to where she lived, knowing that she would recognise the sound of my exhaust. I would do ridiculous speeds through the bends and the long stretch of road that led to her parents' townhouse complex. I was torn between my heart's desire and my own inadequacies, and emotionally I felt crippled, like a blind man searching for light in a world of darkness. The more I stumbled, the harder I fell. The more I fell, the longer I was bound to keep falling.

My perception of love was mixed in with pain and fear of abandonment. I seemed bent on destroying love and running from those who showed me affection. This was my twisted way of expressing a love that was so profoundly beautiful it would drive me to the brink of insanity. With Lana gone from my life, all I wished for was to die a painful death. Pain made me feel alive. Lana had told me that she never wished to see or speak to me again, and I took it very badly. I was set in a destructive pattern of behaviour that would become deeply ingrained in my being. I would run and keep on running.

No sooner had we broken up than Lana hooked up with this guy who came from a wealthy family and who represented everything I wasn't. I tried to be happy for her. In my mind, no woman on this planet deserved to be cursed with the likes of me. I heard that this punk had badmouthed me, however, even after learning about my background.

At this time a friend of mine from school days ran a video shop in Victory Park. He knew I had a score to settle with Lana's new boyfriend, who, as luck would have it, was one of the video shop's clients. I had just arrived at the video shop on my motorbike one day when he and Lana were pulling out. My friend quickly pointed them out to me. I jumped back on my bike and raced after them down the long sweep of Rustenburg Road and all the way to Barry Hertzog Avenue, weaving my way through traffic. I drove up behind them, driving dangerously close to their car, and gestured for them to pull over. Lana recognised me instantly. I remember thinking they looked like frightened chickens. Then I changed down a gear, opened full throttle, tapped through the gears and disappeared into a long line of traffic.

I never saw Lana again.

Chapter 5

Drugs, Sex and Guns

Whenever things in my life fell apart, I would find myself running. Material things meant nothing to me, and time and again I would lose my job and just about everything I possessed. This recurring pattern was usually determined by the amount of drugs I was consuming.

After my break-up with Lana I started using drugs again, but now it was mainly Mandrax. In those days it was popular to pop Obex, smoke weed, drink alcohol and take LSD. It was while jolling at Club Bluebeat one night and tripping on LSD that I met Dennis. We discovered we had a lot in common: we both sold drugs and loved to get high and to party. He used to hang out at a commune in Yeoville. Between Dennis and me, we could get our hands on almost any drug. Most of my customers lived in the northern suburbs of Johannesburg and were part of the South African Jewish community, roughly 200 000 strong, and most of us knew each other either from school or through social events. Almost everybody smoked weed. Through Dennis, I was introduced to a whole new generation of revellers, from punk rockers and college kids to prostitutes and gays. One of Dennis's closest friends was a diehard punk rocker named Brett who played bass for a garage band. As first impressions went, Brett looked like your typical high-school dropout, except that he had one of the meanest Mohicans I'd ever seen. Surprisingly, he had a degree in sound engineering or some shit like that – I don't really remember. What a cool guy.

George the Greek was another of Dennis's friends. He came from a well-to-do Greek family who owned a café close to the coloured areas of Newclare and Bosmont, just west of Joburg. These suburbs were rarely frequented by white folks, and the area boasted some of the city's most notorious gangs, such as the Fast Guns and the Western Boys, who were constantly at war with each other. Fights between these rivals were vicious and brutal, often resulting in violent deaths.

George was one of the few white guys who dared enter these areas. He introduced me to many of the coloured merchants, such as the legendary Oom Bertie from Newclare, who was instrumental in pioneering Mandrax as a smokeable drug. One of his sidekicks, 'Kidnap', was notorious for having engineered the very first high-profile kidnapping in South Africa. The rest of the gang had all done hard time for crimes that varied from hijacking cars and housebreaking to rape and murder, not to mention armed robbery.

As a sales rep with a company car, I had the perfect cover to enter these areas, as all my sales agents were black South Africans. As it happened, one of my areas was an industrial one, actually called Industria, which converged on Newclare, and during my rounds I regularly popped in to score Mandrax from Oom Bertie, who was supplying many of the boys who were pushing drugs on the street corners.

It was in Newclare that I befriended Kaffs, a coloured guy originally from the Cape whose skin was unusually dark. He ranked high in the Fast Guns hierarchy. It wasn't long before I was able to move around the streets of Newclare without fear of being robbed, and I became a regular customer, scoring Mandrax there for all my friends. I even spent a weekend staying over with Kaffs and smoking it up all day.

George lived in a cottage in Melville, but he would come and hang out at the commune in Berea that I'd moved into. It was just off Harrow Road, which linked the highway from the city to the suburbs. Over time, several high-rise apartment blocks had sprung up in the area, and the best known of these were the Metropolitan and the 54-storey concrete tube called Ponte, which was believed to sway slightly when buffeted by strong winds.

Life at the commune was pretty hectic but also a lot of fun. There was a constant flow of diverse people, all of whom had one thing in common: we all loved to get high. If you were one of those who were partying in the early 1980s, you will recall a carefree era similar to the hippie period of the 1960s, where smoking weed and popping acid were part of the new generation of rebellious youth challenging society's norms.

Disgruntled with the South African political system and feeling the weight of the expectations of their parents, in the 1980s more and more teenagers were drawn to the drug culture. Sexual attitudes were liberal. Drugs, sex and rock'n'roll – we lived by them and many of us would die by them, too.

Heroin was virtually unheard of at that time. One of the more fashionable drugs was Wellconal, a small pink tablet that you crushed and diluted with water, and then shot intravenously. Because of its chalky substance, it could block up your veins, causing them eventually to disappear completely and forcing addicts to shoot up in the most unusual places on their bodies. Many junkies died from overdosing. Actually, Wellconal scared the shit out of me. Like heroin, I saw it as a bad-luck drug and one to stay far away from.

By this time I had changed jobs again, and I was working for a company called Jabula Clothing. I was new at the company and had been recruited from my previous job with a promise of better prospects. One condition of my employment, which I'd stipulated when I'd joined, was that I wouldn't have to do any cold canvassing, which I hated, as most days I was either hung over or stoned. My job description was sales representative, but really we sales reps were nothing more than glorified order-takers. All we did was serve our agent. Our target market was your average black factory worker, most of whom couldn't afford to pay cash for things. Most items were marked up at least 300 per cent. The way we operated was that each salesman was allocated an industrial area. Our managers would establish our runs; normally they were required to go through the proprietors of a company and identify a reliable worker who had been employed for several years. This often turned out to be either the 'boss boy', wage clerk or the tea lady. Ideally, huge factories with hundreds of employees were the most economically viable propositions.

If companies refused to allow us in, claiming that we would distract their employees from their work, we would return during lunch break and find an agent inside who was willing to work for us. Each agent would be provided with a colourful catalogue that featured African models showing off our fashion range, which included clothes for the entire family. They would pass our catalogue around to their co-workers and then take orders, which they would either phone through to our company or give us as order sheets during our weekly visits.

I would see and call on 30 to 40 agents a day, covering five different industrial areas a week. I would deliver orders of goods, show the agents our new lines and provide them with new stock. The amount they sold, and the amount of money they collected, determined their income. Their commission was anything from R1 to R50, a sure thing of 10 per cent from R50 to R150, and they got 15 per cent over and above that, which guaranteed them a flat 20 per cent, which we paid out weekly, or when requested by the agent. Some agents preferred to allow their commission to accumulate.

You had to be really vigilant when entering the townships. Sales reps carried a whole range of stock in their station wagons, and there were a few isolated incidents where reps had been robbed of their stock and the cash they carried. On many occasions when an agent had left his employment, I would drive into the township and collect what he was owed and, in certain instances, continue doing the business. During the Sebokeng riots of the mid-1980s I still drove through the townships, even though it could be really scary. Once a mob of angry protesters attempted to attack me, but luckily I always kept the car engine idling and I made my getaway, leaving their disappointed faces covered in a cloud of dust. If they'd caught me, I might have been lynched or had a burning tyre thrown around my neck.

When an agent sold or delivered an item of clothing, they were required to collect half the cost as a deposit from their customers and they were also responsible for collecting the weekly instalments thereafter. There was a daily flow of cash coming in. The more agents you served, the more money in your pocket. (In my case, the more *I* earned, the more I would spend on drugs.) Because I was dealing with factory workers, I would dress very casually, mainly in jeans and a T-shirt, although this was against company policy; reps were expected to dress semi-smart. Still, all my agents, despite my appearance, respected and liked me.

My manager at Jabula Clothing was a real arsehole. He was this tall Afrikaner, built like a rugby player, who was as lazy as hell. His grey curly hair and anaemic pinkish complexion, combined with a glaring lack of fashion sense, reminded me of a circus clown. In short, the guy was a fuck-up. In my circles he would have been a social pariah, and it was hard for me to conceal my dislike of him.

Whenever new salesmen took over a round, some of the agents who had run up huge accounts would disappear. After some investigation by the managers, these salesmen mostly couldn't be traced and so the account would be written off as a bad debt. In my previous job, the salesmen were required to canvass at least two new calls a day for agents, but at Jabula the deal was that I wouldn't have to do this. This became a point of issue when the clown insisted that I canvass. One day, after a heated argument, I was summoned to the boss's office. Sitting in his chair behind an oak table, Len, one of the three shareholders, tried to reason with me. On principle, however, I wouldn't compromise, so they fired me on the spot and told me that I could collect my salary at the end of the month. I got really pissed off and demanded that they pay me my full month's salary right away. The .38-calibre pistol sticking out of my pants might have been enough to convince them that I was capable of hurting them, and, small feat though it was, I walked out that day with a full month's wages in my pocket and my pride intact.

I caught a taxi back to the commune. It wasn't even midday yet and the place was buzzing with activity. When I told my friends and the rest of the gang that I'd been fired, they all cheered.

I had been in and out of quite a few jobs by then, and it was becoming pretty apparent to me that I wasn't exactly cut out to work for anybody. What I knew how to do best was use and sell drugs, and that was the world I inhabited.

A person can only fool himself for so long, though. All the signs were there. It would only be a matter of time before my luck ran out.

For a long time I had been thinking about moving Mandrax on the streets of Durban. George was buying Mandrax in packets of 1 000; in Joburg, the wholesale price was R2 a tablet. Street prices were determined by supply and demand, and varied between R8 and R15. We'd heard that in Durban the prices were double and even triple at times. Our idea was to take one packet of 1 000 tablets, test the market and use the profits to set up shop. We'd have a couple of younger runners do the street-to-street distribution.

The South African government had some strong laws in place in its efforts to combat the smuggling of Mandrax, whose distribution was linked with the then banned African National Congress. It was commonly known that the proceeds from the drug trade were being used to arm the ANC's military wing, Umkhonto we Sizwe. If anyone was caught with a sizeable quantity of Mandrax, you were immediately labelled a dealer and dealing carried prison sentences of up to ten years.

I drove down to Durban on my motorbike, with Dennis and Brett following me with the drugs hidden under the spare wheel in the boot of Dennis's mother's car. We left Joburg at midnight. The agreement was that if I came across a roadblock, I would turn around and come back and warn them. Fortunately, the roads were clear all the way and we arrived in Durban as the sun was rising. It was already getting hot and the humidity clung to our skin.

Dennis and Brett were going to stay at Dennis's sister's flat in the suburbs, and so they went off to check in with her. I took a drive down to the South Coast, clocking speeds of up to 200kph (for some reason the bike's performance always improved at the coast. I would lie on the tank with my feet resting on the rear indicators – what a rush!) My two friends, meanwhile, went into the city, looking to score Mandrax in the hope of finding a connection we could sell our stash to. We'd arranged to meet back at the flat that afternoon. I returned shortly after midday and called in to see my mother, who was by then living in Durban.

In the early 1980s, when I was living in Berea in a furnished apartment, my mother returned from Hungary and, for a brief period, came to live with me. I had seen her very infrequently over the years (once a year was a lot) and the gap between us proved impossible to bridge. It was my sister Joan who kept in more regular touch with her, and she would fill me in on whatever was going on in her life.

The time my mother stayed with me, I nearly went crazy. Her over-protectiveness and sudden displays of love and caring tended to irritate me more than anything else. When I was high on marijuana I could just about tolerate her, but when I wasn't I would experience extreme mood swings. When I was straight or sober, I simply couldn't cope with her. Her incessant questions – where was I going, what time would I be back – to say nothing of the continual advice that poured out of her mouth, drove me mad. Eventually, it got so bad I threw her out of my apartment.

It was soon after this that my mother was introduced to a Hungarian man by the name of Mike, whose wife had committed suicide by dousing herself in petrol and putting a match to her clothes. Two days after they met, Mike sent my mother an air ticket to visit him in Durban, where he lived. It turned out that they were a match made in heaven; my mother moved down to Durban, and they got married.

My mother hated my motorbike and was always warning me of the dangers, but she was happy to see me when I showed up at her door, and she insisted that I stay over that night and join her and Mike for dinner. To make sure that I would come, she promised roast chicken with stuffing.

I met up with Brett and Dennis back at his sister's flat around 5.30pm. I was the first to arrive and I waited outside, sitting on my bike. A woman who was probably in her early thirties, who lived in the same block of flats, walked up to me and asked who I was waiting for. We got chatting and I learnt that she was a divorcée and a high school teacher. When I was at school, I often used to fantasise about fucking my teachers. It was clear that she was interested in me, and so I asked what her flat number was. Then I asked her if she'd like to spend the next day with me at the beach. Just then, my mates arrived, and she quickly leant forward and whispered her flat number in my ear. Just the warmth of her breath on my ear aroused me.

Dennis and Brett seemed awfully pleased with themselves. They had met up with a guy called Flattie and his friend Twigs. Flattie wanted to do a deal: he was willing to buy the entire packet of 1 000 Mandrax tablets, but told them he needed a sample first. I became suspicious and expressed my reservations. I asked them if this Flattie was from Joburg. He was, but Dennis and Brett claimed to have had dealings with him in the past. Still, I felt uneasy. I knew Flattie, too, and I was certainly not as trusting as they were. Anyway, we agreed that at no time would we part with the drugs without money changing hands. I went to the boot of the car and took out a few tablets for them to give to Flattie as samples and off they went to meet with him. I went upstairs to get an education from my new high school teacher. I rang the bell and she opened the door. I started to explain about how I wasn't sure that I could make it to the beach the next day after all when I found myself wrapped in her arms. We didn't even make it to the bedroom, nor did I catch her name. Actually, I don't think she told me.

Somehow I still made it on time for dinner at my mom's place.

Over coffee on Sunday morning, Dennis explained that the deal was set for that night.

My instincts were still telling me that something was wrong. I knew better than to trust Flattie, or his mate Twigs for that matter. Although I didn't know Twigs personally, in the early 1980s he had been a member of Jeffrey Anthony's gang. As a precaution, I insisted that Dennis and Brett show me where Flattie lived with his brother, so they drove me to a high-rise block of flats in the suburb of Morningside. Then we split up and I drove down to the beachfront and spent the day catching a tan and bodysurfing.

Back at the Durban flat, as soon as I saw the expressions on Dennis's and Brett's faces, I knew something was wrong. 'What the fuck happened?' I demanded. They both spoke at the same time. Twigs and Flattie, they told me, had pulled one of the oldest con moves in the book on them. What was even worse was that they had both fallen for it. It turned out that Twigs was acting as the middleman, claiming that the buyer wanted to see the Mandrax before handing over the money and saying that the buyer would only deal through Twigs. Dennis, being a guy who could handle himself pretty well, trusted that Twigs wouldn't dare con him.

Once Twigs had the drugs, he left Dennis in the car and walked into a block of flats deep in Redhill, one of Durban's coloured areas. He never returned. After waiting for over an hour, in an unfamiliar neighbourhood where people were starting to stare at them, they decided to leave and contact Flattie. On the phone, Flattie sounded panicky. He told them the police had raided the Redhill flat and they had locked Twigs up, along with everybody else who had been there. He advised Dennis to keep a low profile. Worried that they might also be apprehended by the cops, Dennis and Brett thought it best that they head straight back up to Joburg.

I told them to go, but said I would stick around in Durban a bit longer. Once they'd left, I thought I would try and investigate what had really happened. I drove to the flat in Morningside where Flattie was supposed to be staying with his brother. The brothers looked nervous when they opened the door to my knock but they invited me in. There were a few of Flattie's friends there. They seemed quite surprised that I had chosen to stay in Durban, but they were very friendly and even offered to let me sleep over if I wanted to, which I actually agreed to do.

In the early hours of the morning, Twigs pitched up. When I confronted him, saying I thought he'd got arrested, he spun me some story about how he'd managed to get away and had come over to Flattie's to celebrate his close shave. He had brought something to smoke. Out came the marijuana and a broken bottle neck. Twigs crushed three Mandrax tablets in with the weed, folded in a piece of paper.

Flattie and Twigs both had a reputation for pulling moves. I knew they were unlikely to have R10 to scratch their arses with, but I held my peace. I didn't ask Twigs where he'd got the money to buy the Mandrax. When the pipe was loaded, I was given the honours of busting it and having the first hit.

The taste was too familiar. I knew, right there and then, as I was rushing out of my mind, that I was smoking my own tablets. We finished smoking the three buttons and Twigs pulled out another two. Before he could crush them this time, I asked to see them. I held the two pills up to the light and said, 'Fuck, you guys, these are my pills.'

Twigs and Flattie looked at each other and then both of them looked at me. It was an uncomfortable situation. Flattie, being the smooth talker, eventually confessed to having pulled a move. My share of that stash was a third anyway, and he ended up convincing me to stay and join up with them. Once we'd sold the Mandrax, he persuaded me, we could move down to the Transkei, where he had a great connection for marijuana. We would use the Mandrax money to purchase a couple of sacks and move the weed in Joburg. Once sold, we would reimburse Brett and Dennis.

To me that seemed fair, so I agreed. Flattie, however, had no intention of following through. In the end we sold about half the stash and used the money for our living expenses. The rest we smoked ourselves.

Having spent most of my teenage years in Johannesburg, I fell in love with the beaches on the South Coast. Living there, I thought, would be the closest thing to living in paradise and I decided to stay on for a while. Flattie and I decided to see if we could find a place on the beach to rent together. We were in luck. I contacted a woman called Mrs Ling, whose daughters had spent some time in Arcadia and had been childhood friends of mine. Rather reluctantly, she agreed to rent us the downstairs playroom of their double-storey house on the beach, but insisted on a deposit and three months' rent in advance. As far as first impressions went, I don't think we did much to convince her that we would be the ideal tenants. Flattie had deep, dark, sullen eyes, sunken cheeks, and long, greasy black hair. In his heyday, standing at over 1.8m tall and extremely well built, he could knock somebody out just by delivering a flat-hand across their face – hence his nickname. But that was long before he became a Mandrax addict. Now he was thin and weak and spent most of his days looking into a broken bottle neck.

Nevertheless, we moved into our new hideaway. Mrs Ling's was the only double-storey house in the area and it commanded a panoramic view of the bay and the shoreline. To gain access to the property, you had to negotiate an almost 90-degree turn in the driveway, which was shaded by a gigantic mango tree. The playroom occupied the entire west end of the house and was divided into two sections by a bar made from bamboo. There was a lounge area with a three-piece lounge suite and a wooden coffee table, and here and there were indoor palms in bright, colourful vases. It also had a three-quarter-size pool table.

From my bed in my corner of the room, through tall arched windows, I had a magnificent view of a large expanse of sea. I would lie there for hours, lost in thought, mesmerised by the sound of waves breaking on the shore. My thoughts often drifted to my childhood and the innocence of my youth. In my final year of high school I had been a lively, energetic young man, who, if I had put my mind to it, could have achieved anything. I had been an all-round sportsman and totally against drugs. Back then, I would never have condoned young people who were involved in the illicit trade, whether using or dealing. And yet, here I was – not only using drugs myself, but also dealing. Cynically, I thought how Janos, my stepfather, would have been proud of the son he never had. I wondered how long it would be before I ended up in prison, or met the fate of so many drug addicts. Death was the ultimate price for this way of life. Then I would think to myself, fuck it, what's the difference whether you die young or old? I mean, we are born and then we die. Whatever transpires in between, in comparison to the frailty, the transience, of human existence, our time on earth is really of no relevance.

At that stage of my life, I hadn't achieved very much. Looking around my new room, my only possessions were my revolver, my motorbike and a suitcase containing a couple of pairs of jeans, some T-shirts and a few pairs of sneakers. Flattie, on the other hand, had acquired two three-litre Ford Cortina bakkies through his unscrupulous shady deals.

The older model had a hidden compartment built into the chassis on either side of the rear wheels, where he could safely hide up to 20kg of weed; the other customised vehicle, which had fitted mag wheels and Michelin tyres, actually belonged to one of Flattie's 'friends'.

I was quickly learning that my new friend and partner in crime only had enemies. He seemed to have fucked over every person he had ever made a drug deal with, myself included. Besides his dubious nature, there was nevertheless something about him I liked. Whether it was his I-don't-give-a-fuck attitude or his tendency to do everything to extremes (like getting fucked out of his head on drugs), he had this ability to manipulate, extort or steal money so convincingly that you simply had to admire his audacity. I wished to fuck I had his balls.

Flattie's most prized possession was a metallic-purple Ford Capri Perana V8 convertible with a supercharger protruding from the bonnet. Fuck, she was a beauty! The only problem was that she guzzled petrol like a thirsty camel that had just crossed the Sahara, so invariably he couldn't afford to drive the thing. When we did take it for a spin, I would practically shit in my pants. What made it more scary was that Flattie was shortsighted, but his ego prevented him from wearing glasses. He often said he'd rather crash than look like a nerd.

His least prized possession was a 750cc Suzuki motorbike that rattled so much it was falling apart. For two guys who were not employed, it probably wasn't difficult to work out that we were involved in some underhand line of work.

After three months living in that beach paradise, it was time for me to go home, and so Flattie and I parted company.

I got back on my motorbike and headed north.

M

Some of the abuses I suffered as a child at the hands of my depraved stepfather and my victimised mother are still, even now, too painful for me even to think about, let alone talk about. Only now, four decades later, have I, for the first time, spoken openly about that part of my life and attempted to examine the impact those abuses had on me.

That frightened little boy still remains imprisoned, crying out, begging to be freed. He calls out to me through the tears I shed whenever I am reminded, by some incident that triggers memories, of a terrifying moment in my childhood. This can happen at any time. I can be reading a book, watching a movie, or watching an affectionate interaction between a child and a parent. I get a knot in my stomach, I start to tremble, tears well up in my eyes, and, once again, I become that same small boy hiding in a dark corner, quivering with terror.

There was a time when this anguish would turn to hatred, anger and resentment. I found myself acting out by being defiant, unpredictable and at times even violent. I didn't care about myself or the consequences of what I did. I was fearless. I was capable of killing. I hated the world and welcomed death. Death, as I saw it, was the ultimate freedom. I was completely incapable of making sense of the cruel and vicious hand life had dealt me – nobody who might have cared enough to listen could have understood. I was alone. It was easier just to block everything out. With practice, I became an expert at disguising my feelings and disconnecting from reality.

My earliest memory of how I reacted to being mistreated as a child was that I would climb and hide in trees. Trees offered a safe refuge for me from the world below. I would imagine myself as a bird, in particular as a swallow, a migratory bird. As a kid I was fascinated by how swiftly they would swoop through the air. Their long, pointed wings and forked tails only heightened their majesty. In one movement they would dive down on insects and feed while in flight. I would visualise myself as a swallow, effortlessly soaring through the vast skies.

One day, when I was about five years old, I decided that the screaming, shouting and the needless beatings were enough. I couldn't take them any more. I climbed to the highest branch of a tree in our front garden, closed my eyes, stretched out my arms like a swallow's wings, and leapt from the top of the tree, wishing with all my heart that I would fly. Instead I landed on our lawn, spraining my ankle and elbow. I cried silent, bitter tears, not from the pain of falling, but from the harsh realisation that there was no escape from the world. I was too scared to tell my parents what I'd done, so I was forced to conceal my injuries. My ankle swelled up so much that I could barely fit my school shoes on and I had to leave my laces untied.

At first, walking without a limp was difficult, but luckily our school was just across the road. With every step I took, it became less painful, and in the end I could walk normally. My arm was another story. Noticing my discomfort, my teacher asked what was wrong and then instructed me to roll up my sleeve. My arm was inflamed and bruised. Hesitantly, I explained that I had fallen out of a tree. The teacher quickly escorted me to the sickbay, where the school nurse bandaged me up, gave me some pills for the pain, and insisted I lie down for a while. I slipped into a deep slumber and only woke up at the end of the school day.

I remember one occasion when Janos and my mother were having an argument in the kitchen. I couldn't have been more than ten years old. The open-plan design allowed me to witness everything. I saw Janos take a fair-sized piece of frozen steak and hit my mom across the face with it. There was a thud, followed by a shriek. My mom was crying hysterically, blood pouring out of her nose, as she begged and pleaded with Janos to leave her alone. By this time Janos had both his hands around her throat. I began trembling and crying, but I ran into the kitchen where I wildly punched and kicked Janos from behind, shouting, 'Leave my mother alone! Leave my mother alone!' and trying to free her at the same time.

Janos released his grip. I was pulling desperately on his trousers as he turned around, swinging his arm. He caught me on the head. I tried to flee towards the front door, which was ajar, thinking that was the best way to avoid his clutches, when he kicked me in the arse so hard that I literally became airborne. I landed against the stair railing, somehow grabbing on and managing to stay on my feet. The pain in my arse was excruciating. After that, I ran for my life and took refuge at the back of the building, near the parking lot, where the rubbish bins were kept. I curled up, crying and holding my backside.

'*Hoekom huil die kleinbaas?*' (Why is the little boss crying?), the night watchman asked as he came over to me. Before I could answer, he had his arms around my shoulders and was hugging me. I hugged him back and just cried and cried. His arms felt strong and his slightly tobacco breath gave me a strong sense of comfort. Here was an elderly man, who knew me by sight but had never engaged in conversation with me, showing me that he cared. This simple gesture of intimacy was something I never experienced with my stepfather. I instantly bonded with that man and I remember wondering why whites and blacks couldn't or weren't allowed to mix. I mean, here was a man showing me compassion like any other normal human being, a man whom white people would refer to as 'boy'. I couldn't understand it.

During those early years, I used to have the most terrifying nightmares. There was one particular dream that stuck with me right into my late teens. I would be walking somewhere at night and there would be this 'thing' lurking in the darkness, always close behind me, almost as if it was waiting to pounce on me. I would begin to run, but, with every step I took, my legs grew heavier as if they were sticking to the ground, until eventually I couldn't run any more. My heart would be pounding. I was too afraid to turn around but I could feel this presence there, almost on top of me. It was at this point that I would wake up screaming.

It was also around this time that I was first introduced to the distinct sweet odour of marijuana. By chance one day I walked into the bathroom, where I found Janos sitting on the side of the bathtub. There was a piece of newspaper unfolded on top of the toilet seat with what looked like dried green leaves on it, mixed with these small greenish-brown seeds. In one hand Janos held a magazine, and with the other he was crushing the leaves and separating them from the seeds.

He ordered me to come in and close the door. Then he meticulously emptied the tobacco from a cigarette, mixed some of it with the leaves and placed the filter in his mouth. He held the magazine close to his face and sucked up the mixture of tobacco and leaves. I was fascinated by the whole ritual. After making sure it was tightly packed, Janos lit up with a match and inhaled deeply. Then he slowly exhaled, and while he did so he grabbed my arm, pulled me closer and blew the smoke in my face. It had a strange sweet scent and I recognised it. I'd smelt it before on numerous occasions behind the school where some of the 'boys' were responsible for disposing of the rubbish.

It was not too long after this incident that I first tried smoking cigarettes. Some of the seniors at school would go behind the ablution blocks and I would join them there. We smoked Lucky Strike. I would drag hard, remembering how Janos had pulled on his cigarette. I couldn't understand why I always coughed and he never did. I kind of enjoyed the dizzy spell when inhaling a lot of smoke.

There was another incident that I could never erase from my mind. Janos liked to play a game in which I had to close my eyes, stretch out one arm and open my hand. Then he would place something in it – anything from an insect to a lizard or a stone – and I would have to guess what it was, identifying whatever it was by touch only. Sometimes it was money, and I would have to guess the amount in order to keep it. On this occasion, he put something soft in my hand; it felt unusually fleshy, almost human. I squeezed it; it was weird and warm. I rolled it around a little but it barely fitted in my palm. Startled, I opened my eyes and there in the palm of my hand was Janos's cock. I got the fright of my life and snatched my hand away. To my stepfather, this was very amusing and he couldn't stop laughing. I can't explain the emotion I felt, whether I was upset about him laughing at me and having made a fool of me, or whether it was something else, but all I know is that it was traumatic and I felt violated.

Hungarians are generally hot-blooded people and quick to lose their tempers, especially after a few drinks. Janos's best friend was a guy named Bandi, also Hungarian, and he had an Afrikaans wife. On the occasion of Bandi's birthday one year, they threw a party and we were invited. Something happened at the party, I don't know what. Perhaps Janos, who was a compulsive womaniser, came on to his friend's wife, because the next thing she was freaking out and asking him to leave.

Janos, being the obstinate person he was, appealed to his friend. '*Bandi, a feleseged kidobot engem bazd meg a kurva anyad nem megvek sehova.*' (Bandi, your wife has thrown me out. Fuck your bitch-mother. I'm not going anywhere.)

'*Ha a felesegem azt akarta hogy menyel akkor job ha el mesz,*' Bandi answered, looking over towards his wife. (If that is what my wife wants, then you should leave. Then it's best that you go.)

Janos was always prepared for anything and he was very strong. Before the poor guy could move, Janos punched him with a pair of Perspex knuckle-dusters, producing a couple of really deep holes on Bandi's bald head. Blood squirted all over the place. Then Janos left the party, dragging my mother by the arm. He drove home and ordered her to wait in the car. He went inside and came out with his double-barrelled shotgun. When they got back to the party, my mom almost got shot in the process of trying to calm Janos down. Fortunately, she managed to convince him that whatever he was planning to do was a bad idea, and they drove back home again.

Janos's sexual appetite stretched as far as my sister Joan, or Babi, as we still called her then, who was around 12 years old at the time I became aware of this.

The two of us shared a room. Our small single beds were about a metre apart, and Babi's was closest to the window, which ran from the floor to the ceiling. The white curtains allowed the moonlight to filter through and bathe the room in its soft light. One night, very late, I happened to be still awake when my stepfather came into the room. I was facing the window when his silhouette suddenly appeared next to my sister's bed. I pretended to be sleeping but I could still see through my half-squinting eyes. Janos waited a while and then he placed his hand over my sister's mouth, waking her up. He moved close to her and I could hear his barely audible whisper although I couldn't make out what he was saying. At the same time his free hand started moving around under the blanket. Joan's body wriggled around as she tried to free herself but she was no match for his strength. From what little I could tell, it was obvious that Janos was hurting her. Terrified I would be next, I shut my eyes tightly. After that, I tried to block what I had seen from my memory.

At first I didn't really understand what had happened, but then my sister started to complain to my mother, who didn't believe her. Then Joan started becoming openly defiant of Janos, who shied away from her. Then it happened again, and when my sister told my mom this time, she confronted Janos about his nocturnal activities. Janos flatly denied it. I was there when this confrontation took place.

'*Hazudsz en lattalak hogy mit csinaltal ez igaz!*' I shouted at him. (You're lying, I saw what you did. It's true!)

Janos was very angry. I could tell by the small vein throbbing in his temple. He wasn't impressed with me.

'*Fogd be a pofad kisz vizilo.*' ('Shut your mouth, you little hippopotamus.)

My stepfather was a nasty specimen, and in a way it felt good to know that somehow I had managed to muster up the courage to stand up to him. All the years of physical and mental abuse had taken their toll. Even as a child, there is just so much a person can endure and Janos had now exposed himself completely. I knew that if my mother failed to take action this time, then it would be up to Joan and me to make sure he never violated us again.

My mother now accepted that something was very wrong. She was friendly with an Italian-German couple, Rosemary and Alfio, who lived up the road from us. She didn't go into too much detail but she asked if my sister could stay with them for a while. They already had two kids, a son and a daughter, Felicia and Flavio. I remember the kids very well because of the mucus they always seemed to have hanging between nose and upper lip and how it gathered dust.

From the very first night she took refuge there, Alfio visited my sister's bedroom and subjected her to the same sexual molestation as Janos had. This went on for a whole month until Joan couldn't take it any more. Although she was afraid my mother wouldn't believe her, she came home and moved back into the bedroom she shared with me. From then on, every night before we went to sleep we would lock the bedroom door firmly from the inside.

It wasn't long after Joan came home that Janos physically abused my mother again. This time there was a *huge* commotion, screaming and crying and the usual back and forth of Hungarian swearing that is too shocking to repeat even now. It ended with Janos slamming the door and going off to some pub to drink. My mom quickly packed a few bags and called a cab. She took us to Marika, our half-sister, who lived just on the other side of town. She left me and Joan there and she herself went off to Cape Town, where she stayed with one of her friends. Staying at my sister's wasn't too bad. Her husband Bela was a very nice guy and he treated us well. We stayed there for about a week before my mother returned. In the meantime, she had told Janos that she would come back only on condition that he moved out.

So finally it was just the three of us: my mom, Joan and me.

I remember it was kite season. The highveld enjoys really warm summers, with late afternoon thunderstorms. August was the windy month. Just before the end of winter and the beginning of spring, the winds would approach. Ever since I can remember, I loved flying kites. I probably built my first kite when I was about five years old. We would use reeds for the frame, which, although not as strong as bamboo, served well enough. In those days, once the light frame was assembled we would cover it in newspaper, mixing flour with water to make glue. Watching your kite take flight as you run holding onto the string, then releasing more string as it gains height and rises higher and higher into the sky, was a quite unbelievable joy for a small boy. I felt a sense of control over nature, and for those moments I would become so enraptured by my kite soaring through the sky; sometimes I would imagine I was a pilot flying an aeroplane, and at others I would be a bird. My passion for kite-making remains with me to this day.

During the 1980s, Mandrax, which is the trade name for methaqualone, was fast becoming the drug of choice in Johannesburg. In the 1960s and early 1970s it was generally prescribed for insomnia, but in 1977 it was taken off the market and classified as a banned substance. The drug is highly addictive, and it has various side effects, especially when mixed or used with alcohol or marijuana. It is physically and psychologically addictive and it causes much physical damage, including deterioration of the bone marrow.

Mandrax also gives you this indescribably intense rush. Smoking it,

I would often black out and fall over, but it was the most incredible sensation. Spit would dribble from my mouth, my eyeballs would roll back in their sockets, and my entire body and all my senses would become numb.

When it was taken off the shelves, crime syndicates continued to manufacture it in garage laboratories, and this became a very profitable enterprise. On almost every second corner in Newclare there were drug pedlars, and territories were tightly defended by the merchants. Gang wars over territory were not uncommon. I became a regular customer in Newclare, and I got to know all the merchants. I'd pull up to one of the corners in my car and a kid would come up to me and ask how many I wanted. It was that easy. They would serve you right there on the spot.

I moved continually between Durban and the highveld, maintaining my Mandrax and weed supply and looking after my customers in the Joburg clubs and suburbs. I was smoking Mandrax more or less on a daily basis, and I joined and then left (or got fired from) various rag trade jobs. The only things that were consistent in my life were dealing and drugging.

There were times, though, when I was clean. During one of these times a guy I had worked with at Jabula Clothing broke away from the company and we got the idea of starting our own company, to be called Indango Clothing. We took on a partner, Antonio, who was the youngest of the three of us. Antonio had no experience in the clothing business, but he somehow persuaded his Italian father to invest in the company. We agreed on R60 000 to get us up and running, although nothing was put in writing. Initially, we were given R20 000, with the balance to follow.

In this line of business, when you are given credit, you need a cash flow to buy stock. Despite things starting off well for us, we soon needed the balance of our start-up capital. Antonio's father was involved in some shady deals. He was buying stolen cars from Europe, which were coming in to South Africa via Swaziland. Apparently, the law was onto him, so when I reminded him about the R40 000 he'd promised us, he told me to make do with what we had. This had not been our deal. Unless he came up with the money, I told him I would walk. Unfortunately, a couple of days after our conversation, Antonio senior left the country. Antonio junior was a party animal and he often came to the office stoned out of his head.

Before long Indango Clothing folded.

One time, when I was living in Yeoville, a good friend of mine, Barney, who lived in Houghton, had ordered a couple of LSD caps for himself and his university friends to celebrate the end of term. On this particular day, close to dusk, Dennis met me at the commune to go along with me on the delivery.

I already had Barney's LSD but we were both craving to smoke Mandrax, so before we went to Houghton we drove to Bertrams, near the Ellis Park rugby stadium, to score. This was an area where whites, coloureds and blacks coexisted peacefully. The part we were heading for was fairly deserted. There were only a few abandoned houses there and an open field with a few old trees. You would always find groups of coloured guys there, gathered around a fire, on the pavement, or just hanging about together, either smoking it up or selling drugs. I was a regular customer and knew most of the merchants. It was usually a quick in-and-out operation.

As we turned the corner, I immediately noticed that the street was deserted. At the end of the street, and stretching right across it, were some fairly big rocks that had obviously recently been placed there, presumably to prevent a car from driving through. Something was amiss.

Anyway, I pulled up next to the house where I usually scored. There was nobody in sight. Dennis gave a whistle and we heard someone shout '*Die boere!*' At exactly that moment, a car turned the corner at high speed. Instinctively, I knew it was the cops. At this time I drove a Cressida station wagon, which was as sluggish as a turtle with three legs, but tonight it had to prove its worth. I accelerated towards the rocks in the road, ramped the pavement, and cut across an open field.

155

The car behind us followed suit – it was a Datsun 1200. The drug police were known for driving those fast little fucking Datsuns. I could make out about five occupants.

My Cressida was an 1800, but, because of its size, I knew there was no way we could outrun them. They would eventually catch up with us, no matter how much of a head start we might have had. In an effort to get away, I jumped red robots, went up one-ways, cut across a double dual road, but still I could not lose them. At one stage the Datsun stopped altogether and three of its occupants got out to make their car lighter and even faster.

Dennis suggested we eat a few of the LSD caps and throw the rest away.

'No way, man,' I said. I still planned on delivering those caps to Barney.

Keeping one hand on the wheel and without slowing down, with the other hand I hid the LSD under my seat, tucked into the leather upholstery out of sight. It wasn't long after that that the cops cut in front of me at a stop street, forcing me to come to a halt. Two of them jumped out of their car, while Dennis quickly rolled up his window, advising me to do the same. It was too late. As I turned to face the cop on my side, he took a punch at me and hit me square in the mouth. At the same time, he gave a shriek and pulled his hand back. Gratifyingly, one of my teeth must have pierced his knuckle; I could see the blood dripping from his wound.

'*You bliksem se moer, ek gaan jou op fok, klim uit die kar*' (You fuck, I'm gonna fuck you up, get out of the car), he cursed, instinctively putting his knuckle to his mouth, blood still dripping. '*Waar is die Mandrax?*' Waving their guns, the cops ordered us out of the car.

I pretended I didn't know what they were talking about. With my hands in the air, my face got slammed onto the bonnet of the car and I was subjected to a thorough frisking. They found nothing on my person, but then they went about searching my car systematically. The rear of this particular model station wagon was like an open boot and you could see into it from outside. That day, the boot was packed full of football uniforms, which must have been a disappointment to them. Meanwhile, the other cop was frisking Dennis. The one nursing his hand was growing impatient. He kept telling his partner we had nothing and they should let us go – and eventually that's what they did. They didn't find the LSD under the driver's seat.

When we arrived at Barney's place, who had been expecting us much earlier, we told him our story. Jokingly, I added that his LSD caps were now going to cost him double.

Every weekend I played football, and before a match we'd always smoke. One Sunday I was running late. I found the time to smoke but not to warm up before the match began. Early into the game, I collided with a defender, Martin, from the opposing side. He was younger than me but a lot heavier. My body went in one direction and all of Martin's weight came down on my leg. There was a loud snapping sound, as if a plank had broken in two. It was so loud that the few spectators sitting in the stands said afterwards they heard my leg break. The tibula and fibula, my right leg this time, had broken clean through. Fuck, I couldn't believe it! A broken leg again.

This was before the days of cellphones, so I lay on the field for at least an hour before the ambulance arrived. I was taken to the new General Hospital, where they wasted no time in getting me all plastered up. I was discharged straight afterwards. An ex-girlfriend, Barbara, from my school days had come with me to the hospital and she insisted that I stay at her parents' home with her in Victory Park. That night was a nightmare: I kept her awake the whole night with my moaning and groaning. It was too much of an imposition on her family, I realised, so I arranged to be moved to the Arcadia cottage in Greenside, where I shared a room with one of the guys staying there. It was far more convenient, and having people there made it much easier for me to move around.

While I was in the Arcadia cottage, I met a woman named Michelle who was a lot older than me. She was also a bit of a nymphomaniac. One night she suggested we go to Sun City with a friend of mine. She borrowed a car and off we went. It wasn't all that much fun for me, hopping around on my crutches, but the night seemed to pass pretty fast. On our way home, late at night, I was in the passenger seat, my friend was driving, and we smoked a Mandrax pipe. After that, Michelle got all horny and wanted to fuck. (This woman wasn't shy. On a previous occasion while I was in bed, and had friends visit me, she gave my mate a blow job in the toilet.)

I slipped my pants down over my full plaster cast and she sat on me and proceeded to fuck me. The driver, who was supposed to be keeping his eyes on the road, obviously had a break in concentration because the next thing we heard was a loud bang and there was flying glass everywhere. Then a fucking head came slamming through the windscreen! We had hit a donkey, can you believe! The driver slammed on the brakes and the donkey went flying over the car into the middle of the road. I was covered in glass and Michelle was screaming her lungs out.

We pulled over about 20m down the road and my friend helped me out of the car. I had just managed to dust the glass off my clothes and was pulling up my pants when a Putco bus came down the road towards us at a helluva speed. By the time the driver saw the donkey lying in the middle of the road, despite desperately slamming on his brakes, it was too late and he drove over the poor animal. The bus then veered off the road, hit the gravel and began to slide straight towards us. I was frozen where I stood, and with my crutches and broken leg I couldn't have moved anyway. I watched helplessly as the headlights, in a cloud of dust, come closer and closer. I began to pray. And then, as if by a miracle, the bus came to a halt literally a couple of metres from us. Another of my lucky escapes, but the most bizarre yet by far!

After about four months I had the full cast removed and was given a half-cast, which enabled me to walk without crutches. During this time I enrolled at the Gordon Flack-Davidson Academy of Design to study fashion design. I also stopped dealing in marijuana. There were several reasons for this, one of them being that Derek and I had had a falling-out over a stash we'd stolen. Catching a bus to the city and back with a half-cast was horrendous, so after two weeks my dream of becoming a clothing designer came to an end. I threw in the towel, something I later deeply regretted.

I got back onto the Joburg-Durban run and my drug habit escalated out of control. At one stage I found myself in Durban with nothing but the clothes on my back and my gun. I had lost all my possessions, including my motorbike. Some of my belongings were in Joburg. I was skin and bone, sleeping in a bus shelter in a coloured area at night and making do during the day. With the last coins in my pocket, I found a phone booth and called Joan.

Joan and Malcolm had got married in 1980, and he and I had always got on well. I didn't see them all that often – mostly when I needed money or help or was in trouble. Joan and I became really close when we lived in Arcadia and, although I was the wild younger brother and was often in trouble, she always looked out for me. In a way, I suppose she really took the place of my mother. Not only did she show me devotion and caring, but she also felt a deep responsibility for me as well. She was always coming to my rescue, a pattern that began in our childhood and continued into our adulthood. Now Joan told me to make my way to Vereeniging, south of Joburg, where she and Malcolm were living. They would fetch me from wherever I managed to get a lift to.

A new shopping centre, Three Rivers, had just been built in Vereeniging. One thing it lacked was a delicatessen, and so Joan and Malcolm had decided to open one there. It was called Deli-World. I was given the responsibility of managing the place. The centre was L-shaped and our shop wasn't in a great position. It was right at the end, which meant that we got no passing trade. We sold an assortment of fresh cold meats, cheeses, chocolates and a variety of mixed nuts and dried fruit. On Sundays in the early hours of the morning, we would drive to Kaufman's Bakery in Joburg, on Louis Botha Avenue, opposite a drive-in fast food place called the Doll's House. There we would pick up many dozens of freshly baked bagels and be back in Vereeniging in time to open up. The bagels were a big hit with our Jewish customers.

Sadly, the delicatessen was doomed not to succeed. For one thing, I started giving credit to some of the African workers who frequented the centre, and for another I would help myself to my favourite foods every day – biltong, rare roast beef, nuts. I just loved the nuts. My sister would argue that I ate all the profits, but this was not strictly true. Unfortunately, we ran at a loss from the day we opened and eventually we were forced to close our doors.

One good thing about living in Vereeniging and working at the deli was that I got clean and I stopped dealing.

In 1983 I moved back to Joburg and stayed with my old school friend Craig in a flat in Berea. Prior to leaving Vereeniging I had organised a job with one of the clothing companies I'd worked for previously. I had always been good at what I did, even when I was stoned. I was given an already established sales round, one that was generating quite a substantial income. Being back in Joburg and reconnecting with my old friends, it was hardly surprising that I started smoking weed again. I seemed to go through these cycles: stop, stay clean for a short while, work, make money, use drugs, lose everything. By now I understood this pattern, and I thought I would limit my smoking to weekends only. On Saturday nights I always went to a club, where I would drink as much as was humanly possible and smoke weed well into the early hours of the morning. At that time there was a quaint club on the edge of the city called DV8, where a lot of punk rockers used to hang out. Everybody was tripping out on LSD and, club-wise, Joburg was happening. People of all ages flocked to the clubs to have a good time.

I remember the first time I ever took LSD was during the day. It was called a microdot, a small, round, hard substance that looked like a slightly compressed lentil. There were six of us and we were raving out of our heads. I remember we walked into this fruit shop. Everything became more colourful and intense. We proceeded to eat the fruit. I don't know what was so funny, but we were hysterical with laughter. Maybe it was the look on the shop owner's face. He couldn't believe our audacity and he did nothing to stop us. I almost died from laughing. We must have looked like raving lunatics. Laughing and provoking the owner, we left the shop without paying. I suppose he was only too happy to see us go.

One night, Craig and I got really fucked out of our heads on Mandrax. I think it had been almost two years since I'd smoked Mandrax. Craig had been going to these African clubs on the far side of the city, where on several occasions he had picked up some hot black chicks. Until then I had never 'crossed the colour bar', but I had often wondered what it would be like, so on this particular night I agreed to go with him.

Once at the club, besides one other white male, we were the only white guys there and the black chicks seemed to hover around us. At first I couldn't actually see myself picking somebody up and taking her home, but as the evening progressed and the drunker I got, the more I entertained the idea. After smoking a joint on the roof later into the evening, Craig picked up two chicks. He introduced me to them at the bar. They acted all shy around us and remained at a distance, giggling and whispering to each other, but never addressing a word to Craig and me. Eventually, we left the club with the two girls. They sat in the back of the car huddled together, but, again, they never uttered a word. When we arrived at the flat, Craig took his chick to his bedroom while I escorted the other one to the lounge, where the lights were pretty dim. She came and sat next to me on the couch. She had make-up plastered all over her face, and her perfume was so strong I thought I might choke. I put my arm around her and my hand came to rest on her breasts. I gave them a slight squeeze but all I could feel was foam. I squeezed a little harder – still nothing, only a padded bra. Although I was drunk and fucked out of my head, this still struck me as strange. I put my other hand on her leg and in one swift movement I pushed it up her skirt and grabbed her crotch. Jesus, fuck! The woman had a huge cock and balls! Shocked, I jumped up so high I almost hit the ceiling. At the same time I pulled out my .38 Special.

'Get the fuck out of here, motherfucker!' I yelled. Grabbing the bitch – I mean, the *guy* – by the scruff of his neck, I dragged him to the door. There, pointing my gun straight in his face, I pulled the door open and threw him outside. Then I ran to the bedroom where Craig was under the covers in a hot embrace with his partner. I couldn't understand why he hadn't noticed that he was with a man, so I shouted at him, 'She's a fucking *man!*' He turned around to face me, mouth agape, his bloodshot eyes widening. I was waving my gun around.

'What?' he responded.

I noticed that he was half-dressed and then I noticed that the person in bed beside him was also topless, except that this person had breasts. Jesus, what was going on? Pointing to the 'thing' next to him, I said, 'You! Get out of here.'

'Are you sure?' Craig said.

'Yours must be a transvestite,' I told him.

By this time the 'thing' was panicking, grabbing her top and scrambling to get off the bed. I helped her out the back door in the kitchen. Then I met up with Craig, who by this time was sitting on the couch in the lounge holding his head in his hands. He seemed to have sobered up very quickly. He looked at me in disbelief, but neither of us uttered a single word. Not then, nor ever after that. We simply erased the night from our minds.

In 1984 riots were breaking out in the townships of Sebokeng, Sharpeville, Katlehong and Evaton in the Vaal Triangle. The trigger was the advent of the tricameral parliament, but it was apparent that these protests marked the beginning of the end of apartheid. The country's economy was in serious trouble, and inflation and interest rates had reached all-time highs. Foreign investors began to withdraw their money and white professionals began to emigrate in big numbers. There was also a rapid decline in the Jewish population, especially in Johannesburg. Estimates showed that about 2 000 were leaving the country each year – and among these were many of my school friends. These were troubled times.

The company I worked for targeted the black market and most of my customers lived in the townships. Early on during the riots I had occasion to go to Sebokeng township. Shops had been burned down, overturned cars lay in the streets, and protestors were everywhere, armed with traditional weapons. When I arrived at my customer's house, he was shocked to see me and expressed fear for my safety. He urged me to leave at once and get the hell out of Sebokeng. He advised me not to come back until things had calmed down.

As I was leaving, a gang of youths noticed me. Wielding their weapons, throwing stones and shouting abuse, they ran after my car. I was thinking, Hey, man, I'm on your side. Fuck apartheid. But I had the sense to know that this probably wasn't the time to tell them. The fact that I was white was all they knew and if they had got their hands on me, I doubt that my political stance, such as it was, would have made a difference to my fate.

My biggest fear was getting necklaced, a form of killing that had become popular in the townships during this time of unrest. People who were seen as government sympathisers or spies were publicly beaten and then had a tyre slung around their neck, which would be doused in petrol. The unfortunate person would then be set alight while he was still alive.

There was chaos in the townships. In contrast, life in the white suburbs was relatively calm and people went about their daily business without being exposed to danger. In this climate of violence and uncertainty, using drugs was one way of closing our eyes and switching off our minds to the many injustices our fellow South Africans endured under apartheid. For me, getting high was an escape from myself. That dark hole into which I'd fallen so deeply had become my sanctuary. Nothing was of any consequence down there. The pain of my past, present and possible future were numbed into oblivion. I had built my own prison and was doing my time as best I could.

During the mid-1980s the escort business was booming in Joburg, and the most prestigious agencies with the hottest girls operated in the city. Prostitution, the world's oldest profession, always attracts a criminal element. Most of the girls were on drugs and many of them turned to selling their bodies to support their addiction. It was a market

I stumbled on purely by accident. One of the girls I'd gone to school with had become an escort, and, through visiting her, I met other prostitutes and I started supplying them with drugs. As a result I spent a lot of time hanging around the escort agencies in town.

The girls were great customers. They always had cash and never asked for credit. The owner of one of the agencies was a Hungarian guy. He knew my family, and his son, with whom he jointly ran the agency, soon became a good friend of mine. He offered me a job as a driver, which also entailed providing protection for the girls. I would take them on house calls and check that the clients were safe. I was also responsible for collecting the fee due to the agency.

There was an incident when a steamer (a term we used for men who paid for sex) got violent with one of our girls. She managed to lock herself in one of the bedrooms in his house. Fortunately for her, there was a phone in the room, so she was able to call for help. Two of us were sent to her rescue. When we arrived, we kicked the door down. In such instances, in my experience, you hit first and ask no questions. As we entered the house, this pot-bellied businessman, half-drunk, came at me, but before he could do anything I pistol-whipped the fucker. Then we found the girl, who was terrified. We let her out of the house and then we ransacked the place, breaking furniture and any other valuable stuff that caught our eye, warning the businessman that if he ever touched another of our girls or reported us to the cops, we would kill him. The guy pissed his pants. He couldn't stop apologising.

I hated men who beat on women. When I raised my gun and was pointing it in his face, suddenly memories of the abuse my mother had suffered at the hands of Janos came to my mind, and all that anger I had felt as a child triggered a psychotic reaction in me. I was about to pull the trigger when my companion grabbed my shoulder.

'Don't shoot, man,' he said. 'Don't shoot.'

I lowered my weapon, but it was touch and go.

A lot of the girls rented houses together, and, when I was not working at the club, I would be at one of the prostitutes' houses, just visiting and doing my usual deliveries. I often smoked with them.

This was how I met Janet. She was a petite girl who had two beautiful kids, nine and eleven years old.

As the supplier, naturally I would have the honours of busting the pipe. One day we had loaded marijuana mixed with two Mandrax in a broken bottle neck, and one of the guys fired me up. After browning the pipe, we added on top what we called 'Cremora' (another two Mandrax). With three burning matches, I sucked and puffed, then had a boss of a hit. Before I released the smoke, Janet put her arm around my neck. Running her fingers through my hair, she pulled me towards her, placed her lips on mine and sucked the smoke from my lungs into hers – fuck, I got an instant erection. (Mandrax is also an aphrodisiac.) Our mouths locked, and the rush, combined with the sexual arousal, was incredible. I placed my hand on Janet's breast, feeling her nipple harden to my touch.

'Hey! What the fuck? Pass us the pipe!' said one of my mates.

For a moment Janet and I had become unaware of all the others. Spit was drooling out of my mouth and my eyes went blurry. All I could think about was fucking her real hard until she screamed from pain and pleasure.

When it came to Janet's turn to hit the bottle neck, I placed my mouth over hers and drew the smoke into mine. Then we left the lounge, went into her bedroom and literally ripped each other's clothes off. Janet was tiny; I lifted her in the air and, while standing, lowered her onto my phallus, her hand guiding me. Fuck, it was great! The bitch was a little nymph – she scratched and clawed at my back and we rolled onto the bed and fucked in every position I knew.

One thing about many of the prostitutes, and this included Janet, was that they were generally clean and they never fucked a steamer without making sure he wore a condom. I took a lustful fancy to Janet and she became my chick. I tried not to think about the guys she was fucking for money. For the next month we saw each other almost every day and fucked each other in as many days.

But then Janet made a fatal mistake. She told me she loved me. The urgency to terminate our relationship and run began to gnaw at me.

One of my regular Mandrax customers had just come out of prison.

Integrating back into society was proving difficult for him and so he reverted to doing the crimes he had done time for. This guy was a professional housebreaker and he would fence stolen goods for Mandrax with me. I was always in the market for gold chains. Whenever we exchanged goods for drugs he would make Janet and me a few pipes. I couldn't help noticing that my new friend in crime had the hots for my bitch. Among his stolen goods was a Winchester single-barrelled shotgun.

One evening, while Janet was taking a bath, I brought up the fact that he was staring at my girl in a way that displayed his desire for her. His first reaction was denial, and he apologised if he had offended me.

'Relax, man,' I told him. 'If you really want her, I'll make you a swap. Ten Mandrax and the shotgun and she's yours.'

We shook hands on the deal.

One morning around 11am, I was at Janet's house. Except for the maid, all the girls were out. I was on my own. I loaded a Mandrax pipe, lit it and took a deep drag, the familiar chemical taste burning my throat and filling my lungs with smoke. My mind went into a spin. As I exhaled, I looked up and out through the window into the back garden. Right at that moment, I saw four plainclothes cops jumping over the wall, their guns strapped to their bodies.

What the fuck, I thought. Their timing couldn't have been worse. I dropped the pipe in the dustbin, ran to the kitchen and made sure the security gate was locked. I yanked the key out of the lock and pushed it into a loaf of bread. Then I ran back to the bedroom and grabbed the dustbin and the folded piece of paper in which I had crushed three Mandrax, enough to get me a prison sentence.

I bolted out the front door with the dustbin and hid it in the garden. My car, a white Ford Laser 1600i, was parked in the carport, but I didn't have enough time to jump in and drive away, so I ran out the front gate and into a block of flats right next door to the house. I caught the lift to the sixth floor, and made my way up the stairs to the roof. From there I had a full view of the house. After about 30 minutes I saw the four cops climb back over the wall again. I sat and waited another 30 minutes before walking back to the house, thinking *Fuck*, that was a close shave! I retrieved the pipe and the folded piece of paper with the Mandrax in it, and finished smoking. Then I got in my car and drove round the block to the house behind the one Janet lived in. Some other prostitutes and their kids lived there.

Two of the girls were sitting on the veranda and they waved at me to indicate that the cops were gone. I wasn't about to take any chances, so I called them over to my car and one of them volunteered to come with me while we talked. I asked her if the cops had found anything on them. She said no, they were lucky, there was nothing in the house, but she was quick to add that it was me the cops were actually looking for. If they spotted my car anywhere in the area, they'd said, they were going to blow it up. My car was easily recognisable. Not only did many of the prostitutes around there know it was mine, but so did all the Mandrax merchants from the streets of Bertrams to the township of Newclare.

It was time to move on or to get a new car. I compromised and had my car spraypainted a metallic charcoal. I also removed the back registration plate. Try and catch me now, you fuckers, I thought. But I avoided the escort agencies for a while.

M

I remember another incident, this time with the drug squad.

For a short while I lived in a flat in Norwood, opposite the Hyperama, with my lifelong friend Morris, the kid I had taken under my wing all those years ago at Arcadia. My merchant from Durban, Glen, had just arrived with two suitcases filled with Durban Poison. In the middle of our lounge we had this heavy wooden rectangular table with an added square section to it that was hollow inside. That day we packed approximately 2 000 rolls into it, wrapped in heavy black plastic bags. Glen was a coloured gangster from Redhill, in Durban, and he was also a Mandrax addict like me, so, naturally, when doing a drug deal, how much better to conclude matters than by smoking a white pipe. Fortunately, a friend of mine, Joseph, was at our spot that day. He drove an 1100cc Kawasaki, so off we went to score some buttons, me riding pillion. Weaving through the traffic, we got to Newclare in record time. We entered from the main road close to Coronation Hospital, which wasn't too far from where we were going to score. When we got to the house where I normally scored, the streets were unusually quiet. I thought it was strange because it was always a hive of activity. One of the kids braved serving us, though, and at the same time he warned me that the cops had just been around. I was not too concerned, as the cops didn't usually hang around, but I remained alert, just in case.

We pulled out of the residential area and headed back to the main intersection. While we were stopped at the traffic light, I noticed an unmarked vehicle without registration plates and realised that it had been following us. Protruding from the centre of the car's roof was a short radio antenna. Drug squad. Fuck. They were onto us. Digging Joseph in the ribs, I told him, 'Don't turn around, the pigs are following us. As soon as the lights change, kick down and let's get the fuck out of here.' The lights turned green, and as we pulled out onto the main road, the cops turned on their siren, overtaking cars until they had fallen in right behind us.

I was shouting at Joseph, 'Go, man, go!', but instead he slowed down and pulled over. So I'm thinking, I have four Mandrax tablets in my hand, here is a window of opportunity to get rid of them. My hands were heavily stained from the resin of when we'd smoked a pipe, it was obvious that I was an addict, and no doubt the cops had also observed us scoring. I knew that even if I managed to dispose of the Mandrax, they could very well force me to take them to my place of residence. I was also carrying my gun and didn't have my ID book on me to prove that I was a licensed gun owner. Over and above this, there were people back at my spot and then there was all that fucking weed there! If I got bust with that shit, I would be charged with dealing. At that time, dealing carried the maximum sentence of seven years.

I still couldn't understand why the fuck Joseph had pulled over, but, as I weighed up the odds, I decided I had to take the fall. Two plainclothes cops jumped out of the car and ordered us off the bike. By now I had slipped the pills into my jeans, pushing them deep into my money pocket. They frisked me and found my gun, which they took away, and instructed me to get in the cop car. They let Joseph go. Once I was in the back seat, the cops told me that I should make it easy on myself and hand over the pills, as they had just seen me score. I dug out the Mandrax and gave it to them. At the police station, I was fingerprinted and charged with possession of four Mandrax tablets. I was allowed the usual one phone call, so I phoned Morris. Joseph had just arrived back at the flat. I told Morris to bring my ID book and come fetch my gun. Morris was there in no time, and I had to sign a letter of authorisation allowing him to carry my gun. Then we arranged that he would meet me in court in the morning and bring bail money. I also instructed him to move all the weed in the flat to a safer spot.

The following morning, I was released on bail. A month down the line, I went to court and was sentenced to a fine of R500 or four months' imprisonment, plus a further eight months' imprisonment, which was conditionally suspended for five years.

I now had a criminal record.

I have to admit that at first it really bothered me. If I was caught again, I would automatically get a minimum of eight months in prison, which in itself, to me, was a fucking long time, plus whatever penalty the other offence carried. Now that the stakes had been raised, I couldn't help thinking that if I had been the driver of the motorbike I would never have pulled over. On the other hand, and also at the forefront of my mind, was the thought that if Joseph had attempted to lose the cops and had opened up the bike, a high-speed chase could have resulted in an accident and our being killed. Fate has a sick way of teaching us lessons.

One day, out of the blue, Morris came to me with this crazy idea, claiming that it was something he had always wanted to do. At that time we were just managing to make ends meet, but somehow we always found money for drugs and gambling. At first, I thought he wanted to do something outrageous, like rob a bottle store. It was a Saturday morning – not the ideal day to pull a robbery.

'So what do you have in mind, china?' I asked him, a bit nervous about what he was going to say.

Morris began to explain that he had always wanted to steal a sheep.

'A sheep.' I looked at him.

'Yes,' Morris replied.

I kept looking at him.

'We could eat from it for a week,' he added.

It was not like people in the city kept sheep in their gardens. To even *see* a sheep we would have to drive out into some rural area. For Morris, however, this was not a problem. He had grown up in Benoni, east of Joburg, and he knew of a couple of farms in that district. So we decided to make an outing of it. We took a six-pack of beers and, before we left, scored a couple of Mandrax, which we smoked. Then, numbed out of our skulls, we took a drive out to Benoni.

Forty minutes later, we found ourselves in the heart of the outlying farming area. After scouting around, we came across a farm that appeared to have a small flock of healthy-looking sheep. The land itself couldn't have been more than about one and a half hectares. There was a long driveway beside a wire fence leading up to the farmhouse, and separating this property from the neighbouring one was a row of trees that stretched to the far end. The plan was to drive halfway up, park the car, and then one of us would go and knock on the front door, while the other would go around the back and knock on the back door. This was Morris's suggestion. The place was quiet; nobody answered either of the knocks and the doors remained firmly shut. Morris then instructed me to go and turn the car around and to keep the engine running. I was beginning to think that this might not have been the first time Morris had pulled such a move. I sat there with the engine idling, looking around to see if anyone was coming.

Then – a sight I will never forget – Morris came running from out of nowhere carrying a full-grown sheep that was almost as big as he was. It was the funniest thing I'd ever seen. As he got closer, his face all red and his eyes about to pop out, he shouted breathlessly, 'Open the back door, open the back door.' I was laughing so hard I could hardly do it, but I leant over the seat, grabbed the handle from the inside and pushed the door open. The sheep was bleating loudly and Morris threw the poor animal onto the back seat where it landed heavily behind the passenger door. He quickly jumped into the car, but, just as I was pulling out of the driveway, a couple of farm labourers came running in our direction. I pulled away as fast as Morris's Toyota Corolla 1300 allowed me to. In the rear-view mirror, I noticed one of them, a woman, writing something in the sand with her finger – the registration of our car, no doubt.

The sheep was all panicky and was bleating loudly. I kept telling Morris to push its head down so that the people in the cars passing us wouldn't see it. The creature must have been terrified, and it promptly shat all over the car. It made me think about how somebody must feel when they're being kidnapped or taken against their will. As we drove through central Benoni, the place was crawling with traffic cops, and I expected to get pulled over any second. But somehow we made it back safely to Joburg, bleating sheep and all.

Our parking spot was directly beneath our flat and right next to the stairway. I quickly went upstairs and opened the front door while Morris followed with the sheep in his arms. We closed it in the kitchen, but before we could decide who was going to kill it, the fucking sheep started making this dreadful me-e-e-eh-ing noise. Morris was quick to suggest that I shoot the fucker. I didn't think this would be a smart move as the noise of the gunshot was bound to attract somebody's attention. Instead I thought I would try and knock it out, so I punched the sheep really hard, square on top of the head. Its legs buckled and it fell to the ground, but within seconds it lifted itself up and resumed the me-e-e-eh-ing noise, which was beginning to drive me crazy. We had to kill it, and kill it fast. Morris refused, saying that there was no way he could slit its throat, although he didn't mind cleaning it once it was dead. So I was left with the task of taking the poor sheep's life.

I took the breadknife, which had a serrated edge but wasn't very sharp. Morris carried the sheep upstairs to the bathtub and, while he held it, I grabbed the animal by its ears, and tilted its neck back. The sheep was looking directly into my eyes; instinctively it knew its death was imminent. I gave it a long look and felt a brief moment of pity. Then I began to saw its neck. It was an arduous and slow process.

The animal's skin was really tough and the breadknife was so blunt it felt like I was sawing through the bark of a tree with a nail file. As the wool parted and I began to cut through the flesh, blood started to spurt all over the place. The sheep was still staring at me, only now that look of fear seemed to have been replaced with something more resigned, even peaceful. Eventually, I cut through most of the tissue in its throat; there was blood everywhere, and all over my face and clothes. A pretty sight I must have been, like some psycho killer or something. Morris then proceeded to skin the creature and take out its intestines, which we put in big black plastic dustbin bags. Then, with an axe, we chopped the sheep into a couple of dozen pieces.

Later that afternoon, we invited a few friends around and had a braai. The meat was still warm when we put it on the fire.

My Durban connection from Redhill delivered weed to my doorstep on a fortnightly basis. The price of Mandrax at the coast was double the street value of Mandrax in Johannesburg, so every time Glen came up I arranged for him to take a couple of packets containing 1 000 tablets each back with him. Eventually, Glen and I became partners. I even managed to organise a stolen .357 Magnum for him. I was now regularly moving the drugs with him to the coast. I also met his family. When I was in Durban, most of our days were spent running around in the coloured areas delivering Mandrax to Glen's runners, who operated on a similar basis to the dealers in the townships of Johannesburg, and collecting money.

Wherever we went, we smoked with whomever a deal was being made. At night we slept in an abandoned house, just like squatters. Glen's addiction was worse than mine, so no matter how well we were doing, our profits went up in smoke. That's the futile existence of a dealer who is also an addict. With all the risks we were taking, at the end of the day we had no money to show for it.

One time, on our return to Durban from a run to Johannesburg, we arrived there after midnight. Glen's chick was with us. She was a young black girl, very pretty. So we went to this roadhouse called the Blue Lagoon, which was always open until the early hours. Glen and his chick went to order us a couple of bunny chows. I got out to stretch my legs and stood leaning against the front of the car, just staring aimlessly out at the ocean. The next thing I heard an altercation break out between Glen and some youngsters. Before anything could even register properly with me, one of these kids came running at me, swinging a baseball bat. What the fuck was going on? I pulled out my .38 Special and, taking a firing stance, shouted at my attacker.

'I'll blow your fucking brains out if you take another step!'

The kid froze in his tracks. I fired a shot in the air. The distraction gave Glen and his chick a chance get away. We all jumped into the car, and, as we drove off, I fired another few rounds into the air just for good measure. Then Glen and I looked at each other, dumbstruck.

'What the hell was that about?'

We shook our heads. I still don't know.

A few weeks after that we did quite a big deal, which turned sour: Glen got ripped off a couple of packets. On this particular night I had planned to visit my mother, who was living close to the nightclub where Glen was going to have a meeting with the people who had conned him. The club was near the harbour and a lot of sailors used to hang out there. He made his own way there because he said he wanted to sort the problem out himself, and so I arranged to stay over at my mom's place. Early the next morning, I went to find Glen at the abandoned house where we'd been sleeping, but he wasn't there. One of his boys told me that the night before, at the club, he had shot somebody at point-blank range with his .357, straight in the face. Glen had gone into hiding.

I went to his parents' house and they were really distraught by the news. Glen was from the old school, a real gangster who lived by a strict code of honour: you fuck with me, you get fucked.

After that there was no point in me sticking around. For all I knew, I could be implicated in a murder, as I was the one who had given Glen the .357 Magnum, so I left Durban in a hurry.

Back in Joburg, I hooked up with another prostitute who I knew from before. She had once hired me as her bodyguard after the violent ex-boyfriend she'd arranged to have stabbed had survived and threatened her with revenge. Wherever she went, I would go. I even moved into the tiny, rather dingy cottage she rented and shared with her huge St Bernard. I hated that dog. He kept dribbling spit all over me.

Like me, she never stayed in one place for too long, and so we moved around a lot, sometimes staying in hotels and occasionally even sleeping in the same bed. I watched her bathe, and there were times when I would be in the room right next door and could hear her fucking some steamer. Through all this we stayed friends and we never mixed business with pleasure. In the end she met a nice Jewish guy, a lawyer, who became her boyfriend and who really loved her. Eventually he convinced her to change her life. She stopped being a hooker and they got married. They both remained clients of mine. Their code names were Burt Reynolds and Goldie Hawn. They lived in the posh suburb of Houghton.

Chapter 6

Dancing With Death

Like clothing styles, drugs go in and out of fashion, too. In the late 1980s cocaine became the drug of choice among Johannesburg's elite. Everybody was 'doing coke' and I saw an opportunity. When I took my first sniff of cocaine, I couldn't quite understand what all the fuss was about. Apart from my gums going numb and a slight feeling of euphoria, it didn't do much for me.

One night when I was at a club, I was approached by a member of the Narcotics Bureau. He knew me by name and he also knew that I dealt drugs. He assured me that he wasn't there to bust me, but told me that, if I wanted, he could supply me with the best coke in town. At first I was sceptical. No way was I going to trust a pig. At the same time, for some reason, my instincts were telling me I *could* trust him, and what better contact to have than somebody in the drug squad? To cut a long story short, we arranged a meeting point – these were always in the parking lot of a shopping mall – and we started doing business. The coke was from Peru, with a slightly yellowish colour to it, and it *was* very good. On top of this, I was getting the shit on credit.

Having an addictive personality, I did everything to the extreme. Before I even realised it, sniffing did nothing for me, and I became hopelessly hooked on freebasing cocaine. The whole ritual of preparation, in anticipation of that first hit, made me a slave of the white powder. How freebasing works is you take cocaine in its powder form, mix it with bicarb and boil it in a spice bottle with a little water. Then you heat it on the stove; once the powder turns to oil, you put a small piece of ice in the water and twirl it around. As the water cools, the oil forms solid rock.

As a drug dealer and an addict, one constantly needs people from all walks of life in your world. Addicts get to know addicts, and the dealers get to know who's doing what. But it's almost impossible to connect with the top guys who are moving kilograms. There's always a second party in between. For me, the ultimate goal was to deal with the top guy. Clubs were good places to meet such people and it was at a club that I hooked up with an old connection of mine, Renaldo, who, years back, had supplied me with LSD and who was now in the cocaine business. We'd first met back when I was running wild in Durban and hanging out with Flattie. Renaldo was a South American Jew who had pulled a heroin stint in Israel and ended up doing a seven-year stretch.

As a rule, I would only take coke on credit in the event that it had been cut or laced with another substance. Generally, I had a good name for moving a lot of drugs, and procuring drugs from different sources was never a problem for me. I was happy to work with my new connection, as he was reliable and never stood (cut or laced) on the coke. In the beginning, and for the first few months, business was good and I was moving a lot of coke. But then I made the fatal mistake of smoking with my customers, some of whom were also my friends. So often when smoking socially, especially doing something as addictive as freebasing, one ends up giving credit. When an addict owes money for drugs, the second he gets his hands on cash, paying his debt is the furthest thing from his mind. He would rather make a score somewhere else than pay the person he owes. Alternatively, if he *does* pay you, in good faith as a dealer you'd be expected to give him more credit, until eventually he will owe you so much that it is almost impossible to collect your money. That is when the dealer resorts to violence.

When all was said and done, I eventually owed Renaldo so much money that he refused to restock me. I kept getting messages on my pager to settle my account. Then the messages became less friendly.

When they found me, he told me, they were going to beat the crap out of me. I had fallen so deep into the shit that the only thing I could do was get out of town. By then I knew it was hopeless. I had lost everything. Once again, all I had were the clothes on my back, my revolver and now a group of very angry drug dealers after me. I did still have my car, but everyone knew what it looked like so I didn't dare drive anywhere. I was desperate.

For some reason, I called my mother and told her that I needed to disappear. She was full of questions, as always, wanting to know what had happened and where I was planning to go. I told her I didn't know. All I knew was that I had to get away. She told me I should sit tight and call her back in an hour. Of all people, my mother contacted Janos, who at that time was the caretaker of a farm about 40 minutes outside Johannesburg. She arranged for him to meet me the following day at the Hillbrow Tower.

I got hold of a girlfriend who used to work at one of the clothing companies I'd repped for. Her name was Charlie. She was also into coke, but not hectically like me. I told her I needed somewhere where I could keep my car out of sight and also hide out for the next 24 hours. She said I could come to her place. Then I scored some Mandrax and weed to help wean myself off coke. Withdrawal can be pretty scary. I still had four grams of coke on me. I explained the situation to Charlie and gave her a gram for her trouble. The other three grams I cooked on her stove and got a nice rock, which I intended to smoke before running away. I was so fucking paranoid that I hid in the toilet at the back of the house, in the domestic quarters, where I smoked till the early hours of the morning.

Sitting on the toilet with my .38 Special in my hand, sweating like a pig, I waited for the sun to rise. Fuck them! If they found me, I decided, I would definitely shoot. There was no way I was going down without a fight.

My rendezvous with Janos was scheduled for 10am.

Charlie dropped me off at the arranged destination. She was a Christian and I could see she was deeply saddened by the state I was in. When she said goodbye, she added, 'I will pray for you.' Little did I know it at the time, but those words would one day not only give me the will to survive but also maybe even save my life. With only the clothes on my back, my drugs in my pocket and my most loyal friend strapped to my side, I waited in the middle of Hillbrow, trying to look normal.

Trying to look normal was difficult, especially when I was convinced that everybody was watching me or out to get me. I had not slept at all. I was unshaven, smelly and totally paranoid. My eyes darted everywhere. I expected something to jump out of the shadows at any second, and my heart was racing. When I was wired I had a habit of clicking my jaw, and I found myself doing this now, too. I kept reassuring myself that I had a gun with five rounds, so what the fuck was I afraid of? The mind is a powerful tool. It does its own calculations. And when it switches into irrational mode, we lose control.

To my relief, I saw Janos pull up in his car. I hadn't seen him since the day I'd so badly wanted to beat him up, but I've never been more happy to see anyone in my life – ironic, I know, considering that I hated him. But here he was, and willing to help me. He gave me a huge bear hug and kissed me on both cheeks. Shit, I thought to myself, don't go turning all weird on me now. It wasn't like I wanted to bond with him or anything. All I said to him was 'Let's just get the fuck out of here.'

The farm, which was really a smallholding, was on about one and a half hectares of ground. Janos stayed in the main house and I was put into a cottage on the property. It had one bedroom, an en-suite bathroom, a kitchenette and a lounge area.

By now, the effects of the cocaine were starting to wear off and, being away from the hustle and bustle of the city, I started to relax. Janos brought out a bottle of *pálinka*, the Hungarian spirit he drank, and after downing a couple of tots I came down from my high. We talked a bit, although it wasn't easy for me, mainly about how his life had been after my mom got rid of him. Actually, it was boring stuff, but I felt the least I could do was to listen. I don't know after how many hours of listening to him blabbering on I finally fell asleep on the couch.

I woke up later that evening to find that Janos had prepared a scrumptious Hungarian dish for us. I couldn't remember when last I had eaten such a good meal. After dinner I took a shower and Janos lent me a pair of pyjamas. They were these really old-fashioned blue-and-white-striped longs, which made me feel like I was in a mental hospital. I told Janos I was going to smoke drugs. He understood and left me to do my thing. I smoked one and a half Mandrax that night, and over the next days I cut down to a quarter. Weaning oneself off makes it so much easier to stop.

Every morning I jogged, and I began to feel fit and strong. There was this open field on the farm, about 30 by 100m, which was covered in weeds and blackjack stalks that were taller than I was. Over the next three months, I cleared the entire field with my bare hands. The labourers on the neighbouring farm, who saw me at work every day, started calling me the White Lion. I stopped drugs, I gained weight, and my mind became clear again.

When there was nothing left for me to do, I contacted an old army buddy whose family were cattle farmers out near Potgietersrus, and he invited me to spend a few months there with him. I said goodbye to Janos and hitched a ride. I got a job as a waiter in town at the local steakhouse. I soon realised that, in this conservative Afrikaner town, I stuck out like a sore thumb. I'd kept my hair reasonably long ever since the army, and this didn't go down well in Afrikaner Weerstandsbeweging (AWB) territory, where most of the young male inhabitants dressed in khaki and had brush cuts. The AWB was a far-right political party, not known to be friendly towards blacks, or Jews for that matter. When customers walked into the steakhouse I could see them whispering, wondering what this long-haired Englishman was doing in the middle of nowhere. I thought sometimes that, if they'd known I was Jewish, too, I might very well have got myself lynched. However, being a waiter there was a lot of fun, but, as with so many of my previous jobs, the inevitable happened.

After about three months of putting up with the manager's shit, I had an argument with him that almost resulted in a fistfight, and I walked out.

I went back to Johannesburg and moved in with Joan and Malcolm, who were by then living in Bedfordview. Having lived for some time in a small town and on a farm, where there was barely any traffic or pollution, it was strange to be back in the city.

The first thing I had to do was go make it right with the people to whom I owed money. I knew that Renaldo had a business on Louis Botha Avenue, so I went there and walked straight into his office. Sitting with him at his desk were two of his cronies. When he saw me, at first he was shocked, but then he gave me the warmest of smiles. It seemed genuine. If anything, Renaldo and I had always been good friends. His boys were asked to leave. We shook hands and hugged. I apologised to him for fucking up but assured him that I planned to make good. I was looking healthy and he was impressed. He told me that, as soon as I was ready, we could do business again.

One of the waiters at the steakhouse in Potgietersrus, Kobus, had cracked a managerial position at Late Nite Al's, a famous steakhouse on Bruma Lake, which wasn't far from Bedfordview. Before he'd left he'd told me that if and when I went back to Joburg I should get in touch with him if I needed a job, so I did, and I started working at Late Nite Al's the very next day. In those days Bruma Lake was a popular entertainment venue. The restaurant, which also had a bar, looked out over the lake, and on certain nights, when they had live music, the place really used to get packed out. Fights were as common as brawls in a sailors' bar and there were two bouncers who worked on the front door. I worked every night and the tips were good.

It was here that I met Sarah-Lee. The instant I laid eyes on her, I wanted to fuck her. When I asked around, I learnt she had a high-school sweetheart but he had gone off to the army. I don't know what arrangements they'd made, but Sarah-Lee seemed to make herself available. She was very sexy and knew how to flaunt her body and strut her stuff. She was very popular with customers and with the other waiters. She was also quite a flirt. To be honest, though, I didn't think she would even give me the time of day.

Most nights I went home after work, while the other waiters would converge on the popular night spots in Yeoville's Rockey Street, places like Dylan's, Speakeasy and one or two others that stayed open till the early hours of the morning.

One night, I could see that Sarah-Lee wasn't her normal self. Although we worked together, we had never officially introduced ourselves, but we'd exchanged bits of small talk now and then. It was almost closing time and all the waiters and waitresses were busy cashing up. I sat down facing her at the table where she was sitting and remarked about her being down in the dumps. We began to talk. She told me that she and her boyfriend had had a tumultuous relationship and that he had now broken it off.

I eventually got around to asking Sarah-Lee on a date, and when she accepted I almost fell off my chair. On our night off we went to a movie together and then decided to go on to Rockey Street. It was around 11.30pm when we got to Dylan's. We sat drinking vodka, lime and lemonade and enjoying each other's company. I found that talking to Sarah-Lee just came naturally, and we were laughing and having fun when in walked our manager, Kobus, and his junior assistant.

They asked if they could join us at our table. Motherfucker, I thought to myself, couldn't they see we wanted to be alone? Reluctantly, I agreed and we shifted up. Sarah-Lee excused herself to go to the ladies', and while she was gone they ordered their drinks and conversation started revolving around work. I was starting to feel agitated. My evening with Sarah-Lee seemed to be taking a turn for the worse. Then Kobus's assistant, who was not much more than a kid, turned to me. 'So, tell me,' he asked, 'is she a good fuck?'

I was shocked at such a direct question. I have always been a very private person, especially with regard to my relationships with women, and this little fucker was about ten years my junior. How disrespectful, I thought. I could feel my blood pressure rising. Trying to control myself, I said angrily, 'Firstly, that's none of your business, and, even if I have fucked her, why the fuck would I tell you?' Just then Sarah-Lee arrived back at the table. It was an awkward moment and I could see she sensed something had happened and that I was uncomfortable. The situation became very tense. I felt like punching the little punk.

I hurriedly finished my drink and motioned to Sarah-Lee that we should leave. We excused ourselves and went across the road to Speakeasy, where the owner was a friend of mine. It wasn't really busy, so we sat around at the bar close to the end next to the wall where there was a poker machine. We had barely got our drinks when another six waitresses from Late Nite Al's pitched up and they came over to join us. Not long after that, Kobus and his assistant arrived, too. By now it was well past midnight and I was on my fourth double vodka, lime and lemonade. I must say I was pretty fucked. Sarah-Lee, who had been drinking only soft drinks all night, was as sober as a tightrope walker. I went to the toilet to relieve myself. As I walked in, there was Kobus washing his hands and face. I ignored him and went about my business. I was really drunk. As Kobus walked out, he made some racial comment about my being Jewish.

I have always been sensitive to any form of prejudice, but especially when it comes to my religion. Not sure if I had heard correctly, I thought, Fuck that, maybe I will let it ride, and so I finished up in the toilet and made my way back to the bar, where Sarah-Lee and two or three of the other waitresses were standing around. And then my blood began to boil. While sipping on my drink, I turned around and on the level below us, staring up at me, was the fucker Kobus. I tried to hold his stare but couldn't, so instead I asked, 'What the fuck are you staring at?' Because the music was pretty loud, I could see that he wasn't sure what I had said, so he moved closer, mouthing 'What?' in an obnoxious way. That was enough for me. I gave him one flat-hand across his face and at the same time I jumped over the railing. A scuffle ensued and the management intervened, asking us to take it outside. So outside we went.

Kobus's friend came with him. 'What the fuck did you say in the toilet?' I asked Kobus. As I spoke, his young sidekick took a punch at me from the side which somehow I managed to dodge. I pulled out my .38 and fired a shot in their direction. The noise of a bullet being discharged at that hour was so loud that it even rattled me. How I missed him I don't know, but they both froze dead in their tracks. Jesus, fuck! I don't know what had possessed me to shoot. I know it was not the alcohol, nor was it fear. Perhaps the long-term use of drugs had caused a chemical imbalance in my brain. Whatever it was, it seemed that my ability to rationalise was in serious question. Could I actually shoot someone? The sickening truth was only too evident. Yes, I could.

The next moment I felt the barrel of a gun against my head and heard the words 'Police! Freeze!' It was two undercover cops, and they were flashing their badges in my face. I had no choice but to hand over my weapon. After questioning them, Kobus and the other guy, who I thought were going to make as much trouble for me as possible, claimed that my weapon had gone off accidentally, and they told the cops there was no problem at all. I was given back my piece and we were told to clear the streets. Kobus and his friend left and I went back into the club to fetch Sarah-Lee. The people in the club were silent. They all knew something had gone down as they'd heard the bang of the gun. I took Sarah-Lee's hand and said, 'We have to leave.' She looked at me questioningly and was a little hesitant to go with me. I said, 'Don't worry, nobody was hurt.' From that point on, I don't remember anything. Rockey Street vodkas were strong.

I woke up around midday, heavily hung over. The events of the early hours of the morning came flooding back into my mind, but for the love of a chocolate milkshake, I could not remember taking Sarah-Lee home. What a disaster our first date had turned out to be. I was convinced there was no way she would ever want to see me again. But one thing was for sure: I wasn't going back to work for Kobus at the steakhouse.

At around 5pm I phoned Late Nite Al's and asked to speak to Sarah-Lee. Relieved to hear her voice, I asked her how she'd managed to get home and apologised for trying to shoot someone on our first date. I assured her that it was not something I was in the habit of doing. Apparently *I* had driven her home ... Fuck! I couldn't believe that, in my paralytic condition, I had got her home safely. Sarah-Lee was quick to inform me that everyone at work was talking about what had happened. Among the waitresses I was a hero (nobody really liked Kobus), but, as far as management was concerned, I was fired and banned from the premises. Fuck it! I didn't care – getting fired was nothing new to me. Then I told Sarah-Lee that I had to see her again, and soon, and to my surprise she replied that she would like that very much.

What the fuck was wrong with me? I couldn't understand it. Why couldn't I keep a job? What was it about authority that I resented and rebelled against? Or was it something far deeper than that? Did I need pain to feel a sense of worth? What was this constant subconscious craving in me that drove me to violence in the hope of being hurt myself? Is that what I was doing? The only form of love my parents ever showed me was through the beatings they gave me. Maybe that was what I grew up learning, and so that was the only thing I knew.

Anyway, I didn't care. Fuck Late Nite Al's, and fuck their job, and if I ever saw that cunt Kobus again, I was going to fuck him up, too. Anyway, what the fuck was I doing being a waiter at 31 years of age? Or any age. Waitering was for pussies. I was a fucking drug dealer, drug addict, what the *fuuuuck* ...

After kissing that career goodbye, I wasted no time in contacting my drug supplier. This time, I vowed, I was going to make money. I was going to stay clean and get my shit together.

Sarah-Lee and I began to date seriously and before long we fell in love. She became my girlfriend. I used to wait for her outside Late Nite Al's to pick her up after closing time. Then one day I got fed up waiting. I walked into the restaurant where I was no longer welcome. Whatever was going to go down, I told myself, I was prepared for it. Sarah-Lee was just finishing cashing up. The employees and African staff were surprised to see me, but for the most part they were friendly, and no mention was made of that almost fatal night. In fact, I was treated to free drinks!

A short while after this, I got a job with Aïda Real Estate in Randburg. It was the perfect cover for me. My time was basically my own and I could still operate my drug business.

Life was good, and money was coming in every day. Instead of smoking the profits, now I was banking them. After five months of not selling a single property, however, I realised that I was about as suited to be a real estate agent as I was to be a waiter, and I left Aïda. I went to work for my brother-in-law, Joan's husband Malcolm, who ran a

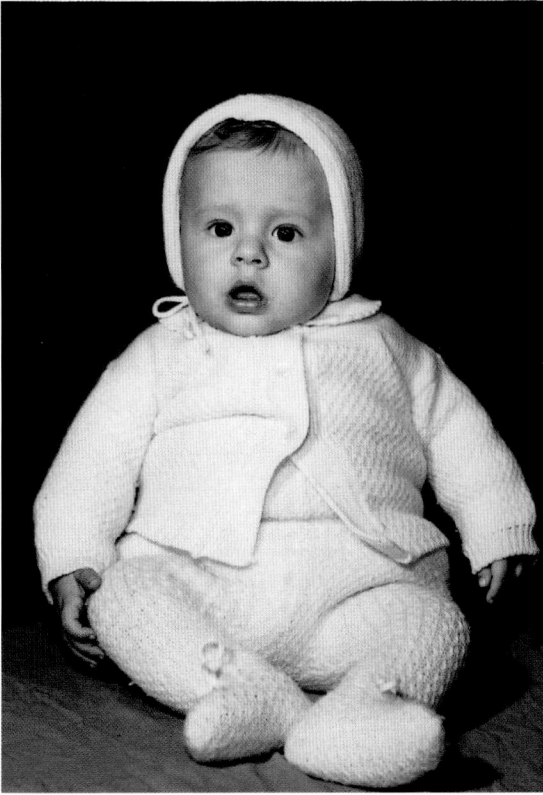

At my most lovable age, surveying the world, around 1960. If I'd known what awaited me, perhaps I would have opted for another life.

My sister Joan's controlling instincts surfaced early. What the hell's she on about? Give me a break, sister.

My mother, Katalin, at the age of 16. This photo was taken in Budapest in 1940.

A happy moment for the Krebs clan. From left are my half-sister Marika, my father Fritz and Mom (holding me), with Joan in the foreground. The smiles hid the grim reality of our dysfunctional family, and my parents soon separated.

Katalin and Janos on holiday in Durban, early 1960s.

Early days at Arcadia: Joan and me with Zsuzsika (Zsuzsi), my niece, in the centre.
This was taken during a family visit in early 1972.

At the annual Arcadia picnic, hosted by the Roth family, held in Vereeniging.

The original wild bunch: my Arcadia brothers, with me in the centre. This photo, which was used in a book called *100 Years of Arc Memories*, was taken on the Arcadia soccer field.

A friend and I with the young son of one of the household staff at Arcadia. This was taken when I was in Standard 9.

I matriculated from King David Victory Park in 1977. That's me on the right.

Joan and I keeping up with the trends, mid-1977. I'm doing my Roger Daltrey impression, while Joan is channelling Joanna Lumley in *The New Avengers*, which was a popular TV show in those days.

At Bikkur Cholim camp in Muizenberg, summer 1975, with my arms around Carol (left) and Babette (right).

In the early 1980s, during one of my wild road trips, I returned to Muizenberg. Here I'm showing my friend Steve who's boss.

My 24th birthday celebration with my girlfriend Dana, at the Turn 'n Tender steakhouse, Greenside, 1984.

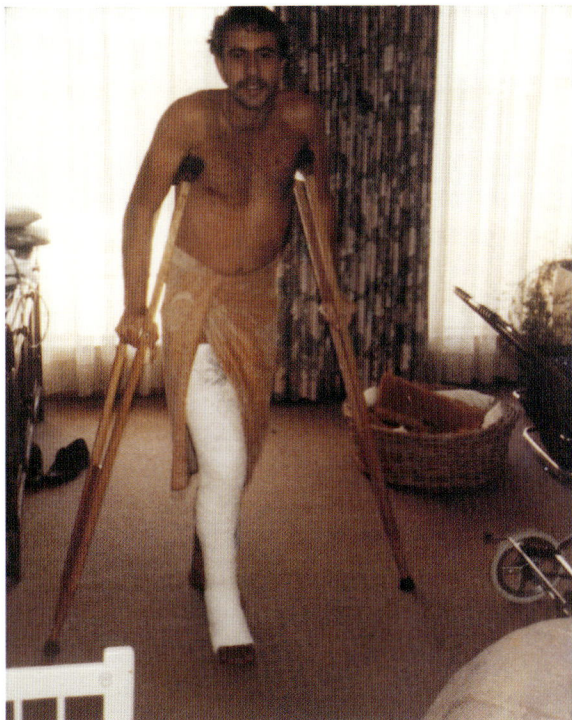

After my motorbike accident, while I was AWOL from the army, at
Joan's place in Vereeniging, December 1979.

Raving out of my head on LSD during that notorious holiday in the Transkei in the
early 1980s. Those were crazy times!

Although my mom put us in Arcadia, she never abandoned us. Even when she went back to Hungary, she kept in touch and made a point of visiting us every few years. Life had been cruel to her, but she always showed us as much love as she could.

Joan and Malcolm on the beach in Cape Town, 1978. They got married in December 1980.

My father Fritz had seen better days when this picture was taken in Vanderbijlpark, in the early 1980s. Over the years, I had some contact with him, but I never felt any affection for the man. When he died, on 22 April 1989, I refused to attend his funeral. Twenty-three years later, to the day, I was released from prison.

company called Stromberg Safety and Security. There wasn't much to the job, as the products pretty much sold themselves. As always, it was juggling the drugs with work that proved the biggest challenge, and it was always work that would come off second best. When an addict wants his fix, he wants it *now*, and so I was often out of town. After about eight months, I resigned. Resigning voluntarily was quite an achievement and it could have been a turning point in my life, considering my record of being fired from most other jobs I'd tried.

Selling drugs was easy money. Although it was illegal, the benefits of selling drugs always outweighed the risks, or, rather, conveniently blinded me to the consequences. I took the risk and most of the time I was lucky. Even as a child, while living at Arcadia, somehow I always managed to outwit or outsmart those in positions of authority – the principal, the matron and the housemothers – no matter what I'd done. It was almost as if I had a guardian angel protecting me.

Being an addict, not to mention my own worst enemy, learning life's lessons the hard way was the pattern of my life. I would repeat the same mistake over and over, which caused me to lose jobs, girlfriends, the respect of my family, basically everything I ever possessed. When was I going to learn my lesson? What would it take for me to understand how destructive drugs were?

But when an addict wants his fix ... Yes, you guessed it. I started freebasing again. The difference this time was that I was doing it behind Sarah-Lee's back.

Just as alcohol is a gateway to marijuana and marijuana to other drugs, sniffing coke eventually leads to freebasing (also known as 'parabatting'), and by then everybody was doing it.

At that stage, I used to sell little envelopes of cocaine in powder form. I did my own cutting. I had customers who were 'sniffers' and others who were 'smokers'. Cooking coke was an art, so, instead of having my customers complain of the return, I started to cook the coke myself and sell it in rock form. At that time, nobody else was selling it already cooked, and so my business began to boom.

Sarah-Lee and I moved into a townhouse in Norwood together. While she continued to waitress at Late Nite Al's, I ran around selling

cocaine. My new girlfriend loved shopping and we were forever buying stuff, new furniture or clothes. During the day, Sarah-Lee would
accompany me on my deliveries. She was a good cover.

Some occurrences in our lives are unforgettable. One such instance,
which still leaves me wondering in utter disbelief, was when I had my
worst freak-out while wired on cocaine.

Fridays and Saturdays were the busiest days in the drug business.
Everybody got high at the weekend. On this night Sarah-Lee and I
planned on going out for a casual dinner and afterwards to Rockey
Street in Yeoville to listen to live music. We were about to leave our
apartment when my pager buzzed. It was Burt Reynolds – for security reasons, all my clients who contacted me on my pager were given
celebrity names. Burt was one of my most celebrated clients, and making a delivery to him was not too far out of our way. Burt and his wife,
Goldie Hawn, lived in a three-storey mansion along the base of a ridge
that divided the north from the northeast of Johannesburg, a winding
road known as Sylvia Pass. The dimly lit road was lined with jacaranda
trees, whose branches met above the road and made it look quite eerie in
a half-light. In season, the trees were a spectacular mass of violet-blue,
trumpet-shaped flowers, which, at the slightest wind, would float to the
ground, transforming the road into a sea of petals. When you drove over
them, they would make a popping noise under your tyres.

Burt's house was enclosed by a concrete wall almost 2.5m high.
Entry to the property was through a solid steel gate. It was early evening and the road was dark and deserted. Sarah-Lee chose to wait in the
car, and even though I was concerned about leaving her there alone,
I knew I'd be back in a few minutes. In the event that she should be
harassed by anybody, I told her to hoot the car horn. I got out of the
car and did a thorough survey of the road. There was nobody in sight.
A drug dealer must be in a constant state of alert. Respecting your
clients' privacy and safety is an absolute priority. Anything less and
you'd be suspected of being a rat. When doing a drop, I would first
circle the block, always keeping a watchful eye in my rear-view mirror
to see whether I had been followed. Once I was sure it was safe I would
make the delivery.

I pressed the electronic buzzer on the gate and Burt's laidback voice crackled through the speaker.

'Is that you?' he said.

I replied, 'Your one and only friendly candyman.'

The gate clicked open. Goldie was waiting for me in the entrance hall. She was wearing a chic white bathrobe that hung loosely on her thin frame. Her small, firm breasts were completely exposed, as was the flimsy see-through G-string that clung tightly to her shaved vagina. Goldie was like a sister to me. If this hadn't been the case, I could very well have fucked her right there on the doorstep. As I walked past her, she murmured, 'He's in the bedroom.'

I walked down the corridor and found Burt. The bed was unmade, items of clothing were lying all over, the windows were closed, and the curtains were drawn. Drug paraphernalia was spread methodically on the surface of the dressing table. The lights had been turned low and the smell of sex and cigarette smoke hung in the air. Burt was wearing faded jeans that looked like they hadn't been washed in a while. His bleached and torn T-shirt showed sweat stains under the arms and his silver-white hair was uncombed. When I walked in, he was standing in front of the mirror, fixed on the reflection of the flame from the two Bic lighters he held in each hand as he concentrated on allowing just enough heat to melt the rock of coke resting on the wire mesh that was fitted to the front of his glass pipe. At his leisure he inhaled the smoke that came out as the substance melted, holding his breath for as long as his lungs permitted. Then he slowly exhaled. Watching him going through the ritual, and knowing that all too familiar feeling of heavenly buzz, my own craving was triggered ...

Burt offered me his pipe, but I declined, explaining that my chick was waiting outside in the car, and adding that we were going out for dinner. I doubt he heard or understood a word I said. He placed the pipe in my hand and sat down on the edge of the bed. He didn't speak exactly, it was more like he breathed the words 'Give me three grams.' Then he insisted I have a hit. Burt was a good ten years my senior and a drug connoisseur from the old school, who remained calm and collected no matter how stoned he was. He kept his own pocket electronic scale to ensure that nobody short-changed him. I was still the only dealer in town who sold his product already cooked. A solid rock with a couple pieces weighed out to 0.7 of a gram, which measured almost three points more than any other dealer's coke when cooked.

Giving in to temptation is the story of my life. My palms sweated and my mouth watered at the thought of having a hit. I reached into the bag that contained 15g of cooked cocaine – each gram was meticulously wrapped and folded into a small paper envelope no more than 2.5cm in diameter. I passed Burt three envelopes, keeping out one for myself. Then I resealed the plastic bag and put it back in my pocket. I opened the envelope, broke the rock in two and hit it in Burt's pipe.

To start with, I was not in the right frame of mind, but it was too late. I sucked the pipe, holding the smoke, and that all too familiar rush was so incredible – as intense as the feeling of ecstasy. Right away, I could also feel myself being overcome with paranoia. Burt, I assumed, was in the bathroom. Nervously, I made my way to the living room, which was in total darkness. Peering through a gap in the curtains, I stared out, surveying everything in sight. I saw the shadows of people moving around on the branches of the trees in the garden. I tried my utmost to clear my mind, trying to convince myself that this was only a figment of my imagination. I even slapped myself in the hope of having a lucid moment. The images were so fucking visual, though, I could swear on my life that what I was seeing was real. The first thought that went through my mind was that Burt had set me up. My heart was pumping and a distant but distinct voice in the back of my mind was telling me to run and get the fuck out of there. I touched the wooden handle of my revolver, as an indication that I was prepared to shoot if anybody tried to apprehend me.

Regaining my confidence, I moved away from the window and saw Goldie standing near the dining room. The light from the passage projected her silhouette across the length of the carpet, giving her shadow the appearance of a prowling creature. It crossed my mind that maybe she was colluding with Burt and that this was part of a conspiracy to trap me.

I had been dealing and using drugs for almost 16 years. The drug squad had a pretty good idea of who was who in the underworld. Being extremely vigilant, so far I had always managed to keep under their radar. I never lived in one area for too long. I was constantly on the move. I even had my cars resprayed from time to time. My instincts were as sharp as those of a wild animal. I was well trained and I could sense danger. When it came to plainclothes police, I could spot them in a crowd. I used to joke that I could smell a pig a mile away.

I wanted another hit before I got out of the house. My eyes locked on Goldie's as I made my way back to their bedroom, and she gave me what appeared to me to be a sinister smile. I could have sworn I was able to read her mind. She disappeared into one of the many other rooms in the house, and when I got to their en-suite bedroom Burt was not there. I did a quick search under the bed, but the base was too low for anybody to crawl under it. I even checked the wardrobe. Burt was not there. Shit. All this time Sarah-Lee was waiting in the road in the car, and I was sure by now she was freaking out. Making my way to the dressing table, where I had left the half of my rock and pipe, I noticed that the rocks were missing and that the resin from the glass pipe had been scratched.

Motherfucker Burt had helped himself to my coke! My hands trembling, I removed the plastic bag from my pocket, opened another small envelope, and carefully loaded the pipe, also adding the remainder of the coke on the dressing table. I melted it and took one fat fucking hit! My brain seemed to come apart at the seams. My jaw started clicking and blowing imaginary smoke in the air, my lips went numb, and my heart beat at such a pace that my entire body shook. As my breathing was growing heavy, Burt came into the room and told me that someone in the street outside had been blowing a car horn repeatedly. Fuck! How was I going to face Sarah-Lee? I was out of my mind. I couldn't feel my feet.

Somehow I tiptoed to the front door and then to the security gate. Without moving my head, my eyes darted in every direction. Shadows of trees and bushes were taking on the forms of human figures and closing in on me. I peeped through a gap in the security gate and saw Sarah-Lee in the car. The inside light was on and there was a plainclothes cop in the driver's seat and two really hefty pigs in the rear, interrogating her. My mind snapped. I turned and went back into the house, but by this point neither Burt nor Goldie was anywhere to be seen.

Convinced they had set me up, I went into the bathroom and flushed all the coke I was carrying down the toilet. I waited a minute or two and then I flushed my pager, too. I removed my revolver from my hip and stealthily made my way to the kitchen, then out the back door and down the concrete stairway that ran at a 45-degree angle to the house. The back yard was paved in slate and there was an outhouse there. Beyond the 3m brick wall that separated Burt's house from his neighbour's was a fence about 3.5m high and topped with razor-sharp barbed wire. Although I cut myself in several places, I clambered over this fence with relative ease and jumped down – a drop of at least 4.5m – into the courtyard of an empty block of flats. The ground was overgrown with weeds and grass and I landed hard. I rolled into an infested damp-smelling pit of rotten foliage and dried branches of some trees that had been chopped down. I imagined being bitten by snakes and spiders. Tripping and crawling, I eventually got through the maze of rubbish and took on the challenge of another high barbed-wire fence, the last obstacle that stood between me getting away from my pursuers. I found my way into the ground floor of the abandoned building, the taste of dust, sweat and dirt clinging to my mouth. I was sweating profusely. I dusted myself off as best I could and adjusted my jeans and revolver. The door to the lobby was half broken off, barely hanging on its hinges. I could hear the noise of traffic. The scene of Sarah-Lee with the cops in the car kept replaying in my mind. Fuck! I couldn't think rationally. All I knew was that my world was caving in and everybody was out to get me.

As my eyes adjusted to the darkness, I could see that the building was in a state of ruin. There was a layer of dust as thick as a rug covering everything. The windows had all been either smashed or removed, and the door handles and any brass or copper accessories had been stolen by vandals. Cardboard boxes and empty beer bottles were scattered all over the show. Squatters were known to seek sanctuary in abandoned buildings, and I wondered if the place was haunted. My instincts were pressing me to get the fuck out of there. Staying close to the wall, I made my way to the lobby. Litter and human faeces were everywhere.

Finally I walked out and onto bustling Louis Botha Avenue.

Breathing in a mix of fresh air and exhaust fumes, I re-evaluated my situation. Thinking that I would make my way back to where I had left my car, acting like any normal pedestrian, I began to stroll in that direction. Then I noticed a car turning into the same street I was heading towards. I saw the driver turn his head and simultaneously throw his car into a U-turn. Convinced that he had recognised me, my adrenaline pumping, I ran across the road, dodging and weaving between the flow of cars. The headlights seemed like eyes, following my every move, and the neon signs of the shop windows along the road made it even more surreal. I removed my shirt, thinking people would think I was a jogger, even though I was wearing jeans.

I found myself doing what I was best at – running. Running for my life. Only this time the enemy was real, or so I thought. Running was so deeply ingrained in me that no matter whether the impetus was friendly or hostile, that moment of escape, the sense of freedom and solace I found in running, was as exhilarating as flying.

All I knew was that there was no way I was going to allow a low-life fucking cop to catch me. I must have run a good 300m on the main road; turning left, I raced down one of the side streets that bordered the suburb of Norwood, predominantly a Jewish area. I took another left turn down a road that, in contrast to the bustle of traffic on the main road, was completely deserted. As I jogged along the road, there wasn't a single vehicle in sight and I felt very vulnerable. Then, in the distance, I saw the headlights of an approaching car. I looked around for a place to hide and my first reaction was to climb up a tree. I dismissed the idea quickly, though; I would be trapped up a tree. Instead I entered the driveway of the nearest house and there I squatted down between two garbage cans. When the car had passed, I slipped out from my hiding place but remained in the shadows until I was able to see the car disappear around the corner.

My throat was dry and I was drenched in sweat. I realised that I was not too far from where one of my clients lived. Cathy was a high-class prostitute who worked from her home. Still in a state of frenzy, I set off in her direction at a brisk pace. I kept looking around, but I believed I had managed to elude my pursuers. On Cathy's street there were cars parked outside almost every house. Diagonally across from her place was a car with two people in it. Paranoia washed over me once again. My heart began to race. I jumped over the wall of the house next to Cathy's, crept over her wall unnoticed and saw that the light in her bedroom was dimmed. Standing there in the shadows, I waited a few minutes, believing that I owed it to Cathy to warn her that the shit had hit the fan and that she was being watched. Very gently, I tapped on the window with the back of my fingers.

'Skin!' I whispered urgently.

A light went on almost immediately and Cathy pulled the curtains open. She was completely naked. 'That was quick,' she greeted me, pushing a hand that clutched a handful of notes through the open window. 'Give me two grams,' she added.

What the fuck was she talking about? Had I just walked into another trap? My first reaction was to punch her in the face, but instead I hissed at her, 'The pigs are parked outside your house across the street!'

'Fuck!' she replied.

Before she could say anything else, I bolted around the back of the house, desperately searching for a way to escape again. In a strange way I felt a certain degree of satisfaction in evading my enemy. I pulled myself up onto a brick wall that was over 2m high and climbed up onto the roof of some domestic quarters, where I lay flat on my stomach. From there I had an excellent view of Cathy's street, and I observed two or three cars pulling over. When I heard their doors slam, I went into survival mode again. It was time to move. Fucking bitch is also involved, I thought to myself. Her time will come. I would bring a few of my friends from Newclare round and teach her a lesson for fucking with me.

Almost in one movement, I got to my feet and leapt into the neighbouring property. I landed on a neat lawn. The dwelling seemed different somehow. There was no clutter of stuff lying about. A grape-vine had been trained in such a way that it offered covering for a car parked underneath it, and there were two fruit trees whose branches had been pruned back. To the side of the house was a washing line with a few items of women's clothing hanging on it. The back door was open and the kitchen light was on. I could hear voices, but I didn't have much time to think. I ran straight into the house. There were two women in the kitchen, an elderly lady and a young girl of about 15. My sudden dramatic entrance, and no doubt my wild appearance, left them open-mouthed and shocked.

I quickly took stock of the situation. This was a mother and her daughter. Seeing my gun holstered down the front of my jeans, at first they just gaped at me. Then the elderly woman plucked up the cour-age to speak. 'Take whatever you want,' she said bravely, taking her daughter's arm and pulling her close. 'Please, all I ask is that you leave us alone!'

I was quite surprised. I had no intention of doing these people any harm. I raised both my arms in protest and said, 'No, no, you don't un-derstand. I'm being chased by robbers.' I could see immediate relief on their frightened faces. 'All I want is to use your phone,' I added politely. Then I explained that 'they' had guns and that I was outnumbered. The mother, logically, suggested that we call the police.

Fuck! What was this woman thinking?

'Please,' I said, 'I don't want to involve the police!'

Registering the seriousness of my tone and probably seeing my ex-pression changing, the woman agreed to do as I felt necessary. The mention of police had sent a chill up my spine. I'd heard the Norwood police had a file on me, and there was no way I could allow this wom-an to call them. I asked if she had a beer to calm my nerves and then asked if she would give me a lift to where I'd left my car. She agreed. She would probably have agreed to anything, just to get me off her property.

The house, although small, was nicely furnished. There were a few antiques, and next to the phone there was a huge old grandfather clock with beautiful, intricate carvings. By now my heart was beating at a normal pace. I was calm and the cocaine seemed to have worn off. I phoned my mate Craig, who was now living in Victory Park. Luck was on my side and he was at home. He told me that Sarah-Lee had contacted him and was on her way to his house, but she was worried as hell. Hearing that she was okay was a great comfort to me and I told Craig to keep her there, that I was on my way.

I had asked my hosts if they would be kind enough to give me a lift to where I had abandoned my car, which was not too far from their house (I wanted to make sure Sarah-Lee hadn't been involved in the attempt to bust me). We drove past Burt's house and everything seemed pretty normal there. Of course my car was gone because Sarah-Lee had driven off in it. I pretended to be shocked, and actually I felt quite bad then asking these women to drive me to Victory Park, which was about 20 minutes' drive away, but they were only too obliging. More than likely they were just too terrified to refuse. I got them to drop me around the corner from Craig's place, just in case they went to the cops, and I pretended to walk into a house nearby. As soon as they disappeared around the corner I made my way to Craig's.

Standing in his entrance hall, I told Craig about my evening. He was in fits of laughter and kept punctuating my story with 'Are you *serious*, Shaun? Fucking hell!' Next thing Sarah-Lee pulled into the driveway in my white Ford Laser. I ran to her, grabbed her in my arms and swung her around in circles.

'Put me down, put me down! Have you gone crazy?' she protested, half-laughing, although she was still upset that I had left her alone in the car for so long. She told me that she'd got fed up waiting for me and had driven around the block. Then she'd gone into Burt and Goldie's house, who had no idea where I'd gone. After that she'd driven over here.

When I related my own version of the story, describing in detail every crazy thing I had imagined and the extreme lengths I'd taken to get away from my pursuers, we simply cracked up laughing.

I went back to visit Cathy shortly afterwards, who was still fairly pissed at me. She told me she had had a steamer at the time and she didn't find my story all that humorous. In fact, she strongly advised me to stop smoking cocaine. The same afternoon I also took a turn past Burt and Goldie, who were somewhat offended by my mistrust and totally amazed by my bizarre behaviour. They, too, felt that maybe it was time for me to stop. What was wrong with these people, I thought. Half the enjoyment was being paranoid; that profound sense of fear and awareness when one became delusional was a high in itself.

By the early 1990s, credit card fraud was becoming a serious problem in South Africa. Crime syndicates were active in printing duplicate copies of people's credit cards and selling them on the black market. One of my close friends had shared with me how easy it was to do this, so I suggested to Sarah-Lee that, while she was at work at the restaurant, she should keep an eye out for businessmen who'd had too much to drink. These guys often lost their cards or neglected to ask their waiter to give them back after they'd paid for their meal.

One Saturday evening, I'd gone to pick up Sarah-Lee after work as usual. As I watched her approach the car I thought she had more of a spring in her step than usual. As she got in, we kissed and at the same time she threw something folded in a piece of paper onto my lap,

'Hey, what's this?' I asked her.

She could hardly conceal her excitement. 'Open it,' she said.

I couldn't believe my eyes. It was a credit card, and not only that – it was a gold one. That night, I must have practised the man's signature a few hundred times until it became like my own.

Being a drug dealer was bad enough, but committing fraud was taking crime to a new level, and this was new to me. I'd always had strong principles while growing up, and until that day I had never resorted to theft. Sure, as kids there'd been the odd occasion when we'd stolen a car just to take it on a joyride, or broken into a movie house and raided the ice-cream chest, but we were kids, and it was all done in the spirit of fun and adventure. This was different. I knew it, but I didn't give a shit.

Sarah-Lee and I decided to dress the part. The first store we hit was

Woolworths, where we bought quite a lot of clothing but didn't overdo it. Because it was our first time, we didn't want to create suspicion. When it came time to pay, I was so nervous I thought I was going to die. The cashier swiped the card on one of those portable credit card machines with a slider and I signed the slip. She checked the signature and thanked me for my purchase.

As we exited the store, Sarah-Lee was hanging onto my arm, squeezing it and smiling up at me like I was her hero. 'Shaun, you're a natural,' she whispered in my ear. This made me feel good, but we didn't stop there. After that we hit all the major stores, then the boutiques, and quite a few restaurants. The restaurants were the easiest targets and we really tipped the waiters well.

One of my friends had a steakhouse, and every two weeks or so they received a list of stolen credit cards, so I kept checking with him to see whether the card Sarah-Lee had stolen had been reported. For the next three months, every day, Sarah-Lee and I literally shopped till we dropped. Our families started asking questions, as we were showering them with gifts. My explanation was that I had pulled off a diamond deal, but I don't think they really believed my story. They kind of understood that it was better that they didn't know where the money was coming from or how I was getting it.

Generally, I avoided bottle stores, but then one day, against my instincts, we strolled into one. It was the first we planned to hit. While we were waiting at the till point to pay, the cashier called the manager and handed the credit card to him. He took it and went to his office which had this one-way mirrored glass portion. As soon as he disappeared behind it, I grabbed Sarah-Lee's hand and we ran. We bolted out of there so fast! I felt sick at the thought of losing the card but instinctively I knew our fun with it was over. We jumped into the car and sped out of the parking lot. At the traffic lights, as I turned I glanced into my rear-view mirror and saw the manager in the middle of the four-lane road running after my car. Motherfucker had balls! I wanted to pull over, stop, jump out and break his face on the pavement.

Sarah-Lee was freaking out and shouting at the same time. 'Drive faster! Drive faster!'

Shit, the guy had definitely seen us. Images of me in an identity parade, with him pointing me out to the police, flashed through my mind. Credit card fraud carried a heavy penalty and each transaction was considered a separate offence. If I was caught I would go to prison for a long time. Suddenly I was overcome with regret and remorse. For me, it had never been about the material things. It was the other stuff that was so fucking thrilling! It was that rush of adrenaline when you're lining up at the till, gambling with your freedom, never knowing when you were going to have to run for your life. I loved it!

Now I knew I was in some serious trouble. Who else could I turn to once again but my family? In fact, Joan and Malcolm weren't that shocked when I told them what had happened. I think they always kind of expected the worst. They'd suspected from the beginning that I was getting up to no good. Right now, though, most importantly, I needed to know whether the guy at the bottle store had managed to get the registration number of Sarah-Lee's car. I looked up the phone number of the bottle store, dialled it, and asked to speak to the manager.

'My name is Detective Botha,' I said. 'I'm calling from Bramley police station. We believe an attempted credit card fraud has just taken place at your store. Is there any chance you could give us a description of the person, and did you manage to get the registration and make of vehicle perhaps?'

Jesus, fuck, he did! The guy not only had the registration number, but also the make of car, *and* he described me and Sarah-Lee down to the clothes we were wearing! Mental images of me being led away in handcuffs went through my mind. The thought of going to jail terrified me. What the *fuck* was I going to do? I couldn't hide at my sister's place. Sarah-Lee's mother was going to have a total freak-out. There was only one solution. I had to get out of the country.

Within two days, I found myself on a flight bound for Budapest. Sarah-Lee stayed behind. In the event that I was caught, she knew I would never implicate her, and vice versa.

I stayed with Marika, my half-sister, who had moved to Budapest many years before. It was winter in Hungary and I didn't go out much. At first Marika was friendly and welcoming, but she wasn't thrilled to be harbouring what she considered a fugitive from justice. I phoned my family and friends back in South Africa almost daily. So far, the police had not been banging on Joan's door, and nor had I appeared on the popular TV show *Police File*, the equivalent of *America's Most Wanted*.

More disturbing, though, was what I was hearing about Sarah-Lee. Apparently, she had been seen leaving the bar after work several times in the company of the same guy. Every time I phoned her she was either too busy to come to the phone or she was not around. Jesus, what was going on? I was sure I was going to lose her, and I couldn't bear the thought. After three weeks I returned to South Africa, convinced I'd be apprehended at the airport. Nothing happened. I couldn't believe my luck. I had actually got away with it. My guardian angel was still watching out for me.

Sarah-Lee had definitely been screwing around, but I decided to let it go. I was just so happy to be back. We moved away from Norwood and into a townhouse in Sandton, in Katherine Road, directly behind the fire station. It might have been a new start for us, but my old lifestyle wasn't about to change yet.

One day I was driving along in my car, on my way to make one of many cocaine deliveries to my regular customers. It was one of those days where anything and everything irritated me. Sarah-Lee sat slouched in the passenger seat beside me. By now we had been together for more than two years – a record for me when it came to relationships – but my relationship with her (and my life for that matter) seemed to be spiralling into an irreversible course of self-destruction once more.

I was running late and exceeding the speed limit. Moreover, I was craving a hit. Bothered by my erratic behaviour, Sarah-Lee and I got into one of the many arguments we had been having recently and which had become more frequent since I had resumed freebasing. In response to her accusations, I took my eyes off the road for a second, just as a car that had been parked at the side of the road edged forward without indicating and made a sharp right turn. Instinctively, I swerved to avoid a collision, but, because of the speed I was doing, when I slammed on the brakes my car went into a skid. The adjoining road ran at a downhill slope and was unusually curved, which made the pavement on that side higher than normal.

I crashed headlong into what felt like a solid wall. There was a loud bang and the sound of crushing metal. I heard Sarah-Lee screaming, shrieking, and saw with terror her contorted frame being pushed beneath the dashboard onto the floor. My head went through the windscreen, but, besides a few small cuts and being severely disoriented, I suffered no visible injuries. However, Sarah-Lee was in serious pain and unable to move. I managed to pull her out of the wreckage and laid her on the pavement.

She was so brave – the desperate look of bewilderment in her eyes expressed the pain and fear she was feeling. I suspected that her back might be broken, and to comfort her I assured her she was going to be okay. In a matter of minutes an ambulance, the police and several people who came to try and assist were on the scene. Sarah-Lee was put on a stretcher and whisked off to the hospital. The medics suggested that I go with her so that I could be checked for concussion, but I insisted I was fine. All I could think of at that moment was cooking up some coke and smoking a big rock. I left Sarah-Lee to be taken to the hospital on her own. A sympathetic bystander kindly offered to give me a ride home.

Sarah-Lee and I had moved again, from Sandton to a townhouse, ironically directly behind King David High School in Victory Park, close to the place where, some 15 years back, I had been introduced to marijuana by Craig and three of our schoolteachers. I was sure they would have been proud of the progress I had made up the addiction ladder. When I got home, I phoned Joan and told her about the accident, and also about Sarah-Lee's condition. I said I planned to be at the hospital in the evening but right now I had a couple of things I needed to do. I asked my sister if she would please inform my girlfriend's mother about what had happened.

I had about 250g of coke stashed at home in a secret compartment.

199

Anxiously, I measured out 10g on my electronic scale, added a proportionate ratio of bicarbonate of soda mixed with a portion of water. I poured it into a small spice bottle. Holding the enticing concoction of liquid up to the light, right there and then I had an epiphany. This was the only true pleasure my flesh desired and responded to. I couldn't remember when last I had had sexual intercourse with Sarah-Lee. I was on the path of no return.

I was an addict.

I placed the spice bottle directly onto a plate on the stove which I slowly heated. Timing and controlling the temperature were crucial so that the chemical reaction caused the cocaine to fizz and rise at the same time. I removed the bottle, shaking it in a clockwise swirling motion. After this the murky substance dropped into the steamed water and disappeared into translucent oil. I proceeded to add a small chunk of ice to allow the solution to cool while still jiggling the bottle in a circular motion. Within ten seconds, a solid white rock crystallised before my eyes. I covered the crest of the bottle with the palm of my hand, turned it upside down, and watched as the rock effortlessly floated out. I looked down at it and I thought, What a beauty. I was truly a master when it came to the art of cooking cocaine.

In a moment of reflection, standing there in my kitchen, I looked back on how my journey into the wretched and sordid world of drugs had begun. In 1977 I was 18 years old and invincible. Smoking marijuana was fashionable and it seemed harmless enough. Little did I realise all those years ago how quickly I would be drawn into the drug culture and its constant temptations. What started off innocently as occasional indulgence would progressively become worse. For 16 years now I had been using drugs, and sometimes I had narrowly escaped the clutches of death. I was always on the move, running not only from myself but also from the law. There was no doubt that the damage to my mind was irreparable; I had become a danger not only to myself but also to anybody and everybody around me. The drugs laid down the rules. They dictated the terms. I was beyond being rational. Whether getting totally fucked out of my head or running, it didn't matter: I was trapped. There was no way out. My days were numbered. Did I care? No, not really. Life had become meaningless for me. I had no purpose. If I ever thought about it, I always reverted to my old thinking: you live and then you die and the length of time we spend on earth makes no difference. What was time anyway?

I was 33 years old. How much lower would I have to sink before I realised the damage I was doing to myself and the people around me? The sick feeling inside me should have told me that things weren't going to end well for me, but, then again, would I have listened?

Then the phone rang, startling me out of my thoughts. Of all things, it was a casting agency, which I had joined a while back in the hope of getting the odd bit of movie or commercial work. As luck would have it, I had been cast as a member of a gang in an Eric Roberts movie that was being shot in South Africa. Fuck, I had completely forgotten that today was the day I was supposed to turn up! The agent reminded me that it was an opportunity of a lifetime.

I was faced with the insoluble dilemma of the typical junkie: in one hand I held a rock of pure cocaine and in the other a promise of success and a better life. Sealing my fate, I decided to have one quick hit and then go to the movie set. After that I would go to the hospital and visit Sarah-Lee. My intentions were genuine. Implementing them was an entirely different matter.

My insatiable craving to get high was continuous, and, as always, it would be victorious over my waning will. Armed with my drug paraphernalia, still shook up from the accident, I headed for the lounge and plonked myself on the dark grey leather sofa. We had a lovely apartment. In the centre of the room was a glass coffee table with a marble base. Adorning the walls were a variety of oil paintings. Near the door, in glazed earthenware pots, were lush green ferns and an indoor palm tree, whose long feathery leaves fanned out over one of the couches and almost touched the ceiling. On the other side of the door was our rectangular glass-topped, wrought-iron dining room table. The pastel-coloured cushions of the eight high-backed chairs arranged around the table matched our roman blinds. On the opposite end to where I was sitting stood two marble pillars on which a single glass shelf was balanced. This was where our telephone and answering machine were.

The apartment was tiled in ivory-white, and here in the lounge we had a white shag carpet.

Leaning forward on the couch, I proceeded to break off a fair-sized chunk of coke from the rock I had just cooked. I loaded it onto the wire mesh that was carefully fitted into the front of my glass pipe. While I was melting it carefully with a Bic lighter, I removed my shoes, undid the buckle of my belt, and loosened my jeans. Then, pipe in my mouth and keeping the flame at enough of a distance that the heat would still melt the coke, I slowly but steadily sucked on the pipe, inhaling the smoke, which I held in my lungs for as long as possible, before gradually releasing it.

The rush that comes with smoking crack cocaine is instantaneous.

There's an all-encompassing flash-like light that jolts your brain and, simultaneously, an intense euphoric feeling that permeates your entire being. This surging sensation has been compared to an orgasm, a mental orgasm. All your senses are heightened. Sounds are magnified and visual images distorted to the point where you actually perceive something that is not there. I fucking *loved* the feeling. When I was at home and high, the minute I had a hit I would sneak around the apartment closing all the windows, securing the doors, and then drawing the curtains shut, ensuring that nobody could see inside.

I had just done all this when the phone rang again. *Fuck.* I got the fright of my life. My heart beating rapidly, I turned down the tone on the telephone, switched on the answering machine and, on tiptoe, made my way to the lounge window. Moving the curtain ever so slightly, I peeped out through the narrow gap. This was an all too familiar scenario for me. Sometimes I would stand there for hours on end, my .38 Special always at hand, my vigil broken only by regular hits on the pipe.

The phone kept ringing. I was so fucked, wired and paranoid I thought that the phone was signalling the cops, so I unplugged it. Needless to say, I didn't make it to the movie set (I never liked Eric Roberts anyway), but, worst of all, I neglected to visit Sarah-Lee at the hospital that night. I continued smoking coke, going through the same rituals, right through a second day and into a third. I felt like a zombie, still chasing that very first rush. I couldn't stop and I didn't want to.

By late afternoon on the third day I had spent a good hour or two crawling around the apartment looking for rocks that might have fallen onto the carpet, in between peering out the window. While I was contemplating cooking more coke I thought I should check my pager for messages. There were hundreds of them, mostly from my customers, but also a few from my sister. Joan warned me in no uncertain terms that if I failed to visit Sarah-Lee at the hospital that evening, she and Malcolm wouldn't, for love nor money, ever speak to me again, and nor would I ever see Sarah-Lee again either. She was ashamed of me, she added.

I had been wearing the same clothes for the past 72 hours. I was so fucking wired, so out of my head, that I didn't even know what time of the day it was. I checked my watch. It was almost 5pm. I had less than two hours to sober up before visiting hours at the hospital. I poured myself a glass of neat whisky, which I drank in gulps, and hurriedly cleaned up. I opened the windows and curtains, allowing light and a fresh breeze to circulate throughout the apartment again. Then I jumped into a bath, which kind of shocked me back to reality. Shaving proved quite tricky, and I cut myself in several spots.

When I was dressed, I took a quick glance at myself in the full-length mirror in our bedroom. Besides the dilated eyes and tiny pupils, I thought I looked reasonably presentable. I grabbed a six-pack of cold beers from the fridge and got into Sarah-Lee's newly sprayed midnight-blue Volkswagen Beetle, my .38 clipped on the inside of my jeans. My gun was my closest friend. It had saved me from many a precarious situation and I never left it behind.

Driving to the hospital was a daunting task. By now it was dark and the headlights of approaching cars looked like meteorites about to collide with me. I had drunk two beers by the time I reached the hospital, and I downed another one in the parking lot for good measure. Between the coke and the alcohol, I felt pretty good, but I was nervous as fucking hell at the prospect of what I was about to deal with.

I wondered who else might be visiting Sarah-Lee. I didn't even know the extent of her injuries. After about 20 minutes I plucked up the courage and made my way through the hospital. I was fucked up.

I hated hospitals anyway; that pervasive sterilised, medicinal smell, compounded by an atmosphere of sick and dying patients, nauseated me. The distance from the elevator to Sarah-Lee's ward, although just a couple of metres, felt like miles. With every step, my feet grew heavier and my heart pounded more loudly in my chest. By now there were only about 20 minutes remaining of visiting hours.

I entered the ward. Sarah-Lee's bed was in the far right-hand corner next to the windows. There were four beds on each side of the spacious room, but not all of them were occupied and only two of the other patients had visitors. The lights were unusually bright, I thought. I felt as if I was on a stage in front of an audience of hundreds of people. It felt like there was a huge spotlight shining directly down on me, with a crowd jeering and shouting and pointing. The words they were shouting weren't clear, but I knew exactly what they meant. Sarah-Lee's family and mine were at her bedside, seated and standing on both sides. Each one of them seemed to turn their heads at exactly the same time and look towards me. The look of disgust, anger and disappointment on their faces made me shrivel inside. I wanted to curl up and die.

My entire life, I was constantly on the run. I was a runaway train. I had always had difficulty with change, and running made me feel safe. This was another of those moments. Right then, I was ready to turn my back and run away, faster than I had ever run in my life, but it was too late.

I couldn't bring myself to look Sarah-Lee directly in the eyes. That poignant, troubled look of disappointment was too much for me. I can still see it to this day. She was on the verge of tears, not because of her injuries, nor because I hadn't visited, but because I was fucked out of my head and she could see it.

None of my girlfriends ever really knew me, *really* knew me. From a young age I had learnt to put up barriers that were impossible to penetrate. Even so, Sarah-Lee had a fairly good idea whenever I was stoned. She had seen how I had been becoming progressively more disconnected. I knew I was breaking her heart.

Some months before the accident, when we were still living in Sandton, I left our apartment at about 10am to pick up a stash of coke. On the way back, while driving on the highway, I rolled up a note, opened the plastic bag that contained the coke and took a snort in each nostril. Small rocks lodged themselves in my nasal passages, while some fell into my lap. Within I was buzzing. As I approached the Sandton turn-off I could have sworn I was being followed, so I stayed on the freeway and for the next eight hours drove around Johannesburg city, snorting and driving at ridiculous speeds, trying to lose the cars I imagined were following me. Sarah-Lee had seen that wired look on my face when I finally returned home that evening. I don't know whether she noticed that I had also clocked about 800km on the speedometer.

Another time, we had a huge argument. In my state of anger, I blurted out that I no longer loved her and that I wanted to break up with her. She went ballistic. She ran into the kitchen and grabbed a knife. In her frenzy she tried to stab me. I thought it was quite funny. Then I pulled out my gun and threatened to shoot her. Naturally, I was bluffing and I thought she would put the knife down. Instead she just kept coming. I ran into our bedroom but Sarah-Lee was right behind me, still wielding the knife. I managed to lock myself in, and she repeatedly stabbed the door, screaming that she was going to kill me.

Even in self-defence it was below me to hit a woman, but what do you do in such an instance? I felt terrible for hitting her, but I did. There is no excuse for manhandling a woman, but I wasn't about to apologise for what I had done. In her state of hysteria, with a knife in her hand, she had been a danger to herself and to me. Eventually she calmed down and we had a heart-to-heart talk. A slight bruise had begun to form under one of her eyes. Sarah-Lee emphasised that I had some choices to make, otherwise we had no future together. Then she went quiet and I could feel the tears building up in my eyes. I let her know that I had to go, I didn't know where. All I knew was that I had to take off. I was struggling to breathe.

Leaving Sarah-Lee, I realised, was going to be a lot more difficult than I had anticipated. Furthermore I was beyond the point of being rational. I found myself driving around aimlessly in the early hours of the morning and then I was parked outside Sarah-Lee's mother's apartment. It was almost 3am when I rang her doorbell. I tried to explain to her mother what had happened, how I couldn't understand what had come over me. She advised me to go home, not before strongly suggesting that Sarah-Lee and I should break up as it was obvious we were having serious problems.

There is something magical about being on the quiet roads at that time in the morning, from when darkness turns to light and the sun's rays begin to engulf the earth. Driving home, I watched in awe as nature reminded me just how insignificant we humans are. When I got there, Sarah-Lee was still awake, but thankfully more composed.

A few weeks, maybe a month before the accident, Sarah-Lee was making dinner in the kitchen and I was pretending to be relaxing in the bedroom. Instead, using a candle, I was busy cooking up some cocaine. She kept coming to the door to ask what I was doing, but she never actually saw. I managed to have one or two hits but she kept interrupting me, so I loaded the whole rock onto my pipe, took a deep breath, lit up, and sucked in the smoke from the melting rock.

From there things went blank. I woke up to find myself lying on my bed. Hovering over me was this strange man. I could feel something cold and metallic on my chest, something disc-shaped that the man appeared to be moving around like he was testing something. I felt peaceful, like I had died and come back to life.

Joan and Malcolm were also there, for some reason, standing at the foot of my bed. I couldn't fathom why they looked so sad and concerned. My nephew Darren, who was about ten years old, was sitting next to me holding my hand. Was I in heaven? Then I noticed Sarah-Lee. She was standing with her arms folded and she seemed to be in a state of shock. Her eyes were bloodshot, as if she had been crying. I on the other hand felt totally serene and calm – what was all the fuss about? Then the doctor informed me that I had had a seizure and was lucky to be alive.

If dying felt so blissful, death would be the last thing I would fear. What I should have been more concerned about was the impact my actions were having on my family. It's not that I never cared or gave it a thought. I really did care, and it pained me, but it was easier to believe that things were beyond my control or, in plain English, that I was an addict with an uncontrollable craving for drugs.

Sarah-Lee and I had been through a lot together. Now it was her turn to look to me for love and support, having survived her own brush with death.

As I approached her hospital bed, nobody greeted me. Despite my feeling of having a harsh spotlight shone on me, I might as well have been invisible. Her family excused themselves and left. Joan muttered something angrily under her breath and poked me sharply in the chest with her finger. 'You're such a fuck-up,' she hissed. 'We need to have a *serious* talk.' She and Malcolm left the ward, too. It was a relief for me. Facing Sarah-Lee was going to be difficult enough anyway.

And then I was alone with my girlfriend.

The alcohol I had consumed had to a large extent helped counteract the effects of smoking the cocaine. Although my conscience was troubling me, I felt alienated from reality and I hadn't slept in days. I knew I was responsible for Sarah-Lee's injuries, but I couldn't bring myself to feel anything. Subconsciously, I think I was already running.

To this day, I have no recollection of the conversation that transpired between Sarah-Lee and me in the hospital that night. All I know is that we agreed that I wouldn't visit her again. Sarah-Lee was stubborn and determined, and two days later she was discharged. Joan and Malcolm accompanied her in the ambulance that brought her home. I hadn't used cocaine since my three-day binge and had spent the days since visiting Sarah-Lee sleeping. Our domestic worker cleaned up the house, making it ready for Sarah-Lee's arrival. Two vertebrae in Sarah-Lee's lower back had been broken in the accident, which meant she would be bedridden for a few weeks. I was warned by my sister that I had better take good care of her.

Actually, it was ridiculous. There was no way the hospital should have discharged her, but Sarah-Lee was adamant. She had insisted that she be allowed to go home because she needed to be around to keep an eye on me and prevent me from slipping further into the abyss.

A few months earlier, we had put down a R50 000 deposit on a townhouse in the fast-developing suburb of Dowerglen, which was still being built. I had responsibilities, and Sarah-Lee didn't want to see me throw everything away for drugs. Ironically, of course, it was the drugs that paid for all the material things we'd acquired, the posh townhouse included.

While she was recovering, I cooked twice a day, served Sarah-Lee her meals, and nursed her. We got into a routine. At times I had to leave her on her own and go shopping at the supermarket, but our domestic worker would be there if she needed any help.

Often in the mornings, while Sarah-Lee slept and I made breakfast, I would cook up some cocaine and smoke the rocks. We had not had sex for some months, which I couldn't attribute to the affects of cocaine alone. Sarah-Lee had lost her sex appeal for me. I wanted sex; I missed the euphoria of it. Masturbating had its moments of pleasure, but I was tired of fucking Kim Basinger in my head. I was on the lookout for somebody else to fulfil my sexual needs. In almost two and a half years of living with her, I had not been unfaithful, let alone contemplated being with another woman.

A part of me loved Sarah-Lee, but the other felt trapped in an existence that represented everything that I was not. I was a free spirit, I trusted nobody, and I found comfort and freedom in my solitude. The concept of marriage was for the emotionally insecure. I couldn't imagine myself fulfilling the role of a husband. I did think about having children, but I was afraid of subjecting them to the life I had endured as a child. I dismissed the idea more quickly than it ever entered my head. Right there and then, I made a decision that I had to leave Sarah-Lee, but now was not the time. If anything, I owed it to her to wait until she was fully recovered. Her recovery took priority. Then, I decided, I would dump her and continue doing what I was best at.

After a few more weeks in bed, Sarah-Lee was able to move around. She was required to wear a full-body brace made out of Perspex. It was constructed in such a way that I would have to pull it open and hold it like that while she negotiated her body into it. It wasn't an easy thing to do. Jesus, fuck! I felt really bad, even more so because she was so brave.

I can still distinctly remember the first time she got out of bed, after a long struggle to slip into the brace, and moved around our apartment. It was like seeing a baby taking its first steps. I was deeply moved and so blown away by her tenacity and determination that I went straight. I knew that I loved her, that she was the one living soul that stood between life and death for me. I stopped smoking cocaine and we started spending evenings at my sister's place playing Scrabble. I was still selling cocaine, the profits of which I kept dumping into the three-bedroomed townhouse we were building.

During the day, in between drug deliveries, Sarah-Lee and I would visit the building site to see how construction was coming along. We were having the room behind the lounge/dining room converted into a Jacuzzi room, which was costing us another R25 000. It was a five-person Jacuzzi, with electronically activated controls; to get the unit into the room, the window frames had to be removed and some of the wall broken away. This should have been an exciting time for any couple, the beginning of a lifetime together, but it was a daunting prospect for me. All this domestic planning was beginning to stifle me. I didn't know yet how I was going to escape, but I knew I wasn't going to be able to go through with it.

Despite all my promises, to myself and to Sarah-Lee, I knew that I was still going to leave her, but it was becoming more and more difficult. I felt trapped in a life that didn't fit me. As a drug dealer, one acquires all sorts of things that addicts pawn or sell for a fix. I had accumulated quite a lot of gold. One of my good friends was a jeweller, and we had her design and make some jewellery for Sarah-Lee – a bracelet that had precious stones and a diamond setting with a matching ring and neck chain. The set was beautiful, impressive in its elegance. But by now red lights were flashing around in my head. Fuck! Before I knew it I would be writing my marriage vows!

I could feel myself being suffocated. My fate was as good as sealed.

Why couldn't I just lead a normal life? When I wrestled with this question in my head, the answers came as easily as they always did. I persuaded myself that there was more to life than conforming to the expectations of society. Besides, I still hadn't discovered my purpose yet, nor the deeper meaning of life.

Eventually, the townhouse complex was completed and we moved into our new home. By now, Sarah-Lee had made almost a complete recovery and was no longer dependent on her brace. We must have given the impression of being the perfect couple, and yet Sarah-Lee and I hadn't been intimate for months – understandably because of her injuries, but that wasn't the only reason. Our new neighbours knew nothing of our dark secrets, and our respective families popped round at different times to see our new place. Sarah-Lee would give them the grand tour. I guess the thing that was on everybody's mind was when we would be tying the knot. Little did they know that I was contemplating my escape, not planning the day when we would walk down the aisle.

The wiring on our Jacuzzi was not finished, which meant that the building electrician had to have access to the townhouse during the day to work on it, so one or both of us had to stay at home. Seeing that I had drug deliveries to make, Sarah-Lee entertained the electrician. When the job was done, the electrician left, but, during the following days, our electricity box kept tripping whenever the washing machine was running at the same time as the Jacuzzi. We called him back to check what the problem was. As it turned out, he needed to rewire the entire circuit board, which would take another whole day. Sarah-Lee volunteered to stay home and supervise. In fact, she was more than obliging.

I went about my business and left the two of them at home. Later that afternoon, I walked in on them relaxing over a cup of tea. I noticed that Sarah-Lee was unusually chirpy, whereas he seemed to feel a bit uncomfortable about my sudden appearance. Fuck, I thought to myself, here's an opportunity being handed to me on a platter! The electrician hurriedly jumped to his feet, said his job was done and excused himself. If the board should trip again, he said, all we needed to do was call. I walked him out to his van. I put my arm on his shoulder, thanked him for his work, and enquired how much I owed him. He told me that he was contracted by the owners of the complex and that there was no charge. In my mind, however, I had already devised his fate.

I invited the guy to join us for a braai on the Sunday, which was going to be our house-warming party, with only our immediate family attending. At first he declined my offer. 'Please,' I said, 'I insist. It allows me to show you my appreciation.' It didn't take much to convince him, and we shook hands.

Sunday could not have come fast enough for me. Sarah-Lee and her mother prepared the salads and baked potatoes, laid the tables and generally saw to everybody's needs. I invited the electrician to help me braai. After a couple of beers, I dropped the bomb. Making sure nobody heard me, I murmured under my breath as my girlfriend walked past us. 'Would you like to fuck her?' As I pointed to Sarah-Lee's sexy ass, the look of guilt on the man's face was something priceless. It was the kind of look rarely captured on camera.

Sarah-Lee was a very beautiful woman. She was slender, bordering on very thin, and she had a great pair of tits. She oozed sensuality. I couldn't help myself. As the electrician, in a slightly drunken state, began stuttering I just started laughing. To save him further embarrassment, I said, 'Listen, I don't blame you, man. She is very fuckable.' His expression went from bewilderment to one of enquiring interest. I confided that Sarah-Lee and I were actually not happy together, and that I was looking for a way to get out of the relationship. If he wanted her, I told him, he could have her. He looked at me in amazement. As far as I was concerned, the day was turning out to be a huge success.

Everyone enjoyed the lunch and the conversation revolved mostly around politics. Apartheid was in the process of being dismantled. Nelson Mandela and FW de Klerk had jointly been awarded the Nobel Peace Prize in 1993, and Mandela was soon to become the first elected black president in our country, democratically voted for by the entire nation. In some views, the future of the white man in South Africa was looking bleak.

I didn't know it then, of course, but my fate and that of my country were indelibly connected.

Meanwhile my plan was falling beautifully into place. The scene was set for the following evening. I would leave the townhouse around 6pm and return around midnight. This would give the fucking electrician sufficient time to make his move. He would arrive unexpectedly, claiming to be looking for me.

The following day around the agreed time, instead of going on my daily drug deliveries, I went to Burt Reynolds' place, where I treated him and Goldie Hawn to a couple of grams of cocaine. The occasion called for a celebration. I was about to become a bachelor again.

My plan was foolproof.

I had learnt from my sources that my electrician friend came from a wealthy Afrikaans family and lived in a mansion in an opulent area just outside Joburg. The only thing that turned Sarah-Lee on more than a stiff cock was a man with a permanently fat wallet. I definitely didn't fit the fat-wallet profile, at least not permanently. Material things had never meant much to me. In her eyes, I was more of a dreamer than anything else, and I had always suspected that she would leave me if something or someone better came along. The thing about drug money is that it is not hard-earned cash. As easily as it is made, spending it or losing it is even easier.

After an evening of heavy freebasing cocaine and drinking with my friends, I was in a stoned, sullen mood. It was well after midnight when I returned to the townhouse where I had left the unsuspecting Sarah-Lee to be seduced by the immoral electrician. I thought that if the seduction failed, the electrician would no doubt confess to Sarah-Lee that it had all been my idea. I was the rogue, he her knight in faded jeans and a shirt that matched his socks. I entered through the garden. Besides the kitchen light, which was on, the rest of the apartment was in darkness. The curtains in the Jacuzzi room were fully drawn, but I couldn't help noticing that the window panes were all misty and covered with water droplets.

I was a little stunned that it had all been so easy, to be honest. Sarah-Lee and I had not yet made love in our new townhouse and yet this motherfucker had already fucked her and, worst of all, in my Jacuzzi! I reminded myself not to forget to drain the water. I didn't even bother going to the bedroom. Instead I poured myself a stiff whisky, put on some music and stretched out on the couch. I found myself reminiscing about the times Sarah-Lee and I had spent together and, quite unexpectedly, I felt a sudden sense of loss and pain that left me feeling sick in my gut. After a few more whiskies the tumult of emotion transformed into cynicism and I laughed to myself as tears streamed from my eyes. I was my own worst enemy. On the one hand I yearned for love, while on the other I ran from it. Would I ever break this pattern?

I woke up in the morning still on the couch in the lounge and feeling like shit. It was almost 10am. Where was Sarah-Lee?

I checked the bedroom. The bed was neatly made and there was a note on it for me, informing me that it was over. The only things she wanted, my girlfriend said, were the tumble dryer, our bed and her jewellery. The request was more than fair, I thought. I would have given her those things anyway. I had really put her through hell. For all I knew, she could have left last night. With or without the electrician, my plan had succeeded. I was relieved and sad at the same time. We had been together for almost three years and yet, in spite of having engineered this situation myself, in an instant the world had become a very lonely place.

Fuck, was I beginning to have regrets? Already? Yes, it seemed so.

I phoned Sarah-Lee's mother's place. No answer. What the fuck was going on? I was heartbroken. I couldn't make sense of how I had allowed myself to push her away. This wasn't a case of when you lose something you realise how important it is to you. My mind was simply fucked up. My head played games ... almost as if my mind and heart were in conflict with each other. *Jesus, fuck.* At that moment I seriously contemplated shooting the electrician. That's how fucked up I was.

That night I managed to get hold of Sarah-Lee's mom, who was always very polite and friendly towards me. She explained that Sarah-Lee was out (with the electrician) and she expected her home only much later. I figured they had gone to a movie or something and estimated that he would drop her at her mother's place at anything between 12 and 1.30am. So I parked outside her mother's townhouse complex, across the road, in the shadows. Around 2am she still hadn't returned. I was fuming with anger, but I decided I should go home. Tomorrow was another day.

After a sleepless night, with all these images of Sarah-Lee being fucked by the electrician in my Jacuzzi playing over and over in my mind, I found it almost impossible to contain myself. Rounding up a few of the guys, beating the shit out of the unlucky electrician, and then taking Sarah-Lee back should be quite easy, I thought. I took a shower, had a cup of coffee, and took a hit on my cocaine pipe. And then, suddenly, it all became crystal clear. It dawned on me that I was single again, with nobody to answer to and that maybe, just maybe, I was better off without her.

Two of my friends, Pete and Jill, who lived in Norwood, had become concerned about my wellbeing. Although Pete enjoyed the occasional hit on a freebase pipe, there were occasions when they wouldn't allow me into their house if they had guests. One night I went round to their place and they told me that if I wanted to smoke I should lock myself in the spare bedroom. I had 20g of rocks on me and I binged for two days. At the end of the second day, I was down to my last rock. My pipe was the brass mouthpiece of a trumpet. I scratched out the residue of all the coke I'd smoked, which made up a full tablespoon of resin, and loaded all of it onto the pipe, placing the rock on top. Then, using two lighters, I lit the pipe. First blowing all the air out of my lungs, I inhaled very slowly, sucking in the smoke.

The next thing I knew, my family was there. I had had another seizure. When Pete came home from work, he said he had found me lying on the kitchen floor, with one of his 13 dogs sitting on my chest, licking my face.

I was rushed to the hospital and once again told by the doctors that I was lucky to be alive. If this was not a warning, then I don't know what it was. Malcolm and Joan were as disappointed as they were concerned, and they insisted I stay with them for a few days and try to clean up my act. They suggested rehab for me, but I declined. I would stop by myself, I told them.

But I was not in control of my life. Far from it.

One morning Joan and I sat talking in her lounge. She told me she thought I should get away from Johannesburg, even if it was just to go on a holiday. She even offered to pay for my ticket.

'Shaun, this life will kill you. You can't go on like this,' she said, taking a tissue and drying her tears. 'Just get away from it all. Please?'

A few days later, as she was thumbing through the pages of a holiday brochure on the Far East that she'd picked up at a travel agency, she looked up at me and smiled. 'What about Thailand?' she said.

I wasn't all that keen, but that night I lay awake thinking about it, and suddenly it didn't seem like such a bad idea. Thailand was where my cocaine dealer was buying his heroin. He had asked me several times to join him in his new enterprise of smuggling 'China White' – pure heroin – to the United States, but I'd wanted nothing to do with it. Heroin had always seemed like a bad-luck drug to me. Now the situation had changed. I was on my own again and I could certainly do with the extra cash. So the next morning I contacted him, explaining that I was planning to go to Thailand on holiday. If he was still interested, I told him, I was ready to get involved.

As it happened, he said, he was about to set up a deal in Bangkok and was only too happy to hear from me. Over the years we had established a good working relationship and we trusted one another.

Fuck it, I thought to myself, against my better judgement, let me kill two birds with one stone. I was in. This could be the beginning of something big. My share of the deal would be approximately US$15 000.

'Book my ticket,' I said to Joan when I got off the phone. 'I'm going to Thailand.'

My sister was right. This life would kill me.

Chapter 7

The Beginning of the Nightmare

It was April 1994, the month in which Thailand celebrated Songkran, the Water Festival. It seemed as good a time as any to take time out from my disintegrating life, to get away from South Africa and to experience another culture. I started my celebrating early by getting drunk on the plane.

It was my first time in Asia, and my initial impressions were a bewildering jumble of sights and smells and noise. Going through Bangkok airport, the place just seemed so foreign to me, although I did notice several Africans entering and exiting the airport building. Once outside, I found a taxi and gave the driver the address I'd been given. He took off into the traffic. The heavy pollution, crowded roads, outdated cars and the sights and smells of different foods being cooked on every corner – I stared in amazement as we drove.

The address turned out to be a hotel somewhere in central Bangkok, graded at barely two stars, if that. I checked in, unpacked, lay down on the bed and fell almost immediately into a deep sleep. That night I had dinner at a restaurant suggested to me by the taxi driver. He came back to pick me up.

'You like girls?' he asked, looking back at me in his rear-view mirror.

He took me to a strip club, where I managed to get myself pretty drunk while watching a live sex show. I partied the whole night. I had not used drugs for over two weeks, but once I began drinking the craving kicked in. I got back to the hotel in the early hours of the morning and slept until lunchtime. When I woke up, I had a shower and hit the streets of Bangkok. I sampled different foods from the many street vendors. Then I caught a taxi and did a bit of sightseeing.

In fact, my airport taxi driver became my personal chauffeur, and he had a whole itinerary planned for my evening. I got so drunk at one club that I got into a fight. I'm not sure whether this was because I was drunk, but the guy I apparently took on was huge and as strong as an ox. He could have been a Turk. We first exchanged blows on the dance floor and we were both promptly thrown out. The Turk was with a friend, who walked up to me and apologised, which I thought was nice of him. He put his hand out to shake mine and as I took it he jerked me forward and head-butted me square on the nose. The motherfucker! I had fallen for one of the oldest tricks in the book. I lashed out with my right leg and caught him in the balls, but after that things got a little hazy. Eventually we were pulled apart by the police. The guy disappeared and I went back into the club. My nose was bleeding, so I went to the toilet and washed my face. I think the manager must have been feeling sorry for me, because he gave me a few drinks on the house. I left the club at 7am and wandered down the street. I was lost. I hadn't the faintest idea where I was staying. I was picked up by the police and eventually we worked out where my hotel was and they escorted me back there.

In the hotel lobby, a couple of taxi drivers I recognised from the day before were sitting around reading newspapers. My sixth sense started to kick in. I became convinced I was being watched. Back in my room I phoned my partner in South Africa and explained that I suspected there was a bit of heat. He told me to stop being paranoid and reassured me that everything would be okay. Afterwards I made contact with the people who were going to deliver the heroin and I was told that they would let me know where and when, which they duly did, several days later.

It was arranged that they would meet me on the fifth floor of my hotel, on the fire escape. We had a code. My contact would say 'Chelsea football team' and I would reply 'Manchester United'. That was the only identification agreed. The man was a Thai. He was short and stocky. He wore his hair Elvis style, and he had these enormous sunglasses that covered almost his entire face and that he never took off for a second – the guy was definitely not taking any chances. We shook hands, and then he pointed further up the fire escape, where I could see what looked like a leather briefcase. He told me in broken English, 'You wait two minutes,' and then he disappeared. I did as he instructed and then I ran up the iron steps and retrieved the case. In my room I inspected it and found that it had two compartments, which I presumed had been specially sewn into it. Anyway, it had been done very professionally. These compartments were where the heroin was hidden. During the past few days I had bought a few gifts for friends and family back in South Africa, which I now put in the bag.

It suddenly struck me that I was sitting with a small bomb in my room and, truth be told, I was as nervous as hell. I wanted to get as far away from the bomb as possible, so that night I went back to the club I'd been in the night before. Before long I got into another fight. The manager recognised me. He was very friendly and gave me free drinks again. At around 3am the police raided the club and wanted to close it. A fierce argument erupted and, in my drunken stupor, I somehow got involved, but the police didn't seem at all interested in me. Eventually, everybody was thrown out of the club except me. The manager then invited me to join him at a bar further down the street for a drink, and there he introduced me to a young Thai lady who, he said, was for me, as a token of his appreciation – no charge, he added. She was a pretty little thing, 18 or thereabouts. I had already discovered that there was something about Thai women that turned me on.

I took her back to the hotel but the night duty clerk refused to let the girl in beyond the lobby. I didn't know what he was carrying on about and I got really pissed off. When he started shouting at me I lost my cool. I jumped over the front desk but, being as drunk as I was, he managed to get away from me. I stumbled after him, knocked over a vase and then just started to throw the furniture around. I don't know where the night clerk went, but once he'd ducked out of sight I took the girl upstairs to my room. In the middle of fucking her, there was a knock on the door. It was the police. I didn't know what they were going on about either, but I took out my wallet and gave them 1 000 Thai baht each. They left and I got back into bed. Eventually, I passed out. When I woke up in the morning, my wallet was gone and so was the girl, but I didn't imagine I would get any sympathy from the hotel management. I called Joan and explained what had happened, and asked her to wire me some money so that I could pay my hotel bill. I had to reschedule my flight because the money would take a day or two to come through.

After settling my bill and re-booking my flight, on 26 April 1994 I was taken by taxi to Don Mueang International Airport. The taxi driver was a slimy-looking man, unshaven and with short greasy hair and a pot belly. He was also an undercover cop, but of course I didn't know that then. While I was sitting in the back seat, he kept staring at me in his rear-view mirror and trying to engage me in light conversation. In the boot of the car were my two suitcases and the leather briefcase containing 2.4kg of heroin in its concealed compartments.

I was nervous but under the circumstances reasonably calm, and I did my best to remain composed. From the moment we left the hotel, I had an uneasy feeling in my gut, a bad feeling. Fuck it, I thought, but I knew there was no turning back, even though by then I was mentally kicking myself for getting involved in this deal. I was scared, too, genuinely scared at the prospect of being caught. In the back of the taxi I chain-smoked and looked at the driver's greasy neck. Was it my imagination or did he also seem tense? And was I imagining it, or was he actually watching me in the rear-view mirror? I don't know. To be honest, I was so caught up in thought that I didn't think there was anything suspicious about the taxi driver *himself*, although his constant staring and chatting were irritating me.

When I got to the airport I paid the driver and called a porter over to take my luggage. As I entered the airport building I said a little prayer. I remember asking G-d to protect me, to close the eyes of the airport security, and to allow me to pass through. I even made a deal with G-d. If I got through, I promised, I would stop using and dealing drugs when I got home. Just this one time, G-d, please, I prayed, let me through. I had never smuggled drugs internationally before, and it was now too late to turn back. I was involved. But the urge to run was almost overpowering.

I made my way to the departure lounge. It was deserted and I found this strange. Why were there were no people around, I wondered. Where were the passengers? For the departure lounge of an international airport to be this quiet I thought was pretty weird. My bags passed uneventfully through the X-ray machine – so that was good. All that was left now was for me to get through customs and the passport check without the heroin being detected. Then that was it; I would be home free. My heart was pounding, but everything was okay so far, so I told myself to stop worrying.

From then on, everything seemed to happen in slow motion. I felt detached from my own body. When the woman at customs asked me for my passport, she didn't make eye contact with me, and this made me more nervous. Perhaps, in retrospect, she was playing for time. Her words were inaudible to me. I knew I must have looked pale, and by now I had the shakes. I kept telling myself to calm down, and to be rational. It was all good, my luggage was through. There was no earthly reason why I shouldn't get through this checkpoint as well.

As I handed over my passport, I suddenly heard a shuffling of feet behind me but I didn't look round. For a single moment, as the woman took the document from me, her eyes and mine locked. I could have sworn there was a look of pity in hers, but I tried to reassure myself. It was okay. It was all okay. I would be on the plane in no time, heading home, to my family, my friends and a life without drugs – just like I'd promised *Hashem*. I hoped He would stick to his end of the bargain.

Out of the corner of my eye I caught some movement and I saw a guy with a walkie-talkie in his hand. Before I could process anything, I was surrounded by heavily armed police dressed in black commando-type uniforms, their weapons drawn.

G-d, what now? My mouth went dry. I could hardly swallow. I felt myself gasping for air, my knees were shaking, and I seemed to have no control over my upper lip. No doubt I had guilt written all over my face. I felt like I was about to die. I could feel my *skin* changing colour.

It felt like the veins in my head were going to burst. I needed a cigarette, but like RIGHT NOW. I needed a cigarette to calm down.

One of the men, who seemed to be in charge, pointed to my luggage, and in broken English demanded to know if it belonged to me.

I remember wondering if this was some kind of a trick question, as I was the only person at the check-in point and obviously the luggage was mine. Before I could even answer, though, one of the cops reached for the leather bag and repeated the words: 'Bag this belong to you?'

For a split second I wondered what would happen if I said no. Juggling with the notion that there was no way they would find the drugs hidden snugly in their secret compartment, I tried to look normal.

'Yes,' I said, 'that bag is mine.'

My heart was pounding, and now my throat was even drier. Why had I ever agreed to do this? What had I been thinking? How had I ever thought I would get away with it?

I was instructed to follow the men in the black uniforms and was led to what I assumed was the airport's security office. I was ushered into a small bare room that had a table and two chairs in it, a typical interrogation room, the one we've all seen in the movies. Except that this was not a movie. It was real and it was happening, and it was happening to me. How could this be? Maybe I was dreaming ...

The walls of the room were a dull yellowish colour, and it struck me that the lights were very bright. There were no windows. Suddenly I felt so small. It was as if I didn't even exist.

First they emptied my personal stuff from the leather case – the gifts for my family were scattered all over the table. Foolishly, I still thought there might be a small chance they wouldn't discover the secret compartments, but this thought was dispelled in the very next second. Without even the slightest hesitation, one of the policemen took a Stanley knife and methodically proceeded to slash the midsection open. I felt like my heart was outside my body, my throat was still parched, and now I also had a queasy feeling in my bowels. Blood pounding in my temples was making me dizzy. Oh G-d. The man started to pull out the plastic bag filled with heroin. Surely this was a bad dream? It was happening on the big screen and I had fallen asleep at the cinema. I wished that was true but I knew it wasn't. This was happening to me, now, and it was my worst nightmare come true. I felt claustrophobic. The room was closing in on me.

When I suddenly received a blow to the head, I realised that it was indeed a nightmare, but a waking one.

There was a lot of activity now, people talking over each other, adding to my confusion. A kit to test the heroin was produced, and I watched as the solution turned purple. There was a triumphant murmur among the cops. The test had proved beyond a shadow of doubt that it was pure heroin, and I had been caught red-handed.

I felt sick. I needed a cigarette. I knew I had to come up with a story fast. I've always been good at talking myself out of sticky situations, only this time it was different. I knew I was in big shit. Minutes later, cameras started flashing in my face. Reporters from the Thai TV stations had appeared as if from nowhere. Perhaps they had been there even before I arrived in the departure lounge. Journalists were shoving and pushing each other out of the way, so eager were they to get a picture of me, and they were relentless. I felt as if I was already facing an execution squad.

Despite all the evidence to the contrary, I kept on telling myself it was all a bad dream. It had to be. This just couldn't be happening – not to me, Shani Krebs! Oh G-d, what about my mother, my sister Joan and my brother-in-law Malcolm? And their kids? What if they were watching this on TV? Could that happen? I covered my face with my hands to block out the invasive cameras. My head sank to my chest. I felt humiliated and ashamed.

Once the parading in front of the cameras was over, I was taken to another room further down the passage, which was secured by several undercover narcotics agents. That greaseball slimy taxi driver, now with a victorious grin on his face, was standing beside the entrance. I noticed he had a police badge clipped to his belt. I wanted to punch him in the face.

In the room was a young American guy, about ten years younger than me. I later learnt that he had been apprehended a few hours earlier with 4kg of heroin hidden in a suitcase. I was questioned by an agent from the Drug Enforcement Administration (DEA). Bizarre as it may sound, it was almost comforting to me that he spoke to me in English and also treated me in a civilised manner. He explained what the procedure would be from here on in. I asked him about my luggage. He told me not to worry; they would bring it to the police station they were taking me to. Then I was cross-examined by the Thai Drug Suppression Unit. It went on for what felt like hours. It seemed like every bit of life was being drained out of me. The bottom line was that I was BUSTED! I knew it, they knew it. I felt numb, sick to my stomach. I wanted to die.

At around 10pm, the American and I were taken in a police vehicle under armed escort to Rachada police station, in central Bangkok. It was a dirty old building, three storeys high, built of reddish-brown brick, with lots of windows. All the lights were on. We were taken upstairs to the second floor and into a large room. It had a lot of tables in it and was a hive of activity.

Then the American and I were split up. I sat around for almost an hour before being subjected to another round of questioning by several different policemen, who asked various questions – which country I was from, my home address, city, age, who I had got the drugs from and how. They examined my passport. They wanted to know who my connection was in South Africa.

I seemed to be more of an object of interest than a criminal, and generally everybody was quite cordial. I didn't know that part of their strategy was to break me down mentally by keeping me awake into the early hours of the morning. Afterwards I was left alone for a long time, and then, at about 2am, I was once again interrogated by somebody in a position of higher authority. This guy spoke relatively good English and he knew his business. He wasn't shy about roughing me up physically either. He was well built, stocky, around 34 – my own age – and had a sinister stare in his eyes. He was not somebody you'd care to bump into in a dark alley, and if you did, you would surely run as fast as you could. When I avoided his direct questions and failed to give him information about my accomplices, I got slapped around. I was hit several times on the head with a telephone directory.

He kept pressing me for the name of my contact in South Africa. I wouldn't give it. I couldn't. I had grown up on the streets of Johannesburg and learnt from a very young age that tittle-tattling was tantamount to informing and was wrong. In adult terms, it carried bad karma, and invariably resulted in death. There was no way that I was going to sell anybody out. This really angered the police. Frustrated, and cursing under his breath, the man began shouting at me in Thai, spitting as he spoke. He had obviously had a long day and no doubt wanted to go home. When he finally slumped back in his chair, I could see by the expression on his face that he knew he wouldn't get any information out of me. Angrily, he had me taken to the cells.

I was badly dehydrated and had a splitter of a headache. I was thrown into a large, dimly lit cell in a musty basement. There were about 14 other people already detained there, mostly Thai and Burmese nationals. The smell of sewage and body odour was nauseating – there was only one overhead ceiling fan. The toilet, which was an area of about two square metres enclosed by a wall just under a metre high, was one of those that was level with the floor – you had to squat over it to relieve yourself. Alongside it was a walled-in tank filled with water. There was a plastic bowl that was for communal use to scoop water to wipe yourself, and you had to flush the toilet manually. There was dried faeces, muck and dirt all over the place, and I could see cockroaches crawling out of every crack. I was sickened and disgusted by the toilet, and wondered how anybody could use it.

The floor of the cell was hard concrete, but in one corner there was a wooden platform that was allocated for sleeping on. I looked around me. The paint on the dirty walls was old and peeling and I could dimly make out traces of graffiti. Directly beneath the ceiling fan, whose slowly rotating blades were doing little against the extreme heat, was a concentration of bodies, everyone trying to be as close as possible to the cooler air.

My new American friend was already in the cell when I arrived. I saw him sitting hunched in the corner alone, wide-eyed and very frightened. When he saw me, he acknowledged me with a blink of his eye. Sleep was the furthest thing from my mind – a million and one thoughts were racing around in my head. Overcome by fear of the unknown, I experienced a flashback to the horrors of my childhood – Janos beating me and afterwards tying me up and locking me in a cupboard. Now here I was, a grown man, back in that small cupboard, choking and struggling to breathe, the old nightmares resurfacing. I wanted to scream, but instead I succumbed to a flow of slow, steady tears. I was weeping, weeping for myself and for my family. What had I done now?

Bars ran the entire length of the cell, and went from floor to ceiling. I found that I could not stay sitting down. Instinctively, no doubt because of the confined space, I started to pace up and down beside the bars, taking in deep breaths and exhaling slowly. After a while I managed to compose myself to a degree, and then I began to prepare myself mentally for whatever lay ahead.

To my surprise, I noticed about half a dozen women prisoners huddled together on the concrete floor a few metres away from the cell I was in. They were trying to sleep, but I could see they were uncomfortable and restless. One of them was moaning in her sleep; another was staring into emptiness. I felt for them, and I wondered what terrible deeds they had done to wind up here. Jail was no place for a woman – it didn't matter who they were. To me, a woman just never fitted the profile of a criminal.

For hours I paced up and down, trying to think. What bothered me most was thinking about my family's reaction. I wondered hopefully whether it was possible that news of my arrest had not reached them. My plane was only due to land in South Africa the next day. I kept imagining their faces when all the passengers had disembarked and I was nowhere to be seen. I knew my sister would be frantic. I could almost *see* her face, the shocked expression when she realised that something was wrong.

I continued to pace, thinking, thinking. Mostly my thoughts were confusing and they rebounded at me off the walls. Nothing made sense. I felt as if my head was going to explode, as if I was losing my grip on reality. I was also getting hot and then cold, but I wasn't sure if this was my craving for a fix to numb my mind, which was the route I had always gone whenever I was faced with a dilemma or an emotional problem, or if I was going into a state of shock. All I knew right then was that I could have killed for a hit on a cocaine pipe, some alcohol, or something, *anything*, to block out what was happening around me. My body started trembling, slowly at first, until I was shaking so much I had to sit down. I was also sweating heavily. I had a cigarette in my hand. My fingers were yellow from nicotine. If I had dragged any harder on that cigarette, I would have swallowed it.

I lost track of time. Night merged into day, and suddenly it was morning. Had I slept, or hadn't I? I didn't know. I wasn't tired, but I felt totally disoriented. I kept wondering if my family was aware that I'd been arrested. Knowing Joan as I did, I knew she would have called the South African embassy to enquire.

As it happened, Joan had indeed contacted the embassy.

I was supposed to have called to tell her I was leaving, and she immediately became concerned when I didn't call. The embassy asked for my name, and, when Joan told them, they said, 'Oh, that guy on the front page of the newspapers? He's been arrested.' Nothing I did really surprised Joan by then, and she hoped that whatever trouble I'd got myself into, it wasn't too serious. If it came to that, she would organise a lawyer.

In the cell they brought us a tiny portion of sloppy white rice porridge. It wasn't that bad, but I had no appetite. One of the Burmese guys came over and told me that if I wanted something else, a policeman would come by later and take orders; if I had the money I could get something from the shops. My stomach was queasy, but I couldn't face going to that toilet. I couldn't even think of food. It was the last thing on my mind. I was more concerned about how I could clean the toilet, how I could organise some detergent and cleaning rags or scrubbing brushes. I had never seen anything so disgusting in my life.

I got talking to the other Burmese guy. He told me he had been in police custody for longer than the law stipulated. He looked in a bad way, his body battered and bruised, his feet in bandages. He said the police had made him stand on ice, attached electrical cables to his groin and sent high-voltage currents through his body until he agreed to sign a confession. The thought of having something like that done to me sent shivers up my spine. There was a limit to the pain one could endure. I would have to spin the authorities a story.

The following morning, the two Burmese nationals were removed from the cell, and as soon as they'd gone I grabbed their spot under the ceiling fan. I told the other prisoners that, as of that moment, I would be occupying that space. I gestured for my American friend to join me, but he declined, and I assumed that he needed to be alone. So I took over the prime place beneath the fan. I thought I had to show that I was taking control, whether I believed it in my heart or not. Nobody argued. Nobody tried to get me to move. I closed my eyes, feeling the cool air on my face.

In an open cell across the way from ours, I saw two Thai girls sitting on the concrete floor. They were shooting heroin, right there in the police cells. I was shocked. There were other girls lying around; they looked like prostitutes on their last legs, thin and ailing. The police were supplying them with drugs. I learnt later that more than likely these girls were paid informers.

I went up to the bars and called out to them. I asked them where they were from and said I was from South Africa. To my surprise, it turned out that three of the girls were South Africans, and we immediately struck up a conversation. I asked them whether they had had any contact with our embassy or if the embassy had any idea they were there. They looked bewildered and told me there was no South African embassy in Thailand. I said I knew for a fact that there was and that I'd already asked the Thai police to contact them for me.

One of the policemen came by just then and went to speak to the prostitutes. As he passed by our cell I called out to him and he stopped. With the aid of graphic gesturing and face-pulling and much pointing at the toilet, and speaking very slowly and deliberately, I did my best to describe what I needed. He looked completely confused. One of the Thai prisoners, who had been observing this, came over and explained to the officer what I was asking for. Then he turned to me and said in broken English: 'You give money, he buy for you now.'

Tucked in my jeans I still had a few dollars. I gave the policeman US$20 and off he went.

I was then summoned upstairs. I told the police officer that I wanted to phone the South African embassy so that they could inform my family back home that I had been arrested. Although his English was poor he seemed to understand. Every Thai knows the word 'embassy'. A translator was sent for and I repeated my request. While he was gone I was instructed to sit down at the table and sign some papers concerning my luggage, which by then had been delivered to the station. The translator came back and told me that the police had already phoned the embassy early that morning and a representative would be coming over at lunchtime.

As I passed the two Thai prostitutes' cell on the way back to mine, I noticed that the girls were shooting up again. I told the South African girls that the translator had told me that a representative from the embassy was coming, and they were very excited.

Back in my cell, I discovered that the policeman had brought everything I'd asked him to buy for me, although there was no change from my US$20, of course. I have never been so pleased to see domestic cleaning products in my life! There was disinfectant, a scrubbing brush and toilet cleaner. I kept my shoes on but set to work cleaning the filthy toilet. There was dried shit everywhere. How could people leave a toilet this way? I scrubbed at the bowl, even scraped it with a spoon. Two Thai guys came to help me. We cleaned everything we could in that toilet section, including the walls and the shower area, until our arms ached. While I was scrubbing I felt a bit weak; I realised I hadn't eaten for about 24 hours and was very hungry. I took a shower and washed my underwear at the same time. The policeman came back again with the rest of my shopping: I had given him another US$30 to buy me some Kentucky Fried Chicken. I was quite amazed that here was a cop acting like he was my butler, but I was beginning to realise that, if you had money, perhaps you could procure almost anything in Thailand.

The events of the past days kept replaying over and over in my mind. Something was wrong; the pieces of the puzzle didn't fit. I was not supposed to get caught. Also, my faith had been severely shaken.

Where had G-d been? *Hashem* had let me down – why? Why now, when He had protected me all these years? In my despair and frustration, I couldn't help but doubt His very existence. All this bullshit about a higher power! The only power was man himself, who relied on his own resilience. Decisions were based on choices, whether right or wrong. Divine intervention wouldn't change anything. I resigned myself to the fact that there was no G-d, and even if there *was* a G-d, He was certainly no friend of mine.

I had always been a spiritual person and I had done my fair share of praying. In the past, always in times of trouble G-d would come to me. I had never had any doubts before, but now I was angry. Angry at myself and angry at Him for letting me down. Prayer was the furthest thing from my mind. I was on my own. I had to keep my wits about me.

At the time of my arrest I weighed almost 88kg. My fitness level was very low. I decided that getting into good physical shape would be key to my survival in this place, so, right away, in between pacing up and down the cell, I started doing push-ups and sit-ups combined with warming-up and stretching exercises. When I rested, I spent a lot of time reflecting on my life and how I had come to be in this situation. I could point fingers at my parents, my teachers, my friends, but at the end of the day, I had only myself to blame. When I really thought about it, it shouldn't have come as a surprise to me that the law had finally caught up with me. This was my karma. It was payback time.

Being the free spirit that I was, it's hard to describe what it felt like to be locked up in a prison cell, but I thought I knew what a caged animal must feel like. Having no idea what was in store for me only compounded my fears. Every time I thought of my family my eyes would fill with tears. How was I going to explain my latest escapade to them when I got home? There was no way I could tell them the truth. They would surely disown me.

Despite the ceiling fan, the air in the cell was stifling. The heat was fast becoming my number one enemy. Every hour I took a shower. Walking back and forth concentrated my mind somewhat and allowed me to draw strength from within. I convinced myself that there would be a way out. I would get bail and flee Thailand to one of the neighbouring countries. Alternatively, there was always the possibility of escape.

My second day in the police cells felt like a week. While I was absorbed in my thoughts, it suddenly struck me that today, 27 April 1994, South Africa was having its first democratic election. Here I was, on the opposite side of the world, locked up in a prison cell, while my country was being set free. Even though my vote would have been unlikely to have made a difference to the outcome, it was a poignant moment for me, mixed with a strong sense of patriotism. That day was a triumph for democracy long in the making.

The monotony of the morning was broken by the relief and excitement of the embassy visit. My hopes were up. Perhaps there was a possibility of bail. A consular officer came to visit me, a very friendly Indian guy who made me feel at ease. He confirmed what I'd imagined, that when I hadn't arrived home as scheduled, my sister had called the embassy in Thailand. She was told that I was on the front page of the *Bangkok Post*, having been caught smuggling drugs. I felt a shooting pain in my heart. I knew how devastated Joan would have been. I felt really ashamed at that moment. What I had put my sister through over the years was unforgivable.

The consular officer didn't bring the best of news. He told me that drug offenders weren't allowed bail and that the embassy had limited power when it came to drug offences committed on Thai soil. Visits to prisoners were conducted purely on diplomatic grounds. There was nothing the embassy could do and neither were they prepared to interfere in the judicial system. He did agree to deliver to my family in South Africa the gifts I had bought for them. Although a lot of my personal things had gone missing from my luggage (clothes, my watch), the gifts were all still there. He also gave me his word that once I had been transferred to a prison, representatives from the embassy would visit regularly.

I was comforted by the visit to a degree. At least the South African government was aware of my arrest. I also knew that my family would be rallying together back home and trying to organise legal representation for me.

The prospect of going to prison scared the shit out of me. I had heard all the stories about male prisoners. I vowed to myself that I would rather die than allow myself to be sodomised. There was no way that I would take shit from anybody. As importantly, I would always stand up for what I believed was right. Like most people, I had a preconceived idea about prison life, gleaned largely from movies, but all I really knew was that prison was a place you don't want to go and that it was definitely not for the faint-hearted.

That night I was overcome with sheer exhaustion. I craved some drugs. I needed to forget. Most of all, I needed to escape from my own thoughts. My thoughts wouldn't leave me alone. They haunted me. I found it impossible to sleep on the concrete and my body ached all over. Over the next few days most of my cellmates were moved, and all the girls were taken to a women's prison. I continued my pacing up and down and exercising. I also began to have conversations with myself in my head, which I found kind of therapeutic.

On the seventh day the American and I were handcuffed and taken to Rachada court under armed escort. This was where all the drug cases went. I stared out of the car window, seeing people walking around freely, and I wondered if I would ever get to taste freedom again. We were met by armed guards with shotguns at the back of court building, escorted through some big steel gates, and then led down a corridor that opened up into a huge hall. Inside it were three cages, like monkey cages, probably 5 or 6m wide and 8m in length, each crammed with 80 to 100 prisoners, all waiting for their cases to be heard. The prisoners were all shackled, and they wore the prison uniform of brown cotton shorts and a slip-on short-sleeved shirt, which hung over the shorts and had pockets on the side. For a horrible moment I thought of the movie *Planet of the Apes*. The screaming, shouting and screeching noises sounded just like monkeys. I felt like I really was on another planet, so far removed was I from what I understood as civilisation.

Guards in light beige uniforms, some with stars on their shoulders to denote their rank, patrolled the cages with batons. The American and I were briskly escorted to the third cage. It was approximately 9am. We were the only foreigners I could see. Again, the toilets were filthy and the only access to clean drinking water was by way of a press water fountain.

After several hours, my name was finally called. The courtroom did not look like a normal court. In the centre, at the back of the room, against the opposite wall to where we came in, there was a long table and a wooden railing in front of it. Sitting at the table was the magistrate, whose attention was on the papers in front of him. I was called by name to the table, told to sit down, and then asked to sign some papers. No one spoke English, but it all seemed like a formality, so I sat and signed. Even at the police station we had filled out hundreds of forms. What was it about the Thais, I wondered, with all the paperwork!

Then I was taken back to the cage, where I managed to find enough space to lie down on a bench. I was tired and scared. This was all so alien. My mind drifted once again to how I had ended up here, and I couldn't help thinking how badly organised the whole trip had been. Somewhere there was a rat. I kept replaying in my mind the moment in the departure hall when I was surrounded by the SWAT team and how they had only had eyes for the leather briefcase. They hadn't bothered to even look at my other luggage. Was it possible they had been tipped off?

Time dragged. I was bored. By 3pm prisoners who had gone through the process were being transported back to their prison. The American and I, handcuffed together, found ourselves with a group of 80 other prisoners loaded like cattle into an armoured prison vehicle. There was not much space and we stood shoulder to shoulder, all of us crammed in the back. Our driver was reckless, speeding around corners so that prisoners were stumbling and falling from side to side. If the truck rolled I reckoned we would all be crushed to death. I calculated that my chances of survival would be better if I found a place in the middle so that if the truck *did* roll, it wouldn't matter to which side – I would only have half a load of bodies on top of me. So I pushed and shoved, dragging my American friend with me to the back of the truck where we stood in the centre.

We didn't crash. Fate had other plans for me.

Chapter 8

A Tiger Among Tigers

After our harrowing ride, a grinding of gears brought the truck almost to a halt as the driver negotiated a turn from the main road into a side street. Dusk was falling. We entered a huge quadrangle with lush green lawns and an array of colourful flowers and tall palm trees. To the left was a car park roofed with corrugated iron with a few cars in it. In the centre, at the end of the winding road, in all its menacing glory, stood a colossus of a building. Running off its sides were towering concrete walls. They stood there, solid and implacable, as if waiting to consume us.

This was Bombat prison.

The crush of men in the prison truck fell silent. Perhaps a collective realisation had suddenly taken hold. What horrors lay behind those walls? We could only imagine, but the fear and apprehension of men doomed to a life of imprisonment now became tangible. As we got closer to the building, the driver took a left turn and the vehicle suddenly gathered momentum. Our bodies swayed over and pressed up against each other. Further on, we took a right turn onto what was now a worn gravel lane. The next thing I knew, the truck came to a sliding halt, filling our nostrils and eyes with dust. I breathed a sigh of relief. We had made it. It seemed like a small miracle. In fact, for me, it was the first miracle of many.

The clanging of keys, opening of locks and banging of heavy-framed steel doors were unfamiliar sounds to me, but soon these sounds would be a constant reminder that I was a prisoner. Pulling my Slazenger sports bag from between my legs, I clutched it tightly to me as the doors of the vehicle swung open. A flow of sweating, broken-spirited bodies shuffled like battle-worn soldiers from the truck in single file. Two guards counted us: '*Ning, song, sam, ci, har, hok, jet, pat, cow, siep*' (one, two, three ...).

We were ushered through a double steel door. On the left-hand side within the frame was a standard-size entrance that opened inwards. Once inside, about 10m ahead, within a spacious corridor, was a similar steel gate structure on the left, forming part of an inner wall that led into the prison itself. Another two guards, dressed in khaki uniforms, stood there next to each other. Each had two gold stars on the collar of his shirt and they had medals pinned to their pockets. Their manner was unfriendly, bordering on aggressive. As they counted us one by one, they pulled our arms and shoved us inside. A few of the guys actually stumbled and fell over and this was the only thing that seemed to lighten the mood of the two guards. In fact, they grinned at each other and laughed like it was really funny. It was getting pretty dark by now. The courtyard where we assembled was lit up by a couple of spotlights. There were offices on either side of what looked like a checkpoint, where a boom was mounted to allow vehicles to pass in and out of the actual prison.

From where I stood, I could see a concrete road stretching about 100m inside the prison compound. On either side there were four decaying double-storey buildings, identical in structure and parallel to each other. This was where the prisoners were housed. We were forced to squat, a position that came naturally to the Thais but not to me. I had to keep standing up to ease the pressure on my calves and thighs. When a high-ranking officer arrived on the scene he immediately walked up to me and in Thai ordered me to sit: '*Nung nung.*' I smiled and with my hand motioned that I couldn't and that my legs were hurting. The officer took a boxing stance and, in a joking fashion, pretended to throw a few punches at me. I took a step back, raised my fists, and in a mocking retaliatory manner, challenged him. He seemed rather impressed by my bravery and, in a friendly tone, asked first in Thai and then in halting English, '*Khun mah jahk ny*? You come from where?'

'South Africa,' I replied.

He looked puzzled. I quickly added 'Johannesburg', but that seemed to confuse him even more.

Smiling, he pointed to my hair. '*Khun dtut pom*' (You cut hair). I had a very long ponytail, so I understood what he meant. Then he asked, '*Khun chawp football?*' (Do you like football?) I nodded. He continued to stare at me thoughtfully for a few minutes, as if he was giving me the 'I'm going to watch you' look, and then, as he left, all the other guards bowed respectfully.

Once again we were each called to a table where they took our names and thumbprints. After that, all 80 of us were lined up into platoon formation of four rows. We were ordered to strip naked and place all our possessions on the floor in front of us. The guards, some of whom were holding batons, sat on plastic chairs waiting for us to file up to them, one by one. Each had a latex rubber glove on one hand. We had to face away from the guard and bend over while he prodded his finger up our rectums and twirled it around to see if there were drugs hidden up our arses. I could have sworn my guard was enjoying himself – whether it was by humiliating us or because he was a pervert, I couldn't tell.

I was shocked. I had only glimpsed scenes like this in books or movies. I saw him casually wipe his hands on a dirty, stained cloth only after every two or three bodies. He prodded away one victim after the next. The Thais bent without resistance. As my turn came closer, I knew there was no way I was going to allow myself to be subjected to such abuse. I had never had anything stuck up my arse, and definitely not another man's finger. Having to stand around naked was undignified in itself. When it came to my turn, I stood facing the guard and I refused to bend over. I said, 'No, no, *no*,' and just stood there, with both my hands covering my private parts. The guard muttered something angrily and pointed at my waist, gesturing for me to bend over. Shaking my head from side to side, I repeated the words. '*No, no!*'

It was obvious he was not impressed, but it didn't look like he planned to relent. Lifting a bamboo stick in a threatening manner, he urged me to bend over. Suddenly, the high-ranking officer who earlier had joked with me arrived on the scene, wanting to know what the commotion was about. The two of them exchanged words and then the guard, still muttering angrily under his breath, gesticulated for me to move on. What a relief! The young American guy followed straight after me, without even acknowledging the guard. It was then that I understood that we Westerners had an advantage over the Thai prisoners.

Besides a couple of items of clothing and basic toiletries, all our belongings were tagged, bagged and taken away to be stored. I managed to hide the last of my US dollars under the cardboard lining of my sports bag. Trousers were not allowed in the prison, so I was forced to cut my Levi's at the knees, and all long-sleeved jersey shirts had to have their sleeves cut off. I didn't have much clothing anyway, as most of it had disappeared from my luggage between the airport and the holding cells. The police were apparently notorious for stealing the belongings of people they arrested, but there was nothing to be done about that. I also kept in my possession a blue beach towel Joan had lent me, and which she'd got as a tenth wedding anniversary gift, and thank goodness I did. That towel would become part of my bedding for the next six months. I had three pairs of underpants, a pair of swimming shorts, three T-shirts and some toiletries – shaving stuff, a toothbrush, dental floss.

Still naked, we stood around for hours before we were allowed to get dressed. Then we were marched round the side of the hospital building, where we were greeted by a well-built Thai prisoner (a trustee) who was responsible for fitting and attaching leg irons to the prisoners. These were thick steel rings with a chain attached to them. First we were put into a steel contraption rather like a vice, and then this lever was pulled down, tightening the steel ring over the bottom of your leg. Once it was in place, the trustee took a 10lb steel hammer and pounded the rings until they closed so tightly it was impossible to slip them off your feet. With every blow of the hammer, I visualised him missing and smashing the bones of my legs.

I was thousands of miles from home and every new stage of what had happened to me so far had seemed more bizarre than the next. But what impacted me most was having to wear shackles. Surely this was a violation of one's rights? It was inhuman. I felt completely demoralised by this indignity, reduced to nothing.

After that, we were taken to Building 1, which was also the check-in point for all new prisoners. By now it was completely dark. We were taken to a cell upstairs, which already held about 50 Thai prisoners. None of us had bedding – there wasn't enough space for everybody – and we all sat around, almost on top of one other. Those of us who wanted to sleep would have to do so in shifts, so, while some of us stood or sat around, others slept. I felt sorry for the American kid. I told him that he could sleep because there was no way I was going to be able to, and that I would keep an eye out in case something went down. We were the only two foreigners there and everybody seemed to be staring at us. In Western culture staring is rude; the Thais don't have a problem with it. In the early part of the evening the American and I got chatting and he told me where he came from, about his family and how he got involved in being a drug mule.

Some time later, I noticed one of the new prisoners, a young boy who had been on the truck with us, being escorted to the toilet by about five Thais. The toilet was at the rear end of the cell, built up off the ground and in a very small enclosure. On each of the corners was a small steel pipe which ran about a metre off the wall. Material torn from plastic rice bags and tied around these pipes acted like a curtain, so you couldn't see anything behind it, but you could hear everything that went on inside.

I thought to myself, this is where the raping starts, but the young boy didn't seem to be protesting. He went inside and the Thais lined up. Then, one by one, they fucked him. There were no screams of protest, and after they were finished I heard splashing water. A minute or so later, the young boy exited the toilet and, looking shamefaced, went to a place at the far end of the cell where some of the other Thais seemed to befriend him. It seemed that everybody wanted a piece of his ass.

After that, a feminine-looking guy was subjected to the same sexual abuse. Without thinking, I made eye contact with one of the guys who had fucked him. He made a gesture to me, pulling his index finger from ear to ear across his throat. The meaning wasn't lost on me and I looked away. Challenging him would be crazy. I was totally outnumbered here. The feminine-looking guy, I couldn't help noticing, also had breasts. Still, I was not about to interfere. I stayed awake most of the night, dozing off from time to time. Everyone was sleeping on top of one another.

Eventually it was morning. All the new arrivals were taken downstairs and again we waited around doing nothing. Finally, we were lined up for haircuts. I wanted to cry when my long ponytail was chopped off and it was back to army style. Since being arrested and held at the police station, I had started growing a moustache. I thought it would make me look different. After the haircut we lined up again at the office, where we were given medical tests, which consisted of our heart rate being listened to, followed by a medic (who was also a prisoner) shoving a wooden spatula into our mouths and looking down our throats. What the fuck he expected to see, I don't know. We also had our eyes tested and then filled out more papers asking whether we had tattoos, any major deformities or any previously broken bones.

At about ten o'clock food arrived in giant aluminium pots. I was starving. I didn't know what kind of food to expect, but I joined the queue anyway. As I got near to the front I was hit by this stinky odour. On close examination, I saw that one of the pots had small pieces of dried fish in it. To me, the smell was disgusting, but the Thais were almost fighting one another to get to it. All it did was make me feel nauseous. In the other pots there was red rice, which looked like it was full of weevils. Hungry as I was, I simply couldn't bring myself to eat. I guessed I wouldn't be having breakfast.

I decided to walk around and familiarise myself with the terrain. What really shocked me were the communal toilets. These were housed in an open shed, and consisted of two rows of ten sunken-in toilets, the back and front rows separated by a low wall, not even a metre high, so you could easily see the person behind you. The toilets themselves were divided by even lower walls. I tried to imagine ten prisoners all taking a crap at the same time, so close they could touch each other, and it made me feel more nauseous than the dried fish had done.

At the rear of the building was the shower area. It looked like a horse trough, about 2m wide and 25m long, and about a metre deep. Running close to the outside wall was an open sewerage system. (I would learn that whatever was flushed down the toilets would work its way along the wall to a vault.) In front of the toilets, where the steps were, was a tank filled with water. Using the plastic bowl the prison provided, each person would manually scoop water to flush his shit and wash his bum. While in a squatting position, you'd use your right hand to scoop the water and your left to wash your ass. Some prisoners used the same bowl to shower, to brush their teeth and to put their food in.

The prisoners who were dressed in blue uniforms were trustees, and they worked for the guards. Actually, most of the work was done by them. The prisoners referred to them as Blue Shirts. In my eyes they were motherfuckers.

Just after midday, we had our fingerprints and our photographs taken and we were each given a prison number. Mine was 562/37. Once all the new prisoners were registered, we were moved to different buildings. I was sent to Building 5 and my American friend to Building 4. We didn't want to get split up, so I went to the guards and asked if we couldn't be together. Earlier in the day, I had befriended another foreigner who had reported sick to the hospital, and through talking to him I'd learnt that Building 4 was full of Westerners. Unfortunately, the guards weren't very accommodating.

Although I had been ordered to go to Building 5, I thought I'd chance it, and so I walked to Building 4 instead. A couple of foreigners came up to greet me, asking where I was from. It really warmed my heart to see that I wasn't entirely alone. I couldn't believe that there were so many Westerners in this Thai jail. It was a real culture shock. The trustee at the gate started shouting at me, insisting that I was supposed to have gone to Building 5 – not that I understood a word he said, but I got the idea. I would have preferred to be with the American kid because I instinctively felt that two were stronger than one. Once again, I experienced that childhood fear of the unknown when changing schools and having to make new friends. I was already a stranger in a strange land. I felt lost and abandoned. And now it felt like I was going to lose my only friend.

I was escorted to Building 5 by the Blue Shirt, and was greeted at the gate by one of Building 5's trustees, and then taken to the Building Chief. The chief was a good-looking man in his early fifties, and by Thai standards relatively tall. He was well groomed and light in complexion. He was also friendly and seemed to show a little understanding towards the prisoners. He welcomed me and put out his hand, which I shook warily. I have always been suspicious of anyone in a position of authority.

The Building Chief wore the standard beige uniform, with stars and a crown on his shoulder straps. The staff of most government departments in Thailand wear uniform, as do bus drivers, conductors and ambulance drivers. In South Africa, prison guards were considered to be on one of the lowest rungs of society's ladder, so I was surprised to see that being a prison guard in Thailand carried some prestige. I was later to learn that the guards were well educated and that some even had university degrees. But they could also pay money, hard cash, for a promotion. It was a very corrupt system.

The Blue Shirt who took me to the Building Chief's office looked healthier than most of the other prisoners, I thought. He had a dark complexion and I noticed he had a dragon tattoo on the inside of his forearm. The man looked rugged, like he had been in prison for a long time. His eyes showed no emotion and his manner was cold and distant. When Thais are in positions of authority, they often display anger and hostility towards foreigners.

'*Phut Thai dai my?*' (Speak Thai, do you?) the Building Chief asked. Having heard the same words about a thousand times by now, I answered, 'I no speak Thai, I speak English.' I don't know why he expected I could speak the language. He instructed the trustee to call a translator, who was there in a matter of minutes. The translator was a prisoner serving a 25-year sentence for smuggling cocaine into Thailand. His name was Tom-Li, and when he introduced himself I was surprised to hear him speak English with an American accent. He seemed to be well educated and he told me he had lived for many years in America. I took an instant liking to him. It felt good to know that there was someone who spoke both English and Thai, because I'd realised that the language barrier was going to be a serious impediment. Things were starting to look up a little. Maybe I wasn't so lost after all. I thought Tom-Li could be my new best friend; that was until I discovered, like a day later, that he was an informer for the DEA. Isn't life just full of surprises? Just when you think things are looking up, you discover you need to look elsewhere.

I didn't know this yet, of course, and as Tom-Li translated for him, the Building Chief took down some notes. He asked which country I was from, asked about my case, what quantity of drugs I had been caught with, my age. He told me he wanted no trouble from me and that I must follow the rules. He didn't like drugs. If I was unhappy about anything I should come and see him. With that, he gestured to us to get out of his office.

After that, I was taken to another office, where there was a prisoner in charge of administration. Again I was asked my name, country, case, how much heroin I'd been caught with, my home address, family details etc. Once I was finished, Tom-Li explained a few things to me. I was then given my cell number, and told that I'd been registered to the paper factory, where I would be required to fill a quota of 50 paper bags a day.

I asked Tom-Li if there were any other foreigners in Building 5. He said there were two Nigerians, an Indian, three Singaporeans and two or three guys from Hong Kong. This information gave me some comfort. He pointed me in the direction where I would find the Nigerian guys, and said he would be available if I needed anything.

As foreign prisoners were 'free' to do what they liked until afternoon lockdown, I thought I might as well get to know my new environment, so I took a walk around. All the buildings in Bombat prison were L-shaped, designed and constructed identically. At the entrance on the right was a small open temple, with four pillars and a terracotta-tiled roof. Inside was a statue of Buddha. To the left was a concrete parade ground with white lines painted on it, demarcating the boundaries of what I thought might be a badminton court.

As I walked further, I passed beneath the first floor of the building, which was on concrete stilts. This was where the guards' office was, and also a first-aid room. Just through the other side to the right was the shower area, with its horse trough. There were a number of factories within the prison, and I would get to know which was which in time. The clothing factory had about 50 sewing machines – old Singers, the ones with the wooden surface. The hum and buzz from the machines going all day was quite irritating. The paper bag factory was just in front of the temple. All foreigners were registered to work there. If you didn't want to work, you could pay a Thai a couple of cigarettes to do your quota for you. Behind the clothing factory, to the left of the back of the building was a small factory where prisoners made the gold paper that the Chinese use for burning at funerals. To prepare the gold paper they used a chemical that was highly toxic.

There was nowhere to sit in the paper bag factory, no chairs, whereas in the gold paper factory they had these wooden benches, which made the place far more comfortable. Shortly after I arrived at the prison, I joined this factory as well as the paper bag one. I thought if I kept my mind occupied I wouldn't think so much about my dire situation. I hated every minute of it, every hour of every day. I probably worked there for three or four weeks before I realised that the other foreigners weren't happy about this. One of them approached me and explained that I was setting a precedent for the prison authorities. Next thing, all foreigners would have to work. So I resigned and my days of therapeutic hard labour came to an abrupt end.

On the whole, the Thais were very friendly and they seemed fascinated by a Western foreigner in their midst. Many shook my hand and wanted to know where I was from. Some even spoke English. Something curious that happened the first time on my walk around, and which was to be repeated many times after that (and has never left my mind), was that often while you were talking to a Thai, he would proceed to pick his nose. He would do this not just casually but with deep intent, as though his finger was scratching his brain, and he would do this for the duration of the conversation. Afterwards he would wipe his fingers on his shorts. It baffled me, and from then on I avoided shaking hands.

The toilets were situated behind the gold paper factory, and next to that was the area allocated for prisoners who wanted to do their own cooking on portable charcoal stoves. I was surprised that prisoners were permitted to cook their own food. It was there that I hooked up with two Nigerian guys, Patrick and Frank. As fellow Africans, we shared a common bond. They were cooking *moola*, which is equivalent to South African mieliepap, and, in a wok, some kind of omelette with chillies. I don't think I've ever smelt anything so delicious in my life.

After introducing themselves, they said, 'You must be real hungry, brother, join us for something to eat.' They dished me a portion of the omelette-chilli concoction, which they served with some bread. They also offered to give me dinner, which they were about to prepare and would bring to the cell that afternoon.

Many of the more privileged prisoners who did their own cooking would keep their food in a *pinto* (three or four metal bowls that fitted snugly into each other; on top went a lid with a handle that held all three bowls together). Some groups had a bigger five-bowl *pinto*, and they would cook up a variety of Thai dishes, all of which contained a lot of chilli. Thai food is very spicy and it took me quite a while to develop a taste for it. They also used a fortune of oil when they cooked, and they had eggs daily, mostly to make omelettes.

Just about all of the prisoners wore flip-flops on their feet. Apparently the footwear was donated by the Chinese and these were one of the few items issued to prisoners twice a year by the authorities. They were all the same brand but came in different colours. We could mark our names on our shoes in pen, and some prisoners would cut a pattern into the sole as identification. Alongside our building was a long, steel-framed, double-shelved shoe rack. In Thai culture, shoes or slippers are not worn indoors, and so we had to leave our flip-flops here before going to our cells in the afternoon. Inmates were forever either taking the wrong pair or stealing each other's flip-flops. Because of the extreme temperatures, wearing flip-flops or sandals was by far the most practical option when it came to shoes, but guys often hurt or cut their feet or toes by accidentally bumping against sharp concrete edges or jutting-out broken pipes.

One morning, I was hurrying past the shower area where the concrete surface was smooth and wet. I was wearing flip-flops. The next thing I knew both my legs were flying in the air. I come crashing to the ground flat on my back. My head hit the concrete with a loud thud. Sitting on the veranda along the side of the clothing factory were a bunch of Thai workers folding paper bags. They all packed up laughing, but I'd hit my head so hard I thought I'd cracked my skull open. I lay there motionless for at least a minute before I could get up. After that I would only wear sneakers, unless I needed to go to the toilet.

After eating with Patrick and Frank, I found that I was exhausted, having not slept the night before, so I went to the temple, where I had dumped my stuff earlier, took off my flip-flops and left them outside. Using my blue towel as a pillow, I lay down and fell asleep almost instantly. It was a troubled sleep, though, and about an hour later I was woken up by one of the Thais for shower time.

Patrick and Frank had given me soap and a shower bowl. When I approached the shower area, I recoiled in horror at the sight of 500 naked convicts watering themselves down at the same time out of what I could only think of as the horse troughs. The sight was beyond description. I had to push myself through the prisoners to get to the water, and when I got there it was the quickest shower of my life. I kept my flip-flops on, and I would continue to do this every time I showered in prison. I made the mistake of putting my soap down – it was there one minute and gone the next. People hung their towels on the barbed-wire fence. I couldn't help noticing that some of the prisoners were urinating right where they were standing in the trough, often pissing on the leg of the person in front of them; some were spitting and blowing their noses with their hands. Guys were brushing their teeth in the same water as others were bending over, naked, doing their washing. Others, while sitting where all the dirty water was flowing past, were cleaning their shackles by shaking them against each other. And everyone was in a rush. Soap was squirting all over the place.

On this my first day in the showers, someone actually had the bloody nerve to pinch my ass! I had no idea who the culprit was, but I turned around and gave everyone in my vicinity a dirty look. It never happened again.

Showering naked in front of so many guys made me feel uncomfortable and exposed. I had grown up with a certain sense of modesty about my body, and was not in the habit of just exposing myself to whomever. Such mass exposure was difficult for me to comprehend. I thought how easily someone could get stabbed there. There were so many people crushed together no one would even notice.

After my speedy shower I went and sat on the veranda next to the clothing factory. This was where most of the foreigners hung out. Then, just before 3pm, a whistle was blown and everybody congregated on the parade ground and lined up in order of their cell numbers. Roll call was conducted and we were then marched upstairs in single file to our cells. As we went we were counted, and at the entrance to the steps each prisoner would be searched. The guards would feel you, frisk you down, probe under your testicles and check your personal belongings. This procedure was to make sure you had no weapons or drugs. I found it humiliating.

After this it was lockdown. Once we were in the cells, we were counted again; in the morning before exiting from our cells, another roll call was conducted. Security was hectic.

M

Being in a foreign prison, unable to speak the language, not to mention being thousands of miles from home, with no regular visitors or access to a telephone, made my suffering and feeling of isolation that much worse. The only visitor I could look forward to was the consular officer from the South African embassy.

When my name was called for a visit on a day when I was not expecting the embassy, I was overcome with excitement and joy. Who on earth could it be, I wondered – perhaps a surprise visit from my family or a friend. I walked eagerly into the visit room, the area that was allocated for official visits, and standing before me was this young man I'd never seen before. He was tall and had a long red beard and a very pale complexion, and he was well dressed. His aura glowed with a lightness of being. I couldn't believe my eyes. What was a rabbi doing way out here? He introduced himself to me as Rabbi Kantor. He was from New York and had been posted to Bangkok to head Chabad House there. He was a good few years younger than me, yet spiritually I knew immediately we were generations apart. His display of compassion and concern for my wellbeing moved me deeply. I remember thinking that, even in the darkest corners of the earth, one could find *Hashem*'s light present. For a moment I wished the walls around me would crumble and the steel bars melt like when Moses parted the Red Sea. For days on end I kept replaying the rabbi's visit in my mind. I was not alone after all. The tribes of Jerusalem extended to wherever one might be.

For now, however, I remained spiritually distant from the powers above.

I met up with an elderly German guy, a tall, grey-haired man in his mid-sixties who was brought in a few days after me. His name was Dieter, and, because we were the only two white foreigners in Building 5, we struck up a friendship. He was very wise and worldly and we got on well. I didn't have anywhere to keep the few things I possessed, so Dieter, made me a suitcase from a cardboard box. It was so well crafted that he started getting orders from other prisoners. Dieter would wear his clothes for days on end. Out of respect for his age, I offered to do his washing for him. Later I learnt that this was not the first time Dieter had been in a Thai prison. He was connected to one of the most powerful Burmese warlords, Khun Sa, also known as the 'Opium King'. In the 1960s, Khun Sa had disappeared into the jungles of eastern Burma with an army of 600 men, where he cultivated opium. At the height of his power, he was producing as much as three quarters of the world's heroin supply. The DEA labelled him the 'Prince of Death'.

My new cell was about three and a half times the size of a double garage and housed 44 prisoners. In the cell were three wooden platforms, which must have been at least 20 years old, and the wood was infested with woodlice and fleas. I got a terrible skin infection that lasted for several months before I managed to get medicine from South Africa. By that time I had scratched myself so badly there were scabs all over my arse. The infection was compounded by a heat rash that produced pimples full of pus all over my body.

Every cell had a room chief whose duty it was to make sure that all new prisoners had a place to sleep. He would allocate you a place at his own discretion. He had to make sure that there was no fighting in the room, that the toilets and the cell were clean, and that there was fresh water available. My room chief's name was Mohammed. He was a Thai Muslim guy, very well built, and very humble and friendly.

The cell was already overcrowded and there was no place for me on the wooden platforms. I was given the spot in front of the steel door, which offered a bit of privacy. I organised a cardboard box which, when folded open, was big enough for my body. I used this as a mattress. I also had Joan's blue beach towel. During the day I would use the towel to dry myself, and at night it was my bedsheet.

In front of the toilet there was a ceramic bowl in which clean drinking water was stored. Resting on the rim was an aluminium cup, which was used by every single prisoner to scoop water and drink. I took one look at this and decided there was no way I was going to drink from that cup.

Once the cell was locked, two guards came around to do the second roll call. For this, we had to sit on the edge of the platforms in a straight line and face the passage. Then each person would count in Thai. Once everyone had counted, the room chief would announce to the guard the number of people in the cell and account for how many people were still in court. For example, he would say, 42 prisoners were there, and two had not come back from court. After roll call, little groups would form in the cell, and everyone started taking out their food. The Thais always ate in groups and they would share their food among the group. They got regular visits and their visitors bought them an abundance of fruit and foodstuffs from the prison canteen. When it comes to food with the Thais, it doesn't matter how much they have, they will invite you and will share their last. It's part of their culture. If you walk past a group of Thais eating, it's customary for them to invite you to join them, either by gesturing with a hand or by saying '*Khun kin cowe*'. Literally, this is an invitation to eat but it can also be interpreted as a greeting. If you aren't going to accept the invitation you would reply, '*Pom kin leow*,' meaning 'I've already eaten (thank you).'

Most Thais had no support, whereas we foreigners were more fortunate. The United Nations donated 25 Thai baht a day to all foreign prisoners; in addition, we would get two eggs each. A prison account was opened for you and you could order food from the prison grocery store, provided you had money in your account. Popular with the prisoners was sliced bread smeared with condensed milk. Another affordable meal, which came in a small packet, was Mama Instant Noodles; all this required was a bit of hot water. We would eat this with canned pilchards.

Several of my Thai cellmates invited me to eat with them, but I had already arranged to eat with Patrick and Frank. They had a spot in the corner of the room and they had an Indian guy they paid to work for them. He helped them cook, washed their dishes, made their beds – which consisted of a couple of blankets sewn together to form a mattress – and did their laundry. His name was Jasbir.

The thing about Thai prisons is that basically you have to pay for everything. The prison provides you with nothing. You don't even get toiletries. Life is much harder for those prisoners who don't have money, and unless you have visitors bringing you stuff, or financial support from your family, you are screwed. Some prisoners are so desperate they go as far as selling their asses. There are many instances of male prisoners, known as lady-boys, who survive by marrying one of the *karjai*s (literally 'big leg'). They provide sexual services. Others wash dishes and clothes, tidy the room etc. Some of the guys are cleaners.

After we had eaten, I went to brush my teeth. Ever since I had had root canal treatment in my early twenties, not a meal had gone by when I didn't floss afterwards. I always had a lot of dental floss with me. Now, here I was, in a Thai prison, in the middle of a room of 40 strangers, flossing my teeth. I was the centre of attention, I can tell you! Everybody was watching me. Some guys even came up to me and asked me what the hell I was doing. I couldn't help but laugh to myself, how something so small could be so amusing to so many.

Lying on an unforgiving concrete floor, with a cardboard box and a towel for a bed, amid an ugly cacophony of shouting voices, each one louder than the next, coming from every side of my own cell and from the cells across the corridor – it was like being at a fish market. There was a constant soundtrack of grown men engaging in trivial conversations purely to pass the time (not that I understood what they were saying, but I could imagine), each one no doubt relating his sad story. Arguments erupted frequently and some ended in violent physical altercations. Knives were drawn at the slightest provocation. There were constant eruptions of bodily noises, of men farting, men coughing. The smells were another assault to my senses – of body odour, prisoners taking a shit, stale cigarette smoke and dirty ashtrays.

I wondered how I was going to I survive. It was like a real-life movie script unfolding around me.

As new prisoners, we were required to wear leg irons for the first two months, and my usual position when I was in the cell was flat on my back, legs shackled, with my flip-flops for a pillow. The Jewish festival of Pesach (Passover) was approaching and I found myself reminiscing and wondering about my family and friends back in South Africa, and about Jewish communities around the world, from Israel to America to Russia, who would be preparing for the Passover. My entire being ached and longed for home and to spend this festival with Joan, Malcolm, their kids Darren and Keri, my mom and Malcolm's parents, Benny and Naomi. Just to think that even these celebrations, which were something we took for granted as a family, were denied to me this year made me feel sad. I hadn't realised before how much they actually meant in my life.

Despairing thoughts looped endlessly through my head, and with each thought I felt the panic rise.

How was I going to get through this? What if I got the death penalty, or a life sentence (equivalent to 100 years)? That was usual for drug offences. I was 34 years old. No way was I going to live to 134. Why was I here? It just made no sense. Fuck, I was confused. I was lonely and lost, and I needed to find a way out. OUT. I had to get out, I had to escape, if not from this life, then from this *Earth*. I was never going to get out of there. If I was going to die in this place eventually anyway, surely death now would be a better option than being reduced to an animal?

Never before had I actually contemplated the idea of suicide, but now I found myself doing just that. Would I go to heaven or would I go to hell? Who gave a fuck anyway? Anywhere had to be better than where I was. Here I am, I thought, in a position to do something about my situation. My destiny was in my own hands, not in the hands of the Thai monarch or the prison authorities, and not in the hands of G-d either. G-d had let me down. During all the time I was dealing drugs and found myself in precarious situations, G-d had always been there to protect me. Now I hated Him. Now I questioned whether *Hashem* even existed.

Was there a part of me that knew that these thoughts were not logical? I don't know.

As far as my family was concerned, they believed the lies I had told the embassy. This was that I had been led to believe I was smuggling forged currency and had had no idea I was actually carrying drugs. My sister Joan believed the story and she was doing everything she could from South Africa to get me out of there. She had a friend who told her he knew of some people, Israelis, who had previously helped two Israeli guys get out of a Thai jail not too far into their sentences. Joan was desperate and she believed in my innocence, and so she managed to make contact with these people and allowed herself to be guided by them. They told her that everything depended on what sentence I received and that, in the meantime, she needed to start acquiring some serious funds.

Around early August, a group of us, about 12 foreigners, were transferred from Bombat to Klong Prem prison, which was just down the road. Late in the afternoon we gathered all our things and were marched down the road from one prison to the other. The entrance was another pair of huge steel gates. We were taken to a security check-point known as the White House, where we were searched thoroughly. Then we were taken to Building 6. In comparison to where I'd been before, this building was enormous. There was a dining hall, basketball court and quite a few factories. To the right of the gate as you walked in there was an area about 30 by 20m square with a fishpond and grass you could sit on. Until we were officially registered, we had to hang out by the fishpond and not mingle with other prisoners. Of course, we attracted the attention of the other foreigners already there, who all wanted to know where we were from.

After registration, each prisoner was allocated to a factory, which was where you were expected to hang out during the day. The factories were dirty and dusty, but one could make oneself relatively comfort-able. I was put into a cell with 30 guys. It had wooden floors that were broken in many places and had cockroaches crawling out from all over. My first night there was quite funny: I'd left my cigarette packet near to where I was sleeping, and in the morning a cockroach had made a hole in it and eaten half my cigarettes.

It was around this time that the people advising Joan, the so-called Israeli liberators, came to visit me. Their plan to begin with, they told me, was to get me a medical pardon. I would see the prison doctors and have some tests done. One of these would be an AIDS test. They had someone inside the lab who would falsify the reports and say that I had AIDS. Of course, there was a hefty fee attached to their services. In the meantime, they arranged to channel some of my own money to me while I was inside.

Shortly after I arrived at Klong Prem, I had been approached by an Australian guy, Daniel Westlake. He asked if I was interested in buying into a private cell with a group of foreigners. The cell I was in was at full capacity. We were lying crammed shoulder to shoulder at night and I was finding it impossible to sleep; I knew it was going to drive me insane. Buying into a private cell seemed like the logical thing to do, although there was a risk that I wouldn't have the 'luxury' of it for long. If Joan's people were to be believed, I might actually have a shot at getting out of there. On the other hand, my case was also coming up soon. There was a slight chance that I would get a 25-year sentence, which meant I would probably stay in Klong Prem, but if I was sentenced to life, which seemed more likely, I would be transferred to Bangkwang Central Prison.

I told the Israeli liberators that I needed more money so that I could buy into the private cell. The money was arranged. I planned to use it to make myself comfortable for as long as I could.

I paid 6 000 Thai baht for my stake in the private cell, which I shared with six other prisoners – British, Australian, Swiss, Pakistani and two Thais. The room had been recently renovated and painted, with new vinyl to cover the floor. There were no cockroaches. Daniel had been there for about two years and he was quite organised. He had a place behind the dining room where he kept his locker and private things.

There were quite a number of Africans in Building 6, from Kenya, Ghana, Nigeria, Liberia and Tanzania, as well as Chinese. Other countries such as Vietnam, Laos, Malaysia, Singapore, Japan and Indonesia were also well represented. And there were many Burmese prisoners.

In comparison to Bombat, Klong Prem prison was paradise. The guys had a lot more freedom. On weekends the area around the basketball court and the walls along the factories would be transformed into a market. Deckchairs and lockers were brought out from the factories and groups of guys would be cooking and selling food, cold drinks and ice creams. In Bombat we used to sit on the concrete floor near the gutter.

Klong Prem was known to have drugs. When we arrived, some of the guys wanted to score some hash or weed, but my priority was to organise a bed. Nothing was free. Some of the Thai junkies would sell their last possessions to get a fix, so organising blankets was relatively easy. By my second day already I had washed the blankets and arranged for one of the Thai guys to make me a bed.

When we left Bombat our personal belongings that had been in storage were returned to us. The US$100 note that I had hidden beneath the cardboard lining of my sports bag was miraculously still there. When moving from one prison to another it's important that you have cash on hand because it can take a month for your prison account to be transferred, and borrowing can be quite expensive.

I was lucky that the Israelis were visiting at that time. They bought me a lot of stuff from the prison canteen and deposited money into my account. Most of the foreigners had support from their families. Getting money into the prison was tricky. The most reliable method was having your own ATM card, which you could give to a guard who, for a fee, would go to the bank and draw cash for you.

Drugs were generally smuggled in by the guards, but sometimes prisoners tried to beat the system by having drugs concealed in food items sent in parcels. These were invariably detected by the guard who was checking them.

Coming from Bombat, and seeing the freedom prisoners enjoyed in Klong Prem, it was like we were on a holiday. I felt my spirits beginning to lift. We would stroll around the yard accosting anyone, Asians or Indians, and asking, 'Hey, man, you got some hash, ganja?' (many Asians understand that word). It was quite funny, but then one of the other foreigners warned us to be careful about drawing unnecessary attention to ourselves.

After living on tinned pilchards and instant noodles for the past few months, the food at Klong Prem was a huge improvement on Bombat. Meals were served in the dining hall and we got two meals a day, not one: breakfast and lunch. Breakfast for foreigners was two boiled eggs each, plus bread you bought yourself from the coffee shop. For lunch we got a lot of sweet potatoes, as well as chicken, but without much meat on the bones. Actually, the chicken was so tough I suspect it wasn't chicken; it might have been wild turkey or something.

The design of Klong Prem was different to that of Bombat. It was based more on an American style, in a T-shape. There was an upstairs and a downstairs, with a lot of smaller rooms. Lockdown was at 4pm and prisoners were let out of their cells at 6.30 in the morning to go to their respective factories.

Just being with foreigners, and not in a cell packed full of Thai inmates, was such a pleasure. Another advantage to having a private cell was that you didn't have to shower with the general population. Every night there was either a game of Scrabble or cards going on. Alternatively, I would read one of the books that circulated around the prison.

Even though I was waiting to be sentenced, and the waiting was a difficult time mentally, at least I was much more comfortable. I bought myself a deckchair and got a locker to put my personal stuff in. I continued to walk around every day, explore, see who worked where. I also started exercising. I managed to get hold of a pair of cheap canvas running shoes, which are called *nang yang*, and I started playing this Thai sport called *takraw*. It's a fast game, played with a round ball made out of rattan. You have to be quite agile and fit to play it, and the Thais were very impressed that a foreigner not only participated in one of their sports but also played well. Within a few weeks I became quite good at it, and we used to play for money.

There was a ping-pong table near the top end of the building, near the transport section, where mechanics repaired the prison buses. You had to pay to play ping-pong – bats and balls had to be bought from the guards – and nobody played just for fun. There was always gambling involved, whatever the activity or sport.

My case was due to be heard in September. I knew that if I got a life sentence I would be moved on return from court to Building 5, which was also the transit building, and after a week there I would be transferred to Bangkwang. So I began packing my things.

A couple of days before my court appearance, Joan arrived in Bangkok. The embassy had let me know she was coming, and her timing also coincided with the annual contact visit. Each prisoner is allowed two visits annually, which can either be taken on separate days or as two visits in one day, one in the morning and one in the afternoon. This is one of the highlights of prison life. The excitement is almost tangible. Spirits are high and generally the guys stay out of trouble, not wanting to forfeit these visits. Usually a few months before, a lot of the guys start working out, wanting to look their best for their wives, girlfriends and families. (There were instances where families who came from abroad and weren't able to visit during the official time of the contact visit would be given special permission, with the support of the relevant embassy, to come at another time during the year.) Marquees are erected for the occasion, and people can buy cooked food, ice cream and cold drinks. Security is also tightened, however, to prevent anybody from trying to escape by posing as one of the visitors. All visitors are thoroughly checked on arrival and are required to carry passports and identity documents. It's a whole long procedure.

Contact visits are one of a few vital support mechanisms for prisoners, but there are upsides to them as well as downsides. On the one hand, it's an opportunity to spend quality time with family and friends, where you can interact freely on a normal basis, but on the other hand, it can also be quite frustrating being with somebody you love and with whom you have been deprived of any form of intimacy for so long. I would learn this in time. For now, though, with my court appearance coming up, I couldn't wait to see my sister.

Tables and chairs for the visit were set out on the lawn near the front gate. The prisoners who were expecting visitors were taken to this area to wait, and so that they could see them coming through the gates. The visitors all come in together, hundreds of them.

It took me a good while to spot my sister, but then, suddenly, there she was. I saw her long blonde hair in the throng as she came around and went through the entrance. I was a fair way away at this point but the moment I saw her, I started walking. I could feel the excitement. I ran towards the entrance and got there just as she was coming in. I couldn't believe it. She was finally here.

Joan looked up and saw me and she just dropped everything, including the two huge bags of foodstuffs she was carrying. I ran towards her and I picked her up and swung her around in my arms. We held onto each other for what seemed like an eternity. I never wanted to let her go. We didn't speak; we couldn't. I just wanted to hold her close. I knew she was crying. I could feel her tears mingling with my own that were rolling unchecked down my cheeks. 'Shaun, are you okay, are you all right?' Just to hear her voice was amazing.

I gently put Joan down. I had so much to tell her, so much to ask, I wanted to know it all. I wanted news, news of my mother, the family, my friends. Then we were both talking at once, Joan asking me over and over again if I was okay. We talked about South Africa and about my court case. We laughed and we cried.

Before somebody goes to court, it is always the same procedure.

In the late afternoon of 27 September 1994 I was called to the office and informed that I would be going to court the next morning. Then I was sent to the White House to have shackles put on my legs. That night in my cell I couldn't sleep, wondering what destiny had planned for me. I was hoping against hope to get a 25-year sentence, but by now I was under no illusions. In Thailand there is no consistency to the law. Anything is possible. It was generally believed that the judges sat around and that a roll of the dice decided the fate of those on whom they passed judgment. Court officials were corrupt. There were cases of people who had actually been acquitted in the first court, but would still be held in prison. Whatever your sentence, the public prosecutor would automatically lodge an appeal, but, unless you paid a minimum of US$10 000, getting a heavy sentence in the second court was guaranteed.

Huddled up with my mates in my cell, I began to prepare myself mentally for the worst. The atmosphere was one of melancholy. Experience had taught us that, so often, one forged a friendship only to find that you or the friend would be sentenced and moved, or else transferred to another prison. Friends came and went like the weather, but, with a sense of separation coming, I was still gloomy.

I got on well with all my cellmates. Nick was a British guy who was doing short time for possession of weed. He was easy-going, always cracking jokes, and very light-hearted. Freddy, my next friend, was more of an introvert. Like me, he was also in for drug trafficking and was a drug addict. Then there was Daniel Westlake, the Australian who had approached me about buying into the cell. He was very quiet and gave the impression of being something of a nerd, but what a great guy he was. I didn't know it then, but he had apparently served time in several prisons around the world and had even managed to escape from one, in Italy. He carried a dozen different passports. In fact, Daniel would later stage one of the most notorious escapes ever, from the very room we shared together. He would be the first foreign prisoner ever to escape from a Thai prison.

My shackles were hurting my ankles. It had been only a couple of months since my first set of silverware had been removed. Now they chafed against the old wounds where the rusty steel rings had rubbed the skin off my ankles.

While shackles may seem inhumane and also a violation of the United Nations' minimum requirements for prisoners, they seem to be part of a psychological orientation that goes beyond the under-standing of anybody who hasn't worn them. Remembering when I first arrived at Bombat, I was so absorbed with the discomfort of the chains, and with the procedure of slipping my underpants and shorts through the rings that held them, that I didn't actually dwell too much on what they represented, namely, the fact that I was in prison.

The night before first court, I couldn't sleep. I could feel my sister's presence, our connection was so strong. I knew she was in Bangkok, and that helped and comforted me.

I was preparing for a move to Bangkwang in a few practical ways. Some of us had Thermos flasks, and I removed the centre piece of mine and hid 7 000 Thai baht inside it. Then I put it back together and sealed it with Superglue. I rolled another 7 000 Thai baht into a small ball, covered it with cellophane, and then, using insulation tape, shaped it into a bullet which I planned to insert up my arse.

The following morning, I was removed from my cell earlier than usual and taken out to the central security point, where there were other prisoners in chains, also going to court. We were all wearing the same brownish khaki shorts and shirts. From there, we were escorted

through a few more security checkpoints and out the front of the prison, where we were greeted by armed guards and put into a prison
transport vehicle with double sets of bars. I had a window seat, so,
while driving to the court, I could watch the people outside, scurrying
around, heading to work, going about their normal morning business.
It evoked a deep sadness in me. Only a few months before, I had been
one of them, running around free. I so longed to be free. It was terribly
painful. I was already so far removed from that world. Even though it
had been only a few months, to me it felt like a lifetime. I kept staring
and imagining what might have been, had I not agreed to smuggle
drugs. I'm such a fuck-up, I thought to myself. Over the last 16 years,
what had I achieved? Nothing. In and out of jobs, I'd lost my business
and had almost destroyed my family, and all through drugs. I hated
myself. What a loser.

And then we were pulling in behind the Rachada courts and being
led in single file into the section where the cages were.

It wasn't too long before I was called, and to my delight there
was Joan. It was so good to see her there. I could feel her support.
She was with the Thai secretary from the embassy, Kun Paem. The
pleasure of seeing her was overshadowed, needless to say, by the fact
that I was waiting to be sentenced. It wasn't like I was bumping into
Joan at Woolworths. Nevertheless, having a family member there to
support me at this tumultuous time was a great source of comfort.

When she saw me shuffle into court, my sister broke down. The
shackles kind of blew her mind. She kept saying, 'You're not an animal, why do they have to chain you?' and, trying to lighten the mood,
I said, 'Oh, these things? This is my jewellery. Instead of arm bracelets,
I have leg bracelets.' We sat next to each other in the courtroom, holding hands. I explained to her that I had had to plead guilty because in
Thailand it was virtually impossible to win a case, even if you *were*
innocent. Once you fell victim to the judicial system, there was no way
out. She didn't understand this – I didn't blame her; it *didn't* make any
sense – and only cried more.

When the judges entered the courtroom, dressed smartly in black
suits, silence fell. The public prosecutor was there, too. It was all very

formal. I watched attentively as the judges read through my files. Two of them conversed. I had a government-appointed lawyer, who spoke no English, and there was no interpreter available. Luckily, Kun Paem could speak a little English. Although I was physically in the court-room, actually I felt like I wasn't there at all. It didn't feel real; it was a dream, like I was watching a movie. One of my nightmares was un-folding in front of me and I couldn't wake up from it. Nothing seemed to be registering in my brain. Thinking back today, it is still a blur.

My lawyer was called up to the bench. I don't know what he said, or even if he said anything at all. Everything was merely a formality, just going through the motions. The procedure was so drawn-out – but for what? Anyone could see that the whole thing was a charade.

I had pleaded guilty, knowing that the penalty was life, but, even so, I don't think I was prepared for the reality of the outcome. I don't even know what I was feeling – confused, angry, disappointed by my naiveté. I was very tense. My legs were shaking and so were my hands. My lips were numb. My heart ached more for my sister than for myself. I wanted it to be over with, for her sake more than mine. I wanted to run or to scream, but I also wanted to be strong for Joan. So I pre-tended to be strong, acting like I was prepared for anything. But can anyone ever actually prepare himself for the thought of spending a life in prison? I knew I would never accept my predicament. I imagined my lawyer saying to the judge, 'Throw the key away on this fuck.' The judges made me think of sentries at the gates of hell.

The next thing I knew, the judges blurted out some words I didn't understand, read from some papers, signed them and passed them to the public prosecutor. Then they got up and walked out. Everything seemed to be happening so fast. Joan and I turned to Kun Paem. We asked her what had been said. She said that, as far as she understood, I had been given the death penalty.

Joan went very pale and sank into her chair. I was in total shock. I asked Kun Paem to check with the lawyer. It can't be the death sentence, I said. She walked over to the lawyer and I watched them exchange some words. I saw him nodding. When she came back to us, she explained that, yes, I had got the death penalty, but, because

I had pleaded guilty, it had been commuted to life, which in Thailand is a sentence of 100 years. I thought to myself: Fuck, that is a death sentence in itself! How am I going to survive 100 years? By now Joan had broken down completely and was mumbling 'It can't be, it can't be, I can't believe it' over and over again.

I was on the verge of tears now myself, but there was no way I was going to break down here. I tried to be strong, to be cheerful and to put up a brave front. I told Joan that there was some way we'd get out of this. There *had* to be a way.

By now our police escorts had informed us that we would have to go downstairs and be put back into the monkey cage. We all went downstairs together for the transfer to Bangkwang. I kept trying to reassure Joan, saying that she shouldn't be too upset, that I had been expecting a life sentence, and that, somehow or sometime, I would get out before the 100 years was up. In spite of my internal torment, I tried to make her smile. She didn't seem very convinced, but I could see she was a bit more relaxed by the fact that I seemed relatively composed.

We stayed in the cages until about lunchtime, and on my return to Klong Prem prison, I was given half an hour to get my stuff together. As soon as they saw me enter the building with my shackles on, all my friends knew I'd got 100 years. If anyone returned to prison still in shackles, it meant death or a life sentence. Anything less and the shackles would have been removed immediately. My things were already packed. I collected my bullet, went to the toilet and stuck my money, covered with Nivea cream, up my arse.

I was moved to Building 5, where my things were searched. They didn't find the money concealed in the flask. After checking in at the office – normal procedure – I was thrown into a small cell with two Nigerians.

One of my new cellmates attempted to talk to me, but talking was the last thing I felt like doing. All I wanted to do was crawl into a corner and cry. In prison, loneliness is like a cancer. Despite being surrounded by hundreds of inmates, at the end of the day you are alone. I was often amazed at how easily complete strangers would share their whole life story with you. I wasn't interested in how they'd got to prison, what crimes they had committed or what sentences they'd received. And at this particular point, I had my own shit to deal with. The Nigerian guy put his hand on my shoulder, saying that he understood what I was going through, adding, by way of comfort perhaps, that he had been in prison for over six years. I had no doubt that he could empathise with my situation, but *fuck* it, man, all I wanted was to be left alone. Over time, I would learn that there exists an understanding between prisoners that reaches beyond the bond of normal friendships.

I felt despondent, lonely and without hope. My thoughts kept turning to where my life had gone so wrong, all the way back to school. Surely schools were places where children got educated? Why had there been no programmes at my school to warn us kids of the consequences of drug use? I had so many questions. And now it seemed I was going to have a lot of time to search for the answers.

While I was waiting to be transferred, my sister managed to organise a contact visit every day. I hated every moment I spent behind bars, and having her there made a world of difference. Joan also had a lot of questions she wanted answers to. For one, she wanted to know how, when I was supposed to be taking a holiday, I had managed to get involved in smuggling drugs across continents. I maintained the lie I had told to the embassy, but for one reason only: to protect my family. If I told Joan the truth, that I had known what I was doing and had smuggled the heroin willingly, I thought she might abandon me.

My problem with drugs more than likely stretched back to when I was in my mother's womb, but no matter how much I wanted to find somewhere else to place the blame, I kept arriving at the same conclusion, namely, that I had only myself to blame. I thought of my father Fritz, and I wished I could blame him for the way I was. After all, he was no better than a criminal himself for neglecting us as children. But I couldn't blame him. We are all gifted with the ability to make our own choices; the rest we leave to fate. So far, I had made one wrong choice after the other, which led me to becoming who I was – a good-for-nothing drug addict and dealer. I knew then, just as I would take a stand when I believed I should, that I needed to take responsibility for my actions. I had to take the bull by the horns and acknowledge who I was and the path I had chosen that had brought me to this point. How I had managed to get away with my former lifestyle for so long had been pure luck. Now I was going to pay the price. When we commit a crime, generally we are aware of the repercussions if we get caught. The question was: how to do the time? I had two choices that I could see: I could either do good time or I could do bad time.

When I was a free man, back home in Joburg, one of my friends had received an 18-month stretch for housebreaking, and I remember thinking, fuck, 18 months is really a long time to be in prison. I heard of somebody else who had done six months, and even *that* had seemed long. Now here I was with this ridiculously long sentence, so disproportionate to the crime I had committed it was laughable, only it wasn't funny. I mean, it wasn't like I had *killed* someone. It just didn't make sense.

It was at dark moments like this that I would feel the urge to get high, to push aside the painful memories, as well as everything that was going on around me, but for some reason things were different now. Somehow it was more important for me first to understand how I had come to be in prison, and then to make a decision as to how I was going to get to where I needed to go. Perhaps G-d could help me answer these questions, or perhaps I had to find the answers on my own. Whichever one it was, right then I needed to feel pain. I needed to *feel* the pain of losing my freedom because this pain made me feel more alive than I had ever felt before. This was the beginning of something I instinctively knew I still had to learn about.

That first night after my sentencing, I didn't sleep, never even shut my eyes. In the cold light of day, it started to dawn on me. I began to understand that this was my retribution. After years and years of ruining the lives of those people I'd sold drugs to, this was my punishment. Surely this was poetic justice! I couldn't cry about the situation. Hard as it was to admit it, I deserved what I got. By accepting that this was my karma, I was going to get through this. An eye for an eye, a tooth for a tooth, a life for a life. I am still alive, I told myself. I must never forget that.

My surroundings became a constant reminder of my reality, but the five dreary days and nights I spent in Building 5, with rusty leg irons attached to my ankles, went by relatively fast. Seeing my sister every day broke the monotony, too. She bought me everything I needed, from clothing and toiletries to luxury items such as chocolates and more chocolates. Everything that enters the prison gets thoroughly checked. The guards use a Stanley knife, cutting food items open, often breaking things. It's really irritating, as it's impossible to eat everything you might have been brought in a single day and food would go stale or off. What pissed me off the most, though, was when one of the guards cut the soles of a pair of Nike running shoes this way! There was nothing anyone could do about this. Respect for prisoners or their property was simply nonexistent.

I was sentenced the same day as the young American who had also been arrested at the airport. He had been carrying 4.5kg of heroin; I had been apprehended with 2.4kg. He received a 25-year jail sentence, while I got 100 years. The difference was that he had cooperated, while I hadn't. The United States also has a prisoner transfer treaty with Thailand, which means that if you are handed down a life sentence, you serve only eight years in a Thai jail and then you are transferred to a prison in your own country. If sentenced to anything less, you have to stay for a minimum period of four years before being transferred. In 1994, over 21 American citizens were arrested in Thailand on drug-related charges. The majority of them received 30-year sentences or less. While the US government finances the war on drugs in Thailand, they go to great lengths to ensure that their nationals are treated with leniency when they get arrested. They even grant their citizens a monthly allowance in the form of a loan.

Day six was when I was due to be transferred to the notorious Bangkwang prison, which is considered among the ten worst prisons in the world.

Besides the money I was carrying in my arse, I also still had the other 7 000 Thai baht hidden in my flask. Having cash on you in a Thai prison is illegal, and if you are caught not only is the money confiscated but also you are shackled and thrown into solitary confinement for a minimum of three to six months. Also, your class is reduced, which affects your chances of a sentence reduction when amnesties are granted. I knew what I was risking, but there was no way I was arriving at a new prison without cash. In this way, I wouldn't have to depend on anyone for anything, and could get organised that much quicker. It was common knowledge that the cost of living in Bangkwang was very high. Not only was I street-smart by then, but I was a quick learner, too.

Another American guy, Cliff, was being moved to Bankwang the same day as me. He was about 1.8m tall, roughly my age, and the spitting image of Burt Reynolds – the actor, not my client back in Johannesburg. It was only the two of us in the prison transport vehicle this time, and about six armed guards. The vehicle had regular plastic-covered seats, like those on an ordinary bus, but the windows had steel bars on them and wire mesh covering the panes. You could still see outside, though, and there was something magical about the streets of Bangkok – from the many street vendors selling their freshly prepared food, the constant flow of pedestrians and the slow-moving traffic to the litter-strewn pavements. It was a world I was no longer part of, and might never get to see again. As we drove through the streets I was overwhelmed by a feeling of great sadness.

It was almost seven months since I was last in civilisation. It felt like years.

Chapter 9

Adapt or Die

We arrived at the Big Tiger – Bangkwang Central Prison, my new home, also known as the Bangkok Hilton.

The driver pulled up in front of the now-familiar steel doors. The guards, armed with their rifles, stood around the truck as we disembarked. I thought it strange that they needed so many guards to prevent two prisoners, shackled *and* handcuffed, from escaping.

The gates opened into a driveway, with administration offices and a waiting room to one side. From there we were led through another set of double steel gates and into an open courtyard with rows of well-trimmed bushes and flowers. The road, on either side of which were the prison visit areas, extended for another 60m or so. Looming over us at the end was the infamous Bangkwang prison tower, where there was another checkpoint with more double steel gates. The security was unbelievable. Once inside, we came to a sort of crossroads: there was a road to the left, a road to the right, and a road straight ahead. On the right, in a fenced-in area, was the section where prisoners received parcels and mail; to the left was the security building; and in between the two there was a sliding gate through which deliveries to the prison were made. Beyond that was the actual prison compound.

We were taken to the security centre, where our things were checked by a couple of Blue Shirts. These trustees, motherfuckers, searched you more thoroughly than the guards did. I had all my stuff packed in two big plastic canvas bags. Our so-called beds, which comprised only blankets anyway, were ripped apart. They went through almost everything, opened my letters, tore open cigarette packets. Among my things were two *takraw* balls. When the Blue Shirt saw them, he smiled and asked me in Thai, '*Khun len dai?*' (Do you play?)

I nodded, and said yes in English.

He seemed pretty impressed and his attitude towards me changed. Then, what I had dreaded most happened: he picked up the flask in which I had hidden my money. He started shaking it and holding it up to the light, examining it closely. Fuck, my heart started beating rapidly. I thought, oh no – I'm definitely going to get bust. At this stage all my things were scattered on the tarmac. I had five cartons of Marlboro cigarettes that Joan had bought for me. Cigarettes are a form of currency in prison, and many inmates have their visitors buy them cigarettes for this reason. Often the price in prison is much higher than the price outside, although sometimes it is lower, depending on supply and demand. Quickly, I bent over, tore open one of my cartons and passed the Blue Shirt two packets. His face lit up. The flask forgotten, he tossed it to one side, where it landed among all my other stuff, and thanked me. Shit, that was a close shave. I was sweating.

After we had repacked all our things, Cliff and I were escorted to Building 2. Being with another person made me feel a lot more secure than if I had been moved on my own. While I was in the other prisons, inmates often spoke about Bangkwang. It was said that if you had money you could procure almost anything.

There was one guard on duty, who was slouched in his chair with his feet propped on the table, and a Blue Shirt standing behind him massaging his neck. He seemed annoyed at first by the intrusion but he turned out to be quite friendly. It was late afternoon already, after lockdown, and close to the end of his shift. He didn't bother to check our stuff, but he asked us, '*Khun mah jahk ny?*' (Where do you come from, you?)

I told him Africa.

'*Machai khun dum,*' he said. At this stage I couldn't really speak

Thai, but I knew that *dum* was 'black' and *khun* was 'person'. The man was fascinated by the fact that I was a white South African, believing that everybody from Africa should have a black skin.

The Blue Shirt escorted us to the office. We walked along a concrete pathway that stretched from one end of the building to the other, to the left of which was a small grass field with some trees and to the right an area where vegetables were grown. Running parallel to the pathway, along the east end wall, was a bakery. I later learnt that an American prisoner, in partnership with one of the guards, had paid for all the bakery equipment, which ran into thousands of dollars. Once the bakery was up and running, the unsuspecting American was transferred to another prison!

My luggage was heavy, and by now the rusty shackles had grazed the skin off the back of my heels, so I was taking strain while walking. After the vegetable patch there was a towel factory, and on the west side of the wall, near the office, was the shower area with the familiar horse troughs. The office area and dining hall were under one roof. In the dining hall I noticed there were these long, steel-framed wooden-topped tables, with benches attached to them. This was where some prisoners ate their meals and where others congregated to write letters, read books or nap on the benches. Just outside the office was a big tree with a cement bench built around it, and behind it was a small building containing the guards' toilets. Further up was an open cemented courtyard with a basketball court in the centre. And finally, beyond that, was the double-storey building where the prisoners were housed.

Lockdown was at 3.30pm, so only a few inmates were still wandering around, mostly workers. The prisoner who was the secretary registered our names and allocated Cliff and me to cell number 45.

Just at that moment, a prisoner who was walking past stopped and introduced himself. His name was Mohammed and he was an Iranian. He welcomed us to Bangkwang. He also offered to keep our baggage for us in his 'house' till the morning and he helped me carry my things. We walked to the rear of the building where, about halfway up the wall, we could see an asbestos roof extending about 4m. The roof sheltered an area that was divided into sections where prisoners kept their lockers. Basically, they had made it into a place where they could hang out during the day. These places were called 'houses' and could be purchased at a price. Your house became your private property. Some of the long-sentence prisoners and the wealthier guys went as far as tiling the floor and even putting in ceilings. Owning such a place was limited to the more privileged prisoners.

Mohammed's house was probably about 4m square. He had a small wooden table with matching stools and two deckchairs. Sitting in one of them was a Saudi Arabian guy, who turned out to be very friendly. The house next door, which was double the size of Mohammed's, was where the Nigerians hung out. Many of them had already gone upstairs. Word had spread that two new foreigners had arrived, so those who were still mingling around wanted to meet us. Everybody was very friendly. It was almost time for everyone to be inside their cells, so they urged us to get a move on, but Cliff and I still wanted to shower. We quickly stripped down to our underwear – as quickly as taking off your shorts and slipping them through your chains will allow. Armed with our toiletries, shower bowl and towels, we made our way to the shower area. It had been a hectic day and I was exhausted. I was looking forward to freshening up with a nice shower. I also couldn't wait to get to the cell so that I could remove the bullet from my rectum.

We placed our toiletries on the edge of the trough and prepared to freshen up. Once our eyes settled on the water, we were both struck speechless. We looked up simultaneously and stared at each other in utter shock. Then we looked back at the water. Besides being unpleasantly murky, stuck to the sides of the tank was a curtain of slimy green fungus and swimming in the water were dozens of small fish and tadpoles. I couldn't believe it. This was polluted water, which was pumped to the prison from the Chao Phraya River across the road. The other prisons we'd been in had at least had clean water! One of the foreigners walked past, and I asked him whether we were expected to wash ourselves in this filthy muck. He told me not to worry, that tomorrow we could organise clean water. The only problem was that you had to pay for it. I wasn't surprised about that part, as I knew by now that nothing in prison is for free. Fortunately, I had money and could live with that.

By the time we finished showering, all the other inmates were already in their cells. I still felt dirty, and in fact my skin was really itchy. Carrying our blankets and toiletries, we made our way upstairs to Room 45, which was also known as the foreigner room. It was about four rooms away from the stairway. The room chief allocated me a spot near the toilet. This toilet was raised off the ground, with a cement wall. When squatting, you were visible from your chest up. Rice bags sewn together were used as a curtain and offered a degree of privacy. There were approximately 21 inmates in this cell, and we had the standard-size beds made from blankets sewn together. Our beds would often overlap. We had no option but to sleep shoulder to shoulder, all crammed together. Sometimes, when inmates changed rooms or someone was moved to another building or transferred to another prison, more space would open up and you could manage a few centimetres between beds.

On my right was a British guy and on my left was an old man of about 65, who was a French Israeli. Sleeping directly opposite me was a Nepalese, next to him were two Singaporeans, and in the corner opposite was an Iranian. Next to him was a Liberian. There were also Burmese, Malaysians, Japanese, Germans, Spanish, Americans and one Chinese guy. Most of these men were drug offenders. Being so far from home, it was of tremendous comfort to me being among people who spoke English. You didn't actually need to speak Thai, in fact, as there were many Thais there who also spoke reasonable English.

Out of a total of 900 prisoners, I was one of almost 200 *farang*s (foreigners), including the Asians.

Through the steel bars of our cell, we could see into the corridor and to the cells opposite ours. Because of overcrowding, prisoners also slept in the corridor, but this privilege was mainly afforded to the Blue Shirts. Then there were also the Thai Big Legs, and some of the Chinese, who had a lot more space. Some of them had beds double the size of those of the people in the cells. They even had foam mattresses that were about two inches thick.

The corridor was noisy as hell. There was a TV outside almost every second cell. I don't know why, but they all turned the volume up high, and each one was on a different channel. Some of the inmates ran businesses in the corridor, one selling coffee, another selling noodle soup with vegetables, and so on; others offered a sort of sweet jelly which they sold cold.

Once I had settled in, I went to the toilet. Getting the bullet out of my arse was extremely unpleasant, as I discovered it had lodged itself sideways. After sticking my finger up and manoeuvring the bullet into an upright position I finally managed to force it out. I then washed the shit off my hands and the bullet, dried it on my towel, unwrapped it and placed the money safely in my pocket. The plastic and the insulation tape I flushed away.

Down the centre of our cell there was enough space to walk to the bars at the front. One of the Chinese guys who slept next to the bars in the corridor asked me in English if I wanted something. I told him I was starving. I wanted two noodle soups, one for me and one for Cliff. He said, no problem, he would order for me. He asked if I had money to pay and I said I did. He seemed surprised, as we all knew money in prison was illegal. When changing prisons, it was extremely risky to smuggle money as the chances of being caught were very high. Bangkwang was the third prison I'd been in and I had learnt the system very fast: if you had money, you had power. Borrowing was also an option, and there were loan sharks in prison, some of whom charged interest, but lending gave them leverage over you. This practice was best avoided, if possible. Anything for free in prison was really very expensive.

A Thai prisoner came to our cell with a tray. He slipped an empty metal bowl through the bars and used a cup to ladle noodles, vegetables and a few fish balls into the bowl. Then, holding the metal bowl against the bar, he poured boiling water over the mixture from a flask, and then placed a lid on top, allowing the noodles a few minutes to soften in the water. He also passed me some chopsticks, a spoon and a small bowl of fresh chillies in soy sauce. It was amazing. A 24-hour takeaway service. The soup was not very filling, but it was tasty. I could feel its warmth lining my stomach.

After my little snack I returned to my space and sat there for a while, familiarising myself with the people who would now become my roommates. There's something very similar about prisoners' eyes. You can see their suffering in the way they look; it's like there's a deep emptiness. I suppose that isn't unexpected. Being so far from home in a foreign prison is really tough, and not having any support or being able to see your families sometimes for years on end is hard. I felt sad. This was how I would look in years to come, I thought. I would get this lost look in my eyes, too.

Eventually I lay down to try and take a little nap, but, no matter how hard I tried, I couldn't sleep in such close proximity to somebody else. It felt like my airspace was being invaded. I stretched out my legs, closed my eyes and allowed my mind to wander. What I really felt like was getting high. While at Klong Prem I had managed to score some hashish, which I didn't really enjoy smoking because it invariably gave me a headache. I preferred to eat it, allowing it to dissolve in my mouth, and it was a far better high that way.

The old French Israeli man on my left had his back facing me. I was just beginning to doze off when he let out the loudest fart you ever heard. Boom! And then another! Fuck, I could feel the heat from his arse, not to mention the disgusting smell that made me want to throw up. I sat up so fast! I tapped him on the shoulder, pointing towards the toilet, and said, 'Go into the toilet if you want to fart.' The old man sat up, too. He was so angry he even lifted his hand to slap me. I couldn't believe his audacity. I put my finger in his face and said, 'Take it easy, old man, you're going to get hurt.' By this time the whole room's attention was on us. He muttered something in Hebrew, no doubt cursing me, but then he rolled over, facing away from me, and went back to sleep. A lot of the guys, specially the non-smokers, used to wear these surgical masks. I thought to myself: tomorrow, at the top of my list of things to do, I have to get some masks made or I will never survive sleeping next to this old man.

It was impossible to get a good night's sleep. I was still not used to the light being on all night in our room, and the hard concrete was very uncomfortable. As always, I tossed and turned the whole night and didn't really sleep much. At 5am the room chief woke us all up. Across the corridor I noticed everybody else was still asleep. The extra early rising was obviously part of our room chief's personal routine. We had to roll up our blankets, push them against the wall, and then, using a straw broom, the chief proceeded to sweep the floors. The guys who smoked used small bottles with lids for ashtrays, and these they emptied in the dustbin, which was next to the steps to the toilet.

By 6am the room chief was finished cleaning and dusting, and we all sat around like idiots until 6.40 when the cell doors were opened. I was not happy about having a prisoner telling me what time to wake up in the morning and then having to sit around idly with no particular purpose before the doors were opened. This was another problem I would have to solve really soon.

At the end of the corridor, by the stairway, was a security gate that was locked every night. Downstairs, at the entrance to the building, was another security gate that was padlocked with chains and a heavy metal bar. Escape would be rather difficult, although I contemplated this many times. It would be pretty much impossible to escape without outside help, I reckoned. In the morning a guard would open the two sets of security gates, then a Blue Shirt, known as a key-boy, would open each cell – first, one on the left, then on the right, then on the left again, and so forth. The prisoners always rushed to get downstairs to start their daily activities. Those prisoners who didn't have any visitors to bring them stuff, or have any financial support, had to work. These were mainly the Thais and the other Asians. They worked as cleaners, dishwashers, laundry boys, ice collectors, water carriers and masseurs. The Thais were also required to work in the factories. They were paid ridiculous wages, which I don't think exceeded more than R30 a month, which wasn't even US$4 in 1994. Some of the wealthier Thais could pay the guard in charge of that particular factory to get out of working.

After being caught in the flow of human traffic to get out of the building, Cliff and I made our way to Mohammed's house, where we had coffee and he offered us breakfast. First on my agenda was organising a locker to keep my stuff in. Second was clean water for drinking and showering. As it turned out, Mohammed, who had been in Bangkwang for about three years already, and was about ten years my junior, was highly resourceful and he had the respect of the guards and prisoners alike. I got talking to the Nigerian guys, Mohammed's neighbours, across the waist-high wooden fence that separated the houses. As fellow Africans, the Nigerians were most welcoming towards me. There were about 40 of them living there. By the time I'd finished my coffee, I had struck up friendships with almost all of them. The first thing they wanted to know was whether I played football. I have to say they were a good bunch of guys. One or two whispered in my ear that there was plenty of heroin if I was so inclined, and credit was no problem. It was hard to resist. I had just received a life sentence. To be honest, I would have loved to have got fucked out of my head. An inner voice was guiding me, however, and I simply said, 'No, thanks, but I wouldn't mind some hashish.'

Bangkwang was a maximum security prison. People here were doing hard time. I realised I would have to be selective about the people I chose as friends. Spending time with the same person, one eventually picks up their habits, and I needed to be acutely aware of this, even in prison. Drugs had almost killed me. Drugs were the reason I was serving a life sentence. Prison was not exactly an environment where one could afford or enjoy to be stoned.

It was vital to me that I do good time. Here was an opportunity for me to choose: I could change my life or fuck it up even more.

After learning that I had cash on me, Mohammed wasted no time and organised me two lockers on the other side of the building, next to the bakery. This happened to be a prime spot, where few of the other foreigners hung out. Next to the bakery was a small furnace with a huge metal tub. This was where the cotton used for the towels was dyed. In charge of this area was a Thai called Somchai, who spoke English reasonably well. There was another horse trough, smaller and square in size, in which the factory workers took their showers. More importantly, there was also clean running water. For 500 Thai baht a month, one of the Thai prisoners who controlled the clean-running water would fill two standard-size plastic dustbins for you to shower from – one in the morning, one in the afternoon. I couldn't wait to take a shower in clean water; that fucking polluted river water had left me scratching all over. For 150 Thai baht I arranged for a Thai to also give me six bottles of clean, boiled drinking water. While I was unpacking my things and putting them into my newly acquired locker, he introduced me to a reliable laundry boy. Every foreigner received a small plastic bag of white rice and an inedible stew every day, which you could sell to the Thais for 150 Thai baht a month. The Thais were given red rice, so our white rice was in demand and one could use it as payment.

By 9am, which was when I was expecting a visit from my sister, I had already unpacked all my things, had a shower and pretty much got myself organised. Mohammed also introduced me to a guy called Lenny, who was from Hong Kong. Lenny spoke English and had done time in an American prison. He cooked Western-style food for some of the other prisoners, and 1 200 Thai baht got you one good meal. Things were looking good. The Hilton was certainly living up to its reputation.

It wasn't too long before the names of those prisoners who had visits were called over the loudspeaker. First, a short announcement was made in Thai, which I didn't understand. Then, after a series of names mispronounced in broken English, I heard mine: 'Alesanda Krebs – lee-myud' (visit). Because there were quite a few of us, we were required to wait at the entrance of Building 2. I was impatient, desperate to spend as much time with Joan as possible before she had to fly back to South Africa. This was her second-last visit. I complained to the guard about having to wait, and he seemed sympathetic. He allowed me to go ahead, without having to wait for the others.

The visit room was a long corridor, with two sets of bars, some wire mesh and a space of about 2m separating the prisoners from their visitors. I don't know why, but I was surprised to see so many foreigners. It was a crazy scene and reminded me of the first day, when I was moved from the police cells to court. Visitors had to shout to the prisoners to be heard, and when the visit room was packed, like it was today, you could hardly hear anything properly.

Buildings 1, 2 and 3 had visits on Mondays and Wednesdays; buildings 4, 5 and 6 had theirs on Tuesdays and Thursdays. Visit days also gave us the opportunity of meeting up with our mates from the other buildings. Magazines and books were exchanged, but, of more interest to us, information was exchanged, too. It was extraordinary how fast news travelled around the prison. It spread like wildfire.

The visit room was also a place where drugs were distributed. Dealers paid inmates to smuggle drugs from the buildings to the visit room. There was a whole underground postal network in place. Messages were written on small pieces of paper, which were folded and stapled and would be discreetly passed from hand to hand until they eventually reached the intended person. Meetings were even arranged at the hospital.

Joan was there waiting for me. I kept up a brave front, telling her about my new friend Mohammed and how he had helped me get organised. I told her there was nothing that she needed to worry about, that in fact this prison was far better than the other two prisons I'd been held in. Joan had arranged with the embassy to send an official letter to the Bangkwang prison authorities requesting the removal of my shackles as soon as possible. My sentencing, as well as the hassle of getting to the prison and having to queue to get inside, had really taken its toll on Joan. My poor sister was an emotional wreck. As much as she wanted to be with me for as long as possible, she also needed to head back home to Johannesburg and her family. The last bit of business left for her to do was to organise a lawyer to handle my appeal. The chance of getting a reduction in my sentence, without bribing the public prosecutor, was extremely remote. The ideal situation would be for me to get my sentence reduced to 25 years. If this happened, I could be moved back to Klong Prem, from where the Israelis had promised they could get me out.

The next day would be Joan's last visit and this reality weighed heavily on both of us. From tomorrow, I would be on my own. It was always difficult saying goodbye at the end of a visit, especially as Joan would break down in tears. We agreed that tomorrow neither of us would cry, and instead of saying goodbye we would say the words, 'See you later.'

My sister's last visit left me unsettled. To this day I can see the expression of sheer helplessness on her face. It broke my heart.

Bangkwang was a money-making machine. Bribery and corruption kept the wheels turning. From the lowest-ranking officer to as high up as the Minister of Justice, everybody got a kickback. Hypothetically speaking, let's say the government budget allocated 200 Thai baht per prisoner per day and at that time there were approximately 300 000 prisoners in Thailand's prisons. The authorities provide food for only 40 per cent of the prisoner population, so if they only use 100 Thai baht a day for a prisoner ... you do the math.

What shocked me more than most things in prison was the number of prisoners who were innocent. In Thailand you can be found guilty by mere association and get the death penalty. Entire families are locked up, parents and their children. For example, you could be in a restaurant while a drug deal is going down at the table next to you. Maybe there's a suitcase containing heroin on the floor beside the table. The next thing, there's a police raid. Nine times out of ten they have information, or else they have set up the whole operation themselves. Every single person, your waiter included, as well as anybody in the vicinity, will be arrested. Chances are, if you plead innocent and try to defend your case in first court, you may well get the death penalty and spend anything up to ten years after that fighting your case. After spending hundreds of thousands of rands, you most likely would still get a life sentence or the death penalty.

I hated the system the more I saw it in operation. Human rights abuses were sickeningly rampant in Thai jails. By now, I hated everything about the country. There was no way I was going to bother learning the language, as this would mean I was accepting my fate, and I wouldn't ever have any use for it once I was free anyway.

There was a section opposite the security office where prisoners waited to receive the food their visitors had brought them. These packages passed through three different checkpoints before landing here. It was also the area where registered mail and parcels were handed out. Receiving parcels from your family and friends abroad was one of the most vital support mechanisms for prisoners. I think it went a long way to keeping you sane. The feeling of seeing a parcel with your name on it was indescribable.

Working in this section was a Thai inmate named Piscet, who was close to 60. He had studied at Oxford University, where he had majored in English. Then, while in Bangkok visiting his family, he had caught a taxi, but unbeknown to him the driver was a drug smuggler. In the boot of the car he had about 2kg of heroin. The police apprehended the driver, but his passenger was also arrested. The poor guy tried to plead his innocence and ended up with a life sentence for his trouble. That's Thai justice for you!

Piscet was in charge of foreign mail, and he was also the official prison translator. He was the only prisoner who was permitted to walk around freely from building to building, as he delivered the mail twice a week. A couple of years later, close to his release, he and a fellow prisoner, a guy from Australia, smuggled a computer into their building. They got caught selling heroin on the internet and eventually got extradited to America.

Whenever a new prisoner arrived in Bangkwang, there was a general curiosity among inmates, especially among Western foreigners. Prison is a lonely place. Friendships are easily forged and just as quickly broken; one day somebody is your best friend and the next he is your sworn enemy. I had to learn this the hard way. Things work differently on the inside. There is no such thing as unconditional friendship. Nothing for nothing. You scratch my back, I scratch yours. I was suspicious of anybody who was too friendly. Now that I was at my third prison, I was more interested in befriending those inmates who worked in key positions and could help make life easier for me.

If the place was a jungle, I was a tiger among tigers.

Like an animal staking out its territory, I did my usual walking around and quickly familiarised myself with my new environment. It was not a pretty picture. There was open sewage and dust and dirt everywhere.

Bangkwang comprised 14 buildings, with six buildings housing a total of 7 000 prisoners. Building 2 housed mainly the offenders who were in for murder, while Building 6 held the drug offenders. Building 7 was the monastery, Building 8 had a furniture factory that prisoners with low sentences worked in, Building 9 was the kitchen, and Building 10 was the punishment building, also known as solitary confinement. Building 12 was the hospital, and Building 14 was the university, where there was also a full-size football field. I'm not sure whether it was Building 11 or 13, but one of these was the pig farm.

Each building was completely walled in, and each was situated on about half a hectare. And each operated independently. They were worlds within worlds. At the entrance to each building was a double set of security gates, which during the day were manned by two guards and two Blue Shirts.

In one of the factories they made picture frames from mother-of-pearl, using sandpaper grinders to smooth the surfaces. The sanding released microscopic particles, and accounted for some of the dust that hung in the air.

The place was terribly overcrowded. Prisoners would sit around all day doing nothing and generally talking shit. The main topic of conversation usually revolved around the crime they had committed and their sentences. Many of the Thais were in Bangkwang because they had committed multiple murders – and their casualness around this fact, their disregard for human life, was something I couldn't get my head around. There was an incident in my cell once where a Thai guy who had killed an entire family got upset with me for killing a mosquito – the Thai Buddhists believe in reincarnation, so the mosquito could be a member of their family reincarnated.

The disparity in the sentences for murder and for drug offences was also something that never failed to astound me. If you are convicted of murder, you will spend anything between seven and fourteen years before you are eligible for parole, while drug offenders remain in prison for anything between 18 and 24 years.

Through time and the effects of exercise, the drugs had worked their way out of my system. The clearer my mind became, the more real was my reality. Survival became my ongoing priority. In fact, this had been the case from the time I arrived in Bombat prison.

While walking around the building close to where my new locker was, I noticed that some of the prisoners had erected awnings, which were attached to the wall, to protect themselves from the sweltering heat. This section of the building we called Chinatown, as it was where a lot of the Chinese guys hung out. Some of them also had houses. Walking further down towards the opposite end of the building, closer to where Mohammed stayed, I saw a group of four guys sitting in deckchairs, their pants pulled down to their knees. As I got closer, I saw they had these weird plastic pump gadgets fitted on their penises. At first I didn't know what they were doing, but then I realised they were busy enlarging their dicks! They were doing this right out in the open, and then they would compare sizes. This was better than the movies!

Further on were the toilets, where there were smaller groups of guys huddled together. These were the junkies shooting up heroin. They used an empty pen cartridge for this: after sucking the diluted heroin into the cartridge, they would attach a surgical needle to it, which was then inserted into the vein. A fellow prisoner then blew on the opposite end of the cartridge, allowing the heroin to enter the bloodstream. Prisoners shared needles freely, without any form of sterilisation. I was sure most of these guys had AIDS. The place was full of addicts, and seeing and being around people taking drugs on such a large scale really frightened me. Bangkwang, I soon realised, was *full* of drugs.

I suppose prisons all around the world tolerate drug trafficking within their walls, but, besides the monetary gains, in Thai prisons the authorities turn a blind eye because they know that drugs subdue prisoners and keep them mellow – a disgruntled prison population can make for a very volatile situation.

The Chinese and the Nigerians controlled the drugs in Bangkwang, and within their organisation they had at least five different syndicates. Whenever a big stash came into the building, it would be divided equally among the dealers. Each had his own customer base and every syndicate operated on a different day. I had barely been in Bangkwang a week – it was around 10am on a Monday morning – when I became aware of how the system operated. During our regular visit days many of the foreigners were at the visit, and those who didn't have regular visits were in the dining hall writing letters. A few Nigerians hung out in the house, while others stood guard at certain posts, keeping a watchful eye. There was always a chance of the building getting raided by outside guards, either from the security section or the Department of Corrections, so whichever syndicate was peddling the heroin that day, one or two guys would be on duty selling. The heroin was put into small papers containing no more than 0.4g.

On this Monday morning I was relaxing in a deckchair in Mohammed's house when three Thai junkies arrived at the entrance to the Nigerians' house. They ordered their papers, and as the Nigerian was about to hand them over, they pulled out knives and robbed him of everything he was holding. It all happened really fast. Apparently it wasn't the first time and it sure wouldn't be the last. With Thais outnumbering foreigners seven to one in Bangkwang, retaliation would be committing suicide.

My second night in the cell, I called for a meeting in which I expressed my disapproval of the room chief waking us up so early. We took a vote and most of the guys supported me; it was decided there and then that the room chief would clean the room only once we had exited. At the same time I changed places with the guy on my right – I wasn't going to be able to sleep next to the old man who farted all the time. My new neighbour was a Singaporean by the name of Jimmy. The poor guy had AIDS. He was covered in pimple-type sores all over his body, which he never stopped scratching. I felt bad for him, but the scratching was terrible. Eventually, I got hold of a cardboard box which I flattened and stood as a partition between our beds.

Because I had started jogging already back at Klong Prem and had played some *takraw*, I was reasonably fit. Sports activities were generally left to the prisoners to organise. First thing in the morning, the basketball enthusiasts would have the concrete court for an hour.

After that, the footballers would take over the pitch. I was soon playing football. Teams were made up of either four or five players. Two teams would square off, while the other teams sat on the sidelines and watched, waiting for their turn. If you were a good player, whenever you arrived at the pitch, players would quickly invite you onto their team. The winner was determined by who scored the first goal. Every time the ball was kicked behind the goal line, the next team to play would count. If by the count of ten there was no goal, both teams would be out and two new teams would come on to play. On Saturdays, Sundays and public holidays, all the footballers would come to play. The Thais love their football, and there were some very talented sportsmen among us in Bangkwang. They were also very competitive, especially when it came to playing against the foreigners.

Despite being physically active, my first days in Bangkwang dragged and the nights were long. I started expressing my inner emotions by composing poetry. I would lie on my bundle of folded blankets and juggle with words. The first poem I wrote I called 'Walls':

> *My life revolves around walls*
> *walls that seem so high that you cannot see the sky,*
> *yet the sky is not so high as the walls seem to touch the sky,*
> *how I wish I could fly.*

Understandably, my spirits were really down, but the deeper I went into my mind, the easier the words began to flow. All the same I felt myself slipping into a state of depression.

I wrote another poem and called it 'Feel the Breeze':

> *This is not about the beginning of the end,*
> *nor is it about the end of the beginning,*
> *this is not about one ways,*
> *nor is it about dead ends,*
> *it's about release,*
> *do you feel the breeze,*
> *I finally feel at ease.*

Suicide wasn't something I'd ever contemplated – Judaism prohibits taking your own life – but now it was a very real option in comparison to what I was facing. I believed I could do it, too. And so I set in motion a plan to take my life.

Believing that the most effective method was death by hanging, I managed to acquire a durable rope, one I estimated would accommodate my weight, and successfully smuggled it into my cell. I recited my prayers, and, just before midnight, said my private goodbyes and begged the forgiveness of my family and friends. I understood that the act of suicide was a selfish one and that ultimately only they would suffer, but I was in a very depressed and hopeless state.

All my cellmates were fast asleep. I took the rope into the toilet and made a hangman's noose. I tied the other end to the bars above the toilet. Then I fitted the rope around my neck and was about to lunge my body out of the toilet, which was at least a metre above ground level, when suddenly I saw a bright light and distorted images, similar to those I had sometimes seen in my nightmares as a child, came flooding into my mind. It was a crazy moment, and the realisation of what I was doing hit me hard. I discovered that my will to live was greater than my desire to die. What the fuck was I thinking? I quickly removed the rope from my neck, untied it, went back to my space and lay down. My heart was pounding. I couldn't believe I had almost taken my life.

I will get through this, I told myself. They will never break me.

The weeks and months that followed my futile attempt at suicide were spent mainly with my head in the clouds. I wrote more poems and became more withdrawn and irritable. And there was no news from home. Letter-writing was the only form of communication that prisoners enjoyed. Building 2's mail arrived every Wednesday and Sunday. When they called the mail over the intercom system and your name was one of those called out, you were overcome with excitement. By November I had written at least four letters to my family and still there was no news from them. I was sick with worry. I could feel it in my gut that something was wrong. In addition, I had not heard a word from my so-called Israeli liberators. Naive as I was then, I trusted people and expected them to come through.

Electrical appliances were illegal in the prison, but they managed to find their way in all the same. Those who could afford them had things like rice boilers, electric frying pans, portable fans and blenders. You could even hire a TV and a video machine so you could watch movies. I managed to acquire a Walkman for 1 200 Thai baht. There were one or two English channels that played my type of music, and whenever I got to the cell, the first thing I did was switch on my Walkman and plug in my earphones. Music has always played an integral part in my life. It does something profound to my soul. But in prison it also made me homesick, especially when I heard one of my favourite songs. These triggered memories of those sentimental moments we all have at some stage of our lives.

In the meantime, the South African consul, Jan Putter, whom I liked a lot, had informed me that our government was in the process of negotiating a prisoner transfer treaty with Thailand, so I put some of my hope in that. The fact that there *were* a few possible avenues still open to me gave me strength to endure the monotony of prison life. I still strongly maintained my innocence, even more so after it had become obvious, to me at least, that I had been set up. There were many such instances where the very people who supplied you with the heroin were working with the police, giving them your identity, what quantity of drugs you were carrying and which hotel you were staying at. In my case, the cops had been onto me already at the hotel or probably, for that matter, from the very moment I'd set foot in Bangkok. It's when you are apprehended at the airport that the charge for exporting carries the death penalty.

In December, while sitting around in the Nigerian house one morning, reminiscing about years gone by, my name was called for a parcel. Finally, some news from home!

I wrote back to share my appreciation with my family:

Dearest Joan, Malcolm, Darren and Keri
Firstly, thank you very much for the two parcels. I truly appreciate it more than you can imagine. The parcel was opened in front of me, two items on your list weren't in them

– two boxes of coffee, though there were a few small boxes of coffee and a blow-up pillow, maybe you forgot to put them in. Firstly, I pigged out on the salami, I fried it and mixed egg with it, then I attacked the cheese with Provita and after that, I had the coffee. It was just like a Southern Sun breakfast. Then I relaxed in a chair and smoked a Camel. I swear, for those moments, it felt like I was sitting in your back garden, you really made my day and it was worth waiting for. Thank you so much.

Lots of love, Shani

December, being the festive season, was a difficult time, not only for me, but also for most prisoners. It was the holidays. That longing to be with one's family or somewhere on the beach was more intense somehow during this time. I could understand why so many inmates turned to drugs. For me, the temptation was always there, but my inner voice kept telling me to stay strong. I had to resist at all costs. My very life depended on it. In Thailand, five days of holidays are given over to New Year, which meant that the prison was closed. There were no visits, no parcels and no letters during those days, and that was fucking depressing, I can tell you.

Several sports events happened over these holidays, all organised by the inmates, the highlight being the football competition, which was based on the same principles of elimination as the FIFA World Cup. Each team collected money, and a guard would buy uniforms and balls – for a fee, of course. Matches started as early as 7am. The tournament was a lot of fun and a break from our normal routine. The guys even placed bets on the games. I made the fatal mistake of being the referee in one of the quarter-final games – the Thais vs the Nigerians. I disallowed a goal the Nigerians scored. Actually, it was quite funny: not only did the players turn on me but so did some of the overenthusiastic Nigerian spectators. I stood my ground, though, and used my yellow card to quell their tempers.

Sport plays a huge role in developing friendships wherever you are, but in prison perhaps more so than anywhere else. There was an unbelievably strong bond among the footballers in Bangkwang. Mostly it was the Thai 'Bad Boys', the samurai, who played. I was one of a few Westerner foreigners who were skilled at the game, so I played for a Thai team. My team made the semifinals, but the tension was too much for our star striker. A goal down at half-time broke his spirit and we went on to lose.

The end of 1994 came and went.

I was still writing poems, and at one stage even considered studying structures and styles of poetry, thinking that somewhere inside me was a Shakespeare struggling to emerge. My poems were private, and when I read them over they usually brought me to tears. I never allowed anybody to read them. As time went on, I struggled to express my thoughts in this way and I began to write less frequently.

Among the many prisoners who spent time in the dining hall was a Burmese guy, whose name was Tin Sei O. He was talented musician, an artist and also a heroin addict. He drew pencil portraits for a fee to support his habit. We became acquainted and I took an immediate liking to him. Fortunately, his English was pretty good. As a Burmese national with a life sentence and no support whatsoever from outside his future was bleak. He would have to serve at least 22 years, and he didn't care what happened to him. Some of the guys in his situation, especially the Asian prisoners, almost had a death wish. I could relate to how Tin Sei O felt, as in a bizarre way death was liberation, the ultimate freedom. This attitude could make for a dangerous environment. There were inmates there with two life sentences, so committing an additional murder wouldn't make a difference to them. They were never going to see the light of day beyond those walls anyway.

For a carton of cigarettes, Tin drew a portrait for me of my sister and my niece Keri. It was a close enough resemblance, with one small mistake that only somebody with an eye for detail would have picked up. Audaciously, and on the spur of the moment, I signed my own name on the drawing, which I then posted home. A month later I received a letter from Joan. They were blown away by 'my' drawing, she said – it was fantastic! Jesus, I thought, what had I done? What if the Israeli thing worked out and I went home in a few months and they asked me to draw more portraits of other members of the family? I had not painted nor drawn anything since some postcards I'd made for the guys back in Bombat prison (and before that not very much since school). For these postcards I had cut the bristles off a toothbrush, attached them to a piece of bamboo and made some sketches using diluted coffee. Now I had a serious problem. The only solution, as far as I could see, was that I would have to learn to draw portraits and that Tin would have to be my teacher.

Tin used the scale system to draw his portraits. He had a piece of hard transparent plastic with horizontal and vertical lines scratched into the surface with a needle. This he would place over the photograph. Then, duplicating the squares on a piece of paper, and using a pencil, he would proceed to draw the portrait.

To get started, Tin gave me a couple of pencils and some other supplies. Within a matter of weeks, I was creating fairly accurate portraits. My models were mainly my family or friends and taken from the photos I had of them. Pencil is not a very versatile medium and, because I was limited to a 2HB pencil, I soon got bored. I then began experimenting with pen, my preference being a Bic ballpoint. In the ensuing months, through the many people I began to correspond with, I asked to be sent stationery and art supplies.

There were some highly skilled craftsmen among the Thai prisoners – tailors, carpenters, plumbers, electricians, bricklayers, you name it, we had them all. Because of the close proximity we all slept in and the discomfort of our so-called beds, a lot of the guys had small fold-up wooden tables, only slightly bigger than an A4 clipboard. I managed to purchase a second-hand one for 150 Thai baht. For the next five years, I used this little table to create many drawings.

In the towel factory there were two very talented tailors. Mondays to Fridays they did their regular jobs, and on weekends they were allowed to do private work. In between making uniforms for the guards, they did many other things – from altering standard-size bedsheets to fit your makeshift bed to fixing a tear in your jean shorts and sewing on buttons. To better handle the extreme heat, I had employed one of them as my personal tailor and he restyled all my T-shirts for me, first cutting the sleeves off at the shoulders and then, if the collar sat too tight around my neck, cutting it into a V-shape. I also had a denim shoulder bag made, which was perfect for carrying my fold-up table and my art materials.

Every afternoon at 2.30 shower time was announced over the intercom, and then around 3:30pm we would be called to go to our cells. There were 50 cells in our building. We weren't allowed to keep anything in our cells, so whatever we took upstairs with us at lockdown we would have to bring down in the morning. Because we spent almost 15 hours of every day in our cells, prisoners took food with them in *pinto*s or plastic containers. The guys also had water coolers in which there was ice to keep their food fresh or their water cold. Two guards and two Blue Shirts would man the door, searching every prisoner as he went into his cell, while the rest of us waited our turn in the stifling heat. It was quite a sight to see, hundreds of prisoners carrying all their stuff in plastic bags. The searches were required by the Department of Corrections, but the guards by and large couldn't be bothered, so the Blue Shirts did most of it. Unless they had information about somebody carrying drugs or weapons, though, these daily afternoon searches weren't very thorough.

Something that surprised me about Thai prisons was that everybody had knives. If you ordered beef from the prison grocery store, the meat you got was buffalo, and because buffalo is so tough the Thais used to chop the meat on a wooden board. And what did they use to do this? Nothing less than a meat cleaver, exactly like the one a butcher uses. Weapons were in abundance.

One afternoon while I was strolling past the shower area, opposite the towel factory, I witnessed an execution-style attack. The victim was a dark-skinned Thai prisoner who was taking a shower. He was from the south of Thailand. The northern Thais are very different from the southern Thais. They speak different dialects and their skin colour is different, too. One of the samurai, armed with a short metal bar, came up behind this guy and he hit him square on the side of the head. He never even saw it coming. His head burst open like a watermelon, and he just slumped to the ground, blood oozing out of his cracked skull. By the time they got him to the hospital, he was dead. Not even a couple days after that, there was another incident. A Thai had taken a broken ketchup bottle and proceeded to cut his own head open in an attempt to stop the guard from taking the bottle away from him. He also threatened to slit his own throat. After some intense negotiating, he eventually surrendered his weapon and he, too, was rushed to hospital. A couple of days later, he returned to the building, his head all bandaged up, but after that there was something really strange about him. He walked very slowly, taking short steps without bending his knees or moving his arms; he seemed to be in a trance.

There was another Thai prisoner who was our very own hobo. He used to lie around on the ground, and never really washed himself either. He was forever eating out of the garbage cans. The poor guy had definitely lost it. The thing was that both these guys had a similar stride. It was obvious that the guy who'd cut his head open had had something done to him at the hospital. I asked one of the other foreigners about this, a guy who had been in Bangkwang for some time, and he told me that when prisoners lost control and became violent they were taken to the hospital, where they were injected with some drug that was so powerful the person would become zombie-like and remain in that state for weeks. We called it the 'Turbo Shot'.

When you are sentenced in first court, the Thai legal system allows an automatic appeal for second court, which can take up to three months. After second court you have exactly one month to submit an appeal. In the event that you are defending your case and the court finds you innocent, the public prosecutor will appeal your sentence. Unless you pay a minimum of US$10 000, the chances are you'll get resentenced in third court to either the death penalty or life, depending on your crime.

My family had hired a lawyer to work on my appeal and we paid her an initial retainer of US$1 000. She neglected to explain the procedure to us, however, and visited me at the prison one and a half months *after* my second court appearance, which meant that it was too late to appeal and so my case was automatically closed. She still had the audacity to ask us for a further US$1 000 to process my appeal. By then I had already been informed by the court that my case was closed – I couldn't believe she was still trying to cheat me. I lost my cool and threatened to inform the embassy and report her to the Bar Association of Thailand. I also demanded that my initial retainer be refunded. It crossed my mind to wonder what might have happened if she had actually done her job. It was very possible that I might have got a reduced sentence. I didn't dwell on this too much, however. The more I thought about it, the more I realised that prison was my destiny.

One day, out of the blue, a friend from Johannesburg popped in for a surprise visit. I can't describe how exciting it was to have somebody visit whom I had seen not too long before. She had brought me some foodstuffs from South Africa and we joked and laughed together. It was just too wonderful to see her. She was a daring kind of girl, so we also discussed her trying to smuggle some alcohol in for me. I told her to buy a pack of six bottles of water, and to remove one of the bottles from the centre of the pack, instructing her how to do this without damaging the plastic cover, and also how to remove the lid without breaking the seal. Then she was to empty out the water and fill the bottle with vodka. I suggested she also bring some other foodstuffs along that would distract the guards from noticing anything unusual. She did as I instructed, and on her next visit the water came through, no problem. I rushed back to the building, really excited. It had been quite a few months since I'd last had a drink. I shared the vodka with two of my cellmates. As the intoxicating liquid made its way to my stomach, I felt a hot flush come over me, prompting an instant craving to get high. My friends laced a cigarette with some heroin and offered it to me. The temptation was almost overwhelming. It took some wrestling with my desire, but, in the end, instead of accepting a quick fix, I settled for some nicotine.

The most common offences that resulted in a prisoner being sent to solitary confinement were fighting or being caught in possession of drugs. In the event that you stabbed somebody, you were given really heavy shackles that weighed over 10kg. Solitary confinement, or Building 10, wasn't a place you wanted to go. All the misfits ended up there. You were locked up on your own 24 hours a day without a ceiling fan or lights. It was a daunting prospect and a punishment I hoped to avoid at all costs. There were many prisoners who had lost their minds in solitary confinement and some had even committed suicide there. When you had completed your punishment in solitary, you were transferred back to the building in groups. As a rule, violent offenders were never moved back to the same building in which they had committed the offence.

One morning, a few of the foreigners were congregated around the office in our building. I couldn't quite make out what the fuss was about, but on closer investigation I worked out that there were some new foreigners – four Nigerians and two Britons – who had been sent to our building from Building 10. One of the British guys was Ryan, the other Peter, and both of them had been arrested on drug-related charges and had been in prison for at least two years. The reason they had gone to solitary confinement was that they had tested positive for heroin in a urine test. Ryan had been living in Thailand for over ten years and had run his own guest house. It makes you wonder why so many foreigners who live in Thailand, and who know that the Thai government imposes the death penalty for drug trafficking, still get involved in smuggling. Had I known the consequences, I would never have come to the damn country.

In room 45 we were already up to 20 inmates. There was no space for more bodies. Ryan and the other guys were put into a Thai room downstairs. The average Thai is smaller than a *farang* and the Thai rooms could have anything up to 26 people to a cell. Having their beds overlapping or sleeping almost on top of each other never seemed to bother them. Thais are affectionate people, too, and for two guys to be walking around holding hands was not suggestive of anything but friendship. One other problem about staying in a Thai room was that a lot of these guys had tuberculosis. Many of the prisoners who had no money smoked a cheap tobacco called *yatung*, which they rolled in regular paper. Each cell had one or two ceiling fans, and, as the air circulated, particles of burning paper would fly around the cell, often landing on your bed and burning holes in your bedsheet. And of course you would breathe the microscopic particles into your lungs.

Ryan wasn't at all happy with his new accommodation. He approached the prison authorities to buy a room, which he wanted to limit to 18 occupants, Western foreigners only. He went about choosing his new roommates. He offered me a place in the cell, which would cost me a one-off payment of 2 000 Thai baht. The money would be put towards buying a new 72cm TV. The prospect of staying only with Western foreigners was enticing. The only problem for me was that more than half of the guys who would be in the room were on heroin. I had a difficult decision to make. Either I remained in an overcrowded cell with Asian foreigners and Jimmy endlessly scratching the sores off his skin, or I could move into a private cell with a room full of junkies. It was still early days, and the threat of relapsing and becoming a heroin addict was a very real one for me. I didn't think I would be able to resist the temptation, so I declined the offer.

Back in Johannesburg, my sister had been forced to get a job so that she could continue to send me money. Without money in a Thai prison, my chances of survival were slim to nil, but all she could afford to send me was R900 a month. In 1995 this would have been about 4 000 Thai baht. One meal a day cost me 1 200 Thai baht, clean shower water was 500, drinking water was 150, cigarettes about 700 for the month, laundry 150, and the remainder went towards odds and ends like the cleaning of the room and the occasional hiring of a video. The money Joan sent me was wired through the Department of Foreign Affairs in Pretoria, and then to the South African embassy in Bangkok, who then either deposited it in my prison account or bought the equivalent in cigarettes. They were always late with these payments, which meant I was forever in debt to my Iranian friend Mohammed. Although he was a good guy, and I always settled my debts, he capitalised on the fact that he helped me: whenever I got a parcel from home I would let him choose something. That was just how things worked in prison.

In the middle of February 1995, the footballers were informed by an official notice that in March the prison would be hosting the annual inter-building tournament. There was great excitement among the sportsmen. Training would begin from 9am next day. This comprised running for at least seven minutes, after which we would loosen up, stretch and do some military-style exercises. I took charge of the exercises. At the time I was still smoking cigarettes, and it was only a year since I had subjected my body to all that drug abuse. Even though I'd been jogging and playing football most days, that first day the training was so intense that later, in the confines of my cell, I broke out in a cold sweat. My body began to shake and ache all over; I covered myself with the towel that I used as a blanket. Once you were locked in your cell, you were on your own. There was no such thing as calling the guards if you got sick.

One of my cellmates noticed that I wasn't well and he gave me two paracetamol tablets. Whenever an inmate was sick and would report to the hospital, it didn't matter what your problem was; the doctor, who was an old retired Chinese man, who I doubted had ever got his medical degree, prescribed paracetamol for everything. It was a joke. Generally, prisoners feared being admitted to the hospital, where at least one patient died every week. It was also believed they performed euthanasia on patients who required expensive medication. Another rumour was that medicines donated by embassies were stolen and sold to private hospitals outside the prisons. I survived the night, but I'd never experienced such a fever in my entire life. Although I'd not slept much, my temperature in the morning seemed to be normal.

That morning, all the footballers, Thais and foreigners, were called to a meeting. We needed to raise at least 20 000 Thai baht to be able to purchase football uniforms for two full teams. Each player was asked to pledge a donation. Alternatively, we could collect and raise money from other prisoners. I was not happy about doing this. It was like borrowing money. One of my Taiwanese friends happily gave me 1 000 Thai baht, and in return he asked me to please make sure his name would be on the list to go to the football field on the opening day. Before I accepted, I thought it would be prudent to check with FIFA, the name of the committee that was arranging everything. I was assured it would be no problem, and so I gave my word. In prison, all you have is your word. Once you fuck somebody over, everybody gets to know about it and your reputation is ruined. The guys avoid you like the plague.

Even though I had confirmed it the day before, my friend's name was not on the list on opening day. What made things worse was that he was all dressed and ready to go. He was really pissed off with me. The chairman of the committee, a fellow foreigner, had let me down, but there was nothing I could do. It ruined my friendship and I ended up giving the guy back his donation.

With the help of the Building Chief, who was a football fanatic, enough funds were raised from the prisoners to support two teams, and the big day arrived. Many of the players had already been wearing their uniforms since the night before. Besides the 22 sportsmen who would go to Building 14, each team was allowed to take 20 spectators along. Those guys who hadn't given a donation towards the uniforms had to pay 100 Thai baht for the day's outing. This money was used to pay for the guards to escort us to the field, for the referee and also for the refreshments for the players. I found it hard to accept that the prisoners had to pay for everything, but that was just the way it was.

Most of the buildings had entered two teams in the competition. There were over 300 Nigerians in Bangkwang at that time, and most of them were keen footballers. Everyone converged on the football field. All the teams marched onto the field in single file, each building's flag held high, and lined up. It was a huge event. A podium had been erected and a microphone set up where the vice-commander of Bangkwang gave his speech. '*Awk kumlekai*' (exercise) and '*sookarpad di*' (health) were the few words I recognised. Obviously he was emphasising how important exercise was in maintaining one's health in prison. The words '*yar septic*' (drugs) also popped up here and there. I kind of chuckled to myself at the hypocrisy of it all. The prison was flooded with drugs, and it was mainly the guards who were were bringing them in! And praising the benefits of exercise and sports was all very well, but it was the prisoners who had to cough up for everything – this grand event included.

Despite the double standards, the system worked. Corruption served its purpose: the guards put money in their pockets and the prisoners enjoyed a better quality of life. Or rather, those who could afford it reaped the benefits of a corrupt system.

Sporting events such as this football tournament were a welcome distraction from the boring daily routine of prison life. It also gave us the opportunity to meet foreigners from other buildings. For the drug dealers, the tournament was an excellent opportunity to distribute their wares and to collect outstanding debts. There were numerous addicts among the foreigners, who would take drugs on credit, promising to pay when their money arrived or their families visited. These debts often ran into the thousands, resulting in their being unable to pay. To avoid being beaten or stabbed, they would secretly get their embassies to request the prison authorities to move them to another building. There were other, more desperate situations where a prisoner who owed money would stab somebody and get himself thrown into solitary confinement in order to get out of paying his debt.

The football competition turned out to be more of an eye-opener for me than anything else. In the quarter-finals there were some irregularities, with teams bribing the referee and resulting in the Building Chief withdrawing both of our teams.

Back home, in the December issue of *You* and *Huisgenoot* magazines an article had appeared about me and the circumstances surrounding my arrest. My sister Joan, who still believed wholeheartedly in my innocence, had earnestly embarked on her mission to campaign for my release. Letters were written to Amnesty International and the International Committee of the Red Cross about the inhumane conditions in Thai jails. Articles had appeared in several newspapers, not only about me, but also about a few South African women who had been arrested around the same time as me. A former Miss South Africa contestant was one of them; another had given birth in the women's prison. In late January and early February, letters from people who had read these articles started pouring in. I received more than 3 000 letters. It was unbelievable. My closest friends would huddle around in a group and help me sort and read through them. My popularity in the building shot up immediately and my status grew to that of celebrity prisoner.

In many of the letters, the majority of which were from women, there were photographs enclosed, some of them showing the letter-writer topless! A few even enclosed their underwear. I soon began to realise that some women on the outside are fascinated by prisoners. Perhaps it was that implied element of danger that was so alluring, but suddenly I was attracting women to me in hordes. A relationship by correspondence was something new for me, although many of the guys had pen pals in different parts of the world. Before prison, the only letters I ever wrote were love letters to my girlfriends. In prison, everything was different, and letters were a lifeline. Who could believe that written words had the power of evoking such intense emotions between two, or several, complete strangers? This was a whole new ball game for me, and something I was only too keen to explore. If nothing else, I decided corresponding by letter would become a pastime, a hobby.

The letters from my sister were a bit different. She would constantly remind me – it was more like nagging – to stay out of trouble and away from drugs.

The year 1995, the year I would turn 36, was a significant one for me on many levels. Not only was I learning about the people with whom I was forced to coexist, but I also discovered a lot about myself. In prison, your strengths are revealed and your weaknesses are exposed. There's no running away from yourself or deceiving yourself about who you are. Through my poetry and art, for the first time in my life I began to find purpose. One of the books I read was Nelson Mandela's *Long Walk to Freedom*. I couldn't believe how ignorant I had been about the plight of black people in my own country. Mr Mandela had sat in prison for 27 years; I had barely finished a year and I felt sorry for myself. His crime was fighting for the rights of his people; mine was that I was a drug dealer, a destroyer of lives. Reading his book was a huge inspiration for me. I thought that if anybody could relate to my unjust incarceration, it could be him. I saw Mr Mandela as my ticket to freedom. I wrote him a letter, which I had smuggled out of the prison to Joan. I urged her to publish it as an open letter in one of the South African newspapers. Nobody wanted to publish it, however. Although my conscience did trouble me regarding my claim of innocence, I justified the lie because of the ridiculous sentence I had been given: 100 years for a first offence. This was virtually unheard of in any Western democratic country. Through the assistance of a mutual family friend, my sister managed to have my letter hand-delivered to Mr Mandela.

In the letter I described the appalling conditions in Thai prisons, the outrageous and arbitrary sentences handed down to drug and other offenders, the corrupt system of using prisoners as labourers in the prison factories, the overcrowded conditions, the poor food, terrible sanitation and the unhygienic water in which prisoners had to wash themselves and their clothing. I hoped that the President would feel compassion for the plight of Africans in the same situation as I was and might intercede on our behalf with the Thai government. It was perplexing to me why a country was so bent on keeping foreigners in its prisons. I couldn't get my head around it. Perhaps it had something to do with the United Nations' provision of a daily subsidy of about 25 Thai baht for each foreign prisoner held there – we prisoners were lucky if we received one fifth of that amount. Perhaps Thailand's corrupt and strict judicial system was a way to leverage stronger political ties with certain Western countries.

Another thing that surprised me, considering all the noise the Thai government made about drugs and the country's drug problem, was that there were no official rehabilitation programmes in the prisons. Instead, there were drugs everywhere. They were so easy to get. The psychological effect on a prisoner of a life sentence in a Thai prison can be devastating, and drugs are an obvious route to dull the pain. This easy access often resulted in people who had never used drugs before turning to them, initially as a method of coping and then very soon becoming addicted. I saw this over and over again in Bangkwang.

In the general run of things, besides the annual inter-building sports events organised by the prison authorities (but paid for by the prisoners), all other recreational actives were organised by the prisoners themselves. The allocated area for these was situated just off the centre of the main yard, adjacent to the towering, ominous 4.5m wall with electrified barbed wire that divided Building 2 from Building 1.

Three of the most popular forms of exercise were football, basketball and jogging. Exercising and some form of game began as soon as we were let out of our cells at around 6.30 in the morning. There was always a game of basketball in progress, which lasted until about 8am, before it got hot. The yard and adjoining court had no covering, and the only protection against the scorching sun was the occasional stray cloud.

At 8am the Thai national anthem echoed through the many speakers strategically positioned around the building. All prisoners had to congregate in the yard for the hoisting of the flag. We foreigners refused to participate and would stay in our houses while this was going on, while some of the Thais would absent themselves by occupying a space in the communal toilet.

When I'd first arrived in prison, the prospect of using the communal toilets was so revolting to me, given the filthy state they were in and the fact that I couldn't take a shit in full view of others, meant that I didn't go to the toilet for eight days. Eventually I was on the verge of bursting. I imagined my intestines and stomach exploding and the pieces spraying in every direction. I hovered by the toilets, hoping to find a moment when there was nobody around, but no such luck. There was a constant flow of people answering nature's call. So, finally, armed with my bucket of water and plastic bowl, and consumed by a feeling of total degradation, I took occupation of one of the end toilets. This meant I had to tolerate only one person at my side rather than two – a small consolation. I had tied a bandana around my nose and mouth, as the stench was unbearable and made me want to throw up. I lowered my shorts and went into a squatting position. Nothing happened. Nothing wanted to come out.

Using both my hands, I pulled the cheeks of my buttocks apart, expecting that this would make it easier to discharge my heavy load. I could feel some movement but whatever was in there was struggling to come out. Because I'd held it in for so long, my faeces had solidified. I kept pushing with all my might, sweating and taking deep breaths with every contraction, and my anus stretched to the limit. The pain was excruciating. I imagined childbirth might feel something like this. The muscles in my calves started to ache. Leaning with one arm on the small wall on the one side to take the pressure off my legs, I was forced to use the other hand to remove the hardened mass that was now protruding from my backside but wouldn't budge any further. I felt nauseous, not only from the rancid odour, but also from the fact that I was using my hands to dislodge shit from my arse. After successfully extracting parts of my hardened stool, my bowels erupted and excrement poured out of me and, to my horror, quickly blocked the toilet, while I frantically tried to flush it down.

I couldn't believe what was happening. Suddenly, I had a severe cramp in one of my calves. Desperately, I scooped water in a crazed attempt to flush everything down. I watched helplessly as everything came up instead. By now I was ankle deep in shit and my leg was cramping painfully. I wanted to cry, it was so repulsive and humiliating, but instead I screamed 'FUCK ME, GEORGE!' and wondered what had I done that was so terrible that I deserved this.

Yes, okay, I knew exactly what I had done: the endless transgressions while I was peddling drugs; the lives I had destroyed; the hell I put my family through; not visiting my girlfriend when she was in hospital because of a car accident I had caused; years of abusing women – the list went on and on. Yes, my immorality had blurred my ability to judge right from wrong, but wasn't there *any* other way I could have redeemed myself than finding myself here, now, standing in a pool of shit? They say G-d works in mysterious ways, and this sure came home to me that day!

When you are serving a life sentence you are forced to coexist with so many people, and, with different cultures all up against each other, problems are bound to arise. I found the Asian way of life, or at least as I experienced it in prison, completely different to the Western way of life. At close quarters, sometimes Asian habits were difficult to handle – the habit of shouting across a room, of blowing your nose with your hands, of spitting. These things freaked me out to the point that I couldn't tolerate the person anywhere near me. I became so irritated with Jimmy, my Singaporean cellmate, that it resulted in me attacking another Singaporean who got too familiar with me.

When I challenged him, he said he was sorry, but, sorry or not, this was prison and he needed to be taught a lesson, so one evening I just let loose. In my experience, people don't always learn respect through dialogue; sometimes one is forced to resort to violence. Half the guys in my cell were angry with me, claiming that it hadn't been necessary for me to hit the guy. Also, fighting was forbidden and punishment was severe. You could very well end up in shackles. Luckily, on this occasion my friend Mohammed paid money to prevent action being taken against me.

Bangkwang was so corrupt that if you had it in for somebody, you could pay the guard to turn a blind eye and hire a samurai to stab that person. The Thai inmates who had double life sentences for multiple murders were mostly total psychos and they would stab you for as little as 500 Thai baht, even if the guards *hadn't* given the green light; some of the samurai were in and out of solitary confinement all the time. They were dangerous and calculating. A one-on-one confrontation was not how they operated; they either came in packs or attacked you when you were most vulnerable. A Thai will always first weigh up the odds. Losing a fight, especially against a foreigner, is a loss of face. We learnt never to underestimate them. As kids, every Thai male learns Muay Thai (kickboxing, or Thai boxing). For a young boy from a poverty-stricken background, Thai boxing is more than just a meal ticket. It's also about honour and tradition.

I quickly discovered how tough the Thai prisoners were. When playing football against them, often our shins would collide. The Thai would walk away without even flinching, while within seconds I would have a big lump and a bruise forming on my shin. From the many years of Thai boxing, their shins were as hard as steel.

In the days after the incident with Jimmy, I really was not happy in my cell. I pleaded with Ryan, who had become my friend, to allow me into the private foreign room after all, which was now referred to as Room 16, or Hong Siephok. In a situation such as this, even though it was Ryan who had organised the room, he would have to discuss a new person with his cellmates first and there would have to be a collective decision. So they had a meeting and the decision was that their room, at its current 16 occupants, was closed. Taking on an extra body would mean that each person, depending on which side of the room I would sleep, would have to give up a few centimetres of his space, and no one was willing to do that. Ryan apologised, but assured me that as soon as somebody moved out, I would be the first in line to move in. I could have kicked myself for being such a fool and not moving in when he'd approached me the first time.

From the time that we were locked up to about 9.30pm, the noise upstairs in the corridor was at ridiculous levels. Between the TVs blaring and people shouting to one other, it was impossible to take an afternoon nap or concentrate on whatever it was that you were doing.

Downstairs, where Room 16 was, it was much quieter. I desperately needed to get out of my room, but I had no choice but to wait.

In between the building that housed the prisoners and the dining hall was an open courtyard with two magnificent trees, which provided an abundance of shade. During the day, many enterprising vendors set up shop here. When you ordered perishable food from the prison grocery store, you would order by the kilogram, but, unless you had an ice cooler and got daily deliveries of ice, it was a problem to keep food fresh. So these vendors, who were all inmates, would portion up fresh beef, chicken, vegetables, etc. and sell them in grams. In other words, you could buy just enough to cook for the day. Different nationalities sold different foods. The Pakistanis, for example, were famous for their *roti* (flatbread), and sometimes they would fill these with scrambled egg and chilli, or else pour sweetened condensed milk over them, which was a nice snack for breakfast. There were a few guys who would barbecue chicken legs, chicken wings and – my favourite – chicken arses (the parson's nose) on skewers. One guy sold lemon juice with crushed ice. It was amazing how this place was a world in itself, a world that functioned completely independently from the outside. If I didn't know better, looking around this courtyard I could very well have believed I was strolling around the streets of Bangkok.

To pass the time, the foreign prisoners would read any novels that were available and doing the rounds, or play board games such as chess, backgammon, Scrabble, Monopoly and Risk.

Among the many foreigners in Bangkwang who had been sentenced to life was a Chinese guy from Hong Kong. His name was Akow and he was a paraplegic. He would manoeuvre his wheelchair from one side of the building to the other with such ease and speed that he was given the nickname 'Schumacher'. I called him 'the Cripple'. I was told that when the Cripple was arrested, he could walk. Then, while he was still in Bombat, he woke up one morning and couldn't. Anyway, my friendship with the Cripple started when he showed an interest in backgammon, a game I enjoyed and was quite skilled at. I organised our first backgammon tournament after I'd been in Bangkwang some months. Akow, who had very little knowledge of the game, wanted to enter the competition but had no money. He promised me that, if I would let him enter, he would pay when his money arrived. Many prisoners found themselves in a similar predicament, where their money from home was delayed and they were forced to borrow or have credit extended to them. The Cripple got knocked out in the first round, but he was determined to lift his game, and after that I would see him playing every day with the Thais. When his money arrived, he came to pay me the 100 Thai baht he owed. I felt bad because he had been knocked out so early and so I wouldn't accept it. From that day on, I had the Cripple's respect.

The key to maintaining one's sanity in prison was to keep one's mind occupied, but playing board games was not really my idea of passing time constructively. I had seriously considered doing a Marketing course through Unisa, but I thought that all the drugs I had done over the years had probably damaged my brain, so I dropped the idea. Art had always been my passion, but I had neglected to pursue it after high school, although I had briefly thought about getting involved in clothing design. Although my present environment was not exactly conducive to being creative, I had time on my hands. What better way to pass the time than doing what you love? I had wasted the past 16 years of my life getting high; now I was merely existing, leading a life with no purpose. Deep inside me I had an overwhelming urge to find a deeper meaning to my existence, to uncover the secret to life. Gradually, I was beginning to understand that it would be through my experiences and what I did with my time here that I would find the answers I sought.

My days started taking on some form of routine. First thing in the morning, when we were let out of our cells, I would jog around the football pitch with a group of about a dozen other regular runners. After that I would shower and get dressed. I drank a cup of coffee and would sometimes eat a couple of slices of white bread that we could buy from the bakery. I would then go find a spot, either in the classroom or the dining hall, depending on my mood, where I would write or respond to letters from my fast-growing pen-pal list or else simply just sit in the dining hall and draw.

In the beginning a few of my good friends from back home had written to me, but as time passed the numbers started to dwindle. My best friend Morris never even bothered to answer my letters, let alone write any to me himself. I could understand that people had their own lives to get on with. Furthest from their minds would be me, Shani Krebs, stuck in a Thai prison on the other side of the world. I'm sure that most of them thought I would never make it and would probably die there, so why bother staying in touch. But I was disappointed in Morris. I wrote to my sister, asking her to tell him, if and when I got out, I was going to kick his arse. Come to think of it, there would be a lot of arses I would be kicking, not just Morris's.

It's strange how grown men turn to childhood hobbies when they find themselves in a situation where they have to depend on their own resources. Stamp collecting was one of these, and it was very popular in prison. Whenever anyone received mail there would be a bunch of inmates pestering you for your stamps; some would even offer you money, while others were happy just to swap. I was receiving so many letters that I would give my stamps to people who were in a position to reciprocate with favours that would be to my advantage.

I normally took my lunch around midday, and then, around 1pm, usually in groups, we would work out at the gym. Because it was a small area and there was an insufficient quantity of weights, each group would have a set time. The weights were nothing more than empty paint cans filled with concrete. We made do with what we had, and the paint cans turned out to be pretty effective. If I wasn't training, I would do one of several things. Because I didn't really have a place of my own besides my locker at the bakery, I often took a nap on top of my locker. The guard in charge of the bakery was Officer Cumning. In the first few months after I arrived at Bangkwang, he was forever chasing us off the lockers or telling us to clean the place up. Then one day the steel bucket that I used to take water with me to the toilet, because there was always a shortage of water to flush, disappeared. On investigating I found that Officer Cumning had confiscated it. I went to his office and retrieved it without his permission. I had just got out of the shower and still had my towel around me when he approached me and angrily demanded that I give it back. I refused and tried to explain that I needed it to carry water to the toilet. Everybody had these fucking buckets; what was his fucking problem? By this time a crowd of Thais had gathered around us. The guard stepped forward and pretended to take a punch at me. I raised my fist and told him, 'Come.'

I could see some of the other foreigners sitting on the lockers watching the scene. I said to them, 'Check this guy's problem.' One of the officer's boys, who was a Thai boxing champion, a little shorter than me and smaller in build, stepped in front of Officer Cumning. Words were exchanged between the two of them, but the Thai never said a word to me. The guard threatened to open a case of insubordination against me. I told him I would open a case against him with the South African embassy. Then the guard just turned around and walked away. The crowd dispersed. Nothing else happened.

The following morning, when I got to my locker, Cumning was waiting for me. Nobody else was around yet. He said to me in English, 'Come, one by one.' I laughed to myself. I couldn't believe he was back here challenging me to a fight. Out of respect, I backed off and told him in Thai, '*Pom yom*' (I surrender). I also apologised. After that, Officer Cumning didn't bother us for a while.

That afternoon, I saw that the Thai guy who had stepped forward threateningly was out training on the field. When I walked past him he challenged me to a sparring session. I accepted and we squared up. He kicked me once or twice really hard, in the ribs and on my shoulder, but at the same time I swept his feet and he landed on his back. I jumped on his chest and with my right hand I delivered three to four blows inches away from his nose. Then I stood back, held out my hand and helped him to his feet. We shook hands and from that point on he became one of my best friends. I named him 'Mike Tyson' and he loved it.

When Ryan came to me one morning to tell me there was a place available in his room, to say I was delighted by the news would be an understatement. I accepted the offer without hesitation. No more Jimmy scratching his scabs, no more noise, and I would be only with Western foreigners. We went to the office and arranged for me to change rooms. My friend Mohammed was kind enough to lend me the 2 000 Thai baht I had to pay upfront.

Inmates were allowed to stay in the cells all day and come and go if they pleased, but this privilege would cost you 1 000 Thai baht a month. If you wanted to go into the cells an hour earlier, you could do that for 500 Thai baht. It was crazy how the guards would make money in every way possible. Posted at the door to the cell was the key-boy, who would let you in and out. It goes without saying that you would also have to keep him happy. Usually a packet of cigarettes every now and again could win you his favour. At 2pm I gave him a Pepsi so that he would let me go upstairs to fetch my bed. I can't begin to tell you how happy I was to be leaving Room 45. I hoped that I would not end up sleeping next to the old French Israeli man who had blasted me with his farts – he had been part of the first group to move to the new foreign room. At 3.30pm as usual it was lockdown. I made my way to my new cell, Room 16. The guys were very welcoming and I was given a spot near the toilet. On my right and left sides were two Nigerians. The space between our beds was about one and a half palm-widths, which was much more space than I had had in Room 45. I was struck by the irony of a white South African ending up between two black guys. One of them snored, and the other didn't use deodorant, but anything was better than Jimmy's scratching and having his scabs floating around the room.

Around July or August, news started filtering through of a possible amnesty in 1996. King Bhumibol Adulyadej would be celebrating his Golden Jubilee on 9 June. Worryingly, though, the prime minister, Chuan Leekpai, had made a speech on TV in which he recommended that drug offenders *shouldn't* be included in the upcoming amnesty. Those of us foreigners whose governments didn't have a prisoner transfer treaty with Thailand depended on sentence reductions through these amnesties.

I panicked. The Golden Jubilee would be the most auspicious occasion on the Royal Thai calendar, and it was imperative that we be included!

It was becoming quite apparent that my Israeli saviours, who had promised to get me out of prison, were not only *not* going to get me released, but had also ripped us off. I had not heard from them for over ten months, so I couldn't rely on their intervention or assistance. I would have to explore every other possible avenue, and so I took it upon myself to do whatever I could for myself and for other South Africans incarcerated in Thai jails. I had approximately ten months to achieve my goal of getting us included in the Jubilee amnesty the following year.

As a prisoner in Thailand, if you are in the court process you are not eligible to benefit from any amnesty, and 'luckily', because of my lawyer's negligence around my automatic appeal, my case had been closed. I didn't know it at the time, but her negligence would turn out to be more of a blessing than a curse.

I began by writing a letter to my sister explaining the situation, and instructing her to draft a letter to the Thai ambassador in South Africa requesting that drug offenders should not be discriminated against and asking that we be included in all future amnesties. In addition I proposed that Joan contact the families of the 12 other South Africans in Thai jails and get their support to stage a demonstration outside the Thai embassy in Pretoria.

Over the next few months I wrote several letters – to the United Nations, Amnesty International, the Pope and the King of Thailand. I also wrote over a thousand letters to people in South Africa who had responded to the articles in *You* and *Huisgenoot* magazines, urging them to write to the King of Thailand and ask for us to be pardoned. Rumours circulated that all foreigners would be pardoned and released because of the importance of the King's Jubilee, and these rumours kept our spirits up.

To my pen pals I wrote letters along these lines:

> *I desperately need to ask a great favour of you. Can you get as*
> *many people as humanly possible to please write to the King*
> *of Thailand, requesting a pardon for all fellow South Africans*

presently incarcerated in Thai prisons, on the auspicious
occasion of his fiftieth anniversary to the throne, which he
will be celebrating on the 9th June 1996. The chance of a
pardon being granted is very likely. Please realise that you'll
be playing a key role in possibly securing our release. I thank
you from the bottom of my heart for the effort you are showing
in this respect. G-d bless you, and your family.

During this time, an organisation called FOSADA (Families of South
African Detainees Abroad) was formed to support South Africans incarcerated in prisons around the world. There were over 600 South
Africans in foreign jails, the majority of whom were in South American
prisons. The organisation was headed by Pam Burgess. Families were
contacted to see if they were willing to demonstrate. None of them
showed an interest. My sister said that she would protest on her own
by pitching a tent outside the embassy, something I couldn't agree to
because she could be risking her life.

An article appeared in the *Daily News* on 16 February 1996 under
the headline 'Plight of the Prisoners':

Local officials are trying to find a solution to nationals in
foreign jails in Thailand where more than ten young South
Africans are in jail for alleged drug offences. The Thai
Government has indicated its willingness to transfer the pris-
oners to South Africa to serve part of their sentences.

It was articles such as these that kept our hopes and our cause alive.
During the Golden Jubilee celebrations, the Thai government expressed
a strong desire to all foreign countries with citizens in Thai prisons to
take their citizens home. The South African government didn't appear
to give a fuck. Their excuse was that South African jails were overcrowded, so why bring back more criminals? Fuck them, I thought.

South Africa was five to six hours behind Thailand. I was forever calculating the time, trying to work out what my family was doing at what time. I would imagine Joan dropping the kids at school, or the family gathered around the dining room table having dinner. I would go so far as to create imaginary conversations they'd be having. I missed them terribly. Thinking of all the years I'd wasted in having so little contact with them in the past saddened me deeply.

Meanwhile, back in my room, my African brothers (who, by the way, turned out to be great guys) had been moved to another building. I now secured my spot in the corner. Sleeping next to me was a youngster from England, Matthew Jones, in his early twenties. He had lived in Bangkok for a year or so. He was a good kid and shared my love of playing football. Prior to coming to prison he had never used hard drugs, but, like so many other foreigners, Matthew had fallen victim and become a heroin addict. I tried to encourage him not to use, but in vain. It killed me to see such a young soul destroying his life. Unfortunately, he had also contracted AIDS, more than likely from sleeping with prostitutes. He had served about six years when his family, with the support of the British government, managed to get him a medical royal pardon and he was released. Before he left, I told him that he now had a second chance in life. With antiretroviral medication he could live for many years and lead a normal life. I hoped that, by regaining his freedom, he would stop drugs and turn his life around.

More than half the guys in my room used heroin. I couldn't blame them and I never judged them. Prison was a place where drugs helped ease the pain and allowed the time to pass quicker. Ryan, who slept next to Matthew, always kept at least 100g up his arse, which he removed every afternoon in the cell and proceeded ritually to cut and make really huge lines to snort. He was a generous bastard and was forever inviting me to join him. Seeing how fucked-up everybody else was, though, turned me against drugs. And not only that – how could I squander on drugs the money my sister was sending me for my food? It would have been really bad karma. By 4pm all the junkies had passed out, some even falling asleep with cigarettes in their mouths. It was like watching a comedy movie.

The room was quiet – there were no TVs blaring. We had run cables from both sides of the room to the main TV, and each person had a jack he could plug his earphones into if he wanted to listen. Because all the channels were in Thai, the foreigners formed a video club. Every day each person contributed 5 Thai baht and the guy in charge would hire movies and a video machine. For those guys who had nothing else to do, watching movies was an excellent way to pass the time. Having been something of a patron of the arts, I had already seen much of what was available when I was on the outside, but some of the more popular movies I would watch again. *The Shawshank Redemption* was one of my favourites.

Having a private cell exposed you to extortion from the guards. The office clerk, who was a prisoner himself and in charge of placing prisoners in their rooms, was a dubious character, and from the beginning I didn't trust him. Every week we were required to pay him 1 000 Thai baht, which he claimed was for the Building Chief. This worked out to about 70 Thai baht per person. It was like paying rent. I talked to Ryan and told him it was fucked that we paid money to the office clerk and not directly to the prison authorities. I know 50 baht wasn't much money, but it was the principle. We were being robbed. Generally, the officers didn't accept bribes from foreign prisoners, their main concern being that we would report them to our embassies. Ryan agreed with me. He asked if I was prepared to take on the responsibility of being the room chief, and I said I was. That night it was discussed with the others in the cell and everybody agreed to my appointment. The following day, I informed the office clerk that I was now in charge of Room 16, and that from then on I would deal directly with the Building Chief regarding any payments that were to be made to the prison authorities. He was not impressed.

For the most part, receiving letters from home was every prisoner's highlight. According to my sister in one of her letters, another article had appeared in a newspaper back home, and this one was claiming that 'all South Africans in Thai jails are going to be released'.

While I was taking a shower one morning, Ryan came running from the back of the building, all excited.

'You better pack your bags,' he told me.

One of the Thais, an ex-policeman, had heard the same story on Thai radio, that all South Africans were going to be released as part of a special deal. I convinced myself that there had to be some truth to the rumour. I hoped with all my heart that it was true. I hated the place, I hated prison, I wanted nothing more than to go home. I had already wasted a year. I believed that I'd learnt my lesson and that I could now become a productive member of society. I wholeheartedly wished that the end was near.

My mom's birthday was on 3 August; it would be her second since my arrest. Whenever it was a family member's birthday I would spend hours on end looking at their photographs. In this way, I felt like I was part of the celebration on that special day. Despite all the difficult things that had gone between us over the years, I had a strong feeling that I was connecting spiritually with my mother.

The South African consular officer now only visited every eight weeks. People from the French embassy came every two weeks and they brought the French prisoners magazines and stamps. The American embassy came every month and gave their citizens vitamins, books, magazines and even Nike running shoes. I thought it was a shame that our embassy did so little for us. When I did see a South African official, and asked about the rumour regarding our possible release, I would be told that they were confident that South Africa would be signing a prisoner transfer treaty with Thailand soon. Every time they visited, the first thing I would ask them was about the treaty and every time the answer was the same.

On 6 August 1995 an article by Ramotena Mabote appeared in the South African *Sunday Times*, in its Metro section, under the headline: 'Mandela Save Me, Begs Drug Runner'. A portion of the letter I had written to President Mandela was reproduced in it.

My sister was doing an amazing job fighting for my release and keeping me visible in the media, and I had Joan to thank for this article. It lifted my spirits, revived my faith and gave me fresh hope. My story was being extensively publicised. Joan would keep me updated on everything she was doing behind the scenes, and she also sent me copies of all the articles that were published in the press. Our prime objective, of course, was to get the prisoner transfer treaty in place, which would benefit all South African prisoners, but, just as importantly, we needed to make sure that drug cases would benefit from the upcoming amnesty in 1996. Joan sent letters pleading our case to President Bill Clinton, Her Majesty Queen Elizabeth II, Archbishop Desmond Tutu, Chief Mangosuthu Buthelezi, the Chief Rabbi Cyril Harris, Tokyo Sexwale (then Gauteng premier) and the Minister of the Interior of Thailand, Banharn Silpa-archa.

For those foreigners whose countries didn't have a prisoner exchange treaty, there was another means of regaining one's freedom. This was by royal decree, which was extended to all prisoners, Thais included. You could submit a personal petition requesting a royal pardon after going through certain channels: first from the relevant prison, then to the Department of Corrections, Ministry of Justice, prime minister's office, and ultimately to the King. It was King Bhumibol himself who made the decision on royal pardons and signed off on them, resulting in either a sentence reduction or an outright pardon. In the 1980s, numerous foreign prisoners had benefited from such clemencies, but, by the 1990s, after a change of government led to a tougher stance on drug offenders, royal pardons had become less frequent.

I was told that I would have to wait at least two or three years after sentencing before I could submit such a petition. In the event that your pardon was rejected, you would have to wait two more years before you could submit another petition. This whole procedure could take anything from three years to five. Submitting a petition for a royal pardon without full support from your own government, however, was pointless. The South African government refused to submit such a letter on our behalf. All they agreed to do was guarantee our travel documents. Other Western democratic countries gave their full support to their prisoners.

Just a couple of months back I had been standing in a toilet with a noose around my neck, ready to take my own life. Now I was full of energy and hope.

My excitement was overshadowed by my nephew Darren's birthday in September and his upcoming Bar Mitzvah on 7 October, a day after my niece Keri's birthday – Jesus, it was tough not being able to celebrate with my family! The more I thought about it, the more I just wanted to get the hell out of Bangkwang. Adapting to prison life wasn't working out for me. Prison is a very dark place. One is reduced to nothing; life can easily become meaningless. Fortunately, unlike many prisoners, my family had not abandoned me, and it was only their efforts sometimes that kept me alive. If I was to get through this, I realised I would have to dig deep. My spirits were like a yo-yo: one minute I was up, the next I was down, and when that happened the vision of a different future was obscured by the towering cement walls.

Chapter 10

My Eyes Were Opening

Prison staff are classified according to rank. All staff wear military-style uniforms and the insignia on their shoulder straps, such as stars, leaves and castles, distinguish their status. At Bangkwang, the Director, who was the number one in charge of the prison, was a C10. The next in line was the Deputy Director, a C9, but also known as the 105, and he basically did the Director's dirty work. Each building had a chief (rank C8). The Building Chiefs sat in their offices most days and seemingly did nothing but dream up ways to extort money from prisoners. The office clerks, who were also prisoners, kept files on everything that went on in the building. They recorded, for example, the roll-call counts, which officers were on duty, prisoner requests, how many inmates had reported sick and needed to go to the hospital, and the arrivals and transfers of prisoners. The Building Chief's sole duty was to sign off on all these files. Beneath him was the second chief, ranked C7. He was virtually a nobody and mostly dealt with general everyday problems. These two chiefs would often be on bad terms simply because the first chief, being the number one, took all the bribes; once you had him in your pocket, there was no need to bribe the second chief.

Beneath the chiefs were the officers in charge of sections. They were ranked C6, and included the factory supervisors, the officer in charge of the actual sleeping quarters, and the officer in charge of the workers who maintained the building. Beneath them were the junior officers, C5s, C4s, C3s and C2s. These guards, or commodores, were stationed at less important posts, but were more involved in the daily running of things. They would also be the ones who smuggled illegal items in and out of the prison, such as money, electrical appliances, CDs, Walkmans and earphones, among other things. The drug dealers would use them to take money out of the prison to their visitors, at a cost of 20 per cent for their services.

Prisoners who enjoyed privileges, such as having their own private room, owning a house or running a business, were required to pay or give a gift on holidays such as Songkran, the Thai New Year, and also on our Western New Year, to the Building Chief, second chief and the officer in charge of the room. Then, depending on your relationship with certain other guards, you might give something to them voluntarily. Failure to do so could result in your sudden and immediate transfer to another building or, worse, to another prison.

Building Chiefs and second chiefs were changed regularly. After serving a term of a year or two, they would be moved either to another building or to a different prison. With every newly appointed chief, there would be a new set of rules; it was like a new government coming to power. Prisoners would drop an envelope on the chief's desk as a sort of welcoming gift, and then the whole process of paying for your privileges would start again.

Absurd as it seems, one is forced to make a life in prison, and I did the best I could. I am the type of person who loses interest if I have to keep doing the same thing for too long, so I had to keep thinking up things to change my routine. I cut my jogging time by half and for the remaining 20 minutes I started an aerobics class. Before long I had over ten members. It was a lot of fun in the beginning, and I made it really tough for the guys, but soon the novelty faded.

My first year really dragged by. All I knew was that I could not give up, and when that first anniversary came round, I would have to try not to be cynical: only another 99 years to go ... I was a survivor. I had to be. I owed it to my family. Knowing my sister was doing everything humanly possible to try to secure my early release kept me going. I remember once thinking to myself that if I had gone to prison when I was a much younger man, I might never have found myself where I was now. This was the last stop before hell. I had my highs and I had my lows, and for the most part the lows were very low. I went through a serious depression. I know it's a cliché, but I felt like a bird whose wings have been clipped. Even writing letters was beginning to bug me. I wanted to have no contact with anybody. The outside world ceased to exist.

In the many letters that I was receiving from family and friends, I had learnt of the upsurge in crime back in South Africa. I was concerned for the safety of my family. Then one day I got the dreaded news that they had been hijacked in their driveway. Thank goodness none of them was hurt. My sister played down the incident, not wanting to upset me, but I could imagine how traumatic it must have been. Joan and I were so alike; neither of us would ever complain to the other. She wanted to make my life in prison as manageable as possible. Every now and again she would send me a parcel containing luxury items such as biltong, dried fruit, nuts, rooibos tea, fish paste, vitamins and clothes. I was always hungry, so any food was welcome. Because of the extreme heat, I was forever breaking out in a rash on the inside of my thighs, so on top of my list of needs was always Canesten cream, an anti-bacterial fungal cream, which helped and soothed. I was so grateful for parcels from home and very happy when they arrived. Everything is relative, though, and on an emotional level I was drowning.

We were grateful for small wonders. My friend Ryan got a Christmas cake around Easter that was laced with hashish. There were probably about 15 foreigners who shared that cake. I ate only a small piece, but I got really high. Some of the other guys in our room really pigged out. We were all on our own mission. The mind is so powerful, independent of the body. For those few hours I could have been anywhere. When I took a walk around the building I would come across some of the other guys and we'd smile at each other and comment on how fucked we were. These may have been lighter moments, but actually prison life is fucked-up. It can make you, but in most cases it will break you. One of the things I hated most was that I had no privacy whatsoever, but at least my accommodation had improved – a small consolation where deprivation was the order of the day.

The communal toilets, which you had to flush manually, were such a freak-out. Twice a year the vaults in which the sewage was stored were emptied. These vaults were situated on the side of the building. There would come a moment when the vaults reached full capacity and the pipes leading into them would start to back up. Opposite my room downstairs was another foreign room in which most of the Nigerians stayed. Early one evening, during lockdown, shit started coming out of their toilet. The guys scrambled to move their beds, piling them on top of each other in the corner of the cell out of reach of the shit. In no time, though, most of their cell was flooded. The sewage reached the corridor and then began to flow into our cell. We piled up a bunch of wet towels along the bottom of the steel security gate to prevent the shit from flooding our room, too. Our Nigerian brothers really had it bad. They shouted, screamed and whistled through the bars at the rear of the cell, hoping to attract the guards on night duty, but to no avail. They shook their steel security gate so hard that pieces of cement dislodged around the frame. The smell was nauseating, and cockroaches came pouring through the toilets in their hundreds. Even the guys in the corridor were scrambling to avoid the floating faeces. It was disgusting. You can't believe what people had flushed down the toilets and was coming back up again. Eventually the guards appeared, wanting to know what the commotion was about. When they realised what the problem was, they went to the side of the building where the sewerage pipes were and, using a steel bar, smashed the concrete pipe that led to the vault. This at least diverted the sewage to the house outside (which happened to be my friend Mohammed's) instead of letting it flow into the cells. He was going to be in for a helluva surprise in the morning!

The vaults were sealed with a big square piece of concrete. When it was time to empty them, a crew of workers and several volunteers would dig up a section of ground in the area where vegetables were grown. They'd dig a trench about 6m long, about 1.5m deep and about the same in width. Then they would remove the concrete lid and take the shit out by means of small buckets attached to ropes. They would empty it into steel drums, which were transported by wheelbarrow to the new pit, where the shit was dumped. When they couldn't reach any further into the vault with their arms, the guys would climb in. They would be chest-high in shit. When the vault had been completely cleaned out and all the shit dumped into the pit, this would be left open for a day or two to dry. The smell would permeate the building.

Every prisoner paid 5 Thai baht to his room chief for this service; once the money had been collected it would be handed in at the office and the money shared among the shit removers, as we called them.

On 25 June 1995 the Rugby World Cup final was broadcast at 10.15pm. It was *so* exciting to watch the hosts, South Africa, winning 15-12 against the All Blacks. I remember the thrilling drop goal in extra time from Joel Stransky that sealed our victory, and I felt such mixed emotions: huge national pride and homesickness, but bitterness, too, that my government was doing nothing for us prisoners on the other side of the world.

A few months after our inter-building football tournament, there was a volleyball competition. Again, the prisoners had to pay for the net, the ball and our uniforms. Building 1 was the only building that had a tennis court, which, for the occasion was converted to a volley-ball court. One of the highlights of this kind of sports event was that we were allowed to take team and individual photographs, which we would post to our families. Needless to say, the photos weren't free; they cost 20 Thai baht per picture.

A contact visit was coming up on 16 December, and my family wanted to come over. I wanted desperately to see them, but for two reasons I talked them out of coming. An Australian prisoner had a sister who came over to visit him quite regularly. On her previous visit she had met up with some people who claimed to be connected to the Thai government. These people had promised her that, with the right amount of money, they could get her brother out. I think she paid them about US$80 000. The Australian had confided in me and told me that there was a chance he would be getting out of prison. I'd even met his sister in the foreign visit room once – a very snice girl, and a brave one, I thought. Then we heard that she had been found dead in her Bangkok hotel room. The cause of death was a heroin overdose. This was a complete bullshit story. The girl had never in her life even smoked a cigarette, never mind used drugs.

There were many cases of foreign tourists being murdered in Thailand or simply just disappearing. I feared for my sister's life. This was the first reason I didn't want my family to come for the December contact visit. In my letters I told Joan that under no circumstances should she come to Thailand, as there was no guarantee of her safety. The sentence for murder in Thailand is less severe than for being caught with drugs and life was cheap. The second reason I told them not to come was because I saw it as a waste of money. The money a ticket would cost would be better put towards my allowance. Reluctantly, Joan and Malcolm agreed with me and they decided not to travel to Thailand.

We were allowed to withdraw only 200 Thai baht per day from our prison account, at a cost of 10 per cent. If you wanted to withdraw a larger amount, you would lose 20 per cent. This went to the owner of the coffee shop, who was also a prisoner. When you consider that there were 900 prisoners in each building, this worked out to a substantial profit. To afford the privilege of running the coffee shop, the owner had to prepare two meals a day for all the guards. Instead of losing the 20 per cent, I arranged with the consular officer to buy me cartons of cigarettes and stamps. Stamps were an excellent form of currency, especially among those prisoners who didn't have regular visits.

I had been in prison for only a year and a half when I learnt of the tragic death of a fellow Arcadian, Mandy, who had been like a sister to me. As a kid, she was the most vivacious and beautiful girl. Mandy had contracted AIDS. I felt really sorry for her, and when I arranged to smuggle the drugs from Thailand, in my mind I had intended for part of the money I was going to make to go towards helping her obtain antiretrovirals. Now she was dead. It pained me deeply, especially being so far away from home.

By the end of 1995, I was completely clean of drugs. Because of my history of addiction, I could sense my sister's concern in the letters she wrote me. She was so afraid that I would fall into my old ways, as drugs were in such abundance in prison. I wrote to her and tried to put her mind at rest:

> *Regarding the money you send me every month, please, Joan, never for one minute think that I am squandering it. I feel bad enough that you are supporting me, never mind still wasting it on something that would be detrimental to my health. I am one hundred per cent clean. I'm very much into my sport and through keeping fit my mind is expanding. I wasted enough years on abusing my body. I even stopped smoking cigarettes on the 13th November 1995. The fitter I become, the more my body is rejecting these foreign substances. Please rest assured, there is no concern for alarm. I'm also keeping out of trouble, understanding how important it is to have a clean record. I cannot afford to do anything irresponsible that would jeopardise my chances of regaining my freedom, nothing is more important.*

What I didn't tell her in this letter was how much I wanted to make my family proud. I had been such a disappointment to them over the years. Now I had a chance to prove that I could be somebody of worth.

There were three of us Jewish guys in Building 2. One was an American journalist who claimed to be investigating the smuggling of drugs out of Thailand for a story and in the process got lumbered with one or two kilos himself. He swore he was innocent. It was a laugh! All convicted felons will tell you they're innocent, although I must say there were a few I met in prison to whom I gave the benefit of the doubt. The other Jew was a Frenchman, and then there were another three Israelis in Building 1, two of whom were on death row after being caught escaping from a prison in Chiang Rai, up in the north of Thailand. The other guy was serving a life sentence. The three of us in Building 2 stuck together and would help each other wherever possible. I actually started learning French, and had two lessons twice a week for an hour. It cost me a carton of cigarettes a month. In the beginning I was quite excited to be learning a new language, although it would probably have been a smarter move to learn Thai. I had set my heart against learning Thai, though, because I was so filled with anger and hatred towards the country that openly violated human rights. I did not want to learn their language. After about three months, my French homework would run into hours and it drained me of so much energy that I found less time to do my art, so I didn't carry on with the lessons for very much longer.

A foreign prison with such a diversity of cultures was the last place I expected to encounter open anti-Semitism. We foreigners were a minority. It didn't matter what religion we were; it was important that we stood united. One day we were standing around and I was chatting to my fellow-Jewish journalist friend, when out of the blue I heard a comment being passed by this German guy to an American. I heard him say something along the lines of that Hitler should have killed all the fucking Jews. At first I thought my ears were playing tricks on me. The journalist and I looked at each other at the same time. We were both shocked. It was quite apparent that the German's statement was directed at us. Immediately my blood pressure shot up. Pointing my finger in the German's face, I blurted out, 'Motherfucker? Careful what you say, or you might find yourself being fucked in the arse. You're forgetting where you are.' The guy went pale. 'Now fuck off,' I said.

Like a little fucking sheep he slipped away and we never said another word to each other. Whenever our paths crossed he would avoid me and walk in the opposite direction.

There were many altercations among the foreigners in Bangkwang and I was learning very quickly that prison friendships were mainly about convenience. If you were of no benefit to me, you weren't worthy of being my friend, and vice versa.

I recall a year earlier, when I was still in Room 45, the day a new prisoner arrived, another American. He was a very laid-back hippie-surfer type of guy, and we became friends. New prisoners often had no money when they arrived, and it was difficult for them to survive. The prison food was barely edible, so, in a way, it was expected that another foreigner would help. One thing I admired about the Nigerians was that they always helped out a fellow African brother. Anyway, I took it upon myself to take care of this guy and I shared with him as much as I could from the parcels I received from home. I stood guarantee with my Chinese chef, Lenny, for his one meal a day. We spent a lot of time chatting about our pasts. I even played chess with him, which was unusual for me; although I was a reasonable contender, I hated the game. It was too slow and my so-called new friend really took his time making his moves. The point is that I valued the friendship and so I made compromises. In the evenings in the corridor outside our cell, every night during the week there was gambling. The Chinese played Mah Jong, the game of a thousand intelligences; the Thais played either Hi/Low, a game in which three dice were used, or the popular card game called Bokkowe (19), which is similar to Black Jack 21. Big money exchanged hands. A prisoner, a Big Leg, was the casino boss. He was the banker and made sure the guards got their share. At the end of the day money circulated among the gamblers, but ultimately the guards were the only winners – for every day the casino was open, they took a percentage. If you wanted to go outside your cell to gamble, you could do that, but it would cost you 100 Thai baht for the evening and you would take your bed into the corridor and only return in the morning when the cells were opened.

I had a Taiwanese friend called Bow, who slept downstairs. He was a professional gambler. In order for him to be able to come upstairs for the night, he would have to be able to find somebody to go downstairs or else there would be a discrepancy in body counts on the roll-call register. Normally when he and a friend came upstairs to gamble, the American and I would go downstairs for the night. The guards did a body count, so it never made a difference on the roll-call register, as long as the numbers corresponded. We would stay in their small private cell that had six occupants. It was like an evening out. We would score some hashish and watch American movies on video. I paid for the new American guy's drugs on the understanding that when his money arrived, he would cover half the cost.

The hashish was ridiculously expensive. Five hundred Thai baht got you a little less than a button-size worth. I couldn't afford it, and anyway all it did was give me a headache and a sore throat. We would smoke it through an empty Coke can. About two months into our friendship, the American's money arrived. If it had been me, the first thing I would have done was settle my debts. Instead, the American stopped speaking to me; it was like I never existed! What the fuck? He owed me money! It was obvious he had been using me. I discovered that it was not the first time he had been in prison either. For a while I left it to see how things would play out, but I'm not the type of person who can keep my mouth shut for too long. After a day or two of suppressing my anger, I caught up with him at his locker by the bakery – a locker which, incidentally, I had organised for him. If and when I'm going to fight, I don't like to get into a verbal confrontation; I'm the first to attack. When I asked him about his debt, he looked at me with this blank stare as if he had no idea what I was talking about. With my wrist twisted in an upright position, I attempted to hit him with an open-palm blow, which can be quite devastating if executed properly. Unfortunately, he was sharper than I gave him credit for and had anticipated the attack. He stepped back, causing me to miss, and simultaneously threw a punch at my jaw. I dodged the punch by millimetres. One of my Chinese friends grabbed me, with both arms enclosing my body, lifted me up in the air and moved me away, preventing the argument from escalating into a serious altercation. I wasn't happy.

'Motherfucker!' I yelled. 'I want my money by tomorrow or I will FUCK YOU UP.'

I wrestled myself free of the Chinaman's grip and, in my highly agitated state, put my foot through the wooden door of the American's locker, leaving a hole in it. Shit, that was not a smart move. In the end I had to pay for the damn thing.

The next day the American gave me my money. It was all rolled up in a bundle. I took it and, being a gentleman, I thanked him and walked away without checking it first. When I counted it, I found that the motherfucker had short-changed me by 30 Thai baht, but I let it go.

I should have known better by then. Everybody was out for themselves only.

Prison gave me the opportunity to change, to better myself as a person. Although different rules apply in prison, our principles shouldn't change. The way we behave on the outside shouldn't be any different from the way we behave inside. Prison is a place where your character is quickly revealed. From then on, I was very selective about who I socialised with. Friends were nothing but a headache. I found myself spending more and more time on my own.

After almost two years in prison, my physical transformation was dramatic. Since my initial arrest, in April 1994, I had lost over 15kg. I was fit and drug-free, but my mind was still not in sync with my body. I was still angry, and my moods changed from day to day. Having grown up in a violent society, my aggression wasn't that easy to suppress, which meant that many of the foreigners disliked or avoided me. They could see I was different. I didn't take shit from anybody. I felt like I was a misfit in a world of misfits.

However, prison is a place where having alliances can save your life, so I selected a few guys to be friends with. I was always watchful, however. My closest ally was my Iranian friend Mohammed. He was exceedingly enterprising and very helpful to me. There was another guy, a youngster maybe ten years my junior, who was from Afghanistan. His name was Ahmed and, like Mohammed, he was also a Muslim. Ahmed became like a brother to me. Among the Nigerians I had many friends and we enjoyed a mutual respect. This comprised our gang, you could say. I also enjoyed the respect of many Thais, Chinese, Nepalese and Burmese.

With the Western foreigners, it was another story. Many of these guys had little or no support from their families, and so they became dependent on others. They were like bums. They never paid their debts and most of them resorted to using drugs. There were forever problems among them. I remember one morning a fight broke out between two

Americans. It was a complete mismatch. One of them was a junkie, white trash (as his fellow countrymen referred to him), and the other guy was a six-foot African American basketball player. Needless to say, the African American beat the shit out of the white trash junkie.

Fighting in prison is strictly prohibited, but, for some reason, when foreigners fought, the authorities turned a blind eye. This had its advantages, but it also set the tone for a dangerous environment. Foreigners would be less patient with each other because they didn't expect reprisals from the prison authorities if they got into it.

M

I have always loved ice cream. It was one of the things I missed most in those early years of my incarceration, especially when it was so hot all the time. When I was moved from Bombat to Klong Prem, they sold ice cream on Saturdays. At least, I thought it was ice cream. I bought a scoop but it turned out to be sorbet – not at all what I was anticipating. I couldn't eat any more, or in fact eat it again. Then, when I was in Bangkwang, there came a time when the prison coffee shop stocked up with Cornetto ice cream. That first time, Mohammed and I were sitting on the lawn. It was around 2.30pm and we were lazing in the shade of a row of trees that ran along the walls. Mohammed bought himself one Cornetto and I bought three! After sharing my love for ice cream with him, he offered to buy me as many as I could eat. We had one of his *luknong*s (boys) running up and down bringing us three Cornettos at a time. I ended up eating 19.

M

I remember an incident that happened once when a new foreigner came to our building from Building 1. He was a Nigerian, an Igbo, and he had been arrested a good five years before me. He was a stocky guy, very dark in complexion, and with a rough skin. He had what we called a typical prison build, i.e. huge arms and chest and no legs – in other words, a strong motherfucker. His name was Okakwu, Okky for short, and he had a reputation for being short-tempered. One day Okky approached me, wanting to swap stamps. I explained to him that I was not a collector and that I had these regular guys I was already giving my stamps to. To my complete surprise, Okky became belligerent. I wasn't sure how to react. I was not about to get into an argument over stamps! In the end I just walked away, but, after that, whenever our paths crossed he would give me dirty looks. I had the sense to ignore him, but the tension was there.

The extreme heat in Bangkok was something I never could get used to, along with the heat rashes I was prone to (as were many of the other prisoners). The rashes were as itchy as hell. Skin diseases spread like wildfire in prison. I was very conscious of my personal hygiene, and so I generally avoided physical contact as much as it was possible in the overcrowded conditions. When somebody got the flu, the whole cell would catch it and then it would spread throughout the building. As a rule, I would wear my cloth surgical mask from the time I entered my cell until I went to sleep. There was a very high incidence of tuberculosis among the prisoners as well, and we were constantly at risk of infection.

By the end of 1995 already I had started sketching with a Bic pen. Most of my drawings were done in black, symbolic of my oppression and suffering. I found myself a place in the dining room where I would spend hours on end every morning, drawing. There were two entrances to the dining area, which was an open-air structure enclosed by fencing, making it relatively cool. The steel-frame tables were topped with narrow wooden beams at half-inch intervals. They were about 5m long, with attached benches to sit on, and they were very heavy. One table could seat up to 30 people. There were 14 tables in the dining room. In the morning, first thing when we were let out of our cells, I would fetch my pillow, which I had had made for me at the towel factory, and take it to the dining room, placing it on the bench where I sat, next to the fence that bordered on the side of the yard where the guys jogged and played football. It was the spot that offered the most light. I had to do this in order to reserve my place, as after 8am the dining room would fill up with people who either ate or wrote letters or slept there on the benches. Exactly above where I sat was a ceiling fan, which provided a bit of extra breeze. The tables were always dirty, so I would always wipe down the surface where I sat.

Thais are inquisitive by nature and they are also culturally quite advanced. In prison there was no privacy; people were forever watching me, especially when I was painting or drawing. At intervals, small groups of Thais would form around me and watch me work. Some would pass comments, such as *'Dee muk'* (very good) or *'Fee mer'* (excellent). At first, I was so self-conscious that it irritated me, to the extent that I struggled to concentrate on my drawing. I would look up angrily and cover my drawing with my hand. I wished everybody would just fuck off and mind their own business. 'What the fuck are you looking at?' I would say morosely, and then I would get some dirty stares in return before they dispersed.

Some of the Thais who ended up in Bangkwang came from the mountains, and many had never seen a foreigner before, so they would often sit and stare blankly at me for what seemed like forever. To overcome my discomfort, I would sometimes imagine that I was the leading actor in a movie and that all the people watching me were part of a film crew. I had a role to play, which I learnt to play exceedingly well, and with time I grew to feel less uncomfortable being watched.

I wrote to my sister about it:

> *It is so hard to draw in this heat as the sweat is running down my face; I have to be so careful not to smudge the picture – that is why my drawings are so unique. Nobody can imagine the conditions I have to work under. Sometimes I have to fight for my place in the dining hall where I sit. People are lying all over the benches and sleeping. There is a crazy psychopath sitting near me talking aloud to himself for hours on end. I feel like bashing his head in. Sitting and facing me is an old man who has TB and does not stop coughing. Man, it*

is like a lunatic asylum here. You think you have problems, I have people leaning over my shoulder staring at me drawing, on my side and in front of me. You would think that they have never seen a foreigner drawing. It is quite an education and if nothing else I'm certainly learning to be patient.

With time, I became more comfortable, realising that the Thais who crowded round every day to watch me draw actually appreciated art. In fact, their admiration for my work became inspiring to me. By now I was painting portraits for friends in different parts of the world, who, in return, were sending me art supplies.

It came to me one night in a vision that, before I would be emancipated, I would go through three levels of evolution: artistically, spiritually and as a person. I knew I had to change. I needed to redeem myself. In my mind there was still too much turmoil, however, that needed to be quieted. The battle raged on inside me.

Besides electrical appliances, money and things that were illegal, we could receive almost anything in the parcels our friends and relatives sent us. For medicines, though, you had to have a prescription. In the event that your family *did* send money, the officer in charge would automatically deposit it in your account. For a prisoner to have cash on him was strictly illegal. One of my friends had sent me a *siddur*, a Jewish prayer book. There were many reasons why I should have been praying. G-d was working miracles all around me, but I was not yet paying close attention. Although I was becoming aware that coming to prison was for my own benefit, I wasn't yet ready to admit it. Instead I clung stubbornly to the belief that a terrible injustice had befallen me. Having convinced my family about my innocence, I started to believe it was true. In my heart I was grateful and gradually I could feel my anger beginning to subside, but I was yet to open that prayer book and pray. In my heart I remained distant from G-d and it would still be a while before I found my way back to him.

My sister Joan had a friend, Edna Ralph, who lived in Manchester in England and was affiliated with Chabad House. She had heard of my plight and, feeling compassion for my situation, initiated contact with me. Edna was deeply spiritual and she started sending me books on Judaism. In her letters she encouraged me to study and read as much as I could. I can honestly say that this was the beginning of my spiritual journey and of my renewed faith in G-d. Edna would walk around Manchester and collect money for 'Eleazer' (my Hebrew name), her new prisoner friend in Bangkok. She sent me £100 every month, and I have to say that the extra funds were a tremendous help and went a long way towards improving my standard of living. I also managed to purchase a lot more art supplies as a result. I was so grateful to her.

One year, the Chabad rabbi deposited 3000 Thai baht into all the Jewish guys' prison accounts for Purim, the Jewish festival in which it is customary to give 'shalach manot' (little parcels of food and fruit) and charity. The money was donated by an affluent Persian Jew who lived in Bangkok. The Israeli prisoners were visited every month by the rabbi, who represented the Israeli embassy. He would bring punnets of kosher food. Although I was not called for these visits, because I was not an Israeli, Rabbi Nechemya always brought an equal portion for me.

In Jewish tradition, it is forbidden to have your body marked. If you are tattooed, you cannot be buried in a Jewish cemetery when you die. I did know this, and part of me was reluctant to defy the tradition, but I did it all the same. For some, a tattoo might symbolise something important; for others, it might be an act of rebellion or merely to be fashionable, part of a trend. I had my first tattoo done when I was in the army, on that infamous New Year's holiday in Cape Town with Gerry, Sam and Mark, when we went to Adams in Woodstock. Mine was an eagle, representing freedom. My second tattoo I had done in Bangkok a few days before I was arrested. I chose a snake with the head of a cobra and the tail of a rattlesnake, implying double danger.

Tattoos are very much part of prison culture, and for the most part are not merely decorative. In prison, tattoos indicate gang membership, and particular tattoos serve to align members of particular gangs.

When I first got to prison, I was surprised to see so many guys with tattoos; some had their entire bodies covered. One very popular symbol was the Thai dragon, which represents supernatural power or some form of magic. Dragons are also associated with wisdom and longevity. The dragon is a central feature of Thai art and literature, and its mythology draws on Indian, Chinese and Japanese legends. Thailand shares a cultural and historical heritage with neighbouring Laos and Cambodia. You will find statues of dragons all over Thailand, particularly outside temples, where they are symbols of protection. In prison, the Thai dragon is associated with the warrior, the way of the samurai. The Thai mafia, or Bad Boys, as we referred to them, had huge dragon tattoos on their backs.

If I was about to spend the rest of my life in prison, I decided that my body ink would become symbolic of my journey: I would have a tattoo done every year until the day of my release. Good tattoo artists, however, were hard to come by, and invariably these artists were one of the Bad Boys. These guys were forever fighting or stabbing each other, resulting in their being sent to solitary confinement, being moved from one building to another, and even being transferred to other prisons.

My very first tattoo in prison was a Thai dragon, which I had done on my left arm in the traditional method, whereby the artist uses a piece of bamboo to which five thin needles are attached. The way these guys work is quite incredible – I had to admire their talent.

Tattooing in prison is strictly forbidden, but on Saturdays and Sundays things were generally more relaxed. Outside guards were on duty over weekends. They were not familiar with the prisoners, so they were either sleeping, watching TV or getting a massage. As long as you were out of sight of the guards, you could usually get away with risking it. In the event that the guards happened to stumble on you while you were being tattooed, they would confiscate the ink and bamboo stick. The tattoo artists normally used ink from a regular pen, which contains lead and can cause skin infections. However, I managed to organise proper tattoo ink and made sure that, when it was my turn, the needles were cleaned with pure alcohol. One couldn't be too careful, with so many of the prisoners having AIDS.

Prison regulations required all prisoners to have short hair, army style. Every building at Bangkwang had at least three barber shops where haircuts were given by prisoners, largely inexperienced guys and not very skilled. In Thai culture, having a haircut is something of a ritual. After having your hair cropped with electric clippers and a switchblade, your ears would then be cleaned. To do this, the barber takes a long thin feather and inserts it deep into your ear. The session ends with a facial massage. In my first two years in Bangkwang I was fortunate to have a hair stylist who had won some international hairdressing competition. I say 'fortunate' because he knew his trade, so that was the upside. On the downside, he was serving time for murder, after apparently running a pair of scissors into a client's throat while cutting the man's hair.

Before I knew about his crime, I would go to him for a trim and a shave. The guy was so popular that guards from other buildings would also come to him. When I learnt what he had done to earn his place in Bangkwang, I never again went near him, or any other barber, for that matter. From then on, I cut my hair myself when I wanted to.

Those of us foreigners who liked to wear our hair long refused to have haircuts. We would argue and say it was for religious purposes, and eventually the guards gave up and allowed us to grow our hair. Before going to prison I'd never grown a beard. I didn't like facial hair. In prison, it really didn't matter what you looked like, and altering your appearance could prove to be interesting. Although a beard never actually suited me, I did get a sense of comfort knowing that if ever I escaped I could simply change my identity by growing facial hair.

Now and again, but admittedly not very often, a prisoner would become eligible for parole after serving his full sentence. Some of these guys had a better life in prison than they did outside, and by the time they were due for release they had become completely institutionalised.

In order to avoid going home, they sometimes resorted to committing murder. I certainly didn't want to be one of their random victims, and avoiding the barber shops was a start.

Chapter 11

`King of the Pen´

By the middle of 1995 my family and I had started working on all the complicated documentation that was needed to apply for a royal pardon. In addition to your application you need letters of support from a high-ranking government official, affidavits from, for example, family, previous employers and friends, as well as a police clearance certificate. You also have to produce all your court papers. Each of these documents has to be translated into Royal Thai. Once everything is in order, three copies have to be made of everything. It is advisable to place each set in a hardbound folder. Then you have to hand them to your embassy, which undertakes to forward the copies to the Thai Ministry of Foreign Affairs under a diplomatic note. From there the petition will be passed on to the Department of Corrections, who checks the details and case history (prisoner class, health, etc.) with the relevant prison. Once the prison authorities have gathered the necessary information, the petition is sent back to the Department of Corrections for recommendation. Only if the petition is approved will it be passed on to the Minister of the Interior for further consideration. The Minister of the Interior then passes it on either to the Prime Minister's office or straight to the Privy Council, who will present the pardon before His Majesty the King's Principal Private Secretary.

This whole long, tedious procedure can be drawn out over years and years, and I'd heard of cases in which pardons were misplaced or lost between departments. Another problem was that if your sentence was reduced as a result of an amnesty, your pardon application had to be returned to the prison in order for your sentence to be adjusted to the new one, and the whole procedure started all over again. Applying for a royal pardon is a serious business, and you really need to involve your embassy and have their support if you hope to succeed. I was advised by other prisoners to rather wait a few years before submitting one, as the chances of having it rejected were high. I was in no rush, but still I believed we needed to get the ball rolling.

By the beginning of 1996 our cell was down to 13 occupants, while in the Thai cells occupancy dropped from around 26 to 21. Many Thais had been transferred to prisons in other provinces, closer to their home towns. With the upcoming amnesty in the King's Jubilee year, it was estimated that 70 000 prisoners were going to be released. This would alleviate the overcrowding to a degree, but it would only be temporary, as new prisoners continued to arrive on a daily basis. We were still not sure if drug cases were going to be included in the amnesty, but there was no shortage of conflicting news and rumours.

On Saturday, 10 February 1996, at 7pm a Thai radio station reported that Thailand wanted to send all foreigners back to their countries as free people, and that they planned to review sentences on a case-by-case basis, either individually or as groups per country. They added that manufacturers of drugs and major offenders would not be included. I was sure I fell into the latter category. The South African embassy confirmed that the Thai government wanted to send us back to our country to serve our sentences in jails there, and they promised that they would do everything in their power to get us home. Empty promises, I thought. There was no doubt in my mind that this was bullshit.

The inter-building football tournament had been held the previous month (January). It was my second since I'd been in Bangkwang, but I could not afford to donate any money, so I volunteered to try and organise uniforms from South Africa. Each team consisted of ten players, one goalkeeper and eleven reserves, making a total of 22 players. I didn't have much time to organise the uniforms, so I quickly drafted a letter to my sister, which one of the guards smuggled out of the prison for me – for a fee, of course – and sent by registered mail. A few weeks later I received a letter from home. One of my friends, Gerald, had stepped forward and bought the uniforms. Joan had already posted them. I couldn't wait to give the guys the good news. Everybody was so excited. Because of my love of football and my support for Premier League champions Manchester United, some of the foreigners, especially the Nigerians, had given me the nickname 'Man U', and my sister was referred to as 'Manchester's sister'.

The B team, which I played for, consisted mainly of Thais. Considering that most of my team-mates were murderers, I felt it appropriate to name our team 'Manslaughter United'. I immersed myself in the business of organising, training and coaching. Here I was, after so many years of addiction and abusing my body, including two seizures in which I had almost lost my life, playing football again – quite an achievement, I thought, considering that certain doctors had told me I would walk with a limp and never play contact sport again.

With a day to go before the opening ceremony, the parcel containing our kit arrived and I breathed a sigh of relief. Gerald had chosen the design of the Kaizer Chiefs' uniform. We were ecstatic.

In the same month as our football tournament, my mother took a trip to Budapest with the aim of appealing to the Hungarian government to intervene in my case. Even though I was a South African citizen, both my parents were Hungarian. You would think the government might have done something to help, but they weren't interested. When they heard I had been arrested for drug trafficking, they wanted nothing to do with me.

Another article about me appeared in *You* magazine, and once again the letters poured in. South African readers were so kind and compassionate, and many of them offered me whatever assistance they could, whether this was money or parcels containing food items. I never accepted any of these offers; I was not comfortable taking help from strangers. One of my prison mates suggested that I ask each person for a donation of US$10. If you multiplied that amount by the thousands of letters I received, I could have become quite a rich prisoner!

I replied to as many correspondents as I could, but after a while this became impractical; I simply could not afford the postage. Instead I used a writing pad with very light, thin paper, and wrote a single page for each person. I would place 20 pages, with the individual's address written in the top right-hand corner, in one envelope, and post this to my sister. Joan would then put each page into an individual envelope and post the letters for me.

I asked each recipient to petition the King of Thailand to include drug cases in the upcoming amnesty. One of the guards started withholding my letters and sending them to the Department of Corrections for censorship. When I got wind of this, I got the South African embassy involved and eventually the letters were returned to me.

Early in 1996 I had a surprise visit from a childhood friend, Colin, who was one of our crew while we were at Arcadia. Colin now lived in Miami. I was touched that he came to visit, and we reminisced about the antics we got up to as teenagers. Colin was one of the group who had bunked out the night we went exploring the construction site of the Johannesburg General Hospital, and the kid who had succeeded in breaking the lock on the three-wheeler bicycle chain.

It's difficult to describe my head space at this time. By constantly striving to convince my sister in my letters that I was okay, it became a form of self-assurance. I mean, how could I be okay? I was depressed, there was no guarantee that we would be included in the amnesty, and we were also thinking about embarking on a hunger strike to draw attention to our cause. Chances were that if we followed through on this threat, we might incur permanent damage to our brains. Not that I had much brain power left – the drugs had probably destroyed most of my brain cells.

Some days I was hopeful and full of energy. On others my future looked bleak. Using drugs again was a real temptation, yet an inner voice tugged at my conscience. I badly needed to prove – not only to my family, but more importantly to myself – that I was a person worthy of more than what drugs had reduced me to. What had happened to my dreams of doing more with my art, perhaps of becoming an art teacher? Where was my dignity? I had only one path to choose, and this was to survive at all costs and become a man people could still respect and maybe even emulate. It was a tall order, but I did have a head start: my morals and principles were still intact, while my faith was in the process of being reawakened. I was street-smart, prison was now my university, and time was on my side. I had plenty of time, but I realised that I couldn't afford to waste a moment.

So much for having one tattoo done a year. By my second year in prison, I already had six. For me they were the physical scars representing the ones you couldn't see, the scars of my own internal war, which continued to rage deep inside me. This deep anger could not be quelled just by yearning for my freedom.

On 15 March 1996, the Singaporean government executed five Thai nationals who had been on death row in prison, even after the Thai government had tried to intervene. This only caused more conflicting rumours to spread. By the beginning of May, only a month before the King could claim to be the longest-reigning monarch in modern history, the rumours were still circulating, some claiming that drug cases were definitely going to be excluded from the forthcoming amnesty, and others that all foreigners would be pardoned and sent home. Many foreign prisoners believed we would be going home; some were even foolish enough to pack their bags in anticipation. I hoped with all my heart that it was true, and secretly I prayed. Whether G-d was listening to my prayers or not, I could not tell, but I was knocking on Heaven's door. Our Father, G-d of Abraham, Isaac and Jacob, let Your light shine upon me, forgive my sins, and set me free ...

The days leading up to the amnesty dragged. I couldn't sleep and the general atmosphere was morbid. Our fate was in the hands of a government that violated a man's right to be a man. The pressure became too much for me and I got really sick. I had diarrhoea for five days.

Initially, I thought this had been caused by eating a rotten egg, but I knew it was really my nerves. I lost a lot of weight but there was no point in going to hospital. In the end one of my Chinese friends gave me some herbal medicine, which cured me.

Meanwhile we heard that Burma and Laos were busy negotiating the exchange of prisoners to celebrate the King's Jubilee, and that Malaysia, on the request of the Thai prime minister, Banharn Silpa-archa, had released 44 Thai prisoners. It was very dispiriting. The South African government seemed not to care about its citizens. Around this time, the deputy director of the Department of Correctional Services in South Africa visited Thailand. Although he only visited the women's prison, he stated publicly that he was appalled by the conditions he saw there and vowed personally to get involved and to try to get us home. This gave us hope once more. All the signs pointed to the likelihood that foreigners would be repatriated. So we sat tight, held our breath and awaited the announcement.

On 5 June 1996, at 10.55am, our Building Chief read out the terms of the amnesty. To our delight, drug cases *were* included in the amnesty and my sentence of 100 years was reduced to 40. Those foreigners who were expecting to go home, however, were terribly disappointed. For them this was an anticlimax, and especially so for those prisoners whose governments were already signatories to a prisoner transfer treaty. To me, however, it was a huge victory, nothing short of a miracle. My family and I had fought tirelessly for this, and I had written thousands of petitions. I had served a little over two years and already my sentence was down to 40. Wow – maybe there was hope after all!

After my sentence reduction, my life took on a whole new meaning. I kept my eyes on the flicker of light I saw at the end of the dark tunnel. Perhaps it wasn't impossible that I might get out after ten years.

Back home, my sister was not so optimistic. To her, 40 years was still a life sentence. She had already had one nervous breakdown. She felt guilty about everything. She was uncomfortable sleeping in her bed while I slept on the floor; she felt terrible eating three meals a day while I had only one. She would break down and cry at the mere mention of my name. Knowing all this broke my heart, but I also needed Joan to be strong. In so many ways, my life was in her hands. If she fell apart, I would be fucked. I depended on her support both emotionally and financially. I believed in a tough approach. Joan had to pull herself together. I bombarded her with mail, hoping that the instructions in my letters would act as a distraction from her sitting around and moping, but I understood that it couldn't have been an easy balance for her to maintain: she worked, she was the mother of two young children who needed her, and she was a wife. Like our own mother, Joan had never employed domestic workers and this compounded her problems, as she also had to take care of everything in her home, from parenting to cleaning. I had to admire her sheer grit and tenacity; without her love and support, I might very well have resorted to drugs again and got involved in all sorts of shit. I was grateful for Joan every day.

Our next step was to move our petition for a royal pardon along. In addition, we had to keep putting pressure on the South African government to sign a prisoner transfer treaty with Thailand.

South African embassy staff usually serve a four-year term, after which they are reassigned either to another country or sent back to South Africa. One day I received a letter from my sister telling me that our ambassador to Thailand wanted the South African prisoners to remain in prison there. He was of the opinion that we deserved what we got. I was devastated by this news, and when the consular officer next visited to introduce his replacement, I couldn't keep my mouth shut. I remember saying, 'Who the hell does he think he is?' and 'Is he voicing his own opinion, or is he speaking on behalf of the South African government?' The consular officer was shocked by my outburst. Five days later, the ambassador himself came to say farewell. He seemed nervous and anxious, and avoided the topic until I confronted him. I asked him whether it was true what I had heard, that he thought we should stay in prison in Thailand and not come home to serve out our sentences in South Africa. He denied saying anything of the sort, emphasising that in fact it was he who had initiated the talks towards a treaty with Thailand. He promised that he would continue fighting for us once he was back in South Africa, as he would still fall under the East Asian section and would continue to be directly involved in the negotiations. I apologised and pretended to be relieved, but I didn't believe him. It was becoming more and more apparent to me that our government couldn't have cared less about us prisoners. I felt ashamed to be a South African. Almost every Western democratic country but mine appeared to be going to great lengths to ensure the wellbeing of their citizens in Thai jails and to arrange for their repatriation. Well, I was definitely not about to give up, and neither was my family. As far as we were concerned, the battle was on.

The new consular officer was not very friendly. She was an Afrikaner woman from Pretoria. On her next visit she didn't bring the stamps and cigarettes I had requested, and, although she did seem apologetic, I knew she just hadn't bothered. For 100 Thai baht you got 90 baht worth of stamps. Initially, when I began writing letters, I also tried to purchase fancy and colourful stamps, covering the entire envelope with them and making it look really attractive. But then I encountered a problem. For some reason my letters were not reaching their destinations. I couldn't understand why they were going missing. All letters, incoming and outgoing, were recorded in a register by the prison authorities. I also kept my own records, which corresponded to theirs, so I knew something was seriously wrong but also that it was not from the prison side. The postal service in Thailand is actually very efficient. It is upsetting for a prisoner, whose only form of communication with the outside world is through letters, to find that the system isn't working. It occurred to me that perhaps the problem was at the post office in South Africa and that perhaps someone there was stealing my fancy stamps and throwing away the letters. Not long before, an A4 envelope containing three of my pen drawings had also gone missing. One of the newspapers back home published a description of the drawings, appealing to the public to return them, but nothing came of it. After this I used the small Thai stamps with a picture of the King's head on them, although the mono colours weren't as eye-catching as the ones I'd used before.

Another time when letters didn't seem to be getting through to their intended recipients, in one of my letters home I complained to my sister about the guard who was in charge of our mail, an officer by the name of Arun. I had long suspected him of withholding my letters. He looked down on all prisoners and hated foreigners in particular. We had heard stories of him sleeping with prisoners' wives, promising to make their husbands' lives easier in prison if they did. Arun hated me and I was 100 per cent sure he was tossing my letters in the bin. I was extremely upset, especially as one of the letters that had disappeared had contained important information regarding my royal pardon.

We prisoners were tired of being victimised by Arun and it was time to get rid of him. In my letter I asked Joan to write an official complaint about him to every government department in Thailand. Seeing that Arun was the one who was censoring our mail, I knew he would read my letter and I knew he would shit himself! Predictable as I thought he would be, one day I was called to the office and there was Arun, on the verge of tears, with my letter in his hands. He couldn't have been friendlier, pleading and begging me not to report him and assuring me that he had never withheld any of my mail. Actually, I forgave him. Using a red pen, I crossed out the instructions to my sister to pursue the matter. Then I signed it and he posted it. After that Arun behaved himself and none of my letters went missing again.

Living with so many people in such a confined space, no matter how positive you are, takes its toll on you. In prison there is always somebody getting in your face. Sometimes it was hard to stay positive, and I really struggled with all the negativity around me, not to mention the drug-taking. I couldn't allow my moods to affect my creativity. For me, art was my escape. I would switch off from my reality and explore worlds unknown. The imagination has no boundaries. My mind became my sanctuary and also my escape. But still the questions kept playing over and over in my head.

Why me? Why am I here?

I was still not getting it. I was getting a second chance at life. And I was also making a difference, even though I might not have realised it. For a start, we had won a victory in the amnesty: drug cases would no longer be discriminated against. But there was still a lot of work to be done. What was it that Jung wrote about the collective unconscious? Something about depression among prisoners being like a generator they are all plugged into at the same time? What was the point of suffering when one had no future? We were all racing against time. Mental breakdowns were common in prison. My biggest fear was of growing old there. I had to dig really deep to keep my head above water. I had to keep telling myself that somewhere along the line, the right door would open. I had to be sure of this or I would crack.

I had had a passion for music since I was ten years old. Cat Stevens, Fleetwood Mac, the Doors, Supertramp, the Bee Gees, the Zombies – these were favourite acts of mine. Some of their songs lived in my head: the Zombies' 'She's Not There', Led Zeppelin's legendary 'Stairway to Heaven', Tommy James' 'Crimson and Clover', the Animals' 'House of the Rising Sun', the Beatles' 'Lucy in the Sky with Diamonds', 'Angie' by the Rolling Stones, Pink Floyd's 'Wish You Were Here' ...

At first I struggled to enjoy listening to music in prison. I would trip out and get really down, as certain songs triggered strong memories, propelling me back in time and space. It was soul-destroying, and all it did was intensify my longings. But I loved music, so I continued to listen to it. I struggled to concentrate on the lyrics, and after a while I would hear only the melody. Sometimes I would lose myself in writing my own words to the music. I had to train myself to listen, but eventually music enabled me to tap into the creative side of my brain, and I reached the point when every drawing or painting I did, I did listening to music.

In one of their parcels, my family sent me cassettes of all my favourite music, as well as personal messages they had recorded for me. They thought this would be a more personal way of communicating than writing letters, especially for my niece and nephew, who were so busy being young that writing letters was a chore for them. A few of the other inmates also used this method of staying in touch, paying the guards a fee to smuggle their cassettes out for them. At first I thought this was a good idea, but the second I heard my sister's voice,

I broke down in tears. I just couldn't listen to the messages. After that I abandoned the idea of recording.

There were 13 South African prisoners in Bangkok, about nine of them in the Bangkok women's prison. My heart went out to these women. The conditions there were far worse than they were in the men's prison. They slept in dreadfully overcrowded cells with up to 100 women in them at a time, maybe even more. They weren't allowed parcels and their letters were limited to one page and maybe one letter a week. I wrote to a few of them, but, because of the restrictions, it took months before they responded. Understanding that their families took priority over anybody else, after a while I stopped writing, and I knew it was selfish of me to expect a letter in reply.

One of my pen pals in South Africa sent me a parcel containing two big pieces of biltong. Unfortunately, they hadn't been vacuum-sealed and had turned all mouldy, but I couldn't bring myself just to throw them away, so I washed the fungus off, sliced off some pieces and fried them in oil. They turned out to be really tasty and I shared them with some of my mates. And, in case you're wondering, I didn't get sick. One thing you learn in prison is never to waste food!

Before my arrest, I had been building a go-kart for my ten-year-old nephew, Darren, which I never got to finish. I loved Darren like he was my own son, and we shared a close bond. Being separated was as difficult for him as it was for me. I could only imagine what it must have been like for those inmates who were fathers and husbands. In my letters I tried to console Darren, and I wrote him lots of short notes, encouraging him with his studies and with other issues or challenges life presented. In spirit, my family was always with me.

With everything that had happened to me thus far, my outlook on life was gradually changing. My eyes were opening and my faith in G-d was slowly being strengthened. As I began evolving, so I began to discover who I was. For the first time in my life I was setting goals and my head was filled with dreams. I was looking to the future and not just living in the moment. I sometimes wondered where I would have been if I had not ended up in prison in Bangkok – more than likely in a prison in South Africa or six feet under in Westpark Cemetery. The more I thought about it, the more grateful I began to feel. I believed that G-d was about to reveal something to me. Prison was saving me from myself and the path of self-destruction I had chosen. I had stopped using drugs, I was fit and healthy, I had a roof over my head. I had developed new interests and there was no shortage of friends – not that I would have invited any of them to a Shabbos dinner! Looking in from the outside, I actually began to consider myself extremely lucky. Life was dictating the terms. I might have been walking on the edge of a precipice, but it was up to me to keep my balance. When I thought of my situation like this, I would find myself smiling and I would allow the sun's rays to brighten my days. Crazy as it seems, I was relatively content. I had made a life for myself within the prison walls.

I enjoyed most days because I was doing what I loved most – being creative. Stimulating my mind was crucial for me to maintain my sanity. The nights were still bad, however. Insomnia had always been a problem for me, and in Bangkwang at night my mind became a battleground for my thoughts, the conscious wrestling with the sub-conscious and causing havoc. For a while I tried meditation, but I had great difficulty clearing my mind and concentrating on a single thought. I guessed I would have to learn to live with it, but insomnia was a bitch. I also knew that there was no way I could take medication, not because it was not available – guys sold Valium like candy – but because I was fighting my own addiction. Replacing street drugs with prescription drugs would have been equally destructive. There were occasions when I did take a Valium, but it affected my thinking for days and induced a chemical depression that I couldn't afford. And sleeping pills scared the shit out of me because the effects were long-lasting.

Having only 13 people in our cell was a real pleasure. I looked forward to being locked up and spending quality time with myself. I didn't socialise much in the cell. After lockdown, first I would take a nap, then listen to my Walkman and draw for hours on end. For entertainment, the guys hired videos every night, but most of the movies I had seen before. Late at night, after watching three or so feature films, they would put on a blue movie, which the Thais referred to as 'sex movies'. In our toilet area, someone had burnt a small hole in the rice-bag curtain at squatting level, so, while you were hunched above the toilet, you could peek through the hole, watch the sex movie and jerk off. One of the Americans would masturbate at least three times whenever we watched a porn movie.

The river water that was pumped into our cells only came at certain times – one hour after lockdown, around 9pm and then again at 5am. The water at the bottom of the tank was thick with mud, and once every two weeks we'd get the room cleaner to empty and clean it. The tank probably held about 60 litres, but whenever there were sex movies we would run out of water by midnight. Often there would be sperm trails down the toilet bowl. This became a problem for me, as I would answer nature's call around 5am, so I organised myself a 25-litre plastic container, which I filled with clean water and carried to my cell every day. I would keep it next to the steps to the toilet.

Masturbation is forbidden in Judaism. Emitting semen in vain is considered a sin, but I thought that, under special conditions, like the one I was in, allowances could be made. I masturbated once a week. For me, the act itself relieves stress, but it leaves me unfulfilled and more frustrated than anything else. Although sex was never an obsession, I longed for intimacy with a woman. Just as I had bottled up my emotions as a child, in prison I needed to supress my sexual desires and push them down into the deepest recesses of my mind.

A rumour that started in the women's prison and then filtered through to us was that there were 300 Thais in South African jails, and that there was a chance of a prisoner exchange between our countries, even though the King's Jubilee had come and gone. I was sceptical. Until something actually happened, I wasn't prepared to believe it. It was amazing how the rumour mill kept churning out stories, and how quickly they spread among prisoners and from one prison to another. Ironically, it was often such stories that sustained our enthusiasm and kept our hopes alive.

One of my South African pen pals, who subsequently became a very good friend of my family, wanted to put on an exhibition of my art and to publish the poems I'd written. It was inspiring to me that somebody out there thought my drawings were worthy of being exhibited. At the time a close friend was due to come and visit me, and I planned to produce as many pieces as possible for him to take back home. I was drawing from eight to ten hours a day. Since the time that my drawings had gone missing in the post, the only other way to get them home was to send them back with people who came to visit from abroad. The contact visit was almost upon us, and I told all my mates I was expecting a friend. My drawings were all ready and safe in a self-made protective envelope.

The first morning, I was dressed and ready early, eagerly waiting to be called. After an hour passed, and my friend hadn't arrived, I gave up. Maybe he'd got lost or was caught in the traffic. There was still the afternoon visit to come. But the afternoon visit came and went with no sign of my friend. I was terribly disappointed. Everybody else who had seen their families came back with loads of food, especially the Thais, and the joy among the prisoners was tangible. I felt a slight touch of jealousy, but still there was hope for the next day's visit. When my friend didn't arrive on the second contact visit day, I cracked up. This was an all-time low for me, and I experienced the first of what I would learn were panic attacks. My chest closed up and I had this sick feeling in my gut. Jesus! I struggled to breathe, I thought I was going to die, or, rather, I *wanted* to die. Then I remembered these breathing exercises we used to do at karate training, where you inhale a long slow breath through your nose, and then slowly exhale through the mouth. I did this repeatedly, while thinking of the night sky, which I had not seen in two years. Slowly I felt myself ease back into a sound frame of mind. My friend never did pitch up. Although it was a terrible letdown, I got over it, and vowed I would never allow myself to get my expectations up for anything ever again. In that way I wouldn't be disappointed.

I became something of a loner in prison. For the most part, I stuck to my own company, enjoying the privacy of being alone, always thinking. Some of the guys who I'd been with from the beginning had turned grey in a short time – something I attributed to them doing too *much* thinking. Distancing myself from the others, I realised, might have come across as my being arrogant and thinking myself better than everyone else, but this was not the case. I always tried to give respect wherever respect was warranted, and I remained honourable in all my dealings with people. I knew I was not well liked, but I didn't give a fuck. It worked just fine for me. Alone, I would lose myself in my art and in writing poetry when I was in the right frame of mind. It was such a beautiful way of expressing myself; even my handwriting began to evolve. I tried to divide my time in a way that none of my interests was neglected, but drawing was my number-one priority. By now I was doing all my creations with a Bic ballpoint pen. Each pen had its own personality. The ink was never consistent in colour; some inks were dark, while others were lighter. When shading in ballpoint, remember that the ball bearing in the tip gradually wears down, causing the flow of ink to increase, which can cause smudge marks if one is not careful. It's a very difficult medium to work with, as you cannot afford to make a mistake. Once the ball bearing was damaged, I would use that particular pen to shade the background; for fine shading and lines I would use a new pen.

My sister had sent me a wall clock and although, sadly, the glass cover had broken in the post, I stuck the clock in the centre of our cell. I would look at it all the time. Time could be man's worst enemy. For some people it dragged, but for others it flew by. I felt like I was passing through time, that time had stood still for me and was now giving me a chance to make up for all the minutes I'd lost.

Takraw season came. I was one of a very few foreigners who played the game, and I loved it. It was a test of agility and strength. The Thais were supremely talented at this sport and the competition was fierce. I made the B team and we were lucky if we won a game. What I enjoyed most was that we played in another building, so I got the chance not only to see what life was like there but also got the opportunity to hook up with some of my friends.

The American who had been arrested at the airport on the same day as me had been carrying over 4kg of heroin. Because he'd cooperated with the police and ratted out his contacts, he was given a 25-year sentence. Motherfucker – I learnt that, the month before, the DEA had collected him from Klong Prem prison, flown him to the US, where he testified in court against his connection, and then returned him to prison in Bangkok. How could he look at himself in the mirror every day, I wondered. In another two years, he would be transferred to an American jail and within two months be paroled. No matter what deal the police might offer me, I could never be a rat. As far as I'm concerned, there's a code of honour among thieves. If you grass on your mates, your punishment is death.

In Thai prisons, every Thai is a potential informer. You are more concerned about your fellow inmates than you are about the guards. I could never quite get my head around this. I despised the prison authorities; they used their people and treated them like slaves, so why the fuck would anyone want to lick a guard's arse? Maybe it was part of Thai culture, but it baffled me. Money got you protection from the guards; they ran the show without having to do very much at all. Even while they were sleeping, which they did most of the day, they had eyes everywhere.

Plans for the proposed exhibition of my art fell through. I was only momentarily disappointed. To tell the truth, I was rather relieved. I was still at a very early stage in my artistic growth, and not yet ready to share my creations with the outside world. They still belonged to the world where they had been created – prison. And what is fame and fortune without one's freedom? The pressure to produce art in time for an exhibition was also too much for me, and once the idea had been shelved, I could continue to draw at my own pace, expressing my feelings without the need to cater for an audience. I was in my element. In fact, the thought of parting with my art almost killed me. My portraits and drawings were my only possessions, and every piece of artwork carried with it a part of my soul. By this stage my art had evolved significantly. I was going through what I referred to as the 'black period'. In quite a few of my pieces I was drawing black and white chequered squares. The squares represented my structured life and also the prison bars.

While I was to some extent settling into prison life, my sister Joan, on the other hand, was still struggling to come to terms with my incarceration. I tried my utmost to put her mind at ease. In one of my letters I wrote to her: 'Don't feel sore about my circumstances. The price I'm paying is very small if one has to take into account how much my life has changed. Don't you see, for the first time, I have direction?'

Joan was making plans to visit in November 1997, and she wanted to bring the whole family this time. Frankly, I didn't think that I could handle seeing the kids. I didn't so much mind if my mom and her husband Mike came, but I also understood that it would be really hard on them. We Hungarians are a passionate bunch and I knew the visit would be really emotional. I didn't want to give the guards the pleasure of seeing us all break down and cry.

Meanwhile we learnt about the dramatic escape from Klong Prem prison by Daniel Westlake, the Australian guy with whom I had shared a cell back in 1994 in Building 6. I couldn't believe it. I had seen him as more of an academic than the adventurous type. I found myself wondering what the chances might have been, if I hadn't been transferred to Bangkwang, of my having escaped with him. I had the greatest respect and admiration for Daniel. Every time I thought about it, and imagined the guards discovering the breakout the following morning when they unlocked the cells, and running around in circles trying to figure out how he'd managed to get away from right under their noses, I chuckled to myself. Good one, Westlake, I thought.

The new consular officer from the South African embassy actually turned out to be quite efficient. She approached her duties to us prisoners with interest and care, and she also helped me send some of my art back to South Africa. It must have been hard for her, and I could sense her frustration at times. She was visiting three different prisons, where every South African prisoner would bombard her with questions, most of them relating to our government's signing a prisoner transfer treaty with Thailand. The truth was, she had no idea what was

going on with this. I think I knew more than she did, as I was constantly receiving updates from home, mostly from Joan, who continued
in her quest to secure my release. She had got as far as meeting with
the Deputy Minister of Foreign Affairs, Aziz Pahad. She was a true
warrior, and her reputation among my friends in prison was growing.
Wherever she went and whomever she met, she would tell them about
my plight. I was getting letters of support from all over the world by
now, and I was writing an average of 70 letters a week myself. I even
received a missive from the Royal Palace of Lesotho, and one from
former South African president FW de Klerk, who expressed his regret
at not being able to help.

On 8 March 1997 another article appeared in the newspapers back
home. This one was in the *Saturday Star*, and it featured two of my pen
sketches, one of which was a portrait of President Mandela. Beneath
the headline 'South Africa's Forgotten Prisoners', journalist David
Capel set the scene for the paper's readers:

> *You arrive in paradise with a pocketful of money and a head-
> ful of dreams. Ten minutes later a dirty prison cell and a
> forty year nightmare are all you have left. Can't happen to
> you? It can. Currently there are one hundred and ninety-two
> South Africans serving prison sentences in various parts of
> the world.*

Our plight as prisoners in Thailand was extensively and regularly publicised, as was the case for other South African citizens in foreign prisons
around the world. It was this that kept my hopes high. To be honest, I
was not expecting to be granted a royal pardon; in fact, I had a feeling
my application would be rejected. But one never knew in prison, where
everything was a gamble – nothing ventured, nothing gained.

And the treaty wasn't off the table yet.

In May 1997 another article appeared in the *Saturday Star*, this one
about the proposed South Africa-Thailand treaty and the possibility of
South African prisoners convicted in Thailand on drug offences being
able to return home to complete their sentences. For once, it looked

like real progress towards this treaty was finally being made and that it might soon be in place. If what they were claiming was true, I would first have to serve eight years in Thailand before I could be transferred back home. As I had already done three, this meant that I would have five years left before I was eligible – not bad after originally being sentenced to 100 years!

Something that I never told anybody was that, at the bottom of one of my lockers, inside a plastic bag, I kept a full set of new clothing, carefully folded – sneakers, socks, a nice pair of shorts and a T-shirt – in the event that, by some miracle, I would be called to go home. When that day came, I would be ready.

I had started to experience severe headaches, and one of my mates suggested I might need glasses. I was reluctant at first to have my eyes checked out at the hospital, which was a place I avoided at all costs. I recall writing to my sister, '*Mense word dood daar*' (People die there). Although I doubted anything fatal could happen during an eye test, the bottom line was that I needed a script and so I had no choice but to go. I duly got a script and posted it to Joan so that she could organise a pair of glasses for me. I hated the thought of wearing glasses because, as far as I was concerned, this reinforced the ageing process, something that I was having difficulty coming to terms with. To cheer myself up, I ordered 'John Lennon' frames, which I thought would be quite cool. Now, when the time came for me to go home, not only would I have new clothes, but I would also be able to see where I was going – headache-free!

By July 1997 my application for a royal pardon was ready, with all the supporting documents attached – all, that is, except for an official letter from the South African government. Our government's stance hadn't changed. All it was willing to do for South African prisoners was to give us a diplomatic letter stating that they would guarantee our travel documents in the event of a pardon being granted. It was disappointing, but not unexpected, and we sent the application to the embassy all the same so they could forward it through the correct channels.

Our government's lack of interest bothered me less because I had realised that there was so much I had to be grateful for: firstly, I was alive and drug-free; secondly, life had become far more meaningful to me; and thirdly, I was undergoing a spiritual awakening. It was becoming clearer to me why I had had to be imprisoned. I had forgiven G-d for having me arrested; G-d was saving me from myself. I said to my sister, 'Joan, I have the support of somebody more powerful than the embassy or the ANC, and that is G-d. My life is in His hands. If it's His will that I am meant to be free, then free I will be.'

The treaty still appeared to be on track, however, and Joan had hired an advocate to draw up a draft document for me so that we would be ready to take advantage as soon as it was signed. Robert McBride, who was in charge of the Directorate for South East Asia at the Department of Foreign Affairs, was also working with my sister towards this end. For the moment, I decided to leave things in their hands.

On the days when it was just too hot to draw, because the sweat would smudge my ink, I would spend the time writing to my pen pals. One of my correspondents was a lady by the name of Christine Read. I'd read an article about her in a nature conservation magazine and, impressed by her passion for the protection and preservation of our wildlife and their habitats, wrote her a letter. I didn't know that her family owned one of the most famous art galleries in Johannesburg. My association with her inspired me to start drawing birds, mainly eagles and owls. Birds of prey had always held a special fascination for me.

It's amazing how people's paths cross in life, often for reasons we can't fully comprehend. We are called upon to play roles in the lives of others, whether we realise or understand it at the time or not. Many people from different parts of the world were lining up to be part of mine. Some would come and go, and others would become lifelong friends. Either way, I remained grateful and felt blessed to have made such wonderful friends on the outside. People of substance don't just land in your lap. Life was teaching me so many lessons.

In December 1997 Joan and Malcolm came to visit me. My mother had decided not to come. It was fantastic to see them. I was showered with gifts, and they brought many messages from friends back home. For that brief period of time, it was almost possible to forget where I was. In prison, though, you come to realise that everything in life is transient and can be taken away from you in a moment – just like the freedom I had taken for granted and which had been so abruptly snatched away from me.

My family's visit was somewhat spoilt for all of us, though, because they were not treated with much respect on their visits to Bangkwang, and the humiliation they experienced meant that they hated every minute they spent in Thailand. Without explanation, the length of normal everyday visits was cut from 90 to 20 minutes. Joan and Malcolm pleaded with the guards for a few extra minutes with me, explaining that they had travelled all the way from Africa to visit me. The guards weren't having any of it. They were downright rude, refusing to allow them even five minutes more, muttering under their breath and gesturing with their hands for my family to leave immediately. We were shocked by their disrespect and disgusting behaviour. It was nothing more than sheer spitefulness and lack of compassion towards foreigners. Even my two contact visits were cut short by half an hour.

With all the gifts and money so many people back home had sent me, I had clothes that would last me for the next ten years and all of my favourite food. I also managed to give my sister about 500 letters, which I had received from friends, to take home with her and keep for me. The difficult part, always, was saying goodbye and it was no easier this time. I found farewells so traumatic I think I would actually have preferred them not to have come, but of course it was wonderful to see them.

On New Year's Eve I was unable to sleep. I greeted 1998 in silent contemplation, thinking about the reality of my situation and wondering what challenges the new year would bring. I thought about how I had spent my entire life running, whether it was chasing a high or fleeing from my past. Now I had stopped running. Instead, I was standing my ground and facing my fears. I was beginning to see myself in a different light as well. I was seeing the real me, a man who was intelligent, sensitive and talented; someone with a renewed will to live and the determination to prove that he was worthy of a second chance.

A few days into the new year, around midnight, Lee Evans, a DJ on a popular late-night radio show on a channel that played foreign songs, dedicated the song 'Free Me' by Roger Daltrey 'to all the foreign prisoners in Room 16 in Bangkwang'. My sister had arranged this just before she and Malcolm had left. It was such a cool gesture and a lot of the guys heard it. A small thing maybe, but such gestures did wonders for our spirits. They reminded us that we weren't forgotten.

A few months later, in April, I heard another dedication while I was sitting drawing and listening to the channel. The DJ announced a song 'dedicated to Shani from Bangkwang from his sister Joan, who says they all love you and are thinking of you'. I got goose bumps all over.

One morning, I woke up and felt a swelling in my nose, like a boil with no head. Over the next two days it got quite big. I tried to squeeze it, but nothing happened, so I took a needle, burnt the tip to sterilise it, and attempted to lance the boil. I squeezed it from inside and out but nothing came out. Then I made another few holes in it, sticking the needle pretty deep into the swollen area. I squeezed as hard as I could, but still nothing more than a drop of discoloured liquid came out onto the toilet paper I was using. About an hour later I got the shivers and shakes and experienced the most severe pain imaginable. The lump in my nose swelled up to the size of a golf ball, disfiguring my face completely. I got permission to go and rest in my cell, where I broke out in such a fever I didn't know how I would make it through to the next day. I was put on antibiotics, and after a few days the thing burst. The pus that oozed out in teaspoon-loads was a bright lime green; I've never seen anything like it in my life. It took two days to drain completely, and left a slight ridge jutting out in the inside of my nose and causing one nostril to be slightly skew.

Sitting on hard surfaces and on my makeshift bed, hunched over my fold-up table and drawing into the early hours of the morning, began to put severe strain on my lower back. It was hurting badly. Among the Thais there were quite a few professional masseurs, and some of the foreigners took advantage of their services. They swore these guys were like miracle healers and would be able to help me, but, even though my back was killing me, I couldn't be persuaded. For some reason I was just not comfortable with a male touching my body. Instead I wrote to my sister, asking her to send me a kidney belt similar to the ones I'd seen delivery scooter drivers use sometimes.

Another morning I took a pair of scissors into the toilet with me, where I proceeded to cut off all my hair. Then I took a razor and shaving foam and shaved myself bald. Being a skinhead was not an image I would have entertained on the outside, but, here in prison, what did it matter? It felt strange and reminded me of being in the army. The next morning hardly anybody recognised me. At first glance, the guys thought I was a new prisoner. Some guys said I looked like a serial killer or somebody straight out of a horror movie. Some of the guards who had always been on at me about trimming my blond curls approved of my new look, and for a long time I kept my clean-shaven style and got used to it.

While my sister was fighting the battle from the outside, I continued doing what I could from the inside. As the first months of 1998 went by, we kept up the pressure and dedicated whatever resources we could to making sure that the world would not forget our plight and that as many people and organisations as possible knew about the appalling conditions under which prisoners had to survive. My logic was that the more noise we made about exposing the conditions in Bankwang and other Thai prisons, the sooner the Thai government would want to get rid of us. In July I drafted a petition and spent two days walking around the building convincing fellow prisoners of the importance of doing this and collecting their signatures. The guards, who had had advance notice of my intentions from their spies, were not happy about it, but I didn't let that deter me.

TO WHOM IT MAY CONCERN

30 July 1998

Dear Sirs
In response to the demands by foreign inmates incarcerated in Bangkwang Prison, the deputy director, Mr Samboon

Pasobret, replied in a letter dated 2/7/98 Ref no MT0905/24 that the Correction Department was currently considering our demands. It has become apparent by the lack of interest on behalf of the authorities that they could not care less and have no intentions of solving the crisis faced by Western foreigners, Asian foreigners and their Thai counterparts. This is obviously an extension of the continued relentless discrimination displayed against foreigners in general.

It has become known that the United Nations and several other countries contribute towards the well-being of incarcerated foreigners in the form of a dietary allotment, as the Thai diet lacks the basic nutrients and is totally alien to what foreigners are accustomed to. We are calling on the United Nations and the other countries to immediately withhold this subsidy, as only a small fraction, if any, is used for the well-being of prisoners. We are requesting that the United Nations sends a delegation to investigate the unbearable conditions that foreigners and Thais alike are forced to endure in Thailand's prisons. We are demanding three square meals a day for all prisoners. This should include Asian and Western foreigners. At present the one meal a day provided by the prison for only Western foreigners consists of a small plastic bag of rice along with an inedible stew that is not fit to sustain an animal.

We are furthermore totally isolated from our families and friends. The only form of communication we enjoy is through the written medium, mainly being letters. Here again, we are constantly intimidated by the authorities who withhold or delay delivery of our mail from our families. We live with the constant fear of not knowing if we will ever see them again, they have also been devastated by our predicament. Why do they have to suffer??? Why do our children have to grow up without hearing their own fathers' voices??? Not only are our lives being destroyed, but you are destroying the lives of our families as well. We are demanding the immediate

355

installation of telephones, as ninety per cent of our suffering and anxiety is over our concern for our families and loved ones. These public telephones should be readily available for the use of both Thai and foreign inmates, under the present economic climate the Telephone Organisation of Thailand would no doubt welcome business that would be generated from the prisons. According to our knowledge the costs of the installation of public telephones is on the onus of the manufacturing company, and the Correction Department would not incur any expenses.

Mr Interior Minister, are you aware of the fact that prisons are institutions where people who have committed crimes are confined for a specific period, with the sole objective of reforming or rehabilitating them, to be eventually released after the expired period of sentence, so that they can resume their role as productive citizens in society? Thai prisons on the other hand are concentration camps where prisoners are treated like animals and are used as slaves for cheap labour, or forgotten and left to die! The instatement of telephones would play a vital role in keeping prisoners reformed and in maintaining their sanity. It would no doubt also reduce the rampant homosexuality which is mainly dominant among Thai inmates.

We are also demanding that the prison upgrades the sanitary conditions, which at present are as primitive as that of the Stone Ages. Prisoners are forced to shower out of horse troughs, which are filled with filthy water pumped from the local river. We demand the installation of hot and cold clean running water. We also call for a proper sewerage system to be constructed. The excretion of prisoners is stored in concrete vaults, which on an annual basis is removed and buried in the prison yard. The general stench of the prison is nauseating. The present open sewerage system emits toxic fumes, which has resulted in many prisoners showing asthmatic symptoms, severe headaches and loss of memory. We are also insisting that the authorities provide toiletries to all prisoners, Asians, Western foreigners and Thai inmates on a fortnightly basis. This should include soap, shampoo, toothpaste, toothbrush, shaving foam, razor blades, washing powder and toilet paper. At present the standard of personal hygiene is shockingly low. These supplies would definitely reduce the already endemic spread of skin diseases.

The Prime Minister, Mr Chuan Leekpai, who earlier in the year appeared briefly on CNN, in an eloquent speech pleaded for foreign investment to help save the already crippling Thai economy. How ironic that foreigners were being treated like animals in his very own prisons. We are calling on the International Community to impose sanctions against Thailand and to initiate an anti-investment campaign along with an anti-tourist campaign. Tourists in Thailand have become the targets of muggers, rapists and murderers. Your lives as tourists are at great risk if you come to Thailand. Thailand supposedly being a democratic country is in the process of amending their constitution, and has claimed it to be a just and fair system. Serving five years in a Thai prison under these conditions would be equivalent to serving fifteen years in any humane Western country's prison. As a first-time offender by any Western judicial standards, having committed the same crime, one would more than likely only receive a suspended sentence or a probationary period and or be expected to perform community work. And for that matter if one has to receive a prison sentence, as a first-time offender it wouldn't be more than three to five years before one was either released or became eligible for parole! While not trying to justify our crime, we believe that a four to five year sentence would be adequate for both Thais and foreigners. We call upon the Thai government to implement a law whereby 1st-time offenders are released or repatriated, irrespective of whether that prisoner's country has a treaty or not. We ask for equal justice for Thais and foreigners alike.

*It was become a common practice for Thailand to procras-
tinate in their negotiations to sign treaties, using this as a
tool to strengthen diplomatic and economic ties. The only
other resource would be for Thailand to hasten their negotiations and to sign treaties of a 4-year transfer period with all
foreign countries who have citizens serving ridiculous sentences in one of the most appalling prisons in the world.
The majority of drug offenders are foreigners. Whenever an
amnesty is decreed the authorities propose to exclude drug
offenders, once again, this is a blatant discrimination against
foreigners, while 99% of convicted drug offenders are first-
time offenders, we ask for leniency and we would like to see
drug offenders included in all future amnesties. According
to the Correction Department, an amnesty has been decreed
for the 5th December 1999 to celebrate the Honourable King
Bhumibol Adulyadej's 72nd Birthday. We would like to see
the first-time offenders, both Thai and foreigners who have
served four to five years or more of their sentence, be released; this would no doubt alleviate the serious over-crowding problem. Your Honourable Majesty, we humbly beg you to
please view all submitted King's Pardons with an open heart
and to consider our situation with mercy and kindness. We
would like to see a fair play of justice for all, irrespective of
nationality, religion or colour. As human beings surely we
deserve a second chance in life. May we take this opportunity of wishing your Highness and the Royal Family health
and happiness in the years to come? Long live the King of
Thailand! It has not been an easy decision but if our demands
are not met, as from the 5th December 1998 we would have
no alternative but to embark on a 'Mass Hunger Strike'. We
ask the international and local news media to please monitor
developments as we the foreigners of Bangkwang Prison fight
with our lives for our basic human rights. May God have
mercy on us! We thank you for your co-operation and we anticipate swift action in redressing the injustices that inmates*

are forced to endure in your prisons!

Yours sincerely
Foreign Inmates Building 2
See list of attached signatures.

I managed to get this petition smuggled out of the prison and sent to a friend in the UK, where it was typed up and distributed to various human rights organisations around the world. I didn't want it to be sent from South Africa, as it would have implicated my family. The way Joan and Malcolm had been treated during their last visit lingered in my mind. From time to time, they had even been threatened and warned not to come to Thailand.

Professor Harry Reicher, chairman of Agudath Yisrael World Organization, one of the human rights organisations to which the petition was sent, presented this letter to the Thai ambassador at the United Nations, leading to a UN investigation into Thai prison conditions. The involvement of the UN was considered a loss of face by the authorities, and their biggest concern was how a letter of such importance had managed to make its way out of the prison in the first place.

They were aware that I had drafted it, and so, from this point on, the guards became more wary of me. My mail was always thoroughly checked, and sometimes delayed and even withheld. In fact, my every move was monitored.

I became known as the 'King of the Pen'. Whenever prisoners had a grievance they would approach me to 'complain'. That was the word they used. I never complained, though, nor was I just another disgruntled prisoner; I was fighting for our basic human rights. That was a crucial difference for me.

The pain in my lower back was getting worse. I had to cut my drawing time in the cell by half and take a stretch break every hour. It got so bad that I even had to stop playing football. Joan had sent me the kidney belt, but it provided only temporary relief. One morning when I woke up I could hardly get up off my bed. My Thai friend Somchai had recommended a masseur, and now he urged me to see him. This man happened to be the descendant of three generations of traditional Thai masseurs. Despite my initial resistance, I was in such pain I thought I would have to give him a try. I was subjected to an hour of complete torture, during which I experienced such pain that I couldn't understand why people had massages. I was only too relieved when he was finished. But then ... I couldn't believe it! The pain was completely gone. It was a miracle! I could move around freely. To be on the safe side, however, I stopped drawing in the cell. Instead, I used the time to study Judaism or write letters, and, rather than sitting hunched over, I would lie in a horizontal position with my pillow resting under my chest. Occasionally I would watch TV. From then on I restricted my drawing to downstairs in the dining room.

My art took me out of myself completely. My moods were of no consequence, and I found I could switch off from my immediate surroundings when I was creating. Art was my natural outlet for expression, and I could see the transformation in my work and how much I was growing. When I was drawing it was like being teleported into another dimension, where the possibilities were infinite.

Letters from home remained my lifeline, but at times they would also bring heartbreaking news. A good friend of mine, Syd, who had been in the army with me, tragically lost his daughter in a car accident. I cannot claim to relate to his pain and loss – the senseless loss of a child must be one of life's worst tragedies – but my heart went out to him. I wished I could convey my condolences to him, if not in person then at least on the telephone. In Thai prisons, there was no access to telephones. It was as ridiculous as it was frustrating, and it became another of my missions to have public telephones installed for prisoners' use.

The consular officer from the South African embassy continued to assist us prisoners wherever she could. When you see somebody on a regular basis, they tend to become familiar, and by now I had begun to think of her as a friend. During one of her visits, she complained about her husband never being at home and how he was off taking deep-sea diving lessons in Phuket (personally, I was sure he was chasing some Thai pussy on the beach). Her confiding this type of information struck me as a bit odd. I can be tactless sometimes, and during this conversation I asked her if she had a healthy sex life. We were in the embassy visit room at the time, with two sets of bars dividing us, one made of thick steel mesh. Well, I thought she was going to fall off her chair, so I hurriedly added something vague about how eating hamburgers every day could get boring after a while ... I could see she was not impressed, though, and she changed the subject.

A couple of days later I got the following letter from her:

> CONSULAR VISIT 29 July 1997
> During the visit on 29th July 1997, I forgot to inform you that I have received the prescription for your glasses. As requested by Mrs. Sacks, the prescription will be forwarded to her for further attention. Please inform me if you wish for the matter to be dealt with in another manner. Following my visit on 25 June 1997.
>
> 1. You are kindly reminded that consular visits to detainees are done on a strictly professional basis.
>
> 2. Please refrain from asking personal questions or making comments which might offend visitors.
>
> Your assistance in this regard is appreciated.

I replied in a letter of my own:

> In response to paragraph three of your letter in which you have requested me to refrain from asking personal questions or making comments which might offend visitors, if I might have unintentionally said anything that struck you as offensive, please accept my sincere apologies. In future I will be more conscientious of subject matters during my conversations with you.

When the consular officer visited the following month, she arrived with her husband! I chuckled to myself – so the man wasn't chasing any pussy around that day. The guy was huge, obviously an ex-rugby player. I guessed he'd come along to check me out, and maybe he thought I would be intimidated by his size. He didn't know who he was taking on. I would have shoved a Bic ballpoint pen through his eye if necessary. In my defence, it had been his wife who had brought up the subject to start with. I was dying to ask him how his diving lessons were coming on, but I refrained, and actually he turned out to be quite a friendly guy. Taking the piss might have given me a moment's satisfaction, but it would have been a bad move on my part. You don't want to be on the wrong side of your embassy!

Chapter 12

Solitary Confinement

In March of 1998 I met a Thai woman by the name of Jai. She and another woman, Sheila, who was Australian, represented a private organisation called One Life at a Time, and they visited the American prisoners in Bangkwang. They were also involved in various other charities. One of the American prisoners, whose locker I had kicked a hole in, had a relationship going with Sheila. Another American, by the name of Eric, who was a sound engineer by profession, had become a good friend of mine. He was a heroin addict and trying to kick the habit, and I helped him out here and there, encouraging him to stay off drugs. To show his gratitude, he told me about Sheila's friend Jai, and said that, if I wanted, he could ask Jai to visit me. I was hesitant at first. It had been almost four years since I had had any real interaction with anyone of the opposite sex – besides my family, of course. Having a regular visitor would also interfere with my drawing time, but what the heck, I thought. What did I have to lose?

Jai was 38 years old and she was quite pretty. She was slim and had long black hair. Her English was good. We agreed that she would visit me every fortnight. Every time she visited she would bring me fresh wholewheat bread and a packet of milk powder. She also offered to fax messages to my family and to bring me faxes from them. At first I had difficulty making conversation, so Jai did most of the talking. With the two sets of bars about a metre apart in the visit room, you had to shout to be heard anyway, and when the room was full it was hard to have a conversation. It was also awkward because the people in your immediate vicinity could hear every word you exchanged.

Jai was nice, though, and I began to look forward to her visits. We also started corresponding with each other, and within a few months our friendship evolved into a relationship. I can't say I loved her, but I did become emotionally dependent on her. There is something uniquely sensual about Asian women, and I was attracted to her physically, too. She had the most delicate hands and her eyes were mesmerising. She had an inner beauty that shone through.

Jai proved to be an indispensable contact between my family and me. She opened a bank account for me, and, through one of the guards, I succeeded in smuggling in an ATM card. I arranged for the embassy to deposit my monthly allowance into Jai's account, and she would then transfer it into the account for which I was now the cardholder.

Whenever I needed money, I would give my card to a guard and he would go to the bank, make a withdrawal, deduct his five per cent and bring the money to me in the prison. This was the most convenient and also the safest way of bringing in cash. From my allowance I would give Jai a running balance, and on her now weekly visits she would bring me such luxury food items as cheese, jam, fruit and ready-made meals. She would also use some of the money to buy me other things, such as art supplies, toiletries and sports equipment. She would post these to me in parcels.

You could say Jai was now officially my girlfriend.

In the middle of the year we were notified, unofficially, that we could request telephone calls to our families. This had to be done through the prison, and then arranged through our embassies, who would first have to get permission from the Department of Corrections. Each embassy also had to supply mobile phones to the relevant prisoners. It was a bit of an involved process, but worth it.

A British guy in my room was one of the first to use this facility. He made a call to his sister and brother in England. I thought he would be happy after talking to them, but in fact he wasn't. On the contrary, he seemed to slip into a deep depression afterwards. I planned to submit my own request and try to organise a call for October, to coincide with my birthday.

For some reason, Jai's friend Sheila disliked me. Without Jai's knowledge, she wrote me a letter, telling me that she and Jai were struggling to make ends meet and that some nights all they had to eat was biscuits. She asked whether there was any chance I could give her some money. Sheila was friendly with the guard, Piscet Shavolit, who was in charge of the foreign section where our mail was censored. He spoke good English and knew me well. I began to realise that Sheila was reading my letters and then telling Jai what was in them. From the beginning, I had been honest with Jai about the many women in different parts of the world with whom I was regularly corresponding (about 50 at that time), and that I had formed an emotional connection with some of them. When Sheila would relay some of the contents of my letters, Jai's response was to say, 'I know, he has already told me.' In my reply to the letter Sheila herself wrote to me, I told her that I sympathised with her and Jai's situation, and that I also admired the work they were doing. At that time, however, I was receiving just under 4000 Thai baht a month, which was barely enough to survive on, and so I was unable to help them with money.

Actually, I was flabbergasted. How could Sheila ask a prisoner for money? I was in *prison*, for heaven's sake, surviving on the charity of my family and friends. Surely she had other means of support?

Sheila had arranged for a company to donate blocks of Philadelphia cream cheese, in their regular foil packaging, to the American prisoners every week. When she visited, she brought a dozen or more packets of cheese with her, which she would give to the surfer guy, her boyfriend, who was supposed to share them with the other foreigners. Instead, he sold the cheese in the building and used the money to buy heroin. So, when I thought about it, Sheila asking me to give her money basically amounted to supporting her junkie boyfriend's addiction. Before

I received Sheila's letter, I had written to the consular officer telling her about the work Jai and Sheila were doing and asking whether it might be possible for her to give them a list of South African companies operating in Thailand, who might be willing to donate money to their organisation to help prisoners. Now I was sorry I had.

One day, Jai came to our visit in tears. She told me that Sheila had told her that I was using drugs and also selling them in prison. This was such crap. If anything, I was the one who was trying to discourage the other prisoners from using. I didn't try to convince Jai otherwise. She was a Thai, and I told her she could find out for herself by asking any of the guards. All the guards knew I played football and was totally anti-drugs.

For some unfathomable reason, Sheila was doing everything in her power to break up my relationship with Jai. After learning that I had contacted the South African embassy to try and secure some sponsorship from South African companies, Sheila took it upon herself to make an appointment to meet with the consular officer and her husband, and she excluded Jai from this meeting. Immediately I smelt a rat. Three of my enemies sitting around the same table spelt real trouble. Jai was also beginning to see an ugly side to her best friend.

Back home, towards the end of the month, Joan drove to Pretoria, as she did every month, to hand in my allowance at the Department of Foreign Affairs. This time, she was informed that they were no longer able to help her wire my money to Bangkok. We had been using this system for four years. Puzzled, she asked what the problem was. She was told that they had it on good information that I was dealing drugs in prison. Joan was completely shocked. She couldn't believe what she was hearing. She knew in her rational mind that it wasn't possible, but, because of my history of drugs, she did have her doubts. She almost had another nervous breakdown. She would now have to deposit my allowance directly into Jai's account, incurring bank transfer fees – all thanks to Sheila. I was really concerned that between Sheila and the embassy they would jeopardise my application for a royal pardon. They had fucked me, good and solid.

In an email that she sent to me via Jai, Joan pleaded with me to stay out of trouble. No more petitions, she said, and no signing any either.

For some reason, our daily ration of white rice was changed to a plastic bag of red rice. We didn't get any explanation, but it made no difference to me, as all my meals were prepared by my Chinese chef, Lenny. The change caused discontent among the other foreigners, though, especially among my African brothers. Okky, the Nigerian who had disliked me ever since I had declined to swap stamps with him, came to me with a petition he had drafted about the rice, which he wanted me to sign. Remembering my sister's plea, I very politely apologised and explained that under normal circumstances my name and signature would have appeared at the top of any petition but since submitting my royal pardon request my family had advised me not to sign anything. Well, Okky freaked out. He threatened me, saying I should watch my back and warning me that there were 'many of them' and that I could very easily walk into a knife. This was the second time I'd almost got into a fight with this guy, first over stamps and now over rice. Fuck you, I thought, but instead I just said, 'Do what you have to do, and I will do what I have to do.'

In order to the keep prisoners in line, the authorities had a prisoner class system. There were six classes or categories: excellent, very good, good, fair, bad, very bad. New prisoners were immediately classified as 'fair', and twice a year prison officials would review and upgrade your class. To give all prisoners an equal chance, when there was an impending amnesty the prison authorities upgraded you so that you would be in a position to benefit fully, although this was usually done for a fee. Your grade determined your sentence reduction, so guards were notorious for extorting money during this process. For example, if you were in the 'excellent' class, you would get a 50 per cent reduction of sentence, while 'very good' would see you receive a third, and so on.

Each class got you different types of privileges. Unless you had 'excellent' class, you could forget about a royal pardon, sentence remission or parole. Thai nationals were paroled when they had three years of their sentences remaining; foreigners were not eligible for parole at all. There were also what they call 'good days': after serving ten years of your sentence, you got two months' credit for every year served.

367

These months were then cut from your sentence closer to the time of your release. Here again, however, foreigners were excluded.

But you could also be downgraded, and one of the things that could make this happen was if you got into a fight.

I turned and walked away from Okky. The last thing I needed was to get into a fight. Apart from a probable downgrade in prisoner class, I could hear my sister saying those famous words 'I told you so ...', and that was enough of a deterrent.

I was still drawing in black ballpoint pen, still in my so-called black period, but I could feel that a shift in my artistic development was imminent. Love has a way of changing one's energy, and now that I had Jai in my life, maybe that also had something to do with it. I looked forward to her visits every Monday. She would also bring news from home; I no longer needed to wait a month for a letter to arrive.

After four long years in prison, I really missed my family, especially my niece Keri and Darren, my nephew. One day I caught a butterfly. I had one of the Thais who worked in the shell factory cast it in a Perspex block for me, and I sent it home as a gift for Keri, along with my football jersey for Darren.

Princess Chulabhorn Mahidol of Thailand was planning a visit to South Africa in February 1999. My sister intended to try to get an audience with the princess so that she could plead my case and request a royal pardon. It was important to keep my cause alive, and it was always at the forefront of our minds that we needed constantly to generate as much publicity as possible. My art was also starting to receive wider interest, and not all the articles in which I featured in South African publications focused solely on my prisoner status. Reproductions of some of my pieces had appeared in the *Sunday Times* and in magazines back home.

August was the month scheduled for my annual contact visit, on the 12th. This time it was going to be different for me: it would be with Jai. For the first time in a long while, I would physically be in the presence of a woman other than my sister. When you have been deprived of physical contact with the opposite sex for an indefinite period, you become highly vulnerable. Prison romances were not uncommon, although it was difficult for me to understand why a woman in the free world would pursue a relationship with a prisoner. Nevertheless, my relationship with Jai did wonders for my spirit. The compassion she displayed was extraordinary. She made me feel wholesome. She renewed my sense of worth. She was every prisoner's dream. And, at this time in my life, she was a lifeline to the outside world.

The night before the contact visit I hardly slept at all. In just over 12 hours I would come face to face with this woman who had come into my life at a time when I was at my lowest, and who had made me feel like a man again. I had not been intimate with a woman for over four years, and there was a strong physical attraction between Jai and me. It's hard to describe the excitement I felt, and I knew Jai felt the same way.

On 12 August we were seated at a table for four, but we had eyes only for each other. We held hands and talked like excited teenagers. All around us were prisoners and their families. The guards were mainly posted at the entrance, where all visitors were thoroughly checked, but they didn't appear to be overly concerned about what was going on in the visit area. Jai had brought a big paper bag filled with foodstuffs, and we positioned it on the table so that it shielded us slightly from view. We kissed and touched each other. My entire body reacted to her touch, but we restrained ourselves. It was awkward being intimate with so many people around, but even so it was still very exciting.

My visit with Jai was over almost as soon as it began. All the kissing and touching left me as frustrated as when I masturbated, and my groin ached. All I could do was fantasise about what it would have been like if we had gone all the way. A prison visit room was not exactly the place I would have wanted to be intimate with my girlfriend, but right now that was the best I could hope for.

M

Over the years, depending on who was in charge, gambling in prison would be either allowed or prohibited. In 1998, every building had opened the upstairs section of the cells and prisoners were allowed to gamble there during the day. We called this area 'the casino'. Prisoners could also pay money to be allowed to stay in their cells during the day, where they were free to sleep all day or generally do whatever they pleased. Some engaged in sexual activities with the lady-boys. Condoms were readily available from our first-aid room, where prisoners were also treated for minor ailments.

Ever since my miraculous massage, and as a result of changing the position I sat in to draw, my back had recovered nicely, and I was once again jogging and playing football. In the afternoons on the lawn near the front gate, I played *takraw* with Arnut, a Thai friend. He had served 12 years for murder and was expecting to be released any day. He spent most of his days exercising and preparing to go home.

Every building had its Thai Bad Boys – Mafia-style youngsters, who ranged in age from 21 to 35. These guys were fearless. Around October one of the Bad Boys ripped off a Chinese heroin dealer to the tune of about 80 000 Thai baht worth of drugs. He paid half of the money to the guards for protection and smuggled the other half out of the prison to his family. For his own protection, he was locked in a cell upstairs for 24 hours. The guards were completely oblivious to what he was actually doing in his cell – which was slowly sawing through the bars with a loose-blade hacksaw he'd taken from the workshop. Nobody knew this except for those who were planning to escape with him.

One morning, Arnut was called for a visit. On his return, I could see he was very upset. I said, '*Mee arrai?*' (What happened?) The police had come, apparently, and he was now being charged with another murder, a murder he had not committed. Worst of all, the police informed him that they had a witness who had implicated him. From the next day, all Arnut did was jog around the building for hours on end. Then, around 27 December, he called me aside and asked if I had a set of new clothing for him. I was excited on his behalf, thinking that maybe he was going home after all. I packed a couple of things for him, and when I handed them over he asked me to take a walk with him. As we walked, he told me about the escape that had been planned.

The break-out was set for New Year's Eve. Did I want to go with him, he asked. This was the type of information I didn't want to know about. Escaping is something that regularly goes through every prisoner's mind, but planning and executing an escape is another story. I toyed with the idea, but, as a foreigner, without outside help the risks were too high, and getting away with it was also highly unlikely. The watchtowers were manned by armed guards, and the chances of getting shot were very real. If I risked it, I would become a fugitive, have to get a new identity, and be running for the rest of my life. As much as I wanted to go, I knew I couldn't. The odds against me were too high.

I tried to talk Arnut out of escaping, but he told me he couldn't face another life sentence.

On the morning of 1 January 1999 our cell doors were not opened at the usual time of 6.40am. Something was amiss. As 7.30 approached there was still no sign of the guards to open up. All we could hear was the murmur of conversation echoing from the other cells. Then it was well past 8am. Nobody could understand the delay. Eventually, at 8.45 the guards opened our cells and news of the escape spread like lightning. Five Thais had got out after sawing through the bars of the cell upstairs. It seemed that they had escaped at different intervals. One of them had been caught near the temple, another in the hospital, and a third had barely made it over the wall in Building 2. My friend Arnut and one other had scaled the perimeter wall and successfully escaped into the night. Needless to say, I pretended I knew nothing about it, but, when I was walking around, some of the Thais pointed their fingers at me, saying '*Puen kun*' (your friend) in a joking manner. I replied '*Pom mai loo jok*' (I don't know him).

On the night of the escape, certain individuals had changed rooms; some had even gone into the corridor to gamble in the casino. These individuals, along with the room chief, were very badly beaten by the guards. Everybody was aware of my friendship with one of the escapees, so I was surprised I wasn't asked any questions but very glad about it. The gamblers in the prison had made odds about when someone would be caught and who it might be.

Never before had anybody escaped from Bangkwang Central Prison. The Big Tiger was not so secure after all. In the ensuing days of the investigation, various officials from the Department of Corrections and Ministry of Justice and even TV news crews visited our building. When this happened, all prisoners were locked in the factories and dining room. There was going to be hell to pay, that was for sure, and many heads would roll. Our Building Chief was removed, for a start, and the officer in charge of the building was transferred to another prison. The Director of the prison was also eventually removed.

After a nationwide manhunt, we heard that one of the two escapees had been found hiding among the reeds in the river. I prayed it was not my friend. To my relief, it was not Arnut. He was still at large.

I said a silent prayer for him that night.

Towards the end of January 1999, our new Building Chief arrived. He was from Building 5 and had a reputation for being strict and incorruptible. All the guys who owned houses or private rooms and enjoyed certain luxuries were concerned. We had paid a lot of money to the previous Building Chiefs for these privileges, and nobody wanted to lose them. I volunteered to approach him. As a foreigner, there was less chance of repercussions than would be the case for a Thai.

Bribing an officer was a serious offence and everyone knew the risks, but I put a 1000 Thai baht note in an envelope and went and knocked on the man's door. I entered, bowed and greeted him. He gestured to me to sit, and as I did so, I slipped the envelope under one of the books on his table. Then I welcomed him to the building and told him that if he needed any help with anything, he could depend on our support. He pulled the envelope out from the under the book and slid it back to me, saying, '*Pom kin kowe young deeor*' (I only eat rice).

The other guys were waiting outside the office. From the look on my face they gathered that my first attempt to bribe our new Building Chief had failed. We waited with trepidation to see what would happen next.

The first rule the new chief enforced was that cells could have only one TV each. This caused a lot of frustration among those prisoners who had their own private sets. Then, on Tuesday morning, 2 February, all the room chiefs in private cells were called to the office. When it came to my turn, I knew what to expect. I pulled up a chair and the chief urged me closer so that I could see what he had attached to his clipboard. It was the roll-call list for every room. He pointed to the list, indicating that all the other rooms had anything from 22 to 25 people in a cell, whereas in my room there were only 16 people. This was not fair, he said. He instructed me to find another four inmates to put in my cell. I tried to negotiate, emphasising that foreigners were physically bigger than Thais. I mentioned the United Nations' regulations and added that, in our culture, it was unacceptable for men to sleep in such close proximity to one another. I threw in the word 'embassy' a few times, which usually carried a lot of weight. In the end we reached a compromise and settled for two new room members, bringing the total in our cell to 18.

Room 17, which was also a foreign room, and housed mainly Africans, also had 18 inmates. The Building Chief didn't even consult with them. He just added four Thai prisoners to their cell without any negotiation. I happened to bump into one of the Nigerians, who asked me how many additional people we had had to put into ours. He was very unhappy at the disparity. The difference was that the foreigners in our room were fortunate in having a few strong embassies, and the prison authorities were more accommodating when it came to Western foreigners. Nigeria didn't even have an embassy in Thailand.

In my experience in prison, the Thais were the biggest racists, and anybody who had a black skin was immediately classified as a Nigerian. The authorities did what they pleased with them, and for the most part treated them like animals. The guy I'd talked to went back to his room and quoted me as having told him that the Building Chief had said that the Nigerians were all animals and that he would do with them as he pleased. You can imagine their reaction! All 40 pissed-off Nigerians descended on the Building Chief's office. Four of the most influential among them, along with a translator, were allowed to go into the office, while the rest waited outside. I was in the middle of eating lunch in a Chinese friend's house when I heard my name being called over the loudspeaker instructing me to report to the office. I covered my food with a plate and innocently made my way there. All the Nigerians were there, looking exceedingly discontented. At that time I really had no idea what the fuck was going on.

As soon as I walked into the office, one of the translators said that the Building Chief wanted to know why I had said that *he* had said that the Nigerians were all animals. I looked around the office at each person standing there. Then I looked at the Building Chief and uttered two words, '*Gore hok*' (They are lying), before walking straight out the door. Nobody said a word. I went back to my Chinese friend's house and tried to finish my lunch, but by then my food was cold and I had lost my appetite. Motherfuckers had taken my words completely out of context! I was mad as hell, not only by them twisting my words, but more by the fact that the Nigerians had gone to the prison authorities instead of speaking to me first.

I left my food and went to look for Okky. He was the Nigerians' leader, and as such he had to take responsibility. By then the group of Nigerians that had congregated outside the office had dispersed. I saw Okky coming out of our coffee shop and I accosted him. 'What the fuck was all that about?' I demanded. 'I never said what your friend quoted me saying.' I then told him what I *had* said and I stuck by it. I also reminded him that we foreigners should settle our own problems and avoid involving the prison authorities. After saying my piece, as I turned around to walk away, Okky called me a fucking arsehole. I spun around to face him. 'What did you say?' I said. He repeated the words. In that instant I lost my cool and I went for him.

Ahmed, my Muslim Afghan friend, happened to be nearby and he grabbed my arm in an attempt to hold me back, but I wriggled free from his grip. I took a few steps towards Okky and lashed out with a kick to the groin, followed by two successive punches to his face. At the same time Okky swung wildly with both arms, missing me completely. We were pulled apart by other foreigners, but by then a large group of onlookers had gathered. Blood was coming out of Okky's mouth and nose. The next thing I knew, he was holding this aluminium stool above his head and running towards me. He looked like he was out to kill.

I turned and ran into the paper bag factory, where Thai prisoners were sitting around folding bags. My eyes were darting all over the show, looking for a weapon. There was nothing I could see and Okky was still coming at me. There was no mistaking his intentions. I could see murder written all over his face. I thought his eyes were going to pop out. I slowed down to a fast walk, allowing him to get closer to me. As soon as he was within arm's reach, I whirled around and leapt at him, grabbing his neck in an arm lock. He still managed to bring the aluminium stool down on the top of my head, opening a wound. I held onto his neck and punched him repeatedly in the face. It took five Blue Shirts to pull us apart. Blood was pouring down my face and my head hurt like hell. I imagined it was quite a deep cut.

I went to the first-aid centre to see whether I needed stitches. The prisoner who was also our resident doctor reassured me that it was only a deep scratch, nothing serious, and he cleaned me up. Relieved, I went to my locker, grabbed a bandana, and as I was tying it around my head, I saw a group of Nigerians, about eight of them, some of whom were the elders from their tribe, coming towards me. What the fuck now, I thought. I was still mad as hell. They indicated that they wanted to talk, but I had nothing to say. They pleaded with me to leave everything as it was and not to continue fighting. The guy who had misquoted me was among them. Pointing my finger at him, I said, 'This was entirely your fault. I never said all that shit.' The guy apologised. Okay, fuck it, I agreed, we'd leave it at that.

Meanwhile, I didn't know it, but almost every guard had left the building in a hurry. I went off to the gym, which was around the corner from where the Nigerians hung out. While I was busy training, about an hour after the fight, Okky and I were called to come to the office immediately. Okky had an entourage of brothers escorting him. Ahmed, my Muslim brother, walked with me. One of the guards had two sets of documents with him. He said the words I dreaded: '*Song kun by dan sip*' (The two of you are going to Building 10).

Actually, it was odd that we were being punished; usually when foreigners fought nothing happened. I wondered whether this was because of my petition or even my association with Arnut. Okky began to protest, but I knew I was guilty, so I just signed the papers and went to pack my things. There was no time to put money up my arse this time so I gave Mohammed 7 000 Thai baht in cash and asked him to send it to me in solitary. We were allowed to take a towel with us, a couple of items of clothing and toiletries. I also took a writing pad, envelope and stamps, my reading glasses, my ice cooler and my prayer books – one a book of psalms and another called *Jewish Thoughts*. I hid my Walkman and earphones among my clothes. I also packed some coffee, Coffeemate and my mug. Okky and I were taken to have shackles fitted and then we were marched to the security section, where we should have been checked but weren't. We were then escorted by two guards to the solitary confinement building, which was situated at the other end of the prison compound.

I'm not sure what was going through my mind. Being a prisoner within the prison was not a good thing, but, then again, how could I claim accurately to be able to explain prison life without having been in solitary? It was almost 3pm by then and close to the end of a prison day. Normally at this time the guards were tired and lazy, and when we arrived they didn't even bother to check our stuff. I was taken upstairs to the second floor and Okky to the third. My cell was dark and dingy. It smelled of damp and dirt. It was about 3m in length and 1.5m in width, with a small wall just under a metre high dividing the toilet area from where I would sleep. The door was of solid steel, with a small square gap just below the centre where things could be passed through. Next to the door was a set of bars covered with a dusty mosquito net that stretched halfway down from the ceiling. There was no light or fan in my cell. The only light was what filtered through from the passage. The cockroaches were the size of my thumb. The key-boy

Around four years into my sentence, circa 1998.

Soon after my first six-month stint in solitary, 1999.

NEWS

Local man's 100 year sentence reduced to 40 by Thai King

David Shapshak

AN ORANGE Grove man serving a 100 year life sentence in a Thai prison for drug trafficking has had his sentence reduced to 40 years by Thailand's monarch.

The amnesty bestowed onto Alexander Krebs, 36, by His Majesty King Bhumibol Adulyadej is in celebration of the King's Coronation Golden Jubilee.

Mr Krebs was arrested in April 1994 for drug trafficking while on holiday in Thailand but maintains his innocence, claiming he was not aware

Seen here before his Thailand trip, Alexander Krebs has spent two years of his recently reduced sentence in a Thai prison for drug trafficking.

he was committing the crime.

Heroin weighing 2,2kg was found sewn into the lining of a bag he had been asked to carry.

A fax from the South African Embassy in Thailand confirms that Mr Kreb's sentence has been commuted.

His sister, Babi Sacks, said she was excited about the reduction, hoping that further reductions may be eventually possible.

Family and friends, who have been in constant touch with Shani – as he is known to them, say he is faring well.

Bishop Desmond Tutu, chairman of the

Truth and Reconciliation Commission and former Anglican Archbishop of Cape Town, and Chief Rabbi Cyril Harris have also written to the King on Shani's behalf.

In his letter, Bishop Tutu wrote of the South African prisoners: "Their family and friends humbly request that these prisoners be deported from Thailand to serve their sentences in South Africa."

Mr Krebs wrote last year to President Nelson Mandela asking him to intervene on behalf of the nine South Africans serving sentences in Thai jails.

"I appeal to you sir, as the only person in

South Africa who can secure our release," Shani wrote.

"You of all people understand what it is like to be robbed of one's freedom. You gave up everything to fight for your freedom, not only your family life, but also your own freedom, because you strongly believed Apartheid was morally wrong, and every South African irrespective of race or colour had a right. I now ask you: Do I have a right?"

An exhibition is being planned for Shani's art work and poetry which he has done during his imprisonment.

One of many articles highlighting my predicament that appeared in South African media. This one was published in the *Tribune* in 1999.

The perimeter wall of Bangkwang prison was studded with guard towers like this. Although manned by armed commodores, duty in the towers was actually a punishment for the guards.

The dragon emerges, circa 2001–2002. Having received a 100-year sentence, I intended to have a new tattoo done each year.

Preparing for a volleyball competition on the tennis court of Building 1, circa 1998. I had shaved my head not long before this, and my hair was just beginning to grow back.

Manslaughter United, the B team of Building 2 for the annual inter-building football tournament, January 1996. The design of our kit was based on the Bafana Bafana uniform of that time.

Relaxing after a tough football practice with my Nigerian brother Jaap.

Keeping fit and healthy, 2005.

In prison, cultural barriers didn't really exist. when I moved to Building 6, in 2010, I joined my new band of friends in their Christmas celebration – my first. This photo was taken in Danny's house.

With my Chinese friend Lim, who cooked for me for ten years. This picture was taken in the garden of Building 4 during an indoor football competition.

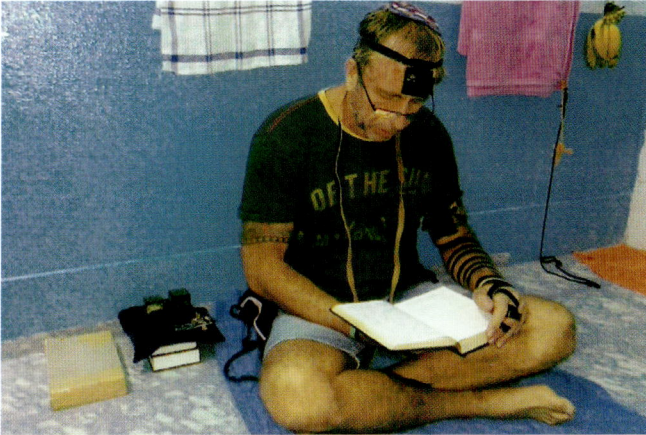

Even during my second stint in solitary, I remained serious about my prayers and Torah study. Although I was locked up for 24 hours a day, with nothing but a towel for my bed and my *siddur* for a pillow, I also understood that *Hashem* was preparing me spiritually and psychologically for my imminent freedom.

Over the years, Joan worked tirelessly to secure my release or a transfer to a South African prison. This picture is from 1997 or 1998.

'Nelson Mandela' (ballpoint pen, 1996). This was part of my 'black period' series.

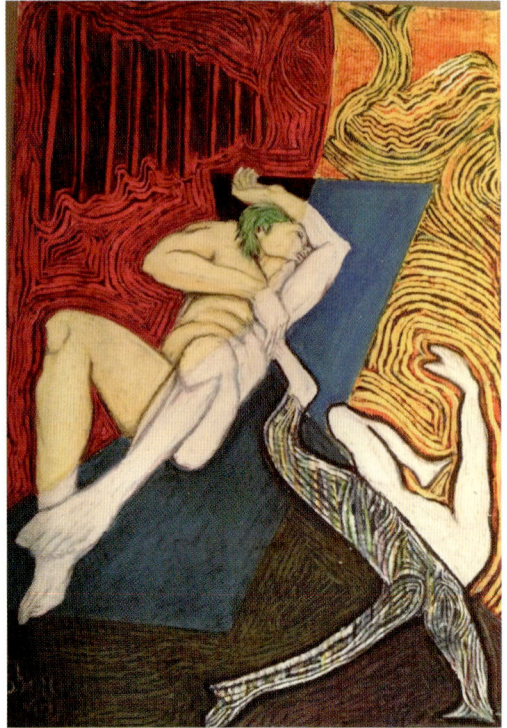

'Freedom of the spirit' (oil pastel, 2000). I created this artwork soon after my first stint in solitary.

'Rabbi Menachem Mendel Schneerson' (handpainted in carbon powder – fine granules of charcoal – with Chinese brushes, 2003). I had a very spiritual experience when I completed this painting. Much later, when I exhibited it in a gallery, some people even asked who the photographer was!

'King Bhumibol Adulyadej' (handpainted in carbon powder, 2002).

'Reflection on still water' (handpainted in carbon powder, circa 2006).

'Lona Misa' (handpainted in carbon powder, circa 2007).

'Fine line this madness' (oil pastel, 2009).

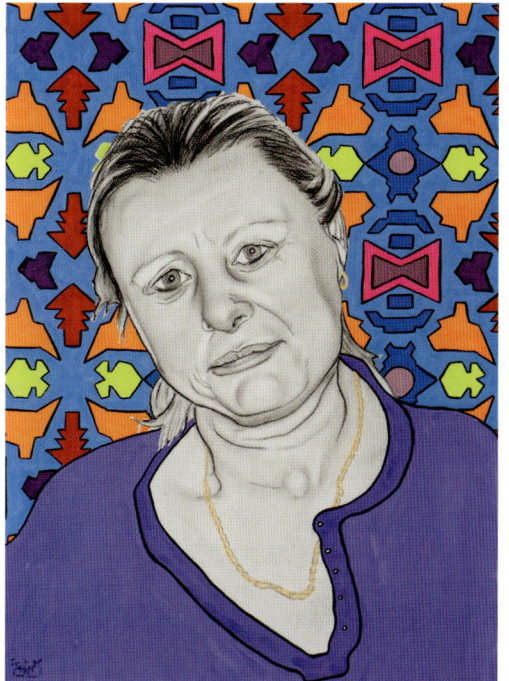

'Joan' (mixed media – charcoal and poster paint – circa 2007). All of Joan's cares and suffering seem to be weighing on her in this picture.

With my nephew Darren and niece Keri during a contact visit, September 2005. Apart from photos, this was the first time I had seen them in 11 years.

With Malcolm and Joan during the September 2005 contact visit.

I was a complete wreck after my five-day ordeal in IDC, but I was free. Elisabeth saw me off at Bangkok's Suvarnabhumi International Airport before my flight back to South Africa.

was normally the last to be locked up, so I asked him to get me a rag, as I needed to clean the cell. There was dust everywhere. What a task it was to clean.

When I was finished, I took a shower in the filthy water. Back at the other building I always wore my underpants when I showered. Now, for the first time in four years, I was entirely on my own and could shower naked. I had forgotten what it was like to have privacy, to be completely alone. In a strange way it felt liberating. Perhaps I would enjoy my solitude. After all, being on your own is not necessarily about being alone, but about how you spend the time with yourself. I slipped on my boxers under my shackles, spread out my towel and lay down. It was hot and virtually airless in the cell. I found the awful mouldy stench suffocating and I could taste dust in my throat. There were spider's webs in the corner of the ceiling and all over the bars. I was sweating profusely, and so I tore off the thin cardboard from the back of my writing pad and used it as a fan. It didn't help much, but it was better than nothing.

Just as it was growing dark, I heard the security gate at the end of the corridor being opened and footsteps coming towards my cell. To my surprise it was one of the guards from Building 2. '*Aleksanda*,' he said.

'*Sa-wat-dee kraup*,' I said excitedly. He passed me a brown envelope through the hole in the door and mentioned Mohammed's name. '*Kap kun kap*,' I repeated. '*Kap kun kap*.'

It was my money! Gee, that was fast! I also had money on my prison card. Among my stationery I had another brown envelope in which I kept my stamps, envelopes, letters and some photos. And, bound in packaging tape, I had also made a hidden compartment there, where I kept my cash. I placed the 7 000 Thai baht inside the compartment. So far, whenever there had been searches, they had never found my money.

That night was a long one. I prayed with all my heart for G-d to give me strength to endure the days ahead. I recited the *Shema Yisrael* in Hebrew, which I knew off by heart. I couldn't sleep. It had been some time since I had last slept on such a hard concrete surface. I got up and paced the length of my cell, up and down. It was a short walk. None the less, after a few hours I was tired and eventually I fell into a light sleep, only to be woken by a huge cockroach running across my face. Fuck, I nearly jumped out of my skin! Cockroaches are such creepy insects, I never could stand them. It was hard to go back to sleep after that, as I was expecting cockroaches to come out of every crack in the wall. The little fuckers were everywhere. Around 5am I relieved myself, brushed my teeth and proceeded to clean the cell properly. Then I paced up and down again. My head was hurting. I sat around until, at about 7.30, I heard the gates at the end of the corridor being opened. The key-boy opened some of the other cells, which I thought was strange as we were all supposed to be locked up, but then I realised that the people who were being let out were the workers who maintained the building. I called the key-boy and asked him to organise, firstly, hot water for me and, secondly, somebody who could do my laundry. Thirty minutes later, a young boy called Sau, meaning 'tiger', came to my cell. His real name was Tanpong. He was from Laos, spoke good Thai and also reasonable English. We agreed that he would be my wash boy and I gave him the clothes I had slept in. I also asked him if there was anybody who could cook my meals. He called Joodt, who was the Building Chief's boy and who also prepared meals for the guards. For a fee of 2 000 Thai baht, Joodt agreed to help me.

While I was waiting and hoping for a visit from Jai, a couple of Nigerians who knew me and had heard I was in Building 10 came and sat outside my cell. I learnt that there were 89 prisoners in the building. The Nigerians couldn't believe that I was in trouble. It felt great to be among friends. I was not so alone after all.

Luckily, Building 10 and Building 2 had the same visit days. Of course Jai had no idea I had been in a fight and had been shackled and thrown into solitary confinement, and she was shocked when she saw me. I tried to reassure her that solitary wasn't as bad as people said. However, I told her, I did need some things urgently. I gave her a list of things to send me in a parcel, among them ankle guards and football socks (to protect my shins and heels from the chafing of the chains) and, most importantly, a hand fan, lots of tobacco and some soap. She had already brought my weekly supplies with her, and after the visit she promised to go to the prison canteen and buy me a whole lot of fruit. She also promised to fax my sister and let her know what had happened.

When I returned to my cell, Tiger, my new wash boy, was waiting at the gate and he helped carry my things upstairs. Every building has its own system of operating, and Building 10 was no exception. A lot of the guys, although they were in punishment, moved around freely during the day, and for the drug dealers it was business as usual. I knew many of the guys in the building from football. Apparently, you could pay to be let out of your cell, but the only problem was that the Building Chief was away on a course for a month, so for the moment I had to return to my cell, where I was locked up. I shared the fruit Jai had brought me with the key-boy and arranged that he would bring me boiled water in the morning for my coffee. If he obliged, I told him, he could join me. I was getting myself organised.

There was no doubt in my mind that the weeks and months ahead – I would be there for at least six months, possibly longer – would be a true test of my physical and mental strength. I also needed to make a plan to get back to Building 2 after serving my punishment because all my things were there. There was very little theft among the inmates, though, so at least I had peace of mind that my stuff would be safe.

It didn't take long for me to realise that solitary was a place that could drive you crazy. My second night was as bad as my first. The heat was intolerable. The lack of air made me feel claustrophobic. I would build up a sweat from trying to fan myself to keep cool. I wanted to cry. Back in the other building I had thought my bed was uncomfortable, but this was so much worse. Memories of my first days in prison came to mind and I found myself reliving those early horrors all over again.

As darkness descended around me, a flicker of light shone through the bars, enabling me to read psalms. It felt like I was conversing with G-d. Here was a lesson waiting to be learnt. It was no longer just about survival. Between 4 and 6pm you could hear the echoing of chains from all over the building. My own rusty shackles had already grazed the skin behind my heels.

Rusty chains reflected your standard of personal hygiene. At the halfway point there was a nylon string attached to the chains, and to clean them you would sit in your shower area, feet slightly apart, and shake your chains back and forth so that they rubbed against each other. After a few days your chains would shine like silver jewellery. To keep them clean, you would do this procedure twice a day. Your chains became an extension of you. Some guys were so obsessive that they added silver rings, so that when they walked, and the chains rubbed against each, they made a distinctive sound.

In the morning, the key-boy arrived with a flask of hot water and his own mug. At the edge of the entrance to my cell, with me on the inside and he on the outside, we drank our coffee and engaged in idle chat as if nothing was out of the ordinary. Boiling water in solitary was a luxury. In appreciation, my new friend would leave my cell door open during the day so that I could at least move freely in the corridor. I was not allowed beyond the steel gates at the end of the corridor, however, but it was better than nothing. Deep down I felt uneasy, almost to the point of being paranoid, thinking about the events that had led me to being here. Why had all the guards left the building straight after my fight with Okky? Now more than ever, I realised, I would have to be extra-vigilant. Prisoners had been known to die in mysterious circumstances, and this was the perfect place for somebody to meet with an accident.

During the course of the morning, several foreigners in the building who knew me came to say hello. One of my good Nigerian friends, a guy by the name of Lawal, a great footballer, was also there, and there was an American I knew, as well as a British guy, both of whom were junkies, and both of whom had the same first name. They were amazed to discover that I had organised to have my cell door left open.

On the same floor as me, but at the opposite end of the corridor, was a Thai prisoner, a white-collar criminal, who had apparently embez-zled millions on the stock exchange. The man lived like a king, but he kept very much to himself. He had actually paid money to stay in solitary confinement, for his own protection. The guy had a TV set, a portable fan, lights and even a foam mattress. He was only in his mid-twenties but he was fat, and he had a pasty-white complexion and an air of superiority about him. He treated the other Thai prisoners badly, and even disrespected the prison authorities. Actually, I was quite shocked by his behaviour and also how he seemed to get away with it. We spoke on occasion, and from what I gathered he was part of a syndicate and was the one who had taken the rap.

At lunchtime Joodt brought me a plate of rice, two fried chicken legs and some vegetables. It was very tasty. A meal like this would cost me 2 000 Thai baht a month. Afterwards, I was sitting quietly, eating fruit, when one of the Thai samurai knocked on my cell door. I knew this boy. He was a bit psycho and extremely dangerous. He had been thrown out of almost every building in Bangkwang and had been in solitary more times than you could count. I knew his last offence had been attacking another inmate with a meat cleaver, and that he had chopped the guy up pretty bad. I beckoned him into my room. He sat down in a squatting position and apologised for intruding. He asked if I would lend him some money, which was obviously for heroin. He was an addict and this made him even more unpredictable. I told him in Thai that I was going to be honest with him: I hated drugs and could not in all conscience give him money for drugs. However, if he didn't have food, he was welcome to join me every day and eat with me, but money I wouldn't give him. 'Toti kartot kun korchai pom,' I said, apologising and asking for his understanding.

He *wai*ed me and said, '*Mai penrai*' (never mind), and thanked me.

It was important for me to make a stand on this issue or every junkie would be knocking on my door.

Nothing changed for the drug dealers in solitary and, as always, the Nigerians were running the show. One of the dealers was locked up for only 20 hours. The dealers paid a commission to the Building Chief, and if they didn't pay, the Building Chief would send a few guys round to threaten them. They would even have someone who wouldn't cooperate stabbed.

Okky had got to hear that I was not locked up and was moving around freely in the corridor. He wrote to the prison authorities, asking why he was locked up while I was allowed out. As a result the poor key-boy was reprimanded and my cell door was locked again. What an asshole – I was not impressed with Okky. So, there I was, locked up again for 24 hours a day. Even so, I didn't feel safe in the place. I began to imagine that perhaps the prison authorities were planning to get rid of me. My suspicions were further heightened when, one afternoon around 3pm, the Director of the prison, along with the guard named Chavoret Jarubwon and his bodyguards, visited Building 10. They came to the second floor. One of the guards opened my cell and called me to come out. The Director was standing about four metres away from me. I greeted him with a bow. Then Chavoret asked me if I had been treated well and if there was anything I would like to ask the Director. It was unusual for the Director to see any prisoner, so I was highly suspicious. I said no, I had nothing to say, and then they left and I was locked up again. I guessed the Director wanted to know exactly who Alexander Krebs was. Shit! I vowed to be even more vigilant from then on.

The following morning, I made a request to go to the hospital. We left at midday. The normal procedure for this was that the prisoners from the other buildings went to the hospital at 9am. The authorities did not want those of us who were in solitary to meet with the other inmates, out of fear of us smuggling contraband. My ulterior motive for asking to be seen by the prison doctor was so that there would be a witness who, if I died, could say that it hadn't been from natural causes. I complained about an infection on my heels where the chains had rubbed the skin off. I also asked for medication for my painful back. In fact, the awkwardness of walking with shackles *was* beginning to take its toll on my lower back, so it wasn't entirely a lie. The medic put Betadene on my heels.

The following day, I received a parcel from Jai containing a lot of tobacco, soap, another towel, a face cloth, the hand fan I'd especially asked her for, and a plastic fold-up mat to sleep on.

After ten days of being locked up for 24 hours a day, I started to lose my mind. I wrote to the prison authorities, asking to be allowed out of my cell to exercise, telling them that I was ready to commit suicide. I was given permission to come out three days a week from 9am to 12pm. It made a huge difference to the lonely days of doing nothing but staring at the four walls. The average punishment for fighting was three months in solitary confinement, but it could take three months just for your case to be heard. Once you were sentenced, your prisoner class would be cut, your visits stopped, and you could expect to be locked up for 24 hours a day.

By now, though, I was into my routine, such as it was, and a structured day did wonders to keep me stable. I would wake up between 4.30 and 5.30am, wash my hands as required by Jewish tradition, and then wash them again, after a thrilling session of squatting on the loo. (When I first got to prison, initially in Bombat, on discovering that there was no toilet paper and we were required to use our hands, the thought of touching my dirty arse sickened me, but now I had got used to it.)

After this, I would daven *Mincha,* the morning service, while on my mat. When I was finished, I would do 500 stomach crunches, a couple of back-stretching exercises and some pelvic thrusts. Then I would shift all my things to one side of my cell, fill my ice cooler with water and washing powder and proceed to wash the walls, wipe down the mosquito screen and the door, and then wash the floor on the empty side. I would then move all my things to the other side of the cell and clean that side. Usually by this time the workers would have been let out of their cells and my wash boy would come to collect my dirty laundry. Once the floor was dry, I would do a couple of loosening-up and stretching exercises, followed by ten sets of 50 push-ups, back and forward windmills and four sets of tricep dips, finishing with 15 minutes of shadow boxing. After that I would wash my hands again and roll up my plastic mat.

Then I began the preparations required for what I was going to wear for the day. I would cover my two canvas bags with a towel to form a kind of table surface and place my clean clothes on top of it. Then I removed my shorts. It was quite an interesting procedure getting them over or under the shackles. Each link of my chains was 4.5cm long and just over 1cm thick and there were 27 links, not to mention the two steel rings clamped around my feet ... I would then brush my teeth, wash the rags I used to clean the floor and then scrub the toilet and shower area clean. Washing my underwear came next (I wasn't comfortable giving these to my wash boy), then my ankle guards and, lastly, my bandana. I had not shaved since being in solitary confinement and my beard was coming on nicely. Finally, I began the arduous task of cleaning my chains, using washing powder and a square of Scotch-Brite, after which I would give the chains a good shake. Once all that was done, I would take a shower in what was river water diluted with lime. Afterwards I would usually be itching all over.

Then I hung my washing on a makeshift line in my cell. Moving across to my sleeping area, I'd take an earbud and clean my ears and bellybutton. Then I would get dressed and give my chains a final shine with a piece of towelling. My chores done for the day, I would stretch out on my mat and take it easy.

Many of the inmates in solitary already knew each other from the other buildings, the visit room or through playing football. The guys who knew me and who were allowed out of their cells would come and sit outside my cell and engage in idle chatter. I didn't really mind because it passed the time, but I was starting to enjoy being on my own.

Some days I would have a breakfast consisting of two fried eggs, bread and biscuits (although getting bread wasn't always predictable). One day Mohammed sent me three loaves of sliced bread; I kept one for myself and the others I shared with some of the guys.

After breakfast, I would clean my teeth and then write a few letters, read for a while or take a nap. Around 2pm my food would be delivered to my cell. This was generally a portion of fried rice, 100g of fried chicken breast and more bread. If there were any vegetables on offer that day, I would arrange to eat some, but usually there were only bones in the stew. My wash boy would then arrive with my clean laundry and push it through the gap in the steel door. At around 4pm I would daven *Mincha*, after which I would read from my book of psalms and try to study a bit of Judaism. I found this quite difficult.

After about 20 minutes my mind would begin to drift. This wasn't a new problem; I lost concentration easily. Often I would think I was reading away, but nothing would be registering. All those years of drug abuse had definitely damaged my mind, and sometimes I wondered whether I would ever be normal again. In fact, I doubted it.

In the late afternoon, for dinner I would have some fruit and some of the things my sister had sent in one of her parcels. I cleaned and flossed my teeth after every meal. I would tidy up here and there, then remove my clothing, wash my 'ankle bracelets' and shower. After I had dried myself I would lie on my mat naked, with only a sarong covering my private parts, and listen to my Walkman. I was so lucky to have risked – and succeeded – smuggling my radio into solitary. Around 7pm I would continue with some letter-writing for about an hour, depending on how tired I was, and then, to tire myself out, I would read from my books on Judaism.

M

I had always suffered from insomnia. Some nights in solitary I would be so exhausted you'd have thought I'd have fallen asleep right away, but I wasn't ever able to enjoy a full night's sleep there. I would lie awake with my eyes closed, conjuring up my own dreams, and eventually drift off, but it was always into a light sleep.

Slowly I was adjusting to this dump. At least I was allowed to go out three times a week to exercise, and on Saturdays, depending on which guard was on duty, I was also let out of my cell for a few hours. After a month, the Building Chief returned from his leave. Through Joodt, my cook, I planned on negotiating with the chief to be let out every day like some of the others – most of whom, admittedly, had been there much longer than me. Naturally, I knew I would have to pay for this privilege but I was prepared to do that. Joodt said I should wait a few days, as I had only been there a month, but I told him I was going crazy. Being locked up for 20 hours a day is not funny.

One afternoon, my white-collar criminal friend arrived back from his afternoon visit carrying two big bags of ready-made food and fruit – man, that guy could eat! By now everybody was locked up. Unbeknown to me (and certainly to him), waiting in the shadows near my door were two samurai armed with knives. The fat man walked past my cell, where I was stretched out on my mat lost in my own thoughts, and I heard what sounded like a scuffle and a grunt-like moan. Then there was a thud, followed by noises like a pig squealing and some more muffled sounds. I jumped up and peeked through the bars and mosquito screen. I could see the man's fat frame stretched out on the floor. Standing over him was one of the young Bad Boys, who couldn't have been more than 21 years old, stabbing him repeatedly in the chest. There was blood everywhere. It was like watching a movie. To tell the truth, I was not really fazed, although it seemed to go on for ever. Eventually, the fat body stopped moving.

The two attackers left quickly, running past my cell, leaving the body lying in a pool of blood. A couple of minutes later, about three or four guards came upstairs with some of the workers. They carried the body out of view of my cell. I could hear the steel door at the opposite end of the corridor being opened, where I knew there was another entrance and a stairway that was only used by the guards. That was how easy it was to assassinate somebody.

I didn't sleep at all that night. In fact, I became totally paranoid, imagining I could be next. I had witnessed the murder, after all. In the morning the key-boy and I drank coffee as usual. He asked me if I had seen what had happened. I told him I had been asleep and had been woken up by what sounded like a fight, but that I hadn't looked to check what was going on. It was not my business. He told me that they had killed 'Oen', the fat one. I asked why. Apparently, his execution had been ordered from outside because he had threatened to bring down the others in his syndicate unless they paid him more money. You didn't have to be a genius to understand how this hit had been arranged. I heard later that the youngster who had done the stabbing was badly beaten by the guards, and that they had broken his hand and leg.

That same morning, I was told by the Building Chief, Mr Sampon Pauksi, that I could come out of my cell, and that I would also be moved upstairs to the third floor on the west side of the building, where the sun set. The cells were much cleaner on that floor and were not so dark and dingy. I slipped the Building Chief an envelope containing some bucks, and that secured me my freedom in solitary.

Upstairs turned out to be great. I discovered that my wash boy was an electrician by trade and was quite a resourceful young man. From the lights in the corridor he ran a cable into my cell and attached a plug. Using some wet rice, I stuck some paper from a magazine around the mosquito screen to hide the cable. One of the workers who was a permanent resident in solitary sold me a light fixture with a globe and I made a lampshade from cardboard. I tied my new lamp to the bars with a piece of string so that it hung about two feet above my mat. In solitary you were not allowed to have a light in your cell. Our floor faced the prison tower, and at night a light in one of our cells could easily be spotted by the guards on duty. Sometimes during the night the guards also patrolled the corridor, and if we heard the steel gates being opened at any point, everybody would quickly switch their lights off. Lady Luck seemed to follow me wherever I went. The next day, a group of inmates who had finished their punishment were being moved back to their buildings. One of them had a portable electric fan, which I bought off him for 500 Thai baht. I also managed to buy two blankets. Life in solitary confinement was turning out to be very different from how I had imagined it.

Besides the inconvenience of the shackles, once I had got myself into a routine, I realised that living alone in a cell and having privacy again was something I could actually get to like. I suppose that, wherever we are in life, it is our present circumstances that will always be the environment that holds challenges and offers growth. This I was learning. No matter what the situation, I embraced the dawning of each day, because in my heart I knew that G-d had a purpose for me. Having faith gave me strength. I had begun to accept that we were born to suffer in order to teach others to appreciate what they have.

My family and friends all over the world continued to send me parcels. From my friend Edna in England I received the *Me'am Lo'ez* volumes of *The Torah Anthology* by Yaakov Culi. This is a widely studied commentary on the *Tanach*. Now that I had light in my cell I could devote more time to studying.

In one of the parcels Joan sent me she included about ten bandanas, which I shared with my wash boy and some of my friends. While he was doing my laundry one day, one of the Bad Boys strolled up to him, pulled the bandana off his head and walked off with it. I was lying in my cell, my newly acquired fan blowing cool air in my face. I was thinking how great life was, even in this confined space. I felt content. I could have been anywhere in the world.

Next thing my boy came charging through my door. He looked really upset.

'*Mi aria, puen?*' (What's up, friend?) I asked him, and he told me what had just happened.

Thais have their own way of dealing with their problems, and as a foreigner it was generally prudent not to interfere. I told him to report the incident to the guards – after all, most of them were snitches – but he was a proud man and he didn't want to involve them. He was look-ing at me like I had the answer. As his boss, I realised that he wanted me to go and retrieve the bandana for him. Fuck it, I told him, let it go. I told him I would give him another one. If I did that, though, it would be perceived as an act of weakness, and, the next thing I knew, the Bad Boys would be helping themselves to my things.

There was an African American guy in solitary by the name of Stan, and he and I had become good friends. I discussed my dilemma with him and he offered to come with me to try and resolve my wash boy's problem. I didn't really want to involve him because I knew that if two of us approached the Bad Boys, this would be considered an act of ag-gression. I agreed that Stan should come with me, but that he would stay out of sight and wait for me at the entrance of the staircase.

The Bad Boys slept in cells on the first floor, and this floor was their turf. Going there was like walking into a hornets' nest. When I got there, there were about 13 of them, sitting around talking, some doing deals, while one or two others were shooting heroin up their veins. The guy who had stolen the bandana was a new face to me. I had never seen him before. I estimated him to be in his late twenties. He was tall and skinny and his eyes were psychotic. As I approached, they all stopped what they were doing – except for the junkies, who carried on shooting up. I lifted my arm with my palm facing the ground. I moved my fingers as if closing my hand. I repeated the action a few times, calling the culprit at the same time to come to me. He ignored me, giving me the who-the-fuck-do-you-think-you-are look. This was not a good sign. I could feel my throat constricting, and I realised that I might very well have to fight the guy.

As I moved forward to confront him, the samurai who had come to me wanting to borrow money walked out of his cell.

'*Aleksander, mi arai?*' (What's up?) he greeted me.

I greeted him back, and then explained to him that one of his gang members had stolen my boy's bandana and that I would like it back. He called the guy in question over and ordered him to give the bandana to me, which he reluctantly did. I thanked my friend, and he told me that if I had any problems in the future I should come directly to him. I breathed a sigh of relief, knowing that the whole picture could have turned very ugly. But this was prison. Unlike my white-collar criminal friend, whose destiny it had been to die, it wasn't my turn yet. I had survived yet another life-threatening situation. Somebody up there was looking after me.

Sometimes in prison you are forced to do things you would normally be terrified of doing. Aggression is fought with aggression, even when the odds are against you. Any wavering can result in death, and every day is a gamble. Unpredictability was a real enemy that lurked inside each and every one of us. Your life was only worth what any given moment dictated. I understood this. I also understood that this phase in my prison existence would not only test me on many levels but would also become of great significance. If nothing else, it would make for an interesting chapter in the book I might one day write – if I survived!

While routine brings a degree of stability to one's life, it can also cause monotony, and by now I was getting bored. I distanced myself from the action. I was reminded of when I was in DB while in the military, which was worse, in my opinion. I was very restless, and

I attributed this to a subconscious yearning to express my feelings through drawing. It had been quite a while since I had last spent any time on my art. On her next visit, I planned to ask Jai to buy me some art supplies. Because of my limited funds, I could only afford some cheap watercolours and an A4 drawing pad, but it would be something.

The thing that continued to give me comfort in solitary confinement was knowing that there were people back in South Africa, and elsewhere, still working tirelessly towards my release. In a letter from my sister, I learnt that, through a friend, our family friend and the well-known philanthropist Bertie Lubner had had my letter to Nelson Mandela hand-delivered to him. This year, 1999, was to be Mandela's last as president. I was convinced that if anyone could empathise with the plight of prisoners, it was Mandela. True to her word, Joan had also somehow managed to give a letter to Princess Chulabhorn Mahidol of Thailand, during her royal visit to South Africa, asking her to intercede on my behalf. We both knew this was a long shot, but neither of us was about to give up. Thinking about and planning for the day I would be released kept me positive and strong. I didn't have any other option.

On Tuesday 23 March 1999, at 2pm, Okky and my cases came up. I was sentenced to three months' solitary confinement and all visitation privileges were withdrawn for that period. My prisoner class was cut from 'excellent' to 'very good'. I felt the sentence was harsh, but, in a country where sentences were generally ridiculous, I reckoned I'd got off lightly. At least I knew that I would be out of solitary by the end of June.

On the same morning, Rabbi Kantor from Chabad House was permitted a special contact visit for all the Jewish inmates. He brought his *tefillin* (phylacteries) with him and each one of us had a chance to put it on. We recited the appropriate blessings, and the *Shema* was incredibly uplifting. He also brought us matzah (unleavened bread), sliced pastrami, turkey, cheese and olives. This was an unbelievable treat. Pesach or Passover started on 1 April. I stopped eating bread, and although my only means of keeping Pesach was by eating matzah, my freedom was in my faith. The irony wasn't lost on me: when the Israelites were being set free from slavery, I was being held captive. And yet spiritually I was freer than ever before in my life.

Mohammed was still sending me white bread every week, but because it was Pesach I would give it away. There was no coffee shop in Building 10, so, unless you had visits, bread was difficult to come by.

Because I had paid extra money to be allowed to stay outside, every day from 1 to 2pm I would exercise. Despite keeping fit, I was constantly tired, my body ached all over (I hoped this wasn't a sign of old age) and I hadn't had a decent night's sleep in five years. Nor had I sat on a comfortable chair. Even my bum got sore.

I had to smuggle some of my letters out because you could be sure every word I wrote was being closely monitored, and Jai's friend Sheila was still up to her tricks. I had no doubt she was still reading them and reporting the contents to the embassy. My sister sent all her letters by registered mail, and registered mail was opened in front of us by Joe, who was one of the guards and in charge of the foreign section, but, personally, I never trusted anybody. For all I knew, even Jai could be working against me. I really hoped this wasn't the case, as I was becoming more and more dependent on her, not only emotionally but also to keep helping me to secure all the daily things I needed. She was my connection to the outside world. Whatever she did, I believed she did out of love. At this stage all I could afford to give Jai was R100 a month, enough to cover her return boat trip to the prison.

I constantly had earache while I was in solitary. I thought that this was probably from the dirty shower water, although there was always the possibility that some insect had crawled down my ear canal. I didn't want to think about that too much. I was eating well, though, and exercising regularly. My hair was getting long again and my beard was filling up.

Most of the guys with us in solitary were killers and had no consciences. Fortunately, after five years in prison, I was already well established in Bangkwang, and I was also feared, mainly for my size and for my reputation as a no-nonsense person. The Thais thought I was some kind of Mafia boss on the outside, and so, as they were all gangsters, I commanded a lot of respect. One day a foreigner, a British guy who owed money to one of the dealers, came to me for protection. He was expecting family to visit from abroad. Word was out that some of the Bad Boys planned to grab him on his return from the visit.

They would seize whatever foodstuffs his visitors had brought him, and chances were that he was also going to be stabbed. The dealer in question was on 24-hour lockdown. He had sent written notes warning this guy to pay his debt or else he would have him taken care of. The British guy ignored his threats and simply scored his heroin from another dealer, whose name was Rusta. This pissed off the first dealer big time. I agreed to get involved, but only because an attack on one foreigner by the Thais could result in an escalation of violence against the rest of us. When the British guy returned from the visit, I met him at the gate, protecting him from whatever ill fate awaited him. We walked up the stairs. The Bad Boys were lounging around waiting for him. Nobody made a move. I escorted him straight to the dealer's cell, as an act of good faith. There I told the British guy to give Rusta half of what he'd got from his visitors, and I also told him that he had to promise to settle his debt. In prison everybody gave credit. At some time or another everybody's money ran out, but you knew also that at some stage you would receive money from your family or friends or wherever. I told Rusta that if he ever had a problem with any of the foreigners, he should call me and not involve the Thais.

Just then, the leader of the Bad Boys appeared. He pointed his finger at the Brit and said in broken English, 'No, Aleksander, today you die.' I warned the Brit that he'd *better* settle his fucking debt or else he would be on his own. Owing money in prison was the cause of a lot of fights. If you didn't pay your debts, word would quickly spread among the inmates that you were a chancer. And once you had a bad reputation, from then on people would avoid you. In prison, good credit makes for good friends.

I was taking a shower in my cell one day when an inmate who had owed me some money for quite some time, and hadn't paid on the due date, knocked on my door. He went on his hands and knees and begged for my understanding. Whenever I lent money I gave it without ever expecting it back, but if you didn't pay, you couldn't ever come and borrow more. Generally, however, I preferred to avoid lending money. It was like buying a headache. When you wanted your money back and it wasn't forthcoming, you could end up looking like the bad guy.

Since the news had spread of my being in solitary confinement, I was receiving parcels from abroad almost every day of the week, which also meant that I got to go out of the building and to see my friends from Building 2 and get the latest news of what was happening over there. For example, I heard that the Building Chief who had sent Okky and me to solitary hadn't lasted very long. He had been removed two weeks after our fight, although that wasn't the specific reason. He had apparently caused so much contention among the prisoners that the authorities feared a riot. Good riddance, I thought.

Meanwhile from back home came some unpleasant news. My sister's boss and close friend, Jol, had got shot up fairly badly in a hold-up that had gone wrong. My brother-in-law Malcolm's father had died. And a good friend of mine, Hilliard, with whom I used to smoke cocaine, had been shot dead by some cocaine dealers. While I could express my sympathy, I was so far removed from their reality that I honestly didn't feel anything. Was I becoming so hardened by my circumstances that I was losing that ability?

My wash boy's time in solitary was up and I decided to do my own laundry. I was now doing a major clean-up of my cell only once a week. I had no reason to complain. In fact I had much to be grateful for. I had learnt to treasure every moment of the present. We exist in the now, which is today, and, for the most part of that moment, I had everything I could wish for. It may not sound like much, but to me it was a blessing. I was a deep thinker and I didn't want to waste my time in solitary. We evolve every day. I wanted to better myself as a person. I tried not to think too far into the future, because anything between now and then might never happen, but neither would I allow myself to dwell on the past. My attention was focused on the now. Every day was a new day and every day was filled with new challenges. True happiness, I was discovering, comes from within. I was also content with the little that I had.

One of my Jewish brothers, the American journalist I'd got quite friendly with, wound up in hospital. I heard he had gone off the rails. Actually, I suspected he was pretending, but one never knew. This place was enough to drive the sanest person crazy!

Around the middle of May, four months into solitary confinement, I started sketching and painting in colour, getting back to my art for the first time in a long time. I can't remember ever feeling more liberated. The transition from expressing myself in only black to colour was a major breakthrough and something that I directly attributed to my spiritual growth.

After five years in Bangkwang, little, if any, progress was being made on the prisoner treaty with Thailand, I was completely fed up with the South African government and their lack of support or even interest in our conditions. We believed that Jackie Selebi, then director-general at Foreign Affairs, had actually shelved negotiations. Whatever the reason for the lack of progress, I advised our embassy that they should only visit if and when I requested them to. European countries were far more civilised, in my opinion, and they actually seemed to care for their citizens. I remember back in 1997, there were two Polish guys who received royal pardons. One of them had been caught with 1kg of heroin but they both got life sentences. The first guy served five years and two months and the other served four years. Like South Africa, Poland didn't have a prisoner transfer treaty with Thailand, but the Polish embassy supported their cause. Rumour had it that a high-ranking Polish official was paid to grease the wheels of their release. Whether this was true or not, I cannot say, but the result was that both prisoners were granted royal pardons and walked free. Stories such as these sickened me and sometimes made me very downhearted.

Even if the embassy wasn't exactly championing my efforts to get a royal pardon, there were still some things I needed them for. Once my time in solitary came to an end, I needed to make sure that I went back to Building 2, and so I wrote to the embassy asking them to request the prison authorities that, on completion of my punishment, I be returned to the building of my origin.

Often I would try to imagine how I would feel when the day came, when they would call my name and say the word '*kabarn*' (go home).

I kept encouraging my sister to go public with my letter to Mandela, even though I knew that the Thai government did not take kindly to negative publicity. There could be two possible outcomes, I reasoned: they could consider me a thorn in their side and get rid of me by granting me a royal pardon; or, they could simply reject my submission for a royal pardon and that would be that. If things went that way, then I would never get out. The odds were 50-50. I was willing to take my chances.

'Let's keep up the negative publicity,' I instructed Joan.

While lying in my cell, my mind would often drift back to my life before Thailand and prison, and especially to certain events that had transpired just before I left South Africa. I had recently received a letter from a prisoner who was doing time in Boksburg. He told me about a fellow inmate named Rufus, who claimed he was a good friend of mine. I wrote back and very rudely told him that Rufus should go fuck himself ...

After Sarah-Lee had moved out, I became even more reckless with my life. It was drugs, sex and more drugs, and everything I owned was walking out of my apartment. As long as I was getting high, I didn't care. After all, they were only material things. It was New Year's Eve and I was out on Rockey Street at one of the many bars there. My mission that night, besides celebrating the coming of another year, was to be on the lookout for some of my customers who owed me money for cocaine. It was in Rockey Street that I met Rufus and his mates. After a couple of drinks, we each popped a cap of LSD, and then Rufus started telling me a story about how, just a couple of nights before, the bouncer across the road had beaten up some harmless kid. The more alcohol we consumed, and as the LSD took effect, the angrier we became about this, so we decided to go teach the bouncer a lesson. I went to my car and, from behind the seat, pulled out my pump-action shotgun. As we walked towards the club, we shouted at the bouncer, 'HEY, MOTHERFUCKER!' The guy took one look at our faces and then, when he saw the gun in my hand, ran for dear life. We tried to chase him, first on foot and then in my car. I let off one or two shots in his direction with my .38 Special. We lost him, probably just as well.

Rufus and I and one of his mates then drove to a club in Rivonia that I knew was frequented by one of the guys who owed me. The three of us marched inside together. I had my .38 tucked neatly into the waistband of my trousers and my shotgun was in my hand against my side. I had to hand the shotgun in at the door. By this time we were all out of our heads. We had a drink and I looked around the club for the guy in question. The cunt took coke on credit and never paid me. Fifty grams was a lot to write off. I couldn't see him anywhere, so we left the club. As Rufus reached my car, he put his beer bottle on the roof of my car and said, 'Shaun, I bet you, you can't shoot it.' He meant it as a joke, but I didn't hesitate. I loaded the shotgun, aimed and fired. The beer bottle disintegrated in a cloud of fragments. Because the parking lot was below road level by a good few metres, the noise of the shot was amplified. Fuck, it was loud!

As I reached my car, in the far corner just near where Rivonia Road passed, five policemen dressed in full riot gear and armed with R4 rifles came jumping down the wall. They proceeded to rush a couple who happened to be parked opposite to where I was, which bought me a couple of seconds to hide the shotgun under my car, close to the front wheel. By now the couple were pointing at me, Rufus and his mate. All five cops ran over, and in seconds we were surrounded. They found the shotgun straight away. Naturally, I claimed ownership but told them the gun had gone off accidentally. I was ordered to follow them, so I climbed back up onto the road with them, one of the cops carrying the shotgun. He went to the passenger side of their car, a yellow Opel Kadett 200is hatchback, while the other four cops hung around, waiting. Then one of them began walking towards me, and as he got closer I pulled out my .38 Special, really just intending to show him that I had another piece. Both firearms were licensed. I'm not sure what *he* was thinking, but the next thing I knew the cop tried to grab the gun out of my hand. In what seemed like less than a split second, there was a shot, there was screaming. My gun fell to the ground, but so did the cop!

I quickly picked up the .38 and slipped it back into my pants as the first cop came running back from the car, still with my shotgun in his hand.

'What's going on?' he shouted.

'He shot himself!' I told him, adding, 'I think he's drunk, officer.'

The policeman shoved my shotgun back at me. 'Fuck off!' he said.

He joined the rest of the policemen crowding around the fallen cop while I jumped down the wall and ran as fast as I could to my car before he changed his mind. Rufus and his mate were nowhere to be seen. As I was driving out of the parking lot they jumped out of the bushes and flagged me down. They were wide-eyed and pale. 'What the fuck happened?' Rufus asked. They had heard the gunshot and the screaming. I told them it had been an accident, but I don't think they believed me. They thought I'd shot the policeman, grabbed back my shotgun and made my escape.

That night we jolled till the early hours of the morning, going from one club to another. Around 7am we picked up this really cool black dude who was a marijuana merchant. We all went back to my town-house in Dowerglen. While the three of them sat in the lounge preparing a joint, I hid my shotgun in the bedroom under my mattress. After smoking a couple of joints, I gave Rufus and his friend some money to go to the bottle store and buy some more booze as soon as it opened. Then I passed out stone cold on the couch. I woke up around 12.30. The black dude was still there.

'Jesus, where the fuck are Rufus and whatshisface?' I said.

It was three hours later; they should have been back long ago. I jumped to my feet, ran straight to my bedroom and lifted up the mattress. The shotgun was gone. I sobered up very quickly.

'Motherfuckers stole my gun,' I told the black dude, who was also supposedly a friend of theirs. He seemed equally concerned. If they weren't back in an hour, I said, I was calling the cops. Then I slipped my .38 Special under the leather couch, lay down and put up my feet up. I tried to watch TV. Actually, I was really worried that the idiots might shoot someone. The next thing, I saw two plainclothes policemen jumping over my garden wall. The glass sliding door leading into the lounge was open but I had security gates that were locked. Gun pointing through the burglar bars, one of the cops shouted: 'Shaun Krebs!' Before I could even answer, he shouted again. 'Don't fucking move! Where's your handgun?' As I tried to get up to show him, he said, 'E-e-e-asy! Real slow, with your left hand give me the gun.'

As soon as the cops were inside the house I had my face pushed up against the wall and the black dude was on the floor face down. We were both thoroughly searched and so was my entire apartment. My stash of cocaine and freebase pipe were well hidden, thank goodness, and they didn't find them. After explaining to them that the black dude had only come to my apartment that morning (I didn't even know his fucking name), they let him go. Apparently, Rufus and whatshisface had been caught jumping a red robot in Rivonia, near where the shooting incident had taken place the night before. They were pulled over and the cops found the shotgun. When Rufus and his mate were threatened with being charged for the shooting of the cop, they had ratted me out. They had even gone so far as to give the cops my home address!

I was taken to the Morningside police station, where I was questioned by the head of the detective branch. I stuck to my version of the story and repeated that I'd suspected that the cop who had grabbed the gun out of my hand the night before had been drinking. It had to have been an accident; why else would they have told me to fuck off? Anyway, they still charged me with attempted murder, as well as with firing a weapon in a built-up area. My guns were confiscated and, after some intense negotiations to establish that I didn't pose a flight risk, I was released on my own recognisance. As I was leaving, I heard my name being called. The voice came from the holding cells – it was Rufus and his mate! They couldn't believe that I was walking out. They asked if I could help bail them out ...?

'Oh, no problem,' I said. 'See you tomorrow.' Like a fucking hole in the head! Did they really think that, after stealing my shotgun, I was going to help them? If anything, I wanted to shoot them with it. I let it go, though. If you hang out with scum, you can't expect any better. I appeared in court and was officially charged. I pleaded not guilty. My case was remanded to February, but by then I had got myself a lawyer.

On the day of my appearance, none of the witnesses, namely, none of the policemen who had been there that night outside the Rivonia club, *including* the guy I supposedly had shot, turned up in court. My case was postponed to 29 April 1994.

Then one night – it was close to midnight, I remember – who should arrive on my doorstep but Rufus, apologising profusely for stealing my shotgun and blaming the other guy. I was slightly intoxicated. No problem, I said. Actually, I was on my way to collect an outstanding debt for cocaine from one of my customers and I said he could come along for the ride. We arrived at the guy's flat. His front door had these French windows so you could see inside. After I'd been ringing the bell, shouting his name and pounding on the door for a few minutes, he finally stumbled down the stairs. He came and stood by the door but refused to open it. So I punched through the glass pane, missing his face by millimetres, and at the same time slashing my finger down to the bone. (It was a deep cut, and fucking painful.) He let us in. There was a lot of blood. He helped me clean my injury and I tied one of those checked dish towels around my finger to stop the bleeding. I needed some booze to numb the pain, so I downed half a bottle of the guy's whisky. After that I was in a much better mood. Then we agreed a deadline for him to pay me, and Rufus and I left. I was supposed to be the bad guy, with intentions to hurt the good guy, yet I was the one who got hurt – what an idiot I was!

Rufus and I went on to Rockey Street and drank ourselves into a stupor. Around 5am my finger really started throbbing. Drunk as lords, we drove to the hospital. Casualty at the Joburg General was busy – surprisingly so, I thought, for that time of the morning – still dealing with victims of accidents and stabbings from the night before. But South Africa has always been a violent society. I was told there would be at least a 40-minute wait before I could see a doctor. Rufus said he was really tired and asked if he could and go sleep in my car. Judaism teaches us that all men are born inherently good, but I must have been born naive as well. I handed over my keys and jokingly said, 'Don't fucking go steal my car!' Rufus laughed, took the keys and off he went. Finally it was my turn. The doctor stitched me up and gave me a prescription for an antibiotic. As I walked out into the parking lot, it was beginning to get light. It was going to be a beautiful day. I looked around. My car was gone!

Motherfucker Rufus!

I couldn't believe how stupid I had been to trust him. I hardly even knew the guy. I ran back into the hospital, found a phone booth and called the police in Norwood to report my car stolen. Then I phoned my sister, and Malcolm came to fetch me straight away. The keys to my apartment were on the same bunch as my car keys and Rufus knew exactly where I lived! When we got to the townhouse complex in Dowerglen and drove down the driveway, I could see the rear lights of my car parked outside and breathed a sigh of relief. At least my car was in one piece; my biggest dread had been Rufus crashing it. As we got closer I saw that my biggest dread was in fact a reality. The whole front on the right side of my car was completely smashed in. How on earth Rufus had managed to drive home like that still baffles me to this day. Then I saw that the back door to the townhouse was wide open, and I knew immediately that my brand-new Kenwood four-in-one hi-fi was probably gone, and my video machine, too. I was right.

Funnily enough, Rufus sold my hi-fi to somebody I knew, so when I put word out on the street that I was looking for him, one of my buddies phoned me and gave me the exact location I would find it. Not wanting any trouble, when I went to retrieve my belongings I took a friend with me who was a policeman. The people who had purchased my music system were shocked when I stealthily entered their property and made my way into their house but retrieved my stuff without incident. Now all I wanted was to find Rufus and put a bullet in him. Just as well for him I didn't find him.

My time in solitary confinement was almost over. Although I enjoyed the privilege of being alone in a cell, life in Building 10 was really boring. When I had only nine days left to go, strangely, a part of me wanted to stay on where I was, which I could have arranged to do, but another part wanted to get back to the general population.

One morning the British guy was called to collect a parcel, but the American guy who had the same first name as him answered the call. Pretending the call was for him, he went and collected the parcel. The British guy had ordered from his friends who had visited him two cartons of Marlboro cigarettes, tuna, soap, instant noodles, a peaked cap and some other items of clothing. His friends had also put in two music cassettes, Queen and the Beatles. The American came back to the building and started walking around selling all the items. After successfully selling most of the stuff off, he then had the nerve to approach the British guy, who had heard he was selling Marlboros but hadn't thought anything of it. Until, that was, the American tried to sell him the two music cassettes! What a lowlife. In prison we all suffer, and stealing from another prisoner is considered very low.

In fact, the British guy lodged a case of theft against the American, and the Building Chief called for a meeting. I was asked to act as the interpreter. To cut a long story short, the Building Chief told the American in no uncertain terms that he had to pay back all the money he'd made, at 500 Thai baht a week, or else ...

As my release day grew closer, I sent a note to Mohammed and two envelopes, one for the Building Chief of Building 2 and the other for the head of security who signed off on the transfer papers. The notes inside said that I was due to return from solitary and wanted to return to Building 2. I then attempted to pay our Building Chief in solitary to make sure that he put my name on the list to transfer back to Building 2, and I had a separate envelope for him. I thought I had covered all possible angles, including asking the consular officer to request the prison authorities to send me back to my building of origin. The chief of solitary declined my envelope, saying I was too late and would only be eligible for the next transfer in three months' time, which would mean I would have to stay a total of nine months with chains on my legs in solitary.

I would have preferred to have made the choice myself and so I was not happy. I became even more determined to leave Building 10. By now I was respected by the guards. My beard was fully grown, which made me look older. Some of the Thais called me 'Rambo' and the foreigners said they thought I looked like Chuck Norris. Generally, the inmates were wary of me to the point of fearing me. If only they knew what a gentle, soft person I really was. It was crazy, though, because if the necessity arose I knew I could kill, just like that, and not feel any remorse whatsoever. Something inside me had died. Sometimes I began to think I was losing it or perhaps that I was taking prison existence too seriously, but that is what prison does to you. The things I had witnessed there in only a few years, many people would not believe. Physically I was powerful and I also had a strong mind. The dragon inside me had awakened. I called myself The Warlord.

I was the only white guy on the third floor. The rest were Nigerians. The Nigerians are a very proud nation and they can be difficult to reason with. Every day there was a problem with them. Aside from my run-in with Okky, which had landed me in solitary, personally I never had a problem with any of the Nigerian guys there, and in fact one of them, Lawal, was a good friend of mine. But the shouting to one another from one cell across three other cells late at night irritated the shit out of me.

Lawal was a dealer, and the same American guy who had ripped off the British guy ripped off Lawal, too. It was Lawal who was freaking out the most, saying that he was going to kill the American, shouting his head off, making a whole performance. I decided to put him to the test, so I went and got a knife from one of the samurai. I rolled it in a dishcloth and the samurai and I went and put it on the floor of the Nigerians' cell. I said to Lawal, 'Go on, take the knife and let's go kill the fucker.' When he opened the cloth and the knife dropped out, he panicked. He said that he was really angry, but that didn't actually mean that he would *kill* the American. I said, 'You got to teach him a lesson, man. This guy has fucked many people over. I will come with you.' Lawal said he would rather just leave it. 'OK,' I said, 'but if you can't do it yourself, my friend here will kill him for you. Just give the order.'

The samurai just stood there, totally expressionless. If Lawal hadn't been black, I swear he would have turned white. He insisted we leave it. No, I told him, this was prison and if you threatened to kill some-body you had better do it, or the chances were that that person might come and kill you.

In those last days, Joodt the chef borrowed a 4-inch black and white TV for me. I was living like a king but still, I had had enough. I needed to get out. I told Joodt that if the Building Chief didn't put my name on the first transfer list, I would let the embassy know just how cor-rupt he was and that he closed his eyes to all the illegal activities in Building 10. This was a dangerous game I was playing, and I knew it. The Building Chief was one of the big Mafia guys, and he could have had me stabbed just like that, but I took my chances.

The next morning, I was summoned to his office. He started telling me how he rode a bicycle to work every day, blah blah blah. I under-stood that he was crying poverty, but I acted dumb. Then he told me that I was on the transfer list and that I would be moving in two days. I thanked him and shook his hand but failed to drop an envelope in his lap. I had given him a chance before and he had tried to fuck me over. Now it was too late.

On the morning of 21 July 1999 I headed back to Building 2, with ten times more stuff than I'd had when I'd arrived there. I was put back in the same cell and got my old sleeping space back. My first day back was a busy one. An army of cockroaches had invaded my lockers, so first I had to clean them. I requested that my shackles be removed, and although I had to pay a bribe for this, they took them off me. What a relief that was – it was an incredible feeling. I felt light and jubilant. I felt like I could fly.

One day, soon after my release from solitary, I was sitting on the lawn near the front gate with Mohammed, eating ice cream. It was just after two in the afternoon when an outside guard walked through the gate carrying a whole lot of papers in his hands. Mohammed jokingly said maybe one of those papers was his royal pardon. 'You wish,' I an-swered. 'Maybe it's mine.' Not even three minutes later Mohammed's name was called out over the loudspeaker. He ran to the office where he was told the magic word '*kabarn*' (go home). It was a moment I will never forget – that look on his face, knowing he was free.

It was close to shower time, so we took our last shower together, as we normally did at that time, while a crowd of his friends and other inmates gathered to bid him farewell. We all helped him pack his stuff. Before he left, Mohammed gave me two lists: one of people who owed him money and another of money that he owed. He left me a wad of foreign currency to settle some of his debts. We agreed that I would buy his house for 30 000 Thai baht. I didn't know then that the money he'd entrusted to me wasn't enough to cover his debts, which also exceeded the value of his house. Mohammed was a staunch Muslim, who prayed every day. We had become as close as brothers. He had helped me out in all my troubled times. There was nobody else that I could depend on as much as I depended on him. It was very emotional for me to see him leave.

When he was ready to go, I walked him to the gate. He promised he would write and send me parcels. I told him that he was a free man now and that he should forget about me and about prison. 'Start your life again, Mohammed,' I told him, 'and may you succeed in everything you do.' We shook hands and Mohammed went on his way. I felt lost.

On her next visit, I asked Jai to email my sister and ask her to urgently organise me US$1 500. The house Mohammed had sold to me would make a huge difference in a place where 900 convicts had to coexist. I could do my art there and also use the house for worshipping. Mohammed had instructed me in a letter to pay out the old French Israeli man, whose name was Simon Dahan, who also lived there, for his share in the house – 10 000 Thai baht – and to ask him to move somewhere else, but I didn't have the heart to throw him out. The man was in his early sixties, and, besides, he was Jewish. I explained to Simon that I would buy his share from him, that the house now belonged to me, but that he was welcome to stay on in it.

I'd noticed that the overhead fan in Mohammed's house was broken, and one of the first things I planned to do was get the electrician in and have it replaced. Things were going smoothly and it felt great to be out of solitary confinement. After months in shackles, though, I was struggling to walk and my knees were giving me a lot of trouble. For some months I'd also been having a lot of toothache, and at the end of August I finally got to see the prison dentist. I hadn't been for a dental checkup for over eight years. I had heard the horror stories about how prison dentists used a hammer and chisel if they had difficulty pulling a tooth out, not that I really believed them. But I had always been terrified of the dentist, so stories like this didn't help my nerves. Twenty-two of us were ordered to line up outside the dentist's room. I was the 19th person in the queue, and I can tell you my hands were sweating. But it was amazing. The whole thing was practically painless. I didn't even feel the injection. Each prisoner got his anaesthetic with a new syringe and needle. As one person came out, so the next person followed. The whole tooth-pulling process took hardly any time at all. Imagine – 20 people having teeth pulled out in 25 minutes flat. Now that should be one for *Guinness Book of Records*!

Mohammed had given me his lockers next to the bakery, which meant that I now had three lockers there. He had also asked me to burn all his letters and documents. While I was doing this, I came across a letter from the Iranian embassy supporting his royal pardon submission. I kept it in order one day to show the world how supportive other countries were of their prisoners, in comparison to the South African government. After reading Mohammed's support letter, I realised how unlikely it was that I would be granted a royal pardon without something similar from the South African embassy. I decided I would do my best to stay positive, if only for my sister's sake, and patiently await the day that I would eventually be released. I was not counting on anybody intervening. In fact, I was expecting to stay in prison for many more years. Joan wanted to hire a Thai lawyer to follow my royal pardon application and apply some pressure, but I was dead against this. In my experience, Thai lawyers were corrupt and crooked. Firstly, they charged a ridiculous fee and, secondly, they could deliberately jeopardise your chances. The lawyer my sister had contacted had already made her all kinds of promises. If your application was rejected, he told her, he knew somebody in the Royal Palace and that, second time round, a royal pardon was guaranteed. I told Joan that I would rather donate the money to the King's charity, and anyway, according to the embassy, my application was already at the Palace.

Round about this time, the Department of Corrections adopted a new policy. Anybody with less than a life sentence was to be moved to prisons in the provinces. One such place where foreigners were going to go was a prison called Klong Pai. It was situated in a valley with a great view in the middle of nowhere, approximately 600km out of Bangkok. In comparison to Bangkwang, apparently it was hell. A lot of Asian foreigners got transferred there, and saying goodbye to our friends, knowing we would probably never see them again, was really hard.

When we heard about this new policy, I immediately wrote to the embassy, asking them to write in turn to the Department of Corrections to ask them not to move us. Apart from anything else, the distance from Bangkok would make it difficult for anybody to visit the foreign prisoners.

In April 1999 Nelson Mandela had stepped down as the first democratically elected president of South Africa, and in June of that year Thabo Mbeki took over the reins. I had a brilliant idea. Businessman and philanthropist Bertie Lubner, who was already actively engaged with my case back home, and was being an incredible help to my sister in her efforts, was a personal friend of Mandela's. Through Bertie I thought I would try to get Mandela to twist Mbeki's arm to write a letter of support for me. It was a faint hope, and deep down I knew it. I don't really know what I was thinking. Who was I, anyway? All I had done was send my own long letter to the great statesman and paint his portrait. I *had* heard that the portrait hung on a wall in President Mandela's house, and I also knew that my letter had been put into his hands, thanks to Bertie. I realised that a letter of endorsement from the new South African president was a long shot, and that a letter from Mandela himself was an even longer one. I was wrong on the first count, but not on the second.

NELSON MANDELA

28 September 1999

Your Excellency

I trust that this letter finds Your Excellency well and in good health. Please receive my best wishes for the well being of yourself, His Majesty and the Kingdom.

Your Excellency, I take the liberty of approaching you on a matter concerning a South African national that is serving sentence in Thailand after being arrested on 26 April 1994 on charges of drug trafficking.

The family, through our Embassy, applied for a Royal Pardon in 1997. As I know the family through mutual acquaintances, I would like to appeal to Your Excellency for any assistance that could be provided in this regard. The particulars of the person concerned are the following:

Alexander Krebs, Prison Number 562/37 and his case number is 3520/94.

Please remain assured, Your Excellency, of our highest consideration.

NR MANDELA

His Excellency Chaun Leekpai
Prime Minister of Thailand

SOUTH AFRICA

407

In order for me to be creative, I need some sort of a routine, and since my return to Building 2, I had had no desire to draw. Instead, every day I would spend hours walking. I knew I would get back to my art but I wasn't ready yet. In the meantime, I arranged, for 2 000 Thai baht, for the carpenter to build me a table with one big sliding drawer and a locker on the side. Because he could only do odd jobs on the weekend, it was going to take a month, but this suited me fine. I moved into my new house. The old man welcomed me, but at first he was not very friendly. With time, however, and as we got to know each other, we became like family.

While I was in solitary I had painted about 50 pictures, all of them on A4-size paper because of the lack of space. Everything had seemed confined and restricted – probably because it was. Even the imagination has its boundaries, I suppose. Now that I was in a different space and felt freer to move around, I ordered A2 paper.

A woman by the name of Norma, who helped and supported some of the ladies at the women's prison, came to visit me, and she offered to take my paintings back to South Africa. She was a godsend and a true Christian, and I couldn't have been more grateful. I was constantly amazed at how helpful people were to me.

When I got out of solitary, there was a new foreigner in Building 2. He was an F-16 jet fighter mechanic from Norway and we became instant friends. Kjell was well over six foot tall and looked like an American footballer. He had been arrested in November 1987 for purchasing about 55 'muscle-growth' pills, which turned out to be a drug called *yaba* (basically methamphetamine mixed with caffeine). He was sentenced to 33 years. Around February/March of 1988, the Norwegian foreign and justice ministers came to Thailand to negotiate a prisoner transfer treaty. They even visited my friend in Lard Yao prison, where he was being held. In June 1988 his prime minister came to sign the treaty. All this took place within a period of seven months. Denmark had also entered into a treaty with Thailand, and

Sweden had also signed one. When I heard these stories it was hard not to feel bitter.

On 15 October 1999 I turned 40. It was my sixth birthday in prison.

My brother-in-law always said life begins at 40, but I don't know about that. To me it sounded quite old. Nevertheless I felt strong and fit. I weighed 80kg, I didn't smoke and I had given up drugs. I might have been getting older but my life had also taken a turn for the better.

During one of the embassy visits, I'd expressed a concern to the consular officer about how, in the impending 1999 amnesty to celebrate the King's birthday in December, if drug cases were cut by half, my sentence would be reduced from 40 years to 20. But this would mean that I would be transferred back to the Klong Prem prison complex, and put in Lard Yao, the section that held prisoners with short sentences. I did not want to go there, I told her. Lard Yao was like the Wild West, something my Norwegian friend had confirmed in the conversations we'd had. Fights were part of everyday life there and one could easily kill somebody or be killed. If this happened, it would mean another life sentence for me. I told her that I needed the embassy's assistance to make sure I was not transferred there.

After what I had thought was a reasonable and logical conversation between us, the consular officer went and reported me to Foreign Affairs, telling them that I had threatened to kill the embassy staff in Bangkok. Talk about a miscommunication! You would think the embassy had more important stuff to deal with, like concentrating their efforts on working towards a treaty with Thailand. I had to defend myself and to clarify what I had actually said and the reasons I'd had for saying it, so I wrote a lengthy letter to the Minister of Foreign Affairs, which began as follows:

> *Dear Sir*
>
> *It was with much concern that it has come to my notice that certain allegations have been made against my person by your Bangkwang staff to third parties. It is my strong hope that the underlying cause is based on a misunderstanding, as otherwise the innuendo that I would blackmail the*

> South African Government by threatening to commit a mur-
> der unless I was helped by the Government, would be quite
> shocking. Particularly for argument's sake, if I did have such
> violent intentions, what would it really benefit me? It would
> seem that the person who is the originator of this slander
> must have read too many detective novels. You can rest as-
> sured that I am not a violent person and wish to be taken as
> such. Hereunder I would like to acquaint you with what was
> really said and which was subsequently twisted and quoted
> out of context ...

I took the opportunity to say a whole lot more, repeating many of the pleas I had made so many times before about the conditions for foreigners in Thai prisons and about the treatment we received. I made a number of very clear and reasonable proposals, among other things, regarding the frequency of embassy visits (which had now been cut back from monthly to only three times a year), medical assistance, pastoral care, the daily allowance for prisoners and the seemingly stalled prisoner transfer treaty between South Africa and Thailand. I held up for comparison what other countries were doing for their citizens.

Needless to say, I didn't receive any reply. Everything we tried fell on deaf ears. I think the furthest my letters got was probably into the nearest dustbin, but I refused to give up. It was a sad state of affairs that the fate of South African prisoners in Thailand remained an unsolved matter.

My sister had managed to raise enough money for me to buy Mohammed's house. Bertie Lubner, along with Dennis Levy from the Chevra Kadisha, had contributed towards this. I was discovering what a shrewd businessman Mohammed was. He had been playing with everybody's money. One of the missionaries who used to visit the prison, whose name was Cosmos, had lent Mohammed 30 000 Thai baht. After he had been released from Bangkwang, and while he was awaiting deportation, Cosmos went to visit Mohammed, who told him about our deal. He also told Cosmos that I would settle the 30-grand debt. Back in the prison, I sold the foreign currency to one of the Chinese, which enabled me to settle some of my friend's debts, but not all of them. One of Mohammed's closest friends was a guy named Chuka, to whom he owed 24 000 Thai baht. Mohammed had not included Chuka's name on the list of people I had to pay, and there were others. In fact, Mohammed left me with a huge headache. Everything he left me cost me more than if I had bought it from someone else. Cosmos came to visit me to discuss the debt. I told him I was sorry, but I couldn't pay him. Mohammed just had too many debts inside the prison, and these were guys I had to live with and whose faces I saw every day. It was not right that Mohammed had ripped them off, but paying them first was the decent thing to do. I told Cosmos my hands were tied. Being the gentleman that he was, Cosmos saw my dilemma and he accepted the situation. In the meantime, I tried my best to settle each person's debt, even if I settled only part of it. Some I couldn't pay at all, but, as everyone in prison knows, that's a risk you take when you lend money.

I couldn't wait to move into my new house. Once my table was built, I planned to get into some serious painting and also to devote more time to studying the Torah. Having a house was a rare privilege, but it also cost a lot of money. Now that I was back in the general population again, when I looked at my time in solitary I realised what a terrible ordeal it had actually been. Solitary confinement is not a healthy environment, especially for one's mind. Being confined in such a small space with a bunch of psychopaths and drug addicts had in fact been really tough on me. In solitary, you were a prisoner within a prison's prison. I didn't ever want to go back there. I had to learn to control myself, to stop trying to change people. I knew that my anger stemmed mainly from the people with whom I had been forced to coexist. These were the worst criminals imaginable. It wasn't that I saw myself as better than anyone else; it was more about having morals and principles. It didn't matter whether you were in prison or outside – there was still a standard one had to keep. I have to say that it wasn't the Thais so much as the foreigners who always seemed to be the problem.

Initially, after his release, Mohammed wrote me three letters from the Immigration Detention Centre (IDC), although I never really expected to hear from him again, nor that he would keep his promise of helping me with my royal pardon. He had spent eight years in this hellhole, and I was sure that the last place he wanted to think about now was prison or anything or anyone associated with it. He was starting a new life as a free man. I bore him no resentment. I was happy for him.

We were now down to 14 in our cell. Lenny our cook had been moved to another prison, so I was eating with another Chinese guy, who was also from Hong Kong. His name was Lim. Most Hong Kong guys spoke reasonable English and seemed more educated than those from mainland China.

Since getting out of solitary, and in the month leading to the December amnesty, my class had been upgraded from 'very good' to 'excellent'. Rumour had it that there was a 50-50 chance that drug cases would be included in this amnesty. I felt confident that we would get it. The day approached that all of us prisoners were so eagerly awaiting: 5 December 1999, the King's birthday.

Calamity! Drug cases were *excluded* from the amnesty. We were shattered. I could have kicked myself. Why hadn't I petitioned the government? One of my reasons, I knew, was that after having been in Building 10, I'd made a private decision to stop fighting the system. It felt like a losing battle anyway. I also had my own house now, and the truth was that I was comfortable and enjoying my privileges and I didn't want anything to mess that up. I was also waiting for an answer to my royal pardon application. Over and above all this, I had become somewhat complacent in the knowledge that some powerful business-men in South Africa were among those who were working towards my release. In fact, I was expecting to go home soon. Plans were being made for my arrival at the airport in Johannesburg.

Dreams are what kept our hopes alive. When they are dashed, as ours were on 5 December, you harden your heart just a little bit more.

Over the preceding months I had begun to cut ties with many of my female correspondents. Jai was my girlfriend and we were almost two years into our relationship, which was complicated to say the least.

It was during this time that I connected with another woman. Her name was Robyn. She had so much compassion, not only for me but also for all of the South Africans who were locked away in Thailand. She got her father involved in putting pressure on the government on our behalf. They even visited the women's prison and provided financial support there.

After meeting Robyn, my feelings for Jai began to change. I no longer envisaged a future with her. Unfortunately, Robyn was married, but I didn't really have any expectations anyway and so I never felt bad about my relationship with her. I was behind bars and could not be a threat in any real way. People come into our lives for reasons that are sometimes beyond our understanding. Perhaps developing feelings for Robyn was only to make me realise that Jai, a Thai woman, was not for me. If Jai met somebody in the outside world, I thought that I would encourage her to make a life for herself with that person. I did not want her to wait for me. My sentence was 40 years. Heaven only knew when I would get out. In any event I never made Jai any promises. I was indebted to her, there was no doubt about that, but the love I felt for her began to evolve into a strong friendship instead. For me anyway, Jai began to feel more like a sister than a girlfriend.

The parents of one of the South African girls in the women's prison came to visit her and they brought a parcel for me from Robyn. It was given to Jai to pass on to me and she went and opened it. It contained a backgammon set, a sweatshirt and a letter, which Jai read. This became obvious at our next visit, when she told me that she suspected Robyn and I were more than just friends. I felt terribly guilty because it was true. I couldn't lie, so I confessed that I did have strong feelings for her. Jai was on the verge of tears. I tried to comfort her by saying that nothing had changed, she was still my best friend. I tried to explain that my needs were great and that one woman could not fulfil them all. In the end, Jai promised to protect our secrets and to continue supporting and visiting me, and Robyn and I continued to correspond, sometimes writing as many as two letters a week to each other. Hers were often 30 pages long.

Not even a month after I had confessed to Jai my feelings for Robyn,

I received an aerogram from Robyn in which she very diplomatically told me that she wished to cut ties with me and that she was going to stop writing. From the tone of her letter, I could see that they were not her words, even though it was her handwriting. I was bewildered. I could not understand what had happened, but my sixth sense was telling me that somehow Jai was responsible. After that, my relationship with Jai took strain. She didn't trust me any more and I didn't trust her. I knew she was going through my parcels and mail from my family and friends. She became unreliable to the point of lying. In a way, though, I understood. I had hurt her and now she was paying me back. All the same, it was hard to get over Robyn, and I was upset that I had been the cause of her ceasing to support the other prisoners.

Even in prison my relationships with women were complicated.

Chapter 13

The Battle Continues

By early 2000, I was painting in different media and developing a diversity of styles, both abstract and realistic. My subject matter varied from nudes to portraits. This was more than likely a reflection of my state of mind, which was all over the place. My family had increased my allowance and my good friend Edna in England was still sending me £100 a month, so I was never short of anything. Most importantly, I was blessed with good health. However, I still felt restless. It was the *not knowing* that ate away at me, the not knowing of when I would be released. It was constantly on my mind. My art was my only salvation. On either side of my new house I had rowdy neighbours. In order to escape the noise and to focus on what I was doing, I would transcend the monotony of a prisoner's dreary existence and enter the spiritual realm where silence became a symphony of calm and peace. There I was among the angels. From above, I watched myself drawing at the table the carpenter had made for me, oblivious to my surroundings. In my mind, only I existed. I imagined that, when we die, we go to a place just like that, where there is no sound. We listen with our eyes, and our hearts are our voices. No words need to be spoken.

One morning I was sitting around at the gym, which was situated near the top end of the building next to a small section cordoned off with barbed wire that was known as the *soy* (punishment cells). There were four of these cells. They had no toilets, electricity or running water. Being locked inside must have been sheer hell. The cells were used to punish prisoners for insubordination or to house those who had committed murder inside the prison or who had attempted to escape. Over the years, it was mainly Thai inmates who were kept there, in what I can only describe as the most inhumane conditions possible.

There were also four houses close to where I was sitting. Everything was open, and you could see from one house into another. One of them, in fact, was the second chief's office. Only a low wall separated them from one another. There was a new guy who had arrived in our building about three weeks before, and I'd heard he was a brilliant artist. I hadn't met or even seen him yet. So anyway, there I was, sitting around not doing anything, and I saw this guy walking towards me. In his hand was a rolled-up piece of paper. I greeted him and asked if I could see what he had drawn. He was very polite. He unrolled the paper and showed me his picture. Well, I was totally amazed. It was a portrait of an old Thai man, half-finished. I had seen some of the other Thai artists use the same medium, but I had never seen anything as perfect or as beautiful as this painting. It looked like a photo. I introduced myself as 'Aleksander'. The new guy's name was Chai Long. Apparently he was in for murder and had got a life sentence. He mentioned that he had heard of me and said he'd like to see my work. I was excited. The medium that he used was carbon powder – fine granules of crushed charcoal. He used a variety of Chinese brushes prepared for different applications.

Before prison I had never heard of this medium. I discovered that Chai Long had a degree in Fine Art and that he had taught art as a profession. He had mastered this ancient Chinese technique from the great grand master of Thailand, who was now in his late eighties. Chai Long was a master himself. I wasted no time in inviting him to come and stay in my house. In return, he agreed to teach me to use carbon powder. I arranged with the carpenter to measure out the space next to my work area and I ordered another table, this one for my new friend.

Chai Long came from a poor family in southern Thailand. He was married and had a son. Through painting for prisoners, he was able to support his family on the outside. I took an instant liking to the guy. We were the same age and were both Librans. He was humble and well-mannered and never said a bad word about anybody. Once the table was ready, he moved in. I watched him work and he tutored me. One advantage I had over Chai Long was that I could draw very well. In my first attempt, I mixed media, using Bic ballpoint pen and charcoal. I was a stickler for detail and quite fancied the picture I had done, but Chai Long was not impressed. To him it was sacrilege. I had violated the sacrosanctity of carbon powder. As a rule, one never mixed carbon powder with another medium – not even pencil, he emphasised. The powder had a life of its own.

It was fascinating to watch him work. I absorbed every action and detail. My next step was to buy my own supplies. My second picture was of an African baby, which I thought came out pretty okay. In appreciation for him teaching me, I had organised that my Chinese chef would cook Chai Long one meal a day, which I paid for. My house became his home. He could help himself to whatever he wanted. Like sport, art broke down any cultural barriers that may have existed between foreigners and Thais. Chai Long became one of my best friends – even murderers have a gentle side to them.

In the meantime, Kjell, the Norwegian, and I also became buddies. Like me, he was an avid backgammon player and he also worked out every day. We had a lot of fun together. Every night he ate a can of tuna straight out of the tin, with a couple of slices of bread, something I couldn't stomach without a topping of mayonnaise or ketchup. Our gym, which consisted of two wooden benches and two concrete weights, was not enough for Kjell to bench, so, between the two of us, we paid the handyman to make us up to 130kg of concrete weights.

The handyman was a Thai-Pakistani Muslim by the name of Pramud. He had been in prison for over ten years, and my heart went out to him. During the 1996 amnesty, his sentence had been reduced to 40 years, like mine. I had been in prison for only two years and had the same sentence as him. From what I heard, he had been found guilty by association and was initially given the death penalty. Whenever a new Building Chief was appointed, he would go to great lengths to upgrade and improve the conditions of the building, and for this Pramud was the man. He constructed buildings, built an office and toilet for the guards, installed concrete lockers for the prisoners and fixed any plumbing problems we had.

There were no English-language TV channels for us foreigners to watch, so, unless we watched videos, there was nothing much on the box to entertain us. Then a Thai prisoner was transferred from Building 1 to our building. He was an electrician by trade and he came up with the idea of installing our own satellite system. Getting a decoder was no problem, but bringing in a satellite dish would be almost impossible. One of the British guys, John, who was an electronics aficionado, happened to have some electronics journals that showed you how to build a satellite dish, so we collected some pieces of scrap metal that we found lying around the prison and John built a 2m dish, which we hid in the roof of the place where the garbage was kept. The decoder was smuggled into the prison by one of the guards and, at the same time, hundreds of metres of aerial cable were also brought in. Cables were run to connect all member rooms. There was an initial membership charge and a monthly subscription fee. John also built boosters so that every room had a clear picture. The remote we kept in our room. We formed a committee to select programmes to accommodate everyone's needs. Pedro, a Dutch guy who was glued to his private TV from the time we got locked up in the afternoon until late into the night, was our committee chairman. Programmes revolved around the news: BBC news was always at 6pm; at 8pm we had either Star movies or HBO; and in between we had a variety of other channels to choose from. On weekends it would be sport. At first our satellite system was the best-kept secret in Bangkwang, but word eventually got out and so we organised two more decoders, one for our Chinese members and the other for a permanent sports channel. It was a full-time operation. We never made money from it, but I can tell you it changed the lives of the foreign prisoners, who would normally be bored out of their heads after we were locked up.

Backgammon was very popular in the prison, even among the Thais; there were inmates who played all day, betting on every game.

I organised a competition of 20 players. Each player paid 100 Thai baht to participate and it was a case of winner takes all. I happened to come third, but it was a lot of fun and the guys thoroughly enjoyed the competition.

During this time I got news from home that my sister had managed to organise government support for my royal pardon. I had no idea from whom, or at what level, but this seemed like a major breakthrough. I struggled to contain myself and wanted to share the good news with everybody, but I couldn't, out of fear of jinxing it. And besides, nothing was in writing, so I kept it to myself.

Guards were always looking to make money from the prisoners. One of them started an email service. It cost 30 Thai baht for two pages, which was not bad considering that this way you avoided going through the prison censorship. For me it was the perfect set-up. And that Australian bitch Sheila was still reading my letters and feeding information to the embassy and, I was sure, adding her lies. I could not understand why she hated me or what had possessed her to decide to make my life difficult.

Parcels from home were still the biggest source of strength for me. Penelope, my ex-girlfriend who had gone on that memorable Transkei summer holiday with me, would send me a package every year on my birthday. Inside it, besides a variety of clothes and foodstuffs, there was always a scrumptious cake. My mom sent me many parcels over the years and she also helped my sister with my monthly allowance. She would buy me things that I never thought of asking for, like sun protection cream, lip balm, ankle stone with oils to soften my heels, special nail clippers to trim my cuticles, earbuds and other items. She would also bake me my favourite pastries. On the day she baked them she would give them to one of the South African women who had befriended her and who travelled regularly to Thailand to buy clothes. A day and a half later, I would be sitting in prison eating freshly baked Hungarian pastries with my friends. My mother's letters, though, depressed me terribly. When I read her words, her pain and longing became too real for me to cope with. I could visualise her small frame and tearful eyes. I preferred it when she didn't write. I could not handle the thought of her going down on her hands and knees, praying for me and crying. I also discovered that my sister had had two nervous breakdowns. It killed me that my family was going through so much pain because of me.

About three years before, I had submitted one of my poems to a competition in England, and it was chosen to be published in an anthology. If it was to be included, though, I was told that I would have to purchase the book – which cost £65. I couldn't believe it. What a scam! Even in the world of literature there were criminals. I wrote to the publishers, saying that if purchasing the anthology was a prerequisite to having my poem published, rather than the merit of the poem itself, then I didn't want my poem to appear in their anthology. They were unmoved. They responded by saying that the poem was on the internet and would be published in another anthology called *Poem of the Century*. They also asked me to send them another poem. I don't know why, but I sent them one called 'The Seagulls Cry'. I never heard from them again, so that was where my career as a poet started and abruptly ended.

Back home, my family was struggling. Malcolm, my brother-in-law, had attempted one business after the other, none of which had succeeded. I wondered whether it was just bad luck or whether it was his destiny to fail. It was a cruel world out there. I prayed for their financial situation to improve, but thinking about them battling made me feel sick to my stomach. Joan and Malcolm had supported me over the past six years even when they could not make ends meet themselves. I was so grateful. All I could give in return was to make them proud of who I was becoming. It was five years now that I was drug-free, and my art compilation stood at 140 pieces. My sister was collecting money for me from people all over the world. The Jewish community of Johannesburg was also rising to the occasion. Still, that feeling of helplessness kept tugging at my conscience.

Thailand had become a popular holiday destination for people from the UK, and there were quite a few British citizens in Thai prisons. Britain was one of the countries that had a prisoner transfer treaty with Thailand, but the conditions of transfer were so unjust – when sent home, prisoners would have to serve half the sentences imposed by the Thai courts – that some British inmates refused to transfer. A group of British guys approached me to draft a letter to their prime minister, Tony Blair. Although we South Africans had it worse, with no prisoner treaty at all, I could empathise with them, so I wrote a letter which I smuggled out to my sister. Joan typed it up and posted it to the parents of the British inmates. After describing the horrendous conditions in Thai prisons, I pointed out how randomly sentencing was done and how ridiculously long sentences were routinely handed down for drug offences. It was absurd that a first-time offender arrested as a drug courier could be given a life sentence, but even more so that the same prisoner, upon repatriation to the UK, would have to serve half of the absurd sentence handed down by the corrupt Thai justice system:

> *... There can be no argument that crime cannot go unpunished, but there can be equally no argument that the punishment must fit the crime. Does our system of justice support the view that sentences ranging from fifty to one hundred years are appropriate for first offending drug couriers? Of course not! The enlightened objective of penal experts is that incarceration should rehabilitate and prepare prisoners for re-integration into normal life. Prolonged sentence[s] in a Thai prison and/or the continuation of such sentences in a British prison would certainly destroy any prospect of being assimilated into any society. The British public does not need protection from repentant first time drug offenders. To throw the key away on us is an untenable sin and cannot possibly be an action of a society that claims to respect human rights and justice. We are not hardened criminals deserving of such savage treatment that requires us to be kept out of society. Our incarceration in an atrocious concentration camp in an alien country has wrought havoc and suffering upon our families. Most societies allow offenders a second chance ...*

Meanwhile, it had increasingly become my view that our South African embassy in Bangkok was actually working against us prisoners. The ambassador himself, JG Janse van Rensburg, had been quoted as saying that we deserved what we got. I suppose if I was in his position I might have had the same sentiments, but to me this was the product of ignorance. Ignorant people have a preconceived notion of criminals, and, while I may have been a prisoner, I never saw myself as a criminal. Yes, I had committed a crime, but everybody deserved their second chance. I wasn't asking for any special treatment. All I wanted was fair play in justice. One day, I vowed, when I was free I would visit this diplomat and enlighten him about the ways of honourable men. By 2000 I had started to understand and accept it was likely that I would remain in prison for a very long time. I had renewed my relationship with G-d and, besides my family, it was He who was giving me the strength to get through my days. Although I could claim to be content in prison, I could never be happy there. Contentment was a far more elevated state of mind than happiness. Happiness we feel from the heart, and it can change from moment to moment. My memories of my life before prison became a dream, and dreams were only for fools. I was alone, and that was my strength.

At the beginning of June about 80 names were called over the loudspeaker, my name among them. We went to the office, where we were told a list of names had come from the Palace. These were applicants for the royal pardon who were due for consideration. We were asked to sign if we still wanted our application to be processed. My name was in the first 20 on the list. If you consider that only three or four people were granted pardons every two years, you will realise just how slim my chances were. I thought the prison authorities were just playing with our minds. False hope had become an instrument of mental torture. I was learning very fast to see things for what they weren't, but it was a difficult balance to maintain.

That same month I got news from home that Joan had been involved in a car accident when another car had jumped a stop street. She had been admitted to hospital with serious injuries to her upper arm, shoulder and knees. Even from her hospital bed my sister continued her campaign for my release. She was one brave and determined sister. One of the things she organised was for a South African television programme, *Third Degree*, to feature my story, and one of their journalists came to Bangkwang to interview me. The 2000 Summer Olympics, which were held in Sydney in September and October, came and went. I watched the closing ceremony on TV, which was truly spectacular. My dream was now to be free and among the spectators at the 2004 Olympics in Athens.

Even with all the publicity surrounding South African prisoners in Thai jails, the ANC government just dragged its feet when it came to a treaty. In January 2001 my sister managed to get a meeting with the Minister of Justice, Penuell Maduna, and she was told at that meeting that the government was reviewing the possibility and that they would keep her posted on developments. Frustratingly, there didn't appear to be any developments or any progress to report. After thinking it over for a while, I proposed to my sister that we should change tactics. Perhaps we could put pressure on the Nigerian government. At that time, no African country had a treaty with Thailand. My thinking was that if Nigeria signed a treaty, then South Africa, the dominant political and economic power on the African continent, might follow suit. I drafted letters to the Nigerian president, highlighting the plight of the over 700 Nigerian prisoners languishing in Thai prisons. We sent copies of the letter to Pope John Paul II and once again to a number of human rights organisations. My sister even went so far as to meet with the Nigerian ambassador to South Africa. Not too long afterwards, we learnt that the Pope had personally contacted the Nigerian president, urging him to look into the situation.

Seeing that the ANC wasn't interested, we then approached the Democratic Alliance, the official opposition party, which was headed by Tony Leon. After months of talks, Mr Leon consulted with his colleague, Hendrick Schmidt, also a member of parliament. This resulted in the Transfer of Convicted Prisoners Draft Bill being submitted to parliament as a private members' legislative proposal by a member of the DA. The Draft Bill was discussed by the committee of Private Members' Bills and Legislative Proposals, during which meeting officials from both the departments of Justice and Correctional Services also made submissions. It was stated that various sections pertaining to the transfer of convicted prisoners were included in the Rome Statute of the International Criminal Court. The Rome Statute had been signed and accepted by South Africa. The need for the acceptance of the Draft Bill, according to the Department of Justice, was therefore questionable. The matter was due to be taken forward and discussed at the next meeting in order to persuade the members of the committee to refer the matter to the Correctional Services Portfolio Committee for their deliberation, and possible acceptance, within the parameters of the latest Correctional Services Amendment Bill, which was currently under discussion. Sadly, parliament rejected the bill.

We tried not to be discouraged. There was still the possibility of a royal pardon for me.

On 7 April 2001 yet another article about South African prisoners appeared in a South African newspaper. This time it was *The Citizen*, and I made the front page. The headline read '500 South African Nationals in Foreign Prisons'. Our plight was being extensively publicised once more. A week earlier, in Botswana, Mariette Bosch, a South African, had become the first white woman to be hanged in a southern African state. The Human Rights Commission requested President Thabo Mbeki to ask Botswana's president Festus Mogae for clemency, but no such plea was forthcoming. (Capital punishment had been abolished in South African in 1995.) If our government was not prepared to intervene on behalf of Mariette Bosch, I thought, what chance did the rest of us have?

On 21 April my sister and niece Keri appeared on a TV talk show, *The Felicia Show*, along with Robert McBride, who had himself been on death row in South Africa. The Mariette Bosch case was a hot topic and the discussion was about bringing back the death penalty. Violent crime had reached an all-time high in South Africa, and this didn't help our cause. The government's argument was: why bring home more criminals when our jails are at capacity with our own? It was becoming more and more apparent that we were fighting a losing battle. We were going to be left to rot in jail far away from home and the support of our families.

In April 2001 Thaksin Shinawatra became Thailand's new prime minister. Among a range of new policies, he also launched a drug suppression campaign. This campaign was popular with his supporters, but the practical result was a dramatic influx of drug offenders into the prisons. The prison population grew and the prisons became crammed. Almost every day saw a new prisoner arriving in shackles. Death row was so overcrowded that we heard they were considering turning part of Building 2 into another death row section. Only a few months after the prime minister's inauguration, four death row inmates were executed. To me, it was terrible to think that one man could change the destiny of another based on his political agenda. To protest the overcrowding, I drafted a petition to the diplomatic representative of the European Union in Thailand. I sent copies to every embassy in Bangkok:

April 2001
To: The Diplomatic Representative of the European Union in Thailand.
Subject: The problem of overcrowding in Bangkwang Prison and other violations of human rights.
CC: Ambassadors of various Foreign Embassies in Thailand.

Dear Sir,
  Citizens of European Union countries as well as various other nationalities who are imprisoned in Bangkwang Central Prison outside Bangkok implore the help of the European Union in demonstration with the Thai authorities, with regard to alleviating the chronic conditions of over-crowding to which we Europeans and foreigners are being subjected.
  Bangkwang is an old prison originally constructed for no more than one thousand prisoners during The Kingdom of

Thailand's wartime alliance with the Empire of Japan. Now due to successive Thai governments' penal policies against small-time narcotics users and handlers, there is possibly an excess of as many as seven to eight thousand prisoners incarcerated here with sentences ranging from over thirty years to one hundred years. From all over Thailand buses are constantly bringing more prisoners and dumping them here without any concern for the fact that there is no space for them.

We Europeans and other nationals are expected to endure the consequently inhuman conditions with equanimity. Unless all European Union countries and other respective Embassies jointly plead with the Thai authorities to observe minimal standards of human decency, human rights abuses will continually prevail unnoticed in Thai prisons.

Due to the influx and the congestion of prisoners, the authorities have imposed electrical restrictions and have also proposed to confiscate privately owned televisions. Even our daily food rations, which consist of a small plastic bag of rice and an inedible stew, have been reduced, which is inadequate even for the consumption of a ten-year-old child. To date we are still forced to take our daily shower in dirty river water. Due to constant negotiations with prison staff we have been able to preserve at least temporarily enough space in our cells for a prisoner to lie down on his back. We sleep shoulder to shoulder packed like sardines. Yet the prison authorities are constantly stacking more people into the already overcrowded sleeping cells. The lack of space and the consequent tension and risk to health (especially from tuberculosis and numerous skin infections) makes our sleeping environment in which we spend 15 hours out of 24, absolutely hellish, a situation synonymous with the Nazi concentration camps and the Soviet gulags.

If only the European Union countries and other foreign Embassies would jointly request that the Thai authorities alleviate the congestion in Bangkwang and be allowed to sleep no more than fifteen people per cell instead of twenty-six. We have no means to measure our cells exactly but we estimate them to be 4½ metres by 9 metres.

As you may be aware, Thailand can be considered a rogue state with regard to its record on otherwise internationally accepted standards of human rights. Cynically the present Prime Minister Thaksin Shinawatra has increased the tempo of executions in order to make space at Bangkwang for the prisoners backed-up in the provinces. Even this elevated culling, however, is inadequate to meet the country's detention requirements.

The problem with raising the issue of United Nations minimum rules as a basis for negotiation with the Thai Government is that Thailand is not a signatory to any major treaty which would affect the practices of their prisons. The Thai Department of Corrections is therefore under no legal obligation to alter its administration of prisons. We the foreign inmates of Bangkwang Prison invite International Human Rights delegations to investigate the precarious living conditions we are subjected to. Such an endeavour should be conducted in the evening when inmates are crammed into the cells as any daytime inspection would be a waste of time.

Our petition was forwarded to the Department of Corrections for consideration. Because Thais generally procrastinated, I didn't expect that any immediate change would be implemented, but I hoped that in the long term something would be done. Even if this happened after I had gone home, at least those who were arrested after me might enjoy better conditions.

It was time for yet another indoor football tournament. Each team consisted of four players and two reserves. I no longer needed to ask my family to send uniforms. Instead we could buy them right there.

Football was huge in Thailand. A person could purchase imitation uniforms of all the popular Premier League teams. The prices were good and the quality was not bad either. Using my money, Jai went to buy the uniforms and then she posted them to me. We would have our kit in three days or less. I loved the competitiveness of the games. I had my own team, made up mainly of Thais. I coached, trained and played; I was not getting any younger, though, and sometimes I struggled to keep up with some of the younger chaps.

Anna-Marie, one of the South African women who came to Thailand to buy clothing, was travelling to Bangkok quite regularly now, and on her visits I would give her examples of my art to take back home. My paintings were my only possessions. Whenever she took them home for me, I would be so nervous, forever emphasising, that, if she took them out of the folder, to please make sure that her hands were clean and that she didn't put the paintings on a wet surface, and, most importantly, to make sure they were kept in a safe place. At times I would give her up to 50 pieces, almost a whole year's work. My mind would only be at ease when I got news from home that my art was safely in the hands of my family.

One day, four religious guys came to visit us Jewish prisoners. One of them, who was about 20 years old, recognised my South African accent. He was the son of a rabbi from the Orange Grove *shul* in Johannesburg, which was the same area where my family lived. Seeing these young men embarking on their spiritual journey so early in their lives got me thinking. How would my life have been if I had never succumbed to the allure that drugs hold for so many of us? But there were too many 'what ifs', and anyway I already knew the answers. It wasn't too late, though. I had to believe that everything that transpires in our lives happens for the greater good. Accepting my situation was the beginning to opening the way to change. I kept returning to this point: I had to take responsibility for my actions. I was being given a second chance. Life was too beautiful to waste and I couldn't allow myself to be consumed by regret, nor should I feel sorrow. My life was no longer my own. My ship was sailing and the promise of a more meaningful life was waiting just beyond the horizon. I could either swim or drown. The choice was mine.

Prison was a world in itself. Thousands of men who had broken the law and committed a crime lived there more or less together. Each had his own story and each had a different life in prison. Some stagnated, others went insane, a few changed their ways, and some men died.

A Ghanaian national who was on death row in Building 1 had his sentence reduced to life imprisonment in the third court. During his time in Building 1, he had acquired quite a few sets of weights, as well as two exercise benches. When he was moved to Building 2, by request of the prison authorities, his weights were brought across. After negotiating with the chief for an area where prisoners could exercise, for US$2 000 they built an office for the second chief with an adjoining room, which would later be given to the General. The area was roughly 4m in width and about 7m in length. A makeshift roof was erected. Two poles with a bar were sunk into the concrete so that we could do chin-ups. Some of us foreigners donated money towards the costs. In comparison to where we had exercised before, it was great. The Ghanaian used more money to buy weights from other buildings, and he soon had quite an effective gym running. Whoever wanted to exercise paid 100 Thai baht a month, while those who had donated money got six months' free.

I was working really hard to develop my artistic skills, expand my mind and reconnect with my roots. It was a long and difficult process and I often found myself getting stuck. Sometimes depression would grab me by the throat, threatening to choke me to death. Those were dark periods. When I thought about how far I had come, I also realised what a long way I still had to go.

Nevertheless, I was making considerable advances with my carbon powder portraits. Chai Long was doing mostly A4-size pictures, but I wanted to paint bigger portraits – on A3 paper. He suggested that this was not practical and that, to maintain the photographic effect, I should keep my portraits small. Being a stubborn fool, I wanted to exploit the full potential of this unique medium. Chai Long had taught me the basics and by now I had extensive experience working with Bic ballpoint pens. My sketching was accurate and I had a good eye for a balanced composition in a drawing. I needed to explore the ideas that came to my mind. How could one place limitations on one's imagination? I was ready to fly. If I had my way, the butterfly would soon soar like an eagle.

In November, I acquired a foam mattress for my bed. Until then my 'mattress' had consisted of about eight blankets, which had gathered a lot of dust and absorbed a fair amount of sweat. In Building 8 they manufactured hard foam mattresses, which cost 1 700 Thai baht each. The foam was 5cm thick and over a metre wide. With my Stanley knife I cut this down to the standard size permitted for every cell. I had a fitted blanket made by one of the tailors. Although slightly hard, it was a thousand times more comfortable than the blankets had been. Jai bought me a new pillow, which was so soft that for the first few nights I couldn't sleep. Comfort was not something I was accustomed to any more.

With the leftover pieces of foam I made cushions for my chair. The Thais in prison did not believe in wasting anything; everything had a function or could be used for some purpose or other, and I learnt from their example. Six years of sleeping on a bunch of folded-up blankets had taken its toll on my body, and my back was a constant worry for me.

I received the news that Arcadia, the Jewish orphanage where Joan and I had spent most of our childhood, was relocating to the Johannesburg suburb of Sandringham because Hollard Insurance Company had bought the property at 22 Oxford Road. The Arc had been home to thousands of kids, who had filtered through its gates since the early 1900s, and the news was hard for me to digest. All the familiar open spaces would now have office blocks erected on them. At least the main building would remain; the plan was that it would be restored and be declared a national monument. We Arcadians were losing part of our heritage, and I was sad to hear it. Gone would be the days when ex-Arcadians would meet there to play football, attend synagogue during the high festivals, or just walk through the grounds reminiscing about our shared childhood.

On 19 October, another four Americans were transferred back to prisons in the US. Two of them had arrived nearly three years after me. They were also drug-related cases. It was so unfair that some foreigners would serve more time than others for committing exactly the same crime, and I struggled with the bitterness this always made me feel. Some of us prisoners had even contemplated holding American prisoners hostage, killing them if we had to, just to attract attention to the unfairness of the Thai justice system. Luckily, we didn't go that far.

Six days before my 41st birthday was Yom Kippur, the Jewish Day of Atonement. I fasted for the first time since my days in Arcadia. It was difficult: the weather was very hot, and praying all day took its toll on me, leaving me dehydrated, run-down and weak. There was always the concern in the back of my mind that, in my state of frailty, I might get into an argument or a fight. During Ramadan, the Muslims would fast for one month. They were not allowed to eat or drink water from dusk to dawn, whereas we Jews abstained from sunset to sunset when we fasted. The guards were very accommodating when it came to religion, allowing many Thais who may well have been Buddhists to convert to Christianity. These guys worshipped with the foreigners. The Muslims were allowed to spend their days in their cells and cook their meals at night.

Meanwhile, I remained hell-bent on mastering the medium of carbon powder. I devoted many months to practising my skills, often stumbling and sometimes becoming frustrated, but I persevered all the same. Eventually I made a breakthrough. I achieved my goal of painting a portrait that was an almost perfect photographic replica. Watching life take form on a blank piece of paper filled me with awe. I would stare at my painting in disbelief. My hands seem to have a mind of their own. This portrait was of the great Lubavitcher Rebbe Menachem Schneerson. It was uncannily lifelike. His very essence seem to come through his eyes. My talent, I believed, was a gift from the angels and something I would never take for granted. I would use my skill to bring joy to others.

I started to mix colour poster paint with the carbon powder. Chai Long was less than impressed, but he couldn't help but be amazed at my creativity and the progress I had made in such a short time. He told me I was his best student ever. Then something strange happened. I was halfway through painting a carbon-powder portrait when he criticised me for doing something wrong. He took the painting from me and worked on it himself to correct my mistake, and he made a complete mess of it. I couldn't believe my eyes. He had deliberately spoilt my picture. It was almost as if he wanted to prevent me from advancing. Maybe he thought that, now that I had mastered the technique, I would have no further use for him.

After this incident I never let him touch any of my paintings again and, unfortunately, our friendship took a turn for the worse. Shortly afterwards, Chai Long got moved to a prison in the provinces. I was upset because there was so much I still wanted to learn from him, but that was prison life – people came and went. Some people make an everlasting impact on your life, while the memory of others fades with time. It is sad in a way, and the loss of Chai Long reminded me of my friends who had died. All we have left of them are our memories and the impressions they made on us.

Chai Long was instrumental in bringing me closer to my dreams of being recognised as artist. I remain indebted to him.

Back home, my family were totally blown away by the pieces of art I was creating. Their opinion was a driving force in my quest to prove my worth. I was no longer a useless drug addict. Not only had I kicked the habit but, importantly, I had also turned my life around. By finding purpose, life had taken on a whole new meaning for me. Did I have any regrets? Yes, I regretted a lot of stuff, mainly having become a junkie in the first place and the people's lives I had destroyed. I also regretted the women I had abused and the hell I had put my family through. Yes, I knew I was a poor excuse for a human being and that I probably deserved to be condemned for life. Forgiveness, like respect, is something that has to be earned. I knew I had a long way to go before I would be fully redeemed, but I was trying.

Whenever new prisoners arrived, whether foreign or Thai, recently arrested or transferred from another prison or building, these prisoners always posed a threat. To get a name or to establish themselves, they would look for fights with prisoners in positions of power, especially the younger boys. I got involved in quite a few such incidents, where I would use a weapon to defuse a situation or prevent it from getting out of hand. Normally, those of us who had done hard time and had been together for years would assist and protect each other in such instances.

In those early years a prisoner could request to have photographs taken. I made a point of taking photos of myself twice a year to send back home. It was important for my family to see that I was healthy and keeping strong. At Easter and Christmas, the Christians would hold celebrations and the missionary workers from outside, headed by Father Oliver, would organise a special contact visit, during which gift packages were handed out. These consisted of toiletries, clothing and foodstuffs. In addition, the prisoners who were the leaders of the church inside the prison would collect money from the Christians and the other inmates to throw a party on Christmas Day.

The guard in charge of the photographic section would come into our building and take photos. When the photos were developed they were placed in an album with reference numbers beside each one. Prisoners could then order as many pictures as they required; one photo cost 20 Thai baht. On one such occasion, photos were taken of prisoners in shackles. In some of the photos the prison walls and the watchtower were visible as well. Somehow these pictures made their way onto the internet. There was an investigation. The guard responsible was removed and prisoners were no longer allowed to take any photos at all.

An ex-Arcadian and a good friend of mine, David Sandler, who lived in Australia, had taken it upon himself to maintain contact through a newsletter, which he circulated to Arcadians around the world. He and I started communicating and, through our correspondence, he encouraged me to think about writing a book about my life. He also contributed funds towards my wellbeing and continued to do this for years. Writing a book was something I planned to do anyway, but at this time my main focus was my art. David started compiling a booklet, and he asked all ex-Arcadians to contribute by writing about

433

their childhood experiences there. I thought it would be fun and nostalgic so I contributed enthusiastically. Once the booklet was printed and posted off, a lot more ex-Arcadians became aware of my situation and started corresponding with me. The stories of the different people were fascinating and inspired David to collect more of them and bring out a sequel. Reminiscing about years gone by was every prisoner's daydream, and writing about them was cathartic. I suggested to David that he should write a book himself.

When Joan and I were living in Arcadia, the children would spend weekends or Sundays with their families. When I was about 16, there were two of us who never had anywhere to go. A Jewish family, the Simons, who lived in Glenhazel, approached Arcadia wanting a male friend for their only son, Clifford, and their three daughters. I was asked if I'd like to go along and meet them. I reluctantly agreed, but, as it turned out, they were the most amazing family and we became very close. Mrs Simon – Phyllis – actually wanted to adopt me. As tempting as it was, I felt it wouldn't be fair on my mother. Only orphans were adopted, and Joan and I weren't orphans. We remained close friends, though, and I spent almost every Sunday and sometimes all weekend at the Simons' house, right up until the time I finished matric. After school, sadly, I lost touch with them. In prison, Phyllis's oldest daughter, Karen, and I started corresponding, and in March 2001 I received the sad news that Phyllis had died of cancer. I was heartbroken at having lost contact with the Simon family and so, in honour of the kindness and love Phyllis had shown me, I painted her portrait and sent it as a gift to her family. If I had allowed them to adopt me, I couldn't help thinking, my life could very well have turned out differently.

David Sandler's Arcadia research and connections triggered so many stories for me, but for the time being my own book would have to be put on hold. I had been commissioned to paint so many portraits that I could see myself being kept busy for at least the next two years. My time was precious, and sometimes there were not enough hours in my day. At this time I also took on two students and was teaching them portraiture. The days would fly by. 'Not a moment to waste' became my motto.

Every time I completed a painting, which could take anything from a week to a month, I would take a day off. On Saturday, which was my Sabbath, I didn't work, and I tried to keep the Sabbath to the best of my ability. Saturday was also football day and the day I spent just generally relaxing. Painting a carbon-powder portrait can be very pressurising, and no two faces are alike. Every portrait I have ever painted has presented a challenge. In between portraits I would do a fun painting or two, in either watercolour or poster paint, and usually these would be abstracts, expressing my inner state of mind and my emotions.

Some four years back I had petitioned to have phones installed in the building. In June 2001 we were informed by the prison authorities that this was finally going to happen. This was a victory for us. The plan was to put two telephones just outside Building 2 on the way to the visit room. Here a new building had been erected, with one section for a computer room and another for an executive conference room. Applications for a telephone card had to go through the embassy. Prisoners would only be allowed to call immediate family, and the embassy had to confirm officially that the number you had submitted was that of a family member. I was over the moon. We would be allowed to call home twice a week, for five minutes at a time. Every building was given a specific day and time. Thirty prisoners would be called at one time, and when we went out we were required to wear our light-blue prison shirts. You could wait up to an hour before it was your turn, but, still, the luxury of being able to talk to your loved ones was great.

In July 2001 we saw the first transfer of two British prisoners, who up until then had refused to be sent home to the UK. Life in a Thai prison was much easier for them. If I had had the choice to serve my time in a South African jail, I would have jumped at the opportunity. Prison is prison; everything is relative. For me, the most important factor would be more the proximity to my family and less the time I would still have to serve behind bars.

My Norwegian friend Kjell also transferred to a prison in Norway. I helped him carry his things to the gate, where we shook hands. We hugged and I wished him well on his way. Another goodbye, and this one was really hard. My eyes filled with tears, of joy and of envy, too.

On the one hand, I was happy that he was one step closer to freedom; on the other, I wished it was me. I vowed to myself that this would be the last person I would allow myself to get close to, and also that never again would I walk anybody to the gate. At that moment I hated our government, and I was ashamed to be South African. To rub salt in the wound, a month and a half after Kjell left I received a letter from him informing me that his prison in Norway was like a five-star hotel compared to Bangkwang. Two weeks later he was granted a royal pardon by the Thai monarch. It was the first time I'd ever heard of somebody being granted a royal pardon *after* they'd been transferred out of a Thai jail. Nevertheless, it was fantastic news. Kjell had served over four years, which was much longer than he would have received in any other country for a similar offence.

Because the increased number of death row inmates had led to severe overcrowding in Building 1, the authorities put into action a plan to convert the downstairs section of Building 2 into another death row section. Prisoners were put to work constructing a steel partition enclosed in wire mesh. It stretched from floor to ceiling and would divide the rooms of death row inmates from those serving life sentences. The area around and near the entrance was cordoned off with barbed-wire security fences. This included half of the outside toilets and the net factory, which was turned into a dining hall. At the front of the building, the downstairs entrance was fenced off from upstairs. The courtyard immediately in front of that, where two big trees offered shade for prisoners wanting to relax beneath them and escape the scorching heat, was also fenced in.

Basically, the idea was to keep the death row inmates apart from the 'lifers'. This was for a number of reasons. Firstly, it was to prevent the distribution of drugs, money, electronic gadgets and other illegal items. Secondly, death row inmates were considered more dangerous than lifers because they had nothing to lose.

Once all the fencing had been erected, six of the first rooms were evacuated and the death row guys from Building 1 took up occupation. Our room was on the same floor, so, to enter and exit the building, we now had to use the rear entrance. Every two months, the steel partition dividing death row would be moved down another room or two to enable more death row inmates to take up residence downstairs. Soon the partition approached our cell. The inmates who had previously occupied the rooms now allocated to death row inmates were relocated upstairs or moved to other buildings. I had hoped that we would be allowed to keep our cell, but no such luck; at this rate, it would be a matter of only a few months before we'd have to move. All the money we had invested in maintaining a private cell was going to be lost.

As the room chief, I was called by the prison authorities well in advance and informed that we should all start looking for other cells upstairs, as there was no way they could give us a private cell, and nor could we stay together. We would have to be split up. I called a cell meeting and explained our fate. None of us wanted to be in a room with 24 occupants or, for that matter, to move upstairs. This meant one thing: we would have to buy another cell. The ideal situation would have been for everybody to contribute, but unfortunately not everyone could afford it. Giving up the luxury of a private room and risking contracting tuberculosis or another disease in an overcrowded cell was a horrible prospect.

Pedro, the Dutchman, had in recent years received a lot of support from people in the Netherlands, and, between him and myself, we reckoned we could raise enough money to buy another room. We agreed 50-50 down the line. I negotiated with the officer in charge of the building and we agreed on a price. According to the prison authorities, we had roughly a month to come up with the money and to choose a room upstairs. Through Jai, I got word to my sister. One thing was for sure – Joan would never let me down. Somehow she always came through for me. Joan contacted various businessmen in South Africa – Bertie Lubner, Benji Schleider and his brother Gabriel, and others – and within ten days US$1 500 was in Jai's account. Pedro, however, proved unable to come up with his share. All he did was make empty promises.

Upstairs it was like a fucking circus, with all the TVs blaring. We were informed by the officer that three rooms remained downstairs: one was three-quarter size; another, Room 11, was a full-size room like the one we currently had; and there was one small room. Ideally, we would want to take a full-size room. Room 11 was occupied by 21 Muslim inmates. It was the perfect spot. Between the Building Chief and the officer, I paid them US$1 000 to vacate it. Never before had a prisoner been so audacious as to move an entire room!

One of the foreigners occupying the room was from Ghana, a great footballer by the name of Keita. He refused to move. The Thai occupants, although reluctant, wouldn't dare oppose the prison authorities, and in a matter of an hour, Room 11 was evacuated except for Keita, who stayed on with us. We took up immediate occupation. From Room 16 we took two of our three overhead fans and then the famous Room 16, known for so many years as the best room in Bangkwang, died. The steel partition was moved forward, cutting our section off from death row.

Our new cell needed renovating. The paint on the walls was discoloured and had mostly peeled off. The vinyl floor was an ugly red colour, broken everywhere and ready for the garbage can. The toilet bowl had obviously been broken and repaired with concrete. It was so dirty that a thick layer of shit had formed a hard crust over the entire surface. It took me two hours to scrape it off with a nail and still it wasn't clean. The repair had been so badly done that when you flushed the toilet the shit struggled to pass through the pipes.

One of the Thai Chinese guys on death row, Ling, who was also a British citizen and spoke excellent English, had spent a fortune fixing up his new cell there. He had even had clean, hot running water installed. The guards were happy to lick Ling's arse and milk him for everything he was worth in the process. Pedro befriended him, and Ling was kind enough to buy us a new toilet bowl. He also helped us order tiles. We hired Thai prisoners to change our toilet bowl and to do the tiling. Because the cement hadn't dried by the time night fell, our cell door was left open so that we could use the toilet in the corridor. I must say I felt strange sleeping with our steel door open.

A couple of days later we had our room painted. They started early in the morning, but even with the extreme heat the paint still hadn't dried by the time we were locked up. The smell of paint was really strong. I wore my cotton surgical mask the whole night but it still didn't prevent me from getting the worst headache I'd had for a while. We used the vinyl from Room 16 and attached our two fans to the ceiling. The rear of our new room faced east, so by the evening it was relatively cool. I kept my spot next to the toilet, and above my head I fitted a fluorescent light with a switch. With the extra money I also bought a colour Sony Wega flat-screen TV for 11 000 Thai baht, as well as a small DVD player. I had a steel shelf made that would fit under my feet at the end of my bed, and that was where I placed my TV.

Pedro never did come up with his share for the room, and after a while I told him to forget about it. In this way I controlled the room and decided who would stay and who wouldn't. I was the boss, and in the end I was very pleased with our new home.

Chapter 14

Murderers Are People, Too

Whenever a new foreign prisoner arrived, I would be called to the office to check whether we would take him into our cell. Invariably, for the first few days I would welcome the new guys into my house. I would feed them and help them get organised. If they didn't have a bed, I would have one made for them, incurring the costs myself. I did this with no expectation, remembering how I had suffered sleeping on a flattened cardboard box when I first came to prison.

Just before Songkran, the Water Festival, a new chief took over Building 2. His name was Mr Prichit Kowmuang. He had a reputation for being strict, so we steeled ourselves for changes. Almost right away he ordered all private TVs to be removed from the cells. Anybody with video machines and other electronic devices had to hand them in. These included electric frying pans and kettles, which meant we would have to cook our meals on a charcoal stove. In addition we weren't allowed to take food into the cells, except drinking water, which was ridiculous, as we spent almost 16 hours a day locked up in our cells. He also stopped us from showering during the day, restricting us to an hour in the morning and an hour in the afternoon just before lock-down. Over and above all this, he wanted to reshuffle our rooms and to mix Thais and foreigners.

When we refused to hand over our electrical equipment, he arranged for the security section to raid our cells. DVDs, Walkmans and CD players found during the raid were confiscated. It seemed that Prichit was hell-bent on making our lives as miserable as he could.

Everybody was in a state of panic. Thais and foreigners alike came to me, urging me to draw up a petition. I drafted one and then walked around the building collecting signatures. My own signature appeared at the top. At night, the petition was passed around upstairs from room to room. One of the Thais who spoke good English also translated it into Thai. The petition was addressed to the Director of the prison, and in it I complained about the new chief in no uncertain terms.

The next morning, I submitted it to the clerk at the office, knowing that it would immediately be taken to Prichit, who would read it and see that we were calling for his removal. After reading it, the chief caught a wobble and ordered a meeting of all foreigners in the dining room. Including the Asian foreigners, there were almost 200 prisoners. The chief gave some speech about how all he was doing was enforcing the rules laid down by the Department of Corrections. We argued our case by pointing out that we were serving life sentences and that we enjoyed certain privileges that the previous Building Chief had been happy to allow. The situation was becoming volatile. Disgruntled prisoners were all muttering at once. A Nigerian who had served over ten years stood up. Pointing his finger at the Building Chief, he said threateningly: 'Do you want peace, or war?' The chief turned pale and abruptly called off the meeting.

The next day, Samuel, the Nigerian, was removed from the building.

An Indian prisoner by the name of Dhawal, whose name means 'light complexion' and who was notorious for writing letters to the United Nations and to human rights organisations complaining of conditions in prison and claiming he had been unjustly imprisoned, apparently then held a private meeting with the Building Chief. Dhawal advised the chief to call in certain individuals and warn them that unless they removed their signatures from the petition, they would be moved to another building. I had no idea that this meeting had taken place, but suddenly many of the Chinese and other foreigners started crossing their names off the petition. I was confused. Then another foreigner, a guy from Mali, came to me very upset, accusing me and seven of my cellmates of removing our signatures. We were all cowards, he said disgustedly. Then he threatened to stab me. Give me a break, I thought. I told him that whatever he'd heard was bullshit, and promised to investigate. To my dismay, I discovered it was true – members of my room *had* removed their names. Fuck, I was annoyed, but in the end I decided it was in the best interests of all to withdraw the petition. When I approached the Building Chief and asked him to give it back to me, he said he'd do this only on condition that I wrote a letter clearly stating the withdrawal of our complaint against him. I agreed and he handed back the petition. Fuck you, I thought, as I walked away. I never wrote that letter.

In the days that followed, the chief didn't leave his office. Then Dhawal paid him another visit, an educational one this time. He explained to him how things were done and also told him that if he sat back and allowed things to run the way they always had, he stood to make a bundle of money. Pretty soon, Mr Prichit seem to get it. The gamblers pulled together and paid the chief 40 000 Thai baht to reopen the casino, and before very long things were back to normal. I had to admit that corruption had its advantages!

Joan's old friend Edna Ralph, who still faithfully walked from door to door in Manchester asking members of the Jewish community for small contributions towards my support, posted me a *mezuzah* – a decorative case, containing a piece of parchment, that is fixed to a doorpost – along with some books on Judaism. The *mezuzah* I attached to the wooden post at the entrance to my house, and inside, on the floor, where I had cemented a hole closed, I scratched the Star of David into the surface. There were other Jews, most of them Israeli guys, spread around in other buildings, but our Jewish fraternity in Building 2 stood at four. We called ourselves the band of Jewish brothers. No matter what our nationalities, we stood united in our faith; we all shared the same forefathers. These guys would hang out in my house and it became our sanctuary, the place where we could relax or pray, and where we would often enter into deep spiritual discussions. There was myself, Simon, the French Israeli man, and Eddie Tutin, a French Jew who had had no knowledge of Judaism until he came to prison. And then there was Roy Stevens.

Roy was an American journalist and an Emmy award-winning television producer, who apparently had produced several anti-drug documentaries. According to him, when he was arrested in Bangkok he was working on a series through which he planned to expose the drug-smuggling networks that operated in the Golden Triangle. Roy really struggled to adjust to prison life, and we watched the painful deterioration of his health and mental state.

On one occasion, Roy took a cigarette and burnt holes in the bed of the fellow American who slept next to him, claiming that the guy was Lucifer. Another time we found him pacing up and down the centre of our cell in the middle of the night, completely naked. He would some-times become belligerent, swearing at and abusing whoever looked in his direction. One night when this happened, we could see he was out of control, and so two of his fellow countrymen pinned him down, hog-tied him and put a sock in his mouth to prevent him from scream-ing. It was clear that he was becoming a danger to himself and to the rest of us. The following morning I was called to the office. By then the prison authorities had heard what had happened from the trustees who patrolled the corridor. Roy was moved out of our cell, and from then on he slept in the corridor.

Back in December 1999 an article had appeared in *The Jewish World* in which the writer described conditions in Bangkwang as horrendous:

> *In their cramped, squalid, stifling hot cells, most prisoners take turns sleeping on the bare cement floor among giant roaches. They use a stinking hole in the corner for a toilet and subsist on a bowl of rice porridge a day. To bathe, they splash water on themselves from troughs filled with untreat-ed sewerage-tainted water from the nearby river.*

While this was probably as fair a description of life in a Thai jail as any, without diminishing or underrating the suffering of other inmates, for me these 'horrendous' conditions had become a way of life. What might have seemed extreme to some had now become the norm for me. And anyway, I had had no choice but to adjust.

The same article went on: 'No money, though, can buy them out of disease or death. AIDS is endemic among the prisoners as junkies are everywhere, pooling syringes.' The writer even quoted me:

> 'G-d works in mysterious ways,' explains 'Kreps' who, with his long, curly hair and pumped-up muscles, resembles a beach surfer. 'If I were outside, I might well be dead by now.' 'Kreps' describes a pre-conviction life of drug addiction and a shoot-out with police back in South Africa. Now he puts on tefillin for daily prayers, keeps Shabbos and eats Kosher. He prays to G-d to add his name to a pending Royal amnesty.

While none of us can predict the future, and while I still looked upon tomorrow with certain trepidation, I had learnt to live in perfect faith. My destiny was in the hands of *Hashem*.

Art is an expression of the inner self, an infinite journey of the mind where the parameters are defined only by the imagination. Every painting became for me a process of discovery. My own inspiration became a means of understanding people and a world that sometimes felt as if it had forsaken me. With each new creation not only did my spirit become more and more free but also, perhaps more importantly, my anger began to dissipate.

But long hours of drawing had taken their toll on my body. My lower back was fucked. It was becoming too much. Massages brought only temporary relief. When I reported sick, after explaining my practice of sitting painting for long hours, the doctor's solution was that I should stop painting! I asked him what he would have me do instead.

Art was my life, I told him. Would he prefer me to do drugs, which had become a favourite pastime for many prisoners? In fact, I had been reporting sick with back pain for two years now. At one stage, a doctor had given me a letter saying I suffered from lower back pain and recommended that I go to the police hospital for physiotherapy. This never happened.

Anyway, I tried to get this doctor to write me a letter recommending that I be allowed an adjustable office chair, but he was not interested. I lost my temper and told him that just because I was a prisoner didn't mean I was an animal. I had my rights. He just laughed at me. He was a young, arrogant prick. I'm not sure what he wrote in the letter he did give me, but when I submitted my request the prison authorities refused the chair on the grounds that illegal things could be smuggled in it.

The staff at the embassy finished their four-year term in 2001, and I had to admit I was delighted to see them leave Bangkok. The new ambassador was Mrs Petho and the consular officer was Miss Naicker. Both were far friendlier than their predecessors and much more compassionate towards us prisoners.

At this stage I was beginning to produce some incredible pieces of art. The last thing I was going to do was stop. I loved painting portraits for people, which I did for free and without expectation. I painted every member of my family. I wished I could see their faces when they accepted delivery of my paintings. Even though they always told me how thrilled they were with them, I wished I could witness their joy in person. With each piece I completed, I felt a sense of accomplishment unlike anything I had ever felt before. My dreams were being realised behind the very walls that reduced men to nothing, where all you were was a number. For some prisoners, coming to prison was the end of their lives, the final chapter. For me, it was the beginning, the beginning of a new life, a life without drugs. When reflecting on my past, which I still did frequently, I could scarcely believe that I had allowed myself to be reduced to the lowlife I became. I was an ex-King David pupil, who had strictly adhered to the traditions of our culture. Where had I gone wrong, and why? What was it that had led me onto that path of self-destruction? I promised myself that if I ever got out of Bangkwang alive, I would never go back to the way I was before.

But what if I was released tomorrow, I thought. Would I be ready to make those changes, to become the man I longed to be?

Actually, the truth was that I was far from ready. I needed to stay in prison, and, in a strange way, I wanted to stay there. The real world was like a great whale waiting to swallow me up. Somehow it was safer behind the high-security walls, where there were no traffic jams, no red traffic lights and no one-ways. Time was no longer an enemy. Time had become my best friend.

After my sister appeared on *The Felicia Show*, she had a meeting with certain representatives of the Department of Foreign Affairs, who advised her to meet with human rights lawyers regarding the injustices and the irregularities of sentencing in Thailand. It was not right that South Africans, in comparison with American, French and Israeli citizens, to mention a few, were spending more time in prison. We had a strong case, but at the same time we had to tread carefully. I did not want to jeopardise the future transfers from Thai prisons of any country's nationals.

Joan met with a human rights lawyer who lived in Ireland, but she seemed more interested in the abolition of the death penalty than in what we were pushing for. I suppose, in her view, the fate of prisoners on death row was more important than my own. Anthony Karstaedt, a barrister from Australia, who was related to us on my brother-in-law's side, volunteered his services, but there was not much he could do except investigate the progress of my royal pardon. On 15 May the Department of Corrections informed him that my application was still in the office of His Majesty the King's private secretary. In fact, this was exciting news, as it had been only three years since I'd submitted my application, and other applications had been known to take five years before receiving an answer.

My sister had also contacted a man in Israel named Harut Lapid, who had become famous for working on behalf of dozens of Israelis wrongfully imprisoned abroad, either for their release or for the improvement of their conditions. Through the assistance of South African

446

businessman Abe Krok, Harut Lapid was flown to South Africa to meet with my sister. Sadly, the meeting was in vain. Harut had never before dealt with the Thai government and said he was therefore not able to take on my case.

It was at these times of setback that I would become quite desperate. In June I told the South African embassy that, if our country would not sign a prisoner treaty with Thailand, I would embark on a hunger strike and I would get the other South Africans in other Thai prisons to join me. I told them I would give them a year. I wanted to plan this properly and get the media involved. My sister was dead against the hunger strike plan, saying that our government did not care in the least and pointing out that, even if I died, it would not change anything.

On 26 June 2001, we were all shaken when a Thai drug offender was executed, and rumours circulated that more death row inmates would soon be killed.

On Friday 17 August 2001, I was called to the gate. My heart was racing as I made my way there, with my Thai friends shouting out '*Aleksander kabarn!*' A few of the foreigners made similar comments – 'You going home, bro.' Actually I *did* think there was a good chance of this happening – after all, I had a personal letter of support from Mr Mandela himself. Although I tried not to allow myself to get over-excited, it wasn't easy to suppress my feelings. Maybe this was the day. Maybe it was my turn to hear that magic word.

At the gate I was greeted by the guard in charge of royal pardons. I felt a lump in my throat. Could it be true? Was I really going home? I tried to read the guard's face, but it was expressionless. Then he told me, in Thai, that my application had been turned down. 'Rejected,' he said. His manner was casual and cold, not that I expected a hug or any words of comfort from him. My heart dropped to my feet. Once I began to process this bad news, my main concern was my sister's reaction. I knew Joan would be devastated. I was more upset for her than for myself. None of my friends could believe it.

The truth was, I never expected to be pardoned, although deep down in my heart I still hoped and wished that I would be. When the reality set in, I felt as if I had been resentenced to life imprisonment. I would have to wait at least two years before I could submit another application.

It seemed that *Hashem* had other plans for me, plans that would only make sense a long way down the road. I knew that day that I was in for a long stretch.

Towards the end August we began to prepare for another football competition. Sometimes there would be about three of these events per year, mostly because the guards made so much money out of them. This time I made a deal with the guard in charge: if supporters paid to attend the games, I would use the gate money to pay the officials. These contests were mostly a lot of fun, but one thing I hated about them was that there were forever problems among the inmates. When we lost a game, fingers were pointed; if someone didn't make the team, an enemy was made. I was getting weary of all the bullshit. Not only did it cost me money, but often it was also a headache. I decided, too, that this would be the last time I financed the uniforms.

After the rejection of my request for an office chair, my sister sent me an exercise wheel. I also started doing lower back exercises with weights. I dropped my weight by a couple of kilos and my back improved radically. When I was drawing, I would stretch every hour. These changes helped me to cope with my chronic back pain.

Jai was still visiting me, but now she came only once a week instead of twice. To be frank, I was running out of conversation. It was a frustrating situation for which there was no short-term solution. I had encouraged her to get on with her life and to try to meet somebody worthy of her love, telling her I was not that man. But she never gave up on me. In fact, Jai taught me what it means to love someone unconditionally. She remained loyal and went to great lengths to make sure all my needs were met. On my mother's 77th birthday, Jai bought her a gift and sent it to her without even telling me.

Seeing that South Africa continued to show little interest in signing a treaty with Thailand, I came up with another idea. I wrote to the

Israeli embassy to enquire about the possibility of my becoming an Israeli citizen. I even offered to join the Israeli army. At that stage I was even ready to relinquish my South African citizenship. The Israelis were not interested, however. Because I was a prisoner, they said, I could not be considered for citizenship. What a shame – even my own tribesmen were turning their backs on me.

On 11 September, at around 7pm, I was lying on my bed reading a book when Roy came running to the bars of our cell, shouting, 'America is being attacked! Check out CNN!' We changed channels hurriedly, just in time to see the second plane crash into the World Trade Center. There was complete silence. Nobody in the cell uttered a word. We were all glued to the TV in a state of total disbelief. It was as if the world had come to an end. It was such a shock. If *America* couldn't prevent a terrorist attack, nobody in the world would be safe. Perhaps a Third World War was not a bad idea, I thought later, cynically; it might be one way of getting out of here.

With all the support I was getting from outside, my standard of living had improved. I was having two big meals a day and fresh fruit every night. The longer I stayed, the more comfortable I became. I was now also the proud owner of a blender and a sandwich maker, which formed part of my collection of electrical appliances. Our satellite TV was up and running smoothly. Life generally was pretty good. Most importantly, I was doing what I loved most – painting – and, although my eyes were deteriorating rapidly, I was producing some of my best pieces of art.

My responsibilities were few and far between, but, even so, being the room chief, and having to deal with all the problems that came with it, was starting to stress me out. I began to suffer from severe mood swings. Often, everybody just seemed to irritate me and my patience dried up. I could feel the frustration building inside me. One night I attacked one of the British guys in my cell, which went against my own rules. A meeting was called, and it was decided that I should take a break and that somebody else should be in charge. Basically, I was voted out. Pedro, the Dutchman, was elected as the new room chief.

I welcomed the break, but I also knew that now our room would deteriorate. A French guy in our cell, whose name was Bruno, had got involved with one of the lady-boys. Pedro also had a hard-on for the lady-boys, so he allowed Bruno's 'wife' to move into our room. At first the lady-boy fitted in well. He even spoke a bit of English. It was strange to watch his actions. Here was a man, thinking he was a woman, surrounded by men. Perhaps for him it was paradise. He would sit on his bed for hours and hours looking at himself in the mirror and applying make-up. At night, just before bedtime, Bruno and his lady-boy would build a tent. They slept at the entrance to the cell and they would tie blankets to the bars and close themselves off completely from prying eyes. Whatever it was that they did, they would do it in the middle of the night. Fortunately, I was at the opposite end of the cell, besides which I never paid them much attention. But I can tell you I was not happy to have this person in our cell, and I wasn't the only one. Whenever the lady-boy used the toilet, he would be in there for far too long, and this pissed everyone off.

The families of the other South African prisoners were also continually contacting the embassy in Thailand regarding our wellbeing and asking about any progress being made towards our repatriation. This put a lot of pressure on the embassy – who never had the answers anyway – and our families were stopped from directly contacting the embassy. All enquiries were to go through the Director-General of the Consular and Agency Services branch of the Department of Foreign Affairs.

My sister was still shaking things up, though, and news of my planned hunger strike had apparently reached our government. I continued to remain positive and focused my energies on my art. I was pumping out portraits. Oblivious to the world around me, I painted and painted. I was convinced that, any day, there was a possibility I would go free, so I didn't want to lose a moment.

During the cold season, which was between November and January, there were spells where the temperature dropped to below 17 °C. During these days I would paint from early morning until well past

1.30pm. When it was hot, by 11am I would be sweating profusely and couldn't work for fear of damaging the painting. The cold season was welcomed by us foreigners, whereas the Thais hated it. Up north in Chiang Rai it got so cold that some prisoners died from exposure. The cold season was so dry that the skin at the tips of my thumbs cracked open, and I also got a rash just below my armpits. My skin would become flaky and sensitive, and the only thing that helped was Ascabiol emulsion (benzyl benzoate); a bottle of this cream could last me for five years. I also suffered from cold feet (even in summer) and I would always sleep with socks on.

I always found it strange to see how, when people are subjected to extreme suffering, they turn to G-d. For me, there was a certain hypocrisy to this. Every Sunday in Bangkwang the Christians would attend a church service in the dining room. Fervently they engaged in song and praises to the Lord. They would go along, Bible in hand, but they never seemed to evolve as people. After church, those who were involved in the distribution of drugs would continue peddling.

I once asked one of the African brothers: 'How can you be the leader of the prison church and still sell heroin? Dealing in drugs got you into prison. You have a life sentence. Surely that would be enough of a deterrent?' He told me frankly that it was the only way he could survive. He had no support; his family could barely take care of themselves. I understood it was not easy, so perhaps his circumstances justified his means.

Thai prisons are tough places in which one's integrity is constantly challenged. Back home, two of my best friends had become born-again Christians. It didn't bother me. Each to his own, I thought. But what I detested was that they constantly tried to convert me. They went as far as to say that, unless I accepted Christ, I would never make it out of prison. I didn't begrudge them their newfound faith; instead I asked them to respect my choices, just as I respected theirs. I was born a Jew and I will die a Jew.

The major Jewish festivals came and went. These were usually sad times, as our festivals are celebrated with the gathering of our families. While locked in the cell, after prayers I would sit on my bed and stare blankly into space. My mind and thoughts would drift to my family. I could visualise them sitting around in the comfort of their home, and no doubt their thoughts, too, were of me. Celebrating festivals in captivity was not the same, and to a degree they lost their spiritual impact. Although I enjoyed a connection with *Hashem*, I felt in my heart that my prayers were becoming more of a routine than anything more meaningful. Praying was a formality, and came out of a sense of guilt and obligation.

On 9 February 2002 came the news that Princess Margaret had died. It was quite significant for me, as I had painted what I believed was a compelling portrait of her, hoping I could evoke some compassion and maybe even get her involved in my case. With her passing, however, that door closed.

Meanwhile our friend Prichit Kowmuang had got into the swing of things, yet he failed to ease the discontent of the prisoners. Many of us were not happy about losing our electronic devices (which hadn't been returned to us). Prichit was not sticking to his end of the bargain. We were paying him money for certain privileges but still he denied us those rights. It reached a point where even the Thais used their influence outside to report the Building Chief to the Department of Corrections. Something must eventually have worked because, after a few months, Prichit was removed.

The new Building Chief had a reputation for loving money and allowing a free-for-all, which also had its disadvantages, but then that's the way the wheels of Bangkwang turned. The 'Big Tiger' could never be tamed.

In 2002 Nigerian president Olusegun Obasanjo signed and ratified a prisoner transfer treaty with Thailand. The Nigerian inmates had been talking about it for months, especially when their consular representative had confirmed that it really was going to happen. When it finally did, the spirits of men who had accepted that they were condemned for life suddenly soared so high – it was something amazing to witness.

It was almost like seeing a dead man coming to life. That night, the Nigerians' cell was abuzz with laughter and conversation. Even the prison authorities changed their attitude towards the Nigerians. In my heart I rejoiced with them, knowing that Joan and I had been instrumental in their liberation. Although our hopes were on South Africa following suit, we also investigated the possibility of South Africans transferring home under the auspices of the Organisation of African Unity (OAU) – soon to be replaced by the African Union (AU) – using the Nigerian treaty somehow. All our attempts to encourage a treaty between the South African and Thai governments were failing dismally.

In May, Bertie Lubner, who never gave up supporting me and my family, wrote to Nelson Mandela, advising him that he was planning to speak to the Deputy Minister of Foreign Affairs, Aziz Pahad, on my behalf: '... Even though I have no responsibility for the young man,' he concluded his letter, 'my conscience does not allow me to stop trying, as a productive and useful life is being wasted locked up.'

In my cell we were a mixed bunch of Western foreigners, and guys came and went. There were four British guys, three Americans, one from the Czech Republic, a German (who would masturbate on his bed in the middle of the night), Simon the French Israeli (who still farted), a Dane, an Estonian, a Slovak and Pedro, who found solace in his lady-boy and drinking. Because we were all serving hard time, we tried to be more tolerant of each other, but this never lasted long. Sooner or later, tempers would flare and arguments erupt. The guy who slept next to me was allowed to be there only because he had stopped smoking, but after a couple of weeks he started again. A hand's-breadth separated our beds. When I objected to his smoking, he gave me a mouthful, and I got so pissed off I threw the TV remote at him and threatened to fuck him up. That seemed to shut him up, but after that we didn't speak to each other for a year.

There were many such incidents, where trivial problems caused rifts between so-called friends. Remember that prison friendships are first and foremost mainly of convenience. It was seldom that one struck up a genuine friendship, although there were exceptions.

In the cell next to ours, and also across the way, were the Nigerian rooms. We had a rule that because there were so many Nigerians, and they were forever in trouble and being transferred from one building to another, our room was strictly limited to 'white boys'. This had nothing to do with being racist. But if you took one Nigerian into your cell, then every time another arrived, the prison authorities would shove them in your room and none of us wanted to compromise that hand's-breadth of space. This rule caused a lot of resentment towards me, especially as I was a white South African. The Nigerians were also forever at each other's throats, shouting the worst abuse imaginable. It got so bad sometimes that we would bang our fists on the wall for them to tone it down.

The Slovak guy, Ivan Zavadinka, who was gay, slept opposite me. His mother was from Budapest and we spent quite a lot of time brushing up on our Hungarian. He was tall, good-looking, intelligent and generally liked by everybody. One Sunday night – it was 2 June – he complained about severe pains in his solar plexus area. We were locked up and there was nothing we could do. Many a prisoner had died in the cells because it took the guards so long to open up, and there were no emergency procedures in place. If you had a heart attack or a stroke, all you could do was hope to die quickly and peacefully. Anyway, Ivan's friend, who was the guy from the Czech Republic and who slept next to him, gave him a bottle of freshly squeezed lemon juice, which seemed to ease his pain. I went to sleep. Around 3am I woke up and noticed Ivan on his hands and knees crawling to the toilet. He was in terrible pain. I helped him up and out of the toilet. For the next four hours until they opened our cell, he lay on his bed curled up in agony. It was heartbreaking to watch.

When our cells were finally opened at 6.30am we carried Ivan downstairs. After the necessary paperwork was filled out, he was loaded onto one of the four-wheeled flat wheelbarrows that the food containers were carried on. That morning, when Jai visited, I asked her to call the Slovak embassy to inform them that Ivan had been hospitalised. The following day, Tuesday, we got the news that Ivan had died from a burst ulcer. The guard who told me actually laughed. We foreigners were totally shocked. A few days later I learnt that, on arrival at the hospital, he had been admitted but the doctor hadn't even attended to him. A medic had given him a couple of paracetamol and let him go to sleep. The fuckers had simply let him die. I was so fucking angry. These people had no respect for life. Here was a beautiful human being, still in the prime of his life, and, just like that, he was gone. I could not understand nor believe that fate had anything to do with it. As a gesture of goodwill, I painted Ivan's portrait and had it posted to his mother. I wanted her to know that Ivan was a gentleman and well liked by everybody, and that his death was mourned by Thai and foreign prisoners alike.

The Thais have a traditional home-brew, an alcoholic beverage called *lao*. There are two kinds of *lao*. To brew the first kind, they dry sliced bread by laying it out in the sun, thereby gathering natural yeast from the air. The bread is then soaked in water and sealed in a plastic bag with small holes poked in the sides, allowing air to enter. The bag is kept in a dark place. After a week or so, when mould has set in, the bag is placed in a container and three litres of water and half a kilo of sugar are added. This allows fermentation to set in. After five days the mix turns to alcohol. The stuff tastes terrible, and I'd heard stories of prisoners going blind from drinking it. The first time I drank it was with a Dane who brewed his own. Within ten minutes I had severe stomach cramps. I ran to the toilet and my insides literally poured out of me.

The second method of making *lao* involves using yeast with fruit, water and sugar. This yields a much better and stronger form of the drink, and two cups will still knock you for a loop. *Lao* was usually brewed before Songkran and New Year, when there were five days of holidays. Alcohol was strictly forbidden in prison and yeast was harder to come by than heroin. The problem was that drinking invariably led to violence. We would go to extreme measures to hide the alcohol. At one stage the guards were so strict that we actually buried the containers it was brewing in. After lockdown the guards would walk around the building checking all the water containers. If they found alcohol, they would pour it down the drain.

On 12 September 2002, my sister drafted a letter to the Minister of Foreign Affairs, Nkosazana Dlamini-Zuma:

There is the matter of prisoners having the right to request a pardon from the King of Thailand. Generally the Thai authority only recommends the pardon to the King if the resident embassy supports the application or provides a 'no objection' (to the pardon) letter. It is my belief that such a letter from the embassy would assist in the reduction of some of the sentences of South African prisoners held there, and it would be sufficiently neutral not to have any repercussions.

I humbly request that consideration be given to allowing our embassies to provide 'no objection' letters. I attach for your information a letter of support from the Islamic Republic of Iran (also known to have a hardline attitude towards drugs – people are executed in Iran for drugs) for one of their prisoners requesting a pardon. As you will note, my request above does not even go this far.

On 6 October 2002, my niece Keri, Joan's daughter, wrote to Nelson Mandela:

Dr Mr Mandela
My name is Keri Sacks, I am a thirteen year old and I have a wonderful Uncle who has been in prison for 9 years (nine).
He is a kind hearted man from what I can remember. His life is so wasted in a prison.
My Mom and Gran are so devastated especially my Gran who is seventy-eight years old.

She is worried she may die before she sees him a free man again.

I truly would like to see you for just five minutes to explain my sad story.

I know you have many requests like this one, but please consider my request, it would mean so much to me.

I thank you for reading this letter and I look forward to hearing from you. You could tell Mr Lubner what you decide to do and he could tell me.

In Grateful Anticipation

Keri Sacks

Meanwhile another eight Americans were transferred back to the US. While America financed the war on drugs in Thailand, when it came to their own nationals, they did everything to ensure their safe return home and early release. While I was happy for anybody who regained their freedom, I was bitter about the injustice of it all. We needed a new strategy.

At this time, the rand was weakening against the dollar, which meant I was getting fewer Thai baht. Fortunately, there was always somebody who stepped up to help out. My mother even contributed a portion of her pension money to provide for my needs in prison.

Notwithstanding the conditions, in comparison to the majority of prisoners I enjoyed a much higher standard of living. By now I employed the services of five 'boys': I had one who did my washing, another who would change my sheets and take my bed into the sun once a week, and I had a water boy, who would carry and collect clean water for my daily showers. In my cell, I employed the services of a professional masseur, who gave me a foot massage every night just before I went to sleep. Lastly, I had a boy who carried my portable electric fan and water cooler to the cell when we were locked up in the afternoon. Having all these luxuries, and knowing that I wasn't short of anything, gave me peace of mind. In my heart I was beginning to accept my fate. I learnt a very important lesson in prison – that peace of mind is the single most important element to allow you to succeed in all your endeavours. This was clearly evident in the pieces of art I was producing. My eyes were worsening, though, and I was already on +200-strength reading glasses.

Rumours were surfacing that drug cases would no longer be considered for royal pardons. If this was true, it would be a terrible blow for many of us whose only chance of freedom was through a royal pardon. I had grown accustomed to hearing all these rumours and, unless something was in writing, I usually didn't give them much thought. This particular one bothered a lot of the prisoners, though.

I was going through my most prolific artistic phase. I would allow nothing to stand between me and my dreams, and I continued to escape into my own world where my thoughts converged with my desires. I created my own paradise.

Despite the new government's clampdown on drugs, with the introduction of cellphones, which were illegal in prison, the drug trade in Bangkwang continued to thrive. *Yaba* was the drug of choice for many prisoners. Increasingly, people who were busted on the outside with large amounts of drugs would inform the police that they were working for bosses inside Bangkwang. They would give the police phone numbers, names and even tell them which buildings these 'bosses' were in. This led to regular raids by the police, who arrived with sniffer dogs.

Bangkwang Central Prison is a million-dollar enterprise. The amount of money that passes through its gates is unbelievable. In addition, the prison factories are a significant source of revenue for the government. The position of Prison Director is a powerful and lucrative one. Besides being of sufficiently senior rank to qualify, the officer who is considered for this position has to pay huge amounts of money to the director of the Department of Corrections and to the Minister of Justice.

The Director is the man responsible for the prison's budget and for allocating money for the prisoners' food. Our Director would cut costs wherever possible. One of the buildings at Bangkwang was a pig farm. Here pigs were slaughtered and the meat supplied to the prison kitchen. This provided food for only about 40 per cent of the prison population, but that was all the Director would allocate in funds. The rest he pocketed himself. He also received kickbacks from all the factories.

Bangkwang went through phases when restrictions were alternately eased or tightened, which usually happened whenever a new Director took over the prison. It is similar to what happens when a new government comes into power. Rules were changed, new visions articulated, and sometimes buildings were even renovated. In 2002, for example, our annual contact visit was cancelled.

Many things were illegal in prison. Money was one, electrical appliances another. Searches happened fairly regularly. These could be conducted by the inside guards, which comprised the Bangkwang security section together with guards from our own building, or, every now and again, by the Department of Corrections. They would often invite a police and military contingent to take part in the raid. These raids were more serious, and when they happened prisoners would be warned to hide their money and anything electrical they happened to have. Sometimes the warning came 20 minutes before the raid, and suddenly everybody would be scrambling and running around trying to hide their things. Money would be rolled up and wrapped in plastic bags, and buried in the sand. We'd put our electrical appliances into rice bags, marked with our names. The guards would open one of the solitary cells for us and we'd store our goods there until the raid was over. If it was the outside guards who caught prisoners with money or electronics, it would be a loss of face for the Building Chief in question, as it would be clear that he was corrupt, and he would be punished.

It was quite ironic, really; the whole system was riddled with corruption, but as long as it was done clandestinely that was okay.

Notwithstanding the new government's stern line on drugs on the outside, it was business as usual on the inside. The only difference was that we were on constant alert.

On 11 December, Aziz Pahad, on behalf of Mr Mandela (and thanks to Bertie Lubner), took my case to His Majesty King Bhumibol Adulyadej of Thailand. He beseeched him to grant me a royal pardon. The Royal Palace replied in a letter stating that my application for clemency was still in the decision process. It seemed that my pardon had not, in fact, been rejected and that an administrative error had been made!

I was not to learn about this until January 2003, and as soon as I could I related these developments to the consular officer, mentioning also that Mr Mandela had personally supported my application. Mrs Pheto was only too eager to follow up. More rumours were circulating, one of which was that Prime Minister Thaksin Shinawatra had called on all foreign governments to sign treaties and to take their citizens out of Thai jails. Once again, I allowed myself to hope. The signs were all favourable. There was no doubt in my mind that if our government really wanted to liberate us, they could do so. There were 14 South African prisoners in Thailand at that time, most of whom had been arrested in 1994. Close on ten years was a long time by any standards.

At the end of December of that year – I remember it was a Tuesday, not my regular visit day – Tony Leon and his beautiful wife came to visit me. I was humbled that a prominent politician had not only taken the time to come and meet me, but had also, prior to his visit, made several attempts to influence certain cabinet members to work towards a treaty. Unfortunately, nothing materialised from his efforts.

During the days and nights leading up to 27 March 2003, the day they were due to be transferred back to their home country, the Nigerians couldn't sleep. All they talked about was their transfer. Their excitement was tangible. They were all busy gathering their things together and packing their bags. Some packed only basic essentials and a few sets of clothing, while others took their DVD players, movies and MP3s. After all, they were still going to prison in Nigeria and not about to be released altogether. Even so, they were one step closer to freedom. And anything was possible in Nigeria, a country where corruption was as rife as it was in Thailand.

That Tuesday morning, 321 Nigerians made their exodus back to the land of their birth. Two aeroplanes were chartered to transfer them back home. About 30 guys, many of them dressed in traditional attire, walked through the gates of Building 2. The balance was made up of prisoners from other buildings and also from Klong Prem. Irrespective of skin colour or nationality, we were all brothers. I had forged strong friendships with quite a few of the Nigerians, and I shared their joy. I hoped and prayed that now a window of opportunity would open for the South African government to follow Nigeria's example.

After the Nigerians left, the prison quietened down considerably. It was something of an anticlimax, I suppose. The number of foreigners had dwindled, and, where foreigners had once dominated in football, this was no longer the case.

The owner of the gym had managed to get onto the transfer list. When he left, he gave the gym to another African, Dikor, who was from Mali. I was a member of the gym, and, although I paid my monthly fee of 100 Thai baht, it hardly ever worked out that I got full value because I played football on most days. If I did weight training two months out of the year, it was a lot. Dikor, who spoke fluent French, was a very good friend of Simon, the French Israeli guy.

In September we heard that Catherine Mnyengeza, who was serving a 35-year sentence at the women's prison, had tragically passed away. She was still in the prime of life, and we were friends, corresponding regularly. She was nine years into her sentence when she died. If South Africa had had a prisoner transfer treaty in place, she would have been eligible for transfer after four years, paroled and would have received proper medical attention. She would, in all likelihood, still be alive. Our embassy had done nothing to help Catherine. In fact, as far as I was concerned, they had murdered her. Her tragic and sudden demise cast an ever greater shadow over us South Africans and the uncertainty of our fate. In her honour, I painted a vase with orchids, which I have dedicated to her memory. In a letter I subsequently wrote to President Mbeki, I asked him: 'How many of us must meet the same fate as Catherine before you take the necessary steps to repatriate your citizens?'

It seemed that Catherine's death had, in fact, rattled our government. On 6 November I was informed by the authorities that I should prepare myself for an audience with the Director of the prison on the 10th. I had no idea what was going on. That morning, when I walked out of the gates of Building 2, there were balloons and Thai and South African flags lining the road that led from the main gate. My heart was pounding. What the fuck was going on? Was I going home? I wished and I prayed. I was escorted by two guards to Building 14, which was the university building. The Director at the time was Mr Pittaya Sangkanakin, whose goal in life seemed to be to rid the prison of corruption and drugs. He had built a television studio in Building 14 so that prisoners could learn to be camera operators. The studio made it possible to televise live events – mainly our annual football competition. Teams were no longer allowed to take supporters with them because drugs would be exchanged and distributed to the other buildings during matches. Prisoners could now watch every match on a big colour TV in the dining rooms of their own buildings. Alternatively, for those who had private TVs, they could watch the games in the comfort of their houses.

When I arrived at Building 14, I was told that my embassy would be coming, so I sat and waited. Eventually, the ambassador, attaché, consular officer and a delegation of South African government members arrived. It was all very formal. I was introduced to the Commissioner of Corrections, Mr Linda Mti, who informed me that the purpose of his visit to Thailand was to exchange ideas and discuss policies between the respective departments and to review the possibility of a prisoner transfer treaty between our countries.

We were ushered into the studio, where the conversation was being televised and broadcast live to the buildings. We discussed different aspects of prison. I couldn't believe this was happening. Here I was, sitting in on talks on the fate of South African prisoners with members of the South African government and the Prison Director. My hopes reached an all-time high; this was by far the greatest breakthrough we could have hoped for.

For days afterwards, I couldn't sleep. My head was buzzing with visions of my arrival at Johannesburg airport. After my visit that week with Jai, she emailed the good news to my family back home. I emphasised that now was the time to keep up the pressure and to get as much publicity as possible regarding our predicament.

M

Birthdays in prison are the most depressing days of the year, and I always became melancholy when mine came around. I was growing old alone – not exactly what most people envisage for themselves. People got married, had kids and then grandchildren. That was how things were normally done. Why had my life turned out so differently? Why do the choices we make have to determine our lives?

On 15 October 2003 I 'celebrated' my tenth birthday behind bars. I was 43. I had asked Jai to bring me 17 Big Macs, which she did, and I shared them with my cellmates. The guys were grateful and wished me well. The only meaning my birthday held for me these days was the knowledge that my family were thinking of me possibly a little bit more on 15 October than on any other day.

I got two pieces of disturbing news around this time. The first came via my sister: my stepbrother Wessels had committed suicide. He'd stuck a shotgun in his mouth and blown his head off. Fuck, he must have been a deeply disturbed soul to do something so drastic. I was shocked. The second piece of news was that Bertie Lubner had had a quadruple bypass. I was sad to hear this; in my view the man was a saint: he was fighting for my release and now he was fighting for his life. Bertie was devoted to my cause, but still with the understanding that I was innocent of the crimes I'd been accused of. I felt very guilty for having deceived such a decent man. I wanted to tell him the truth, but I couldn't bring myself to. We twist the truth to protect ourselves, and so I remained silent.

Whenever renovations were done in Bangkwang, you could be assured that the Director would be pocketing most of the funds allocated for the project. In 2004 the foreign and Thai visit rooms were upgraded. We no longer needed to shout to our visitors through the two sets of bars and a walkway about a metre and a half wide. Glass partitions were erected on the visitors' side and telephones were installed. It was a far better system and it made our visits more pleasant; at least now we could have a conversation without everybody hearing what we were saying.

Plans were also under way to demolish Building 1 and to put up an American-type high-security building with state-of-the-art surveillance systems, closed-circuit TV, electronically operated security gates, etc. But first Building 5 had to be renovated and transformed into a high-security block to accommodate all the death row inmates from Building 1. Prisoners with sentences below 33 years would be moved to the provinces, while the lifers would be split up and absorbed into the other buildings. During the demolition of Building 1, besides the noise of machinery all day long, a blanket of dust descended on Building 2, making our lives miserable, not to mention it being a health hazard.

With the group transferred from Building 1 was an Israeli named Shlomo Cohen. He had murdered his wife in a Bangkok hotel, chopped her into pieces, and then attempted to put her through a blender. When this didn't work, he put her dismembered body parts in a suitcase, which he threw in a river. His case had been extensively publicised on Thai television, so we knew about him and expected to see him at Bangkwang sooner or later. As a fellow Jew, I welcomed him to stay with me. Although I thought his crime was a most heinous one, who was I to judge him? The drugs I had transported would have destroyed, and maybe even killed, many people. I was no better than a murderer myself. The only prisoners I would discriminate against would be the paedophiles.

Shlomo turned out to be your typical Israeli, but he was a nice enough guy. I was no longer making use of my Chinese chef; ten years of his oily food had almost killed me. I was now cooking my own meals. Shlomo immediately took over the cooking and introduced me to some tasty Israeli dishes. He was also quite the comedian, and at first we got on pretty well.

Shlomo stayed with me for three months, during which time he told me his life story. He left out the details of the murder of his wife, about which I never asked. I don't especially like Israelis; for some reason I never have, and I imagine I never will. After a while, Shlomo started getting on my nerves. Actually, the man was beginning to drive me insane. It didn't matter what the subject was; he always knew better. He wore thick-rimmed glasses, and one of his eyes was slightly squint, so it looked like he was forever staring at me. It gave me the creeps, besides which I couldn't help imagining him cutting up his wife – all the blood in the bath, on his hands, and possibly even on his glasses and face.

One day we had an argument and I asked him to leave my house. He seemed baffled. I added, 'Fuck off, already.'

But Shlomo was the type of guy you couldn't remain angry with for long. He came from a big family, and his three siblings took turns to visit him every year, so he was not short of anything. Obviously, though, he had his own demons to deal with, and I could see he was a troubled soul. The murder of his wife, the mother of his two sons, haunted him every minute of the day. Love is a strange animal, and it can bring out the worst in any man. In the cell, Shlomo slept at the opposite end of the room to me, but in fact the guy hardly slept at all. He was pale and grew thinner by the day. I was sure his conscience troubled him immensely. One night I went to sleep early. I drank a lot of water during the night and, as I was also a restless sleeper, I would visit the toilet often. Around 11.30 I noticed Shlomo was fast asleep; then again, around 1am, on my next visit to the toilet, I saw that he hadn't moved. He was still in exactly the same position. Much later, after tossing and turning and being unable to sleep, I thought I would check on him. He still hadn't moved. Rather odd, I thought. When I got up at 4.45am, he was in exactly the same position. It was very strange, but I thought I would first do my morning ablutions routine and finish davening *Shacharis* before I took any action.

I strolled over to his bed and shook his leg, softly calling his name: 'Shlomo, Shlomo.' He too didn't budge. What a heavy sleeper, I thought, dead to the world. Then a Dutch guy, Mikhail, who was an amateur Thai boxer, came over to Shlomo's bed. He too was concerned, and I told him I thought something was seriously wrong. Mikhail said he had seen Shlomo counting out a handful of pills on his bed last night. Well, then, it was obvious: Shlomo had taken an overdose. We could see he was breathing, but there was not much we could do except wait till they opened our cell.

Some of our other cell members were surfacing by now. One was

Philip, Mikhail's friend and co-accused, who came over and started slapping Shlomo around, trying to wake him up, but to no avail. Philip said that when they opened the door he would take Shlomo to his house and let him sleep it off for the day. 'No fucking way,' I told him. 'This is a matter for the authority to deal with.'

I called the key-boy in the corridor and told him in Thai that Shlomo had taken a lot of medicine and I thought he was dead. Fortunately, the key-boy managed to alert one of the guards and our cells were opened earlier than usual. Shlomo was put into a wheelchair, which had by now replaced the wheelbarrow as the regular emergency mode of transport to the hospital. Later that day we got news that, when they couldn't revive him at Bangkwang, he had been rushed by ambulance to Lard Yao prison hospital. He was still alive. If I had listened to Philip that morning, Shlomo might very well have died.

During my visit with Jai, I asked her if she would go to Lard Yao and check up on Shlomo, and see if there was anything he needed. Amazingly, Shlomo survived his attempted suicide. He had taken 100 Valium tablets, and that's a lot of pills. *Hashem* wasn't going to let him get off that easily. A troubled conscience was worse than a life sentence. Jai, bless her soul, visited Shlomo regularly until he returned to Building 2 about a month later. He was very pale, but he joined the gym and it wasn't long before he regained his health.

Besides being Jewish, and although he was Sephardic and I was an Ashkenazi, Shlomo and I had one other thing in common: our love of movies. Between my family, Jai and the movies I bought from the guards, I had accumulated an extensive collection. Among them was the *Saw* series. I managed to watch 30 minutes of the first one, but it was far too gruesome for my liking. Shlomo, on the other hand, enjoyed them thoroughly and watched each movie with such intent I imagined he was looking for new ways to chop up his next victim.

In the third court, Shlomo received a 33-year sentence for the murder of his wife.

Over the years, Akow the Cripple had devoted almost all his time to playing backgammon, and he had improved dramatically, until he was eventually playing against the top-ranking players. Joseph, an

Israeli cellmate, was one of the champions and they often played in my house. As a rule, I never got involved in a big game, but I enjoyed gambling. Whenever the Cripple played, he would attract a crowd taking side bets. The Cripple generally played very safe, never leaving a piece open if he could, whereas Joseph was more of a chancer and would risk pieces being hit. On one occasion, a fierce game between the two of them was under way and, as usual, a crowd had gathered to watch. Joseph was down over ten grand. I watched a few games and was getting frustrated by all the mistakes Joseph was making, so I offered to sit in and play the Cripple myself, hoping to win back my Jewish brother's money. So Joseph and I partnered up. Unfortunately for us, the dice went in the Cripple's favour. He threw double after double. Whatever dice he needed to kill me and close his house at the same time, he did on every throw, causing me to lose every game. Within an hour I dropped an additional eight grand. This was so unlike me – why I got involved, I don't know. I was pissed off, especially as the Cripple would laugh happily every time he caught me. In the end, I decided to cut my losses and come back fighting another day. Luckily, I kept a pool of money that I'd won gambling on the English Premier League, which I used to pay for certain of the privileges I enjoyed. Handing the money over to the Cripple, who had won it fair and square, hurt my pride more than anything else. Joseph had lost I don't know how many thousands over the months to the Cripple. In his view, *Hashem* may have taken away the Cripple's use of his legs, but in return He had blessed him with luck.

Actually, the Cripple was kicking everybody's arse. There were other times when I played him, but, although I won some of the games, I never won the money back that he had taken off me that day with Joseph.

For those with addictions, temptation was always there in prison, enticing you to take a chance. Compulsive gamblers were as bad as, if not worse than, drug addicts. It seemed like a more difficult habit to kick, but at the end of the day it boiled down to the same thing: you have to reach deep to overcome your vices.

Here I'm reminded of a saying by the poet William Blake, who wrote something about 'the road of excess leads to the palace of wisdom'. In my own interpretation, moderation is the key to maintaining a balanced lifestyle. However, in my own *experience*, abstinence is the only answer. My addiction had not only almost killed me, but it had also destroyed the lives of so many of the people around me. Perhaps Blake meant: why subject yourself to the evils and destructive forces of life before you arrive at the conclusion of your misguided choices?

On the Thai news channel, we were riveted by the dramatic account of a robbery that had gone down in Phuket. Three Russians had held up a bank, and in the course of events a Thai security guard had been shot and killed. A nationwide hunt for the robbers was under way. After a few days, they were apprehended while trying to make their escape in a small boat. During the arrest, one of the Russians was shot in the leg. Whenever a foreigner was arrested and appeared on TV, we all knew that it was only a matter of time before we would get to meet him. The last stop was always Bangkwang.

The Russians were tried and sentenced; one was sentenced to death; the second received a life sentence; and the driver of the getaway vehicle was sentenced to 33 years. Because of the notoriety surrounding their case, and out of fear of the Russians attempting an escape, the prison authorities split them up. Yegor came to Building 2, Felix was thrown into Building 6, and the third guy was put on death row in Building 1. Naturally we welcomed Yegor into our room.

When Pittaya Sangkanakin took over as Director of Bangkwang, he put a stop to all private enterprise in the prison. The guys who sold coffee and soup in the corridor at night and food during the day had to cease their business activities. The Director didn't want prisoners making money off prisoners, he said; if you disobeyed the regulations, you faced the prospect of being moved to another prison. Dikor, the guy who now ran the gym, and also enjoyed the luxury of a private room and house, became nervous. He wanted to sell the gym. I was not interested. The gym was a headache. Every month you had to run after members to collect their money. Dikor was asking for 10 000 Thai baht, which wasn't much, considering how much it had cost to build the place, but none of the other foreigners was interested in buying it either, mainly out of fear of being moved. Yegor the Russian was keen, though, as he worked out every day. Many foreigners used the facility, including me when I wasn't playing football, and losing it would be a huge blow. Exercise was a vital part of relieving stress and preventing depression in prison, and for many inmates it was a form of self-rehabilitation. The foreigners pleaded with me to change my mind. I was the only one who could save the gym, they said, and not get into trouble. Yegor came to me with the suggestion of us being partners and, after giving it some thought, I reluctantly agreed. Knowing how desperate Dikor was, I offered him 8 000 Thai baht, which he grabbed. And so the alleged Russian bank robber and I became the proud owners of the gym.

In Thailand at this time, there was another very high-profile criminal case in the news. It related to the daring theft, in 1989, of a large quantity of jewels from the palace of Saudi Arabia's Crown Prince, Faisal ibn Abdulaziz Al Saud, in Riyadh. The thief was a Thai worker, and among the stolen items was a rare blue diamond. The estimated value of the jewels taken in the heist was over US$20 million, and the case became known as the 'Blue Diamond Affair'. The Thai worker managed to get the gems back to Thailand, to his home district of Lampang in the north. Lieutenant General Chalor Kerdthes of the Royal Thai Police was assigned to the case. The worker was arrested and some of the jewels were recovered. Kerdthes himself took the jewels back to Saudi Arabia to return them, but it was discovered that they were fakes – including the blue diamond. Two diplomats, one of whom was Abdullah al-Besri, and a third person were assigned by the Saudi government to travel to Thailand to investigate and to try and track down the real jewels; they were joined there, in November 1989, by a Saudi Arabian businessman close to the Saudi royal family. On 4 January 1990 the businessman was gunned down by masked assassins outside his home, and the following month al-Besri was assassinated in Bangkok, as were two other Saudi diplomats. The Thai police

469

apparently managed to find the jeweller who had swapped the real jewels for the fakes, but before this could be established, the jeweller's wife and son were killed in an accident.

The real facts of the case remain a mystery and the jewels have never been recovered, but in 1994 General Kerdthes was arrested on suspicion of the murder of the jeweller's wife and son. He was tried, found guilty and sentenced to life on one of the charges.

After his arrest, the General was first held at Bangkok Special Prison, but in 2002 he was moved to Bangkwang and put in Building 2 – my building. The prisoners referred to him as 'Par Chalor' (father Chalor), and the respect he commanded from guards and prisoners alike was extraordinary. This was a man who was once at the helm of the country's police force, responsible for the arrest and assassination of many perpetrators of crime, and now here he was, no better than your common criminal and the equal of any one of us inmates.

The General was a short, stout man in his sixties. He was slightly balding and had some difficulty in walking. The authorities gave him a house to stay in, and he immediately recruited an entourage of more than ten bodyguards. In the corridor opposite our cell was another room, which had a toilet, a shower area and a curtained-off section where a person could sleep comfortably and enjoy a bit of privacy. This was where the General stayed. Since death row had taken up most of the downstairs section, there were only three rooms at the rear entrance now. The first, as you walked in on the left, was a three-quarter-size room. This was the 'TB room'. Prisoners who had been hospitalised and treated for tuberculosis would stay here temporarily before being integrated into the general population. Next to theirs was my room, which was a full-size room, and opposite was a small room where six Chinese guys slept. In the corridor there were another 12 prisoners, some Thais, Singaporeans, Taiwanese and my Chinese friend Akow the Cripple. There was also the key-boy, a real motherfucker Thai informer. On many occasions when we were raided by outside guards, they neglected to notice the small section of rooms we occupied. It was a perfect place for the General.

Within a week of the General's arrival, two of his boys were put in my cell without my knowledge. By this time I had resumed my position as room chief. Normally, the office would first call me, to get my approval or else to negotiate about whether I would take somebody into the cell. When I approached the office clerk to ask why he had put these guys in my room without first checking with me, he appeared slightly nervous. Then he told me he was acting on the General's instructions.

Our cell was a private room and restricted mainly to foreigners. We were at that stage at our limit of 16 people, so an extra two would mean less space between our beds. I found myself in a dilemma. I had been in prison for close on ten years. I was well established and respected by all. Some of the Thais even called me 'Mafia'. If I didn't take a stand on this issue, the General would keep putting his boys in our room and eventually we foreigners would be forced out. If it came to a showdown, being the minority meant that we would have no chance.

I made a decision.

I was not sure whether I was being brave or just plain stupid, but I went to the General, greeted him in the traditional Thai way, and then, in English, told him I would like to speak to him in private. I addressed him as 'General', not feeling comfortable calling him 'Par Chalor'. The General, who could come and go as he pleased, suggested we go to his cell. Very humbly, I introduced myself, but he told me he knew who I was and knew that I owned the gym. I said I knew who he was, too, and told him I had the utmost respect for him. Then I explained to him about our room and informed him that, in fact, I had bought it. It was a private room, I said, and strictly for foreigners. Even though we did have a few Thais in with us, I was the one who decided who could stay in the room. If the General wanted somebody in my room, I added, he should talk to me. To my surprise, the General was most amiable and agreed to respect my wishes. As we shook hands, I cautioned him that if I had any problems with his two boys, it was he who would have to resolve the issue. He laughed and put his arm on my shoulder saying, '*Mai mi punhar*' (No problem).

One of the Thais the General put in our room was a captain in the police force. He spoke English, but he was arrogant and rude, and his toilet manners were disgusting. He would blow his nose with his fingers and then flick the snot into the toilet, which more often than not landed on the side of the toilet bowl. He would also spit these huge blobs of slimy green phlegm and not flush them away. I was especially irritated because I slept right next to the toilet. The other Thai, an elderly man in his late fifties, had a permanent cough, and I suspected he had tuberculosis. The atmosphere in the room changed after their arrival. Nobody liked them, not even the Thais we already had with us to make up our quota of 16 in the cell. The Thais slept on one side of the room next to each other in the corner. Their beds, no wider than 50cm, were pushed together with no space in between, whereas we foreigners had up to two or three hand's-breadths between our beds. I felt bad about their space, but I'd explained that we could not give them any more than that because we foreigners were paying a monthly rent to the Building Chief for the privilege of having a bit more space. What can I say? This was prison, and money talks. Nevertheless the Thais seemed quite content sleeping like that, on top of one another, and accepted that this was just how things were.

After a month of clenching my teeth and biting my tongue, I finally cracked. When the Thai policeman kicked the bottom of my bed on his way to the toilet for about the fiftieth time, without ever bothering to apologise, I'd had enough. 'Come on, man, watch where you're going,' I said, pointing my finger at him. He looked at me contemptuously and mumbled something in Thai under his breath. I wanted to jump up and beat him to a pulp – we were roughly the same age and size – but I let it go out of respect for the General. Instead I went to the General the next day and expressed my annoyance, and referred to his friend's lack of manners.

The General looked at me. Then he took his thumb and slid it across his throat. I took this to mean that I had his permission to deal with the policeman personally. It would cost me money, but what a pleasure it would be to get rid of him. I wasted no time. I went straight to the Building Chief, dropped him an envelope, and gave the names of the two individuals. I made it clear that those guys should be moved out of our cell right away or else, for sure, there would be boxing that night.

The General's main bodyguard was a man named Shamlong, who was also a policeman. He became a staunch friend and would, I think, have given his life for me. Within days of the General settling in, he had his own mobile phone, and he had his house organised, which formed part of my gym. It was a small place: inside he had a table and a chair, a three-quarter-size foam mattress and a locker for his clothing.

Late one afternoon, the Director of the prison, together with a handful of senior officers and a television crew from Channel Three, a local news channel, came to our section. Although we were already on lockdown, the steel doors were opened. From my cell, where I stood leaning against the bars, we watched the proceedings. Everybody knew the General. He was a popular and colourful political figure, both loved and feared by the people of Thailand. My girlfriend Jai knew him well, in fact, and had interviewed him on several occasions. As I watched them all exchange greetings, I could see that even the Director had great respect for the man. The TV crew came into the corridor and filmed the General's quarters. The police were more powerful than the government and the General was known to be a close friend of the Crown Prince of Thailand himself.

The General's house was situated right at the back of the building, with a clear view of the front gate. Anybody who approached from the gate would be in the General's line of vision. He would sit there and brazenly talk on his mobile. Even when one of the guards walked past, the General would continue with his conversation, making no attempt to hide the fact that he was on the phone. Mobile phones were strictly forbidden, and if you were caught with one, you would be shackled and thrown into solitary. As a precaution, I started calling a mobile phone a 'dog', as most of the Thais understood the words 'mobile' or 'cellphone'. So 'dog' became the code word we began to use.

Things were changing in our building. With the General's presence, the guards' power was being undermined. Within two months of his arrival, mobile phones were everywhere. This was a whole new era in our prison existence. As the room chief, I made it a rule that no dogs would be tolerated in our cell. If we were caught, the prison authorities would take away the privilege of a private room and either put us in a different room or even go so far as to move us to another building. There were a few incidents where, when a room was raided, a dog was thrown into the rubbish bin. When it was retrieved, if nobody owned up, every person from that cell was moved. I was adamant about enforcing this rule. My room had cost me a lot of money, and, besides, I wasn't about to risk losing the comfort of a private cell and choosing who got to share it with me.

The second chief in Building 2 was replaced by a new officer named Adun. He was a short, stocky, dark-skinned man from the south, and known to be a no-nonsense commodore. On his second day in our building, I was summoned to his office. He wanted to know why there were only 16 people in our cell and pointed out that the Thai rooms held up to 20 prisoners. I couldn't tell him that I was paying corruption money to his boss, the Building Chief, so I pitched the usual argument, never failing to drop in the word 'embassy' a couple of times. He wasn't particularly impressed, but he didn't push the case. Then he asked me if anyone in my room had a mobile phone. I assured him that no one did, not that I would have said anything even if somebody had one.

Simon, the French Israeli guy, was now well into his sixties. He was short, only about 1.5m tall, but he had a huge stomach and weighed 90kg. He tied his long grey hair up in a ponytail, which made him look like a Mafia hitman. He was a tough old man with a short temper. We had stayed together for almost four years now, and in this time I had got to understand him, and we became like brothers. Simon had been caught with 12kg of heroin when he was arrested, and I'd heard that this was not his first trip to Thailand.

Simon smoked cigarettes and ate unhealthily. For most of the day he sat around in his deckchair. He was due to be transferred to an Israeli prison, but there was a delay on the part of the Israeli embassy, which really stressed him out. It seemed that his government, like the South African government, didn't give a shit about prisoners. Our families were the only ones who cared about us. This was the stark truth.

On 10 May it was Shabbos, and around 12.45am I heard muffled noises coming from Simon's bed. He was moaning and his body was convulsing. One of the Thais who slept opposite him came to wake me up. Something was seriously wrong. I wasn't sure what to do, so we tried to sit Simon up. His eyes darted desperately from side to side as he attempted to speak, but nothing came out except incoherent noises. His left side, from his shoulder to his feet had become completely paralysed. He had had a stroke. We gave him water, and then four or five of us massaged his arms and legs, and gently rubbed his chest area. I whispered in his ear, 'Hold on, Simon, don't let go, hold on.' I recited the *Shema Yisrael* and begged *Hashem* to spare him. He had a wife and grandchildren waiting for him in Israel. Prison was the last place any man, no matter how bad, should die. It broke my heart to watch, but what made it worse was that there was nothing I could do. If the Israeli government had been more efficient, Simon would have been transferred a year earlier and might never even have had a stroke.

The following morning, Simon was taken to the hospital. Fortunately, on Monday morning Jai and I had our regular visit and I immediately informed her about Simon. I asked her to call Rabbi Kantor. Thanks to Jai, after that Simon was taken by ambulance to the police hospital, where the medical care was of international standard. That afternoon, I was called to the office and asked to pack Simon's things. He didn't have many belongings, so I put all his stuff into a small sports bag. I knew I would never see him again, but I believed, knowing how strong he was and how close to his freedom, that he would make it back to Israel.

No sooner had Simon left than a young South African guy by the name of Jonnie Ratchett arrived. Jonnie had been arrested a couple of months earlier. I asked Jai to visit him during the initial days of his incarceration, so through Jai I knew when his court case was coming up. She told him that when he came to Bangkwang he should ask to come to Building 2.

Jonnie arrived on 14 May 2003. His father was a British citizen and his mother was South African. Soon after he was arrested he discovered that South Africa had no treaty in place with Thailand regarding prisoners, so he relinquished his citizenship and became a British subject. My heart went out to him. He was 26 years old and, according to him, innocently accused. His wife, a Thai prostitute and the mother of his child, had also been detained and they were both sentenced to life.

I took Jonnie into my house, and he took over Simon's spot. Jonnie was like a breath of fresh air in my life, and his youth and innocence rubbed off on all of us. He and I became instant friends. After all, he was a kindred spirit.

Jai was amazing. She visited all the South African inmates and acted as a go-between for them and their families. From the £100 I received from Edna in Manchester most months, I would give half to Jai. This would cover her transport costs, and often she would use the money to buy fresh fruit for the other South Africans and myself.

The head of the Blue Shirts was a Thai Muslim prisoner, also an ex-cop, and a murderer. His name was Somsak and he came from the south. He answered directly to Adun, the second chief, who assigned him to spy on the General and his boys. One of the General's boys, Aporn, had a locker outside my house. Somsak started patrolling our area during the day; he was even watching me. Word got back to the General that Somsak was watching him and had reported that the General and his boys were the main distributors in the building of mobile phones. Mobile phones had become big business and, naturally, it was the guards who brought them in. One afternoon, about two hours after lockdown, while I was using the toilet, I looked out the bars into the adjoining houses, where I saw about 30 commodores. Some were from Bangkwang, the others from the Department of Corrections. I realised we were about to be raided. I had time only to warn Joseph, who had a cellphone on him. Seconds later, I heard the steel gates to our section being opened. The guards charged inside. The General was in his room. A thorough check was conducted of the corridor, the Chinese room and the General's section, and they bust the General with a mobile, which was confiscated. Luckily, our own room was not searched or they would surely have bust Joseph. The next day, the

General was not happy, but he understood that from then on he would have to be more vigilant and could no longer use his mobile so openly.

At the request of the General, I allowed one of his boys to stay in our room. He slept at the entrance, right next to the steel door. One morning at around 5am, when I was finishing up in the toilet, I noticed the General crawling on his hands and knees out of his section across the corridor towards our cell. As he reached the door, the Thai guy in our cell slipped him something wrapped in plastic. I knew it was a dog. There was nothing I could do about the General keeping his telephone in my room, but I did tell the Thai guy that, in the event that our room was raided, he would have to take responsibility.

With the introduction of mobile phones, thanks to the General, apart from the upsurge of drug activity both inside and outside the prison, the atmosphere became far more relaxed. For prisoners to have instant contact with their families made a big difference to their lives. Times were good. The casino was running, drugs were openly being used, and home-brewed alcohol was flowing. The 'Big Tiger' was not as fierce as its reputation would have you believe. As long as the guards were making their money, the wheels of Bangkwang would never stop turning. Life was so good that many of us became complacent. The informers were still feeding information to the prison authorities.

It was just a matter of time before there would be another clampdown.

On the home front, my family continued to campaign on my behalf. Every possible avenue to secure my release was being pursued. Benji Schleider had become a friend of the family. While he was in London in August, and staying at the Royal Garden Hotel, coincidentally Princess Maha Chakri Sirindhorn, second of the Thai King's daughters, was in London, too. On one of Her Royal Highness's shopping trips to Bond Street, Benji spotted her in Grays Antique Market. Very respectfully, he managed to approach the Princess and discussed my situation with her. She promised to look into the matter.

Meanwhile we had heard that a general amnesty was going to be granted in August, on the occasion of Her Majesty the Queen's sixth-cycle birthday, and that all prisoners would benefit. It was said that drug cases would be included, but this time there was a catch for those prisoners. A royal decree was passed stipulating that, if the cases for those drug offenders who had been sentenced to more than eight years had not been final by the time of the *previous* royal decree granting an amnesty (which had been in 1999), these prisoners would not be eligible to benefit from the August amnesty. If this was true, it would be a terrible blow for all new drug offenders.

In the August amnesty my sentence dropped from 40 years down to 36, plus a few months. While I knew I could never survive 33 years in prison, at least there was movement in the right direction. Slowly, my sentence was being reduced. Rumour had it that there was another big amnesty coming up in 2006. Hope kept being dangled in our faces like a carrot on a string. All the same, it was hope that kept me going.

My art remained my escape, the world where I found peace and purpose. There were no walls in that world, and no pain. There my sprit could soar like an eagle gliding through the sky. I became the sculptor of my own destiny. My art was more than just painting pretty pictures; it was about redemption, taking back what I had lost, and holding on to my faith.

One morning, out of the blue, and just before shower time, four guards and Somsak, the Blue Shirts' head, raided the locker belonging to Aporn, the General's dog handler. They also searched the surrounding garden, poking into the soil with metal poles. The guards weren't really interested and did their checking half-heartedly. It was almost the end of their day and the last thing they wanted to do was work, but Somsak, who was a prisoner himself, was hell-bent on busting Aporn with a mobile phone. Knowing that Adun was behind him, his position had gone to his head. In any event, for all their efforts they found nothing.

Somsak stayed upstairs and he slept in the corridor. He slept late every morning and only came downstairs around 7.45am, in time for the national anthem at 8, whereas everybody else would come out an hour earlier. On the morning of 13 October 2004, I had just settled down to paint (it was around 7.30) when I heard the most bloodcurdling screaming coming from upstairs. The screams lasted only about a minute but seemed to go on for much longer. By the time I came around the other side of the building, I saw a group of about eight prisoners walking briskly out of the building, Aporn among them. They came straight towards me and I couldn't help but notice their eyes. All of the guys seemed highly charged and their eyes were bloodshot. Translated: these prisoners were in kill mode. If you are ever unlucky enough to look into a person's eyes just after they have committed a murder, I'd advise you to run. You will have just seen what a psychotic killer looks like. I saw that look that morning.

Somsak was carried down by some of the room cleaners. He had stab wounds to every part of his upper abdomen. Blood was pouring out of him. His eyes were already on the brink of lifelessness. He was loaded onto a wheelbarrow and rushed to the hospital, but he died before he even got there. I honestly can't say that I felt any sympathy for the man; he had broken the code of silence. An informer's end is death, no matter what. The fucker deserved what he got.

It scared me that I could be so cold and callous, but I was. What was becoming of me? Prison can turn a man's heart to stone. Was *I* capable of committing murder, I wondered, and not for the first time. The frightening truth lay in my conscience. If provoked, I had no doubt I could take a life at the snap of a finger. May *Hashem* forgive me for what I knew then.

Whenever a Blue Shirt approached us, we foreigners would whisper to each other, 'Watch out – here comes the CIA.' It made me sick knowing that prisoners were informing on prisoners, and that there was nothing you could do about it. When Somsak was murdered, I knew things would change. Kill one to teach the rest. Apparently Somsak was stabbed 36 times. His death brought a wave of fear to the other Blue Shirts, and being a trustee was no longer as glamorous as before. A statement had been made and its message was clear: you inform, you die. The guards could not protect you. Every Blue Shirt knew that they would now have a target on their backs.

A morbid atmosphere permeated Building 2. Aporn was taken away and charged with Somsak's murder. He was shackled with heavy rail-way chains and thrown into solitary confinement. Soon after that, the second chief, Adun, was promoted to Building Chief. We didn't know it, but our problems were just beginning.

On my birthday on 15 October, my eleventh in prison, I was awake at the crack of dawn, cheerful and ready to take on the day. I was 45 years old. When our cells were opened, I made my way to my house. As I entered, I was confronted by a pool of sewage. My house was ankle deep in watered-down human waste. They say when you stand in shit it's meant to be lucky, but I'm not so sure about that. I started scooping and throwing out the water. Jonnie arrived, took one look at the mess and disappeared. The smell was disgusting and soon had me choking. I had to get a plumber in. The sewerage pipe had blocked and the pressure that had built up was so strong that the water was leaking through the concrete walls. Well, that was my gift for my birthday. I expected a shit-load of luck to come my way!

Mikhail was by then quite a good friend of mine. Interestingly, he and Philip, who was Australian, had both been arrested on suspicion, but had been found to have no drugs on them. In the first court they were acquitted. When this happens, the public prosecutor appeals your sentence and, unless you pay money, the chances are you will receive a prison sentence in the second court. Mikhail and Philip believed they had a strong case and their lawyer advised them not to pay. They waited two years for second court, where they were both given life sentences. They would have to wait for third court, which could take up to another eight years.

When they came to Bangkwang, Philip was placed in Building 6 and Mikhail came to Building 2. About a year later, Philip got into an altercation with a fellow prisoner and that was how he came to move to our building.

The General used to work out in my gym. One of the Iranians, Reza, a murder offender, was a 4th dan. Reza had done time with the General back at Special prison, and now he became his personal trainer. One day, the General was relaxing on one of the benches in the gym when Philip, who had been in Building 2 for only a couple of days, walked in. He wanted to use the bench and rudely signalled with his hand that the General should clear off. In Thai the gesture and accompanying words '*by by*' (go go) say it all. Even to an ordinary prisoner this is highly disrespectful.

The General got up, never said a word, and walked away. All this happened while I was in my house, drawing. About an hour later, the General's right-hand man, and my good friend, came to me to tell me what had happened. He said they wanted to stab Philip. As I was the leader of the foreigners, they first wanted to run it past me. Although Philip had a reputation for being an obnoxious fuck and was forever starting shit with the weaker guys, I couldn't allow an attack on a foreigner. Philip had no idea that his life was in danger. I explained to my friend that Philip was new in our building and he didn't know who the General was. Even so, he argued, Philip had disrespected an old man. I was in a difficult position. Surely a peaceful solution would be better, so I told him I would sort it out with the General, and we agreed upon that.

I found Philip walking around on the grass patch near the front gate. When I told him what was going down, he turned white. I suggested that he follow me to the General's house and apologise. First I spoke to the General, explaining that Philip was very sorry and hadn't known who he was. Philip reiterated his apology and simultaneously put his hand out to shake the General's hand. The General was not impressed, but, because of my relationship with him, he said, 'No problem.' But he didn't accept Philip's hand. Instead, with his own hand, he brushed Philip off. I pulled Philip away by his arm, thanked the General and quickly led the Australian away before the General changed his mind.

Aporn, before he murdered Somsak, taught me how to make *lau* (whiskey), or – my own personal term of endearment for it – 'love juice'. The parcel guard, Suchin, was different from the other guards; he spoke good English and he knew which foreigners used drugs and which didn't. He never really checked the contents of my parcels, which made it easier for me to bring in the key ingredient you needed as a brewmaster: yeast. I would share the yeast with the Thais who formed part of our drinking circle, giving them two or three tablespoons from which they could make at least nine litres. In return I asked for one litre of their best. I also gave the General yeast, and his boys were great whisky makers. I was one of the only people in Bangkwang who always had a supply of yeast, and this bought me a lot of friends. As a rule, I didn't sell it; if I had it, I was happy to share.

My relationship with the General was good. There were occasions when we even sat and had a drink together. Anytime I wanted to use the General's mobile, I could. Among his crew was a Thai boxer, Weenai. He was bigger than the average Thai. He and I had a mutual respect for each other. I had discovered in getting to know the Thais that some of them were really amazing, sincere and genuine people; if you respected them, and behaved properly, they would do anything for you. I was learning more and more to be friends with them. The Thais were more resilient than the foreigners, and they accepted the hardships of prison life without complaining.

During this time, I started drinking on weekends. My relationship with Jai was taking strain. She had started lying about small things and had neglected to carry out certain of my requests that were important to me, like depositing my allowance and lying that she had when she hadn't. We were definitely growing apart, and my feelings for her were becoming increasingly Platonic. Still, it was a complicated situation and, irrespective of my own cooling feelings for Jai, I remained indebted to her; she was not only helping me but also many of my friends who had nobody in Thailand.

While lifting weights one day, I strained myself doing chest, and felt a vein pop out of my arse. I was told I had 'rissidoeing' (haemorrhoids). It was damn uncomfortable. I couldn't remember when last I had used toilet paper to wipe my arse, so whenever I flushed, using my hand I would feel this vein and it really bothered me. I was too scared to go to the hospital, even though I heard it was quite a quick procedure to sort out. Somebody advised me to get a cream. I tried to push it back with my finger, but it kept popping out whenever I squatted. After a month of waiting, I eventually got some cream from home, but it didn't help. Then my Thai friend Somchai, who slept in my room, introduced me to this cactus-type plant that grew like a weed; each piece was about 5cm in length and about the thickness of my baby finger. Every day I was required to eat three pieces. First I had to wash them well, then trim off the four rough edges before chopping them into small pieces. I then had to take a segment of a naartjie (tangerine), split it open along the edge, take out the seeds, and fit as much of the cactus into the naartjie as possible. Then I had to close it and swallow it whole. If the cactus came in contact with my tongue or mouth, Somchai cautioned, it would leave me incredibly itchy, so I had to be careful. After 12 days of performing this tedious ritual, my haemorrhoids disappeared completely. I repeated the process every three months and never suffered from haemorrhoids again.

Meanwhile, the Director's administration was proposing stopping prisoners receiving parcels and foodstuffs from visitors, the reason being that there had been a few incidents where the prison authorities had detected drugs in parcels and food brought by visitors. There was also a serious clampdown on guards who were suspected of bringing drugs inside, and some of these guards were transferred to other prisons. The price of heroin increased tenfold. Somehow, though, drugs still worked their way into the system, but on a smaller scale.

On the parcel issue, it was time to draw swords. Apart from cutting off a lifeline of support to many of us, it did not make sense to stop parcels from being sent to the prisoners. First of all, the prison didn't supply the prisoners with anything. We paid for our own food, medicines and even drinking water. The things we received in parcels from our families and loved ones were necessities, and parcels were the only tangible contact we had with them. Some of our families couldn't afford the airfare to come and visit us, but they felt good knowing that we could receive some small luxuries to make a difference to our existence. What did the prison authorities hope to gain? Just because a few individuals abused the privilege and smuggled drugs, why punish us all? Once again I drafted a petition expressing our grievances, distributed it to every building, collected signatures and submitted it to the Director. Surprisingly, he withdrew his recommendation and eased the pressure. If it hadn't been for my initiative, life in Bangkwang would have been much more difficult for everyone.

Joseph, the Israeli backgammon player who had been so soundly beaten by the Cripple, slept opposite me. He and his co-accused had escaped from Chiang Rai prison, but had been caught, rearrested and given the death penalty. For seven years they had sat on death row, with leg irons welded round their ankles. Then, with the support of the Israeli government, through a royal decree their sentences were reduced to life imprisonment, which was how Joseph had come to our building.

Late one night, at around 1am, the sounds of a muffled conversation woke me from my sleep. It happened again the next night. After a few nights of puzzlement I realised Joseph had a mobile phone, a dog. The next day I spoke to him about it, thinking that I would reprimand him and ban him from bringing his mobile into the room. I did not want to run the risks that being caught with a dog carried. When Joseph first arrived from Building 1, I had invited him to stay in my house with Simon and me, on condition that he stopped using heroin, which he did. He turned out to be a great guy, actually, and he was the one who introduced me to gambling on football. Joseph was from the old school, where there was still honour among men who had chosen a life of crime. When I spoke to him about the phone, very diplomatically and respectfully, he explained to me that in fact there was nothing I could do to prevent the guys from using mobiles in the room. If I tried to stop them, he said, I would make a lot of enemies. He added, 'Don't you want to speak to your family?'

Obviously, he was right. How could I even try to prevent the inmates from having instant contact with their families? Joseph had one of those small Panasonics and a SIM card (code word 'biscuit'). His friends on the outside would text him airtime numbers from a pop-up voucher.

On weekends, the General's house and the area behind it became like the post office. Guys were ducking and diving behind their locker doors all day, phoning their families. People would happily allow you to use their mobiles ('bark the dog') and airtime was easily arranged. Every 500 Thai baht cost you an extra 50 Thai baht. It was another way of bringing revenue into the prison without having to go through the guards. I remember the first text message I ever sent was to my friend Melanie in Pretoria. It read: 'Hello'.

When I took ownership of the gym, our membership stood at 15. I employed the services of two Thai boys to unpack and pack the weights away every day. We also had to pay the guard 500 Thai baht a month, after expenses. The profit left was worth one football. If the gym was going to run profitably, we needed to get more members to join. So I had this idea. Everybody liked to watch themselves in the mirror when they trained, but the gym had only two mirrors, both of which were small and badly cracked. Through one of the guards I arranged to buy four big mirrors, ordering them from the furniture factory in Building 8. Within a week of fitting them in the gym our membership increased to 30 paying members. I also organised permission for the guys on death row to work out between 8 and 9am. Actually, I ran the gym single-handedly; my Russian partner Yegor sat back and did bugger all. Being a people person, and knowing how important it was to keep busy – not that I had all that much time on my hands – I didn't really mind. I also offered a special for senior citizens and only charged these older guys half-price.

Much as I was beginning to like some of the Thais – and some were already close friends – they had some personal hygiene habits I could never quite get my head around. Sometimes when you would be working out in the gym, and looking at yourself in the mirror from about 3m away, a Thai guy would come and stand close to the mirror right in front of you, squeeze his blackheads, pick his nose, then wipe his nails on the edge of the wooden frame, not in the least perturbed that you were watching him. It amazed me every time one of them did this.

It was hard to prevent people from training in the gym for free. If I saw somebody who was not a member working out for the first time, I wouldn't say anything. If he came back the next day, I would tell him that the use of the gym was strictly for members, but that he was welcome to join – at a fee, of course. There were also some guards who worked out; naturally I could not charge them. With the profits I made, I would buy footballs, *takraw* balls and even ping-pong balls. I was one of the fortunate ones who had support from home, so I used the money I generated from the gym to benefit prisoners by buying sports equipment.

Being the owner of the gym also enhanced my position as leader of the foreigners. Among the Thais there were some really big gangsters, and these guys had a lot of influence. I would allow them to train for free, mostly out of respect, but also because they all had bodyguards. So while the boss didn't have to pay to train, he paid for six or seven of his boys to use the gym. There was an incident where one of the Thai Bad Boys took a 5kg weight and smashed it on the head of one of the other prisoners with whom he had had a falling-out, opening quite a deep gash. I did not witness the attack, but whenever there was a fight, every second person who walked past you would say, or ask, whether you had seen or heard about what happened. One of my boys who worked in the gym came running to tell me.

In the gym we had dumbbells, weights, bars, any of which could be used as a weapon. The investigating guard submitted the 5kg weight as evidence as the weapon used in the attack. It was sent out with a report to the security section. My greatest concern was that they might close the gym down, but thankfully this didn't happen. I was called to the inquiry, but the guard in charge only asked me to please monitor the weights and generally to be more vigilant. After that, every afternoon when my boys packed the weights away, I was careful to do a count.

One day, a Frenchman arrived from a prison in the provinces. In our cell we had decided that whenever a new person came, until they paid their 2 000 Thai baht, they would have to sleep among the Thais without any space between their beds.

On his first night, as the new guy passed my bed, he muttered in his

French accent, 'I want the same space as you.'

'All in good time, my friend,' I told him. 'It took me almost ten years and a lot of money to enjoy this privilege.'

All he had was a couple of soiled blankets. Without his knowledge, I ordered one of my boys to wash his blankets, dry them, buy another two blankets and make him a bed, which was ready by the time he came to the cell that afternoon. He looked at his bed, not sure if it was for him.

'It's yours,' I said.

I couldn't believe my ears. The guy moaned about my gift, saying that he'd never asked for help. I actually found myself apologising for my good deed, and saying that one of the requirements of being in our cell was that he have a bed. I didn't get upset, though. When I extended help, it was always unconditional. With time, most of us took a liking to the Frenchman.

Jonnie the South African, on the other hand, was likeable, easygoing and always had a smile on his face. He and the Russian and the Frenchman became good friends, and all three of them would hang out in my house.

By now there were at least two dogs in our cell. Jonnie and one of the British guys wanted the three of us to club in and buy one. We paid 18 000 Thai baht for a Nokia and I took on the responsibility of hiding it and bringing it in and out of the room, which was quite dangerous. Before we entered, there would be a guard at the gate checking our bags and frisking our bodies. Because of the power I had by now, whenever we entered I would briskly walk past the guard without pausing to give him time to search my bag or my body, and I was never called back. You have to remember that most of these guards had, at one stage or another, taken a bribe from me. I wasn't about to allow myself to be searched.

I took the cardboard tube from a roll of toilet paper and made a small box with it, about the size of a cigarette packet. I used Super Glue to stick the box under and against the edge of one of my lockers, and this was where I would hide the dog. Having a phone was still extremely dangerous and had to be kept a secret, especially from the Thais, whom one couldn't trust. Despite the good friendships I had forged with some of them, the Thai mentality remained very strange to me: if a Thai could benefit from you in some way, he would be your best friend, but the second there was no advantage to be gained, he didn't know you and wouldn't give you the time of day.

I went through stages of contentment, but often depression crept in. It would take me by surprise, throwing me completely off balance. The scorching heat didn't help matters, and when I was in this low state of mind, often I wouldn't paint for weeks on end and I would neglect my Jewish studies. Sometimes I hit such a low that not only did I lose my will to live but I also thought I was losing my mind. I became short-tempered and everybody irritated the fuck out of me. And, more often than not, I would take my bad moods out on Jai. She once remarked that my tongue was quicker than my brain, and she was right. The smallest thing would upset me, and then I would say the most hurtful things without considering the other person's feelings. When I saw that I'd upset the person, I would be quick to apologise, and I couldn't understand it when the recipient of my verbal attack wasn't as quick to forgive. The truth was, I really *did* care, but I just couldn't control my mouth. The abuse would spurt out of me with such ferocity that I frightened even myself. The anger that I thought had dissipated over the years was still there, festering inside me like a cancer.

I needed some answers, and so, as I certainly wasn't going to find them in my head, I looked to G-d. I assumed He knew my mind was troubled. During one of my many conversations with Him, through my inner voice He asked me these questions: 'Eleazer, if I were to grant you your physical freedom, redeemed as you are, would you be able to resist becoming a slave of your own desire? Why would you be any different from what you were before coming to prison? If you are ready to fulfil My purpose, I will open the steel gates of hell.' His voice was audible in its silence. If I answered yes, I had no doubt the way would be open, but this truth still remained: I was not ready. The gates to freedom were only an obstruction of my mind; my time behind these walls was of greater significance than my liberation.

When a baby is born prematurely, there are all sorts of complications, so I thought of this as an analogy and I answered no. I was not ready. Time would be the deciding factor. With every day that passed, I would grow from strength to strength, so I told *Hashem* I was not ready. Once I understood that I would be staying indefinitely in prison, I began to be more at peace with myself.

The authorities had decided to install a telephone in every building, to replace those we had been using at the computer room outside the building. That first system had become a logistical nightmare and a security risk, with so many prisoners leaving the building to make calls. This new system would be far more practical. Of course I had a mobile by then, but in order not to arouse suspicion I applied through the embassy for a prison telephone card, which permitted me two five-minute calls a week. Scratchcard vouchers were available through the coffee shop. To call South Africa cost me 40 Thai baht for five minutes. Scratchcards came in fifties and hundreds. The problem was that, some months, a telephone card holder could only buy the 100 Thai baht cards. There was always a shortage of fifties. The owner of the coffee shop, who was a Taiwanese, would organise extra scratchcards and share them out, mostly among his Chinese friends. Seeing that we had been together for so long, and that he was also a member of my drinking circle, he helped me out, too. Whenever there was a shortage I would make a lot of noise, write petitions and demand extra, but it was all a bluff. I was in contact with my sister on a daily basis barking the dog, so when I called her from the office for my five-minute session, we would have nothing to talk about!

Keeping an account of the weights in the gym was a headache, but it was a necessary exercise – we *were* a bunch of criminals, after all. There was an incident where one of the prisoners removed a set of dumbbells, took them to his locker on the other side of the building, and just kept them. But my biggest problem came when new prisoners arrived. They would walk around the building familiarising themselves with the environment, just as I had done years before. The gym was probably the main attraction. I couldn't allow people to exercise for free; it wasn't fair to the paying members. So some of those who wanted to train but didn't want to pay would occasionally help themselves. Weights would frequently disappear and the equipment would also wear out quickly or get broken. I can't tell you how often I had to do repairs or replace equipment.

By now we had about 40 Thai Bad Boys among us. These gangsters had committed offences such as being caught with drugs, being found with mobiles, and being involved in stabbings. Building 10 was at capacity, and there was a waiting list to get into solitary, so they would be moved around from building to building until such time as a cell became available. Some Building Chiefs simply wouldn't accept them in their buildings. Adun, our Building Chief, never discriminated. He accepted anyone, no matter what their record,

Most of these guys were avid footballers. I discovered that, except for not valuing life the way we Westerners do, they were really no different to me, and we definitely had football in common. They, too, were warriors, and they wore dragon tattoos proudly all over their bodies. By this stage I had more than 15 tattoos and planned on covering both my arms. The only problem was that the tattoo artist never stayed in the building for more than a month or two. The guy who did the 'Skull with Bandana' on my right shoulder died of TB.

The gym ran pretty smoothly, though, but with all the Bad Boys it was inevitable that there would be trouble sooner or later. Six of them started hanging out there, just sitting around smoking and using the weights and making a nuisance of themselves. One day I had no choice but to confront them, and they left reluctantly. The next morning, they were back. This was an outright challenge. I had to bear in mind that these guys were dangerous, unpredictable and couldn't give a fuck, so, instead of confronting them for a second time, I never said a word, but the next morning I kept the gym closed. When the gym was closed, the exercise benches, the bars and weights were piled in a heap, chained together and covered with a tarpaulin. The gym was an open area and also a throughway to the houses next to the *soy* or punishment room. In front of the gym was a concrete water storage pool, which was used to breed catfish. The pool was enclosed by a thick concrete wall roughly half a metre high, which prisoners could sit on. I couldn't stop them from sitting there.

Four Bad Boys arrived at the gym. It was still pretty early, and, seeing that the weights were locked up, they started sparring with each other. Then I arrived. I explained the membership story once again. One of them threw a punch at me, which I blocked, at the same time delivering a kick to his groin, stopping just millimetres from impact. Surprised, he made some remark about me knowing Thai boxing. I told him in Thai that I didn't want any problems and asked them politely to leave. The Bad Boys left, and from then on they never bothered me. I guessed they'd asked around about me.

Weekends were holidays, and this meant a couple of days of relaxation for the guards. They didn't bother the prisoners; they'd be sleeping or getting a massage. One of guards who used to work in death row in Building 1 was transferred to Building 2. His name was Veesarnou and he was a real motherfucker. His first Saturday on duty, the Frenchman and I were sitting quietly in my house drinking our home-brew from Coke cans. Usually we would drop an envelope to the guard who sat near our section and ask him to '*peet tar*' (close your eyes). So the Frenchman and I were on our second can of wine, but, because we were wary of Veesarnou, we would hold the cans under the table out of sight. Veesarnou sneaked up on us through the Nigerian house and must have seen something to arouse his suspicion, or else he just thought we were up to something. The wall separating our houses was just over a metre high, and pushed up on the Nigerian side were wooden lockers, so it was difficult for him to lean over completely. He wasn't tall, either. Anyway, he popped his head over and asked, '*Khun tum aria?*' (What are you doing?)

I don't know what possessed me – I don't think I realised how strong the wine was – but I told him that today was a holiday. '*Won ni won jud,*' I said. '*Kun ropkoen tummai.*' (You're disturbing us, why?)

He was taken aback by my cheek, but before he could answer, I asked him, '*Ar yu torai?* (How old are you?) *Pom cisiep qua*' (I'm forty plus).

He didn't answer. With every word that came out of my mouth, I got braver. I told Veesarnou that I'd been there for almost ten years and did he have any idea how we foreigners suffered in a Thai prison.

In the end he just walked away. He'd probably heard quite enough. The Frenchman was beside himself; he had no idea where such balls came from. I was drunk, that was where. The guardhouse where Veesarnou sat was opposite the Nigerian house, and in full view of mine. He summoned a few Thais to his office and asked them who I was. I was known as being one of the Big Legs. I wasn't too concerned about the Thais, as I was known as the leader of the foreigners. Not long afterwards, one of the Thais who was close to me came to warn me that Veesarnou hadn't been impressed by my behavioiur and there was a good chance I would be reported to the Building Chief on Monday. This also wasn't a problem for me, as the chief was deeply corrupt. The prison authorities are strange: if you are doing something that's illegal and you don't bring it to their attention, they will close their eyes to it, but once they actually see what's going on, then you are likely to be punished for it. Why make unnecessary trouble, I thought, so I went to Veesarnou and apologised, admitting that I'd been drinking. He waffled something or other, but respected the fact that I had come forward, and so the matter was dropped.

It became apparent that Ling, who had been on death row while Veesarnou was in Building 1, was working with the guards. Ling had also established a strong friendship with Pedro from our cell. As a rule, I was suspicious of everybody, but for some reason Ling acted more like a foreigner than a Thai, and generally the foreigners never informed.

Around this time, after visits and while waiting in the area where prisoners received foodstuffs from their visitors, a Western foreigner who was on death row in Building 1, and who knew Ling well, enlightened me about him. He told me that Ling was a rat and that he had been transferred to Building 2 because his life was in danger in Building 1. I shared this information with the 'dog handlers' in our cell. We would have to be extra-vigilant. Ling was the only death row prisoner who was allowed to move around freely during the day and mingle with the lifers. He spent time in the house next door to mine with my Chinese chef, and he also hung out for hours with Veesarnou. I definitely smelt a rat, and from then on I started to dislike Ling.

Our new office clerk was a Thai prisoner by the name of Keng. He spoke English and he was part of my fast-growing new circle of drinking friends. Keng controlled all the administration and day-to-day running of the building, and this included the prison cells. Every time I made wine, I would drop Keng a litre. Booze became a currency that bought you loyalty. Veesarnou had been there only a month when Keng informed me that Veesarnou had a list of people he suspected of having mobile phones and that my name was on top of the list, followed by three other members of my cell. Veesarnou summoned me to the office. He told me he knew I had a mobile phone, but said that if I handed it over I wouldn't be punished. I acted shocked, and flatly denied the allegation. Angrily, I added that whoever had told him more than likely had one himself, and that was who he should be investigating, not me.

The Nokia mobile we'd bought was a second-hand job. The screen was cracked and the zero key didn't always register. We couldn't exactly send it for repairs, and my friend John, the electronics expert, couldn't risk repairing it either. So, using a small screwdriver, I took the machine apart myself and managed to fix the key. Because I took most of the risk in keeping the dog, I felt it was only right that I should use it more than the others, but the ideal situation would have been for me to have my own mobile phone. The problem was that the Thais were the ones distributing them. This was doubly dangerous, because they would sell you a mobile and then inform on you. Buying a phone from the guards, on the other hand, opened the door to having money constantly extorted from you.

One of the other foreigners managed to smuggle in a dog concealed in a container of peanut butter sent in a parcel. This was also risky; since the new drug laws and the clampdown in the prison, all items in our parcels were now thoroughly checked. The parcel area was divided into two sections, with one end for the Thais and the other for the foreigners. One guard, Suchin, controlled and checked the foreign parcels and registered mail, while another, Watcherine, checked the Thais.

Arranging things from home was much easier now, as I would just SMS my sister or call her. I was feeling increasingly unhappy having to share a mobile. Our British co-conspirator would speak for hours on end, which irritated me a lot. I've always been an independent person, and I hate having to rely on somebody or to wait for someone else. Unfortunately, I couldn't afford my own dog, so I arranged for my sister to send me one. I instructed her to conceal it in a portable radio but I emphasised that it was imperative it be done professionally. At that time Joan worked at a place called Delta TV. I knew they'd have technicians who would be able to organise this for me. About a week before its expected arrival, I told Suchin that a radio would be arriving for me in a parcel, and at the same time I dropped him an envelope. He was not altogether happy, because the Director had tightened up on things. I also had to take care of the Blue Shirts who were posted at the gate entrance of our building.

The moment of truth arrived. I was called over the loudspeaker to collect my package. I was extremely nervous. What if Suchin had decided not to give me the radio and to keep it overnight to check whether anything was concealed inside it? If he found the mobile, I had no doubt he would report me, which would mean six months in solitary. Armed with my plastic carrier bag, I made my way to the parcel area. The Blue Shirt, Weechai, would be waiting for me. It was around 9am. Trying to act natural, I greeted Suchin. My box was there. I recognised the brown wrapping paper and my sister's handwriting. I whispered to Suchin that it was the radio I'd been waiting for. My knees were weak and my hands were shaking. I kept telling myself to relax or for sure Suchin would sense something. Taking a Stanley knife, he cut the box open. There were a few other odds and ends in the parcel, things like Dettol, soap, some dishcloths, tennis socks, Provita biscuits and toothpaste, all of which he handed to me first. Then Suchin looked around discreetly to make sure nobody was watching him. He took out the radio, examined it to make sure that it had not been tampered with, and then opened the battery compartment. He lifted the radio up and started to shake it. *Fuck*, I wanted to drop down dead. I was praying that Joan had concealed the cellphone properly. When nothing seemed amiss, Suchin passed it to me. It was not very big, so I put it in my plastic bag, pushing it down under the other items.

When I arrived at our gate, the guard was stretched out on his chair, feet on the table, watching a replay of a football match. Weechai, who I had paid for this, looked into the plastic bag and pretended to be checking through the stuff. He allowed me to pass. I took a deep sigh of relief. I had made it. As I walked along the concrete path that led to the main office I felt the spring come back into my step. I was smiling from ear to ear. Lady Luck was on my side today. When I got to my house I locked the radio away, and no sooner had I done so than I was called for a visit. It was a Wednesday, the day Jai would bring me a whole roast chicken and potato salad, as well as my normal weekly food order.

Hidden in one of my lockers were two 3-litre containers with wine brewing – today called for a celebration. As they did every Wednesday, Jonnie, Yegor and the Frenchman came to my house for lunch. My Chinese chef, who was cooking for me again, had made us a platter of dim sum. After lunch, we topped up our mugs with wine and I broke the news of what I had pulled off. I hadn't told anybody about my plan until then, as one never knew who one's friends really were. I took out the radio and Jonnie volunteered to dismantle it. To my surprise and dismay, there was no phone to be found. What was going on? It *had* to be there! In frustration I took the radio and smashed it on the concrete floor ... and out fell the mobile. It had been so well hidden and covered in black carbon paper that none of us had been able to detect it. It was a Nokia 7250i, one of the first phones with a camera and internet connection. The jack to charge it was the same as for the other Nokia we had, which I had sold to the British guy for much less than we'd bought it for, on the understanding that we would share the jack. It was not an ideal situation, though, so again through my sister I ordered a jack from home. I advised her to cut the cable about two inches from the jack, making it easier to conceal. My idea was to hide it in a vacuum-sealed packet of sliced biltong, so I suggested Joan send me three packets of 1kg each, gambling that the guard would cut open only one of the packets and that it wouldn't be the one that contained the jack. The odds were two to one. As it turned out, that was exactly what happened. I managed to get my own charger. I had taken a hell of a chance, but what was life without taking risks?

In the cell there were four of us with private TVs, so from the main plug, which had two or three adaptors attached to it, we ran our own extension cables. I took the adaptor from a CD player, cut the cable and attached the jack for my mobile phone. Every night before I went to sleep, I would charge my phone for the next day.

Pedro, who had had his pardon rejected way back in 2001, a month before my own, had heard that Queen Beatrix of the Netherlands had visited the King of Thailand early in January 2004. A month later, he and a Ghanaian who was married to a Dutch woman were granted royal pardons and were released. Pedro's sleeping spot in the corner was taken by Mikhail. Meanwhile Joseph convinced me to bring Philip into our cell because he felt sorry for him, as he was in a room with 22 Thais. Philip was a strange fucker who came from a tough background. He slept on the floor and drank his own urine. He had another bad habit that really pissed me off: he would lie on the floor and let out these really loud and rather offensive farts. Thank goodness I didn't sleep near him. Well, that's prison – it takes all types to make up the zoo.

Mikhail also had a Nokia, the same as the one we shared before I got my own dog. One afternoon, about an hour and a half after lockdown, I was sitting on my bed with my back resting against the wall. On my lap I had a file in which I was using Joseph's dog, a Panasonic. I had earphones in my ears, pretending to be reading and listening to music, but instead I was busy texting with about ten people at the same time. I was so caught up in what I was doing, I never even heard the steel doors to the downstairs section being opened. Mikhail's instincts were so sharp, though, that within seconds he was in the toilet flushing his phone down. The British guy also flushed his phone, but, by the time I realised what was going on, it was too late. The guards were standing by the bars, armed with batons, and instructing everybody to stay where they were. Mikhail casually came out of the toilet, while somehow I managed to roll the earphones around the mobile and slip it into my underpants, between my testicles and anus. Our cell door was opened and we were ordered to exit one by one while a guard stood by the door subjecting each person to a thorough body search as they passed. Fuck, I nearly shat in my pants. I literally started shaking and for once didn't even have time to say a prayer. In my hand I took my key-ring and a dishcloth that I used to wipe the sweat. There were six keys attached to a string long enough to fit around my wrist. I was the last to exit. One of the guards started frisking me around my shoulders, and under my arms. As he got to my waist, I deliberately dropped the keys; the guard noticed and also heard them hit the floor. In that split second, hoping that the distraction would break his concentration, I bent down and, as I picked up my keys, apologised and walked away so that he never got the chance to search my private parts. Whether by divine intervention or a stroke of luck, I succeeded in avoiding what could have turned out to be something of a disaster. The punishment for being found in possession of a mobile was six months in solitary confinement in shackles.

Luckily for us, they didn't find anything in the entire downstairs section, although I'm not sure how well they searched the General. There was no way he wouldn't have had a mobile with him.

The raid had been organised by Bangkwang's own security section, so they weren't as thorough as outside guards; I suspect our room had been their prime target. I was sorry for Mikhail and the British guy, who had lost their mobiles down the toilet, and which by then had probably made their way through the sewer system into the vaults where the shit was stored. While we waited outside for the guards to finish their search, Joseph stayed far away from me, but he kept staring at me questioningly, his eyes expressing his concern about the fate of his mobile. I gave him a wink. Slightly perplexed, he returned a smile of acknowledgement, obviously hoping that somehow all was not lost.

The guards had ransacked our cells. Our belongings were thrown all over the show, beds were taken apart and pillows torn open. What pissed me off the most was that they had walked all over our beds with their shoes. After we had brought some semblance of order to the room, Joseph came and sat on my bed. By then I'd already slipped the dog out of my underpants and wrapped it in my dishcloth. I smiled at him. Then I slid the dog over to him. He stared at it in disbelief and I could see that he simply couldn't comprehend how, firstly, I had managed not to get caught, and, secondly, that I hadn't had to dispose of it. Talk about defying the odds! Somebody up there must love me. Our other cellmates were equally impressed, but I declined to give my secret away. All I said was that I had left the dog in the side pocket of my haversack and hoped for the best.

Chapter 15

The Dog, a Prisoner's Best Friend

Nothing had come of Linda Mti's visit to Bangkwang in 2003. In my view, the whole thing had been a huge waste of taxpayers' money. Mti's vision of signing a prisoner transfer treaty with Thailand had started to take shape when the Minister of Correctional Services, Ben Skosana, publicly announced that his department was looking at drafting a policy to enable the government to repatriate the more than 600 South Africans held in prisons around the world. However, following South Africa's national election in April 2004, Ngconde Balfour replaced Skosana at Correctional Services. Balfour was said to be addressing the issue of transfer treaties. With all these public announcements, one would think that something was being done to turn them into policy, but in fact nothing materialised. I couldn't understand it. What was going on? Did our government really not give a fuck about its citizens?

Almost a year back, the ambassador, Mrs Pheto, had expressed an interest in using my art as part of the celebrations to mark South Africa's ten years of democracy in 2004. She had even commissioned me to do paintings of the Thai King and Queen. This was exciting for me, and inspiring, besides which I thought that perhaps some public exposure of my talent would attract attention to our plight. In the beginning my hopes were high. Perhaps the Thai government, in an act of good faith and to strengthen diplomatic ties with South Africa, would even release all of us South Africans held in Thai prisons on the milestone occasion of ten years of democracy in my home country. I knew it was a long shot, but it was this kind of dream that sustained my enthusiasm and helped me to endure prison life.

When the Indian Ocean tsunami hit at the end of December 2004, I was already barking my dog regularly. Concerned friends who had never been in Thailand kept asking me questions, like whether we were safe and if the tidal wave had reached the prison. We were so far inland I thought this was funny. Some of the prisoners in Bangkwang, however, lost family members, and my heart went out to them.

Meanwhile, with the clampdown and rising prices of drugs, alcohol had become the favourite high, but yeast had become increasingly difficult to bring into the prison. Suchin had gone on a course and Watcherine had taken over the foreign parcels. He was no pushover, and it would be hard to deceive him. Joan, who had no idea we were making wine from the yeast (she thought we were using it for baking!), agreed to send me some from home. My instructions this time were for her to buy a variety of spice and tea sachets, as well as different brands of yeast, which came in similar-size packets, and to put them all in a plastic bag, the logic being that Watcherine would recognise the tea and not bother to check the individual packets. My logic was spot-on. It worked like a charm, and from then on I had people from different parts of the world all sending me 'tea' in their parcels. My Russian friend Yegor also got clever. He had his family send him packets of instant soup; in the same-size packaging they also sent him sachets of yeast, which he sold for up to 2 000 Thai baht.

Yegor had bought a small house behind the second chief's office and in front of the gym, but he had failed to drop an envelope for the Building Chief. This was standard procedure; if you owned property, you paid the 'tax'. If you ignored this rule, which, by the way, was also a direct disrespect for the officer, you would quickly find yourself in trouble. Any violation of the rules would mean your immediate removal to another building. The guards would go so far as to set you up and they would seize your property and sell it off themselves. When Yegor first arrived, he seemed like an amiable guy and he and I became good friends. He spent a lot of time in my house with Jonnie, eating our lunches and drinking our wine. His wife often posted him parcels, but Yegor never shared anything with us. He would rather have cockroaches and ants eat his food than hand it around. It wasn't that I wanted or expected anything from him, but in appreciation of our hospitality and for the use of the dog, I thought it would have been nice of him just to offer.

One night in the cell, soon after lockdown, I had not even unpacked my haversack when I saw Yegor waving to me. He held up his hand and made a sign – baby finger stretched out and thumb up – that he wanted to use the dog. I chose to ignore him and didn't respond. In prison, one hand washes the other and Yegor needed to learn that. That night, when I gave him the dog much later than I usually did, he sensed that something was wrong. Another problem with Yegor was that when he spoke on the phone it was very loudly; you could hear him in the corridor. The key-boy was permanently on the lookout to bust somebody. I warned Yegor a few times to be careful and also told him that I was not his 'boy', that I was doing him a favour.

Anyway, a few days later Yegor, Mikhail and myself were walking to the cell when out of the blue Yegor said to me, 'Why is it that all Jews are stingy?'

What fucking chutzpah!

'Yegor,' I said, 'in my life I have never met a selfish Jew, but you know what, though – I have met one fucking stingy Russian.' Before he could say anything, I went on to add that the entire Jewish religion revolves around charity and doing good deeds. It's impossible that a Jew could be stingy. Yegor had no comeback to that, but his days of using my dog were over.

After this unpleasant incident, we barely spoke to each other. Then Yegor's house was raided by the building guards. They had been aware that he was selling yeast, but all they found was the leftover stub of a marijuana joint. This was something you could normally pay your way out of, but they were after Yegor's house. He was in trouble and he knew it. He came to me and told me he was selling his share of the gym to Philip for 8 000 Thai baht, thereby doubling his investment. He knew Philip and I were not on speaking terms either, and that I would pay in the money because I could never have Philip as my partner. That afternoon, Yegor was moved to Building 3. In a way, I was sorry to see him go, but, after his anti-Semitic comment, I got a bad taste in my mouth whenever I saw him.

Shortly after Somsak was murdered, the General was transferred to the hospital, where he was given a single cell formerly used to isolate the crazies. I was sad to see him leave for many reasons. I had no doubt, though, that security would be tightened in Building 2, and I was right. After the General left, Veesarnou became obsessed with clearing all mobile phones out of the building, and regular raids were conducted upstairs. Guards who found phones were offered the reward of promotion.

Sleeping in the centre of the cell was another British guy whom we'd nicknamed 'Flea' because he was so thin. He was a junkie and a talented musician and I really liked him. Flea was a dog keeper. This meant that the owner of the dog paid him money to risk bringing it into the cell at lockdown and taking it out in the morning, so usually Flea himself only got to bark the dog around midnight. Believe it or not, Flea would hide the dog up his rectum, first covering it with two condoms, which were freely available from our first-aid room. One morning, around 1am, I was woken by the sound of muffled conversation. The sounds were coming from Flea's direction. If *I* could hear him, there was no doubt he could be heard in the corridor and the key-boy was the number-one informer. He had already ratted out every dog handler in the corridor, and those guys were now sleeping in solitary. Anyway, Flea had a blanket over his head and was lying on his back, one leg pulled up and the other crossed over the top with his foot vibrating. How fucking obvious can you be? The following morning I reprimanded him, explaining that he was endangering all of his cellmates and that he should be more considerate. That night, again I had to get out of bed and kick Flea to lower his voice. He was due to transfer to a British prison soon and didn't give a shit.

Every morning, I was the first to wake up and the first to exit. When the steel doors at the entrance to the building were opened, the guard would hand the keys to the key-boy, who would then open the individual cells. The guard would either walk away or wait outside. I would always be waiting at the door to get out. A couple of days after I had warned Flea, the steel doors to the downstairs section were opened slightly earlier than usual. I thought it strange, but did not suspect anything out of the ordinary. I stood waiting, with my haversack over my shoulder, my water cooler in one hand and my dog, which was in a small zip-up pouch, in the other. This time the key-boy didn't open the first cell; he came straight to ours. By the time I realised what was going on, three guards had rushed past me into our cell, Veesarnou leading the charge. I stood to one side, letting them through. Flea was still fast asleep. The guards went straight to him, while I got the fuck out of there as fast as possible. I quickly went to my house and hid the dog in its kennel (hiding place). Then I went back to the cell. They had caught Flea red-handed. Before they took him away to be shackled, I told him that he couldn't say I hadn't warned him. I also told him that when they investigated his case, if they asked him where he'd bought the dog, he should say that Commodore Veesarnou had sold it to him for 10 000 Thai baht. He should say that he'd paid the money but then Veesarnou wanted another 5 000, which he'd refused. And that was why Veesarnou came to catch him.

Flea had nothing to lose, and so he did exactly what I'd advised. Veesarnou was investigated. I don't know what the outcome was, but, after that, his attitude towards prisoners changed drastically. And he never bothered our cell again.

As with so many things in life, good things never last too long. In prison, things could change from one moment to the next. Not too long after Flea got busted, around midday one day a group of three Thai civilians, dressed casually and accompanied by Veesarnou, were seen walking around the building. They were looking up at the roof. Then they went into the cells. The office clerk, Keng, who was my friend, was well informed of everything that was happening in the building, so I went and sat around outside the office, hoping that he would make conversation with me. When he saw me, he came over and asked, 'Whatz up?' This was what he always said. '*Min dun*' (The same), I replied. Then, switching to English, I pointed to Veesarnou's group, who seemed to have finished their surveillance, and asked what was going on.

Keng told me they were installing signal blockers, which meant we would soon be unable to use our mobiles. News travelled around the building like wildfire. The dog handlers were devastated. Within a week, machines were installed outside every third room, in the corridor in the centre of the ceiling, and also at three-room intervals on every corner of the building just under the roof. In no time, the system was up and running. The prices of mobile phones dropped dramatically. There was no way you could get a signal inside the cell, but outside and away from the building, down the other end where Chinatown was, one could still bark the dog. The property prices on that side immediately shot up. The houses were open and only small walls divided one from the other. It was risky, though, because anybody walking past could see what you were doing. Mikhail had his place there, and he would climb right into his locker (a small cupboard), close the door and use the dog in there. It was a tight squeeze and very uncomfortable, especially with the heat. Shlomo also had a house there and was kind enough to allow me to use the dog in the event of an emergency. For me, the risk was too high, and from then on it was only occasionally, maybe on a Saturday, that I would call my sister. Fortunately, I still had my two five-minute calls a week at the office.

Some of the dog handlers would still bring their dogs to the cell every night, hoping that by some miracle they could get a signal, but it was no use. To be suddenly cut off from the outside world was quite traumatic for us. The atmosphere became tense and the dog handlers walked around with long faces. Arguments broke out and led to fistfights.

The signal blockers were housed in protective boxes. Each machine had a green light and a red light. Red meant the machine was not working, and green that it was. If both lights were on at the same time, it meant the machine was faulty.

There is always a positive side to every negative. With the installation of the signal blockers came benefits, one of which was that I started to get a good night's sleep. Another was that I was no longer putting myself at risk of being caught on a mobile phone, and, instead of spending all night texting, I got back into reading books. There was only so much TV I could watch.

After about three months, the system started to break down. As if by a miracle, the red and green lights kept coming on at the same time, and this allowed us to reconnect with our families.

At 3.30pm, the usual time for lockdown, when we entered the cells a guard and two Blue Shirts would stand at the door. One by one, they would check our things. Prisoners carried their food in steel *pinto*s, and plastic bags were filled with items they planned to use to pass the time during the night, which might include listening to music on an MP3 player or watching a DVD. Regardless of our choice of entertainment, our things were all thoroughly searched. Some guards were lazy and would let you pass without checking, and it was always prudent to find out who was on the evening shift. If it was one of the more stringent guards, one who liked to conduct a full body search, for example, then I wouldn't risk walking the dog.

Watching movies was always a favourite pastime for most of the foreigners, and this led to the formation of a movie club. My DVD collection now stood at well over 600 titles. I also loved a good series. My all-time favourites were *The Sopranos*, *Prison Break* and *Heroes*, although *Heroes* kind of lost the plot by season two. One or two guys had DVD machines that you could hire for a night for 100 Thai baht, including a movie. Almost every day I had people come and ask if they could borrow my DVDs. I gave them with pleasure, the only condition being that they looked after them and made sure they didn't get scratched. As always, though, there were those who would abuse the privilege, and these guys got blacklisted.

One thing that was impossible to avoid in prison was swearing. Every second word that came out of your mouth was 'fuck' or 'motherfucker'. We prisoners were an embittered species and swearing somehow empowered us and made us feel better about ourselves. It was our way of keeping the hatred and anger alive. As I evolved spiritually, this

505

became a real concern to me. My new year's resolution would invariably be to stop swearing, but actually, if the truth be told, this was more difficult even than stopping smoking. They say effort produces results, but only time would prove whether that was true.

Changing times kept biting us in the arse. Another new Director, who liked to be referred to as Commander Sophon Thitithammapruek, had somehow heard about our illegal satellite TV, and an order was sent to our Building Chief to remove and break both the decoder and the satellite dish. The guards from our building were not very happy about this, as they also enjoyed watching TV during their night shifts, but there was nothing to be done but obey the order. The Blue Shirts were given the honour of breaking our dish and smashing the decoders. Life after that became unpleasant, especially for us football fans, who avidly followed European football and the English Premier League. We were locked up in our cells for over 15 hours a day, and boredom and depression walked hand in hand. The nights were hot and long. I had watched many of my own movies more than once. Shlomo and I organised more of the latest movies and TV series to be sent to us from home. Our families would send the discs to one of the guards I'd befriended, and he would smuggle them in for us for a fee. Whenever I watched, I would connect the main TV to my own so that everybody else could watch, too.

Sophon was also a bit of a nutcase. He began to use the closed-circuit TV to broadcast his multiple rules and regulations. During the day, his voice could be heard booming over the loudspeakers and on all the TVs. When you asked any Thai who watched what he was saying, they all responded, 'Mai sumkan' (Not important). Anyway, Sophon kept tightening the screws, and everyone agreed he needed to be stopped.

Building 1 had by then been reduced to rubble, but work had suddenly been suspended. Once again, Thais and foreigners alike appealed to me to petition the Commander to have the UBC satellite TV installed legally through the prison. I drafted a letter and distributed a copy to every building, instructing the prisoners to collect as many signatures as possible. The plan was that we would all submit our petitions on the same day.

506

13 October 2004

The Commander
Mr Sophon Thitithammapruek
Bangkwang Central

Dear Sir

We the foreign and Thai inmates in Building 2 are appealing to you for your consideration, to please allow the reintroduction of some of the UBC channels on the Bangkwang cable TV. Primarily we are asking for a news channel, either BBC or CNN, and a movie and sports channel. Since your inauguration you have instituted many changes, making life increasingly difficult for all prisoners. There have been three stress-related deaths and one murder in Building 2 alone, all a direct result of these changes. The prison is over-crowded, tensions are running high, we still don't have clean running water to shower with. The coffee shops are continuously without stock and we are unable to supply our daily needs. The prison does not provide any official rehabilitational programmes to prevent the mental and physical deterioration of prisoners, nor any organised events or representational forums to air our grievances. We cannot follow any of the local Thai TV networks because of the language barriers. UBC was the only form of entertainment that enabled us to pass time without going crazy. How many more prisoners must die before you ease the pressure and begin to meet the United Nations minimum requirement regulations for prisoners? Must we keep reminding you that we are serving life sentences; we are not short-term prisoners. We kindly ask you for your understanding and to allow UBC to be transmitted to all buildings for the benefit of everyone, as well as the Thai inmates, many in number, who are trying to learn to speak English. We are also calling on you to introduce medical emergency procedures, to supply proper medical equipment due to all the buildings, to train prisoners in CPR

and other emergency procedures to prevent further avoidable
fatalities. You don't even have an emergency fire evacuation
plan. Unless we start seeing some improvements to our living
conditions and an easing of the unrelenting pressure you have
imposed, we will be compelled to petition for your resignation
and early retirement.
   Discontented foreign and Thai inmates
   Building 2

A month after submitting our petition to have the satellite TV rein-
stated, we were informed that the Ministry of Education would donate
all the equipment to get the satellite TV up and running. Not even two
months later, four big satellite dishes were erected in Building 14 and
every building was hooked up. We foreigners were given an English
movie channel and a series channel. The others were all in Thai. There
was also the National Geographic channel and a sports channel. Even
though the guards operated and monopolised the satellite TV, this was
a huge victory.

In the middle of 2005 the Department of Corrections ordered the
seizure of all electronics. We had to bag and tag everything and give
them up. Even our frying pans had to be handed in. The reason for this
was that, apparently, the electricity bill was far too high. This was a big
blow. Without our electronics, life would be sheer hell. Even in prison
we had grown to take things for granted. Now that we were going to be
deprived of these simple luxuries, everybody panicked. We felt we had
no choice but to fight for our rights, and to remind the prison authorities that even though we were the prisoners, we also had power in our
numbers. The last thing they could afford was a riot.

   Towards the end of July, I drafted one of my by now famous petitions,
addressed to the director-general of the Department of Corrections, requesting the restoration of our rights to use electronic equipment. My
tone was respectful, as usual, but I also threw in the not very thinly

veiled threat of letting our embassies, the media and human rights organisations know about this latest indignity.

Eddie Tutin, our self-proclaimed French Jew, had become a Blue Shirt. For the past four years he had been in and out of hospital, after having been wrongly diagnosed, not once but three times, with tuberculosis. He began losing a lot of weight and complained of severe chest pains. He was eventually sent to the police hospital, where they detected cancer in its final stages. He was brought back to Bangkwang, but his condition had deteriorated to the extent that there was nothing that could be done for him. Too weak to survive in a general population, Eddie was admitted to hospital, where he would take his last breath and succumb to the unrelenting clutches of cancer. A fellow Frenchman volunteered to nurse him in those final stages, when even Eddie's bowel movements were beyond his control. His embassy had done nothing to repatriate him. I didn't have a lot of sympathy for Eddie. He had stooped too low when he became a Blue Shirt. He worked for the prison authorities and had become an informer. Yes, fate might have dealt him a cruel hand as far as his health went, but such is life – you reap what you sow.

The last time I'd seen my sister was way back before the new millennium, but my family were planning to visit me in October 2005. Their primary reason for coming was personally to deliver my second application for a royal pardon, to put it directly into the hands of the King's Principal Secretary at the Palace. Jai had already translated it into Royal Thai for me. Normally, after a pardon has been rejected, a prisoner must wait a minimum of two years before applying again. I had waited four years to submit a new application, my logic being that when the European Union countries had their citizens transferred back to prisons in their own countries, the Thai government would only accept a minimum of 14 years for that prisoner to be resentenced in his own country. This meant that, by the time my pardon would be considered, I would have served close to 14 years.

It was all about timing. I was confident that the second time around I would be lucky.

My niece Keri and nephew Darren would also be coming. I had not seen them for 11 years. My mom was advised not to come because it would be too traumatic for her. Whenever there was a contact visit coming up, prisoners would prepare themselves physically and mentally. It was not so much for myself that I did this, but more for my family. I felt it was important for their peace of mind if they knew, and could see, that I was strong and healthy. If I suffered, and I certainly did, I suffered in silence. My pain was not theirs to bear. Their own anguish was already deeply manifested, and my complaining would only compound it. Even so, I knew it was going to be hard to conceal my emotions. I loved my nephew like my own son, and my niece had been a mere toddler when I was arrested. I had only got to know Keri through our correspondence.

Two contact visits of one and a half hours each hardly constituted a family reunion, but it was all we had and we would have to make the most of it. There would be a million questions I wanted to ask, and I had no doubt they shared the same curiosity. Time restrictions always frustrated me. One minute you were sitting there and the next it was time to say goodbye. The system was cruel – inhuman, actually. My family would have had to cross oceans to be with me, and it was miserable to think that we would see each other for such a limited time. An ex-Arcadian and good friend by the name of Peter Hough, who lived between Canada and Australia, had provided financial help to make their visit possible and I was enormously grateful for his generosity. There were some amazing people out there, many of whom didn't even know me personally. They came from Australia, Canada, England, Israel and South Africa. Most of my old friends never bothered to send me so much as a letter. I think they had written me off for dead, believing that I would never make it out of prison alive. It is true what they say: 'In times of trouble real friends are precious and far in between.' I was attracting a whole new crowd of friends, wholesome and compassionate people who didn't judge but only wanted to help and to make my life as bearable as possible. Some did this unconditionally, while others who might have had some sort of expectation would ultimately be disappointed. However, this never diminished my gratitude; instead it opened my heart to others.

For days before the expected arrival of Joan, Malcolm and the kids, I was extremely anxious. I couldn't sleep a wink and my excitement was tangible. Our first meeting would be in the foreign visit room, with no physical contact but at least a chance to break the ice. I had prepared myself physically, but, when it comes to a man's emotions, you are only as strong as the moment dictates. Nothing can prepare you for what may unfold.

The day arrived and I made my way to the visit room, my heart beating rapidly and my palms sweating. And there they all were. Darren was so tall! And Keri, who would be celebrating her 16th birthday in Bangkok that weekend, had blossomed into a beautiful girl. She was the spitting image of her mother when Joan was young. My lower lip began to quiver and my throat went dry. Pull yourself together, I kept telling myself. I was a hero to my family – I had survived more than ten years in prison. Tears were forming in my eyes; the floodgates were ready to burst. Breathe in, breathe out, I willed myself. Breathe in, breathe out. I had a role to play and the cameras were rolling. Take 1. Action.

I smiled so hard I thought my face would crack, but my joy was real. I could not believe how much the kids had grown, which made the years I'd spent in prison suddenly seem a lot longer than ten. I fought the tears back, and we joked and laughed, while all the time a thousand questions were racing through my mind. All of them were lost in the moment. Ten years was an awful lot of time to catch up. As we talked and got to know each other, those years simply fell away. I was so impressed with the kids. They were intelligent, well mannered and, above all, loving and caring towards me.

Our first contact visit was deeply rewarding. The second and final visit was strained, however. Jai joined us for this visit. Until coming to Bangkok, my sister had never met Jai, although they had emailed each other and spoken over the phone. By now Joan loved her like a sister, and for everything she meant to me, but, when they finally met, Jai was not the woman Joan had imagined her to be. I wasn't sure whether it was something about Jai or whether it was just the cultural barrier, but, as much as she tried, Joan just couldn't warm to her. Jai sat next to me and we held hands. We were seven years into a relationship that still hadn't been consummated. Sadly, her hands were as cold as my heart was for her; I no longer felt anything for Jai except gratitude. We are told that everything happens for a reason, and she and I were not meant to be.

My family and I had agreed before our last visit that, when they departed, we would not shed tears but would rejoice in the joy of our reunion, knowing that it was only a matter of time before I would eventually be free. So once again we said our goodbyes.

On their last day in Thailand, they delivered my petition requesting a royal pardon to the Palace. Now all I could do was wait. I was at the mercy of the King.

Despite the high risk that went with them, mobile phones became big business in the prison, and this continued into 2006. The guards were still smuggling them in. When they caught one of us with a dog, they would simply resell it in another building. Prisoners were now communicating with each other by phone from one building to another, ordering drugs and mobiles. On a weekend, the Bad Boys would arrange to wait at a specific time at the wall dividing our building, with scouts placed at strategic positions just in case one of the guards decided to walk around. Then, seemingly out of nowhere, a package would come flying over the wall.

The price of mobiles and drugs fluctuated from building to building. Because security was far more lax in Building 3, for example, drugs were more freely available there. Prisoners were beating the system from every angle.

In another attempt to curb the problem, the prison authorities installed closed-circuit television to monitor inmates and watch for illegal activities, and certain cells were targeted, ours being one of them. The first day the closed-circuit system was operational, we had a pretty good idea that our friend Veesarnou would be monitoring our cell. The incident with Flea, I'm sure, was still fresh in his mind. We were bound to be the target of his revenge. At lockdown, when we entered the cell, every member of our room lined up, our backs facing the closed-circuit camera. We pulled our shorts to our knees and bent over, flashing our brown eyes at the camera. It was really funny. Even so, that night most of us were extremely uncomfortable with the idea that our every move was being watched by the guards. Two days later, one of the guys climbed up on the security door and turned the camera towards the ceiling. I don't know what we were thinking. As the room chief, the following morning I was summoned to the office and severely scolded by Veesarnou, who warned me that, if we so much as touched the camera again, he would send each and every one of us to another building.

Still, the guys in the room were not happy. Using the dog under these circumstances would be extremely dicey, so once again I drafted a petition complaining about the cameras being invasive. We all signed it, but, after giving it some thought, I decided not to hand it in. I believed it would only draw more attention to our room. So Big Brother won that round.

I developed a method of blocking myself out of the field of vision of the closed-circuit TV cameras. I would take a sarong, attach a string to it, and tie it to a nail in the wall. Then I tucked the sarong under my bed, which successfully cut me off from everybody's vision up to my chest. Whenever I used the dog to make a call, I would lie on my left side with my back to the corridor, the dog resting under my ear and against my pillow. I would pretend to be sleeping. When I was texting I held a book with my left hand and with my right I typed away. I kept emphasising the risk and reminding the other guys who had dogs to be careful, as our room was always being watched.

✹

The date of His Majesty the King's 60th anniversary on the throne was 9 June 2006, and so another amnesty was in sight. Once again, however, the Thai government proposed to exclude drug cases. I was so tired of them using us as an excuse to strengthen their own political ambitions that, this time around, I decided I was going to throw all I could muster against them. One thing I had learnt about the Thais: the more you ask for, the better your chances are of getting something – maybe not all that you ask for, but something. So, besides reminding them not to discriminate against drug cases, I would now also call for the abolition of the death penalty, knowing full well that they would never do this, but hoping that, while I wouldn't win on the death penalty, I might be luckier when it came to the inclusion of drug cases in the amnesty. History was repeating itself once more, even here in prison. I drew up the petition and had it distributed to every building – same scenario. The petition demanded three things: first, the abolition of the death penalty; second, a general reduction in sentences; and third, an end to the discrimination drug offenders faced from the Thai judiciary. The petition this time was for the attention of the Minister of Justice, General Chidchai Wanasathit.

In 2006 I met a new foreigner on death row. We first connected at the parcel area. He was in for murder, and although he claimed to be innocent, suspicious circumstances surrounded his story. He was accused of killing a Swiss businessman while having an affair with the man's Thai wife. We struck up an immediate friendship and would often bump into each other either collecting parcels or at the registered mail section. In the course of one of our conversations, he told me that he owned property in northern Thailand, but ran the risk of losing it. He asked me whether I knew a good lawyer who could help him. I didn't, but I offered to ask Jai to find him a lawyer. I didn't particularly want to act as a go-between, so I suggested that Jai visit him herself and then he could deal with her directly. After all, what are friends for? Jai had helped out many of my friends. To cut a long story short, Jai organised a lawyer and sorted out his property problem. She started visiting this guy regularly. I knew about these visits and I was quick to hear an opportunity knocking. It might sound diabolical, but I saw in this new friendship a chance to pawn Jai off. Jai and my new friend seemed to hit it off pretty well in any case.

One day after his visit with Jai, we met up at the usual place. He congratulated me on how well I'd 'trained' Jai; she was so efficient, reliable and trustworthy. I didn't suspect anything. I was genuinely happy that Jai was making a difference to his life. I trusted Jai and didn't think for a moment that she would leave me. I sat my new friend down and explained that, as fond as he was of Jai, he should remember that she was still my girlfriend. In the event that I might soon be going home, however, if he played his cards right, I said he could take Jai over from me. There was no way I was going to have a future with her, I said. And so we had a gentleman's agreement. He would respect the boundaries for now, but in the end it was up to him.

I had no idea that he and Jai were already communicating during the night. In the weeks that followed, I noticed a huge change in Jai. She was glowing, and almost every week she wore a new outfit. I myself was not in a good space at this time, and I couldn't quite put my finger on her newfound happiness. Then, during one of my visits with her, out of the corner of my eye I saw the death row guy approaching. I didn't acknowledge his presence, but I knew he was standing behind me. Jai's eyes moved hesitantly from me to him and back to me. Finally, I turned around and offered him the phone, asking him if he wanted to speak to Jai. He declined and Jai also brushed it off, saying she would see him the following day. I insisted that they speak to each other, but Jai refused. He had an embassy visit that was at the entrance to the visit room, and, when the visit ended, Jai left and so did I.

By now I definitely suspected something, so I went next door to the Thai visit room, from where I could get a full view of the foreign section. Clearly, Jai had only pretended to leave, because there she was, coming back to meet him. In an instant my blood pressure shot sky high. I went back to the foreign visit room and caught the lovebirds in the act, talking to each other on the phone. When they saw me, they both turned white. I grabbed the phone from my so-called friend and he disappeared very quickly.

'What the hell is going on?' I screamed at Jai. A heated argument erupted between us. Finally, Jai confessed that she and the death row guy had fallen in love. This was what I had wished for, and even planned for, so it should have been perfect. I *wanted* to get rid of Jai, but I didn't anticipate that it would happen so soon, and now that it was happening I broke down in tears. Jai cried, too.

Our relationship was over.

The bastard had told Jai what I'd said about him taking over from me when I eventually left prison. I wanted to kill him. Jai was terribly hurt, and she stormed out of the visit room. I discovered that I was devastated. Until that moment I hadn't fully realised just how emotionally dependent I had become on her. She was my best and closest friend. It was hard for me to come to terms with what had transpired. I couldn't cope with it. I wanted to take my life. I had been here before so many times; it was the same story, over and over, like the revival of an old movie. I struggled to pull myself together, but found myself slipping into a dark hole. What is it about human nature that in order to appreciate the value of something, we have to experience the loss of it first? I was a victim of my own heartlessness. Things got so bad that I had to see the prison psychologist, who prescribed a 50mg sleeping tablet. Sleep I got, but the tablet also put me into a semi-comatose state for days on end, so in fact it only made me feel worse.

Jai visited me on two more occasions, but only to clear up some financial matters. During these visits, concealed in my underpants, I carried a small knife, hoping that I would see my former friend. I wanted to cut his face so that every time he looked in the mirror he would remember me. The authorities became aware of the tension between us, and for his own protection he was given permission to have all his visits in a Thai visit room. When I saw Jai, I broke down. I still loved her, but it was too late. She had found somebody better than me. I simply had to accept that.

I found solace in my art, painting a series of colourful abstracts that helped me to understand and process the pain I felt. Time passed, but my emotional wounds would take much longer to heal.

Not too long down the road, I got a note via the underground prison postal delivery service, from one prisoner's hand to another. The note read: 'Shani, I wanted you to know Jai and I have decided to get married, I'm sorry.' They got married in a ceremony held in the foreign visit room, in the passage that divided the prisoners from the visitors. My initial pain when Jai left me, which had turned from sadness into anger, was beginning to ease. Now I tried to feel happiness for her. All those years when I had encouraged her to find another man, I did not expect that man to be another prisoner, and my friend at that.

Anyway, Jai's new husband's trial came up, and in the second court he was resentenced to 15 years – strange.

Still nursing a broken heart, I found myself becoming more and more dependent on alcohol. It relieved my pain. By then I had become quite the connoisseur and had gained a name for making an excellent wine. Yeast was still coming in from friends all over the world. One of these friends was Zelda, who lived in Dubai and regularly sent me parcels. I texted her on my dog, requesting a whole bunch of yeast. Some of the yeast came in tins; some was hidden in with tea bags. She'd also included a 500g container, which she'd emptied of its original contents, filled with yeast, and then resealed and packed with other foodstuffs and items. When I was called to collect the package, yeast was leaking out of the parcel. Watcherine lifted the box, looked at me questioningly and, in Thai, made some comment about me making wine, which was illegal.

'Pom mai loo,' (I don't know) I answered blankly.

He cut the box open and there was yeast everywhere. He became so preoccupied with dusting off every particle from the other items he handed to me that he failed to detect the hidden yeast. He was clearly annoyed, but, because I'd been in Bangkwang so long, he let it go. I had a good laugh with the guys when I shared my story.

For the next year I made wine every weekend. After playing football on Saturdays and Sundays I would pour the wine into empty plastic water bottles. One cup was strong enough to make you tipsy. As the day progressed, while the music blared, I had friends in and out of my house, coming by for a drink. At lunchtime we would have a braai (barbecue). We would use one of the portable clay stoves you could purchase from the coffee shop. Prisoners who didn't have electric frying pans made use of these stoves. The coffee shop also stocked charcoal.

Eventually, I was drinking even during the week, busy drowning my sorrows. I was letting myself go. My break-up with Jai had made me weak. Twelve years into my imprisonment and I had found a new vice. Was there a difference, drugs being one thing, and alcohol another? Surely my prolonged incarceration, in the light of so many other foreigners going home, justified my drinking? I knew I could never go back to drugs, but was what I was doing now any different?

I was struggling to come to terms with my predicament. I understood that I was not ready to be part of the free world yet, but I longed for nothing else. I was bored with the mundanities of prison life; the same routine every day was suffocating me. I needed to spread my wings. Alcohol dulled the pain and gave me a false sense of confidence. The only problem was, when I woke up the next morning, besides having a heavy head, my reality was no different. In fact, it depressed me even more. There was no getting away from it: they say once an addict, always an addict. I was disappointed in myself. My emotions were playing havoc with my mind. Whether it was to celebrate or to numb the pain, I had so many excuses to justify my drinking. It was far easier to escape than to face my problems. So often in life we become our own worst enemy. I knew this, so what was wrong with me? I had come such a long way and now I had fallen. Love can either make a man or it can break him, that's for sure.

There was a stage where I would have more than 24 litres of wine brewing on a given day. One day I got this idea to bottle some for Shabbos: keep it for a month or two and it would be like drinking a vintage, I thought. Using bottles that I purchased from the coffee shop, I cleaned them out and filled them with wine that I'd made from grape juice. Then I stuck them in the back of the locker where I kept a supply of tinned food, among other things. Two days later, when we were let out of our cells in the morning, as I rounded the corner before my house I detected a strong smell of wine. I stepped up my pace. When I entered the house I saw immediately that wine had leaked out of the locker and had dribbled all over the floor. The pressure in the bottles had caused them to explode. Fortunately, the guards were too lazy to walk around at night; a search might have led to unnecessary attention.

Sometimes I would begin drinking early in the morning, which led to occasions where I got into a physical altercation with another prisoner. Alcohol clouds your judgement, and after a few drinks I would get very aggressive.

One day I attacked my Chinese neighbour, Lim, the man who had been my cook for ten years. I was in the wrong. Every time we drank, I would turn my music up. I didn't realise that the volume was driving poor Lim mad. Music was my thing; it not only opened my mind but it also stimulated my creativity. To be honest, I never considered my neighbours. I just presumed that they also enjoyed some rock'n'roll. On this particular day, Lim gave me a dirty look that triggered something inside me. There was this anger festering deep within me waiting to surface and, when it did, it was ugly to the point of being scary. I could kill; I felt it inside me. The anger was like a cancer. Was I losing my mind and becoming a psychopath? Self-rehabilitation in a jungle of criminals was not easy, and I was failing badly.

Although I continued to produce some amazing pieces of art, the drinking started to affect my mind. I became lazy and eventually stopped painting. For some reason, whether lack of exercise or the excessive drinking, the joints in my ankles could hardly bend. I had the most excruciating pain, and there were days when I struggled to walk. After having a blood test, which was sent to an outside laboratory, I was told that because of a build-up of uric acid in my blood, crystals had formed around my joints. I had developed gout. It was crazy to think that in prison one could become an alcoholic, but it looked like that was the way I was going. I needed to evaluate the situation. Nothing was more important than my health. The only way I could stop drinking was to stop making wine.

I managed to obtain a homeopathic remedy from home called *Urtica urens* (stinging nettle), which I took three times a day. Within three weeks the pain in my joints had subsided and I got my life back on track. It seemed that, no matter where I was, there was only one way I was going to learn life's lessons: the hard way. It was the story of my life.

On the occasion of the 60th anniversary of the King's accession to the throne, we were granted the amnesty. The death penalty, however, was not abolished.

Chapter 16

Touched By Angels

From the table where I sat and worked every morning, I had a view of the Chinese houses. About 10m away was the communal toilet. Lost in thought one day, I was sitting there staring into space, not really concentrating on anything. The toilet had one occupant at the time, a Thai prisoner who was new in our building. He had spent time in solitary confinement for stabbing another prisoner and he still had his shackles on. I was not paying attention when another Thai came up from behind him and, with a meat cleaver, delivered two swift blows to his shoulder, almost taking off his arm. I believe it was a retaliation attack ordered from another building. Revenge stabbings were common. Every few months we heard about a murder in one of the other buildings. The Thais were dangerous, and one had to be careful. The mere fact of being a *farang* gave you some degree of respect, so generally Thais didn't interfere with us foreigners. And if you stayed clear of the underhand dealings that went on all the time, you were reasonably safe. However, if you disrespected one of them, it wouldn't be long before every single Thai in the building would know that you were bad-mannered, and from then on you would have difficulty getting anything done. One could never become complacent.

The year 2007, my 13th in prison, was a tough one for me. After losing Jai, I really struggled to get through my days. I promised myself that I would never become emotionally dependent on anybody again. I found myself living more and more in my head.

Often with the intake of new prisoners came new trends. An Estonian prisoner who had been on death row for seven years had his sentence commuted to life in third court, and was transferred to Building 2. He and Shlomo became good friends. The Estonian was a bodybuilding enthusiast and weighed almost 100kg. At 1.8m tall, he towered over me. He had some interesting ideas on muscle building and would do certain routines on the weights. At the time I weighed about 80kg and it made sense to me to build muscle. Having got bored with playing football and my daily walking programme, I embarked on a vigorous gymming course. I started drinking protein shakes and eating three meals a day. Soon I had lifted my weight to 90kg. I was working out five days a week and had developed really nice arms; I thought I was in great shape.

For the enterprising prisoner, art was a means of making money. There were several talented Thai artists in Bangkwang who painted portraits for a fee. Whenever I was asked by an inmate to do somebody's portrait, I would name a ridiculous price, firstly, because I never had the time, and, secondly, because frankly I couldn't be bothered. Early into my incarceration I did paint a few pictures for some of my closest friends in jail, but after a while I stopped. Every building had guys who were artists or interested in art, but I gained the reputation of being the Number 1 Portrait Artist in Bangkwang.

That year, the prison introduced a programme called 'Art for All'. Rather than being part of the rehabilitation process of prisoners, it was yet another scheme devised only to benefit the prison. The prison supplied all the art equipment, but there was a condition: anything you painted belonged to the prison. Art pieces would be exhibited outside and the proceeds would go to expanding the programme. The rest, needless to say, would go into the pockets of the prison authorities.

In Building 2, the bakery was converted into a studio for the prisoners. Drinking in Building 2 had become a serious problem, and the authorities suspected that the bakery commodore was selling yeast to the prisoners. So they closed the bakery and transferred the supervisor, who was a prisoner, to another prison. I thought it was really funny because they were so off course: it was me who was bringing the yeast in, and had been for a while. Ironic, really, when you think about it – with all the shit the bakery guard used to give us, we screwed him, even if it was indirectly. What can I say? Karma is a bitch.

Once a week an art teacher from outside would come and give basic art lessons to any prisoner who wanted to learn. All the prison artists knew each other already, and we were friends. Whenever one of us needed supplies, we would help each other out. I taught many of my fellow inmates the finer points of using carbon powder. Usually, when we wanted to send our paintings out with our visitors, all we had to do was make a request. This would be signed by the Building Chief and his subordinate in charge of foreigners – a simple procedure.

I had painted several nudes for one of my correspondents, who owned the Lisa King Gallery in Cape Town. She was keen to assist me and wanted to show my work to another gallery she thought could be interested in representing me. So I wrote the usual request and handed it to my friend who worked in the office, who translated it into Thai. Not much later, I was called to the office and informed by the new Building Chief that I could no longer send my paintings out and that they were now the property of the prison. This was the same arsehole who had chopped down every tree around Building 2, including the two beautiful ones beside death row that had offered shade to the prisoners. I don't think he realised who he was fucking with, but first I tried to reason with him, explaining that I had nothing to do with the Art for All programme, and that in fact I personally supplied a lot of the students with paper and other items. He remained steadfast and refused me permission.

I had visitors arriving from South Africa in two days' time to whom I was planning to give some of my pieces to take back home for me. I immediately drafted a petition on behalf of all the artists and threatened the prison authorities that we would inform every embassy in Bangkok about their proposed policy to steal our paintings. All the artists signed the petition. I submitted it and waited, knowing that I would have rattled the Building Chief's cage. I had barely walked away when my name was called over the loudspeaker. I strolled back slowly. I was ushered into the chief's office, whose whole demeanour had changed. Without wasting any time, he offered me a deal. He would give me, but only me, permission to send out my art, he told me, on condition that I withdrew the petition. I don't know what he was thinking, but there was no way I was going to do that. Just on principle I wouldn't do it. I wasn't about to sell out my mates. So I told him it was all or nothing. I gave you a chance this morning, motherfucker, I thought to myself. Now you will suffer the consequences.

So the petition was sent out to the Director. At midday I was once again summoned to the office. All the other artists had gathered around, waiting for me, and from the expression on their faces I could see that we had won. I was really happy, as I knew that a lot of these guys had no support from outside and the only way they could survive was by the portraits they painted and sold to other prisoners.

There were rumours that the Thai government's deeply controversial 'War on Drugs' programme, which had led to the deaths of more than 2 500 people allegedly involved in the trade, was set to be relaunched by the new government led by Samak Sundaravej, which had come to power in early 2008. According to foreign news reports, during a three-month period in 2003, thousands of Thais on police blacklists had been shot, allegedly on government orders. Some of those killed apparently had no involvement in drugs, according to the government's Narcotics Control Board. The government had not set a target for the new anti-drug campaign, though the Minister of the Interior, Chalerm Yubamrung, had been reported as suggesting a tough line similar to the previous 'war' might be taken.

Early in 2009 there was a raid by the army, police and Department of Corrections. We had been warned to hand in all our electrical equipment a week before, so I took my dog and hid it in the lid of the water boiler. Then I packed all my other things in a cardboard box and tied it up with string. The authorities locked our stuff in the *soy* rooms next to the gym. After three days, the Building Chief informed us that all the equipment we had handed in was going to be moved to a safer location outside Building 2. I immediately became suspicious and assumed that our electrical equipment wasn't going to be returned to us, so I insisted on taking everything back, as did some of the other prisoners. Two days later, soon after lockdown, they raided us. There were more than 100 commodores. They came armed with steel bolt-cutters, broke all the locks on our lockers and proceeded to do their checks.

From my cell I could see them in the Nigerian house. They ransacked everything. They then moved on to my house, broke open all the locks and proceeded to do a thorough search. My dog was hidden in the same locker where I kept my DVD machine and I was as nervous as hell. There were at least six guards searching my house. Besides all the electronics I had, there were also two plastic protein powder containers filled with wine that was still brewing. I didn't mind losing the electronics; it was my dog I really didn't want to lose. After a while, I got so nervous I couldn't bear to watch any longer. I expected the worst, but hoped for the best. As always in times of trouble, I needed help from the powers above. I prayed to G-d and asked Him to close their eyes to where the dog was hidden. The anxiety was contagious and nobody really slept that night.

The following morning, when I got to my house, it looked like a bomb had gone off in it. Everything was strewn all over the place, even the foodstuffs. My hi-fi and speakers, blender, toaster, sandwich maker, DVD player and every single DVD I had collected was gone. Luckily, my iPod, which had been given to me by a good friend and correspondent, Adi Fredman, which was in the top drawer of my desk, hadn't been found.

My heart was beating rapidly. If they had found my dog, I would be moved to solitary confinement immediately. Making sure nobody was watching me – everybody in the other houses was preoccupied with sorting out their own stuff – I checked to see if the dog was in its kennel. When I felt with my hands that it was there, I cannot describe my excitement. I breathed a sigh of relief. Once again, I had outwitted the authority.

My house was a mess. The bastards had taken one of my backgammon sets, stolen 2 000 Thai baht worth of stamps and 10 000 baht in cash that I had hidden in a book. They also took my books on semi-nude photography. One thing that surprised me was that, although they had obviously detected the wine – one of the containers had been opened – they hadn't thrown it away. This was prison, nothing was sure; your situation could change from one moment to the next. There was nothing you could do. At least I still had my dog; that was all that mattered. My guardian angels were still keeping an eye on me.

We had to do something, however. I discussed various courses of action with the other foreigners, emphasising that the first thing we should all do was complain to our embassies. It wasn't that I was hopeful we would get anything back, but it might deter future raids. Later that morning one of the Blue Shirts came to me. Apparently, one of the guards who had raided the previous night was head of security, and he had been on duty in our building after the raid. He had told the Blue Shirt: '*Aleksander tam lao dee*' (Alexander makes good wine).

The South African consular staff, when they heard what had transpired, were supportive and wrote a letter to the Department of Corrections asking what had happened to my personal belongings. The Department of Corrections always preferred not to have any negative publicity or to get on the wrong side of the embassy. The official response was unequivocal: I had been found to be in possession of illegal items, and under no circumstances would these be returned. This didn't surprise me. It was the response I had expected. Many prisoners had lost their things. And everybody knew that when you bought an electronic gadget, it was a gamble as to how long you would enjoy the privilege of using it.

Over the years, the Cripple had become an integral person in the lives of many of us inmates. He had spent the past 14 years gambling his life away on just about everything, from backgammon to football to death row executions. You name it, he would put his money on it. The Cripple slept in front of our cell. Whenever he was up on his winnings, he became irritably loud and arrogant; when he lost and was down and out, you never heard a squeak out of him. Money in prison meant power. Most of the Asians had a similar mentality. You would know exactly when a person's money had arrived from home by their tone of voice. One warm April afternoon in 2008, soon after we were locked in our cells, the Cripple buckled over and had a heart attack. Fortunately, the key-boy managed to alert a passing guard and the Cripple was loaded onto the wheelchair and rushed to the hospital. For a few days we didn't hear anything and, to tell the truth, I kind of forgot about him. Then, after about a week, I asked one of the Chinese if they had any news; I thought maybe the Cripple had died. I was told that he was now paralysed down his left side but that, by some extraordinary miracle, he had regained mobility in his legs. The Cripple was now hopping around on crutches!

The motherfucker, I thought to myself. He had been faking his paralysis for 14 years! On the one hand, you had to admire the man. I was sure he was gambling on the possibility of being granted a medical royal pardon. On the other hand, more dangerously, he was gambling with fate. A true gambler to the end. At least he was alive. I decided to go and visit my old rival, so I filed a request saying I had an ear infection and needed to see the doctor. When I reached the ward, the Cripple spotted me before I saw him. Excitedly, he pulled himself up with one arm and waved me over. In a half-stutter he called, 'Alec! Alec!' Next to his bed was a single crutch. As I reached him he said to me in broken Thai, '*Do, do, pom dun dai*' (Look, look, I can walk). Then he hopped off his bed, grabbed his crutch with one hand, the other arm dangling lifelessly against his body, and hopped along the ward. It reminded me of when I had a broken leg and my friends called me 'Hopalong Cassidy'. I smiled at the Cripple and, pointing my finger at him, said '*Kun zig zag*,' which was Thai slang for being deceitful. He pretended not to hear me. I then added, '*Kun keng muck*' (You are very strong).

But the Cripple would never be the same again. He now had a speech impediment and had lost about 60 per cent movement on his left side. His tenacity was impressive, though. When he returned to the building, hopping around on one leg with the aid of his crutch, he was determined to regain his strength.

One day in early August 2008, after eating almost a whole kilo of buffalo, rice, potatoes and broccoli topped with cheese sauce for lunch, I was relaxing on my deckchair, as I usually did after lunch, when suddenly I got this severe pain in my chest. It went shooting right through to my back. At first I thought maybe it was indigestion, so I struggled to get to the toilet. Nothing happened. The pain got worse, and then I collapsed in my house. Shlomo happened to come by to visit me and saw me sprawled out, pale and in pain. I told Shlomo that I thought I was having a heart attack, so he ran to the office to inform the authorities. They were reasonably quick to react. With the help of my Nigerian brothers, I was loaded into a wheelchair and shipped off to the hospital. It seemed like we crossed oceans to get there. I can't really say what was going through my mind. I had heard that when people are close to death their whole lives flash before them, but all I could think of was that prison was not the place where I wanted to die. Did we ever get to choose? Surely this couldn't be *Hashem*'s plan for me? What about my poor mother, whom I hadn't seen since before my arrest; she lived for the day that I would be free. My death in here would surely kill her.

When we reached the hospital, I was taken to one of the rooms that was used as a theatre. While I was lying there, one of the nurses came to ask me what the problem was. The pain was really bad; I honestly thought I was going to die. At that moment, I thought of my family and tears began to run down my cheeks. I was thinking how hard it would be for them to accept my passing. '*Mai tong wrong hai*' (Don't cry), the nurse told me. She seemed sympathetic, even understanding in the way she looked at me, but I don't think she could relate to what was going through my mind. I began to recite the *Shema Yisrael*, begging *Hashem* that I was not ready to die, not here, not in prison and not now. There was still so much I wanted to do and to see, so many dreams to fulfil.

An electrocardiogram was conducted and the doctor made a diagnosis of atrial fibrillation, a common form of cardiac arrhythmia. I was admitted to the hospital and put on a drug called atenolol, which slows down the heart. I was given a bed close to where the medics cooked their meals. Prison hospital was a depressing place. Nobody really cared about you. Even the doctors were prisoners; I knew for a fact that two of them had murdered their wives. Imagine being treated by a killer. Could they have any empathy at all, I wondered. It was something I couldn't quite come to grips with: from saving lives to taking a life. How did that work? And now my life was in these doctors' hands.

I was told I would have to stay in hospital for at least ten days so that they could monitor my condition. The atenolol had dropped my pulse to 16 beats per minute; I was also given aspirin to thin the blood. The one doctor explained how it came about that I had an irregular heartbeat, and he pointed out that the chance of my having a stroke was very high unless I changed my eating habits. He suggested I cut out all oily foods, coffee, meat and anything fatty, and bring down my cholesterol level. That night I couldn't sleep, not only because I couldn't remember when last I had slept in a bed, but also because something happens to a man when he has a near-death experience.

The medics who worked in the hospital cooked for themselves, while the patients who didn't have money had to eat the prison food. The smell of food, as well as being surrounded by so many sick people, some of them on their last legs, was very depressing. Prisoners were dying here; the death rate in prison hospitals was high. I decided I couldn't stay there another day. I needed to get back to the building. So I told one of the orderlies that I wanted to see the doctor, who agreed to discharge me the following day.

Behind the main reception area of the hospital were two fishponds the size of tennis courts and a beautiful lush green garden with banana trees. I was starving. Situated near the back was a flat-roofed building that housed the second chief's office and a small coffee shop that handled the food ordered for the hospital workers and prepared meals for the guards. One of my mates, a foreigner who worked at the hospital in the pharmacy section, arranged a meal for me. For the rest of the day, I paced up and down a path between the two fishponds. I felt myself beginning to relax. Just being out in the fresh air in the garden reminded me of home.

The next morning, I returned to the building. I immediately changed my diet and from then on ate only steamed vegetables and salads. In fact, I started a salad club. There were four of us. One person ordered either a kilo of tomatoes, carrots, green peppers or long beans every third day; the rest – lettuce, cucumber, baby corn, etc. – I provided. This enabled each member to have a healthy-sized plastic bag of salad every day for three days of the week. I would prepare up to ten packets a day and give the balance to my friends. The rest I would keep in two of my coolers, in which I kept two bricks of ice. My weight dropped from 90 to 73kg within a month. I stopped gymming completely and instead jogged five days a week. I also went back to playing football. And I stopped drinking alcohol.

At the end of August, after attending the Beijing Olympics, my long-time friend Penelope, along with her new boyfriend Ivan, popped in for a visit. Penelope had been sending me parcels every year for my birthday since my arrest. Ivan and I had an instant connection, and it was great to see Penelope again. They stayed a couple of days in Bangkok and visited me every day, buying me a fortune in healthy foods, such as almonds, raisins, prunes and healthy crackers. They could not have come at a better time. They also deposited a substantial amount of money in my prison account. It gave me such a big lift. It was wonderful to know that there were people who genuinely cared. When they left, Ivan vowed that he was going to make it his life's mission to try and secure my release. He also promised me that if there was anything I needed, he would take care of it.

Before Ivan and Penelope's visit, I had heard that a friend of mine from school, who lived in the US, had met with certain Israeli politicians to find out whether there was any possibility of my being granted Israeli citizenship. Apparently, a former head girl from King David, who had been my contemporary, had also attended the talks. I was constantly amazed; the world was such a small place. I had friends all over. Sadly, the Israelis wouldn't budge. There was no way they would agree to giving a foreign prisoner citizenship.

Since Jai had left me, I hardly had any visits, which in fact I didn't mind. However, occasionally there were people who came from abroad to see me. One such instance was that of the Fishers, an Australian couple and their daughter. They had read my stories in the Arcadia book, and, while they were travelling in Thailand, decided to come and meet me. They were very nice and compassionate towards my circumstances. I think people generally are fascinated by prisoners and the whole concept of prison. And they were especially intrigued by the fact that I was Jewish, as not many Jews were serving life sentences in prisons.

Louise, the wife, and I started communicating by letter and, later, on Facebook. She told me that she had a heart condition, and had had a pacemaker inserted, and still managed to lead a relatively normal life. I was inspired by her. Everybody has a story, and so often, when we get to hear the difficulties others face, it gives us a different perspective on our own lives. Prison may have been tough, but people on the outside faced their own challenges.

People kept surfacing from all over. Another one was Sandra from Canada, who happened to be the daughter of the *Chazan* (Cantor) who during my childhood took the service at Arcadia on the High Holy Festivals. Sandra and I became very close, and she would do almost anything for me. I was blessed in so many ways. All these people had one common goal: to do everything they could to make my life as easy as possible in prison. And they achieved it. For me, it was not so much about the material things they sent; it was more about knowing that people cared – we Jews took care of each other. When it came to the people outside, I was still living a lie, however. I wondered whether, if they knew I was guilty of the crimes I was accused of, they would still be as understanding and considerate towards me. I so wanted them to know the truth, that I was guilty, that I had known about the heroin I was smuggling out of Thailand, but I couldn't say anything. It was not the right time.

Around this time I was also privileged to be introduced to a group of British women who lived in Bangkok and who had undertaken to visit British prisoners. Among them were Bev Bolton, Yvonne Ziegler (who was in fact Australian) and Gale Isobel Bailey. Bev used to visit a young British prisoner who had been arrested at the age of 21. Hearing that I had no regular visits, Bev also came to see me whenever she had the time, and we became good friends. After the death of her husband, Bev returned to England, but we maintained our friendship through correspondence. She wrote the most beautiful and inspiring letters.

Yvonne, who used to work for the Australian consulate, was asked by Louise Fisher to visit me on my birthday and to bring me a chocolate cake – what a nice surprise that was! Birthdays, as I've mentioned before, were a depressing time for most of us prisoners. When I saw Yvonne with a cake, bringing wishes from my family and my friend Louise, I became quite tearful. These women were simply amazing. At their own expense and in their own time, they had taken it upon themselves to help out prisoners, emailing, messaging their families and helping with money transfers. Whenever there was a birthday, they would bring cakes, wear party hats and sing 'Happy Birthday' in the visit room. I could only admire them. I don't think they quite understood the happiness they brought, or the difference they made to us.

On one such occasion, a friend of the British women, also an Australian, whose half-brother had done time in Klong Prem, was in Thailand to celebrate her birthday. They all met at Yvonne's apartment for the occasion. With them was a Swiss lady by the name of Elisabeth, who apparently had also been visiting prisoners for some years and was at that time coincidentally visiting one of the South Africans in the women's prison. Before going out for lunch, they planned first to come to Bangkwang. Knowing that I had hardly any visits, Yvonne and Gayle suggested that Elisabeth visit me while they saw the British prisoners, to which Elisabeth reluctantly agreed. What was the point, she argued, of a one-off visit? Anyway, she came to see me. Apparently, she already knew who I was and had seen some of my artwork. When I arrived at the visit room, I had no idea who it was that was looking for me. Elisabeth was seated near the front, her back turned to me. There were quite a few visitors waiting for prisoners by then. I walked past her and down the entire length of the visit room without recognising anybody. At the end of the visit room were two senior ladies. I waved to them enquiringly and pointed my finger at myself. Puzzled, they shook their heads. Obviously, there had been a mistake so I decided to head back to the building.

Then, as I approached the last group of visitors, I saw this very pretty woman smile at me. I picked up the phone and she followed suit.

'Hi,' I said.

'Hello,' she answered in a beautiful Swiss accent.

'Are you here for me?' I asked.

'Yes,' she replied. Then she went on to explain how it had come about that she'd come to visit me.

I don't know what it was, but this woman made such an impact on me that, after the visit, I couldn't think of anything else but her. That night, using my dog, I contacted another South African woman, Anke, who had visited me several times soon after my heart condition was diagnosed. Anke also lived in Bangkok and was seeing some of the ladies in the women's prison. I asked her for Elisabeth's phone number. After plucking up the courage, I phoned her. In the interim, unbeknown to me, Elisabeth had emailed my sister and told Joan about her visit to me that day, and also about the impact I had made on her. At first, she was somewhat shocked by my call and not all that impressed that Anke had given me her number without consulting her first.

Our conversation was slightly strained. I think both of us were hesitant to admit that there had been an immediate connection, but, for both of us, it was love at first sight. I'm not sure whether it was because of my situation and my vulnerability, but I had this ability to connect with people on a deep level. Whether this was a blessing or a curse, I'm not sure, but in this instance I considered it a blessing. People seemed to come into my life when I most needed them.

Elisabeth was married, but separated from her husband. She was different from anyone I'd ever met and I fell instantly in love. She gave all of herself unconditionally. From then on, she started visiting me every week and she also took control of my finances. She not only became my girlfriend, but she also became my best friend, too. Having been with Jai and never having been able to be physical with her, I anticipated that, with time, my relationship with Elisabeth would also become complicated. What I hoped for was that I might be released and at least get the opportunity to see whether we'd be compatible under different circumstances.

Meanwhile, Ivan stayed true to his word. In early 2009 he hired a so-called top lawyer in Israel to investigate the possibility of Israeli citizenship for me. I was told that this lawyer had made great progress, but now required a personal letter from me to the President of Israel, giving him a bit of background on my situation and explaining why I wanted to become an Israeli citizen. I had been down this road before, but nevertheless I wrote to the president, Shimon Peres. I went right back to the beginning, to my mother's family in Hungary and their persecution by the Nazis. I told the president how my parents had managed to flee Hungary. I told him that circumstances had prescribed that I be brought up in a Jewish orphanage, and how, as a young boy and man, I had embraced my Jewish heritage, how important this was to me and how it informed my life:

> ... *My reason for contacting your office is primarily to appeal to your government to grant me Israeli citizenship. As a young man I dreamt of making* aliyah, *unfortunately the unkind vicissitudes of my fortunes prevented me from making this journey. Besides being abandoned by my own Government, I have for many years had an overwhelming desire to return to my religious roots, to learn Torah and to start a new life in Eretz Israel.*
>
> *During my incarceration I have upheld our traditions and not given up practising Judaism. I daven three times a day and observe Shabbat to the best of my ability and within the limitations of my environment ...*

I sent it off and hoped that Ivan's lawyer knew what he was doing. It was almost 15 years since I'd been stopped from boarding that plane back to South Africa, and here I was, still hoping, still trying, still seizing every opportunity that came my way to get out of Bangkwang. And back in South Africa my sister Joan continued to do her part, although she had been banging her head against a wall for so long it was a wonder she still had the strength to persevere. We were getting nowhere with the South African government, so perhaps Ivan could pull something off. I wasn't about to jump up and down with joy or excitement just yet, though. The Israelis were a stubborn bunch and they had already rejected me. In my view, every Jew had the right to live in Israel.

I'd reached a point where helping new prisoners had become more of a headache than anything else. Those of us who had done hard time were set in our ways now. I became withdrawn and generally kept to myself, minding my own business and trying my best to get through my day. My clock had stopped ticking. Time was killing me. South Africa was nowhere near even considering a prisoner transfer treaty. By then I had become the longest-serving Western foreigner in Bangkwang prison. Even the guards were baffled as to why I was still there, thinking that I must be some big Mafia boss. I accepted that depression was something I would have to deal with on a regular basis, but survival was a priority. I had a story to tell and my audience was out there somewhere.

Sometimes someone would ask me, '*Aleksanda, young mai karbarn?*' (Yet not gone home?), to which I would jokingly respond by saying that Bangkwang was my home. But at the same time I would feel a deep sadness. It is difficult to describe the depth of my longing after 15 years locked up in a foreign country. It took all the courage I had to stay positive and believe that my prolonged imprisonment was for my ultimate good.

Daily life did not change. During the week, we would receive letters and parcels, fights would erupt, stabbings occurred, and the occasional murder was committed. Directors, Building Chiefs and guards were constantly being reshuffled. Alterations to the buildings were carried out from time to time – the walls of Building 2 had been painted for the third time, which of course we prisoners paid for – occasionally royal pardons were granted, sentences were reduced, Thai prisoners were paroled, and foreigners were transferred home. The FIFA World Cup, to be played in South Africa in 2010, was fast approaching.

There was already talk from the commodores that on 5 December 2011, when the King celebrated his 84th birthday, there would be a general amnesty. Giving prisoners amnesties was considered a way of attracting good karma; His Majesty was a benevolent and kind monarch, and many prisoners had benefited from this over the years. When you consider the hardships we had to endure daily in prison, two years was still a long time to wait, so I tried to put December 2011 out of my mind.

M

The Thai New Year, Songkran (the Water Festival), which fell on 12 April every year, had become an annual drinking festivity. There is a very festive vibe in Bangkok at this time, with thousands of people, most of them armed with water pistols, hitting the streets and running round wetting and squirting everybody in sight. In prison, the Thai prisoners and the guards upheld the tradition, and they would walk around the building grabbing prisoners and throwing them into the fishpond. This would go on throughout the day.

Thais would eat in groups, sometimes up to ten or more. Everybody contributed to meals. Huddled around on the floor with numerous dishes of food, these were occasions when prisoners could enjoy a moment of true companionship. Eating was a time of sharing, a time to bond and to lose yourself in conversation – a time to forget you're a prisoner.

Songkran was always a significant milestone for me, as it had been the time of year I had come to Thailand, and April was the month I had been arrested. By April 2010, I had served 15 years in prison. After benefiting from several amnesties, my sentence had come down to 24 years, with nine still to go. I didn't know quite how I had survived 15 years. These days, when I prayed, I reminded *Hashem* that I was strong and would be able to resist temptation in all its forms. I was ready for my freedom.

At the beginning of the year my friend Edna in Manchester had sent me a photo of a Chassidic rabbi she wanted me to paint, but for some reason I just hadn't got round to doing it. Somehow, whenever I was commissioned to do a painting, I don't know why, perhaps because of the pressure of having to do something to order, my creativity would desert me. After ten months, I'd only just finished sketching the rabbi's picture. In between, I'd managed to do a few paintings in hard charcoal, nothing too exciting. For the past months, to be honest, I hadn't been in a good space, and the truth was I didn't care if I died. My lack of enthusiasm could be seen in some of my abstract paintings. I had been doing abstracts for some years by then; art for me was also about having fun, and I used these as a means of stretching my mind and embracing my imagination.

Despite davening three times a day and reminding *Hashem* that I believed I was strong enough now to embrace my freedom, and to fulfil my dreams and His purpose for me, I'd largely lost my connection to the Man above. My prayers were becoming routine and I was praying more out of a sense of obligation than anything else. It was hard not to lose hope, hard not to be negative. If it hadn't been for my dog, man's best friend in prison, I reckon I would have gone out of my mind.

From my correspondence, and from friends I'd been in touch with on my dog, I had heard about a website called Facebook. Apparently, this was a cyber-social network for people to interact with each other or to reconnect with friends around the world. I could access this site from my dog. One of the other foreigners had set up his own website, which he used as a platform to inform people about his predicament. The site gave his postal address, and this had allowed many friends he'd lost touch with over the years to contact him.

I realised that I had missed out on so much over the years, but now, being a dog handler myself, I wanted very much to be part of this new technology. After enquiring from my sister about the possibility of having my own Facebook page, she decided to create an open group, which she called 'Shani Krebs – Captivated Artist'. The main function was to keep people updated on my situation, in the hope that some of my friends would write to me or make contact. In the beginning, one or two popped up here and there, but over time more and more people joined the group.

Later, I set up my own Facebook account, using the pseudonym 'Zor Krebsowitz'. The reason for a pseudonym was that Chavoret, the guard in charge of foreigners, and who was also the executioner, had his own Facebook page and I couldn't risk exposure. For my profile picture, I used a photo of the masked Zorro on his horse, rapier drawn. Facebook was an amazing resource. I reconnected with friends I had forgotten existed, and also made new friends, most of them women. The only problem was that my Nokia took ages to open and post messages. I would stay up late at night and into the early hours of the morning surfing the net.

Then calamity struck. The defective signal blockers were replaced with a new computerised system. The new system didn't block the signal; instead it could pinpoint the exact location and room from where a dog was being barked. Within a few weeks of the system being operational, we had a reprieve, but not from the prison authorities: one of the Big Legs on death row organised for his boy to cut the cable. There was so much wiring, it would take months before the authorities could locate the break. Prisoners are of necessity resourceful people.

Despite all the crackdowns and restrictions, the drug problem in Thailand had reached uncontrollable proportions. There were regular scenes on TV where some raving lunatic had taken a hostage, usually a woman, and was wielding a knife and threatening to take the victim's life. The TV reporter on hand would keep mentioning the words '*yah septic*' (drugs), so you knew that the perpetrator was on drugs. This kind of constant publicity reinforced the Thai government's hard line on drugs and their policy of not granting amnesty to drug offenders in prison. This was further compounded by the fact that there were Thai prisoners who had served full life sentences but who, after regaining their freedom, would soon resort to criminal activities and be rearrested. Some had even been back to prison for the third time.

It was crazy. I vowed that, once I regained my own freedom, I would never see prison walls again.

At the suggestion of one of the ladies who was a regular visitor to the prison, Elisabeth and a friend decided to go to the hospital where the King was being treated for a prolonged illness. Daily prayers were said there and gifts were presented to the monarch. On occasion, when the King felt strong enough, he would come outside and greet the many well-wishers. Most of his visitors were Thais, so whenever foreigners came to the hospital, they were thought to be important dignitaries. When Elisabeth and her companion arrived, they attracted a certain amount of attention, including that of the Grand Chamberlain (aka the right arm of the King), who worked in the Bureau of the Royal Household and had remained loyal to the King for 60 years. He was fluent in both French and English and had lived in Lausanne, the city where Elisabeth grew up.

That night, when barking the dog, Elisabeth excitedly told me what had transpired. She came up with the idea of a gift I could give the King. I could make up a folder in which we would put photographs of the portrait I had painted of the King and include some of my other pieces of art. We also chose a prayer from the Book of Psalms and I wrote a personal message to the King wishing him a speedy recovery. Seeing that Elisabeth had a special relationship with one of the South African woman prisoners, whom she had been visiting for some years, we included her, too.

The following week, Elisabeth and her friend went to the hospital again, this time to hand over our gift to the King. On their arrival, they were taken to a special section where only diplomats were allowed to make presentations to the King. The two women were swamped by journalists, and a television crew who happened to be there filmed and interviewed them. The folder was beautifully made up, and everyone who saw it was very impressed. The gift was recorded in a ledger and one of the officials of the Palace assured Elisabeth that he would personally hand it to the King. Besides my family, I never told any of my friends in prison of this breakthrough, believing that it might jinx any chance of something positive happening for me as a result. In my eyes, this was the closest we had come to getting the King's personal attention. I hoped and prayed that he would get to see and read the contents of the folder and would view my recently submitted royal pardon. For once, perhaps this was not such a long shot.

One morning in July, while immersed in my art, as if from a distance I heard my name being called over the loudspeaker. There was nothing unusual in this; in prison, whenever you had mail, parcels or visits, or if the prison authorities needed to see you for some reason, you were always called on the intercom system. Often I would be so focused on my painting that I could be called several times and still it wouldn't register. Eventually one of my mates would tell me. Whenever I was so engrossed in my art, and I had to stop painting, it would take me anything up to an hour to come back to earth. This was one of those mornings. On my way to the office, as I passed the gym, I walked into what was obviously the conclusion of a violent altercation between three prisoners. Nothing seemed to register in my brain. I felt as if I was an outsider, visiting from another dimension. The dispersing crowd was slowly moving away, and as they did, I saw one of the guys who'd obviously been in the fight lying out on the concrete floor in front of me. Blood was spurting out of a wound on the side of his head. As I passed by him, the sun's rays caught his face, transforming the colour of his blood into shades of radiant vermilion. This triggered an unusual and vivid image in my mind: I saw bright red roses, rows and rows of rose bushes that seemed to stretch to infinity. In the foreground was a sensuous girl with long black hair, dressed in a silky white dress that hung loosely to her knees as she glided effortlessly through the air. What a sight it was, and what a great painting I thought it would make.

I walked on to the office to see what it was that I'd been summoned for this time.

One of my closest friends, and an ally for many years, was Ahmed Ratib, a Muslim from Afghanistan who had been in and out of almost every building in Bangkwang. Ahmed was a true warrior and was one of the inmates who had no outside support. Despite this, he, like me, had survived 15 years in prison. Although he was ten years younger than me, his suffering was evident by his hair having turned grey. Actually, I couldn't talk because by now I was balding. Recently Ahmed had survived a knife attack by two Thais and he had been transferred back to Building 2. I had not seen him for a while, as he hardly ever got visitors, and I was very pleased to see him again. Ahmed helped out with the cooking, and on weekends he made *roti* with barbecued chicken breasts.

For some reason, the prison authorities had not detected that the cables of the signal blocking system had been tampered with. When the system was installed, they monitored the screen around the clock, which resulted in many dog handlers being caught, but, as with everything, the novelty soon wore off. The cables were eventually repaired, but we had some time in between.

I decided to purchase a new dog. It was a lot safer to buy one through a foreigner than from a Thai. Ahmed, who was involved in all sorts of underhand dealings, found a new dog for me. I bought it for two reasons. Firstly, an upgrade was long overdue, but that wasn't my only reason. There were two Israelis, Itzik and Avi, who had recently been arrested on drug-related charges and placed in Building 4. A third Israeli, an old man, was in Building 3. The first two Israelis had heard about me while they were in the other prison – I was known as the Jewish South African who had been there for 16 years – and eventually I got to meet them. On first impression, the two of them seemed like really nice guys. They wore their yarmulkes and claimed to be very religious. Prison had this effect on people, and inmates would often turn to G-d. Faith had its way of working miracles. In their case, the change was rather sudden, it seemed to me; they went from one extreme to the other. It was too much, too soon. My own spiritual journey had started with certain acknowledgements. First I had to change from within, take responsibility for my actions, and accept wholeheartedly that whatever transpired in my life was for the greater good. Remorse without sincerity never warrants forgiveness. I began to suspect that the two Israeli guys had a hidden agenda.

Shlomo came up with the bright idea of having all the Israelis housed under one roof, and, on the request of the Israeli embassy, the prison authorities agreed to this proposal. The three new Israelis would all come to Building 2. The two guys in Building 4 apparently shared a dog with somebody else, so, when they moved, they would need a dog of their own. As my fellow brothers of faith, I felt it would be my duty to accommodate them, and my plan was to give them my old dog. When you changed buildings you were always thoroughly searched, so trying to smuggle a dog across would be suicidal.

Being united with your own tribesmen strengthened your position as an individual and I was looking forward to enlarging our Jewish brotherhood. Security in Building 4, where Itzik and his co-accused Avi were housed, was far more lax than ours and dogs were cheaper there. Itzik had a better command of the English language than Avi and I really liked him, even though when talking to him you couldn't get a word in edgeways. I didn't know if this was an Israeli thing or whether he just had a certain energy about him.

They were expecting to get moved any day, so I asked Itzik if he could buy and smuggle in a jack for my dog when they got transferred. I needed a spare.

Shlomo was in his element when they finally arrived in Building 2. He welcomed them into his house, and I welcomed them into our cell. Itzik would sleep directly opposite me with the old man, while Avi would sleep next to me. With the addition of the two of them, now we would be 14. Until then, Shlomo had been the only smoker in our cell. Now I discovered that all three of them smoked. This was going to make life unpleasant for the other members of the cell, who were all anti-smoking. A while back, I had tried to convert our cell into a non-smoking room, but Shlomo had refused, claiming that we were being selfish and not considering him. I had to give him credit, though, because he did compromise and only smoked three or four cigarettes while we were locked up. On the Israelis' arrival I explained the problem to the three of them and asked them politely, for the 15 hours that we were all cooped up in the cell together, to please cut down on their smoking. Smoking had been banned in public places in many countries, and everyone knew that second-hand smoke was known to cause cancer. All I was asking them for was a little consideration.

Itzik had managed to smuggle the jack I'd asked for into our building, and I paid him for it straight away. The guard at our gate was the infamous Mr Somporm. He was only about 1.5m tall, but, since his appointment to the gate, he had bust many prisoners carrying drugs and dogs – even biscuits. How Itzik got past him, I don't know – we drug dealers had our ways of eluding the guards – but anyway I was impressed.

Within minutes of arriving in our building, Itzik was already making enquiries about the availability of a dog. I was quick to enlighten him. As newcomers, the three Israelis would be closely watched by Veesarnou and his spies, the Blue Shirts, who informed indiscriminately on their fellow inmates in order to find favour with the guards. The risks were great. The key-boy informer now slept where the General used to stay, but he would walk around in the corridor to see who was doing what. In addition to all this, the closed-circuit cameras in our cell monitored our every move. I told them they needed to sit tight for at least two to three weeks. I didn't mention yet the spare dog that I planned to give them. Instead, I offered to send text messages for them if there was something important they needed to communicate to someone outside.

Itzik's wife and two little boys were living in Bangkok with the rabbi, and through the Israeli embassy he had organised permission for his wife and kids to visit every day and bring him food, as he claimed to be kosher. He was entitled to have his visits in the embassy section, which was at the entrance to the foreign visit room.

For my entire life, I had always been wary of people who are too friendly. Itzik was one of these people; he was over-familiar from the beginning. On his second day he already was pressing my buttons. He asked me to organise him a locker, preferably close to where Shlomo had his house. By that stage, as a rule, I had stopped assisting newcomers. Besides the fact that nobody ever appreciated a helping hand, the next thing you knew you'd find you'd adopted a next of kin. Anyway, I made an exception for the Israelis; after all, these guys were now my new friends. One of the Thai guys owned a locker right near Shlomo's place, and, as a favour and because it was me, he gave me the best price possible. Itzik, in his broken Thai and disrespectful manner, then tried to bargain the guy down to a cheaper price. The Thai's irritation was more than obvious, but Itzik just couldn't see it. So I winked at my Thai friend and, with my hand behind Itzik's back, gestured that I would pay the balance.

That Friday, the very first afternoon of their arrival, soon after lockdown I was davening *Mincha* when Itzik was on my bed with his wife's phone number in his hand, asking me to message her to wish her good Shabbos and to tell her that he loved her. There were other instructions about things he wanted her to bring on her following visit. I really didn't mind helping, as I knew from experience how important it was for us prisoners to have contact with our families, but it was a bit intrusive all the same. Avi, who slept next to me, also woke up early to daven *Shacharis*. Because we slept so close to one another, and although we are required to recite certain prayers in an audible tone, I always prayed in silence so as not to disturb the person next to me. When I was finished praying, I would go back to sleep for an hour before the cell was opened. Avi, I soon discovered, prayed pretty loudly and he also made other noises with his throat and was forever blowing his nose. I had no doubt that it wouldn't be long before the guy would drive me crazy. I was already getting irritated.

Because it was Shabbos, Itzik didn't ask me to bark the dog, but first thing Sunday morning, he was at my house asking to bark. Inside my house and against the wall I had two sets of lockers, on top of which were another two. Behind the lockers and in between the walls of our houses was enough space for you to sit and bark the dog without being seen by people walking past. Because I'd bark the dog at night in the cell, and because of the danger of using it during the day, I never risked using it then myself, but I was happy to help Itzik, Avi and the old man out, so I offered to facilitate them every Sunday until such time as things were more relaxed. Itzik did not care much for protocol. In the days that followed, every day he asked me to bark the dog. In the cell, he harassed me with ridiculous messages like 'Tell my wife I love her and miss her.' He was constantly coming to sit on my bed.

I then made it very clear to him that I didn't socialise inside the cell. My time there was the only quality time I had away from the noise and goings-on of the prison. It was the time when I got lost in my head, and now Itzik was invading my space.

To avoid disturbing everybody in the room, all four of the Israelis would congregate on Shlomo's bed, talk for hours and smoke. At first they limited their smoking; then, as the days passed and they became more comfortable in their surroundings, their conversation became louder, their smoking increased and they adopted an 'I couldn't give a fuck' attitude. By the fourth day Avi was driving me mad, so I moved him to the other side of the room.

With the signal detector system fully operational, whenever I wanted to bark the dog I had to do so during the day on the other side of the building. Now that I had two dogs, I wanted to check the accuracy of the machines that supposedly picked up the signal and pinpointed your location. In a worst-case scenario, if there was a check I would flush my dog down the toilet – which reminded me of the time when Philip, the Australian, had flushed Joseph's dog down the toilet. This was during a raid on the downstairs section. As always, we'd heard the security gates being unlocked. The guards rushed past our cell to the Chinese room, which they searched thoroughly. Philip, who was by now squatting in the toilet, completely panicked and flushed the dog. Meanwhile the guards didn't even come into our cell. Philip was the laughing stock of the room. For somebody who acted like he was some notorious gangster, for him to have disposed of his dog, and not even his *own* dog at that, was such a laugh.

So I barked my dog in the cell, but all the time I was very nervous and fully expected to be raided in the morning when the guards had picked up my signal. Nothing happened. Perhaps the machine was not as accurate as we had been led to believe, or perhaps it was just that the guards on duty weren't paying attention. That very afternoon, soon after lockdown, the cell next door to ours, which was part of death row, was raided. The guards had entered from the other side and bust one of the guys with a dog. There was every possibility that when I had been barking the dog the night before, the machine may have pinpointed the cell next door. I felt bad, but maybe it had just confirmed my suspicion that the system wasn't as accurate as we'd been led to believe.

Several cellmates came to me complaining about the Israelis and their smoking. Being the room chief, I thought the best way to handle the situation was to call a meeting where each person in the cell could express their grievances and offer suggestions for a solution. Soon after lockdown and roll call, I addressed the guys, explaining that since the Israelis had arrived there had been a certain amount of discontent regarding the smoking and level of noise. When we were locked up in our cells, each of us enjoyed a degree of peace and tranquillity, whether this involved watching TV, writing letters, reading a book or engaging in prayer or meditation. Those of us who had done hard time found the Israelis' lack of consideration irritating to the point of being disrespectful. As newcomers, they needed to fit in with our way of life, and not the other way around. Each person said his piece. Nobody was rude, and the general consensus was that the Israelis should cut down on their smoking or smoke in the toilet and not on their beds. When Itzik and Avi spoke in their defence, they were obnoxious. They said simply that if they wanted to smoke, they would smoke.

Itzik was on my back every day, wanting to bark the dog. I couldn't believe the attitude of these guys. Here were two Jews who claimed to be religious and who were davening three times a day, and yet I wondered if they actually understood the biblical injunction to 'love thy neighbour as thyself'. Being in a private cell was also a privilege, and it was something they were taking for granted. I really couldn't take it any more, so I basically told Itzik to fuck off and leave me alone. Reiterating my cellmates' sentiments, I added that they, the Israelis, made me feel ashamed to be Jewish.

The next evening, soon after roll call, Itzik sat on his bed, legs folded, and stared straight at me in a challenging manner. Then he lit up a cigarette and blew the smoke in my direction. This was a direct act of defiance and disrespect, but I wasn't prepared to react. Instead, I fitted my surgical mask around my mouth and nose and ignored him, pretending his actions didn't bother me. I continued doing whatever it was I was preoccupied with. The following day, the Russian guy who slept next to Shlomo and who, when the Israelis sat together on Shlomo's bed, was subjected to more smoke than anybody else, approached me. He complained bitterly about their habits, and especially about Itzik's cocky attitude. He told me he wanted to fuck him up. I thought this was a great idea and would save me the trouble, so I encouraged him to do it and added that, in the event that the prison authorities got involved, we would all testify that Itzik threw the first punch.

That night, Avi went into the toilet and conducted a conversation with himself, pretending to be speaking on the dog. He was quite loud, and his voice would be audible to the Thais in the cell next door. I was at this stage the only person in our cell who was a dog handler, and I was convinced he was doing this deliberately to arouse suspicion. When he emerged from the toilet, I was standing at the end of my bed waiting to go and urinate. The little shit was half my size, but as he passed me, he bumped into me. He pulled his shoulders back and gave me this menacing look. I couldn't help but laugh to myself, knowing that with one punch I could knock him out.

The tension in the cell was mounting. I wanted nothing to do with these bloody Israelis. Besides, my 50th birthday was coming up – half a century! – and I considered it something of a miracle that I had made it so far. Fifty was a milestone in itself, and if you think about my past and how I never envisaged even making it past 30, I decided it was cause for celebration and that I was going to celebrate in style. My birthday fell on a Friday, so celebrating on the day wasn't an option, as drinking during the week was far too risky. In preparation, I made 24 litres of wine and decided to have two parties, one on Wednesday for all my cellmates, and the other on Saturday, for my drinking buddies.

I discussed with Shlomo the problem we were all having with his fellow countrymen. He was not too happy with them, either. I told him in no uncertain terms that I didn't want to speak to them and that they should avoid me at all costs. Shlomo understood, and I'm sure he conveyed my message. The Friday night a week before my birthday, about an hour before Shabbos, I was sitting on my bed with an open folder in front of me texting a friend of mine. Itzik had been watching me; he knew I was barking the dog. The next thing I knew, he was on my bed on all fours asking me to please send an SMS to his wife. Talk about being thick-skinned. I gave him a dirty look and told him to fuck off. He climbed off my bed and blurted out a volley of abuse. I put my dog in a small zip-up bag and placed it in my underwear. Itzik then called me a fucking South African. I'm not one for verbal confrontation, so I jumped up and rushed him. Ahmed and Donald, who slept next to me, grabbed me and tried to hold me back, but I broke free. By this time Itzik had made his way to Shlomo's bed. I pursued him. Avi tried to block my way, saying something stupid like 'Take it easy'. I lashed out and hit him first. He staggered to the side. Then Shlomo tried to prevent me from getting to Itzik. I told him I would fuck him up as well. I was mad as hell. I caught Itzik in the corner on Shlomo's bed and I started punching his head. He kicked wildly and scratched my face, but I kept going. It took six of my cellmates to wrestle me off him or I would more than likely have killed the fucker.

With all the commotion going on, somebody from the corridor had alerted the guards, who entered our cell carrying batons. I was ordered out of the cell and made to wait in the corridor while the commodores investigated what had just happened. My face was bleeding where I'd been scratched. One of my fingers was turning blue and swollen. I thought it was probably broken from punching Itzik's hard head. We were both warned that if we didn't stop fighting we would be removed from the cell and placed in separate rooms. I was so mad I still wanted to break him in pieces, but I agreed to call it a day. After the guards left, Ahmed and the Russian came and sat on my bed. I was pissed off with the Russian, too; I thought he was supposed to be the one who was going to sort Itzik out.

In preparation for my pre-birthday lunch on the Wednesday, Elisabeth bought ready-prepared food from the prison canteen on her visit, plus three trays of prawns (not kosher, but a real treat for some), ten packets of sticky rice and some spicy Thai dishes. Ahmed started early in the morning preparing the dough, and we had marinated 4kg of chicken breasts the evening before. I ordered 100 dim sum from my Chinese neighbour. One of the lady-boys who made meals for the guards had steamed two deliciously prepared fresh sea fish and barbequed 30 chicken drumsticks. Cold drinks I purchased from the coffee shops.

There were about 14 of us for lunch. It was a real feast and everybody enjoyed themselves; in fact, there was so much food that I had to give some to my neighbours. The night before my birthday I stayed up almost all night barking the dog.

Friday 15 October dawned and I was 50 years old. I didn't feel much older than the day of my arrest, actually. While I was relaxing and drinking my coffee, Ahmed arrived with a folded piece of A3 paper. He embraced me and wished me happy birthday. I unrolled the sheet of paper; to my surprise, one of the Thai artists had drawn a portrait of me in pencil crayon. There were birthday wishes written all over the page from prisoners and guards. One of the guys had even composed a poem for me. I was so deeply touched I almost broke down. It was the nicest gift I'd ever been given in my life. Even behind these forsaken concrete walls, such poignant moments did happen sometimes, and we were all the richer for them.

I was expecting at least 20 people for my Saturday party. My first priority was to pay the guard on duty to close his eyes. My next mission was to transfer the wine from containers into plastic bottles. I made my favourite fried rice and another rice dish with buffalo, which I'd cooked for four hours the previous day. Ahmed made his *roti* and barbecued his chicken breasts as usual, to be served with baby marrows, onions, chillies, tomatoes and mushrooms. I made a gravy. The lady-boy barbecued drumsticks and chicken wings for us. By 11am my friends were beginning to arrive, everyone in party mood. I was the barman, filling plastic cups with wine and passing them around. Many of the guys got really drunk. One of them puked all over and passed out in the drain running in front of my house. I got really drunk my-self, for that matter, but we all had a great time.

My 50th birthday was probably the most memorable prison birthday to date, and the most short-lived.

Chapter 17

A Change of Fate

We are taught that, at some stage or another, all good things come to an end, but bad times can be equally fleeting. It all depends on you. A change of attitude opens other possibilities. Positivity attracts, while negativity repels. I tried to keep my negative thoughts at bay as far as the South African government was concerned. They had failed in their duty to alleviate the injustice that South African citizens were suffering at the hands of a foreign government. All my hopes and positive thoughts I now pinned on becoming an Israeli national. In Israel I would be with my own people, Jews like me who cared for one another. Whether I was being delusional or not, time would tell. And the Israelis in my cell weren't doing their country proud, that was for sure.

The day after my fight with Itzik and Avi, while I was quietly enjoying my coffee, Ahmed came running to the house. Apparently a group of Bad Boys who were my friends had heard about the fight and had congregated outside Shlomo's house. They were ready to attack and stab Itzik. One of the outside guards summoned me to the office and asked me to defuse what could become a dangerous situation. I went and told my Thai friends to leave the Israeli guys alone. Then the same guard, whom I had known for years, asked me how best we could come to a peaceful solution. I told him that there was no way Itzik and I could stay in the same cell. Either they would have to move him out of the cell or they'd have to move me. Seeing that he was new in the building and that not only had I been there for much longer but I also owned the cell, Itzik was moved to a Thai room upstairs. I was still at the office when Itzik came up to me and threatened to inform on me to the prison authorities and to tell them that I had a dog. I couldn't believe the man's chutzpah! I had just saved his life! Anyway, I told him to go ahead. I had connections. Some of the biggest Thai gangsters were my friends. I could arrange a surprise party for his wife. Furthermore, his family's phone number was registered on my phone. In the event that he did inform and the authorities were made aware of my dog, I would simply tell them it belonged to him.

I walked away. The guy was a rat. I would decide later what course of action to take. In the meantime, I banned him from using the gym. When Itzik was removed from our room everybody was happy. Even his own countrymen didn't like him. A few days before our incident, Itzik had threatened Tovia, the old Israeli guy, who was in his mid-sixties. In the days that followed, Itzik was advised by a few foreigners that, for his own safety, it would be wise for him to request a transfer to another building.

Monday morning came, and as usual Elisabeth was the first to arrive. I would be waiting at the gate, so that as soon as I was called for a visit I could hurry out of the building. Elisabeth and I were chatting when Itzik's wife arrived. She came into the visit room and, without bothering to greet Elisabeth, took the phone straight out of her hand. She launched into telling me the sad story that Itzik's father had died. With tears in her eyes, she pleaded with me to allow Itzik to bark the dog that night. I explained to her that Itzik and I had had a fight and were no longer on speaking terms. In an instant she turned stone cold, said 'Oh' and gave the phone back to Elisabeth. Then she walked away. I couldn't believe how rude she was.

About 40 minutes into our visit I saw the rabbi arrive with a fellow Israeli, carrying the plastic bags of kosher foodstuffs they brought with them whenever they visited. Normally the rabbi's visit would coincide with Shabbos. Our weekly parcels of bread rolls and pastries would arrive either on a Thursday or Friday, and, because they were sent by post, they weren't very fresh on arrival. When they were steamed, however, the bread rolls were actually quite delicious. Whenever the rabbi visited, he always brought me the same food package the Israeli guys received. This normally consisted of freshly baked bread rolls, coleslaw, fried chicken and potatoes, an aubergine dish, tomato and paprika, and hummus with pita bread. Shlomo would bring my package, and on his return he would swap my fresh rolls from the rabbi with the stale ones we'd received through the post in the parcels. Can you believe it?

Earlier in the year, on Pesach, Shlomo had collected my package as usual. Every year, for as far back as I could remember, I had received four boxes of matzah from the rabbi, along with all the above-mentioned dishes, plus other traditional Pesach foods. The package was always really big. Only when I got back to my house did I notice that I had only one box of matzah. I immediately went back to Shlomo's house to enquire where the rest had gone. I could only wonder what else he might have helped himself to. It baffled me that a Jew would steal food from a fellow Jew. Prison may bring out the worst in a man, but for me such behaviour must have been deeply ingrained in his character. Being a prisoner was not an excuse to behave badly; rather, it offered an opportunity to better yourself as a person. Shlomo claimed that while waiting in the parcel area for everybody's stuff, he had mistakenly given my matzah to his mates from the other building. I was dumbfounded. I couldn't believe what he had done. Then he gave me half of his matzah.

Anyway, while I was chatting to Elisabeth I was told that the rabbi was also there to see me. He brought with him the good news that the Israeli Minister of the Interior had agreed to grant me citizenship. It was a strange feeling. Only a few days ago I had had a fight with the Israelis and now I was being considered to take on a new identity. If it actually happened, I was going to be the first Jewish prisoner in the history of Israel to be granted citizenship. Although it was not yet official, it was definitely on the cards. I was really excited, as there were some foreigners whose transfers were currently being prepared; the next transfer meeting between Thailand and interested parties was scheduled for April 2011. Once the Thais agreed on the terms of the treaty, the process usually took about three months before you would be moved. Israeli marshals would be sent to escort me. This meant I could be in an Israeli prison by as early as July or August of 2011. Where others had failed, my friend Ivan had achieved the impossible.

News travelled quickly around the prison. My friends were really happy for me. With it not yet being confirmed, I didn't want to jeopardise my chances, so I could not tell the South African embassy what was being planned. I also learnt, that in the event that I did not inform my country of origin of a change of citizenship, I would automatically relinquish my existing citizenship. On the other hand, I could hold dual citizenship. My primary objective, however, was to get out of Thailand. Once I was in Israel, I imagined I would soon be paroled. I cannot describe the excitement I felt after all these years of people trying to secure my release. I could almost taste my freedom.

So often we get caught up in the moment, forgetting where we are. There was still the danger that everyday prison life presented, and I had to remember that I had made it this far. The last stretch was going to be the hardest.

As fortune would have it, there was a new Director of the prison. Once again, we braced ourselves for new rules. I knew the system by now and, as I predicted, one of the first regulations the new Director instituted was that all prisoners who slept in the corridors, except for the Blue Shirts, had to be moved into the cells. Seventy per cent of the occupants who stayed in the corridors were Chinese. Their foam mattresses were over one metre in width, because space was not a problem in the corridor. Room 15, which was opposite my cell, and which was also privately owned by the Chinese, was being confiscated. Chen Ming, the owner, was a long-time friend and also a member of my gym. He asked me if he could come and stay in my cell. A few of the other Chinese from upstairs also approached me. Their alternative was that they would have to move into a Thai room. This put me on the spot. The new rule was causing a lot of discontent, especially among the Chinese who had enjoyed the luxury of sleeping in the corridor for more than a decade, where space was never an issue and one could walk around freely. Now, just to start with, they would have to cut their beds to the standard 65cm width. This was like a punishment for them. Because of my long-standing relationship with the commodores and the staff who controlled the cells, nobody from the corridor had yet been placed in our cell by the authorities, but suddenly the problem with the Chinese became mine. The difficulty was that if I allowed one of the Chinese into my cell, I would almost certainly be asked to accommodate more. Within no time they would have taken over.

Firstly, the agreement was that our cell was for Western foreigners only. Secondly, none of us was willing to give up our extra space. More importantly, the Chinese tended to speak very loudly to one another – to shout, you could say – and it could get unpleasantly irritating. Lastly, most of the Chinese guys smoked, and I definitely didn't want to subject myself and my cellmates to more of a health hazard than already existed in our room. I decided that I had to take a firm stance on this issue, and so, as politely as possible, I explained to Chen Ming that for the above reasons, unfortunately, none of them could move into our room.

For the most part, in all my time in prison, I had enjoyed good friendships with most of the Chinese inmates. One of my longest-standing allies was a Taiwanese guy who had been arrested way back in 1992. His name was Paul and he owned the coffee shop. He was a true gentleman and had helped me out on many occasions. Nevertheless, a disgruntled bunch of Chinese got together and wrote a petition to the Director, complaining about our cell, Room 11 and the Nigerian cell upstairs, Room 45. The Chinese were now having to be squeezed into already overcrowded rooms while we, the Western foreigners, enjoyed the comforts of no more than 12 people to a cell. They had up to 24 prisoners in theirs.

I was called to the office, where the guard in charge of the building showed me the petition with all the signatories. He asked me what I suggested we should do. I clarified our reasons, as I had done on so many occasions, and also pointed out that we paid for this privilege. It was not our problem; it was his. I tried to do this in a calm manner, but I was quite agitated. The Chinese had openly challenged my power. As I was leaving the office, I raised my fist and said to the guard, '*Boksing di*' (I accept the challenge). He responded by pulling his forefinger across his throat while giving me a cynical smile. I interpreted his action as permission to stab. I let my cellmates know what had transpired and strongly suggested that we should attack the Chinese. I even approached the Nigerians, who were few in number at the moment because so many of them had benefited from the transfer treaty. Nobody agreed with me. Nobody thought we needed to resort to such extremes. I knew, though, that if I didn't retaliate in some way, it would be the ultimate loss of face, and my power would be in question, so I planned my own revenge.

I decided I would attack the leader who had instigated the petition – none other than my friend Chen Ming. I removed the steel shaft from a broken portable fan, got one of my friends at the workshop to grind it to a sharp point, and then spent days smoothing it with sandpaper, transforming it into a deadly weapon. I placed it on the table where I painted, right next to a pile of books on Judaism, and sat back to wait for the right opportunity.

Over the years in Bangkwang, there had been an explosion in the number of feral cats, most of which carried infections. Certain prisoners got attached to the creatures and would keep them as pets and feed them. There was so much interbreeding that, every now and again, the guards would have the prisoners catch as many cats as they could, at least the homeless ones. They were bagged and removed from the building. Wherever there are cats, there are rats. In front of my studio I had placed a piece of concrete, 2m in length and about half a metre in width, that was so heavy it took at least two prisoners to move it. One morning I noticed fresh soil being burrowed from underneath it. Understanding that it must be a rat, on investigating we discovered not one rat but a huge litter of the fuckers. As the mother rat bolted, one of the guys kicked it so hard that it hit the concrete wall and lay there unconscious. The babies were fed to the cats. After that, whenever we saw places where fresh soil had been turned over, which was almost on a daily basis, about six or seven of us, armed with bamboo batons, would cordon off the area while two prisoners moved the concrete. As the rats tried to escape we would hit them, and, in the event that they got past us, we would run after them. It must have been quite a funny sight, if a bit gruesome, but it had to be done. In a matter of two months, we killed over 40 rats – and, contrary to rumours, nobody ate them.

On 6 November 2010, it was a Saturday afternoon, around 2.45, and I was taking my shower directly opposite my house where I'd built a concrete platform for my five plastic dustbins filled with clean water. Next to me on the left, my Chinese neighbours had a similar area where they showered, and next to them there were more Chinese. As usual, the casino had been in full swing the whole day and now, around closing time, the Chinese were all gathered around shouting to each other. Their shouting irritated the shit out of me – no doubt they had won money. Chen Ming was standing among them and he was the loudest. After two weeks of planning and giving them the evil eye, I could no longer contain myself. It was now or never. So I shouted out some general words of abuse in Thai, but not directed specifically to any one person. I had just finished showering and, my towel around my waist and still dripping with water, I made my way to my house. They continued talking very loudly and I shouted more words of abuse like 'aheer', and 'yet care'. These are very offensive swear words.

I noticed Chen Ming getting really upset. He started shouting something threatening at me in Thai and began to move towards my house. No doubt he was coming to fight. Instinctively I knew this was the chance I had been waiting for. I looked around for my steel shank so that I could finally teach him a lesson. But I couldn't find my weapon! It was nowhere. Chen Ming was about to come through my small wooden gate; there was no time to try to find it. All I could see on the table was a small screwdriver, so I snatched it up and leapt at him, still in my towel. I was aiming to stab him in his neck, a quick couple of pokes that would take him down, but at the last second I slipped. Chen

Ming was at least ten years younger than me, well built but not as big. He had anticipated my attack and, because I'd slipped, managed to block the screwdriver. I caught him in his hand and grazed his head, and he quickly backed away.

Then all hell seemed to break loose. I can't exactly say how many of them there were, but I could account for at least five Chinese. Some were picking up rocks from the garden; others had bamboo sticks and were throwing them at me.

Our houses were enclosed by a row of concrete lockers that stretched all the way from the Nigerians down to the last of six houses. I had stacked my water coolers on top of them. In each cooler was a block of ice, water bottles and fruit. Even these they were throwing at me. I turned to grab the piece of bamboo I kept to kill rats and one of the rocks hit me in the back. Armed with my screwdriver and bamboo stick, I ran outside shouting, 'Come, motherfuckers! Come!'

Then suddenly a couple of guards appeared, as if from nowhere. They had batons and they came running at us at quite a pace. As soon as I saw them, I quickly put the screwdriver in a cardboard box that was an arm's length away on one of the lockers. Just as I released it and was removing my arm, I felt a hand touching my arm and saw one of the guards retrieving the screwdriver. Chen Ming was bleeding from his forehead and hand, and I had quite a deep cut on my back. We were escorted by the guards to the office building, where the prison medic cleaned our wounds. Chen Ming, who was sitting a short distance away from me, kept saying, 'You die – sure.'

The guards on duty that day were not the regular guards from Building 2. I was ushered into the office and kept there while Chen Ming was allowed to leave. Everybody was locked up and they kept me there for at least another 40 minutes. During that time one of the guards went outside to report the incident. Because this was my second fight in less than a month, and out of fear that the fight would escalate into a gang war, the guards decided that I should be moved to another building. I was given a choice of any building, so I chose Building 6. Then I was escorted to my cell, where my cellmates helped me fold up my bed and pack my stuff. My TV set I gave to the old Israeli guy in return for his

38cm laptop/TV/DVD. I gave the gym to Donald, a Burmese guy who was the leader of the church. We then went to my house. By now I had about 20 lockers, all filled with stuff I had accumulated over the past 16 years. I emptied four of my water containers, dried them out and packed my things inside them, but I couldn't take everything. There was just too much stuff. I had become a compulsive hoarder.

My only real possessions of value were my paintings. I had only recently finished the portrait of the Chassidic rabbi commissioned by Edna, and I was working on another of Jim Morrison from The Doors. Fortunately, all my other paintings were safely in South Africa. Thinking that I might transfer to Israel in a few months, I gave all my art supplies to the Russian, and I left my spare dog for Avi and the other two Israelis to share. My new dog I hid in my underpants. If anything, I should have given my spare to Ahmed, but, since Pakistan (where his mother lived) had signed a treaty with Thailand, he was expecting to transfer any time. I know I hurt his feelings, though; it was one of those mistakes you make on the spur of the moment. Ahmed would have given his life for me, whereas the Israelis would have stabbed me in the back without a backward glance.

My house and all the other possessions I left behind I gave to the Israelis – another mistake, I realised in the days to follow.

Apart from my immediate cellmates, I never got the chance to say goodbye to the many Thais whom I had made friends with, and with whom I had coexisted for so many years. Everything was happening so fast. It took four of those wheelbarrow-type carts to transport my things. Saying goodbye and leaving what had become my home and comfort zone was suddenly devastating to me. I broke down in tears and bawled like a baby. What was I holding onto? I had always imagined that when I was released I would be able to take my departure at my own pace, saying goodbye to everybody and shaking their hands. Apart from my fight in 1999, until the Israelis arrived I had a clean record. I was now being forcibly removed, thrown out, for misconduct. I couldn't bring myself to believe that this was for the greater good of things. But it had happened, and, as with so many other things in life, we don't get to choose or necessarily accept the terms.

Four guards escorted me, pushing the carts, which we parked outside Building 6. Nobody checked or searched me on my way in. I carried with me my bed, a haversack containing toiletries and other personal items like my *siddur* and *tefillin*, a writing pad and a clipboard file. The rest of my belongings I was told I could collect in the morning.

It was around 5pm when I arrived. All the inmates had long since been locked up, but the entrance to the cells was open. I was put in a Thai room, which was also known as a transit cell for new arrivals. There were 18 Thais in the room, so not much space. I was given a spot near the door and squeezed my bed between two Thais. In fact, our beds overlapped and we were shoulder to shoulder.

Once I had settled down I went into the toilet, removed the dog from my underpants and barked my sister. It was early in South Africa. They were five hours behind Thailand. I didn't want to risk barking for too long. I was now in unfamiliar terrain and I knew that getting bust with a dog would only spell disaster for me. Hurriedly, I informed Joan about the fight, told her that I was now in Building 6 and asked her to please call Elisabeth and tell her what had happened. Elisabeth should visit me on Tuesday, which was the official visit day for Building 6, and not on Monday.

I then went and lay on my bed. Looking around, I recognised some of the Thais who had at one stage or another been in Building 2. Nobody ever got moved on a weekend unless it was a serious fight. My reputation preceded me. I was well liked and known for my integrity and no-bullshit attitude. The Thais saw me as a Big Leg. If you had money, you warranted respect. Respect came in two forms: there was the assumed respect and then there was the respect you earned. I had earned mine, not only by putting in the years but also by being honourable in my dealings with all prisoners. I didn't take shit from anybody, and I not only stood up for our rights but also fought for them, too. That night I struggled to sleep. I was restless and uneasy. I couldn't help wondering whether my arrogance would in the end be my downfall.

They say a change of scenery can do wonders, and I had probably been in the same building for far too long, bored and frustrated with seeing the same faces day in and day out. Perhaps this move would be for the better.

About ten months earlier, I had attended an inter-building four-a-side football tournament. There I had met one of the new foreigners, a guy in his mid-twenties named Dani, who was in Building 6. He was from Kazakhstan and seemed like a really nice guy. At that time, we were only nine foreigners in our cell, and I had suggested to him that, in the event he wanted to change buildings and transfer to Building 2, he would be welcome to stay in my house and would also be guaranteed a spot in our private cell.

I already knew all the foreigners in Building 6, and when the cell was opened in the morning I immediately went looking for Dani, hoping he would help me out with a place to stay. Some of the foreigners were shocked to see me, no doubt wondering what I was doing in their building on a Sunday morning. While I was waiting for Dani, who slept late, the British guys invited me for coffee. Eventually, when Dani came down he welcomed me with open arms.

Previously, Dani had stayed with an Iranian and an Israeli. The Israeli had won his case and the Iranian had been granted a royal pardon after having served only seven years of his life sentence. Dani now stayed on his own. Times were bad, he said, and he was struggling to survive. In return for his hospitality, I offered to take care of all his meals. In addition, I also agreed to pay some of the debts he incurred.

Building 6 had a lot of Chinese inmates, one of whom was my good friend Paul, who used to own the coffee shop in Building 2. About a year before, when Building 2 was raided by the Department of Corrections, from what I could gather they had been acting on information and had specifically targeted the coffee shop. Paul kept a lot of money with him. Nobody ever suspected that the prison authorities would raid the coffee shop, so it was a safe place to hide your money. The Chinese also ran the casino, and large amounts of cash circulated among the big gamblers. During that early-morning raid, Paul was the only one who was removed from his cell. He was taken downstairs and told to open the shop. The authorities seized 700 000 Thai baht that morning, 200 000 of which was Paul's own money. The balance belonged to his Chinese friends. Paul was never officially charged and, needless to say, the money simply disappeared. After that he was transferred to Building 6. Over the past year, with the help of his family, he had paid his friends back to the last baht.

Paul welcomed me as well, and he gave me two lockers to use in the meantime, with an option to buy them. The Chinese were all connected or knew each other, but, after learning about what had happened with me, Paul assured me there would be no revenge attacks. He would personally write to Chen Ming, he said, and for the sake of peace I also agreed to apologise. I was transferring to Israel soon; with my freedom so close, what did I have to lose by saying I was sorry? The truth was that I would stand to lose the most.

There were three foreign rooms in Building 6. One was a Nigerian full-sized cell like the one I'd had in Building 2; the second was a Western foreigners' cell, which was a three-quarter-size room; and the third was a small room occupied mainly by Pakistanis. In the Western foreign room were a Dutchman, who was Jonnie's co-accused and had basically taken the rap, two Brits, an Australian, Dani, a Chinese, a Nepalese and a Burmese. There was not much space for a ninth person.

Dani agreed to let me stay with him in his house. Because I wasn't sure whether I could trust him completely, or whether he would freak out about my having a dog, I kept my mobile phone a secret. With the help of Dani and some of the other foreigners, I collected my belongings, which were still parked outside the entrance to Building 6. One of the young guards on duty half-heartedly checked my stuff. The guys were amazed at all the things I had, my excuse being that I'd been in prison for so long. Dani's house was a lot smaller than mine had been. He gave me three lockers and half of a fourth one to store the things that I would use on a daily basis. The rest I stored in Paul's locker, which was at the other end of this warehouse-type hangar that had about 20 houses, mostly owned by Chinese.

Another good friend of mine, a guy from Tanzania by the name of Dodi, also a fellow footballer and who had previously stayed in

Building 2, had extended an invitation for me to stay in the Nigerian room, but only on the condition that I never barked the dog. The foreigners told me that they would have a meeting before they decided whether I could stay in their cell or not. It was a Sunday, so nothing could be done till Monday anyway. I would have to stay another night in the Thai room. I was not too perturbed about anything. In a sense, the change of environment was proving to be a distraction from the pressures and responsibilities I had had in Building 2, where I had got caught up in a structured routine that subconsciously had affected my way of thinking. While it got me through the day, and time passed relatively quickly, I had lost my spontaneity. Everything I did had to have a reason.

Dani had no chairs or cushions, and so we sat on a vinyl-covered concrete floor and ate our meals around a fold-up wooden table. First on my to-do list was to have a couple of cushions made, I decided. I have a small bum, and it got sore very easily. Monday morning arrived and I brought my bed outside first thing and put it in Dani's house, not being sure where I was going to sleep that night. But soon after having coffee and taking my regular morning shower, Steve (the Brit) and the Dutchman, who was also the room chief, came to me and said that the foreigners had unanimously agreed to give me a place in their cell. I was humbled by their enthusiasm to accommodate me, realising that I was now a guest in this building and among inmates who would be my new friends.

On Tuesday morning, Elisabeth visited me. She was somewhat taken aback by what had transpired. I don't think she quite believed I was capable of stabbing somebody. After the visit, while waiting to collect my foodstuffs, I bumped into some of the guys from Building 2. Apparently on Sunday morning my house had been looted. The Thais came in and took whatever they could get their hands on. I couldn't see how this could have happened unless the prison authorities had instigated it. Something was wrong.

After three days, I told Dani about the dog. It was his house and I had to respect that. In the event that I transferred to an Israeli prison, I told him, I would leave the dog for him. Luckily, Dani didn't have a problem with it. We both knew the risks involved, and I assured him that in the event that the dog was found by the prison authorities, I would take responsibility. In the meantime, we needed to find a good hiding place for it.

On Wednesday morning, I was called for a parcel around the same time that Building 2 finished their visit. The guys went mad when they saw me, hugging me and shaking my hands, and actually it was great to see them. Then I was told that, the day before, while the Israelis were sitting in my house, about ten samurai came with knives and threatened them, forcing them to pack their things and get out. At first, they thought I had arranged the attack, which obviously I hadn't done. The whole situation could have been avoided if the Israelis had gone to the prison authorities first thing on Monday morning and explained that I'd given them my house, and at the same time either pledged or dropped an envelope with at least 10 000 Thai baht to the Building Chief. This was a Thai jail, where nothing was for free. If you wanted to own property, you paid the tax. All the same, I was sorry for the Israelis, and I blamed Shlomo, who should have advised them.

After speaking to my friends, on my return to my new building, I had barely unpacked the contents of my parcel when I was called over the loudspeaker to go to the gate. Waiting for me was the commodore in charge of our rooms and the foreigners from Building 2. The commodore took me aside and told me that the Israelis had been seen using a mobile in my house, so they, the authorities, had put a stop to it. He also told me that no charges would be brought against me for the stabbing. In return, he advised that I should not get involved in the matter of the Israelis and my house. I agreed and we shook hands. In the same vein, I urged him to make sure that the Israelis wouldn't have any further problems. Making a deal with the prison authorities was out of character for me, but I didn't feel guilty because the Israelis had already fucked up. Anyway, I was now in another building and there was not much I could do. My getting involved might be more of a danger to them than anything else.

On Thursday morning, after my visit, I bumped into one of the main samurai who had threatened the Israelis. I refrained from asking about the incident and let him do all the talking. He said he was sorry that I'd left Building 2 and for what had happened with the Chinese, adding that I should have got him to stab Chen Ming. This guy's name was Tor. He was a youngster of about 29, tattooed all over and extremely dangerous. He was also a great footballer. There had been an incident a while back when Tor had attacked one of the British guys who was disliked by both Thais and foreigners. Single-handedly that time, I went to the British guy's rescue and made sure they didn't stab him. If I had not interfered, other foreigners would have run the risk of being attacked by Thais. I helped the Brit more out of a sense of duty than anything else. Anyway, I made it clear to Tor that the Israelis were my friends and that I didn't want them to have a problem. He understood and we shook hands. I felt confident that they would be safe.

Later I learnt that three Chinese were put into my old cell, and that Shlomo had taken on the responsibility of room chief. I received a letter from Donald, my Burmese friend to whom I'd given my gym, saying he needed some cash to buy the weights that belonged to the Estonian. When the Estonian went home he gave the weights to Shlomo, who was now selling them. I sent Donald a note to tell him that I would sort it out with Shlomo and that he shouldn't worry.

For as far back as I could remember, the occupants of Building 6 took their sport very seriously. They had their own football league and I was quickly recruited into one of the Thai teams. We played matches every day. Soon the days became weeks. In the afternoons I would indulge in a game of backgammon with another good friend of mine, Rashid from Pakistan. I got word through Paul that Chen Ming had accepted my apology and that there wouldn't be retaliation. Even though I was pleased and my mind was more at ease now, I still couldn't afford to relax. I remained as vigilant as I had been since the first day I'd walked into prison.

The foreigners in Building 6 were a smaller group and more unified than we were in Building 2. They were also more relaxed and friendly, forever joking and making fun of each other. I realised I was far too serious. As a rule, I avoided joking. With time, I would become more comfortable and accept that things could be done differently. In the cell I slept next to Steve, and on my other side was a Chinese guy. Five of my eight new cellmates smoked, but out of consideration for me they all cut down. The atmosphere was quite different here and gradually I became a lot more chilled.

Christmas was fast approaching, and every year the boys from Building 6 celebrated in style. The group of British women would provide the food. For my part, I offered to make some wine. I found myself wanting to participate in their festivities. This had nothing to do with a Jew celebrating Christmas; it was about embracing my new friends, crossing cultural barriers and breaking the chains of bondage that had held me captive for so many years. It was about letting go of all the hatred and anger inside me and which surfaced at the slightest provocation.

Christmas Day arrived. The guys had gone to great lengths to make the day special. At lunchtime a traditional English breakfast was served and we all wore Christmas hats. One of the Chinese distilled pure vodka and sold one litre for 1 000 Thai baht. Mixing it with my own brew made for quite a potent concoction. The Christians were headed by Tony, a Ghanaian, who had been arrested two years before me but had only come to Bangkwang in 1995. They held their church service and gifts were even handed out, donated by Father Oliver, head of the mission. Thai and foreign prisoners all participated in the festivities. Everybody lent a hand in the preparation and food was in abundance. We had a great time and even went so far to have the occasion photographed. I drank far too much, but I wasn't the only one, and at lockdown we all staggered up to our cells. During roll call, instead of calling out numbers, which we always did in English, one or two of us blurted out words like 'Leave me alone', 'Go away' and 'Get the fuck out of here'. The guard just presumed we were counting in English. It was difficult to keep a straight face, and as soon as the guard had ticked off his register and turned around to go to the next cell, we all burst out laughing.

Dani and me soon became close. He was a good kid, tough, honourable and street-smart. He reminded me of myself when I was young. Still high on alcohol, that afternoon Dani and I connived to pull some jack-arsed stunts on our cellmates, which turned into a free-for-all wrestling match. We had this game, which the Australian and I played with each other, where one of us would lift our chin, exposing our Adam's apple, and the other person, using both hands, would flick the Adam's apple with as much force as possible, using both index fingers. We called this game 'Double-barrelled shotgun'. The Thais who saw us playing it thought we were lunatics. So there we were, drunk as lords on Christmas Day, in a free-for-all wrestling match. Punches were flying. At one point I had the Australian in a headlock without realising that he was choking. He punched me in the face. Things were getting a little too serious, so I released my grip and then they all turned on me. I don't recall much after that. Exhaustion got the better of me. Either I tapped out or passed out, I don't know, but apparently I puked all over the bed of one of the British guys, which couldn't have been much fun for him. When I woke up in the morning, besides having a hangover, my entire body ached. The knuckles on my right hand were so swollen you couldn't see the bone. Understandably, the British guy was really pissed off at me. I apologised and offered to have his sheets and blankets washed. I guessed it was the least I could do.

Wednesday 12 January 2011. The Israeli consular representative, Mr Eli Gil, and Rabbi Nechemia Wilhelm visited all the Israelis. I was also called. When it was my turn to speak to the consular representative, who looked, I thought, more like a gangster than a government representative, smilingly he waved a passport at me.

It was official. I was an Israeli.

Did I feel a sense of pride? I really can't say. I think I was more thrilled by having the opportunity of making *aliyah* (return to the Holy Land) and the prospect of starting a new life in another country. Mr Gil instructed me to write a letter to the Prison Director, Mr Veesarnou Parchon Chi, informing him of my change of nationality and putting in my request to be transferred to a prison in Israel. I was told my travel documents were in order and the transfer process was already in motion. After almost 17 years of knocking on doors that briefly opened and then slammed shut in our faces, for the first time the light at the end of the tunnel was truly bright. Our prayers had been answered. Through the visit guard, Mr Gil sent me my transfer papers as well as a copy of my new passport. I was impressed with the speed at which the Israelis were doing things.

On my return to Building 6 I decided that I would start getting rid of my things right away, but I couldn't wait to bark the dog and let my family and friends know that in a matter of months I would be in an Israeli prison waiting to be paroled. My lifelong friend, Sharon Friedman, had arranged a house for me to stay in on the beach in an area known as Afridar in Ashkelon, south of Tel Aviv. She would also give me a position at her school, the English Studio, where I would teach English. It all seemed like a dream, but then I believed in dreams. Dreams give a man hope, and without hope there is no reason to live. I could visualise myself taking long walks on the beach, watching the sunset, swimming in the sea, cleaning myself of all the prison filth that had clung to me for so many years.

For my first two weeks in Building 6, I never dared to bark the dog. Eyes were everywhere. I could feel I was being watched. In the house next to Dani's were two Blue Shirts, and although I was in their football team, one could never be too careful. The Building Chief was a nutcase. He walked around looking to catch anybody using the dog or taking drugs. If he caught you, you could pay him money and the problem would disappear, but I didn't even want to take that chance, although there were even some cells that paid a monthly fee to him in order to use the dog freely.

The anticipation of my imminent transfer and eventual freedom was liberating. In my mind I was free already. Everything I had endured had made this moment that much more worthwhile. Freedom was something I would never again take for granted. I had not been creative for some time, and I yearned to express myself creatively again. I also needed to stimulate my mind or else I knew the months would really drag, so I started to write my story. Every morning I tried to devote a few hours to writing.

Considering that I would be going to Israel soon, I got as comfortable as possible. One of the Thais who worked in the clothing factory used offcuts to make me five fairly big pillows to sit on. Dani cooked most of our meals. In the afternoons I played backgammon with Rashid. And, eventually, at night I barked the dog. The dog was my lifeline. Steve, who slept on my right, was romantically involved with a girl in England and he spent most nights writing letters to her. After I introduced him to my dog, however, it took his love affair to another level. Still, my days were long, and in my mind I kept visualising life on the outside, over and over. Even my dreams became fused – prison and life in the free world merged into one. It was a happy picture, the reality of which, of course, was still to be seen. As we moved through time, so the day dictated its own terms.

I filled out my transfer papers and, through one of my visitors, had them delivered to the Israeli embassy, who in turn forwarded them to the Ministry of Foreign Affairs in Israel. Everything was falling into place. Steve and the Dutchman were also in the process of transferring, so the three of us had something else in common now. I found it hard to focus on my book, and the writing was slow. The only thing I looked forward to was barking the dog, which I would do till the early hours of the morning. I slept very little and took naps in the afternoon instead. In the house next to Dani's on the right was a Chinese. He was very loud and often woke me up. At first I couldn't be bothered getting upset, but, as the weeks turned to months, he really started to get on my nerves.

The guards in Building 6 carried out regular checks. The prison was flooded with mobile phones and drugs and this was a constant thorn in the side of the authorities. The favourite times for raids were straight after roll call in the afternoon or else early in the morning just before our cells were opened. Sometimes we were raided twice a week. They even came to our houses. I had barely been in Building 6 a month when, on a routine check headed by the Building Chief, the chief said to me, not once but twice, in English: 'Pay money, no check.' I was flabbergasted. In all my years in Bangkwang I had never come across a guard who openly asked for money. Normally they used prisoners to ask you. These prisoners were referred to as their *looknong* (boys). This man was greedy and he had a reputation for loving money.

The year before, while I was still in Building 2, we'd heard about a serious incident that had occurred in Building 6. A Blue Shirt had informed on one of the Bad Boys for having a mobile. The guards bust the Bad Boy. After being threatened, the Blue Shirt ran into the office, thinking that he would be safe with the guards. About 30 Bad Boys followed him straight into the office. Some jumped over and through the counter while others pushed their way through the doors. They threatened the guards, who ran away, and then they assaulted and stabbed the Blue Shirt. Within minutes, 100 guards armed with batons and shields rushed into the building. The culprits, who numbered up to 35 prisoners, were rounded up and beaten. They were stripped, had their heads shaved and had their arms tied behind their backs. In their underwear, they were marched in single file out of Building 6 to the area where prisoners had shackles fitted. I was sitting right there at the time, waiting to collect a parcel. From there, they were taken to Building 8 and locked up in single cells. The ringleader, who had also been involved in other murders, was taken aside and beaten so badly that he died. I never saw any of those boys again.

On 18 February 2011 an article about me appeared in the Israeli newspaper *Yedioth Ahronoth* under the headline 'Just Like a Mafia State'. My story had caused disagreement in Israel and had even triggered political tension in the cabinet. Apparently there was some anger in the Ministry of Foreign Affairs over the decision of the Minister of the Interior, Eli Yishay, to grant me Israeli citizenship:

> *The aim of the process is to enable him to be transferred to a prison in Israel and his release here.*
>
> *In an unprecedented decision the Minister of the Interior Eli Yishay's decided to grant Israeli citizenship to a South African citizen serving a twenty-four year term of imprisonment in a Thai jail for dealing in drugs. High-level officials in the foreign office were strongly against the decision but their objection was overruled. Recently the prisoner received his*

Israeli passport that will enable him to be transferred to an Israeli prison and lead to his release in a short time after arriving here. High-ranking officials in the foreign office argue that the issue of an Israeli passport to a South African drug dealer makes Israel look like a Mafia state.

Shani Alexander Krebs, aged fifty-two, was arrested in 1994 in Thailand after he was caught smuggling a large amount of drugs. He was sentenced to life imprisonment but his sentence was later reduced to twenty-four years by the King. He has currently served seventeen of them and has seven years left to serve. This makes him the longest-serving foreign citizen imprisoned in a Thai jail. During the last two years, Krebs and his family, with the help of Chabad Thailand, have been campaigning to receive Israeli citizenship. According to the law, a Jew can only gain Israeli citizenship if he makes Aliyah and comes to live in Israel. Exceptions are made only in extreme circumstances or for humanitarian reasons. This is the first time that the Minister of the Interior has allowed a foreign prisoner to become an Israeli citizen while he sits in a foreign jail.

Krebs approached Minister Eli Yishay and requested him to grant him citizenship in order to enable him to serve the remainder of his sentence in Israel. Rabbi of Chabad Bangkok, Nehemiah Wilhelm, awarded the Jewish prisoner patronage after he stated that he is in the process of 'Chazarah be-tshuva'. Krebs showed remorse for his actions and stated that he had been completely rehabilitated. The Rabbi approached Minister Eli Yishay and brought to his attention the terrible conditions Krebs is living in. Minister Yishay was convinced and granted him citizenship. The professional level within the foreign office were dead against the decision and tried to overturn it but to no avail. Yishay also convinced the Minister of Internal Security, Yitzhak Aharonovitch, to agree to Krebs being transferred to serve time in Israel. The foreign office received orders to hand Krebs his passport. High-ranking

*officials in the foreign office voiced their objection to Minister
of Foreign Affairs, Avigdor Lieberman, but were turned down.*

*Recently the Consul in Bangkok visited Krebs in his Thai
jail and informed him that he is now an Israeli citizen.*

*Negotiations are underway with Thai authorities regarding
his transfer to Israel. High-ranking officials in the foreign
office said 'Israel does not need to import drug dealers even
if he is "chazarah be-tshuva" was the response from the
Ministry of the Interior'. Minister Eli Yishay decided to grant
citizenship to Krebs by the law of return, even though strong
opposition exists, after representatives of the Ministry of the
Interior vouched for Krebs and claimed that he is on the path
to rehabilitation.'*

A couple of weeks later, while in Israel, Rabbi Nechemya was invited to
appear on a radio talk show. There was growing controversy surrounding the issue of my citizenship.

Meanwhile the lawyer working on my case advised my family to
deactivate my Facebook page, as all eyes were on me.

Because of the many limitations confinement imposed, my relationship
with Elisabeth was often shaky. We argued a lot, mostly about ridiculous
things, and every so often we would break up. It may sound ridiculous
even to say that we were in relationship, but we were. It had been love
at first sight for both of us, although that didn't make it any easier.

During one of our break-ups I had connected on Facebook with a
girl, Jessica, who had been my junior at school. She had got married,
had children and now lived in America. One thing led to the next and,
in between making up with Elisabeth, Jessica and I also fell in love. It
got so intense that we ended up having phone sex. I know it sounds
crazy, but there I was – in love with two women, neither of whom
I could touch. Elisabeth fulfilled more of my emotional needs and
Jessica my fantasy physical needs.

One day, when I had been up till the early hours of the morning having cyber-sex with Jessica, I woke up at 5am as usual, but having hardly slept at all. I fulfilled my customary morning rituals of *vassing* (hand washing) and davening, after which, knowing that the cells would be opened soon, I rolled up my bed, packed all my things, lay on the floor with my head resting on the bed, and went back to sleep. No sooner had I shut my eyes than I heard the bottom door being unbolted and the sound of footsteps coming up the stairs. The timing was odd, but I thought it was probaby nothing more than one of the sporadic checks we had grown accustomed to.

This time there were about eight commodores, four of whom were in black combat uniform – and they had weapons. They all approached our cell and simultaneously called my name in Thai. *Fuck*, my heart dropped to my feet. I got up from the floor and made my way towards the bars.

Then I heard the words: '*Yai reun jam*' (Change prison).

Two weeks earlier there had been a similar incident where the regular big drug dealers who were still involved in dealing from within the prison were extracted from different buildings. I was stunned. I wasn't one of those guys. What was going on? The first thing that came to my mind was Elisabeth. It was our anniversary and she was due to visit me that morning.

After being shackled, and carrying my bag over my shoulder, I shuffled my feet along. The restricting chains represented more than just punishment. They symbolised the inhumanity of imprisonment. As I passed Building 2, standing by the gate were three guys, also shackled and with their travel bags. One of them was Chen Ming; the other was Donald. The third guy I didn't know. Things were getting interesting. Wherever we were going, my enemy and I were about to embark on the same journey. It was a little after 7am. There were about 24 of us on the bus. The guys looked half-asleep, their hair ruffled and with long faces. We had all been pulled out of bed, with not even the chance to brush our teeth, let alone eat something.

The Thais knew our destination. We were being moved to the notorious Khao Bin prison, which is near the city of Ratchaburi. This would be my fourth prison in Thailand. I had hastily left a note for Dani, instructing him to ask Elisabeth to contact the South African embassy. It was 19 April, the first day of Pesach, so the Israeli embassy would be closed. I couldn't believe that my departure from Bangkwang coincided with the exodus of the Jews from Egypt. The symbolism was uncanny. Although I was chained, I believed with all my heart that the powers above would work in my favour. Once the South African embassy learnt what had happened, I had no doubt I would be brought back to Bangkwang within the week.

On the bus I sat next to a Nigerian by the name of Oteng Samuel, the only other foreigner. Chen Ming was sitting a few seats behind me. Six months had passed since our fight. I got up from my seat, shuffled in my chains back to where he was sitting and, at the same time as I greeted him, I extended my hand. He took it and we shook hands, understanding without having to speak that the matter was put to rest.

The trip to Khao Bin took three hours.

When I had been there for two days, I put my thoughts and experiences down in writing in my diary. I wrote the words with Jessica in my heart and my mind:

'I can't think of nothing else but you. I'm lying on the concrete floor in another prison with 24 other prisoners sleeping shoulder to shoulder, there is a lot of noise, the guys don't stop smoking. Although alien to my new surroundings, prisons don't differ insofar that I remain confined. Being comfortable is another matter entirely. Knowing how much you love me will give me the strength to overcome this ordeal. I remember you writing in one of your letters "Once in a lifetime you need someone special, a person who changes your way of thinking, who touches your heart and soul and makes each day seem a little more exciting than before." It's now Wednesday, my second day in Khao Bin prison and all that keeps me going are my thoughts of you. When we arrived here yesterday I was checked very thoroughly and my address book was confiscated with your contact details. There was also the incident where I was instructed to remove my gold earring. It was a difficult latch and I couldn't get it out and this really pissed the guards off. So much so that they bought a pair of pliers and wanted to cut it out of my ear. I protested and eventually managed to get it out. While they were checking me, they found the charger for my mobile. It was the adaptor used for a CD player that had been modified. I just acted dumb and said it was for a CD player. After that we were marched to Building 4 where we were given an hour's lecture by the Director. During this time, I kept dozing off, and really struggled to listen to the shit he was talking. He couldn't stop looking at me and at the end of the talk, motioning with his forefinger, instructed me to cut my hair. And if I failed to do so, waving a baton, he threatened to have me beaten. I had no choice but to acquiesce. The blond curly locks cascaded down my shoulders. It never bothered me, as my mind was so preoccupied thinking of the two women I loved. My heart longs for one and my body longs for the tender touch of the other. I am missing you something terrible. I promised myself to write to you every day [in this diary], even if only a paragraph. Today I wrote a petition asking the Director to transfer eight of us back to Bangkok as we are innocent and have been unjustly accused of dealing drugs in the prison. All we can do now is wait for the embassy. The food isn't great, I have a running stomach and my entire body is sore from sleeping on the concrete. I miss reading your letters and hearing you express your love. I was moved here with another foreigner, much younger than me, but quite the athlete. He is a Nigerian. We hooked up and decided to stick together. Our group has grown to six members and during the day we hang out in the dining room. There is no prison canteen and one cannot buy anything besides the regular plastic bags of food. I smuggled in 6 000 Thai baht but it is basically worthless. One of the main features of Khao Bin prison is the mobile phone signal jammers that operate around the clock. These jammers are to prevent inmates from doing drug deals from behind bars, a problem that became worse after many of the biggest drug dealers were moved from other prisons and relocated to Khao Bin. It's really crazy as there is only one spot in the entire building where it is possible to get a signal. The owners of the dogs are generous enough to allow us a minute or two to speak to our families. It's bizarre as some mornings there is a queue of about 30 prisoners waiting to call. I wish I could hear your voice, but I know a few seconds would only intensify our need and desire.

574

'Today is Thursday 21st April. It's really tough here. We are in the punishment building, we are approximately 160 inmates, supposedly all the big dealers from every prison in Bangkok. I have since learnt that it's approximately only ten. The rest such as myself and many others were scapegoats. If all the big players were moved out of Bangkok it would cripple the prisons financially. (A lot of the dealers from Bangkwang had actually paid money to the guard in charge of transfers to keep them in Bangkwang, from where they can continue to sell drugs on the outside.) The battle continues and today I made my second petition asking the prison authorities to allow inmates to receive parcels. This has caused quite a stir among the guards. Around 2.45pm I was called over the loudspeaker, saying that I had a visit, and that it was a lawyer. Well you cannot imagine my excitement, I ran to the office thinking my nightmare was over, only to learn that my address book had been returned. Otherwise our days are very boring and the heat is unbearable. You are in my thoughts every waking moment and I keep thinking of what must be going through your head and if you miss me a fraction of how much I miss you, then you must be going out of your mind too. I still cannot believe how intense things got between us, and it just continues to grow. I imagine my sister called you to let you know that I was moved to another prison. In my cell we are now twenty-five Thais. I still don't have a bed but managed to acquire a blanket which is very thin, but better than nothing. My time in the cells is very difficult and there is a constant murmur of convicts from different groups around the cell. It is fucking crazy, yet I'm not perturbed in the least. I know in my heart of hearts that *Hashem* has a reason for sending me to hell, hopefully I can make the difference and there is a lesson to be learnt. I'm praying that the embassy, be the SA or the Israeli, are doing something to have me transferred back to anywhere in Bangkok. It's ridiculous that I was transferred out here; I hope Dani isn't abusing my dog.

'Today is Friday 22nd and as usual my head is filled with thoughts of you. My longing to hear your voice intensifies. Fridays are the only days that Building 4 in Ratchaburi Khao Bin are allowed visits. We were all hoping that at least one of us in the group would get a visit.

After taking a shower, I tried to try to connect with Elisabeth. One of the Big Legs who had done time with me in Bangkwang allowed me to bark the dog. Liz never recognised my voice at first and when she did, she told me I was going to be moved to Klong Prem's Lard Yao prison on Monday. I couldn't contain my excitement and share the good news with some of my friends who half-heartedly believed me.'

Chapter 18

Raining, Cats and Dogs

Once you are moved to Khao Bin, it's regarded as going to hell. Nobody gets out of there alive. I spent most of the morning of my fifth day there walking around collecting signatures for the parcel petition. This attracted a lot of attention from the commodores. It seemed to make them nervous. Around 12.30 I went to the office to complain that there was no water to shower with. The day before, the second chief had told me that since I'd arrived at Khao Bin, he'd had a permanent headache. 'Likewise,' I replied. When I left the office I decided to walk up and down the driveway, which was in a horseshoe shape. After I'd done about four laps I was called to the office and informed that I should gather my belongings. I was to be moved to Klong Prem. I wasn't happy that my mates were going to have to suffer while I was going to a better prison, but all the same I was relieved. Actually, I didn't quite believe it. I quickly ran to pack my things, said my farewells, and was then escorted out of the building and taken to be shackled.

The drive to Klong Prem prison was a long one. I stood and stared out of the window, watching the flow of pedestrians and people in the cars and buses going by. It was a strange feeling, wondering what those people's lives were like. Eventually we got to Klong Prem at about 4pm. I was subjected to a thorough search, and this time the good-luck R10 note that my sister Joan had sent me was confiscated.

I was taken to Building 2, where I was thoroughly searched again and also questioned by the Building Chief and four other guards. One of them wanted to know if there was gambling going on in Khao Bin prison. I told him I wasn't sure but that I personally had not seen any gambling in the short time I was there, which was a lie. They played Hi-Lo in Khao Bin, which is a game played with three dice. The stakes for one throw ran into millions of Thai baht. Some of the guys at Khao Bin were thought to be among the biggest drug dealers in Thailand, and their business continued behind its walls.

While I was being searched, one of the trustees found where I had hidden my money, but the guy was decent and he just slipped it back in its place. After the search, I was placed in what I assumed was death row. I was still suspected of being a big fish. I was hoping to get into a cell with some other guys who might be barking dogs, but instead I was locked up on my own.

The next day I discovered I was actually locked in solitary confinement. Inmates in solitary are held indoors for 23 hours and allowed out for an hour each morning between 11 and 12. The Building Chief was kind enough to give me a TV to watch, and, even though it had only one channel, just having the TV as background noise made me feel less lonely. I had no bedding whatsoever besides my towel. The concrete floor of the cell was covered in old vinyl, which offered a bit of comfort but not much.

I asked one of the trustees to call a foreigner to come and see me; any foreigner, I said, it didn't matter who. I just needed somebody to help me. So along came this guy from Ukraine. He was a strange dude. I asked him if he could arrange drinking water for me, some washing powder and a bed or blanket or anything I could make a bed from, promising to pay back whatever expenses he incurred. He said he would see what he could do, but that was the last I heard from him. Fortunately, some of the Thai inmates were far more compassionate, and they helped me out with drinking water, at least.

Later on, I managed to bark the dog and called Elisabeth, who had heard through her sources that the reason I'd been moved was because I was connected with the big drug dealers. She sounded as if she doubted me. I explained what I suspected had happened, but not because I needed to defend myself. One of my friends, the Burmese guy Donald, who was in charge of the church in Building 2 at Bangkwang and who spent most of his days reading his Bible and teaching English to other prisoners, had also been moved to Khao Bin.

I was fervently hoping that the embassy would come and see me after the weekend, so that, with their support, I could try to insist on being moved back to Bankwang. It was imperative that I be able to clear my name. Also, I didn't think I could survive in Klong Prem, as prisoners there were not allowed to receive parcels. Neither were they allowed foodstuffs from visitors, nor to prepare their own meals. In fact, the system in Klong Prem was completely different to that in Bangkwang.

I paced the corridor for over three hours. Later on, my new Thai friend, Jib, allowed me to bark the dog for a few minutes. When I heard my sister's voice, it brought tears to my eyes. Although I knew that in America Jessica would be asleep, I still hoped there was a chance we could speak. I needed to hear her voice, to be assured of her love. She didn't answer her phone, but I managed to leave her a message, which I hoped would give us both the strength to get through what lay ahead.

My entire body ached. I had not slept for almost a week. I was kind of at peace knowing that a connection with Jessica had been made, but at the same time my longing for her intensified. I lay on my bed, watching the rotating fans on the ceiling and wondering what was going through her mind. It was going to be almost impossible to contact her regularly, if at all. There were three dog handlers that I knew of, but they were virtually unapproachable. I hoped that I would be moved back to the general population soon. Apparently, there were a lot of foreigners in Building 5. I had to admit, though, that I wasn't finding it too bad in solitary confinement. The privacy was welcome.

With no clocks around anywhere, I lost all concept of time. The only means of telling the time was my body clock, which responded to nature's call at 5am and was as regular as clockwork. Monday came and went, with neither of the two embassies, the South African nor the Israeli, coming to visit. I heard that the South African embassy was closed that day, so I presumed the Israeli one must have been as well. During the hour that I was allowed to leave my cell, I met up with an Italian guy. He was very friendly and later brought me some fruit juice, two litres of drinking water and some washing powder. I was very grateful. One of my Thai neighbours showed me how he rinsed his washing: put your clothes in an ordinary plastic bag, fill it with water and a little fabric softener and shake. I felt as though I was back in the fucking army. Anyway, his method worked pretty well.

I spent a lot of time writing in my diary. I couldn't help feeling frustrated and melancholy at the same time. It was hard to accept where I found myself now.

Tuesday 26 April 2011 marked exactly 17 years, to the day, that I had spent within the corrupt Thai prison system.

'Here I am in another prison all on my own,' I wrote in my diary. 'It's kind of reminiscent of creation. We are born into this world alone, and depart from it on our own. Ironically I have always, or at least for the most part, been a solitary person. I spoke to Elisabeth today, who will be visiting me tomorrow. A part of me does genuinely love her, but it's different to what I feel for you [Jessica]. I know she would have a major freak out if she heard me say that I loved her as a sister. I can never tell her about us. I've managed to separate the two of you from my mind and heart. I love you and can only wonder about our fate. Strangely my cell no is 34, exactly the age I was when I was arrested. Perhaps it's a sign of a miracle about to happen.'

I managed to figured out how to tell the time. When I moved the TV out of tune, as the picture jumped around the time was briefly displayed up in the left-hand corner; it wasn't exactly visible there, but then it dropped down to the side near the centre, and, with the aid of my spectacles, I could make out the time.

The next day, Wednesday 27 April, I was called for a visit around 9.45am. This prison had some really strict regulations. Whenever you left the building, you were thoroughly searched; then, halfway to the visit room, there was another checkpoint, where you had to remove your shirt and pass through a metal-detecting walkway; and finally you were searched again by the White Shirts.

Elisabeth arrived around 10am and it was great to see her. If I'd still been at Bangkwang, we would have had our contact visit that day, but that would have to be put on hold for now. It seemed that anybody who got involved with me emotionally had to go through hell. The visit was only 30 minutes, so we had to try and get as much said as possible. I knew in my heart that I loved Elisabeth with a very deep love, but I felt torn between her and Jessica. What the fuck was that about? Did I still hate women, and were they only objects of desire to be done with as I pleased and disposed of when I wanted? My relationships with each of these women were very different. I felt like I was living two lives, and the lines blurred between what I felt for whom. Some days my conscience really troubled me, but then I would convince myself that my circumstances justified my behaviour. My mind was very focused on Jessica at this time, especially when I was alone in my cell and writing in my diary.

I began to find myself adapting to a different prison lifestyle. I still had not had a visit from either of the embassies. The longer I stayed in solitary, the more used to it I became. I felt almost content there. The dilemma I faced was whether to try to move to Building 5 in Klong Prem or to stay where I was. Each had its own disadvantages. I also knew that I should try to get back to Bangkwang, because all my things were there. If I stayed here, how was I going to get them? I supposed it wasn't really up to me where I went anyway. Only G-d knew what was in store for me.

After only a few days there, Klong Prem prison, I decided, was the rear of a donkey's arse. The place was designed to make your life as difficult as possible – although it was better than Khao Bin. If it hadn't been for Elisabeth going to the embassy, no doubt I would still have been there. I finally managed to connect with Jessica and it made me so happy. Hearing her voice was amazing. As was becoming my habit now, I wrote to her in my diary:

'... my little sex goddess, you sounded a little sleepy but ever so sexy. Babe, you are also at the forefront of my thoughts. Hearing you declare your undying love for me meant the world, and will give me the strength to endure the days until we speak again. I so much crave to reconnect on a deeper emotional level with you. Unfortunately we are restricted from doing so, because of our limited time. Earlier on I was lying on my back, immersed in thoughts of you and I had all these conversations with you in my head. There is so much I want to say to you ...'

On 29 April, at around midday, I managed to phone Elisabeth again. I had been in solitary confinement for almost a full week. Elisabeth mentioned that the rabbi was planning to come and see me, but she couldn't tell me when. Then, while I was eating lunch, I was called for a visit. It was the rabbi. According to him, the Department of Corrections had acknowledged that they had made a mistake in moving me out of Bangkwang in the first place and they seemed apologetic. He couldn't tell me much more than that. I hoped and prayed that I would be transferred back there. Apart from anything else, Bangkwang was a far more relaxed prison, and, after so many years there, it had become my home. Some of my friends there were like family.

Because it was the weekend, we were not allowed outside for our daily one-hour exercise session, and I was struggling to remain cheerful. I could feel depression threatening at the edge of my mind. When or indeed *whether* I was actually going to be transferred was also causing me some anxiety. As the days passed I became more and more restless. Not knowing my fate was killing me. I didn't even feel like writing in my diary any more. Life was starting to take on a dreary monotony.

April turned into May and I was beginning to feel emotionally and physically detached from the rest of the world, which I guess is the purpose of being held in solitary confinement. Once again I was a prisoner within a prison. My body ached all over and I found it virtually impossible to grow accustomed to sleeping on the concrete. My mind was not functioning normally. So many thoughts raced erratically through my brain, with a part of me wondering whether this whole move from one prison to another might even be part of a conspiracy orchestrated by the Israeli embassy.

At midday on 2 May I was told that Osama bin Laden had been killed. The news was all in Thai, so, frustratingly, I couldn't really follow it or get all the details.

At around 3pm we were raided by almost 100 guards, who did a thorough check of the entire building. Fortunately, the guys in solitary had been warned a few hours in advance and they all managed to hide their dogs and chargers, whereas the guys outside were not so fortunate. Over 100 mobiles were seized.

On two different occasions I was woken up in the early hours of the morning by noises that sounded like somebody rattling their shackles, the way the chains sound when you're cleaning them. I thought it was strange, but even stranger was that the noise seemed to be coming from the corner of my room, sort of from the ceiling. Half-asleep, I didn't give it much thought, and just assumed it was coming from the cell next door. The second time I heard the noise something about it was different. There was the noise of the chains again, but this time I felt what I can only describe as a presence. I laughed to myself – maybe there was a ghost around. But fuck, it was weird all the same.

Then, on 11 May, I was moved from cell 34 to a newly painted one, number 38. When I was chatting to my Thai friend Jib, he casually asked me whether I'd heard the ghost in my old cell. He told me that, about three years before, a guy who came from northern Thailand, one of the mountain people, had been sentenced to death and was put in cell 34. He had hanged himself from the bars. From time to time prisoners who occupied that cell thought they heard his ghost ...

At the end of May, I was still in solitary in Klong Prem. I wrote to the Director of the Department of Corrections, Mr Sudhiklom Chartchi, requesting that I be transferred back to Bangkwang. At the same time I put in a request to the Israeli embassy, asking to be allowed to receive the following items: two blankets, one bedsheet, one normal pillow and one round long pillow (known as a sausage). I really needed a bed. We could order blankets through the coffee shop, but as we were allowed to spend only 200 Thai baht a day and a blanket cost 100 Thai baht, that left only 100 Thai baht for food. And the blankets they sold were so thin anyway I'd have had to buy at least 20 just to be comfortable.

Just to get out of the building and to break the boredom, I found a reason to visit the hospital. In Klong Prem you couldn't order fresh vegetables, and I was obliged to eat the oily food they sold us in plastic bags. I was afraid this would lead to my having heart problems again, and I was beginning to experience discomfort similar to what I'd experienced just before my first episode, which was now about three years back. I wanted to ask a doctor if I could go back on aspirin. Since being in solitary, I had lost 5kg.

At the hospital I met two foreigners, an Australian and a Canadian, who were serving short sentences. They seemed stressed and in fact rather overwhelmed by my friendliness – not surprisingly, as I learnt later on that they were both paedophiles!

While I was at the hospital, a group of women prisoners was marched in. Among them was a Western woman wearing a surgical mask. For some reason I thought she might be the South African-Russian girl named Nina Chetchkov. Male prisoners and women prisoners are forbidden to talk to each other, and anyway she didn't notice me. I doubted that she would recognise me. While we were waiting for the doctors to return from lunch, I saw the girls sitting a short distance from me. I walked part of the way across to them and called out to the woman, asking if her name was Nina. She didn't respond, only gave me a glance as if she thought I might be crazy. I walked away, not wanting to attract the attention of the woman guard. A little later, a few of the women prisoners, 'Nina' included, walked past where I was sitting on their way to the toilet. When they came back, she couldn't have been more than a couple of metres away from me.

'Hey,' I said. 'I'm South African. It's me, Alexander.'

'I'm Nina,' she smiled, her eyes lighting up as she removed her mask.

It was quite an emotional moment. Nina and I had corresponded maybe some 15 years back and here we both were – still a long way from home.

All the doctors took lunch from 12 to 2pm. While I was waiting, I asked one of the medical orderlies to fit me in early, as I had not eaten. He rudely replied that if I could not wait, I should return to the building. The rest of the group that had come with me from Building 2 had long since gone back, but one of the White Shirts had been instructed to remain behind with me. Out of spite, he left my name for last, so I saw the doctor only around 5pm. I'd been there since 9 in the morning.

We normally got locked up at 3pm, so while I was still patiently waiting to see the doctor, two guards came rushing into the hospital reception area, searching for me, thinking that I might have escaped. They were not impressed with the hospital when they saw me still sitting waiting to be attended to, and in fact asked me to report the incident to the embassy.

I still didn't have proper bedding and so I arranged with Elisabeth, on her Wednesday visit, to buy me five new towels which I would use to make a bed. She could buy these at the prison shop, and they would be delivered to the building at about 1pm. That night, tossing and turning on the concrete, I actually dreamt about the towels. Even my dreams were becoming boring.

On Friday 27 May I finally had a visit from the Israeli embassy. The rabbi came along too, with his sidekick Chai. It was a good visit, but a sobering one. The rabbi informed me that I might not be able to go back to Bangkwang. I had been moved, he said, because I had been categorised as dangerous, and the suspicion that I had been dealing drugs in prison was sticking to me. I was also suspected of having a mobile phone. That I had a dog was true, but the rest was all hogwash and I told the rabbi.

When I first arrived at Klong Prem, there were five of us in my section of solitary confinement, two of whom were on death row and had shackles permanently welded onto their legs. We were locked up for 23 hours a day. I had arrived there fairly late in the afternoon, when all the other prisoners were already locked up. Although it was a punishment section, the rooms also had guys in them from the general population, which meant that we would be let out around 6.30am and then they would get locked up at the same time as us in the afternoon, around 3pm.

My first morning when I had a cell to myself, when we were woken, after the other guys had been let out, we were required to take our personal possessions – beds, plates, cutlery, books, whatever you wanted – into the corridor. Our cells were locked and the electricity was switched off. One of the cells would be left open so that we could use the toilets during the day. Just outside the solitary section, in the passage, were two or three tables where the guards would lounge around.

It was a Saturday morning, so there was only one commodore on duty. Between the five of us, three of the guys had dogs. They would use them quite freely, and the guards paid no attention. Jib also had a dog, but, because he had ordered several executions from within the prison, some of the outside guards would pay him regular visits hoping to catch him with his dog and extort money from him.

In that first week, I built a hiding place in my cell and I agreed to keep Jib's dog for him in the early hours of the evening, when it was customary for the guards to raid our cells. Naturally, I was taking a huge risk, but my hiding place was an excellent one and I felt reasonably confident. That evening, while watching *Thailand's Got Talent* on TV, Jib, who slept diagonally across the corridor from me, gave a whistle, signalling that he wanted his dog. Using a mirror, we would watch to see what the guards were doing. They were approximately 40m away but couldn't access our section without opening the security gate. This became our routine: Jib would signal to me that he was ready, then I would take the dog out of its hiding place and put it in a plastic bag with the charger. Then I would lie flat on my stomach close up to my steel-cage door, at the bottom of which were bars, so I could actually reach out into the corridor. Jib would then shoot a long length of string across to me, with a little metal ring attached to an elastic, a distance of about 7m. I would stretch my arm out and, still lying on my stomach, retrieve the metal ring with the string, and quickly tie it around the plastic bag with the dog inside it. Using my mirror, I would look again to make sure the coast was clear. (The first time I went through this rigmarole, I can tell you it was quite a nerve-racking operation.) Then I'd release the plastic bag and Jib would haul it in as quickly as possible. I would peek in the mirror one more time to see if the coast was still clear, but, even if it wasn't, it would have been too late because Jib by then was already hauling it in. Jib would bark the dog till morning, and I would go back to do whatever it was I was doing – either reading or watching TV. In exchange for keeping the dog for Jib, he would allow me an hour on Saturdays and Sundays to call my family. The risk was definitely worth it. Because of the time difference between Thailand and North America, and Jessica's own personal circumstances at home, this wasn't always easy for us, but we set a time on a Saturday when I would call her. These conversations were intense and passionate.

One night, when Jib was busy hauling in the phone, one of the cats that lived in solitary started grabbing the plastic bag and trying to pull it just as a guard walked past in the corridor. I don't know if we were more scared of the cat snapping the string or of the guard catching Jib in a highly illegal act. We were both shitting ourselves. What if the cat broke the string and ran off with the phone? I was hysterical; I couldn't help laughing, but more from nerves than anything else. Luckily for us, the cat ran off and the commodore was none the wiser.

Some of the guys would just wrap the charger in a cloth and throw it across the corridor. Sometimes it would fall short, and the guy who wanted to use it couldn't reach it; it was also difficult to throw because you couldn't swing your arm properly. You had to sort of flick it. There were instances where a guard would quietly be watching the whole operation; after a while, he would open the security door, sneak up to the cell and listen. When he was satisfied that someone was using a mobile, as he'd suspected, his face would suddenly appear at the bars and he would demand that the phone be handed over, or else he would just open the cell door, march in, do a thorough search and confiscate both mobile and charger. When the guards confiscated a phone, some of them would hang on to it and sell it to a guard in another building; those who were less corrupt would actually take a baton and smash the dog in front of you. This was always such a sad moment, because a dog cost in the vicinity of 40 000 to 200 000 Thai baht.

Despite the ongoing national crackdown on mobiles and drugs, both continued to circulate among inmates and it was largely business as usual. Ironically, the dealers were probably doing more business selling drugs inside prison than they ever did outside. But there were consequences, of course. Numerous dealers who were caught outside the prison would give information about their contacts behind bars, and then these inmates would be rounded up and a new civilian case would be opened; in addition, they would be either thrown into solitary confinement or moved to another building.

It was well over a month now that I had been in solitary. Although a comfortable bed was not yet a reality and I wasn't getting much sleep, I was surprisingly content. I began to understand that *Hashem* was preparing me for my freedom. I had been reduced from being in a position of power in Building 2 in Bangkwang, where I had stayed for over 16 years, and then to being a guest in Building 6, and now to here, where I had nothing. Not even a bed. It was humbling. My relationship with G-d had strengthened. Every morning I would put on my *tefillin* and daven. I was back to davening three times a day. I found sometimes that I didn't really care any more whether I went back to Bangkwang or stayed where I was.

I had also acquired a pencil, an eraser and a ruler, and I had started thinking about designing my own pack of cards. I was quite excited at the prospect of expressing myself through drawing again. I decided I would use prison as my theme and depict on the cards some of the depressing faces among Klong Prem's inmates. It was really such a stressful prison. Nobody ever seemed to smile there. Everybody looked depressed.

My sentence was down to 21 years and seven months. This meant that there was a chance I was going to be released in 2012, but I didn't know where I was going or when. And a lot depended on the amnesty that would be granted on 5 December, on the occasion of the King's birthday.

On 9 May our Building Chief came around, accompanied by his usual entourage. At first I thought they were mounting another full-scale search, but this time I was wrong. The chief had come to tell us he was being replaced by the chief from Building 3. He looked very upset to be moving on from Building 2. No doubt this had something to do with the fact that Building 2 housed some of the richest Big Legs in Klong Prem, from whom he was extorting a lot of money. I told him I was really sorry to see him go, and in fact he was a nice guy and more understanding of prisoners than a lot of the others. He said his goodbyes and left; not even 30 minutes later, our new Building Chief arrived, pitching up with the same entourage as his predecessor.

As it turned out, I knew the new guy from Bombat prison, from when I was arrested way back in 1994. He had been one of the guards who had welcomed a truckload of prisoners to Bombat. He was bald, and back then I had nicknamed him 'Kojak' (his real name was Mr Shavolit Pubping, and his peers called him Bobby). He was quite a boorish man, but conscientious when it came to his duties and strict with those who didn't find favour with his pocket. When he walked into our section and saw me there, he came straight up to me. He turned to the other guards and in Thai told them he knew me and that I was very dangerous, and, according to the drug enforcement agencies, that I was involved in selling drugs in the prison.

In return, I greeted him respectfully and then, also in Thai, said, '*Sawadi Kap wanna Kojak, Khun yung mai prokarsiel*' (Hello, Chief Kojak, I see you haven't retired yet). He wasn't impressed, and pretended not to hear what I'd said. Anyway, he didn't respond. I guess he didn't like his nickname. What I'd done was bordering on being over-familiar and may even have belittled him in front of the guards and the prisoners. He had his sidekick with him, a man named Santi. He was a sadist, who enjoyed inflicting physical pain on prisoners. Santi's favourite way of spreading fear was to make prisoners lie on their backs and then, using a bamboo cane, to strike them on the soles of their bare feet. He also used to kick, punch and beat prisoners. What sickened me the most was that Santi was extremely corrupt. My friend Somsak had once actually given him a piece of land to get him to close his eyes to us using a mobile phone.

Later that afternoon, when he was in the corridor, I walked up to Kojak and asked why he had said what he did. I told him that it wasn't true. And although I was in solitary, I still hadn't been told why I was being punished or what I had done wrong. I had not violated any of the prison regulations. Kojak smiled and said in English, 'Joking.' At the same time, he stretched out his hand and I shook it. Then he asked me why I was in Klong Prem. I told him I didn't know.

The next morning there was a major reshuffle in our section. All the normal prisoners who occupied cells in the punishment section had to pack their things and were moved to normal cells. There were others who were also on permanent lockdown, and these people were all moved to our section, bringing us to a total of 16 in solitary confinement. During the move we were pounced on by the prison search party known as '*Moodang*' (Red Caps). Through my own stupidity I was still holding the Bluetooth earpiece of Jib's cellphone. Being a foreigner, I didn't expect a thorough search of my person, so I hid the piece between my thigh and my right testicle. We were all lined up in the centre of the corridor while two of the 30 Red Caps searched each prisoner from head to toe. At the same time, a guard ran a metal detector between our legs, in our pockets etc. I was wearing cut-off denims and, thinking quickly, I placed a tube of lip-ice in my right pocket as a deliberate distraction. It worked. It caught their attention, as it was meant to do. After they were done feeling my balls and ass, I then pretended to assume they were finished with me and tried to push past them, but I was roughly pulled back.

'*Bi-nai?*' (Where are you going?) one of the Red Caps said.

I tried to act dumb and began moving away again, but the trustee pulled me back by the arm. I was instructed to drop my pants. Silently I started praying, asking G-d to close their eyes. And can you believe it – when I pulled my underpants open, showing them my cock, they didn't see the earpiece hidden there. I was told to get dressed and move on, and I allowed myself to breathe one heavy sigh of relief.

The next time we had to entertain the Red Caps was only a few mornings later. This time they raided our cells, taking out our bedding, ripping it apart and rummaging through all our belongings. I was really shitting myself, as Jib's dog was in its regular hiding place, but luckily they didn't find it.

These military-style raids continued almost daily, and at first this was extremely frustrating for me. I found it difficult to control myself. I just wanted to lash out all the time. Then, with time, as strange as it seems, even these raids in a sense became normal. On the positive side, though, once the Red Caps had searched through everything, they would leave, and immediately after they'd gone we would take out our dogs and bark them.

On Tuesday 24 May I was called for an embassy visit. I could see that Anna, the consular officer, was kind of shocked by my appearance. I hadn't shaved for two weeks, and I was going grey on my face. I can't have looked very happy. Anna asked me to please shave, but I explained that you couldn't purchase shaving cream in this fucked-up place, and anyway you could pay up to 5 000 Thai baht for a can. It was unbelievable how expensive things were there. She was very sympathetic and promised to follow up with the Department of Corrections, and to ask to have me transferred back to Bangkwang. In the meantime, she said she would at least request to have me taken out of solitary. I wasn't holding my breath. Nothing seemed to be going my way.

The more I thought about it, the more I realised that coming to prison was not only my destiny but also an opportunity to change. With all the chaos around me, in spite of everything, I felt quite peaceful.

A month later, Eli Gil, the consular representative from the Israeli embassy, the rabbi and the Thai secretary visited me. There was a lot of mumbling, some of it word for word the same stuff Mr Gil had told me six months before, when he had made such a big deal about me being issued an Israeli passport and telling me that all the documentation on their side was ready. The consular officer admitted that, when they had sent my transfer documents to Israel, they had somehow neglected to include my official release date. Now they were waiting for the Thais to give them this last piece of information, but it seemed they were struggling to obtain it from the Department of Corrections. Gil also muttered some incoherent words about having spoken to Sam Goldstein, our lawyer in Israel, but actually it was all crap. The man was lying through his teeth.

At that point I became very emotional and told Gil that unless I was in the next transfer meeting I would refuse to go to Israel. Gil didn't defend himself against my verbal attack, which only made him look even more guilty. Instead he remained cordial and promised to make it his priority to speed up things.

On the matter of my being transferred back to Bangkwang, however, he had no news for me, only that he had forwarded my request letter to the Director of the Department of Corrections. During my outburst, I was almost on the verge of tears, I was so angry. As prisoners, we really had no control over anything that happened on the outside. I was completely dependent on other people, which I found incredibly frustrating.

I could see that the rabbi genuinely had my best interests at heart, but I was quickly losing faith in Mr Gil. I wasn't planning to hold him to his promise, because I believed there was no way he was going to keep it. In fact, I was beginning to believe that the Israeli government had concluded that transferring a South African drug dealer to a prison in Israel, not to mention granting him citizenship, would be a bad move politically after all. Well, I would have to wait and see. I had no other choice.

In solitary in Klong Prem, I found I had little desire to draw or paint. Even my attempt at making my own set of cards fell hopelessly short of the standard I had reached before. In my bleaker moments I couldn't help wondering whether this was another test, or whether the angels had taken back my talent. I wasn't one for sitting around doing nothing for too long, and the only other way to express myself was through poetry, and so I would let my pen lead the way:

POEM 1 (in Solitary)
Wall, walls and more walls. Adorned in steel, like a platoon
of stark imposing monoliths conspiring to escort you beyond
the veil.
Blindfolded in an all-encompassing sinister shred of the sun,
moon and stars, all rolled up in one.
Strapped in a straitjacket to a runaway train with a one-way
ticket to the nearest tow-away zone.
In suspended animation, a portrait of distorted faces reflected
in the hall of mirrors, parallel the ebb and flow of the awak-
ening tides.

From a bird's-eye view, the bridge between madness and sanity is a dark place of 1000 serpents juggling lost souls.
Through men of a pure heart congregating along the Wailing Wall an avalanche of blessings fall down the end of a rainbow.
Self-expression bottled in a jar of Jell-O, high on Ritalin, kids are nothing more than puppets on a string mimicking their parents marking time.
While in the name of global enterprise pharmaceutical giants live the American dream.
Amy Winehouse majestically rode the white horse, straight into rock and rolls legendary club of 27.
In the process of opening our eyes to the ways of the world, Adam and Eve uncovered the very secret that sustains life, Like a mountain of fireworks all going off at once.
Words were drawn, boundaries were crossed. It's friendship such as yours that restore our faith in the human spirit.
Swallow a snake, wrestle a crocodile, in the land where the scales of justice sway to the momentum of a rusty pendulum ultimately the righteous will always prevail.
Listen to the pouring rain, listening to it pour ...

One day, I think it was Sunday 26 June, I felt really homesick, not that nostalgic feeling that borders on euphoric emotion, but one where your entire perception of the world changes. This feeling turned into something more frightening. The walls and floor, and in fact everything, seemed to come alive and take on a menacing appearance, as if at any moment I'd be swallowed up by them. Scared to close my eyes, I turned up the volume on my TV, which usually had a soothing and calming effect on me, but this time it didn't work.

I looked at myself in a mirror and saw an old, white-bearded man. Then the old man with the white beard started going psycho on me. He seemed to be mumbling under his breath about how fed-up he was with prison life, and some bullshit about fulfilling his purpose once he was free. Most of it was incoherent, and the rest made little or no sense. At first I ignored my white-bearded other self, but when he produced a blade, I started to become concerned. I proposed a deal with him: either you shave that fucking white beard of yours, which makes you look like some lost vagrant, or else you lose the blade. I hoped he would agree to the former, which thankfully he did. He shaved his beard. After that, everything seemed to get back on track. The blade was put in a safe place and we began to coexist peacefully. I guess solitary confinement has its way of fucking with your mind.

The visit with the Israeli embassy kept playing over and over in my head like a never-ending silent movie, and a deep feeling of bitterness persisted. The problem with society, and with people in general, is a preconceived notion about prisoners: people think that all prisoners are uneducated and rotten to the core. In my 17 years of incarceration I had come to realise that this was far from the truth. Prison changes a man, and the lessons we learn during our confinement behind those high walls a 'normal' person in the free world wouldn't grasp in two lifetimes. Once you have been caught for breaking the law, you can expect to be discriminated against for the rest of your natural life. Convicts are a condemned species. Forget about second chances. Nobody really gives a fuck.

Still, I desperately waited for news from the Israeli embassy, but nothing was forthcoming. It seemed to me that they were deliberately delaying the signing of my documents. I found myself sliding deeper and deeper into a state of depression, not helped by Elisabeth's departure for Switzerland and her annual holiday. A feeling of hopelessness consumed me. This was compounded by what I could only think might have been hypertension. My spirit felt crushed, physically crushed. One day I almost choked on my own breath, and I could feel my chest closing up. The pain reached as far as my lower back. I know that when I am very stressed I tend to overreact, but this time I thought I was having a stroke. Then, as if an angel had descended from heaven, I remembered something my friend Jenny had written in one of her letters to me. Overcome with a sense of urgency, I scrambled through my things and found an envelope with her familiar handwriting on it. At this point I could sense myself falling over the edge, barely managing to stay afloat. I think I might have been on the border of insanity. Jenny's words pulled me back to life:

> At this point in time, as you read this, ask yourself for a sincere intuitive response to this question: how much energy and focus am I putting into accessing the full range of my inner guidance, my inner knowing, and my commitment to my highest path of unified intent? Who do you truly want to be as a free man, what kind of man? What do you wish to work on when you're free? Apply this in whatever way, to whatever ways your mind takes you, pray for the real Shani to be set free, to follow his noblest path. Find yourself in yourself alone, in the stillest, humblest, most peaceful place in yourself.

That night I wrote in my diary: 'I kind of understand now, what it means, or feels like, to be insane. I was there; I crossed over, but fought my way back. Medication, psychologist, is not always the answer.'

Although I gradually began to feel stronger mentally, my chest pains got worse and I started having panic attacks. My mouth would become dry and my arms and my lips would go numb. One night, the discomfort in my chest area was severe. Believing that I was having a heart attack, I banged my hands on the floor and tried sticking my arms out of the bars, gesturing to the guards to come. I could see with my mirror the guard just standing there, watching me, and then simply walking away. Later, one of my friends shouted for the guards, telling them that the *farang* was dying. I knew I wasn't really dying, but my chest had closed again and I was very pale. When the guards eventually came to my cell and saw me lying there sprawled out on my back, I told them in Thai, '*Hoorchai mi-panha*' (heart trouble), and they said they would call the doctor.

Almost two hours later, the so-called doctor arrived. The guard didn't even open the cell door. I had to go to the bars and stick my hand through, and place one of my fingers in a small electronic gadget, which I think took my pulse and temperature. Then the doctor stuck his stethoscope through the slit in the steel door and listened to my chest, for no more than two seconds. He turned around and, after saying, 'You are very strong,' gave me two sachets of electrolyte beverage powder and an energy drink for sportsmen. I couldn't believe it. There I was, in serious trouble, and that was the best they could do? Really, they didn't give a shit.

I did some slow breathing exercises and said the *Shema Yisrael* over and over. Later I decided that I would stop drinking Birdy, a popular canned coffee drink – maybe that was what had caused my heart palpitations. Generally, though, I had noticed how my health was deteriorating. I was no longer used to oily food and I missed having my fresh vegetables.

When I had been to the hospital to get aspirin, I had met a Jewish guy there, Bevan Rabinowitz, an American citizen who was in Building 6. He seemed okay and suggested I should try to be moved to his building, as there were a lot of foreigners there. I submitted a request to be let out of solitary, explaining that when I had first arrived at Klong Prem I was extremely fit and strong but that, since being deprived of regular exercise and a healthy diet, my physical and mental state was rapidly going downhill.

That afternoon, after we were locked up, the Building Chief came to the punishment section and asked me to make a list of the foods I could eat. He said he was going to try to help get them for me. At least I knew he had read my request, but I wasn't putting any bets on the rest.

One weekend in July, a high-ranking military official, rumoured to be a general in the Thai Air Force, was brought into solitary. He must have been in his late forties. When he arrived he was escorted by some really senior military guys. Every day after that, at least three times a day, and at odd hours, they would come and remove him from his cell, take him outside and give him a serious working-over. It was crazy what they were doing to him. I later heard that apparently he was in the Royal Guard and was supposed to have embezzled a large sum of the Crown Prince's money. The general was really suffering. When he first arrived, he must have weighed about 90kg, but soon he was looking thin and sick. Still they continued torturing him, sometimes during the day in front of other prisoners. One day, they brought him a model of a small aeroplane made out of steel, something that kids would play on in a park, and he was forced to sit in it while prisoners gathered around and jeered. Most of the prisoners laughed at him, but I really pitied the man, and in fact I admired his strength. It was very unusual for the military to be allowed into the prison, but these guys were here every day, even filming what they were doing to this general.

Around 8pm one evening, the lights in the corridors were switched off and I could see the soldiers at the general's cell. They dragged him out, rolled him up in a blanket, hoisted him onto their shoulders and, shouting out military orders, carried him away. I was convinced that he was either dead or that they were taking him somewhere to be killed, but I was wrong. Next morning I discovered that, in Thailand, when someone is wrapped in a blanket and taken against their will, it means the person is going to be executed, Mafia-style. What they had done the previous evening was intended to scare the shit out of the guy. Apparently they carried him some distance, shouting abuse and threats of death all the way. When they reached their destination, Building 7, which was the prison kitchen, they threw him in the pond where he had to endure heaven knows what forms of torture. For two nights in a row after that, the general was forced to crawl on all fours while other inmates shouted at him and kicked him.

I started jogging in the corridor, and after two weeks of exercise my spirits were lifted. Although I was still having strange sensations every now and again in my heart region, I stopped taking the aspirin. I hated taking pills of any sort and preferred to get healthy through exercise and eating properly.

At the end of the month I was called to Room 5, which was at the halfway checkpoint to the visit room and was also the office of the second in command of the prison. My request to the Director of the Department of Corrections had been reviewed, and apparently he wanted to know certain facts regarding my heart condition, diet etc. In the air-conditioned room there were two guards and a translator, and I could see they had a copy of my request. After they had read it through, they subjected me to a series of questions about why I wanted to be transferred back to Bangkwang.

The next day, when I related the story to my Italian friend, he thought it was a very good sign. He was convinced that I would transfer back to Bangkwang as early as the following week. I went back to my cell and waited.

By the middle of August I was still in solitary confinement, but oddly enough I found myself in a better space. This could have been due to the fact that I'd been reading a lot, and healthwise I felt more or less okay. I tried to be patient.

One day, during my one-hour walk, I managed to say a few words to the Air Force general. I discovered that his name was Porcupine and also that he spoke relatively good English. Despite the rough treatment that was constantly meted out to him, his spirits seemed high. I presumed that the money he had embezzled was safely tucked away somewhere and that was what kept him going.

M

The month of October saw nature at its deadliest in Thailand. Continuous rain caused severe flooding that reached catastrophic proportions. Out of 70 or so cities in the country, more than 50 were flooded. Very badly affected was the city of Ayutthaya, about 75km north of Bangkok, which was completely inundated. One of the prisons there was so badly flooded that 5000 inmates had to be relocated to other prisons. Two hundred of these were transferred to Klong Prem, where they were put into Building 5. Two hundred of Building 5's inmates were then moved to our building. This was significant because, ever since the inauguration of the new government, the prime minister, Yingluck Shinawatra, had vowed to crack down on drug distributors, insisting that, once they were arrested, they would be isolated completely from other inmates, more specifically in order to restrict their access to mobile phones.

By the middle of the month, the upstairs section of our building was vacated, and razor-sharp barbed-wire and wire mesh were installed, as well as new steel gates. Our section, approximately 14 of us, among them the most notorious drug smugglers in the kingdom, was supposed to move upstairs, where we would be included among all the new major drug dealers who had recently been arrested. It seemed that the policy of isolating us drug dealers might be suspended indefinitely.

Despite the hopeful meeting I'd had with the second in command after my request to be moved, nothing had happened. My new friend Porcupine was still being subjected to bouts of public humiliation. I heard a story that once he had been taken outside the prison and forced to beg for money on the street in front of a government building, while the military stayed out of view and filmed him. While Porcupine was in a sitting position, his knees folded, and begging as instructed by his military handlers, out of the blue a security guard from the government building suddenly appeared. The guard asked him what the hell he was doing there, and he began kicking him in the face and beating Porcupine with his baton. Luckily for him, his military escort came to his rescue, slapping the unsuspecting security guard and informing him that his victim was in fact a general. Apologising profusely, the guard scurried off like a rat. He must have been very confused!

Another day, while we were outside for our daily walk in the yard, the ice delivery arrived. It was announced over the loudspeaker that the ice would be delayed and that we should all gather around the parade ground. Here Porcupine had to square off with an inmate who weighed about 120kg. They each had to carry five blocks of ice, one block being the size of two and a half standard bricks, from the delivery truck to a point about 20m away, then run back and collect another five blocks. They had to repeat the exercise until there were no blocks of ice remaining on the cart. While this was going on, the military were filming and one of the other prisoners gave a running commentary over the loudspeaker. I felt really sorry for Porcupine, who lost the race – but not by much, I have to say.

While many Thais were clearly amused by the spectacle – almost to the point of hilarity – I did not find it funny. Public humiliation of others is distasteful to me, and so I chose not to participate.

In October I received the news that the Israeli Minister of Justice had at last signed my transfer papers. I also heard that a copy of my second petition requesting a royal pardon had been forwarded to the Palace. My mind was running wild. Imagine if I got a royal pardon *before* the amnesty in December, or managed to get transferred to Israel? I was hopeful and in fairly high spirits, just knowing that something was going on behind the scenes, even though, as on so many other occasions, nothing concrete might materialise. Without hope, it was difficult to remain sane in prison. Even false hope was better than no hope.

On Tuesday 11 October, what started out as a glorious day also brought some sadness for me. That day, my closest friend in Klong Prem, Jib, whose full name was Somsak Metwong, took his last breath. Jib was a notorious gangster, a former Thai boxing champion, and also one of the most honourable fellow criminals I had had the privilege to meet. He succumbed to the powers above after doing what he loved best – boxing. Unfortunately, at 45, and having been on death row for six years (and shackled for the entire duration), Jib was no longer the invincible fighter of 20 years before. During our usual workout in the yard, Jib was called to have a sparring session with one of the new inmates, who was also a formidable Thai boxer. A lot of the other prisoners congregated to watch them working out. I was actually quite stunned to see that Jib managed to go a full five rounds, and I knew that he would be exhausted. It was also an incredibly hot day.

Since I had arrived in solitary, I had offered my services as a masseur to anybody who needed them, and I would give Jib a half-hour massage almost every day. As I watched the sparring session, I imagined that, after this workout, he might be needing more than a massage. He could even end up in hospital.

We went back to our cells, and Jib joined us about 40 minutes later. He didn't look good, and soon broke into a cold sweat. Then he collapsed right next to me. I assumed that, besides having over-exerted himself, he was probably suffering from heat exhaustion. He complained of pains in his chest. I suggested he drink a lot of water. Then I proceeded to give him a light massage around the top of his chest and shoulders, and within five minutes Jib was half-asleep. I left him to sleep until our cells were opened at around 1.30. He got up and stumbled towards his cell, where he lay down on the vinyl-covered floor. In the meantime, I rolled his makeshift bed together and put it in his cell, and I persuaded him to let me help him onto it. Then he asked me for two atenelol tablets, which I gave him with a cup of water. He asked to be left alone, as he was going to retire for the afternoon, and requested that I shut the cell door.

I left his cell but I didn't close the door, thinking that I would check on him as soon as I had packed my own things away. When I returned, Jib was lying on his stomach. His body was twisted in an unusual position and he seemed to be convulsing. I quickly turned him on his side, calling out his name. His face was changing colour as I watched him, and it seemed that his eyes were going to pop out of their sockets. He was grunting like a pig being choked to death. I was so shocked I didn't know what to do. I kept shaking him, trying to bring him back from wherever he was. I shouted for the key-boy, whose name was Pong. 'Call the guards!' I called. 'Jib seems seriously ill!'

When they heard me shouting, four of the other guys in solitary came to his room and hurriedly lifted him. I took his right arm and shoulder and together we ran out of the cell, carrying Jib between us. By the time we reached the front gate and put him in a wheelchair, I could see in his face that his life was slipping away. I tried to find a pulse but felt nothing. I hoped for the best, but in my heart I knew he was gone.

Even though Jib always seemed remorseful for all the murders he had committed, he told me he had never killed anybody who didn't deserve it. It seems that no man is above retribution. The distance from our building to the hospital was about 1.5km. In the days that followed,

I learnt that the guard who had supposedly rushed him to hospital had stopped for some time at the White House, the control centre of the prison. It was almost as if they had deliberately killed him.

In prison, friends come and friends go and it isn't wise ever to get too close to anybody. I mourned my friend for exactly 22 hours.

Chapter 19

Amnesty!

Amnesty countdown. 15 October, my birthday, believe it or not, was a wonderful day. It was only 52 days to the amnesty and I was 52 years old. On this day, I thought of all the people who had a special place in my heart – mainly my family, of course, whom I continued to miss with a deep longing.

On the morning of 19 October, four of the original five of our group were moved into the general prison population, leaving me still in solitary confinement. By now, after almost six full months, I was fed up with the place, fed up with the stench and filth in the corridors, the ash and cigarette butts (almost everyone smoked), and the almost suffocating smell of cat urine and cat shit. It reached the point where I couldn't bear it any longer, and I went to the guards and asked them to supply me with cleaning materials. I also requested that some of the guys be let out of their cells to help me clean. They didn't seem to have a problem with this and we were supplied with scrubbing brushes, buckets and hard straw brooms. There were ten of us who set to work. We scrubbed the entire section, including the walls on both sides of the corridor.

While we were hard at it, the military arrived for Porcupine, who, as usual, was forced to endure yet another bout of humiliation. Besides helping us sweep with the filthy water, he had to do push-ups and roll around in the soapy water. Along with another inmate, I was busy sweeping the waste water into one of the empty cells, where one of the other guys was using a tin can to scoop the water into the sunken toilet. Porcupine came across to me. 'Alex, give me the broom,' he said. Porcupine was expected to work himself, to the point of dropping. I refused to give it to him and told him he should rest. All this time the military guys – there were about five of them – were looking on and one was filming us with a video camera. Porcupine wanted the broom so that he could do the work instead of me, but I told him no way. During our brief exchange of words, I heard one of the soldiers say in Thai, 'Get this shot with the foreigner,' so there I was being filmed with Porcupine scooping water into an empty cell. I wondered if the Crown Prince of Thailand, or at least his subordinates, were conscientiously watching these daily videos and what they made of this piece.

Once we had finished cleaning, I very politely asked everybody to please keep the corridor clean and to use ashtrays instead of throwing their cigarette butts all over the place. The following morning, when we were let out into the corridor, I was quite impressed that they seemed to have listened to me. It was a small victory, but a victory nevertheless for the one non-smoker among them.

Prisoners generally tend to be very selfish. They think only of themselves, and some of the guys I was obliged to live with were really very dirty. I think I washed my hands about 100 times a day. I don't know if I suffer from OCD, but the filth in Klong Prem really got to me. I would even wash my hands after shaking somebody else's.

After our major clean-up, there were hardly any cat shit deposits along the corridor walls, but every few days I took to sprinkling washing powder along there just to make sure. The responsibility for cleaning the corridor was the key-boy's, and he was also in charge of opening and closing the cells every day. First he would sweep the area, and then he would take an old blanket, roll it up and put water on it. Then he would push it along the floor with a T-shaped, wedged broom. This blanket was so dirty and smelly I'm quite sure it was never washed. Eventually, I took it upon myself to start cleaning the corridors in the afternoons.

Every morning, my cell and one of the Big Legs' cells would be opened first, and there was always cat shit somewhere along the corridor. I would pick it up with a piece of cardboard and some tissue (as the Thais call toilet paper) and afterwards, clean the area with a rag and some washing powder. Then I would sprinkle water all over the corridor and, using the blanket and broom method, would start mopping. I would work from the outside, along the edge of the square, working my way to the middle. When the key-boy cleaned the cat shit, the problem was that he always left some residue behind. The urine he never wiped up at all, so he would simply mop it and spread it around the corridor. Then, once he was finished, he would just fold the wet blanket up and hang it in one of the empty cells, which I called the spare room. The blanket smelt disgusting, and its damp stench turned into an intolerable odour. I don't think there is anything worse that a mixture of stale urine and cat shit, but the key-boy seemed completely immune. He would perform the same mopping ritual every morning without even the twitch of a nostril. I couldn't understand it.

In the afternoon, after I had done my laundry, as quickly and as inconspicuously as possible, I would give the blanket a thorough scrub, wash and rinse. Then I would open it out and hang it up on one of the shower curtain rails in the spare cell.

Pauporesor was a term used by the drug police. It was the name given to those inmates who were suspected of doing drug business outside the prison. Some of these guys had been in solitary confinement for up to two years already. One Friday morning towards the end of October, all the *pauporesor* guys were told that, in a month, they would be let out of solitary. One of them asked the prison authorities, 'What about *tarnchad*?' (foreigner). The guards called me and said that if I wanted to come out of solitary, they would let me. At that point, it was so overcrowded outside that I told them I would rather stay where I was for the time being. We still had the extra 200 from Building 5 and, added to that, the authorities had closed off one large area at the rear of the building as well as the indoor football field, which was in a big warehouse. For once, I agreed with the guard. More importantly, for once, it was my choice: solitary was best for me, and it would keep me out of trouble.

One day after our exercise session between 10 and 11am, I was sitting and chatting with my Italian friend and one of the Nigerians who had temporarily been moved from Building 5. His name was John, and he told me about an incident that had taken place the previous year in Bombat prison. Over the past couple of years, there had been an influx of Iranian prisoners, all of whom had been caught smuggling 'ice' (methamphetamine), or 'numkem'. The problem started in one of the predominantly Muslim cells. Out of about 58 in the cell, 40 were Iranians. One of the Thai Muslims, a Malay, was praying when two of the Iranians were engaged in conversation. The Thai Muslim asked them to keep quiet, but the Iranians ignored him. An argument ensued, which very quickly erupted into a fight. During the night things remained calm, but the following morning the Malay was seen sharpening a piece of bamboo. One of the Iranians got to hear about this, and he was also warned not to go near the shower area. As the day progressed, absentmindedly he walked past or through the area where the Malay was hanging out. Apparently, the Malay crept up beside of him, and thrust the bamboo spear through the front of his forehead. It exited at the back of his head. (While this might sound like a slight exaggeration, I did remember hearing the same story while I was in Bangkwang.)

A couple of Iranians then pounced on the Malay and beat the shit out of him. The next thing, the entire building of about 500 inmates turned on what were no more than 80 Iranians. With the odds of five to one, it turned into a real bloodbath.

It was time for me to get back to the punishment section, so I said goodbye to John the Nigerian and my Italian friend. On my way in, I saw that the food was arriving. The food system in Klong Prem worked differently from Bangkwang. There was a menu of maybe 50 or 60 dishes to choose from, most of which were Thai – very oily and spicy – and prepared by the wives of the guards. The food was put into plastic bags. The average price of one bag was 25 Thai baht. There were all sorts of dishes – macaroni and chicken, ginger with black mushrooms and chicken, and my favourite, *som tum thai*. This was made from raw papaya and dried shrimps, tomatoes, green beans and a chilli sauce. It was prepared in a mortar and eaten raw – very tasty. A lot of Thai food is delicious, and everything contains chillies. You could also get a salad, which most of the foreigners used to order.

No sooner was I back in my cell than I heard that both my Italian friend and John were being transferred to Bangkwang. We said our goodbyes and I tried not to feel bitter. It was I who had suggested and encouraged the Italian to change prisons because life in Bangkwang was much easier than in Klong Prem. Now all I could do was wait for my turn.

The main news story on TV was still all about the floods. The heavy monsoon rains that had been drenching the country since mid-July had wreaked havoc all over South-East Asia, and parts of Thailand were experiencing the worst floods in 50 years. Villages, historic temples, farms and factories were inundated. It was estimated that at least 300 people had died so far, and rescue workers and emergency services worked night and day to prevent a humanitarian disaster. About 8.2 million people were affected and the loss to the economy was enormous. What amazed me was the fighting spirit of the Thai people. Many of them had lost everything, and yet they seemed always to be smiling. Flooding of course wasn't unusual in Thailand, and it was the low-lying villages that always got hit the worst, but I'd never seen anything like this in my entire life.

According to the International Committee of the Red Cross, who were having daily meetings with the Department of Corrections to ensure the welfare of prisoners, Bangkwang was still dry. The prison had managed to keep the waters from entering, while the surrounding area was inundated. At least I knew my things were safe, and dry – if only for the moment.

On Wednesday 26 October our cells weren't opened at the usual time. Instead, a handheld bell was rung an hour earlier. After about 30 minutes there was a flurry of activity, but it was hard to guess what was happening. Using my mirror and pointing it outside the bars, I could see some of the guards busy ushering prisoners along the corridor. Inmates being transferred was not an unusual occurrence, but in fact an evacuation was in progress. About 140 guys from our building were moved, and they were allowed to take with them only the clothes on their backs. It seemed that all the life-sentence and death row prisoners were being transferred to other prisons, and later that morning I learnt that almost all the women had been evacuated from the women's prison as well. And apparently all death row inmates from Bangkwang had also been moved, to Khao Bin.

Since the start of the floods, water and food supplies had dwindled. Fortunately I had managed to stock up and to secure a lot more drinking water. The atmosphere in the prison was one of apprehension. Some days there was no food delivered, and our other orders were incomplete. There was another mass exodus of evacuees one morning, 300 prisoners in total, and not because of the floodwaters, but because of the shortage of food. We were right to be worried: no food deliveries could reach us. To make sure we didn't starve and to avoid a possible riot, the Department of Corrections took the decision to relocate prisoners instead. As no one was allowed to take his personal possessions, we assumed this was a temporary measure until things returned to normal.

My breakfast that morning consisted of two almonds, one date and a small carton of soy milk. I still had some cans of pilchards in tomato sauce, a can of tuna and a bag of oats, but I was trying to ration myself. I had also saved a small loaf of raisin bread that I planned to eat for Shabbos.

We were now down to 400 prisoners and I suspected we might be moved upstairs in the event that the floodwaters began to seep into the prison. Bangkok was built on marshland, after all, and water would rise up through the ground. Walls and barricades would not prevent the prison from flooding. I kept having visions of the rising water filling up my cell, with me standing on the television. There was an eerie stillness about the place, with none of the usual hum and buzz of muffled conversations.

I decided to put in a second request to be let out of solitary confinement. I've never been a pessimistic person, but, as things stood, I somehow couldn't envisage the King being in the mood to celebrate his birthday in December when almost his entire kingdom was under water. It was very possible that we would not get an amnesty, but I kept that thought to myself.

The days passed slowly, and every few days more prisoners were relocated, until only 270 inmates remained in Building 2. For a while, things looked like they were getting back to normal, and we were told that we could start placing our regular food orders once again. These came intermittently, however, and the flooding continued to disrupt supplies. I was thankful, at least, that I had a dry floor to sleep on and a roof over my head, compared to some of the misery I watched on TV. It was ironic, when you think about it: prison seemed like not a bad place to be.

In November, we heard that half of Bangkwang prison had also been evacuated and that the rest were expect to be moved soon. I couldn't help wondering anxiously about the possessions I still had there, mainly photographs and letters. Then we heard that the floodwaters had reached the outside walls of Klong Prem and that the water was at knee height. Chatuchak, the district where Klong Prem prison is situated, was declared a high-alert risk area, and some of the guards began wearing gumboots. Those inmates who were evacuated had left all their personal belongings in their cells, and almost every day the guys in my section would ask the key-boy to unlock these cells so that they could pilfer whatever they could. I was quite relieved I was still there, only imagining how quickly my things would have disappeared. After more than six months in solitary, I had accumulated quite a lot of possessions. I was really shocked at the behaviour of some of the Thais who were with me in solitary. They displayed no consideration for others, and did not respect the property of even their fellow prisoners. Beds disappeared, as did toiletries and any foodstuffs they found lying around.

Meanwhile, my friend Porcupine, whose real name I had discovered was Turkit Junsaung, was still being put through a vigorous exercise session every day. I had to admire the man; at 55, his endurance levels were remarkably high.

When I first arrived in Klong Prem and was placed in solitary confinement, I received a letter from an ex-King Davidian, Ian M, who was at least eight years my junior. When he heard of my plight, he offered to help me with whatever I needed. After assuring him that all my needs were provided for, and thanking him for his offer, I did suggest that there was one thing he might do: this was to contact my sister and to be of moral support to her, as I knew she was struggling emotionally. Ian came through for Joan, and he and his family developed a strong friendship with mine. Through a friend in Israel, he arranged a prayer from a prominent Kabbalah rabbi, a prayer that I would have to repeat ten times a day. It went like this:

> *Master of the Universe who can do everything, (release) and redeem Eleazer Ben Katelyn like the blink of an eye, immediately in the merit of the Tzaddik, the foundation of the world. In the same way you released Daniel from the Lion's den, so too, release Eleazer Ben Katelyn immediately (in the blink of an eye). And then we will thank you with song and music and rejoicing of thanks and joy.*

I wondered what makes a man do something so great for another man he barely knows, never judging or condemning, and I reached the conclusion that such men are messengers of *Hashem*.

I said this prayer five times in the morning and five times in the evening as part of my morning and evening prayer ritual, after reading from the Book of Psalms. I never thought or believed that, through this prayer, I would be physically released from prison. Instead, I understood that the prayer was part of something far more profound. It wasn't clear yet what this was, but I knew in time I would understand why I'd been told to recite it.

The King of Thailand celebrates his birthday in cycles of 12, so 2011 was a huge occasion and, the natural disaster of the flooding notwithstanding, we anticipated that there would be an amnesty. What we didn't know was what reduction drug cases would get, although usually we were granted considerably less than offences such as murder, rape or robbery, etc. In Thailand, there was no guarantee of anything. Things changed from day to day; governments were overthrown by the military; the Red Shirts were fighting the Yellow Shirts; and every so often the country teetered on the brink of civil war. And now the flooding had injected more uncertainty. Rumours of an amnesty continued to circulate, however, and gave us a glimmer of hope.

The one Western foreigner left in my section was an Eastern European guy. He was not my best friend, but beggars can't always be choosers, and so sometimes we would hang out together. He seemed quite knowledgeable about the internet and how you could make money on it. Health products, he told me, and vitamins and the like, were sure money-makers. Everything depended on the volume of traffic you were able to attract to your website. The idea was to outsource all the responsibilities to a network of agents, who would do all the work for you. Talking to him, I realised that this was an area I had no knowledge about, but I felt that it might be exciting to explore it once I was free. It was at times like this that I longed for my freedom. I longed to be part of the progress the world had made over the past 18 years while I had been deprived of my freedom. I couldn't even begin to imagine how much I had missed and lost. The thought scared me. How would I cope? Would I fit into society? Would people accept me, or would they always stare at me with wary eyes? During these years in prison, I had come to realise that women, particularly, were completely fascinated by me, but was this only because they saw me as wild and dangerous, someone who associated with criminals?

I would have to wait and see. Only time would tell, time forever being the deciding factor.

M

With 26 days to go to the amnesty, we heard that a first group of prisoners who were to benefit from the amnesty and be eligible for release had been called to have their pictures and fingerprints taken. These were prisoners who had three years and less remaining of their sentences. I, on the other hand, had four and a half – another missed opportunity, this time by only a year, for an earlier release. Bad luck seemed to follow me like my own shadow.

Despite my jogging and playing the occasional game of soccer, my health was still troubling me, and the continued lack of vegetables gave me the most anxiety, especially when it came to my heart. One of my friends in solitary, a Thai baht multi-millionaire, gave me a small cabbage and some green beans one morning. I was quite taken aback, considering that no supplies were coming either in or out of the prison just then. Amazing what you can do with ready cash.

On 11 November, at around 6pm I suffered another severe pain in my chest and collapsed to the concrete floor, where I lay clutching my chest and struggling to breathe. At the same time as I was gasping for air, I broke out in a cold sweat. What was more terrifying to me than the excruciating pain was the fact that I was totally helpless. It's true what they say: my whole life did flash past me. I thought this must be how somebody feels when they are about to die. I kept saying to G-d that this wasn't the way it was meant to end. *Surely* this wasn't the way? I was so close to being released, with only a few more months to go. Oh G-d, I said, this can't be!

The pain kept getting worse. I was a caged animal, trapped and left to die. I felt myself slipping and sliding, deeper and deeper into darkness. Was I having a heart attack? Fuck, I didn't know! All I knew for certain was that I didn't want to die here, alone, in this dreadful place.

How I managed it I don't know, but I found a large envelope, put it over my face and breathed into it. I breathed in and out for almost an hour before the pain slowly started to subside. While I forced myself to breathe into my makeshift paper bag, I focused my attention on the TV set that was on in my cell. There was a David Attenborough wild-life programme on, in which he was following a school of dolphins in some ocean or other. I remember thinking what a beautiful sight this was, and that if by chance I *should* die, at least I would die smiling. I imagined myself swimming with the dolphins, and this seemed to have a calming effect on me. It helped regulate my breathing until the pain in my chest gradually lessened.

One Sunday morning, a strange thing happened. It was around 9.30 and I was in the spare cell barking the dog – talking to my family, in fact. There was a prisoner who was locked up 24 hours a day, but because he was a diabetic he had to be taken every day to the hospital to get his insulin shot. Because the area around the hospital had been flooded, on this particular morning the insulin was brought to his cell. The commodore who accompanied the medic was notorious for trying to catch prisoners with illegal items. He entered the solitary section looking like a prisioner. Right outside the diabetic prisoner's cell was another prisoner, fast asleep, with his mobile phone hidden in his pillow. At the precise moment that the guards approached the cell, the light on this guy's mobile starting flashing, signalling an incoming call, and of course the guard noticed it right away. Talk about bad luck or bad timing. As everyone knew, the punishment for being caught with a mobile was severe. You would be put into these huge chains and locked up for 24 hours a day in solitary for at least six months. No fan in your cell, no TV, no nothing. These guys don't get to come out at all.

I quickly removed my biscuit from the dog, hid it in my mouth, and then hastily hid the dog under some of the cleaning equipment. Then I went to see what the commotion was about. I must have been as white as a sheet. I immediately saw the mobile in the guard's hand. Now we would definitely be raided; there would be a complete shakedown of our entire section. The poor guy with the mobile was marched outside, returning later shackled with 10kg chains. Punishment in that place was swift and severe.

The Building Chief punished everyone in our section by confiscating our TV sets and taking away the hour's walking time in the prison yard. For some unfathomable reason, I was the only person in the entire punishment section who *wasn't* punished. When the Building

Chief made the announcement, I responded by saying, '*Pom khun dee*' (I'm a good person), at which his wingman, Santi, gave me a dirty look and, pointing with two of his fingers at my face, said, 'I know that you have a mobile.' I laughed. Because I didn't have a mobile. I had *access* to a mobile, sure, and the guards knew it. With the amnesty coming up, I was taking great care not to violate any regulation.

Later in the morning we were raided by the Red Caps, but this search was very casual and more of a formality than anything else. Just after they'd gone, I was called to the office and told that my request to come out of solitary had been approved. It was 14 November 2011. For a second, I couldn't believe what I was hearing and I had to ask the guard to repeat what he'd said. Having been a prisoner in the prison's prison, the thought of being let out was almost like being released from prison altogether. I couldn't stop smiling. I just buzzed around the building. Almost every fifth person would ask me in Thai, '*Awk lao?*' (Out already?)

'*Chai wan nee pom long*' (Yes, this day I out), I replied.

'*Chok dee*' (Good luck), they would say, smiling back.

I stayed outside till about 1pm, light-headed, excited and happy. Every day seemed to be bringing me closer to my freedom. In the meantime, though, I needed to find a place to stay and a locker to keep my things in.

One of the Thai Mafia guys had become a good friend of mine. His name was Wichan and he had been born in Kanchanaburi, in western Thailand, the only son of a street fighter who had abandoned his family when Wichan was five years old. His mother inherited an 8ha farm, and she harvested rice, vegetables and fruit. During his school years, Wichan excelled at athletics and academically was rated among the top ten students. He also showed strong leadership qualities from a young age. But, as was the case with so many Thai teenagers, when he left school he took to the streets, and, as the years passed, he began his own protection racket. Before long, Wichan was feared and respected by all, and he very quickly advanced up the hierarchy of the local Mafia.

By this time, he had been involved in many gunfights with his enemies, his rise to power beginning when he shot the leaders of his rival gangs (although none of them actually died). Word soon spread and, at age 19, Wichan was approached by an army general to be his personal bodyguard. Then one day he was given his first professional assignment, for which he would get approximately US$10 000. He was required to go to Phuket, where a contract had been taken out on a local businessman. He was given a photograph of the target and had to arrive a couple of days before, first to survey the area and then follow the businessman around. Apparently the businessman and five of his work colleagues were due to attend a meeting at a posh restaurant at a certain time. Without any disguise or anything, Wichan walked into the restaurant, went up to the table where the men were sitting talking, called out the guy's name and, as the man turned around to see who was calling him, shot him at point-blank range with a .45 Colt. One bullet to the centre of his forehead. There was screaming and shouting, and people scattering in all directions, and amid the panic and chaos, Wichan made his escape. A close friend of his was outside waiting for him on a motorbike.

That was Wichan's first murder, and the first of many.

Being spiritual, after he had murdered someone Wichan would buy a basket of food and take it to the temple, where he would offer the gift to the monks and pray for his victim's family. In this way, he told me, he cleared his conscience. When I asked if he felt any pity for his victims, he said he felt nothing. He was only interested in the money. From the money he made for this first hit, Wichan gave a small portion to his friends and some went to his mother. In fact Wichan continued to support his mother for a long time without her knowing what he actually did for a living.

Over the next two years, Wichan assassinated more than 20 people. A single bullet to the temple became his trademark. All of these hits were ordered by the army general he worked for, who was a big Mafia guy himself. When he was 20 years old, Wichan had his entire body tattooed, from his toes all the way to his head, except for his face. It took months. Sometimes there were two tattoo artists working on his body at the same time. At age 21, all Thai men are called up to do two years of military training, and, after he had completed his basic training, Wichan became a sniper. During the next two years he continued to kill whenever he was commissioned.

Among his victims was a prominent politician in Bangkok, for which he got US$20000. The fact that he was in the army helped him escape detection. After the army, he moved around from province to province, staying with close associates in different places. He became an independent agent, working for the highest bidder. By this time, Wichan had a reputation that stretched throughout the kingdom. Although he was much younger than other Mafia bosses, he was respected as their equal. With the killing of the politician, however, because it had been executed in Wichan's trademark style, he became the number-one suspect, even though there had been no witnesses and no evidence had been found to link him to the killing. Nevertheless he was now listed as one of Thailand's ten Most Wanted.

When he was 25, Wichan was commissioned to kill a deputy mayor in a city about 600km west of Bangkok. After assassinating his victim, as he was making his escape, he noticed a young boy watching him from about 30m away. There was no doubt that the boy had witnessed the murder, but Wichan thought that at that distance he would not have been able to identify him, so he left. At that time, Wichan was staying in a rented apartment on the 20th floor of a high-rise building. Two months later, at around 9.30am, while he was still fast asleep, 15 members of one of Thailand's elite police units kicked down his door, rushed in and apprehended him. The young witness had clearly had better vision than Wichan had thought.

Wichan had two handguns in his possession, an 11mm Colt and a 9mm Beretta. He immediately called the army general, who instructed him not to talk and told him to just take it easy. The police held and interrogated him for 15 days, at the end of which he still pleaded innocent. He was given bail. In the meantime, the young boy who, it turned out, *had* witnessed the assassination but was the only witness, was intimidated and threated with death. Wichan's lawyers also paid off the public prosecutor, which is common practice in Thailand to win a case. All charges were dropped and Wichan was released.

A couple of years later, Wichan met the girl of his dreams. She was the book-keeper at a reputable company. His mother asked her family if they could be married, and, at an elaborate ceremony, which was attended by the general and a variety of friends and acquaintances from the army, the police and the Mafia, Wichan and his bride tied the knot. This was a pivotal moment in his life, and he told me he couldn't ever remember a time when he was as happy as he was that day. There and then he decided to stop killing. After a year, his wife bore him a beautiful son.

Things weren't going so well for his mother, however, who had run into financial difficulty. She needed to sell their house, although Wichan was against this because it had been their family home for many years. He made a commitment to his mother that he would alleviate her financial problems. He called the army general, saying he needed work; if anything came up, the general should let Wichan know. The general contacted a friend of his, another general, who was in the police, and who was under investigation for illegal casino activities. The army general enquired whether he knew anyone who might want someone assassinated. The police general was only too happy to oblige, and he ordered the murder of the government official who was spearheading the investigation against him.

Wichan's fee was 2 million Thai baht (US$70 000). The hit was to take place about 400km outside Bangkok, in the province of Isan. The police general had organised an apartment where Wichan, along with his getaway motorbike friend, would wait for the call. The call came around lunchtime, and Wichan made his way to the government official's residence, where he found him relaxing in a deckchair beside the pool. The first bullet caught him in the centre of his forehead, and this was followed by four shots into his body. After hearing the shots, two bodyguards came running out, but by this time Wichan and his friend had already made their escape.

'*Yibloy*' (Done already), Wichan said when he phoned the police general, and the money was duly wired to his account.

In fact, I remembered this particular incident well, because it took place when I was already in prison. It was *very* big news.

For about a month nothing happened, and Wichan expected to get away with this crime, as he'd gotten away with all the other murders he'd committed. Then, out of the blue, the police general calmly informed him that he was now the prime suspect in the case, as the bullets he had used in many of his other killings matched those found at the latest crime scene. Before he could react, members of the Special Forces surrounded his mother's house, but they didn't find Wichan there. By then he was hiding with one of his associates in an apartment in Sukhumvit Soi 4 in Bangkok's red-light district. Then, at the suggestion of the general, he and his friend left Bangkok and hid out at Ko Samui, where he blended in with the holiday-makers. They'd been there about a week when he received another call from the general, who told him that the police knew where he was. Wichan drove on his own to a cabin in the mountains about 120km away, where he hoped nobody would find him. His luck, however, was about to run out. Two days later, early in the morning, the police descended on the cabin. Wichan tried to run but was quickly apprehended. Apparently his friend had been caught, and, after being badly tortured and beaten up, he had given away Wichan's hiding place.

Wichan confessed to the murder, but once he appeared in court he retracted his confession. He was then flown to Bangkok in a private plane. For the next week the story was in the headlines every day in every major newspaper in Thailand. Wichan was charged for the two murders and taken to a special high-security prison. Three days later, the police general was also arrested. He, too, pleaded innocent but still managed to get bail. Wichan pleaded guilty to the murder of the government official but not to the killing of the deputy mayor. Basically, what happened was that he entered into a plea bargain with the prosecutor because the killing of the government official was so high-profile that the police really just wanted to close the case.

While out on bail, and after many court appearances, he was sentenced to life imprisonment on 12 November 2008 and transferred to Klong Prem, Building 2, where his reputation had preceded him. Everybody knew Wichan. He was infamous among all the inmates, who both feared and respected him. In prison he ran a protection racket and was boss of the casino in Building 2, where, on a good day, there would be up to 7 million Thai baht on the table. At the end of the day, after paying the guards, he would pocket about 100 000 Thai baht, some of which he shared with his boys, and some of which he sent to his associates on the outside, most of whom in fact had no idea he was even in prison.

After Wichan had made a small fortune, one of the prisoners videoed the casino operation inside the prison and sent it to the Department of Corrections, who launched a full-scale search of Building 2. They found over 200 mobiles and a whole load of money, literally millions, which they confiscated. They also found a bag full of phones in the Building Chief's office; the chief was keeping the phones safe for their owners – at a price, of course.

In the time Wichan had been in Klong Prem, he had never had a single visitor. His mother did not know where he was, although sometimes he used to call her, and even send her money. In the prison he controlled his boys with an iron fist, and if one of them stepped out of line or used drugs, which he was totally against, he would beat them up, often using a baton. The authorities always turned a blind eye. In the general amnesty of 2010 his sentence was reduced to 40 years, and in 2011 he was given a one-third reduction. Now he had 28 years to go.

About three years back, during a big clampdown in Klong Prem, all the Big Legs were transferred to other prisons. With his main source of income cut off, Wichan decided to turn over a new leaf. He started praying and generally tried to behave like a gentleman. He claimed he regretted having killed all those people. His wife was still waiting for him, and his kid, who was seven years old by the time I got to know Wichan, was apparently very artistic. There was a good chance he would become eligible for parole in August 2014; if he did get out, his plan was to become a farmer and breed fighting chickens.

I met Wichan when I was transferred from Khao Bin prison to Klong Prem and thrown into solitary confinement. During the first few days that I was there, he and I had a serious problem, which almost resulted in a physical altercation. As I didn't really know anybody in the prison,

I backed down after he challenged me. Over the weeks that followed, however, we eventually exchanged a few words. One day, he asked me if I could box and challenged me to a friendly fight. After that, we started sparring with each other every afternoon and became friends.

When I eventually came out of solitary, it was Wichan who gave me a place to stay and a locker for my stuff. During this time I personally witnessed his transformation and I truly believed he deserved a second chance. To me, he would always remain a brother.

After solitary, I moved into the general population and my new room was cell number 95. Frankly, this cell, which had belonged to some of the guys who had been evacuated, was in a hell of a state; it was full of dust and spider's webs. The key-boy for the section helped me remove all of the previous inmates' personal belongings. I was told by Santi that I could stay on my own in the meantime, but as soon as the evacuees returned I would have to find two inmates to stay in there with me. I was hoping that by then we would have received the amnesty and, if it was a one-fifth reduction, I would be home by January.

It took me about four hours to clean the cell and unpack my things. The euphoria of being out of solitary was kind of overwhelming. At first I couldn't sleep and dozed off around midnight, only to wake up at 3am, tossing and turning. Then, as I was dozing off again, I was woken by a huge cockroach crawling over my face. I nearly had a heart attack. First on my list of things to do, I decided then and there, was to seal the netting, which had gaps all around it where insects could come and go freely in and out of the cell.

I found a spot that looked like a good place to hang out, in an area that had previously been assigned to death row inmates. There was generally quite a lot of space. The section was like a reasonably large dining hall with long concrete tables and benches placed at right angles to each other. Some guys kept all their belongings in cardboard boxes under or along a table. There were packs of bottled water stacked all around the place, and at the entrance there was a hot water machine. Further along the rear was an area where the guys showered, and just to the left of that was a shack where the toilets were – surprisingly, these were all Western-type toilets with seats. After all my years in prison, this really posed a problem for me. I had become so accustomed to squatting that, when using the seat, I had to stand on it to find my balance. One time I slipped off in the middle of having a crap!

Beside this area, closer to where the tables were, was a row of tiled concrete basins where you could wash your dishes. There were also a couple of taps, which was far more civilised than what you had at Bangkwang.

On my first full day outside of solitary, I noticed that there were a couple of guys around the building who played backgammon, and I looked forward to finding someone I could play with. Jesus, it was quite strange, being in the sunlight again. One guy gave me a deckchair and I sat in it for a long time, just revelling in the unusual sensation of the sun's rays on my skin.

Every morning I would go for a jog, and then I would work out at the gym, which consisted of a couple of benches and one or two shoulder and chest machines. Then I would take a shower, collect my dirty laundry and give it to my new wash boy – a welcome change from having to do all my own laundry every day. In fact, the skin on my hands was raw and peeling from the harsh chemicals in the washing powder. In solitary, your food was delivered to your cell. Now I had to get used to lining up for it. Some days I would really get pissed off because some of the Thais would just come and push their way to the front. I didn't say anything, though. I wanted to avoid any sort of confrontation.

I had taken to washing my food with hot water. Every day I ordered a salad, two corns on the cob, and some vegetable stirfry (which wasn't too bad, but also had to be rinsed), but the bulk of my meal would be fruit. I would get a punnet of papino, grapes, pineapple and sometimes a mango. Most of the food was cold by the time we got it, so some of the guys would steam it up. After we had eaten, I would relax in my deckchair and even doze off for 30 minutes or so. There was really not much to do, and keeping my mind occupied was rather difficult, but, as the days went by, I got into something of a routine, and I would catch a game of backgammon here and there.

Between 2.30 and 3pm they would announce on the loudspeaker which floor, upstairs or downstairs, would have to enter their cells first. As we passed through the passage, the guards would do the usual checking – they'd frisk us and search through our things. Once we were locked in the cell I would take a short nap and then get up and shower. Then I would put on a clean pair of boxers and T-shirt and daven the afternoon prayer that is said before sunset. Afterwards I would eat my fruit, and then it was teeth-cleaning time, which was still something of an obsession for me. Sometimes I'd watch a little TV or read a book or write a letter, and then around 9.30 I would daven *Ma'ariv* (the evening prayer).

I would lie quietly on my bed thinking about my freedom and my hopefully imminent release, and I'd wonder when the other prisoners were going to return. I kept trying to imagine what life would be like on the outside, what my friends looked like, whether they were even alive. Some of them I hadn't heard from during my entire incarceration. What was the new South Africa like, and how would I fit into it? From what I'd heard it was crime-ridden, but what exactly did that tell me – was it safe to walk in the streets?

On 30 November 2011 I experienced quite a fast vibration in my heart. This lasted approximately a minute, but it kept recurring, so I decided to report sick. At the hospital they did an ECG, which was performed by a prisoner who worked there. Once I had the results I had to wait to see a doctor. I explained that I had been diagnosed with a heart condition, atrial fibrillation, back in 2008, and I told the doctor that if he could prescribe some blood-thinning aspirin, that was what was needed for my heart to beat regularly again. The doctor examined my ECG scan and confidently pronounced my heart rate as too slow. I asked him what his area of expertise was and he told me he was an ear specialist! I just laughed and told him I needed to see another doctor. One thing I was sure of was that my heart wasn't beating slowly; it was beating too fast. I waited for another three hours before I was finally seen by another doctor, who said that all I had experienced was heart palpitations and that in fact the ECG scan showed my heart to be normal. But he gave me aspirin and prescribed propranolol as well, which I should take only if the palpitations recurred.

With the date for the King's amnesty now so very close, no wonder my heart was over-excited.

For some time now I had been rather troubled by something my sister had planted in my mind: for some reason, Joan believed that I would never get out of prison alive. I never discussed this with her, as that would have been like inviting a bad omen to materialise, but now I couldn't help wondering to myself whether I *would* actually ever make it out of Klong Prem. Freedom seemed tantalisingly close, but too much hoping always seemed to have a way of turning on me. Then I would pull myself together and decide that there was *no way* I was fucking going to die, and it didn't matter what anyone thought. I would make it out of prison alive!

After months of counting down to the crucial news that would affect my life so profoundly, Sunday 4 December arrived – one day before the official announcement of the amnesty. Well, at least I had made it to the amnesty, I thought. So far, so good. The atmosphere in the building was exhilarating, and the news we wanted to hear had already begun filtering through. The documents had apparently arrived at the prison, but the official announcement was only to be made the next day, on the King's birthday. However, everybody seemed to know that drug cases were going to be given a one-sixth reduction. If this was true, it meant that I would have approximately five months of my sentence left to serve. Although I had been hoping for a one-fifth reduction, I was over the moon with one sixth.

From being sentenced to life imprisonment, and then having to endure years of not knowing, finally I could start counting the months and weeks to my freedom. Let the final countdown begin! This countdown was *real*.

It's hard to find the words to describe what I was feeling. It was like a dream. My head felt light and my heart raced (in a good way). I don't think I had ever before experienced such an emotion. Happiness normally comes in waves, but this feeling had a permanence about it that lifted me so high I could almost fly. I wanted to scream and shout so that all the world would hear me.

I was going home!

When the news filtered through, I managed to call Joan to share it with my family. There were shouts and tears of joy at the other end of the line. I'd never heard my sister so excited. I imagined my mother's joy, too, when she was told that she would see her only son in just a few months. Our nightmare was finally coming to an end. Suddenly that light at the end of the tunnel was brighter than it had ever been.

My time on the phone was very restricted, but I did manage to phone some of my friends and share the news with them. Joan would put it up on my Facebook page, though, and soon all my friends around the world would know that it wouldn't be long now before I was a free man. That night, alone in my cell, I recited the Master of the Universe prayer, the one I had been reciting ten times a day. It slowly dawned on me that it had nothing to do with being physically released from prison; it was all about being spiritually free. Of course it was. During my prayers that night, I was far more attentive and aware somehow, and I felt the closest I had ever felt to G-d. I thought about my mother who, for the past 17 and a half years, had gone down on her hands and knees every single night and prayed to G-d that the day would come when she would see her only son again. I always believed that I would be released in G-d's time, and, over all the years I'd been locked up, I had kept telling Joan that *Hashem* had the perfect time for each and every one of us. And now here was mine: this was *my* time. I was going to make it, I knew I was. I couldn't stop thanking Him.

My excitement was tangible. I could feel it and taste it. I tried to force myself to read, but it was so difficult to concentrate that eventually I gave up and lay staring at the ceiling, thinking about life on the outside. One of the first things I wanted to do was sit at a pavement coffee shop and just watch people walking by. I was going to experience everything as if I was experiencing it for the first time.

M

Amnesty or not, it was business as usual in Klong Prem. After all, only a handful of us would be going home; the rest, although with reduced sentences, still had to face the harsh reality of doing a long stretch of time. As a distraction, besides having my head in the clouds, I would spend between two to four hours a day playing backgammon.

The next weekend, something happened that dampened our spirits. On the Sunday, one of the Thai inmates in solitary confinement committed suicide. There were six Thais in the same cell; at around 1am one of them went to the toilet and found this guy strung up with the nylon drawstring from his shorts. They shouted for the guards and there was a huge commotion. The guards came in, looked through the door, and told the guys that under no circumstances should they remove the body. They would come and take care of it in the morning.

I couldn't understand why this guy took his life, as he was one of those who was going to benefit from the amnesty. Perhaps, after being in prison for so many years, the thought of going into the outside world was too frightening for him to contemplate. It made me apprehensive about my impending release. I had become institutionalised, too, but my longing for freedom only intensified with each passing day that brought me closer to my release.

On 21 December I was called for an embassy visit. Normally I would make my way to the visit area by myself, but today a guard came to escort me. And instead of going to a normal embassy room, I was taken to the office where the administration guards worked. There, to my surprise, I was greeted by Douglas Gibson, the South African ambassador himself. He had come to say goodbye to me because his four-year term in Thailand was up. I was glad to see him; something that had been very much on my mind was whether I was still a South African citizen. He confirmed that I was.

Christmas came and went, and then, on Monday 26 December, we had a major check at 5.45am. This time, the guards opened each cell and instructed us to come out and squat, while one or two guards did a thorough search of our cells. Unfortunately for me, the guard checking my cell was an arsehole who for some reason had an intense dislike of *farang*s. I was nervous because I had two SIM cards hidden away, as well as my stabbing knife. They turned my room upside down and this guard found my knife.

'What is this?' he asked as he called me back in.

I explained to him that I used the knife to cut fruit.

He looked at me sceptically. The length and shape of the blade were nothing like a normal fruit-cutting knife and both of us knew it.

After the check we were all taken outside, and made to sit while the second in command of the prison (the 105) gave us a lecture. He asked in a joking manner where we had hidden our mobile phones, as they had found nothing among our belongings (except my knife, which, I noted uneasily, he was holding in his hand). He then called one of the senior commodores from our building and asked who the knife belonged to. The commodore pointed at me and said, '*Tarnchad*' (foreigner).

Being caught with a dangerous weapon was as bad as being caught with a dog. Shackles and solitary confinement. I had been out in the general population for only a month and a half. I heard the guard ask whether I kept a knife to commit suicide. I laughed and repeated what I'd said earlier, that I used it to cut fruit. All the prisoners had a chuckle at that – the guard, too. I hoped they would just let it go for once. Later I was teased by the guards, who kept asking me why I had to cut my fruit with a sword; some even went so far as to ask me who I wanted to stab. It became quite the joke, but of course everyone understood that the knife was for self-protection. I breathed a huge sigh of relief when it became clear that they weren't going to take the matter any further.

That night, a group of about 50 of the prisoners who had been evacuated during the floods returned. They seemed really jubilant. It was just my luck that three of them used to occupy the cell that I was in. I had made a deal with the guard that I could stay on my own until they came back, and now one of the guards came and negotiated with me. Would I take two of them into the cell? I didn't really have a say, but I said that I could only stay with non-smokers. Both prisoners were serving death sentences for murder. One had been in prison for only three months, the other for three years, and I would be going home in five months. I didn't understand the logic.

These guys had come from Khao Bin. They were tired and hadn't eaten anything. Fortunately, because of orders that we hadn't received at the beginning of the floods, I had extra food that had arrived that day, so I shared my supper with them. They seemed okay and I thought we would get on just fine. Neither of them complained about my having the space in front of the TV. I felt really strange sharing the small cell and being in such close proximity with two strangers. The two of them showered after supper, and it wasn't long before they were sound asleep.

Around midnight I was woken by loud snoring. I started moaning out loud – oh nooo ... not snoring! The other guy woke up and we looked at each other disgruntledly. If there is anything I hate, it's snoring. There was no way I was going to get any sleep. I wasn't happy at all. Not only had they invaded my space, but now one of them was going to torture me with his fucking snoring. Whenever he snored, I would knock him (which he had given me permission to do), but still I felt uncomfortable. I didn't really like to wake anybody up, and besides, this had originally been their cell, after all.

On the positive side, I welcomed their company because it might help the time pass more quickly.

A few days later, the Israeli consul came to visit. I could tell that Eli Gil didn't feel comfortable in my presence, but frankly I wasn't very happy with the Israelis either. I knew they had deliberately drawn out the procedures to transfer me to Israel, knowing that I would benefit from the amnesty and would be released in the coming months anyway. Now he wanted to know if I still wanted to transfer to a prison in Israel. I asked him when the next prisoner transfer meeting would be held. Usually, these meetings were in either March or April. I estimated that my day of release would be near the end of April 2012. Gil said the next meeting would be in July 2012, which only confirmed for me that they had never intended to take me back to Israel.

I looked him straight in the eyes and said, 'Where's the logic in that? I'll be home by April. Why would I want to wait until July?' I was thinking, just to fuck him around, that I would still go to Israel. I could just imagine all the excuses he would have to come up with. In the end, though, I told him I would be going home to South Africa to be with my family. But, I couldn't resist adding, I still wanted my Israeli passport.

Over the past month a tomcat had been patrolling the corridors late at night and howling like a crying baby, so loudly that it woke virtually everybody up. It was driving us crazy. My Eastern European friend and I conspired to kill it. We decided that we would give it the propranolol that had been prescribed for my heart palpitations, mixed in with some tinned fish. One night, the creature's yowling woke us up as usual, and we sprang up, ready to put our plan into action. My accomplice pushed the fish mixture into the corridor and we went back to sleep. The next morning, we heard that one of the cats had died. Excitedly, we went to see if it was true, and we couldn't believe our eyes: we had killed a cat all right, but it was the wrong one!

With my freedom imminent, I spent the better part of most days daydreaming, dreaming of the future. While a new chapter in my life might be starting, there was still no escaping the past. My joy was overshadowed by the sadness of knowing that I was leaving my friends behind. Unlike at Bangkwang, where we had a party every year to celebrate New Year, nothing exciting had been planned in Klong Prem for Songkran. I didn't mind because I knew I'd be celebrating something much more exciting in a few months' time.

My new cellmates turned out to be okay. One of them was a taxi driver who was in for murdering a woman and her daughter. Besides snoring, he would also sometimes talk in his sleep, waking me at odd hours. Early on New Year's morning, while I was on the toilet in the cell, with the curtains drawn, one of my cellmates kept asking me to hurry up.

'*Rew, rew*' (Quickly, quickly), he said urgently.

'*Bab neung*' (One minute), I responded.

What this guy didn't seem to understand was that I was in the middle of relieving my own bowels; it's not like you can just switch off. Anyway, I starting flushing and washing my ass, but before I had finished, while I was still squatting over the sunken toilet and before I had a chance to stand up and pull up my pants, this Thai pushed into the toilet, dropped his pants in a single motion and let rip before he'd even squatted. My face was almost up against the wall and some of his shit came spraying onto my bare feet.

What a freak-out! I screamed at him, '*Khun baa!*' (You're crazy), holding my nose and breathing desperately through my mouth and flushing my feet with water all at the same time. Then I bolted out of there in a flash, trying not to puke and add to the disgusting chaos. Once safely away, I burst out laughing, whether from shock or the flashes of the scene that were replaying in my mind, I don't know. After that, whenever I saw this guy, we would look at each other and pack up laughing. That was a New Year I was certainly never going to forget.

My New Year's resolution that year wasn't actually to stop swearing (it hadn't worked too well when I'd tried it before), but to try and limit it to the best of my ability. I didn't want to go home and still pepper my conversation with 'motherfucker' or 'fuck' every five seconds, like all foreigners in prison did. I wondered how successful I'd be.

During my last few months in prison, I had learnt from a recently arrested Nigerian that, of the original 300 who had transferred back to Nigeria in 2003, 60 had since returned to Thailand and been caught smuggling 'ice' (methamphetamine). Now they were awaiting trial in Bombat prison. This had angered the Thai government and had put a strain on Thailand's relations with Nigeria.

In February, two months before my release, I was told by a Facebook friend and a correspondent of mine that Joan had got divorced. I was shocked. Joan, not wanting to upset me, had kept it a secret. My brother-in-law Malcolm and I had always been close. It would be strange, after his involvement over all the years, to think of him not being part of the celebration.

With a new year came a new wave of clampdowns in Thailand's prisons. In early February almost every TV channel carried stories about this.

Five hundred prisoners, the Big Legs, were to be moved to Khao Bin, and before long, in a combined operation, the army, the Black Shirts and the Department of Corrections raided several prisons. Bangkwang and Klong Prem were high on their list. Many mobiles and drugs were seized. These crackdowns were all very well, but what the government didn't realise was that every time such a major move went down, they were handing the guards an opportunity to extort money from the dealers. The dealers could pay anything from 200 000 to 1 million Thai baht not to be part of the move, so that they could continue with their business of selling drugs.

The Minister of Justice announced plans for the building of a new prison called Supermax, intended to house only drug offenders. When I heard this, I couldn't help thinking about the time in Bangkwang, more than 12 years back, when they had closed down Building 1 and moved all the prisoners into the other buildings. They had demolished the building with a view to constructing a high-security block similar to American prisons. The demolition started with great enthusiasm, but once the building had been reduced to rubble, the whole operation ceased. Weeks and then months passed, and nothing happened. When we enquired why construction had been halted, we were told that the Director of the prison had stolen all the money. And the funny part of it was that, although he lost that job, he got another one straight afterwards, and a promotion, too, to Deputy Director of the Department of Corrections! I could just imagine where the money allocated for this new Supermax would go – straight into the pockets of all those corrupt officials who ran this million-dollar kingdom.

In early February the Thai footballers approached me to ask whether they could draft a petition in my name requesting the prison authorities to reopen the indoor football pitch. If the Thais used their names, there was a chance of their being moved to another building. Foreigners had more chance of getting things done, largely because of the authorities' fear of pissing off our embassies if they declined a reasonable request. About 30 of the footballers had already signed the petition.

One thing I had to give the prison authorities was that they did encourage sports activities, and sometimes they even participated themselves. Soon after the petition was submitted, our request was granted. We started using the indoor court to play football once more. It was a very happy day for all of us.

M

One afternoon I received a visit from Renee Aaron from the South African embassy. She told me she was going to start processing my temporary travel documents and would need me to sign some papers, have my fingerprints taken and also a photo. On the same day, the prison confirmed my official release date.

On 22 April 2012 I would be walking out of prison.

What a feeling! I could hardly wait to bark the dog and tell my sister. My Facebook group page, 'Shani Krebs – Captivated Artist', was already alive with activity in anticipation of my return. By the time I managed to speak to her, Joan had already heard the news from both the Israeli and the South African embassies. Even though this was only a confirmation of what we already knew, hearing it made official was still music to my ears. Silently, I celebrated and thanked *Hashem*.

But I knew very well that I wasn't free yet and that anything could happen between then and April. I was not so naive as to think that my path was clear. For one thing, my heart was still giving me trouble, and there was also always the possibility of getting into an altercation or even of being stabbed, so I knew I had to be extra-vigilant and try to control the events around me as much as I could. I'd come so far. It wouldn't be wise to become arrogant or overconfident now. I would continue to be my humble self, and, although swallowing shit was something I only did in extreme circumstances, if I had to turn the other cheek, I resolved that that was what I would do.

On Valentine's Day I was called to have my photo and fingerprints taken. On my way out, a lot of the Thais kept saying the words to me '*Khun karbarn, khun karbarn*' (Going home, going home). I couldn't help smiling. How many years had I waited to hear those very words?

On 6 March 2012 (with 46 days to freedom), just after 7 in the morning and after the cells had been opened, I had another attack, a pain in my chest so severe this time that I couldn't move. Everyone had gone by then. I was lying on the floor breathing into a plastic bag when the key-boy saw me and went to call the guards. I told him he shouldn't worry, I was sure I would be okay, but the next thing I knew, the Building Chief arrived – my friend Kojak – who insisted that I go to the hospital. They brought me a wheelchair, which I declined. Instead, I walked to the hospital with one of the guards as my escort. I arrived there just before 8am and waited about 20 minutes before I was put onto oxygen. During the wait, I paced up and down, breathing in and out slowly. Once the oxygen mask was removed, I waited almost four hours for a doctor, but no one came. I got frustrated and told the guard I wasn't going to wait any longer.

'*Kun pen tuk churn*' (You are emergency, you have to wait), he said.

'*Tuk churn sum cher mong lao, pom boeer lao*' (The emergency was three hours ago and I am beginning to get bored), I responded.

I returned to the building without having seen the doctor. I decided I would just have to take my chances with my heart from then on, at least until I was safely back in my home country.

Remembering my sister's advice of long ago, and which she had recently reiterated, about finding a corner somewhere quiet and staying out of trouble, I found just such a place. This was a bench just outside the main office, and most days that was where I would sit, either by myself or with my Eastern European not-so-good friend. We amused ourselves by sharing jokes or criticising every second person who walked past. The office was in full view of where we sat.

One morning, there was a serious altercation in the dining room and the culprits were brought to the office. One of them was a foreigner, a Malay guy from Singapore, and the other one was a Thai. Four of the guards really got stuck into the foreigner with batons and boots. Strangely, or maybe not so strangely, I wasn't fazed at all. I had been surrounded by violence for so many years, and had witnessed so many beatings, that by now it just seemed to be part of everyday life. The foreigner was taken outside, shackled and thrown into solitary confinement. The Thai was also beaten, but not badly, and then let go.

One day in the middle of March, an Israeli guy on death row was transferred from Bangkwang. He arrived late in the afternoon, so I didn't have much chance to really talk to him. It was Shabbos, and I managed to help him out with food and give him a case of drinking water before he was taken to his cell and locked up for the night. I had met this guy previously, around early January 2011, when he and his co-accused were sent to Bangkwang from the very building that I was now in. They had been thrown into Building 10, where he had stayed up until now. We had met on several occasions back then in the foreign visit room and had struck up a friendship. Seeing him arrive here only a month or so before I was going home seemed really cruel. I couldn't wait to see him again so that he could update me on all the goings-on back in Bangkwang. When we hooked up the next day, we walked for hours, talking mostly about Bangkwang. I learnt that the room I had bought had been broken up because one of the Israelis had been caught barking the dog there. It was no longer a foreign room and the authorities had put several Thais in there to keep an eye on things. The other new thing was that, on 16 March, all deliveries of fresh food from the grocery store at Bangkwang had been stopped. They would now be implementing the same system that we had at Klong Prem, with prisoners having to order ready-made food that was delivered in plastic bags.

On 22 March I had a contact visit with Elisabeth. I never thought I would see the day, as it was a year ago that I had been so abruptly moved to Khao Bin just a week before our contact visit. But now here we were, and I was really happy to see my girlfriend. When I entered the area allocated for our families and friends, I was directed to one of the corners that was strictly for the foreigners. Here they had these long tables with wooden benches that were not only dirty but also quite rough. When Elisabeth arrived, I sneaked her to the Thai section where there were nice round tables and plastic chairs. We found a spot almost in the centre of everyone. While we were sitting there, the two prisoners who were the photographers for the day took a few photos of us. In one, I was giving Elisabeth a kiss. The next thing I knew we were surrounded by four or five guards.

'*Joop tee nee my dia.* No keesing arroud,' one guard reprimanded us. Then he wanted to know why a foreigner was in the Thai section.

I responded by saying, '*Pom mai chai farang*' (I am not a foreigner). '*Pom kun Thai*' (I'm a Thai national).

He looked at me, quite bewildered, and for a minute I thought he was going to grab me by the throat and suffocate me. I needed to explain, and quickly.

'*Pom yoo teenee sip baat pee lao*' (I've stayed here 18 years already and I was not comfortable in the foreign section and I prefer to stay where I am now), I hurriedly added.

'*Yoo sabai sabai*' (Enjoy your stay), he answered.

With these words, and by not forcing me to move, the commodore was actually giving me respect and acknowledging that I had done a long time in prison. After that, Elisabeth and I were left alone. Just being together, and holding Elisabeth's hand, was the most incredible feeling. This was a day we had both dreamed about. We wanted nothing more than to be in each other's physical presence. Just to be. For once we weren't shouting to each other through double sets of bars, and neither were we talking to each other on phones divided by glass partitions. Here we were, like two ordinary people, just being together. What a beautiful moment. Naturally, most of our conversation revolved around my imminent freedom and our joint excitement about that reality. But in our hearts we both knew that, with my freedom, would come a time of separation for us, and we were torn by the thought that we would not consummate our love in those initial days of me being a free man.

Elisabeth had been my girlfriend and regular visitor for almost two and a half years now, and in that time we had experienced a lot together. It had been an emotional roller-coaster ride for both of us. She had her own issues and I had mine. I also still had my secret relationship with Jessica, which was passionate and exciting, but Jessica was far away and Elisabeth was a physical and loving presence in my life. And she was here, now, holding my hand. Neither of us was quite geared to deal with the other, and it was a relationship that had been complicated from the outset. We both understood that, initially, my adjusting to normal society and starting a new life would be challenging for me, but even above that, and before I could consider getting into a serious relationship, I needed to be on my own, to experience everything I had missed and to take a good look at whatever life would now offer me. Finding my feet wasn't going to be easy, and being in a relationship, with Elisabeth or anybody else, was not a good idea. We both knew this in our hearts.

On Tuesday 3 April 2012, with just 19 days to go, the South African embassy visited me. I met Gregory, the police attaché, who had been newly appointed to this position. He said he was there to ensure my safe return to South Africa, and he was able to reassure me that everything was running smoothly. The following day, Rabbi Nechemya came to visit, but the prison authorities wouldn't allow him to see me because the South African embassy had come the day before. Also, I had been told by the prison authorities at Klong Prem that I had to choose between one of the two embassies. This was ridiculous because I was now a dual citizen, but in fact I wasn't all that bothered. I would have liked to have seen the rabbi, though, as it was just before Pesach, the last I would spend in this dump.

During this time the Israeli guy and I really bonded. He ate with me and I basically shared everything with him. We also worked out in the gym daily, and in the short time we were able to spend together we became like brothers. Most days we took long walks together and just talked and talked, sharing stories and adventures from our childhoods. We'd both be counting down the days to my release, both of us with mixed feelings about not seeing each other again. I felt sad because I knew his suffering would continue for years to come. Friends had come and gone in prison, and I had always been careful about getting too close to anyone, but somehow, when it came to members of my own tribe, it was different. The comradeship you experience with a fellow inmate is unlike anything you would ever encounter in the free world.

On Saturday 21 April, the day before my scheduled release, I hardly slept a wink. My excitement and longings were driving me round the bend. Time began to drag, and yet it was passing through me so fast

I felt I was losing my balance. I couldn't wait to share my joy with Jessica, and, at our appointed time I called her. No answer. I called and called. Still no answer. In between calling her number I phoned Elisabeth and my sister, but it was Jessica I really longed to speak to. I dialled her number again. What the fuck was going on? This was the most important moment in my life. Something was amiss. I was worried sick. I needed her now more than ever. After over an hour of trying to reach her, I had to give the dog back as there were other inmates waiting to bark.

Why wasn't Jessica picking up? I tried to put my worry aside and focus on the most important day I was about to enjoy in 18 years.

Chapter 20

Going Home

At last it was 22 April, the day I would wipe the dust of prison off my shoes once and for all and begin my journey homeward.

The process was not a straightforward one, however, and certainly not as simple as getting a cab to the airport and waving goodbye. But nothing could dampen my spirits. My joy was almost tangible and my million-dollar smile said it all. While waiting for my police escort on the veranda of the White House, I paced up and down for the almost two hours it took for them to come and collect me. The officers would accompany me to the Immigration Detention Centre (IDC), the last stop before my freedom. While I waited and paced, I looked around at the familiar buildings. Prison might have been the place I had spent almost 18 years – I was just four days short – but I'd always known I never actually belonged there, in the sense of it being the place where I lived and died. In fact, it was now horribly unfamiliar, and I grew impatient. I needed to take the first steps that would lead me to my new life, my real life.

While I waited, a group of about 100 prisoners was brought to the control centre. These guys, who only had a couple of months left before they would also be released, were part of a workers' gang that did odd jobs outside the prison. They all wore the same dark green uniform, and their blank stares conveyed the hopelessness that you'll see in almost every prisoner's eyes. For some of these men, the prospect of starting a life on the outside was scary and intimidating. Many of them enjoyed a better life within the confines of the prison walls. I could empathise with the way they felt and I recognised that look in their eyes. Although I was excited about leaving prison, I was also apprehensive, and my mind was a turmoil of questions.

How would people react to me? How would I respond to them? What if all the anger and bitterness I'd supressed for years suddenly erupted? Was I a walking time-bomb ready to explode at the slightest provocation? What if I killed someone ...?

No, I told myself, that was not me. And, in the free world, the rules were different. Or were they?

Also at the forefront of my mind was the thought of finally fulfilling a secret desire, once more performing the sacred act of sex. This was a primal need, a longing that the years of enforced celibacy could never quell. It raged like a burning fire inside me and tugged at my soul. I longed for intimacy, but was I willing to surrender myself for a moment of lust? I wasn't sure. I felt pure, almost like a virgin. While I was in prison my dreams were frequently about being with a woman. There was kissing and touching, but then as soon as I was about to enter her, I invariably woke up, often in a cold sweat. The questions I now would have to grapple with were many. Would I still run from love? Would I even *find* love? And what about children? Would the experience of parenthood be something I could embrace? There were just too many questions, and I certainly wasn't going to find the answers in my head that day. Slow down, I said to myself. One step at a time.

When my police escort turned up, I paused and took one last look around. 'You thought you would beat me,' I whispered to the thick prison walls, 'but I always knew you wouldn't. I won, didn't I?' Then I thanked G-d for allowing me to make it. I was about 120 hours away from boarding a plane bound for South Africa.

The distance to the main gate was about 500m. My short walk to freedom began. As I made my way, I started to count my steps. I walked through four checkpoints. It was Sunday, so things around the prison were very relaxed, as prisoners weren't allowed to leave their buildings.

Hardly any of the guards at Klong Prem knew me, so my release was of little interest to them, and no one took much notice of my departure. Still, in a sense it was a nostalgic moment. After all, between Bangkwang and Klong Prem, prison had been my home for almost two decades. I had watched five football World Cups behind prison walls. It felt like a force was beckoning me backwards, telling me not to leave, but I knew it was time. Time to put distance between us.

The guards didn't bother to check me as I walked steadily towards the outside world. It would have been a different story if I was being released from Bangkwang, where I had gained the respect of almost every guard there and had forged so many strong friendships. It would have been extremely emotional to have had to say my farewells. At the thought of all my friends, I could feel my eyes fill with tears. That morning, as I walked out of prison and inhaled my first breath of freedom, strange though it may sound, I think I left a part of my soul behind.

The huge steel gates were ahead of me. This was the moment of truth. They slowly opened and I passed through them. When they clanged shut behind me for the last time, I stood dead still for a few seconds, taking deep breaths, just savouring the moment.

My silent reverie was soon shattered.

'*Mar, mar*' (come, come). It was one of the cops, urging me impatiently forward. Time to move on. He was right, of course, although I put my own interpretation on his words. It definitely *was* time to move on, no doubt about that, time to put prison life behind me.

I lifted the two bags that I was carrying, one containing all the letters I had accumulated over the past year, and the other with a change of clothing and some toiletries. I followed the cop to his car and jumped into the passenger seat. As we pulled away, I was startled by a buzzing noise coming from the dashboard, which sounded like an alarm going off. The driver pointed towards my seat. At first I thought he was telling me there was a bomb underneath it, but eventually I got it: the noise had something to do with the seatbelt, so I clipped it in and the noise stopped. I certainly had a few things to learn in the outside world – starting right now.

In the back seat was a Thai woman. She was a lot younger than my police escort, and her hair was bright red, almost orange. She was slightly plumpish and reasonably pretty. After 18 years of deprivation, all women, irrespective of age, were attractive to me. I noticed that she was wearing a low-cut blouse that partly exposed her breasts, and I just couldn't help staring. I thought that maybe the grey-haired cop, who must have been beyond retirement age and anyway looked rather timid and frail, might very well be her father.

After some small talk, I asked him if he had a phone I could use, adding that I had my own SIM card but needed some airtime. He passed me his phone and said, no problem, I could call as long as it was local. I phoned Elisabeth, but, disappointingly, she didn't pick up. We stopped at a store and I took out my wallet and handed the cop a 100 Thai baht note so I could top up my airtime. When I called my sister and told her where I was calling from, using a dog freely and out in the open, her excitement was palpable. I quickly explained that I was being taken to the Narcotics Suppression Bureau (NSB) where I would be held overnight before being taken to the IDC the following morning. I asked Joan to contact Elisabeth and let her know where I was, because I knew she was expecting me to be moved straight to the IDC.

The IDC was notorious for its harsh conditions and extreme over-crowding, but I didn't care. Nothing could get me down that day. I was free; I had done my time. As we turned and twisted our way through the crowded streets of Bangkok, despite the vibrant colours, the crush of people on all sides, and the constantly flashing neon lights, nothing was actually registering in my brain. I could have been staring at a blank wall, for all I knew. There was too much visual information for me suddenly to process.

We arrived at our destination and drove round to the back of the NSB building, where I was taken through a side entrance that led to the holding cells. I was directed to a single cell. I dropped my bags on the floor and, as they locked me in, took the opportunity of asking the cop if I could use his mobile again. This time I managed to get hold of Elisabeth, who by then had spoken to my sister. She had got directions to the NSB from a café owner and arrived to see me at about 2pm. She brought my going-home clothes with her, a mobile phone, some food and some money, all of which she passed to me through the bars of my cell. The cop started telling me that visiting hours were only between 4 and 5pm and that Elisabeth could either wait at the reception or return later. While trying to reason with him, I slipped him a 1 000 Thai baht bill (old habits die hard). Elisabeth decided to wait, but within five minutes the cop was back anyway. He told me to pack my things – he was taking me to the IDC. I realised that the whole object of bringing me to the NSB first was to get some money out of me, but it just made me smile. I didn't mind paying. Every moment was bringing me closer to boarding the plane.

Elisabeth and I sat in the back of the police vehicle like two love-birds with our own chauffeur. We were so overjoyed it felt like we were going on honeymoon. Clasping each other's hands, we taked excitedly about how I felt to be free. Disbelief was one of the emotions we both shared. At one stage, we had discussed her flying home with me, but even though for a while I was in two minds about it, I knew this would be a bad idea. I was far from ready to maintain a serious relationship. Quite apart from the emotional side, it just wasn't practical. First I needed to be free, totally free, not only to deal with the whole adjustment process, but also free to explore and live a life.

I was a different person now. I was no longer the Shani Krebs who had left South Africa for a quick holiday in Thailand in April 1994. My mind had become conditioned to an environment of survival, where I was in a constant state of alertness. The psychological transformation from a prison mindset to something completely different was too vast to contemplate. I had always been of the belief that marriage was for the emotionally insecure, that in a sense marriage was a worse institution than prison. Before I could even consider a relationship with a woman, let alone marriage, I would first have to become financially independent. There were too many factors conspiring against me and Elisabeth, and we both knew it. And besides, there was that all-too-familiar silent voice tugging at my subconscious: 'Here's your chance. This time it is easier than it was before. Run while you still can – *run*.'

Would Elisabeth ever understand that, while I did love her, I was incapable of loving?

We phoned Joan again from the car. She was so excited to hear my voice for the second time that day that she cried from happiness. I had to keep her updated on my every move, while she in turn was busy posting developments on my Facebook page so that my over 1 000 Facebook friends, who were all eagerly monitoring my release, knew what was happening, too.

From the outside, the IDC looked nothing like a prison. We pulled into a narrow parking lot that ran parallel to the entrance, which had a huge blue steel sliding gate. There were no guards that I could see. The policeman pressed a buzzer and then proceeded to slide the gate open himself. The next thing, a loud alarm went off; it was almost like an evacuation fire alarm. The noise brought me back to reality as I mentally prepared myself to confront whatever lurked behind this new gate. Elisabeth was not allowed beyond this point, so we hugged and kissed briefly and arranged that she would visit me on Wednesday.

I was greeted by two immigration police, who were in civilian clothes and looked like detainees themselves. We walked into an open courtyard, directly in front of which was an office. Inside, sitting around a couple of tables, were four or five more police, also wearing civilian clothes, except for one. Just to the right of the door, I could see a whole lot of bags and a few suitcases, so it seemed we weren't allowed to take our personal possessions inside with us. I also saw a variety of different-coloured sandals and shoes scattered around.

I could hear conversations and activity echoing from all over, upstairs and downstairs. To the left of the office was a double doorway that led into a passage that gave access to the rear of the building, where the women detainees were housed. Outside in the courtyard there were three large wooden tables and benches, which I assumed were for official visitors, such as representatives from embassies, lawyers and immediate family. Behind this was a small cafeteria that sold things like basic toiletries, fresh bread, water and some groceries. Above it was a gated stairway that led upstairs to where the majority of the male detainees were held in cells under heavy security.

I wasn't subjected to any checking and was ushered to the last cell on the ground floor. I was instructed by one of the policemen to leave my bags outside the cell, which didn't please me, and, after an argument that got a little heated, I was allowed to take one of them in with me. I chose the bag that contained my toiletries, change of clothing and my mobile phone. The cell wasn't bad, about 3 by 6m, and it looked relatively well maintained. I would be sharing it with 13 other detainees. One of them, a Western foreigner, immediately approached me and introduced himself.

'Hey, I'm Mark, where are you from?'

'I'm from South Africa,' I said.

'Really? So am I!' he replied. 'What a coincidence.'

Mark went on to explain that his visa had expired and he had to pay a fine, but unfortunately he didn't have the money. To be honest, my mind was so preoccupied with my own thoughts that nothing much of what he said registered. I was vaguely aware of his mouth moving, but that was about all. While he was still jabbering on I took my place right by the door and near the overhead fan. Then I took stock. There was a group of about six Pakistanis, who had United Nations refugee status and were being relocated to families in the US, two Nigerians and three Laotians, one of whom was a beautiful woman in her late twenties. I was startled when I noticed her. Why was a woman here, locked up with a whole bunch of men? Then I realised that 'she' was actually a 'he', a lady-boy. This should be interesting, I thought to myself. I took out my towel and spread it on the floor. Then I took out the fake Blackberry Elisabeth had bought for me. After figuring out how to work it, I called home once again and also phoned a few friends to update them on where I was. It was really exciting sharing my joy, and everyone I spoke to was thrilled for me. Elisabeth had also bought me quite a lot of food – bread, cheese, fruit, nuts and chocolates. I invited the South African guy to eat with me, and then anybody else who felt like joining in. Naturally I invited the young lady as well, and she happily joined us. She didn't speak much English, but we struck up a conversation. She told me she was a dancer at a club in Phuket and had overstayed her visa. Besides her prominent Adam's apple and masculine voice, there was no way at first glance you could tell that she wasn't a woman. Her name was Thong. After we had all eaten, I was busy cleaning my teeth when Thong came and asked me if she could use my phone. I said 'with pleasure'. She came and sat next to me, so close that her leg was touching mine. I became aroused, and when she'd finished using the phone, I asked her if she would give me a massage. She agreed, so I lay back and put my leg on hers. I was wearing a pair of short jeans that were slightly loose, and, as she started to massage me, she slipped her hand up and under my thigh, almost caressing my balls. I felt myself getting hard. While she rubbed my leg, I played with her hair and, whispering, asked her if she enjoyed sucking cock. She gave me a seductive smile and gently squeezed my balls. I couldn't believe that my body was reacting in such a manner. Could it be that after so many years of sexual deprivation I had become gay? How could I be turned on by a man with breasts? Well, hey, I thought to myself, maybe it would be an interesting experience.

Mark, my new friend and fellow South African, was still busy eating, but I could tell he was fascinated by what was going on.

'Hey, Mark,' I asked jokingly, 'would you like a blow job?'

He seemed kind of nauseated by the thought and hurriedly said he had a girl in America whom he'd met on Facebook and fallen in love with, so he would give it a miss. It was really funny. Perhaps if he had been in prison as long as I had, he might have felt differently. I mean, after all, who goes to Thailand without getting laid by a transvestite?

I thought I would settle for a blow job. I longed for intimacy but drew the line at a lady-boy. But I decided that I would keep an open mind and just see how things unfolded. So far, IDC was proving to be a lot more interesting than I'd anticipated.

After all the excitement of the day, compounded by the hot weather, I thought I would take a shower. I half-undressed and then, first securing my towel around my waist, removed my shorts. Out of the corner of my eye I could see the lady-boy watching me. Shower bowl in hand, I made my way through to the back of the cell where there was a doorway (without a door) into the so-called shower room. This consisted of a water trough on the left-hand side running the length of the room

– similar to the ones in prison. The difference here was that this area was tiled and had clean running water. On the right-hand side there were five Western-style toilets, completely walled in for privacy. The downside was that all the doors had been removed.

I slipped off my underwear. As I'd expected, the lady-boy had followed me, and, as she passed me, she gently touched my neck and ran her hand down my back onto my arse, sending shivers up my spine. I hung my towel over the wall of the toilet. I was naked. The lady-boy took her place in the end toilet and started removing her clothes. While scooping water over myself, I turned and faced her, and began to soap myself, while she stripped down to her skimpy hot pants. My hand moved over my cock. I was fully erect. Her breasts were small and her protruding nipples were enticing.

She watched me as I showered, touching herself, caressing her breasts, all the time never taking her eyes off me. Then she took her thumb, pointed it towards her mouth and slowly mimed something unmistakable. It was an instant turn-off for me. I couldn't help it, but I just burst out laughing. I knew there was no way I could go through with it. So much for my first blow job as an almost-free man!

Things were getting a bit weird, even for me. I finished my shower and left the pretty lady-boy there in the toilet.

It was dark already when, at around 7pm, one of the Nigerians and I were called to the office, where we joined a queue of about 20 new detainees all waiting to get registered. They ranged from young children to entire families, who were obviously illegal immigrants from neighbouring countries. While taking my place at the back of the queue, I suddenly remembered I was in an open courtyard. I looked up to the heavens. The vast open skies had come alive with millions of bright, shining, luminous stars. I felt a knot in my stomach and tears welled up in my eyes. For 18 years I had been deprived of the simple soul-nurturing pleasure of seeing the stars and the moon. I was mesmerised by the sight and thrilled by the idea that, in a matter of five short days, the night sky would once again be part of my everyday existence. I must have been staring for quite some time, because suddenly I noticed that everybody else was looking up at the sky, trying to see what

I found so fascinating. They looked at me enquiringly, as if they were asking me to point out what it was that I was seeing that they couldn't. Yes, they were looking upwards, but they couldn't possibly have seen what I was seeing, or felt what I was feeling. They might as well have looked with closed eyes.

I pointed to the stars and said, '*Siep pat pee pom mai hen* (Eighteen years I never see). '*Pom hue krang nai reenjum*' (I stayed in prison).

I'm not sure if they even understood Thai, as they still looked bewildered. I smiled to myself and thought, I'm alive again. There's a whole new world out there, and it's been waiting for me all this time. My breath grew heavy with excitement and I knew there and then that I could never allow myself to ever take anything for granted again, especially my freedom. No amount of money was worth losing one's freedom for. I said a silent prayer of thanks to *Hashem*.

Eventually I got to the front of the queue. I had my photo taken and was given a copy pasted on a small card, which was now my IDC identity card. When we were returned to the cell, I was instructed to get my stuff. The Nigerian and I were being moved upstairs. I tried to argue, as I dreaded the prospect of being thrown into one of the overcrowded cells upstairs, where the likelihood of getting into a fight was very real. It was not that I feared fighting. I had nothing to prove to these strangers who were going to be my companions for the next few days, but I had a whole new life waiting for me and I didn't want anything to jeopardise that. My arguments fell on deaf ears, and once were were out in the courtyard again, with all our belongings, we were asked if we had mobile phones. If we did, we would have to hand them over. I hadn't been prepared for this. My dog was in my bag, the one they were already searching. Anyway, I decided it was best to cooperate, so I handed the phone to the guard, who also took away things like my deodorant, aftershave, my mirror and my belt. These items were put in a big brown envelope for safekeeping. We were then taken to the third floor. The first cell on the left was for all African foreigners, so my Nigerian friend was put in there.

Although I had just met the Nigerian guy, and so he wasn't strictly speaking my friend, calling all fellow prisoners 'my friend' was a habit

I'd picked up from the Thais. In prison, irrespective of whether you're a foreigner or a Thai, whether you knew somebody's name or not, invariably you would refer to them as *puen* (friend). So this made all of us 'friends'.

There was a lot of noise coming from the African cell and I could actually feel the body heat. It was obviously very overcrowded. I was placed in the cell next door. When I entered, it felt like there was no air in there at all. I felt claustrophobic. There were bodies everywhere. At a glance I estimated at least 80 Western detainees, with many Koreans, Chinese and Singaporeans. I was taken into a small room within the big cell where I was introduced to the room chief, a Chinese guy who spoke good English. He had been in IDC for several years already. He was starting to take out this huge ledger to register my name when three Chinese guys approached me, calling my name. 'Hey, Alesanda *puen!*' Their eyes lit up as smiles stretched across their faces. Wow, I couldn't believe my eyes. I knew all of them! About 13 years back, we had not only stayed together in Building 2 but had also been good friends. I felt a warmth in my heart, knowing that for the next five days I would be among people who knew me, rather than among strangers.

The Chinese guys invited me to stay in their private room. Some of them had been waiting a month already for their visas and travel documents. However, this didn't seem to dampen their spirits too much, nor mine. What we had all been through was nothing in comparison to a few weeks, or days, in IDC. My new cellmates were only too keen to help me in whatever way I needed, and what I needed most was a dog. So when I was offered the use of a mobile, for however long I needed it, I became instantly cheerful. I decided I could live with the squalid conditions, even with only two toilets among us, both of which were broken. Shit would leak out when you flushed and float past your feet where you were taking a shower. Temperatures soared over 40 degrees, but nothing was going to detract from my good mood, and even the ugliness of my surroundings took on a much brighter hue now that I was among friends.

I took advantage of the mobile to try calling Jessica again, and finally I got to hear her voice. I felt a flood of relief wash through me.

When I asked her what had happened, and was she all right, she was apologetic and a bit surprised at my tone. Her son had fallen ill, she said, and she'd switched her phone off. Naturally, I was sorry about her son, but still—! I thought she could at least have messaged me, at this of all times in my life. Right there and then, I decided that I would have to dump her. I tore up all her letters. It made my load lighter for one thing, and my conscience clearer for another. Jessica had fucked up and she would pay the price. Second chances were earned; they weren't just afforded.

By the fourth day in IDC, I had broken out in a rash along both arms, and I had these pus-filled pimples that were incredibly itchy. These few days felt more like months – the thrill of being a free man was temporarily stifled by the insufferable conditions.

On Friday 27 April, early in the morning, a list of names was brought to our cell of those people who were going to be deported. My name was among them. Everything was on schedule.

I went through a whole range of different emotions during those last hours of counting down the time. I was spinning out of my head, jumbled thoughts bombarding me from the deepest recesses of my mind. I kept looking compulsively at my new Swatch watch, which hung as uncomfortably on my wrist as did the jeans around my waist. I stared at its face as the seconds and minutes ticked past. I could *see* time moving, and yet for me time stood still. And rising up from the pit of my stomach was that all too familiar feeling of nervousness that I remembered from the first time I walked into prison. The moment was drawing closer, the moment I had dreamed about, waking and sleeping. It was real, *too* real. My brain struggled to absorb it.

I couldn't help wondering what it was going to be like to see my mother again. I had suffered terrible trauma at the hands of my parents during my childhood. I had never talked about it, not to anyone, but over the years I had done my fair share of reflecting and trying to process it all. Somehow, somewhere in my heart I had learnt to forgive my mother, and during the past 18 years she had certainly tried to make up for lost time. But was that enough? Would it change anything? Truthfully, I doubted that it would. All the same, knowing that her remaining years were probably few, I was determined to show her as much love as I was capable of. That was the best I could do.

That evening, around 8pm, the steel doors of our cell were opened and those of us who were on the list were called to go downstairs. My things were all packed. I thanked my friends from IDC and said good-bye. There was no room in my heart for sentimentality. All I wanted to do was get the hell out of there, and, hey, it was my turn now to turn my back on the battle-scarred faces of men who lived in four-walled city-towns.

It was my turn.

I walked lightly down the stairs.

Acknowledgements

Where to begin and how to thank the many thousands of people who encouraged and supported me for almost two decades of my imprisonment? Thank you to my family – my mom Katalin, Mike, Joan, Malcolm, Darren and Keri. Without your unconditional love and devotion, I might never have made it out alive to write this book.

Joan Sacks, my sister, who never judged nor questioned my actions, but remained loyal and made it her life's mission to get me out of prison, putting her family and her own life aside and providing for my every need: I may not show you love, but please know that I'm eternally grateful for the love and caring you have shown me all my life. Thank you.

Vicky Klevansky (RIP), who was like the father I never had.

To Jeff Nathan, who was willing to give up his own freedom to see me free. Not many people I know have as much heart as you. Love you, brother.

Darren and Keri Sacks, my nephew and niece, whose lives were changed forever. Thank you for your support and for never giving up on me when I had almost given up on myself.

To Alison Lowry, my editor and now friend for life, 300 000 handwritten words later, you managed to put it all together and still maintain my voice throughout. Well done and thank you. I would like to dedicate the book to Alison's daughter, Tiffany, who, like me, was a warrior, but tragically lost her life to an accidental drug overdose at the tender age of 18.

Ian and Pam Jacobson, you guys were amazing. You came into my life at a time when death was knocking at my door. I am grateful to both of you for making such a huge difference to my life in prison. Thank you.

Mark Cohen and his wife Sandi: I thank you from the bottom of my heart for everything you did for me. Words cannot express my gratitude.

Peter Hough, fellow Arcadian and brother: whenever I reached out you came through for me. Your kindness and generosity have touched me deep in my heart.

Abe (RIP) and Rosie Krok, and Solly Krok. What can I say? Knowing people such as yourselves has been more than an honour and a privilege. Thank you for coming through for me when you did.

Bertie Lubner, you were part of my journey from those initial years. When all hope seemed lost, you were one of the people who gave me strength to endure my suffering. I always said to Joan, 'If anybody can get me out of here it's Bertie Lubner.' Thank you so much.

Doc and Edna Ralph, I am deeply indebted for your support and, more importantly, for helping me to renew my faith in *Hashem* (G-d).

Nelson Rolihlahla Mandela (RIP), a man loved and respected by all. You stood for equality and freedom and had the courage of your convictions. As a prisoner, I was inspired by everything you epitomised. Many a lesson I learnt from you. Thank you for your personal letter supporting my royal pardon application.

David Sandler, a fellow Arcadian and a brother who brought so many of us ex-Arcs together from different parts of the world. Your support and correspondence over the course of my incarceration were tremendously uplifting.

Angsana Yamakanon. When I think of the times we shared and your unconditional love, you were not only an inspiration, but an angel. You renewed my self-worth and taught me that no man is an island. Without you I could never have attained the standard I achieved in my artistic development. *Kob kun krab.*

Elisabeth Grimm. Our paths crossed for reasons I did not understand at first, but then with time I realised that you were another angel, whose extended love and friendship not only inspired me but carried me through in my darkest moments. You are always in my heart.

Rabbi Yosef Chaim Kantor. I would like to thank you not only for your friendship but for also being a spiritual mentor. Your visits were a source of strength on so many levels. May *Hashem* always be with you.

Morris Landsman (RIP), my best friend and brother, you were always there for me, no matter what. We brought out the worst and the best in each other. I miss you more than anything, although your spirit will always live on in those who had the privilege of having their lives touched by you. I'm so sorry that you aren't here to enjoy my freedom with me.

Jackie Benjamin. We loved, we shared, we learnt – a time in my life I will never forget. Thank you for not only being an inspiration but also my number one fan.

To Jeremy Boraine and the team from Jonathan Ball Publishers, who had the foresight to approach me even before I had started writing my book. Thank you for having faith and believing in my story. Thank you Alfred LeMaitre, for your copyediting skills. It was great working with you, even though we only spoke on the telephone.

Thank you to Anne Brest, whose computer skills and assistance in putting the manuscript together were much appreciated.

To the following people, please know that the order of names does not diminish in any way the importance and gratitude I feel towards each and every one of you. I am touched in my heart beyond words. A big *'Yasher Keach'* and sincere thanks: Adrian Rosenberg, Alik Dresner, Randy Shiff, Vicky Klevansky (RIP), Sandy Lipshitz, Rob and Sharon Nisbett, Beverly and Jon Davimes, Louise Fisher, Yvonne Ziegler, Gale Isobel Bailey, Bev Boulton, Rabbi Nechemya Wilhelm, Dr Henk van Staen, Leo and Jane Niedermayr, Alon Ossip, Tony Chaskelson, Adi Fredman, Monty Koppel, Brian Leftin, Shirley Roth, Joel Costa, Les Durbach, Sharon Friedman, Denis Rubenstein, Derek Rosmarin, Barry Aaron, Peter Aaron, Melvyn Gutkin, Neville Sacks, Peta Ann Cohen, Howard Sundy, Kelly and Marcia Schlesinger, Cato Pastoll, Grant Port, Mark John Sher, Gail Smith, Peter and Karen Hohenstein, Wendy Kirsch, Dr Dean Lutrin, Saul Colley and Susan Ruttenberg, Brett Schlesinger, Barbara Jochelson and Pam Burgess (RIP).

Kevin Port, Ilan Saffer, Larry Miller, Wendy Rosenberg, Riekie Robinson, Rabbi Shain, Ian and Lana Meltzer, Anke van Niekerk, Laurie Fineberg, Jules Gordon, Michele and Hans Roelofsen, Leanne and Ty Micinilio, Carmen Upiter, Barbara Gavin, Robyn Woolf, Malcolm Spence (RIP), Anna Marie de Ridder, Gavin Cohen, Benji Schleider,

Gabriel Schleider, Carol Kirshon, Trevor Pearlman, Philippa Sklaar, Norma Payne, Douglas Cohen, Lauren Witkin, Roy Levin, Ellen Levy, Tony Mark, Sandy Meltz, Jenny Arkles, Christine Read, Ekie Litvin, Roy Lotkin, Florentina Savedra, Zsuzsi and Kristi Gurics, Zelda van Rooyen, Karen Lotis (RIP) and Katherine Sprietzer.

Hazel Friedman, Debora Patta, Dormer Csaba, Jane Abbott, Mark Franz, Laura Sher, Colleen Kanowitz, Sergio Nocera, Erwin Verhoeven, Bernadine Stein, Hilary Vogel, Selma Richter Habecker, Sue Wyche, Hilary Shill, Melanie Rosen, Elize Aimes, Derick Berold, Patricia Gerber, Belinda West, Lucy McDermid, Anton Schutte, Errol and Dianne Ballen, Paul Marc Ephron, Mike Leeb, Larry Wainstein, David Cato, Mandy Harnoy, Shelley van der Hoven, Juliana Sanviso, Denis Goffinet, Raven Randall, Trevor Romain, Karl and Anna-Marie Lechky, Levana Mizrachi, Salomie Green, Charlene Lewison, Robynne Pozniak, Carole Herson, Debbie Stein, Janine Goodson, Melanie Scheepers, Chris and Jackie Burgess, Charmaine Chatkin, Gil Lang, Stephen Sacks, Barbara Jochelson, Karen Page, Somchai, Alan Deshowitz, Athena Botolous, Danya Medow, Seline Kasner, Michelle Levenstein, Gisele and Beverley Winick, Aubrey and Heather Scheider, Myra Woolf, Howard and Gail Rybko, Coreen Lourens, Tanya Shenfield Schwartz, Anthony Mark, David Givechy, Nanda and Vidia Govender, Delene Kleyn, Irwin and Janice Schaffer, Salome Green.

Special thanks to the following: FW de Klerk, Pik Botha, Desmond Tutu, Tony Leon, Robert McBride, Aziz Pahad, Professor Harry Reicher, Harut Lapid (RIP), Ambassador Goris, Ambassador Douglas Gibson, Ambassador Pheto, Anna Mokoko and Jan Putter.

To all those people who took the time to write to me, I want to thank you. Your words of encouragement gave me the strength to endure those long lonely days that almost swallowed me alive. Sadly, it was impossible to reply to all of you who wrote to me – please forgive me.

Lastly, to all my friends in prison, keep your minds occupied, stay fit and know that dreams come true. Another day in paradise.

Shani Krebs
February 2014